MOSES MONTEFIORE

MOSES MONTEFIORE

Jewish Liberator · Imperial Hero

ABIGAIL GREEN

THE BELKNAP PRESS OF
HARVARD UNIVERSITY PRESS

Cambridge, Massachusetts, and London, England 2010

Library of Congress Cataloging-in-Publication Data

Green, Abigail.
Moses Montefiore : Jewish liberator, imperial hero / Abigail Green.
p. cm.
Includes bibliographical references and index.
ISBN 978-0-674-04880-5 (cloth : alk. paper)
1. Montefiore, Moses, Sir, 1784–1885.
2. Jews—Great Britain—Biography.
3. Philanthropists—Great Britain—Biography.
I. Title.
DS135.E6M7334 2010
305.892′4041092—dc22
[B]   2009034174

Contents

Maps

Illustrations

Preface

My mother was born a Sebag-Montefiore, and with a different family background I would not have written this book. But bias is unavoidable for historians, and while my personal connection with Montefiore has inevitably shaped the outcome I hope this biography is not the poorer for it. I have striven to avoid both the pitfalls of hagiography—exemplified by Lucien Wolf's and Paul Goodman's accounts of Montefiore—and the wildly revisionist stance taken more recently by Moshe Samet. My goal is neither to praise nor to damn Montefiore, but to assess his life and achievements in terms of the times in which he lived.

Ultimately, I suspect this book is more influenced by my own training as a professional historian, working on nineteenth-century German history, than by any sense of family loyalty. Coming from outside the world of Jewish studies, I have brought with me a different set of preoccupations and intellectual baggage. This is in some ways a weakness, and I am indebted to those who have corrected my errors and helped introduce me to a new field. Exposure to such a rich and stimulating array of secondary literatures has transformed my horizons as a historian. I hope, however, that my background in "mainstream" European history has also been an asset: enabling me to integrate Montefiore into the broad currents of nineteenth-century politics and society, and to interpret his life in new ways.

It must be every historian's dream to work on a subject that is at once as important and as historiographically neglected as Montefiore. Geographically and chronologically, it has also been a vast project; I did not fully appreciate the scale of the challenge when I first took it on. To compensate for the destruction of most of Montefiore's personal archive, I have drawn on primary material in private, institutional, and state archives scattered through Britain, France, Italy, Israel, Morocco, Turkey, Romania, Russia, and the United States and newspaper reports in the British, French, German, Polish, Romanian, North American, and Hebrew-language press. Access to such a broad range of sources would have been impossible without extensive financial support. I am very grateful to the British Academy, the Lucius N. Littauer Foundation, the Memorial Foundation for Jewish Culture, the Oxford University Research Development Fund, and the Jeffrey Fund at Brasenose College for the funding they so generously provided toward my travel and research costs, to the Hebrew and Jewish Studies Unit at Oxford for supporting some of my illustration costs, and to the Oxford University History Faculty for allowing me an extra term's research leave.

The sheer quantity of material generated by and about Montefiore has left me heavily reliant on research assistants. Special mention should be made of Anne Giebel, who brought her considerable enthusiasm and intelligence to bear on the *Allgemeine Zeitung des Judentums*, the French Jewish press, and other material in Paris. I am also very grateful to Asaf Pink for his work deciphering nineteenth-century Hebrew manuscripts, and to my husband, Boaz Brosh, for his help translating them. Kursad Akpinar did excellent work in the Ottoman archives, and I have felt personally enriched by our interaction. Avital Erez and Yael Ronen did invaluable work on the Hebrew-language press, and Tehila Pink on North American Jewish newspapers. I am also grateful to Michael Clark for his work with English newspapers, Mohammed and Assia Kenbib for their help with Moroccan material, Sergei Kusnetsov for his work in the St. Petersburg archives, Svetlana Rukhelman for her Russian translations, and Marius Turda for his work in Bucharest libraries. Thanks are due too to Stephanie Douglas for Yiddish translation, Agnes Erdos for transliteration, Ursula Fuks for identifying material in the Polish press, Aleksandr Lokshin for identifying documents in Moscow, Bendict Rundell for Polish translation, and Katherine Smith for help with the Safi Affair appeal. Finally, I am grateful to Douglas Banin for his help in exploring Montefiore's involvement with Freemasonry. Without the practical support of Sue Henderson and Lucy Hodson in the History Faculty and of Julia Palejowska at Brasenose, organizing all this would have been impossible.

It has been both a privilege and a great pleasure to work through the Montefiore family papers while staying with my cousins Robert and Anita Sebag-Montefiore in Switzerland. I have loved having the opportunity to know them better and I am delighted these documents have now found a home at the Oxford Centre for Hebrew and Jewish Studies. I also greatly appreciated my regular visits with Adolf Schischa, who showed me his collection and shared with me his extensive knowledge of Montefiore. Meeting him has been a rare and rich experience; my thanks to Ezra Kahn for the introduction. I am grateful too to my great-aunt Ruth Sebag-Montefiore for sharing with me Adelaide Sebag's travel diary and other Montefioriana: she is the only person I have ever heard refer to Montefiore as "Uncle Moses." Many thanks too to Rabbi Abraham Levy, for allowing me to see Montefiore's personal Bible, and to Raphael Loewe for sharing some reflections and recollections. Finally, I am grateful to the Board of Deputies for permission to use their archives and for the permission of Her Majesty Queen Elizabeth II to use the Royal Archives.

In addition, I would like to thank Melanie Aspey at the Rothschild Archive; Miriam Rodrigues-Pereira at the Spanish and Portuguese Jews' Congregation; Piet van Boxel, César Merchan-Hamann, Milena Seidler, and Noa Dagan at the Oxford Centre for Hebrew and Jewish Studies; Ezra Kahn, Kay Roberg, and Aron Prys at the London School of Jewish Studies; Chris Woolgar of the Hartley Library in Southampton; and the many librarians and archivists who helped me over the years. I am grateful to all those at Cambridge University Library; the Hebrew National University Library, the Central Archives for the History of the Jewish People, and the Central Zionist Archives in Jerusalem; the British Library, the Evangelical Alliance, the Guildhall Library, the Jewish Museum, the Mocatta Library (University College London), the London Metropolitan Archives, and the National Archives in London; the Biblioteca Nacional de España in Madrid; Brasenose College Library, the Bodleian Library, the History Faculty Library, and the Leopold Muller Memorial Library in Oxford; the Alliance Israélite Universelle, the Archives Nationales, and the Ministère des Affaires Etrangères in Paris; the Archivio di Stato di Roma, Archivio Segreto Vaticano, and the Communita Israelitica di Roma in Rome. Researching this book has entailed a lot of travel, and in this context I would particularly like to thank Rahel Kostanien and Simonas Dovidovičius in Lithuania; Rafi Elmaleh, Sylvie Ohnona, and Simone and Elie Tordjman in Morocco; and Naim Guleryuz in Turkey.

Many historians have taken the time to read my work on Montefiore, and this book is much the better for their input. Discussions with Vincent Viaene have been critical in formulating my views on "Jewish internationalism," while David Rechter has been throughout an invaluable sounding board for my ideas. Besides my anonymous Harvard University Press reviewers, I am grateful to Amira Bennison, Olga Borovaya, Francesca Bregoli, Glenn Dynner, Robert Evans, the late Jonathan Frankel, Michele Klein, Ron Nettler, Peter Pulzer, William Thomas, and Steve Zipperstein for their comments on individual chapters. Above all, I am grateful to Peter Claus, François Guesnet, Derek Penslar, Michael Silber, and Yaron Tsur for their help with the draft manuscript, which in all cases, and for a variety of reasons, went well beyond what I might reasonably have hoped. Various slices through this project have been presented in Cambridge, Jerusalem, Leuven, Oxford, and Southampton; at the conferences on "Jews and Empire" and "Jews beyond the Nation" held in Southampton and Berlin; a symposium on the history of humanitarian intervention held at Peterhouse College, Cambridge; and within the framework of the "Jewish Community and Social Development in Europe" project based at the Rothschild Archive: all provided useful input. I have also benefited from conversations with Israel Bartal, David Feldman, Sander Gillman, Ruth Harris, Raphael Loewe, Brad Sabin-Hill, and Oliver Zimmer, while Eitan Bar-Yosef, Tim Blanning, Christopher Clark, David Devries, Uri Dromi, Lucien Gubbay, the late John Klier, Hana Lifschitz, Simon Sebag-Montefiore, David Sorkin, and Jonathan Steinberg provided various forms of support and advice. More generally, my life is enriched by the wider community of historians at Oxford and particularly by my immediate colleagues in Brasenose: Martin Ingram has been a tower of strength, while Lesley Abrams, Rowena Archer, and Andy Boyle have, at different times, been wonderful colleagues. Brasenose has, in a wider sense, proved to be a warm and supportive environment, and I am privileged to be a part of it.

This book has taken longer to write than I expected, and the process has not always been a smooth one. Throughout, Niall Ferguson has been an intellectual inspiration and a true friend, providing critical support at various junctures. If his influence was barely discernible in my first book, I hope he will see more of himself in this one. It was thanks to Niall that the Wylie Agency took on this book at a particularly difficult time: I am enormously grateful to Andrew Wylie, Scott Moyers, and Sarah Chalfant for all they have done for me, and for helping to make it happen. Kathleen McDermott at Harvard University Press has been an enthusiastic, hands-on editor, and I have enjoyed seeing the end-product come together with her.

The arrival of our daughter Hannah has delayed the publication of this book, but she has transformed my world, and the chapters I have written since her birth are immeasurably the better for it. My brother and both my parents have given me love and support through difficult times, as have (in different ways) Ivana Rosenzweig and Natasha Cica. My mother has, more recently, provided critical childcare, while Emma Purves has been the kind of friend who makes parenting much easier. My husband, Boaz, has always believed in this project. He has worked through documents, traveled with me in Montefiore's footsteps, and given all kinds of practical advice and encouragement. I cannot imagine having written it without him. There is a sense in which this book is for all my family, but it is, of course, particularly for Boaz and Hannah.

Note to Readers

The nature of both source material and subject matter has made it difficult to adopt hard-and-fast rules with regard to the spelling of both personal names and place-names, although where possible I have adopted the spellings in *Webster's Biographical* and *Webster's Geographical Dictionaries*. For the sake of simplicity, I have preferred to anglicize Hebrew and Yiddish names (Elijah, Isaac, Israel, etc.), except where the primary source material suggests otherwise. In such cases I have adopted the style used in the primary sources (for example, Moise Racah, Moshe Sachs), and where this spelling is conflicting I used my own judgment. In the notes, I have used the Littman Library of Jewish Civilization system for the transliteration of Hebrew-language sources. Where possible, I have also adopted this system for the transliteration of Hebrew words in the main text, but to make life easier for the reader I have preferred not to use a diacritical for the letter *chet*, and where quotations use alternative renderings, I have left the original. Turkish and Arabic names and words are likewise rendered without diacriticals, as in Montefiore's time.

Many of the places described in this book have been known by several names. For eastern European towns, I have adopted the Jewish usage with alternative versions in brackets: for example, Vilna (Vilnius), Vilkomir (Ukmergé). Where nineteenth-century place-names are very well established, I have adopted the anglicized version current in Montefiore's day, with an alternative version in brackets at first usage: for example, Constantinople (Istanbul); Mogador (Essaouira); Smyrna (Izmir). Exceptionally, I have retained the Italian Livorno for Montefiore's birthplace rather than the English Leghorn, in order to emphasize his foreign origins.

Finally, two sources of Montefiore's diaries are distinguished in the Abbreviations and Notes because of the great difference in their relative value. Louis Loewe's two-volume edition contains both his own heavily edited version of the diaries and excerpts of the original manuscript versions or original letters reproduced therein. The latter, which are obviously of greater value, are identified by the abbreviation LDMS.

MOSES MONTEFIORE

Introduction

Outside Jewish circles, Moses Montefiore (1784–1885) is now a forgotten figure. Yet every year in August hundreds—sometimes even thousands—of ultra-Orthodox Haredi Jews descend on the shabby-genteel seaside resort of Ramsgate to mark the anniversary of his death. To those unfamiliar with Ramsgate's history, they must seem an incongruous presence. With its Regency terraces, eighteenth-century harbor, and semidetached sprawl, this is a quintessentially English town. But the mausoleum that Montefiore shares here with his wife, Judith, is one of the few places in western Europe that can be described as an authentically Jewish religious site.

Montefiore's tomb is accessed via a neglected rural footpath that once led directly to his home on the East Cliff. Now it runs steeply down from a typically suburban English close. Nothing remains here of the Lady Judith Montefiore Theological College, the imposing neo-Tudor complex that Montefiore built to perpetuate his vision of traditional Jewish religiosity in an English key. Farther down the hill, the little synagogue is hidden from view by trees and bushes. The mausoleum itself is a modest white building. The doors are stiff, and the interior is dark and musty, lit only from the entrance and a small stained-glass window at the apex of the dome. Modeled on the Tomb of Rachel near Bethlehem, it feels out of place here, better suited to the baking heat of the desert than to the gray drizzle of an English summer's day. The mausoleum is locked for much of the year. On the anniversary of Montefiore's death large sheets of silver foil are spread over the graves, with a folding table for candles and a small pile of prayer books. There is a steady trickle of men in black hats, kaftans, and sidelocks making their way down the path. Many have brought families, and there are plenty of harried-looking women with children in push-chairs. At first both men and

1

women light candles inside; then, as the site becomes busier, the women stay outside, praying and chatting. The tomb soon contains a solid mass of men in black. In this enclosed space, the walls reverberate with prayer; even from the outside the religious intensity is palpable.

This wave of enthusiasm for Montefiore is a relatively recent phenomenon. It has been orchestrated to some extent by religious hard-liners seeking to wrest control of the site from the Sephardi community to which Montefiore belonged. Led by members of the anti-Zionist Satmar sect, this particular strand of the Haredi community sees ultra-Orthodoxy as the future of British Jewry in an age of assimilation. They wish to appropriate Montefiore's legacy both to honor the man and to perpetuate their way of life. Many of the old Jewish communities on the south coast have died out, and Ramsgate is no exception. Defeated by demography, the Sephardim have invested Montefiore's legacy in educating a new generation of Anglo-Jewish rabbis in London. They admire Montefiore as a Jewish leader; they are too self-consciously enlightened to revere him as a holy man. It is the kind of controversy that he himself would have recognized: a quarrel about money underpinned by radically divergent religious views, rooted in conflicting ideologies of tradition and change. In death as in life, Montefiore remains torn between the two.

Montefiore was one of the first truly global celebrities. A humanitarian, philanthropist, and campaigner for Jewish emancipation, his fame stretched from the Great Plains of Kansas, through the elegant drawing rooms of Victorian London and prerevolutionary St. Petersburg, to the gold fields of Australia, the Old City of Jerusalem, and the *mellah* (Jewish quarter) of Marrakesh. In an age when the global public sphere first became a reality, his centennial birthday celebrations captured the imagination of the world.

Born into London's Sephardi merchant elite, Montefiore made his fortune on the Stock Exchange at the dawn of the modern financial age. At forty he was already a very wealthy man. For the next fifty years he crisscrossed the globe in his efforts to improve the lot of nineteenth-century Jewry, disregarding the dangers of piracy, cholera, and war, overcoming his age and physical infirmities. These activities played a critical role in the crystallization of modern Jewish consciousness: bridging the gap between the informal influence exerted by eighteenth-century Jewish financiers in the courts of Christian princes and Muslim sultans, and the more formalized lobbying efforts of international Jewish organizations and other groups in our own era.

HARPER'S WEEKLY.

JOURNAL OF CIVILIZATION.

Vol. XXVII.—No. 1400.
Copyright, 1883, by Harper & Brothers.

NEW YORK, SATURDAY, OCTOBER 20, 1883.

TEN CENTS A COPY.
$4.00 PER YEAR, IN ADVANCE.

SIR MOSES MONTEFIORE, THE OLD MAN BENEFICENT.—From the Portrait by G. Richmond, R.A.—[See Page 662.]

Global celebrity: the American Harper's Weekly *marks Montefiore's ninety-ninth birthday, October 20, 1883.*

In the heyday of the British Empire, Montefiore provided leadership and inspiration to Jews throughout North America, Australasia, and the West Indies. He was a symbol of hope to Jews throughout eastern Europe and the Middle East, who lived with inequality, insecurity, and often oppression. In Morocco, Persia, and the Ottoman Empire, Montefiore's defense of Jewish rights dovetailed with British foreign policy and imperial ideology, epitomizing the grand humanitarian campaigns of the Anglo-Saxon world. His support for the struggling Jewish community in Palestine has led many to see him as a founding father of modern Israel, while his pioneering approach to the problem of Jewish persecution helped transform the international response to abuses of human rights.

Montefiore is a towering figure in modern Jewish history, comparable perhaps to Moses Mendelssohn, Theodor Herzl, or David Ben-Gurion; yet there is, surprisingly, no serious, archivally rooted biography of him.[1] Montefiore was, moreover, an obsessive record keeper. He kept letter books of his correspondence, ordering and archiving the flood of mail he received over the years. Besides account books and travelogues, he was the author of eighty-five diaries, which he kept under lock and key.[2] Upon Montefiore's death, his writings were transferred to the Judith College library, where his collaborator and friend Louis Loewe spent two years putting together a much-abridged edition of the diaries. At Montefiore's request this drew explicitly on Judith's travel journals, but it also exploited Loewe's own recollections and the vast archive that Montefiore had assembled.

Lucien Wolf—historian, Jewish activist, and author of the authorized biography published to mark Montefiore's centenary—was the only man apart from Loewe to have any knowledge of this material. He concluded that Loewe had "failed altogether to extract . . . the valuable political and social information" contained in the Montefiore diaries.[3] But only a few years later Montefiore's nephew and heir, Sir Joseph Sebag-Montefiore, ordered the destruction of his entire archive. It is said that the bonfires at Ramsgate burnt for days.[4]

The man entrusted with burning Montefiore's papers was Rabbi Hermann Shandel, who served Montefiore as minister, reader, and ritual slaughterer. Appalled by his complicity in this act of destruction, Shandel secretly saved some twenty files from the flames. In the 1930s his son-in-law, Rabbi Solomon Lipson, began to sell off this collection. Some pieces found their way back to members of the Montefiore family, who had built up small personal collections of memorabilia. Others were bought by the scholar and collector Adolf Schischa, who arrived in London as a penniless Jewish refugee from Vienna in 1938 and set about gathering together the scattered and neglected relics of a rapidly vanishing Jewish past.

   From the perspective of the twenty-first century the actions of Sir Joseph seem inexplicable. Oral tradition has it that he acted in deference to Montefiore's own wishes: adored in his lifetime, Montefiore had no desire to be worshipped and made into a plaster saint. An alternative tradition hints that there were things in the diaries that the family wished to hide. George Collard, who claims illegitimate descent from Montefiore, has even suggested that documents connecting Montefiore with a young man reared in an orphanage in the Essex town of Brentwood lie buried in his grave.[5]

   In fact Sir Joseph seems to have conducted a primitive weeding exercise. A collection of papers still kept in the family reflects above all the things that mattered to him. It includes personal correspondence, Sir Joseph's own letters to Montefiore, a few pages torn from Montefiore's diaries, and communications from internationally famous political figures like Lord Palmerston, Sir Robert Peel, French prime minister François Guizot, Prince Carol of Romania, the prominent Ottoman reformer Fuad Pasha, and Count Pavel Kiselev, confidant of Tsar Nicholas I. Tellingly, the vast bulk of these documents is in English.

   Letters and diaries also survived outside the family. Loewe died a year after completing his work on the Montefiore diaries, but someone knew enough about the material to conduct a further weeding exercise. This was most probably the Romanian Zionist Rabbi Moses Gaster. A brilliant, eccentric, quarrelsome man, he served as leader of the Spanish and Portuguese Jews' Congregation in London for decades and as principal of the Judith College until it closed in 1896. Thanks perhaps to Gaster, the Sephardi community acquired an apparently random collection of Montefioriana to supplement the material that Montefiore himself had entrusted to them: key documents including the invaluable Census of Palestine Jewry and a wealth of congratulatory addresses, many of them beautifully illuminated and enclosed in extravagant presentation cases of silver, velvet, and rotting silk.

   The existence of guilty secrets may possibly explain the burning of Montefiore's diaries, but they cannot excuse the wanton destruction of his entire archive. Very few of these documents were in any sense personal. The overwhelming majority were mundane letters from rabbis and Jewish communal leaders—full of flowery language, usually written in Hebrew, utterly uncontroversial. Montefiore himself was incapable of understanding most of them; Sir Joseph may simply have failed to grasp their significance. Unable to anticipate either the Holocaust or the mass emigration of Jews from Arab lands, he cannot have known that so many of the communities in contact with Montefiore would disappear almost without trace during the next hundred years. Had it survived, this archive would have provided a doorway to this lost world.

Even without it, Montefiore's life remains the best window we are likely to have onto the Jewish nineteenth century. With relatives scattered throughout western Europe, he knew the hopes and frustrations of wealthy Jews in Britain, France, and Germany, torn between community and nation as they struggled for acceptance and equality. He knew, too, the more uncertain condition of their Italian counterparts, who lived still in the shadow of the Inquisition as they embraced the nationalist dream.

Through his travels and web of correspondents, Montefiore encountered the Jewish world in all its rich diversity: the Jews of tsarist Russia, at the crossroads between tradition and modernity; the Jews of Morocco, caught between their loyalty to the sultan and the promise of equality brought by Western imperialism; the Jews of Romania, victims of a violent and intolerant nationalism; the devout and divided Jews of Palestine, unsettled by the winds of change.

Montefiore's life reminds us that Jewish history is never simply about the Jews, but always about their relationship with the rest of society. In Britain, his ties with Quakers, Evangelicals, antislavery campaigners, and Christian Zionists helped to place the cause of Jewish relief at the heart of a wider humanitarian campaign for civil rights and religious liberty. The dilemmas he faced in implementing his philanthropic vision in Palestine foreshadowed many of the problems encountered today by charities and nongovernmental organizations managing aid projects in the developing world: allegations of corruption among local officials, the clash between Western and traditional values, the difficulties of managing projects from afar. Indeed, Montefiore exemplifies the achievements of a whole generation of moral crusaders, who mobilized international civil society in unprecedented ways and shaped the values of the world in which we live.

The questions that preoccupied Montefiore—religious inequality, racial prejudice, the fate of refugees, and the persecution of minorities— sometimes seemed peripheral to contemporaries. They have proved centrally important ever since. Through Montefiore, we can trace their origins and the long-term evolution of interfaith relations in the Muslim "East" and Christian "West." Here, we see the origins of Zionism and the rise of international Jewish consciousness, European penetration of Palestine, and the making of the modern Middle East.

Wherever he went, Montefiore encountered Jewish communities in the throes of a confrontation with modernity that posed the same chal-

1. Captain in Surrey Militia, 1805.
2. Carrying despatches of the Battle of Navarino.
3. First Visit to the East, 1827.
4. Presented to Mehemet Ali in Egypt.
5. Interview with the Emperor Nicholas of Russia.
6. Travelling in the Desert.

THE CAREER OF SIR MOSES MONTEFIORE.

Montefiore's life was the stuff of legend: the Illustrated London News *celebrated the extraordinary career of a centenarian on November 3, 1883.*
(By permission of the Bodleian Library, University of Oxford: N.2288.b.6)

lenges: emancipation, assimilation, the conflict between religious reform and fundamentalist Orthodoxy, the rise of anti-Semitism, and the first faint stirrings of Jewish nationalism. His story bridges the Ashkenazi-Sephardi divide in Jewish history, presenting the transformation of Jewish life in Europe, the Middle East, and the New World as part of a single global phenomenon. For the changing nature of Jewish identity in the West and the impact of these changes on Jews elsewhere were complementary facets of a global transition to modernity, testifying to both the unity and the diversity of the Jewish world.

Chapter 1

Livorno and London

Livorno. 1784. A bustling, thriving port, famed throughout the mercantile world for its dominant role in trade between the Atlantic, the Mediterranean, and the Levant. A magnet for entrepreneurs from East and West. A cosmopolitan, exotic place, where respectable European traders in breeches and wigs rubbed shoulders with their more colorful oriental counterparts, dressed in the turbans and flowing robes of contemporary cliché. The harbor a forest of masts and rigging, its parade of tall ships serviced by an armada of little boats. Sea glittering, seagulls shrieking, the stink of fish and the bleating of livestock; smartly dressed officials taking issue with shabby clerks; porters hollering, sailors shouting. European visitors never failed to comment on the clamor of a hundred tongues and costumes they encountered here: Spaniards, Italians, Germans, Greeks, Turks, Jews, Muscovites, Armenians, and Moors. They traded in everything from silk, cotton, and goat's hair, through gold, pearls, and precious stones, to leather, tobacco, dried cod, dates, saffron, and caviar.

"How cheerfully I elbowed my way through this riot of nations," wrote the German poet Ernst Moritz Arndt when he visited Livorno in the 1790s; "such a tumult and chaos of busy, active life as energise this little place . . . The tone is free and uninhibited, as it is in every lively sea town."[1] Freedom, indeed, was the attraction of Livorno. Men of all nations benefited from the port's status as a tax haven, but, as the historian Edward Gibbon noted, the real charm of Livorno lay in the fact that "it is actually the people who enjoy complete freedom. Every nation can arrive here and live according to their religion and under the protection of their own laws . . . This is the veritable land of Canaan for the Jews, who experience here a mildness unknown in the rest of Italy. The interests of commerce have almost silenced the conversionist spirit of the Church of Rome."[2]

Religious toleration, in other words, was the secret of Livorno's success. In the 1590s, at the height of the Inquisition, the Medicis had issued a charter known as *la Livornina*, which acted as a siren call to the persecuted Jews of Italy and the Iberian Peninsula.[3] Everyone in Livorno had a right to absolute freedom and security of goods and person; a right to acquire property of all kinds; and, crucially, a right to live free of inquisition even if they were Jews who had previously lived disguised as Christians in other states. By the 1780s Livorno allowed Jews a say in municipal government—not to mention a host of privileges, ranging from the right to graduate at the University of Pisa to guarantees of fair treatment at law. All this, at a time when Jews elsewhere in Italy were locked up in ghettos, banned from most trades and professions, and stigmatized by wearing the degrading Jewish badge.[4] Thanks to *la Livornina*, the port at Livorno flourished, and Jews came flocking.

In 1752 about a fifth of the major commercial houses in Livorno belonged to Jews, who made up a third of the town's inhabitants. The 20,000-strong community played such an important role in Livorno's business life that the whole port reportedly observed Saturday—the Jewish Sabbath—as a day of rest.[5] Yet contemporary perceptions of Jewish wealth were exaggerated.[6] Roughly half the community survived on poor relief, and only about a third could afford to pay tax at all.[7]

By the eighteenth century Livorno boasted the largest Jewish community in Italy, and one of the most important in Europe. The Jews of Livorno even spoke their own dialect—Italian, corrupted with Hebrew and Portuguese. By all accounts this dialect was a fair reflection of the community's mixed heritage: "vivacious, clear and precise . . . pure for the lowliest expressions . . . colorful like people's garments and spicy like their food. It possessed the style of the Bible with something of Spanish pomposity and of Tuscan graciousness. But the use (and misuse) of imagery, proverbs, quaint sayings was still Oriental."[8] In short, the Jews of Livorno typified the mix of cultures that made up the Western Jewish diaspora, known collectively as Sephardim (from the Hebrew word for Spain).

The Sephardim were descended from the Jews of Spain and Portugal, who had flourished under Muslim rule but faced conversion or expulsion as a result of the Christian reconquest of the Iberian Peninsula. Even before the expulsion of 1492, some Spanish Jews converted to Christianity in the face of pogroms and socioeconomic pressures; others took refuge in Portugal, only to be confronted with mass forced conversion in 1497. "New Christians" in both countries remained a distinct

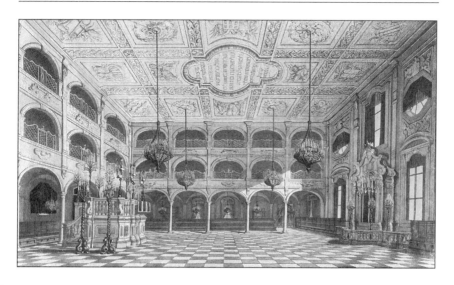

The interior of the synagogue at Livorno around the time of Montefiore's birth: hand-colored engraving by Ferdinando Fambrino, after Ornabano Roselli, 1793. (By permission of Nicolas Sapieha/Art Resource, New York)

social group, specializing in particular economic activities and marrying among themselves. Some were genuine converts; many remained secret Jews. The Inquisition, instituted in the Iberian Peninsula to root out their heresies, only isolated these so-called *conversos* further. It promoted the growth of a subculture based on secret, family-centered transmission of Judaism, and fostered a strong sense of group identity among those who—tellingly—called themselves "men of the Nation." *Conversos* fled all over western Europe and the New World in search of religious freedom and economic opportunity.[9] Whenever they felt safe to do so, they jettisoned their "Christian" identity and reentered the Jewish community. Their Iberian background and international connections left them well placed to take advantage of the transformation of the European economy that followed the discovery of the Americas. The thriving western Italian port of Livorno was an obvious destination.

In due course the "men of the Nation" in Livorno were joined by Jews from elsewhere in Italy and by Sephardim from North Africa and the Levant. The latter were also descendants of the Jews expelled from Spain, many of whom took refuge in Morocco and the Ottoman Empire, where they enjoyed the relative toleration of Islam. At first the Iberian exiles looked down on indigenous Jews in these places and established their own communities. With time a rich fusion of the two cultures emerged, in which the Sephardim retained the upper hand. Once again, their Iberian background and connections stood them in good stead, enabling them to mediate both diplomatically and commercially between Christian and Muslim worlds. The Sephardim of the Ottoman Empire played a key role in Mediterranean commerce, while their counterparts in Morocco dominated trade with the West. In the eighteenth century they, too, began to settle in the ports of northwestern Europe, the western Mediterranean, and the Atlantic seaboard. Like the *conversos* of an earlier generation, they were attracted to Livorno—now a respected center of Jewish learning, a magnet for famous rabbis, and home to one of the most influential Hebrew printing presses in the world.

In Livorno the Jewish "nation" operated to some extent as an autonomous community, but it was also integrated into the life of the town. Jewish merchants thronged the coffeehouses of the elegant Via Ferdinanda, with their gaily painted walls and dazzling display of mirrors.[10] Mingling with traders and businessmen of every description, they loitered around the marble-topped tables, making contacts and cutting deals amid the tinkle of silver on fine porcelain. Wealthy Jews were even free to buy villas in the suburbs and surrounding countryside. Most still chose to live among their own in the ten streets that made up the town's Jewish quarter. Here, as elsewhere in Livorno, the buildings were tall and cheerfully painted. "Four, five, yes some even six, seven stories high," they blocked out the bright Tuscan sunlight so that the narrow streets below remained cool and shady. In just such a house opposite the synagogue in the Via Reale, a son was born to a young Jewish couple from England on October 24, 1784. Joseph Elias and Rachel Montefiore had been married for barely a year. The boy was their first child, and, in keeping with Sephardi custom, they called him Moses Haim after his paternal grandfather, Moses Vita (Haim) Montefiore—a native of Livorno who had left for England some thirty years earlier.[11]

The Montefiores were an old Italian Jewish family who had married into the Sephardi diaspora.[12] Italian Jews customarily took the name of the town from which they came, and the Montefiores were no exception. Probably they lived at some point in the northern Italian hill town of Montefiore Conca, whence they took the rampant lion and palm tree *(fiore)* that figure in an early coat of arms.[13] They may even have passed through Montefiore dell'Asso, with its charming views of the Adriatic. Either way, by the mid-fifteenth century they had moved on, via Ravenna, to Pesaro, acting as bankers to the dukes of Malatesta in the 1460s. When the popes took over, the Montefiores resettled in Rimini, where they stayed for nearly 150 years. Some then moved to Ancona, where in 1630 one Leone Montefiore gave a curtain, embroidered by his wife Rachel, to hang before the ark in the synagogue.[14] By the late seventeenth century, members of the Ancona branch of the Montefiore family had already settled in Livorno.[15] In about 1690 a prosperous merchant, Isaac Vita Montefiore, took his nephew Judah from Ancona into business with him. Judah married a member of the wealthy Medina family, and they had four children. The eldest, Moses Vita Montefiore, was born in Livorno in 1712.

After 1715 Livorno faced growing competition from other Mediterranean ports. By the middle years of the century, it was experiencing a structural crisis.[16] It is hardly surprising, then, that a young, enterprising Jewish merchant like Moses Vita Montefiore contemplated moving elsewhere. At a time when between half and two-thirds of all ships arriving in Livorno were British, London was the obvious place for him to go.[17]

Like Livorno, London was a major center for the Sephardi diaspora. Just as *la Livornina* had attracted the secret Jews of Spain and Portugal, so the readmission of Jews to England in 1656 encouraged *conversos* to settle in London. Here they could live undisturbed by the discriminatory legal and social structures established in most European countries to constrain and control the Jewish community. But though free, they were not necessarily welcome. In 1753 attempts to facilitate the naturalization process for foreign-born Jewish merchants like Moses Vita provoked loud opposition and revealed deep-rooted fears about the Jewish presence. The motives behind this outcry may have been political and economic, but the prejudices it revealed were religious.[18]

Perhaps as a result, the Sephardim remained cosmopolitan, with relatives in ports throughout the Mediterranean and even across the Atlantic. Jewish family ties were, quite literally, the lifeblood of early capitalism, and the Western Sephardi diaspora became pioneers of international trade. In an age without a developed banking system, Jewish merchants knew they could rely on their relatives, friends, and business partners overseas. If necessary, they could even appeal for justice in Jewish courts. And so Jewish businessmen played a central role in commerce between London and Livorno, dominating the trade in coral and diamonds that ran between Livorno, London, and India.[19]

This network made life easier for Moses Vita when he arrived in London. In the early 1740s he began to establish contacts there—no doubt building on his relationship with the fabulously wealthy financier, Sir Solomon de Medina.[20] By 1744 Moses Vita had already joined the Spanish and Portuguese synagogue at Bevis Marks. But it is not until 1754 that we find him permanently established in Philpot Lane, Fenchurch Street.[21] He had married Esther Racah, the daughter of a Moorish merchant, before leaving Livorno. In 1760 Moses Vita was prosperous enough to be included among the 800 merchants who presented loyal addresses to George III on his accession, on which glorious occasion he was allowed to kiss the king's hand.

It is likely that Moses Vita's move to London was part of a wider family strategy. His brother Joseph already lived there, and two more brothers, David and Eliezer, subsequently followed.[22] Another cousin, Jeuda di Moise Montefiore, settled briefly in London.[23] Almost certainly, the Montefiores of London continued to work closely with the Montefiores of Livorno. In 1755 Moses Vita was active in the coral-diamond trade—possibly in partnership with his brother-in-law Moise Haim Racah, a coral merchant based in Livorno.[24] Moses Vita also imported other Italian commodities. Conversely, by 1790 trade with London dominated the affairs of Lazzero Montefiore of Livorno, although he retained business interests in Dublin, Tripoli, Smyrna (Izmir), Sicily, Genoa, and Ancona.[25]

The two branches of the Montefiore family kept in regular contact. In the next generation their business ties were cemented by several marriages—designed, among other things, to keep the money in the family. Judah Montefiore, the eldest of Moses Vita's seventeen children, was born and bred in Livorno. He subsequently married his first cousin Reina, daughter of Moses Vita's brother Eliezer, who was now based in London. In 1782 Reina accompanied Moses Vita's son Samuel and daughter Jayley to Livorno, where Samuel was due to marry his cousin Esther Montefiore and Jayley to marry another cousin, Massahod Montefiore.[26] On their arrival, Samuel, Jayley, and Reina were greeted by Samuel's younger brother Joseph Elias, who may well have been acting as his father's agent.[27] Joseph had been born in 1759 and was now in his early twenties. He returned with Samuel and Esther to England a few months later, before setting out once more for Livorno, this time accompanied by his young, pregnant bride Rachel and her sixteen-year-old brother, Moses Mocatta. Here they stayed with Joseph's maternal uncle Moise Racah; it was an unpretentious house, small but with a good garden.[28]

These sea journeys were not to be taken lightly. In a diary he kept on the way to Livorno in 1783, Samuel Montefiore described the daily rigors of storm and seasickness, regularly punctuated by Jayley's faints and Reina's prolonged fits of hysterics. The voyage culminated in a devastating encounter with a small whirlwind shortly before they arrived in Livorno, during which the tiller ropes broke and poor Samuel was "knocked about like a ball from one side of the Cabbin to another."[29] For Joseph and Rachel traveling back to London with baby Moses, it must have been even worse—not least because Rachel refused to hand Moses over to a wet nurse and insisted on keeping kosher throughout the journey.

She subsequently recalled that Moses had been "a beautiful, strong, and very tall child, but yet on our return journey to England, during a severe winter, I was unwilling to entrust him to a stranger; I myself acted as his nurse, and many and many a time I felt the greatest discomfort through not having more than a cup of coffee, bread and butter, and a few eggs for my diet . . . No meat of any description . . . passed my lips; my husband and myself being strict observers of the Scriptural injunctions as to diet." But Moses thrived, and she considered her sufferings amply repaid. "What I thought a great privation, in no way affected the state of my health, nor that of the child; and I feel at present the greatest satisfaction on account of my having strictly adhered to that which I thought right."[30]

Rachel was clearly a woman of character. She withstood the rigors of a long sea journey rather better than her sisters-in-law, and she prided herself on fulfilling what she saw as her religious duty. Her portraits show a woman not particularly pretty: solidly built, with a warm and intelligent twinkle in her eye, which in later years matured into a gaze of tolerant affection. In the context of late eighteenth-century Jewish London, however, she had more than a touch of class.

Rachel Montefiore was descended from two of England's oldest Jewish families.[31] Her father's family, the Mocattas, claimed to have arrived in Spain as early as the eighth century. After the expulsion of 1492, they lived for some time as *conversos* before settling in the Jewish communities of Venice and Amsterdam. In the seventeenth century, the Amsterdam Mocattas were among the first to leave for England. The original Moses Mocatta came to London sometime between 1656 and 1671.

These new Jewish arrivals from Amsterdam were soon followed by other Sephardim from the West Indies, and by New Christians from France and the Iberian Peninsula and its colonies.[32] They established a synagogue and in 1663 drew up statutes for the congregation. These reflected the insecure position of early Jewish immigrants and the difficulties of establishing congregational structures in a city where there were no precedents, and where many Jews were recent *conversos* unused to the disciplines of Jewish communal life.

There were barely 500 Sephardim in London at the end of the seventeenth century.[33] By this time they had been joined by Jews of German origin from Holland, Poland, and the Holy Roman Empire, known as Ashkenazim. In the 1750s, when Moses Vita Montefiore settled in London, there were roughly 2,000 Sephardim in England, compared with about 6,000 Ashkenazim.[34] Yet throughout the eighteenth century, almost all the really wealthy and powerful Jews in London came from the Spanish and Portuguese community and (if they were religious) attended its synagogue in Bevis Marks. Most of the wealthier Sephardim were financiers and merchants, trading with the help of friends and relatives scattered across Europe and the New World.

In 1710 Abraham Mocatta, the younger of Moses Mocatta's two sons, became one of the twelve Jews officially allowed to operate as brokers on the Stock Exchange. He was a successful merchant, specializing in precious metal broking and, in 1735, was appointed permanent broker to the East India Company.[35] By the 1740s he was already selling more silver to the East India Company than any of his Jewish rivals, and possibly acted as broker when it purchased large amounts of silver from the Bank of England. During the rebellion led by Bonnie Prince Charlie in 1745, Abraham Mocatta joined with other prominent London merchants in a deputation to George II, assuring him of their support. Abraham had no sons, but his daughters made good marriages. In 1749 he resigned his brokership to his grandson, Abraham Lumbrozo de Mattos, and took the boy into business with him. When Abraham the elder died in 1751, Abraham the younger took his name, becoming Abraham Lumbrozo de Mattos Mocatta: father of Rachel and grandfather of Moses Montefiore.

This Abraham was only eighteen when he took over the family firm, but he rapidly rebuilt his grandfather's business empire. In 1759 he married the wealthy Esther Lamego, who brought him a dowry of £5,000—well over £600,000 by today's standards, although life was cheaper then.[36] A year later Abraham entered into partnership with Alexander Isaac Keyser, an Ashkenazi Jew. Mocatta & Keyser became key players in the London precious metals market. During the first five years of their partnership, the East India Company bought almost all its silver from the firm. When Alexander Keyser died in 1779, Abraham took another Ashkenazi partner, Asher Goldsmid. By 1790 the new firm of Mocatta & Goldsmid was selling silver to the East India Company worth several hundred thousand pounds. When he died in 1800, Abraham Mocatta left £150,000—today he would have been a multimillionaire several times over.[37]

Precious metal brokers in London like Abraham Mocatta functioned as the connecting link between the various branches of British trade in precious metals with the Iberian Peninsula, the Spanish and Portuguese colonies of South America, the precious metal market in Amsterdam, and those countries to which Britain exported silver and gold, notably India, the Baltic, and the Levant. Crucially, they mediated between importers of precious metals from the Western Hemisphere (often Sephardim) and merchants trading in bills of exchange and precious metals between London and Amsterdam, who tended to be Ashkenazim. Abraham Mocatta's choice of business partners enabled his firm to straddle the two sides of this process. It was a farsighted decision at a time when relations between Sephardi and Ashkenazi Jews in London were far from friendly.

The Sephardim regarded themselves as the elite of London's Jewish community. As late as 1772 the Mahamad, as their governing body was called, refused permission for a Sephardi-Ashkenazi marriage in Bevis Marks. On other occasions the Mahamad allowed such marriages but referred to the bride simply as *Tudesca* (German).[38] There was more to this designation than pride in their status as firstcomers; in fact it reflected profound cultural contempt. The Sephardim of London came largely from families that had lived as Christians for decades if not centuries—at once rejected by and assimilated into the gentile society of the Iberian Peninsula. When they arrived in ports like Amsterdam and London to reintegrate into Jewish society, they found they had relatively little in common with the historically segregated Ashkenazi Jews of northern Europe.[39] Put crudely: for many Sephardim, Judaism was a religion; for the Ashkenazim it remained an all-embracing way of life. Only in the second half of the eighteenth century did this dichotomy begin to break down, with the emergence of an acculturated Ashkenazi elite in cities like London, Amsterdam, and Berlin.

The fact that the English Sephardim tended to be wealthier than their Ashkenazi brethren added an element of snobbery to the relationship. Not all Sephardi Jews were rich merchants. In 1800 only about half the Sephardim in London could afford to pay any kind of synagogue membership fee. Equally, not all Ashkenazim were immigrant pawnbrokers or peddlers, speaking in broken English and dealing in old clothes, secondhand watches, and—more disreputably—stolen goods. London's Ashkenazi community inevitably boasted a growing elite of merchants, gem dealers, stockbrokers, and loan contractors. Still, there was enough truth in the stereotype to feed prejudices.

The contrast between the two communities made a vivid impression on Johann Wilhelm von Archenholz, a Prussian who visited England in the 1780s. Archenholz declared himself "astonished at the prodigious difference between the Portuguese and German Jews . . . Dress, language, manners, cleanliness, are all in favour of the former, who indeed can scarcely be distinguished from Christians. This extends even to their prejudices and their publick worship: the features peculiar to the whole race are the only peculiarity they have in common." The German Jews, however, appeared to him "the very refuse of human nature . . . All the children of Israel, who are obliged to quit Holland and Germany, take refuge in England, where they live by roguery; if they themselves do not steal, they at least help to conceal and to dispose of the plunder."[40]

As Archenholz noted, rich Sephardim like the Mocattas rapidly adopted a comfortably English way of life. They played cards in coffee-houses, attended the theater and the opera, visited fashionable resorts like Brighton, and purchased lavish country estates.[41] Over time, the Ashkenazim began to do the same, causing Chief Rabbi Hart Lyon to lament the moral decay of eighteenth century Anglo-Jewry: "All our endeavours are to associate with the Gentiles and to be like them . . . the women wear wigs and the young ones go even further and wear décolleté dresses open two spans low in front and back. Their whole aim is not to appear like daughters of Israel . . . We see that [our neighbors] live happily, that their commerce dominates the world, and we want to be like them, dress as they dress, talk as they talk, and want to make everybody forget that we are Jews."[42]

Lyon was right to be alarmed. As a result of this behavior, some Jews disappeared into English society altogether. Assimilation was particularly rife among wealthy Sephardi financiers, for whom conversion had always been the final barrier to total social acceptance.[43] Assimilation caused the number of Jewish marriages held in the Spanish and Portuguese synagogue to plummet by 43 percent between 1740 and 1800, despite the continued influx of newcomers like the Montefiores.[44]

As the daughter of Abraham Lumbrozo de Mattos Mocatta, Rachel Montefiore belonged to this wealthy and acculturated milieu. But as we have seen, she was far from assimilated, and her portraits suggest that she dressed modestly. Since Rachel was barely twenty when she returned from Livorno, her determined Jewish observance probably reflected a religious background. Both the observance and the background were things she shared with her husband. Very little survives relating to the life of Joseph Elias Montefiore, but we do have a certificate confirming his competence as a ritual slaughterer of poultry.[45] Presumably Joseph found this necessary in order to keep kosher while traveling on business.

As early as 1777, then, Joseph Montefiore had already settled on his path in life as a merchant specializing in Italian goods, notably Carrara

marbles and Livorno straw hats.[46] Years later Rachel Montefiore recalled: "When I first went to Marseilles & Leghorn [Livorno] I had the
pleasure to see your dear Father so much esteemed & welcomed by all
that knew him & had transacted business with him."[47] From this, it
would seem that in these early years Joseph was a regular visitor in both
places, and probably in other Mediterranean ports as well.

Joseph's marriage to the wealthy and well-connected Rachel must
have helped him considerably. It may also reflect a business relationship
between Moses Vita Montefiore and Abraham Lumbrozo de Mattos
Mocatta. Links between the two families were cemented shortly afterward by a marriage between Rachel's sister Grace and Joseph's recently
widowed brother Samuel. Rachel's own marriage settlement was generous, but not sensationally so.[48] Her dowry consisted of £1,500, of which
£1,000 was to be settled on her and her children and the remainder
made available for Joseph's use. In addition to this, Rachel's father gave
Joseph £200, and Joseph's father gave him £300 on the day of the wedding. Finally, Rachel could expect to receive a share of her grandfather
Isaac Lamego's estate upon the death of her mother. She subsequently
inherited £8,000 upon her father's death in 1800.[49]

At first things seem to have gone well for the couple. In the 1790s Joseph felt able to commission a family portrait. Awkwardly painted, it
shows him as a slightly stout paterfamilias, seated confidently with his
legs akimbo, one arm around his eldest son. Rachel is all ostentation
in blue silk, a bouffant wig and an overelaborate bonnet; her two little
girls are dressed to match. The younger of the two boys has a slightly
truculent expression, but Moses looks out at us curiously, his elbow
resting on an open book. The furniture is sparse but elegant. A portrait
hanging above the family gestures toward their respectable past.

The war and upheaval caused by the French Revolution render this
snapshot of Georgian prosperity a little misleading. In the mid-1790s
Joseph traded both on his own and in partnership with one of the Mocattas, but if he dealt heavily in Livorno straw hats, Joseph must have
struggled to cope with the decline in their popularity: imports plunged
from 15,972 dozen in 1782 to 1,602 dozen in 1800. Yet the communal
accounts at Bevis Marks suggest that Joseph's income increased fairly
steadily during this period. In 1788 his income-related synagogue membership fee, known as *finta*, was assessed at £1; in 1791, it rose to £1
10s; in 1794 it rose to £2, falling a little in 1797 to £1 6s 8d, before rising to £3 in 1800.[50] This last increase placed Joseph comfortably in the
upper half of fee-paying members; on his death in 1804 he left between
£9,000 and £10,000.[51] Although this paled beside the fortune left by
his father-in-law, it still represented a respectable £650,000 in today's

Mr. and Mrs. Joseph Elias Montefiore and four of their children, from a
pastel by R. Jelgerhuis. Moses is standing next to his father. (Courtesy of
the Montefiore Endowment, University College London Library Services, Special
Collections)

money. When we consider that as late as 1839 only 14 percent of all
adult males left property worth £20 or more, it is clear that Joseph was
comfortably off.[52]

Rachel's fond memories suggest that the Montefiores had a happy
marriage. The names they gave their children tell us something of their
shared values. Moses, Esther, Abraham, Sarah, Abigail, Rebecca, the
first six, were traditionally biblical; Justina, the next born, was perhaps
a loose translation from the Hebrew; Horatio, the youngest, was named
after Nelson and his sensational victory on the Nile. Perhaps with time
the Montefiores began to feel a little less Jewish and a little more British;
perhaps they were merely swept up in the patriotic fever of 1798. Either
way, they provided a warm and affectionate home for their three sons
and five daughters. The family lived at a number of addresses in the City

before moving in 1800 to 3 Kennington Terrace, Vauxhall—down the road from Rachel's brother Moses.[53]

Tragedy struck two years later when careless sixteen-year-old Esther allowed her dress to catch fire. We do not know how quickly she died or if any of her family witnessed the horrific accident. Joseph certainly never recovered. Moses later recalled that his father had been "of a most cheerful disposition, but after he had the misfortune to lose one of his daughters at a fire which occurred in his house, he was never seen to smile."[54] For Moses, too, Esther's death must have been devastating: she was nearest to him in age, and they probably shared the sense of responsibility common to older children in large families.

Rachel was close to all her children, but Moses appears to have been her favorite. In 1823 she wrote to him: "I shall only be looking forward like a child for the future pleasure [of seeing you] as every hour that I have spent with you has been the happiest of my life."[55] Tellingly, Moses was the only one of her children to be mentioned by name in a letter she wrote shortly before her death, addressed to "my dear Sir Moses & all my dear children." After expressing love, gratitude, and a pious hope that they would meet again in the world to come, Rachel added the following postscript: "My dear Moses Believe me your presence has always given me the pleasure next to that of an Angel & I am grateful for every hour that I have enjoyed of your society."[56]

What else we know about Moses Montefiore's childhood and upbringing relies on the secondhand accounts of his official biographer, Lucien Wolf, and his collaborator Louis Loewe.[57] His parents apparently sent him to a small private school, where he learned useful business skills: reading, writing, arithmetic, and probably French—which he continued to study in later life, when his French was as good as (if not better than) that of his more conventionally well-educated wife, Judith.[58] But both Loewe and Wolf are more interested in the moral development and Jewish feeling of the young Moses than in his practical education. Loewe tells us that "[a]fter he had completed his elementary studies, he . . . began to evince a great desire to cultivate his mind, independently of his class lessons. He was observed to copy short moral sentences from books falling into his hands, or interesting accounts of important events, which he endeavoured to commit to memory."[59] This was the beginning of a lifelong habit: as an adult Montefiore also peppered his diaries with religious quotations and moral exhortations.

Wolf, meanwhile, stresses the inspirational influence of his father's brother Joshua Montefiore and his mother's brother Moses Mocatta. From the former, Moses derived a passion for travel and adventure;

from the latter, a love of his people. Moses Mocatta was a Jewish scholar of some distinction, and it is highly likely that the Montefiore children received their religious education at his hands. Moses, however, seems to have emerged with little Hebrew and no Talmud.[60] Probably the young Moses identified with his biblical namesake. Like many other Jewish boys of the same name, he must have thrilled to hear about the Exodus from Egypt and the revelation on Mount Sinai; perhaps it gave him a stronger sense of Jewish destiny and moral purpose.

The role that Wolf attributes to his other uncle is rather more credible. Throughout his life, Moses apparently retained "a vivid recollection of his dashing 'Uncle Josh,' whose laced red coat and pigtail, and cocked hat and sword, together with his fund of tremendous anecdote, rendered him a huge favourite with his nephews."[61] The adventurous Joshua Montefiore was exactly the kind of man likely to capture the imagination of his young nephew. He was one of the few survivors of a disastrous expedition to settle the island of Bolama, off the coast of West Africa, during which some settlers were hacked to pieces by enraged tribesmen and most of the rest died of fever.[62] Nothing is more probable than that on his return Joshua regaled his nephews with colorful tales of his encounters with native Kings, brutal Portuguese colonizers, and exotic wildlife.

By focusing on these English uncles, Wolf underplays the wider importance of Montefiore's international family network in shaping his worldview. A hundred years after his birth, *The Times* would declare: "he has been the victorious defender of persecuted Jews because he was the perfect English gentleman."[63] In terms of his background, nothing could be further from the truth. On his mother's side, Moses may have had deep roots in Anglo-Jewish society, but he was also the son of a second-generation Italian immigrant. He himself was born in Italy—not by chance, but because his family retained close ties with their Italian relatives and his father traveled extensively there on business.

Moses' uncles and aunts were scattered across the Western Hemisphere.[64] Joseph Montefiore's brother Judah and sister Jayley remained in Livorno, while another sister, Sarah, married Abraham Israel of Gibraltar in 1776. Two of Joseph's brothers, Eliezer and Jacob Montefiore, settled in Barbados—although Eliezer returned to London in 1813. Two of Joseph's sisters, Reyna and Rachel, married Jews from the West Indies. Even Moses' unmarried aunt Lydia Montefiore ended up in Marseilles, presumably because she had relatives there.[65] We cannot know how much contact there was among various members of the Montefiore family, but Joseph almost certainly corresponded with his brothers and sisters overseas, and some probably visited him and his growing family.

The young Moses belonged to the cosmopolitan world of London's Sephardi community. For all their anglicized airs and graces, the Spanish and Portuguese Jews' Congregation remained foreign in certain key respects. Tellingly, they continued to conduct their official business in Portuguese, although many spoke Italian or Judeo-Spanish, and some Arabic. As a child attending the synagogue in Bevis Marks, he would have been familiar with the Turkish-style dress of Moroccan peddlers, or the turban and robes of North African scholars.[66]

Rachel and Joseph spoke English to one another, yet both parents nurtured in Moses a strong awareness of his Italian origins and the ties of affection linking him to relatives overseas. In the only surviving letter to his Livornese uncle and godfather, Moise Racah, the nine-year-old Moses wrote: "I should not have so long delayed writing you had it [sic] not been hoping to do it in a language [Italian?] that would save the troble of an Interpreter, but as yet am not able, for many times have I ardently whished to return You & dear Aunt that Gratitude, which Your Kindness to me in my infancy demands & which my dear Father & Mother have often told me was in the Extreme . . . I hope in God after I have gone through my Studies to Embrace & thank you & dear Aunt in Person."[67]

Even at this tender age, Moses understood that he belonged to an international network and took it for granted that travel—at least as far as Italy—would play a part in his adult life. This cosmopolitan orientation was his birthright as a Montefiore and a child of the Sephardi diaspora.

Montefiore's immediate family background in London and Livorno added an important element to this heritage. Both were port cities in which Jews could lead lives relatively free of discrimination and oppressive legislation.[68] Theirs was a situation of almost unique privilege. Jews in the United States and in British colonies, like the West Indies, were treated as equal citizens, but in the Old World there were very few places—perhaps only Amsterdam—where Jews were as comfortably off as they were in London and Livorno. Moses Montefiore inevitably had quite different expectations of life and a wholly different understanding of the place of Jews in society from those he would have acquired growing up in the ghettos and shtetls of Germany and eastern Europe, or living as a Jew in the lands of Islam under the Pact of Umar.

Chapter 2

Making a Fortune

Few things better capture the unusual flavor of Montefiore's social experience at this stage in his life than the grand reception held near the little village of Roehampton to mark Nelson's victory at Trafalgar. This charming spot in rural Surrey was the site of Benjamin Goldsmid's country mansion. He and his brother Abraham dominated the money markets between 1797 and 1810, when the government financed Britain's wars with France through the issue of some £400 million worth of bonds, known as Exchequer Bills.[1] The Bank of England advanced about £70 million directly, and the Goldsmids handled most of the rest. They were fabulously wealthy and lived accordingly.

Benjamin had rebuilt the house from scratch "on a scale of magnificence and beauty equal to any Nobleman's country seat." In blunt terms, it was overdone. There were thirty well-furbished bedrooms; a red morocco-leather breakfast room replete with chandelier, gilt cornices, and family portraits; a grand staircase "ornamented with Bronze Figures"; and a marble vestibule decorated with Corinthian pillars, opening onto a large terrace with a splendidly landscaped view. But Benjamin was not ashamed of his Jewish origins. Besides "a choice and tremendous collection of the most famous Roman and English Classics," his library featured the Torah scroll that he and his family used for prayer.[2]

In these lavish surroundings, Benjamin was in the habit of entertaining largely. His victory celebrations after the battles of Aboukir and Trafalgar were second to none. Here, the "first characters of distinction in this Kingdom" mingled with friends and family, enjoying music and dancing, masques and fireworks, as an army of servants plied them with rare kosher meats, exotic fruits, and fine wine. Young and on the make, the twenty-year-old Montefiore was apparently "a frequent guest at the palatial residences of the Goldsmids," whose third brother, Asher, was the business partner of his Mocatta relatives.[3] So it is safe to assume that Montefiore was also at Roehampton for the Trafalgar celebrations of 1805, enjoying the sensational hospitality and recalling sentimentally his own encounter with the national hero.

The house that Nelson shared with his lover Emma Hamilton during his last periods of shore leave was close to Abraham Goldsmid's country home in Surrey. Emma used to sing and make music with the refined Goldsmid daughters, and the couple often visited Abraham at Morden Hall. We know that on at least one occasion Nelson also dined with Asher, when it fell to Montefiore to sing the long Jewish Grace after Meals.[4] With printshops filled with images of "Noble Nelson" and crowds mobbing the admiral whenever he ventured into London, singing the grace was a signal honor. To a young man from a family of Nelson enthusiasts, it must have been thrilling.

The early 1800s were make-or-break years for Montefiore. He began his career the hard way, working for a wholesale tea merchant and grocer in Kennington before transferring to a countinghouse in the City.[5] The hours were late, and in later life Montefiore often spoke of how hard he worked in these early days. Sometimes he "had to take letters to the post on the stroke of midnight. There were no copying machines, and all letters had to be copied by hand. He also spoke of the great distance he had to walk every night from the city to Kennington Terrace, during the cold winter months as well as in the summer time."[6] But things could have been much worse; for Rachel made sure that Montefiore always had something tasty to eat upon his return, when he regularly astonished her with his "onslaughts upon cold boiled beef—his favorite dish as long as he lived—after fifteen hours work and a six mile walk."[7] Besides, with his international connections and rich relations Montefiore cannot have expected to spend his career as an anonymous countinghouse clerk.

He could hardly have chosen a more exciting moment to enter the world of high finance. In the eighteenth century, Britain had developed the most efficient financial system in the world to fund an increasingly global military presence. This relied upon a combination of relatively cheap and centralized tax collection, parliamentary control of the budget, a stable system of public borrowing through funded national debt, and a monetary system centering upon the Bank of England's guaranteed convertibility of notes into gold. After the French Revolution in 1789, however, public expenditure to fund expanding British military commitments grew inexorably. It rose from £18 million a year in 1793 to £100 million a year in 1815, and the national debt soared from £240 million to £900 million by the end of the Napoleonic era. In 1797 the

Bank of England was forced to suspend payments, putting an end to the gold standard and prompting serious inflation.

These developments created new opportunities for men who knew how to exploit them.[8] While Britain's European rivals struggled to cope with the impact of wars fought all over the Continent, City merchants quietly increased their share of global trade.[9] War made for an atmosphere of intense excitement, patriotism, and uncertainty as the City waited with bated breath for news of victories and setbacks. This mood encouraged unprecedented financial activity, accompanied by general instability in the money markets and a sharp rise in bankruptcies.[10] It was an era when fortunes were made and lost on the Stock Exchange as never before.

After a short period working as a clerk, Montefiore opted to follow his rich connections into the City. In 1803 he became a member of the London Stock Exchange with the support of Thomas J. Ellis, Jos. Pulley, and his uncle Moses Mocatta.[11] In theory, stockbrokers needed a license granted by the Court of Mayor and Aldermen.[12] Some 700 licensed brokers operated on the Stock Exchange, but the number of Jews was limited to 12. In practice, there was no penalty for acting as an unlicensed broker, and about two-thirds of all brokers did so—partly because it was cheaper but also because it gave them greater latitude. Most acted as principals as well. A relatively high proportion were Jews, and Montefiore was one of them.[13] He seems also to have taken on other kinds of business, enrolling as a Lloyds underwriter in 1803.[14]

Montefiore was still finding his feet when his father died a year later. With four unmarried sisters and two younger brothers, Montefiore was now head of a large family. No doubt his inheritance came in useful, but the loss of Joseph so soon after Esther's appalling death must have been a hard blow for all of them. Rachel in particular may have struggled to cope. As the firstborn Montefiore probably supported his mother emotionally in this difficult period. Their closeness during her early widowhood probably does much to explain the depth of her attachment to her eldest son. Rachel's brother, Moses Mocatta, had already sponsored Montefiore's entrée into the business world; he now took the young man under his wing in other ways.

Montefiore started out doing business in John's Coffee House, but from 1805 until at least 1809 he was working from Grigsby's, where Mocatta & Goldsmid also operated.[15] Coffeehouses like John's and Grigsby's played a vital role in London's economy. They supplied their clients with newspapers, a meeting point in which to conduct business transactions, and an opportunity to mix with others in the same line of trade. One visitor to London in the 1790s was moved to comment that the English lived "in a very remarkable manner. They rise late and spend most of the morning, either in walking about town or sitting in the coffee-houses. There they not only read the newspapers but transact business. Associations, insurances, bets, the trade in foreign bills; all these things are not only talked of, but executed in these public places . . . An English coffee-house has no resemblance to a French or German one. You neither see billiards nor backgammon tables; you do not even hear the least noise; everybody speaks in a low tone for fear of disturbing the company."[16]

We should picture Montefiore in these early years moving between the hushed seriousness of Grigsby's and the more chaotic atmosphere of the Stock Exchange. Here clerks perched in the upstairs gallery overlooking the fray—and occasionally dropped things on the unsuspecting brokers below, shouting and swearing six to the dozen as they fought their way through the crowd. The uproar was, by all accounts, tremendous: "Tickets—Tickets—South-Sea Stock for the opening—Navy-bills—Bank Stock for the rescounters—Long Annuities—(*here the waiter calls* Chance—Chance—Chance—*Mr. Chance is not here, Sir he is over at his office*—Here Tickets for August—Omnium gatherum for September— Scrip for the third payment—3 per Cent consolidated, gentlemen—Here Mr. Full *(whispers a friend, but is overheard)* they are all BULLS by G-d, but I'll be d-d if they have any of my Stock, I'll go to Bath, and not come near them till the rescounters—Here Bank Circulation, who buys Bank Circulation . . ."[17]

Montefiore showed a flair for business; soon he was dealing in large sums. But only three years after joining the Stock Exchange his business collapsed, when he fell victim to a massive fraud perpetrated by Elkin Daniels.[18] Montefiore's losses amounted to £30,000—the equivalent of nearly £2 million in today's money.[19] The General Purposes Committee of the Stock Exchange considered the incident a "Matter of great Importance" and discussed it three times between October 1806 and January 1807.[20] It would take him ten years to pay off the debt in full.[21]

This was an almost crushing blow. Still smarting decades later, Montefiore regularly noted in his diary the anniversary of the day when Daniels "robbed me of all and more than I had. Blessed be the Almighty, that He has not suffered my enemies to triumph over me."[22] His family responsibilities added to his worries, but Montefiore's reputation and credit seem to have remained intact: the General Purposes Committee would eventually conclude that his conduct did him "great honour."[23] Montefiore also recovered surprisingly quickly. Less than six years later, he took an office at 9 Birchin Lane and began to issue a rule book—both indications of greater stability.[24] Together with his uncle Moses Mocatta,

Montefiore recommended his younger brother Abraham for membership in the Stock Exchange that year, and in April the two founded a
partnership under the name of Montefiore Brothers.[25]

Abraham was some four years younger than Montefiore. Like all
brothers, they must have fought and laughed their way through childhood, their endless squabbles masking a profound familiarity. But by
1812 Abraham was the black sheep of the family; he had married the
daughter of a Christian stockbroker in a scandalous runaway match.
Rachel's staunch religious observance makes her distress easy to imagine, although intermarriage and apostasy were by no means unheard of
in their elite Jewish circle.[26] Cut off by his Jewish relatives and friends in
a world in which connections were everything, Abraham faced disaster.

His native ability may have been sufficient to pull him through. Lucien
Wolf's centennial biography tells us that Abraham had already realized
a small fortune in the silk trade before joining forces with Montefiore.[27]
This is certainly possible, for Abraham was a remarkably driven man
with a real appetite and talent for business. As late as 1823, when his
energies were already undermined by ill health, Rachel complained that
she had not seen her son for some time; "such a house of Business as he
is in where every room is occupied with it I cannot but think the visits of
an Old Woman must be intruding."[28] Elsewhere, however, Wolf suggests
that things went badly for Abraham. Indeed, in a later article Wolf
claimed that Abraham and his wife were "almost starving in obscure
lodgings in Islington" when Montefiore sought them out and "despite
the frowns of the world" took his errant younger brother into business
with him.[29] That the partnership was part of a wider reconciliation between Abraham and his Jewish circle testifies to Montefiore's personal
standing within the community. Perhaps Abraham's wife eventually underwent some form of conversion; more probably she died.[30] Her daughter would eventually convert and marry a Jewish cousin, while the firm
of Montefiore Brothers flourished.[31]

The year 1812 also marked Montefiore's marriage to Judith Barent-
Cohen, the daughter of a wealthy Ashkenazi merchant.[32] The union
proved a stroke of luck in more ways than one: Judith's brother-in-law
was none other than the up-and-coming Nathan Rothschild. Montefiore's marriage is customarily viewed as the turning point in his recovery from the catastrophe of 1806. In fact he must have been pretty well
established to make the marriage in the first place. When Rothschild
asked to marry Judith's sister Hannah in 1806, her father, Levi, made
certain that his future son-in-law owned at least £10,000, and insisted

on a thorough examination of his books. "If, instead of giving me one of your daughters, you could give me all, it would be the best stroke of business you had ever done," the exasperated Rothschild is said to have replied.[33]

Levi was dead now, but if Judith's relatives had regarded Montefiore as a bad prospect they would never have permitted the marriage. Hannah married Rothschild with a settlement of £3,248 14s 6d, and Judith brought Moses nearly as much, having been left £3,200 in her father's will.[34] This was serious money. Nice Jewish girls like Judith and Hannah did not throw themselves away. Bevis Marks membership records indicate that Montefiore had indeed turned the corner financially by 1812. In August 1806 he was assessed to pay a very low *finta* of only 16s 8d, but by August 1809 this had risen to £1 16s 8d, and by September 1811 to £3 3s 4d—placing him just in the upper half of *finta*-paying members.[35] By 1812 he very probably did have the required £10,000.

The Barent-Cohens belonged to London's Ashkenazi elite and were well networked with leading families like the Goldsmids, many of whom shared their Dutch background. Sephardi-Ashkenazi marriages were still rare, but they no longer carried quite the frisson attached to them thirty years earlier.[36] For Montefiore and Judith, with their family ties to both sides of the Mocatta-Goldsmid business nexus, the social and financial benefits of a "mixed" marriage should have been obvious. Montefiore, for one, was eager to cultivate this extended network. Many of his Sephardi relatives had been Freemasons, but he now chose to join the Moira Lodge, a stronghold of Ashkenazi Jews, into which his brother-in-law Rothschild had been initiated a decade earlier.[37]

Marriage in such circles was always about money and connections. Montefiore and Judith were fortunate that their union was underpinned by shared values and genuine affection. Both were in their late twenties, a nuptial age entirely usual among the British middle classes, who liked to be settled on a path in life before choosing a life partner.[38] Standing six feet three inches in his stocking feet, Montefiore had fine features, fashionably curling (reddish) hair, and an intelligent, somewhat calculating expression.[39] A portrait of the young couple suggests that Judith was considerably shorter. His height must have given him confidence, and there is a fondness in Montefiore's eyes as he gazes down at his young bride that is oddly touching; dressed in brilliant blue with a generous bosom, she looks admiring if a little hesitant. Two other portraits of Judith survive from this period. The first shows a very pretty woman with huge dark eyes set in a perfect, oval face, framed to pleasing effect by attractively tumbling black curls.[40] In the second, her face is longer and thinner, her eyes more thoughtful.[41]

Judith and Montefiore as a young couple, probably painted around the time of their marriage. (Courtesy of Robert Sebag-Montefiore; photograph by Lykke Stjernswärd)

Of course, there were cultural differences. Judith's father was a German speaker; Montefiore's spoke Italian. The Barent-Cohens must also have had greater pretensions to gentility; because Judith had received private lessons in English literature, music, singing, French, German and Italian.[42] None of these differences seems to have mattered much; the couple made a point of giving equally to Sephardi and Ashkenazi charities, and Montefiore used jokingly to refer to his oh-so-German wife as "my liebe Frau."[43] What perhaps mattered more was their shared life experience.

Judith was not the eldest child, but like Montefiore she had been forced into a position of family responsibility. Four years earlier she had shared the burden of nursing her father, Levi, during his final illness; once he died, Judith's redoubtable mother, Lydia, depended heavily on her daughter.[44] Judith apparently recognized in her husband a similar family feeling, commenting on her wedding day that Montefiore's "fraternal and filial affection gained in me an interest and solicitude for his welfare at a very early period of my acquaintance with him, which, joined to many other good qualities and attention towards me, ripened into a sincere ardent sentiment."[45]

In other ways, too, they had much in common. Like Montefiore, Judith had received a secular education, but she could also read and translate correctly the Hebrew language of her prayers and the weekly Torah portion read on Shabbat.[46] Like Montefiore, she had been brought up to honor her religious tradition. Levi was sufficiently orthodox to correspond with a learned rabbi in Prague about whether an observant Jew could open an umbrella on the Sabbath.[47] In her will, Lydia would urge her children to copy their father's example: "Now my dear children I have a grand point to say & as it is my last wish, I hope you will abide by it, as it is for all your good, which is, that I Beg & pray you to not to forget that you are Jews & keep your Religion, & always have in your memory your Father who is in Heaven & take example from him, then I am sure you all will be good, & the Almighty will bless you all."[48]

Judith, at least, did not disappoint her. On the first Friday night of her married life, she felt a pious sense of occasion at fulfilling her new duties as a Jewish wife. "[O]n lighting the candles in the evening with my mother, according to her wish and what is taught us, I experienced a new sensation of devotion and solicitude to act right. I trust that God Almighty will direct us how to perform that which is most pleasing to him. I do not know any circumstances more pleasing to me than to perceive that my dear Monte is religiously inclined."[49] She was, in short, delighted by her marriage. Whenever Montefiore spoke of their wedding day, he fondly remembered "how 'Judy'—as he always called her afterwards—told him 'she could not for her very life squeeze a tear out of her eye, though for appearance's sake she tried her best.'"[50] But Lydia found it harder to part with her daughter.

The newlyweds spent the first week of their married life in the bride's home. "We propose leaving Angel Court to-morrow, for Mrs. Montefiore's at Vauxhall," Judith wrote. "I do not know if my dear mother will permit us to leave her quite so soon. Whenever we do it will be a trial to me. The idea of leaving one's home and friends with whom one has been nurtured from infancy, brings reflections affecting and serious, but when again we reflect it is to go with such a friend as a husband we trust will prove, it becomes consoling." Judith's fears were justified. In the event, Lydia "would not suffer" the couple to leave, and they had to stay a few days longer than intended.[51]

Lydia's reluctance to let her daughter go must have caused tensions, but the couple spent a happy week rejoicing in their newfound domesticity with a tight-knit circle of relatives. The wedding itself had been celebrated in grand style with a dinner attended by some eighty or ninety people. It proved impossible to invite all Lydia's grandchildren to the party, so Judith and Moses spent the next day playing with their nephews and nieces, before taking dinner with "all our sisters and a few select friends." On Saturday, Mr. and Mrs. Moses Montefiore proudly attended synagogue together for the first time, accompanied by close relatives from both families. There they "said our prayers most fervently" before returning home to receive a string of congratulatory morning visitors. It was, Judith felt, "a very happy day. Thank God!"[52]

Montefiore's marriage to Judith came at a crucial time in his business

career. Within days of their wedding, Judith noted in her diary: "The
Loan being contracted for this morning, my dear husband was induced
to attend to business, as he is greatly concerned at such a period, although it is rather unusual to attend to business within seven days after
marriage. However, as this is a matter of consequence, he was perfectly
right."[53] Shortly afterward the couple set off to spend a few days in the
country, but Montefiore's mind was elsewhere. After dutifully admiring
Canterbury cathedral and visiting the sights in various south coast resorts, he cut the honeymoon short. Judith proved understanding: "My
Monte discreetly has made up his mind not to prolong our excursion, as
his business is going on rather briskly, and consequently he wishes to be
on the spot, being more anxious now than ever in this respect."[54]

All this indicates that Montefiore was doing pretty well financially, but
he soon began to do even better. The dramatic improvement in his affairs owed a great deal to his new brother-in-law, Nathan Mayer Rothschild. Rothschild corresponded regularly with his brothers on the Continent, Amschel, Salomon, Carl, and James. They wrote to one another
in *Judendeutsch,* a German Jewish dialect written in Hebrew script.
These letters, which are exceptionally hard to decipher, have now been
translated into English. Together with new material from the Montefiore
family, they enable us to reconstruct the relationship between Montefiore and his famous brother-in-law for the first time.

   Eight years older than Montefiore, Rothschild arrived in England from
Frankfurt in 1799 and settled in Manchester, where he established himself as a successful textile merchant.[55] He rapidly diversified and, after
Napoleon's imposition of a blockade on British trade with the Continent in 1805–06, continued his export business as a smuggler. But Rothschild's real talents lay elsewhere: by 1808 he was beginning to establish
himself as a banker. In 1811 Rothschild closed his Manchester office
and moved definitively to London to pursue this new career.

   His timing could hardly have been better. Wellington's victories in the
Iberian Peninsula and British financing of the Grand Alliance against
Napoleon after 1812 made the British government's need for money
more acute than ever. British forces on the Continent needed hard cur-
rency, and Napoleon's continental blockade made this difficult to come
by. The death of Francis Baring and the bankruptcy of Abraham Goldsmid in 1810 left the City temporarily leaderless. The enterprising Rothschild stepped into this breach.

   In 1810 at the latest, Rothschild and his brothers became involved in smuggling gold bullion from England into France.[56] This enterprise entailed making large purchases of bullion on the London market, and in January 1814 Nathan Rothschild was officially charged with providing up to £600,000 in gold and silver coins to finance the advance of Wellington's armies. By the middle of May 1814 the British government owed him some £1,167,000. It was risky work, but government contacts brought lucrative opportunities. Between 1811 and 1815 Britain subsidized its continental allies to the tune of some £42 million, and the Rothschilds secured a dominant share of this business. So useful did they prove that the British prime minister, Lord Liverpool, was moved to say of Nathan to Lord Castlereagh: "I do not know what we should have done without him last year [1814]."[57] When Montefiore married Judith in 1812, Rothschild was well on the way to making his extraordinary fortune—but by no means there yet.

The two men were contrasting characters. Rothschild was famously slapdash, prompting his father to warn him: "When people see that you are not orderly . . . they will do business with you only in order to cheat you."[58] Montefiore was meticulous. When traveling abroad, he would record to the minute exactly how long each stage of the journey took, exactly when they reached every major town, and exactly how much everything cost.[59] His approach to business was equally thorough. In later years, Loewe frequently accompanied Montefiore on visits to foreign branches of the Imperial Continental Gas Association. Loewe "often wondered at his minute knowledge of every item entered in the books of the respective offices."[60]

Rothschild was daring, imaginative, and a risk-taker. His rival Alexander Baring commented in 1824: "I must candidly confess that I have not the nerve for his operations . . . he is in money and funds what Bonaparte was in war, and if any sudden shake comes, he will fall to the ground like the other."[61] Montefiore was more cautious. According to Wolf, he took to heart the advice of a Scottish friend: "Always remember that it is better to earn a pound, than toss for two."[62] He could be innovative in business, but his innovations tended to be technical. He was, for instance, one of the first to issue weekly price lists of stocks quoted on the Exchange.[63]

Rothschild was a workaholic. In 1816 he famously declared: "I do not read books, I do not play cards, my only pleasure is my business."[64] He also advised his children "to give mind, and soul, and heart, and body, and everything to business; that is the way to be happy."[65] Montefiore was also no slouch when it came to business. "I cannot fully reconcile my mind to this gentlemanly way of living," he wrote to his brother-in-law on a trip to Paris in 1814, "and ardently wish to be once more in the bustle of the Stock Exchange."[66] Yet Montefiore did find time in his life for other activities.

Between 1809 and 1814 he was a captain in the Surrey Militia.[67] There was nothing unusual about volunteer service, and Montefiore appears to have enjoyed what he experienced of military life. He took lessons in playing the bugle and felt duly disappointed when the company voted to disband. Together with Judith, he enjoyed playing cards and socializing with friends and family.[68] At home, they studied French together, besides reading the classics and other improving literature.[69] The couple used also to visit the village of Smithembottom in Surrey, where they "greatly enjoyed the walk over the hills, while forming pleasing anticipations of the future; and they always found on their return to the little inn, an excellent dinner which their servants had brought with them from London—never forgetting, by the order of their master, a few bottles of his choice wine."[70] The food at least was kosher, but Montefiore's lifelong love of port suggests that he worried less about the provenance of wine.[71]

Despite—maybe because of—their differences, Montefiore and Rothschild hit it off immediately. Shortly after their marriage, the Montefiores moved to 4 New Court, St. Swithin's Lane, where they lived next door to Nathan and Hannah.[72] Here the Rothschilds and Montefiores found themselves in the throbbing heart of a city known to contemporaries as "the centre of the trade of the whole world."[73]

For all its prestigious commercial buildings—including the Royal Exchange, the Guildhall, and the Bank of England—the City was by no means a grand place. It was too old, chaotic, and dirty for that: a maze of winding lanes, crammed with desperate, ragged men, women, and children living alongside struggling laborers, brash seamen, respectable shopkeepers, and wealthy financiers. But it was exciting and cosmopolitan too. The writer Thomas Addison was probably not alone in feeling "secret satisfaction as an Englishman to see so rich an assembly of countrymen and foreigners making this metropolis a kind of emporium for the whole earth."[74] So thriving was its economy, so hectic its thoroughfares, that strangers could only stand and stare.

"If I looked with any feeling of wonder on the throngs of the west-end," wrote Richard Rush after visiting the City in 1817, "more cause is there for it here. The shops stand, side by side, for entire miles. The accumulation of things, is amazing; it would seem impossible that there can be purchasers for them all, until you consider what multitudes there are to buy; then, you are disposed to ask how the buyers can all be supplied. In the middle of the streets, coal wagons and others as large, carts, trucks, vehicles of every sort, loaded in every way, are passing. They are in two close lines, like great tides, going reverse ways, and reaching farther than the eye can see."[75]

Surrounded by this hustle and bustle, Montefiore must have felt himself at the center of things. Thanks to his friendship with Rothschild, he really was. Not long after the move to New Court, Montefiore began to benefit substantially from Rothschild's financial expertise. According to Loewe, by 1813 Montefiore was "in constant intercourse with Mr. N. M. Rothschild, through whose prudence and judicious recommendations with regard to the Bullion Market and Foreign Exchanges, he [was] enabled not only to avoid hazardous monetary transactions, but also to make successful ventures in these difficult times."[76] Montefiore was deeply grateful. On August 31, 1813, he added a codicil to his will giving Nathan and Hannah Rothschild £5 each for a ring and "entreating them to continue to my dear Judith the friendship & regard, they have so kindly favoured us with; this is my last & most earnest wish."[77] Apart from Judith, Rachel, and Abraham, they were the only personal beneficiaries.

By 1814 Rothschild was allowing Montefiore to become even more closely involved in his affairs. In addition to their direct involvement in Britain's subsidies to its continental allies, the Rothschilds sought to profit indirectly by speculating on the fluctuations in bond prices. Like exchange rates, these were very sensitive to international transfers and wider political developments. The French invasion of Russia in 1812 caused Russian bonds to plummet from 65 percent of face value in February to 25 percent in October, but news of the retreat from Moscow prompted a rally, followed by another fall after Napoleon's victories in Saxony.[78] As an Allied victory seemed increasingly likely, Russian bonds rose again, but with the outcome still uncertain it made sense to try to buy them cheaply if one thought the Allies were likely to win. With this in mind, Rothschild sent Montefiore to Paris in March 1814 to stay with his brothers James and Salomon de Rothschild shortly before Napoleon's first abdication. But Montefiore was too late. He reported that Russian Paper (bonds), which was 90 when he arrived, had now risen to 100. He would buy £2,000 worth if the price dropped again to 90, but was unenthusiastic at the prospect, concluding: "alas, this is all I can say with respect to the object of my excursion to this City.[79]

Judith, however, relished the opportunity to visit Notre Dame, the new national Museum, and the sights of Paris. She explained to Hannah Rothschild that she could not disapprove Montefiore's decision to return home "when M. reminds me, it is time unprofitably passed but he acknowledges after some little argument it is not entirely without profit the period we have spent here; for we do not allow an hour to dwindle away without being gratified with grand sights which this place richly affords."[80]

As Rothschild's close associate and neighbor, Montefiore found himself at the heart of the thrilling events of 1815. He never tired of recalling the day when Rothschild woke him at five in the morning with the news that Napoleon had escaped.

> Hastily dressing himself, he received instructions what sales to effect on the Exchange, and then Mr. Rothschild went to communicate his information to the Ministry. A French courier had brought the news, too precious to be entrusted to the usual pigeon post, and when in the evening, he was given a packet of despatches for the correspondents from whom he had come, Mr. Rothschild asked him, as he filled a stirrup-cup, if he knew what news he brought. The man answered "No." "Napoleon has escaped from Elba and is now in France," announced Mr. Rothschild. For a moment the man looked incredulous. Then waving his glass, he shouted "Vive l'Empereur!" and enthusiastically tossed off a bumper. As the courier took his leave Rothschild turned to his brother-in-law and said reflectively, "If that is the temper of the French I for[e]see we shall have some trouble yet."[81]

This legendary incident highlights the dramatic interplay between events on the Continent and individual fortunes on the Stock Exchange. We even have a relatively contemporary account of how Rothschild and Montefiore exploited this kind of sensitive information. According to City legend, if Rothschild knew of news likely to make the funds rise, he would commission his broker—in this period, Montefiore—to sell half a million. As news spread that Rothschild was bearing the market, "Men looked doubtingly at one another; a general panic spread; bad news was looked for; and these united agencies sunk the price 2 or 3 percent. This was the result expected; and other brokers, not usually employed by him, bought all they could at the reduced rate. By the time this was accomplished, the good news had arrived, the pressure ceased; the funds arose instantly; and Mr. Rothschild reaped his reward."[82]

Montefiore undoubtedly derived substantial benefits from acting as Nathan Rothschild's broker, not least in terms of commission. In 1816, for instance, Montefiore Brothers sold £150,000 in Exchequer Bills received by Nathan Rothschild from John Herries, commissary in chief of the British government.[83] Montefiore had finally purchased his broker's medal in 1815, and on all this business he would have received the customary commission of one-eighth of one percent. Nathan Rothschild's

The Royal Exchange, 1821. Moses Montefiore and Nathan Mayer Roth-schild are in the foreground. (Reproduced with the permission of The Rothschild Archive, London)

brothers worried that he was too generous in the terms on which he did business with the Montefiores. In a letter dated August 1816, Nathan's youngest brother, James, wrote him from Paris: "I note with great satis-faction that you have bought £400,000 stocks, but tell me, are you get-ting commission on it and, if not, where is your profit? That is the most important thing. Or are you working for Montefiore?"[84]

Commission was always welcome to a broker, but Montefiore must have found Rothschild's government contacts at least equally useful. Acting on Herries' advice in 1816, Rothschild invested almost all the firm's capital in 3 percent consols—a form of perpetual government bond—at prices of about 65.1 and 61.5, a move that yielded him a profit of £250,000 when they rose above 82 after July 1817.[85] It seems almost certain that Montefiore profited from this excellent tip. James de Roth-schild for one thought that Nathan was too indiscreet when dealing with his London associates: "Everyone is saying to me, 'you are being secre-tive and your brother tells everything to those who want to hear him.' Please, dear Nathan, if you send me a courier with an offer [of stock] then at least don't tell everybody about it."[86] It is telling that both Moses and Abraham became seriously rich during precisely this period. In Sep-tember 1815 Moses Montefiore was assessed to pay *finta* of £8 13s 4d to the Spanish and Portuguese Synagogue, and Abraham to pay £8 10s.

This levy was steep, but still not the top of the range. By 1819, however, Moses was paying £25 and Abraham £23 6s 8d, placing them among the very wealthiest of the Sephardi elite.[87]

The years 1815–1817 proved decisive for the relationship between Rothschild and the Montefiore brothers. On August 23, 1815, the widowed Abraham Montefiore married Nathan's sister Henrietta, thereby strengthening the connection. Henrietta was a strong character, pushy and often downright rude. She and the grasping Abraham were a well-matched pair. Henrietta's brother Salomon complained in 1817 that they were too mean to "sacrifice a shilling and to offer her brother a piece of blackened glass for the occasion of the eclipse of the sun."[88]

When Henrietta and Abraham visited Paris in the spring of that year, they were intent on muscling in on Rothschild business operations. James was appalled by their behavior. "I paid Montefiore all due respect and attention," he complained to Nathan, "but unfortunately I did not give him millions and, worse still, I did not talk to him about *rentes*, for how could I possibly know that this man had come here in order to make a spec as they say now? I had no idea at all and I thought all along he had come to Paris to amuse himself."[89]

James had no objection to using Abraham as a broker, but he advised Nathan not to involve his brothers-in-law in the rest of his affairs. If Nathan stuck to doing business with his blood family, James told him, "you will soon find out who your friends really are, because as soon as the arse lickers see there is nothing more to gain, they will fall away like blood suckers when they have drunk too much blood." Six months later, Abraham's visit to Paris continued to rankle. "You write that when [Abraham] is rich enough, with God's help, you will be thanked [but I say] your children are more likely to be given a glass of water," James wrote to Nathan that December. He signed off "with good wishes from your loving brother who, like all brothers, is the one person you can rely on and whose loyalty and righteousness is more proven than that of a brother-in-law already counting on our brother Amschel's *inheritance* and working out the quickest way to join us."[90]

To some extent these tensions were part of a wider problem. Nathan's brothers undoubtedly resented members of their extended family in London for seeking to interfere in family affairs. Writing from Amsterdam to his brothers James and Salomon in Paris, Carl von Rothschild complained: "Nathan was on his own for too long and has attached himself too closely to others."[91] In 1817 James was therefore delighted to hear from Salomon that he "did not know London any more. Not only that people like [Abraham] Montefiore and Salomon Cohen are no longer discussing the letters, but that not even [Meyer] Davidson is getting them any more."[92] And indeed, 1817 was something of a turning point in Nathan Rothschild's business practice, marking a decision to focus on the family firm at the expense of his new London relatives.

Moses Montefiore appears to have been more circumspect than the other Rothschild brothers-in-law. Indeed, Salomon went out of his way to describe Moses as "a fundamentally honest, fine man."[93] The fact that Moses and Abraham had dissolved their partnership in November 1816 may have distanced him from his younger brother's ill-judged activities.[94] An often-quoted letter written in early 1818 suggests that Nathan and Moses remained on very friendly terms. "I am very happy to learn you make as good a Bear as you formerly did a Bull," he wrote to his brother-in-law Rothschild; "you must have had some difficulty with my brother Abraham, indeed it is quite a new character for both, it has one great advantage that while Consoles continue at or above 82 there can be very little to fear, you have beat your antagonists so frequently that I am surprised there are any to be found in the Stock Exchange to oppose you in any considerable operation."[95] Retrospectively, however, the impact of Abraham's behavior appeared little short of disastrous. When Rothschild died in 1836, Montefiore wrote bitterly: "NMR was a great & honored friend to Jud & I until Henrietta arrived in England & married Abraham. They may God forgive them destroyed the kind feeling which preceedingly subsisted."[96]

Yet Rothschild and Montefiore remained associates throughout the 1820s, famously founding the Alliance Assurance Company together in 1824. In 1818 Montefiore seems to have taken responsibility for dealing with a shipment of merchandise from Leipzig on behalf of the Rothschilds.[97] In 1822 he led a consortium of brokers managing the subscription to a £6.6 million loan in 5 percent Russian government bonds issued by the Rothschilds.[98] He himself took at least £9,350 of the original subscription to this loan and a further £25,012 in April 1824—not to mention £81,606 in French *rentes* and rather smaller amounts of Spanish and Colombian stock.[99]

All this activity caused Montefiore to lodge in the public imagination as Nathan's sidekick. Physically, the two men could hardly have been more different. Montefiore was tall and fairly good-looking; he had filled out physically and gained in confidence as a result of his worldly success. In one cartoon dating from 1818, he surveys the world with a self-satisfied expression. His gaze is commanding, his chest thrust forward, and his shoulders pushed back as he clasps his hands behind him under the tail of his smart blue coat. Rothschild, in contrast, was short and fat, "a very common-looking person with heavy features, flabby pendant lips, and projected fish eye . . . stout, awkward and ungainly."[100]

Wealthy and worldly: caricature of Moses Montefiore as a successful young businessman, from Richard Dighton's City Characters *(London, 1818). (Courtesy of the City of London, London Metropolitan Archives)*

The physical disparities appealed to caricaturists. Alongside the numerous images of Nathan's squat figure dominating the Exchange, there are several of him and Montefiore.

The years immediately after Waterloo were hard for Britain. The country emerged from the war with too much paper money in circulation and artificially high prices—partly a result of inflation and partly a consequence of Napoleon's continental blockade. With military demands on the economy falling, stagnation and deflation were a real threat.[101] The return of large numbers of demobilized soldiers and sailors only added to the country's problems.

At first the chancellor of the Exchequer, Nicholas Vansittart, tried to manage government finances just as he had done in wartime—through new loans. To guarantee lower prices, he kept the money markets artificially high by borrowing money from loan contractors to buy government stock. Rothschild was a key player in this system, but by 1818 both he and Vansittart were under attack. There were growing pressures from all sides for a resumption of gold payments at the old parity by the Bank of England and a return to tighter money markets. These pressures came partly from key members of the government, like the Canningite William Huskisson, but also from the landed gentry and from some Whigs, for whom the gold standard represented "ethical" fiscal policy.

In 1818 the prime minister, Lord Liverpool, received an anonymous letter warning him that

> the Capitalists of the Money Market . . . have set their faces against your Plan because it serves not their purpose or puts Money in their Pockets. The Jew interest alias Mr. Rothschild are disappointed and straining every nerve to defeat your objects.
>
> It is a deplorable Circumstance that in so great a Country as this, Your Lordship & Colleagues should be the Sport [&] the caprice of a Jew Party, it is truly lamentable.[102]

This insinuating epistle demonstrates clearly how polemics over the resumption of cash payments fed into deeper fears about the new economy and the dominant place of Jews—especially Rothschild—within it. While most Jews scraped a living in low-status street trades, the wealthy few were disproportionately associated with the money markets at a time when financial capitalism was new enough to be mistrusted. Whether they dealt in stocks, shares, or stolen goods, Jews were now instinctively identified with the unscrupulous pursuit of wealth at the expense of decent Christians.[103]

Rothschild was believed to be the central cog of the new financial system—the "pillar of 'Change" depicted in a famous caricature.[104] "Who hold the balance of the world?" asked Byron in the twelfth canto of his *Don Juan*. His answer was: "Jew Rothschild, and his fellow Christian Baring."[105] This anti-Rothschild feeling inevitably had an effect on Nathan's brother-in-law Moses Montefiore. A hostile political cartoon from the mid-1820s, lampooning Rothschild for bankrolling the reactionary states of the Holy Alliance, depicts him and Montefiore talking together in French—something we can be sure the German Rothschild and the Anglo-Italian Montefiore never did.[106] But the cartoonist was not interested in accuracy: he sought merely to emphasize their Jewishness and, by implication, their foreignness in an English setting. Ironically, despite their much-vaunted closeness, after 1817 things between Montefiore and Rothschild were no longer what they had once been.

Chapter 3

A World beyond Business

In 1816 a couple of well-to-do English tourists went shopping for a top-of-the-range traveling carriage from the famous Parisian coachmaker Beaupré.[1] Like so many of their fellow countrymen in the aftermath of Waterloo, Montefiore and Judith proposed to tour France and Italy, exploring the art and culture denied them by two decades of war. Such a vehicle was the only way to avoid the chaos, overcrowding, and discomfort of stagecoach travel. Montefiore and Judith would have looked for strength, easy rolling, steadiness, and safety for persons and luggage —and what one nineteenth-century traveler described as "the general stateliness of effect to be obtained for the abashing of plebeian beholders."[2] They would also have been concerned about storage, exploring cupboards beneath the seats, secret drawers under front windows, and pockets hidden in the vehicle's padded lining, where they could keep their valuables safe from dust and prying eyes. Finally, they would have worried about comfort: cushions that did not slip, rounded corners, well-constructed blinds, and closely fitted windows that would protect them from drafts. At 4,072 francs, the price was steep. But money was no object when it came to choosing the little apartment that would be their home for the next few months.

For Montefiore the carriage was an investment and a new beginning. With a fortune behind them and no children (as yet) to care for, he and Judith could afford to have fun. The expedition was such a success that they returned a year later, visiting Scotland in 1821 before embarking on a third major European tour in 1823. A journey to Ireland in 1825 was essentially a business trip, but even here they found time for a little sightseeing. Montefiore had acquired what Judith called a "mania for travelling."[3] It was a passion he would nurture for the rest of his life.

Underpinning this enthusiasm lay shifting priorities. Montefiore's first

trip to the Continent had been undertaken on Rothschild business.
When it proved unproductive, he insisted on returning home. The pull
of the City was weaker now: in his mid-thirties, Montefiore no longer
found this "gentlemanly way of living" so unattractive.[4] Privately, he
was beginning to question the materialism of the business world; his
1820 diary begins with a few lines from Shakespeare and a popular
poem expressing similar sentiments:

> *With moderate blessings be content*
> *Nor idly grasp at every shade,*
> *Peace, competence, a life well spent,*
> *Are blessings that can never fade;*
> *And he that weakly sighs for more*
> *Augments his misery, not his store.*[5]

These lines represented an aspiration—one that contrasted starkly
with popular stereotypes of the grasping Jewish financier and, indeed,
the traditions of his own family. Montefiore remained a towering figure
on 'Change. His frequent trips abroad allowed him time and space to
cultivate other sides of his personality, refashioning himself as a certain
kind of English gentleman. With Judith he visited churches, museums,
palaces, and charitable institutions, marveled at the wonders of nature,
and struggled with the boredom and discomfort of endlessly long coach
journeys. Judith's travel diaries and a handful of surviving letters give an
unexpectedly intimate insight into their life as a couple.[6]

Even money and a first-rate carriage could not always guarantee luxury. On one memorable night, Judith reported, "The cieling [*sic*] of our
chamber was covered with cobwebs and soot . . . the sound of rats and
mice amused our ears and the smoke from the kitchen was most refresh-
ing."[7] They learned to cope. Arriving in 1821 at Kimone in Ireland to
find the best rooms in the hotel occupied, Judith commented cheerfully
that "the fine situation amply compensated for the smallness of the
room, had but the dinner been tolerable, however the consolation was
we had experienced much worse. It will not do always to have the best.
We should become spoild *Children*."[8]

Impatient and quick-tempered, her husband sometimes failed to share
this resignation. In 1823, when a mix-up occurred on their departure
from London, he showed "a little *warmth*."[9] Two days later things were
even worse. "Mun [Montefiore] not in the best of *tems*. [tempers],"
wrote Judith, "perhaps being called earlier than usual or some unac-
countable something incidental to us capricious mortals, produced the
answer. 'do not speak to me for I am very cross.'"[10] Yet there are hints
that he also possessed an unexpected sense of humor. "[W]e observed

on the outside of Churches large images with a cross some of gild, others of Marble," Judith informed Hannah after their journey from Dunkirk to Paris in 1814; "every now & then M. said here we are coming to another Jesus."[11] Some years later, when they passed through Wolverhampton, Judith noted: "The inhabitants have not the most agreeable appearance but they have the character for loyalty & patriotism . . . in our Evening walk thro the churchyard and its environs we happened to meet two or three wrangling couples so Montefiore said he must mark them down for another quality, that of quarrelsome."[12]

Montefiore was less sociable than Judith—"ever reluctant to form new acquaintance," as she put it. But he enjoyed a glass of wine and was not above having fun with new friends made while traveling. During their stay on the Isle of Man in 1821, Judith recorded a little disapprovingly: "Mr. & Mrs. Richardson came to tea & remained till 2 o'clock in the morning, rather too *jovial* a party to please me." Few of these traveling acquaintances were Jewish.[13]

Both showed an appreciation of wild and magnificent scenery, but Montefiore appears to have been particularly susceptible. In 1821 he was "much inclined" to buy a property on the Isle of Man. Judith thought it too remote, "a desirable habitation to many who have not the blessing of a numerous relationship across the seas." Still, she enjoyed the "stupendous rocks & innumerable waterfalls" of the pass of Glencoe, and presents us with a rather startling image of Montefiore at the summit of a Scottish mountain "seated . . . in a picturesque manner with his Tartan wrapt round him."[14]

Nevertheless the couple were not altogether typical English tourists. Whereas Montefiore's parents had gone out of their way to avoid non-kosher meat, Judith wrote pragmatically to her sister from Verona that they were "well pleased with the Cookery, when a slice of bacon does not cover the [incorrectly slaughtered] roasted Poultry in that case Mr Mazzara [their traveling companion] contrives to finish the dish."[15] On Saturdays she and Montefiore struck a similar balance. They never traveled on the Sabbath and always made a point of saying their prayers and reading the weekly Torah portion together—even if Montefiore made little effort to pray as part of the religious quorum of ten Jewish men, known as a *minyan*.[16] Their interest in foreign Jewish communities was at best spasmodic.[17] Yet their Jewishness did color their traveling experience in that, unlike most British tourists, they had family abroad.

In 1818 Montefiore and Judith visited Livorno together, where they met one of his uncles and two of his cousins.[18] Montefiore had turned away from the cosmopolitan traditions of his father's family when he chose to become a stockbroker rather than a merchant. Nevertheless he

retained a sense of connection with his origins, writing to Nathan Rothschild that he had "made a short visit to Leghorn [Livorno] to bid adieu
(most probably for ever) to my birth place." To Rothschild, Montefiore
acknowledged the beauty of the surrounding scenery and the benefits of
life in a town where "with four or five hundred a year a family may live
very genteel & keep a carriage." But he felt himself a foreigner, concluding that "with all these advantages, an Englishman would frequently
sigh after his native land."[19]

These trips to the Continent saw the birth of two significant friendships.
When staying in Marseilles in 1816, the Montefiores made the acquaintance of an Italian Catholic called Mazzara, a gifted amateur artist and
Hebraicist. He proved an engaging companion and accompanied them
on several subsequent trips.[20] The three seem to have shared similar
tastes in literature, enlivening their evenings with, among other works,
Torquato Tasso's *Aminta* and Conyers Middleton's *Life of Cicero* as
they traveled in 1823 through northern France.[21] In 1818 the Montefiores even stayed with Mazzara and his wife in Rome, and they always
visited these old friends when passing through the Eternal City. Mazzara
in turn visited England at least twice.[22]

The second lifelong friendship Montefiore formed in these years was
with a young Quaker doctor, Thomas Hodgkin.[23] Like Jews, Quakers
were a relatively closed group, who, because they could marry only their
coreligionists, were heavily interrelated. Like Jews, they were socially
and culturally distinctive, wearing plain, old-fashioned dress and using
the outmoded "thee" form in conversation. As Protestant Dissenters,
they suffered from a similar range of civil disabilities and tended to enter
similar professions. Hodgkin, however, showed a precocious interest in
science. His upbringing in Quaker Tottenham and his medical training
in Edinburgh brought him into contact with a host of intellectually sophisticated and philanthropically engaged individuals: the bookseller
and mineralogist William Phipps; the antislavery activists William Wilberforce, Zachary Macaulay, and Thomas Fowell Buxton; the philanthropist William Allen; the socialist Robert Owen; and the prison reformer Elizabeth Fry. So enthused was Hodgkin by their passion for
reforming the world that at the age of twenty he wrote "An Essay on the
Promotion of Civilization," in which he declared: "my life's aim will
be to protect the primitive aboriginal people of all continents of the
world."[24]

Montefiore and the serious young Quaker took to each other immediately. They first met in Paris in September 1823, when Henrietta Mon-

tefiore employed Hodgkin to look after her sick husband. Henrietta, Hodgkin, and Abraham then traveled south to Rome, in the hope that warmer weather would improve his condition. Judith and Montefiore took a less direct route, and Hodgkin was delighted when they finally arrived. "It is a great satisfaction to me that his [Abraham's] brother Moses is here," he wrote to his mother. "I have mentioned meeting him at Paris when I was much pleased with him. & I am certainly not less so now that I have a fuller opportunity of becoming acquainted with him."[25]

By this time Abraham was in a bad way. On their departure from Paris, Hodgkin had hoped that Abraham's lungs were still sufficiently free of tuberculosis for much to be achieved though strict diet and regular exercise.[26] But Abraham found the journey difficult and on reaching Rome began to cough blood once more. Henrietta was beside herself with anxiety. She refused to leave her husband's bedside, and both she and Abraham urged the Montefiores to remain with them. This they were glad to do. "The idea that Montefiore's Society may be a consolation in his present state induces us to consent," wrote Judith in her diary.[27] Judith, Montefiore, Abraham, and Henrietta were soon joined by Solomon Sebag, the Moroccan husband of the Montefiores' sister Sarah.

It was a difficult time for all concerned. As Abraham's condition worsened, tensions between Henrietta and Hodgkin became acute. On their arrival in Rome, Henrietta had consulted two eminent Italian doctors, who—inevitably—disagreed with Hodgkin over the best treatment. Henrietta was desperate, and their more interventionist approach probably appealed to her restless nature. She dismissed Hodgkin in January 1824.

Judith and Montefiore had little sympathy for Henrietta's behavior. Both "found him [Dr. Hodgkin] a great acquisition to our domestic circle both in sensible information and kind attentions & only regret he should not please those to whom it is most requisite."[28] Hodgkin was comforted by their support, telling his parents: "I may flatter myself that I retain on the separation so much of the good will & good opinion of Moses Montefiore & other members of the family who are here as will counteract any unfavourable report."[29] Sure enough, when Hodgkin's father visited the Montefiores in London a month later, he declared himself "highly gratified by the encomiums which he & his amiable Wife passed upon thee."[30]

In point of fact, there was nothing either Hodgkin or anyone else could do for Abraham, who died in August 1824 at Lyon. News of his younger brother's death prompted Montefiore to reflect on his own mortality. He copied into his diary the following lines from the book of Psalms:

Seize the transient hour
Improve each moment as it flies
Life a short summer—man a flower
He dies, alas! How soon he dies.[31]

Both Mazzara and Hodgkin were highly intelligent and cultivated men. When they finally met in 1859, they found much to admire in each other, Hodgkin describing Mazzara in his notebook as "a remarkable man with a good head."[32] Hodgkin, who has gone down in history as the discoverer of Hodgkin's lymphoma, had a first-class mind and knew what he was talking about. Historians have tended to dismiss Montefiore intellectually, and in later life he proudly declared himself "'a know nothing'—wise only, as he frequently added, in this, 'that he knew it.'"[33] Yet his friendships with men like Hodgkin and Mazzara should give us pause for thought. Judith's diaries refer frequently to books the couple read together, and Montefiore's personal library was extensive, revealing a particular (and wholly unsurprising) predilection for travel books.[34] He may have been no intellectual, but he could hold his own in conversation with those who were—and enjoy it.

These friendships are indicative of the way in which Montefiore's social circle had expanded by the 1820s. When he married in 1812, neither he nor Judith invited a single Christian guest.[35] When he became a Freemason, he chose a lodge that may have been Jewish enough to serve kosher food but probably afforded fewer possibilities for Christian networking.[36] By 1817, however, Montefiore was seeking to carve a place for himself in English society. That year he purchased a house in the country, and in 1819 he applied for a coat of arms. He described himself in the application as "Moses Montefiore of New Court, St. Swithin's Lane, City of London, and of Tinley Lodge, near Tunbridge, co. Kent, Esquire, Captain in 3rd Surrey Local Militia."[37] He chose to model his coat of arms as closely as possible on the original armorial bearings of the Italian Montefiores.[38]

Of course, his life continued to be punctuated by Judaism. An entry in his 1820 diary provides an account of how Montefiore spent his days: "With God's blessing,—Rise, say prayers at 7 o'clock. Breakfast at 9. Attend the Stock Exchange, if in London, 10. Dinner 5. Read, write and learn, if possible, Hebrew and French, 6. Read Bible and say prayers, 10. Then retire. Monday and Thursday mornings attend Synagogue [when the first part of the weekly Torah portion is read]." This was more than could be said for many financiers. Indeed, Loewe tells us that "[h]owever profitable or urgent the business may have been, the moment the time drew near, when it was necessary to prepare for the Sabbath or solemn festivals, Moses Montefiore quitted his office, and nothing could ever induce him to remain." There are hints, too, of a more profound religiosity.[39]

In 1815 Montefiore was nominated *gabbai,* or treasurer, of the Sephardi community.[40] Such positions were hard to fill, and the Spanish and Portuguese Congregation had started fining those who refused to take office. The time-consuming post of *gabbai* was particularly unpopular, not least because the incumbent had to pay a £600 deposit.[41] Montefiore's willingness to fill it at the height of his business career indicates a degree of commitment to the synagogue at Bevis Marks. Communal officials were often lax in attending meetings, and for these shortcomings, too, the congregation had been forced to implement financial penalties. In 1818 Montefiore was elected president of the synagogue's governing body, known as the Mahamad. He did not attend a single meeting during the first two months of his presidency; for the rest of his year in office he was absent more often than not.[42] When he did come, he was usually responding to a summons to make up a quorum. By September 1819 it had become clear that this state of affairs could not continue. "[H]aving observed the difficulty which has lately been experienced in forming a competent Mahamad owing to the number of Gentlemen who have paid their fines in lieu of serving the office, and having at Heart the welfare of our Kaal [community]," Montefiore and four others offered their services as communal officials with the intention of taking the post more seriously.[43] He never missed another meeting.

His membership of the burial society is still more striking. This was an honor reserved for the truly pious: a religious duty of the first order, but also a burden. Jews are buried as soon as possible, and as a *lavadore* Montefiore would have been regularly called upon to help purify and prepare the corpse by washing it, dressing it, and watching over it the night before the funeral. Nor did he neglect the death rituals of his own family. When his mother-in-law died in 1817, Montefiore visited Judith's brothers as they sat *shiva* and attended every congregational meeting during the prescribed week of mourning "with a view of devoting the rest of the day to the furtherance of some good cause." On the anniversary of his father's death in 1821, Montefiore went to Bevis Marks to offer the customary mourner's *kaddish* prayer and then visited his father's tomb. He distributed gifts to "the poor and needy" and "passed the whole of the day in fasting and religious meditation."[44]

This blend of ritual and charity was characteristic. In 1822, for instance, Montefiore had the honor to complete a scroll of the Torah in his own hand on the eve of Yom Kippur, the holiest day in the Jewish calendar.[45] Disseminating the Torah is a prime religious obligation among Jews, and finishing a Torah scroll is regarded as a great *mitzvah,* or good deed. Montefiore marked the experience by "offering on the following day £140 for the benefit of various charitable institutions of his community." A year later he made a far more substantial donation in the form of thirteen houses in Cock Court, Jewry Street, as almshouses for the Sephardi poor.[46] But Judith had always grasped that for her husband religion and philanthropy were integrally linked, noting shortly after their marriage that his was "that sort of religion which he possesses that in my opinion is most essential—a fellow feeling and benevolence."[47]

This degree of religious commitment meant that the Montefiores continued to socialize primarily with Jewish friends and family. Judith's entries for December 1825 are littered with references to visits with Hannah at New Court, dinners with Miss Mocatta in Finsbury Square, family parties to mark her sister Esther's wedding anniversary, and tea with Rachel Montefiore in Kennington.[48] Yet by the time of their visit to Edinburgh in 1821, Montefiore was sufficiently well connected to be invited to a public dinner held to mark the coronation of George IV at the Waterloo Hotel, where, according to Judith, "he met with great Politeness from Sir John Hay to whom we had letters; & the Lord provost who sent to take wine with him: there was a seat reserved at the top of the table for him. Mun was also greatly pleased at meeting in his opposite number at Dinner a Major Carle who was Major of the volunteer Corps to which Mun formerly belonged."[49]

Montefiore's involvement with several landmark new businesses in the 1820s underlines his integration into this wider social world.[50] All three companies bridged the confessional divide, bringing Montefiore into contact with radical political and social activists, whose religious beliefs put them outside the mainstream. The first of these businesses was the Alliance British and Foreign Life and Fire Assurance Company. According to one tradition, Nathan Rothschild was prompted to found the company by a chance encounter with Benjamin Gompertz—husband of Montefiore's sister Abigail, former business partner of his younger brother Horatio, and a connection of the Barent Cohen family. Gompertz was a brilliant mathematician and the author of an important paper on life contingencies relating to the insurance business. And yet, a distraught Gompertz explained to Rothschild, the post he had applied for as actuary of a large insurance firm had gone to a less qualified candidate just because Gompertz was Jewish. "Vat! Not take you because of your religion! Mine Gott! Den I vil make a bigger office for you den any of dem," Nathan Rothschild is said to have replied.[51]

Whether the Alliance really had its origins in religious discrimination is open to question—although Gompertz was the only official mentioned by name in the original prospectus. Montefiore also claimed credit for the idea, recounting that he happened upon Rothschild on his way to draw dividends from a newly established insurance company.[52] The two men had discussed the business, realized that their friends could supply a useful clientele, and—"mainly at the suggestion of Montefiore"—resolved to found a new insurance company with a larger share capital and more influential board of directors than any yet established. Gompertz's involvement was an advantage, but in planning to mobilize their business network Montefiore and Rothschild did not have their sights set simply on Jews. When the Alliance was founded in 1824, three of its five presidents—Francis Baring, Samuel Gurney, and John Irving—came from leading Christian businesses.

Baring had just been made a partner in Baring Brothers, Rothschild's main rivals in the business of government loans; and Irving was a partner in the firm Reid Irving.[53] Despite their origins in finance, both families were well integrated into England's social and political elite. Members of the Baring family included the baronet Sir Thomas Baring and the M.P. Alexander Baring; Irving was a member of Parliament in his own right. With Baring and Irving on board, Rothschild and Montefiore had the financial establishment in their pocket.

Sam Gurney brought rather different connections to the Alliance. He was a founding member of Richardson, Overend, Gurney & Co., the City's leading bill brokers. As one contemporary wrote, "He appears to have been bred and born in the money market, for all his relatives and friends are bankers in the provinces; and Essex and Suffolk boast of some of their wealthiest people bearing his name."[54] Like Hodgkin, Gurney was a Quaker. Dressed in his dark-brown Quaker's coat and white broad-brim beaver hat, he cut a distinctive figure in the City and was almost as well known as a philanthropist as he was as a businessman. Gurney was active in the cause of prison reform, spearheaded by his sister Elizabeth Fry and his brother-in-law Thomas Fowell Buxton, M.P. He was also a member of the Anti-Slavery Society established by Buxton, Wilberforce, and others. Buxton himself became auditor of the Alliance, and the Quaker firm Hoare, Barnett & Co. acted as its bankers. Thus Alliance Assurance depended almost as much on the Quaker Gurney and his brother-in-law Buxton as it did on the Jew Montefiore and his brother-in-law Rothschild. The union between Jewish and Dissenting business interests had not been formed overnight. There is evidence of friendly relations between Montefiore and Gurney as early as 1821, and Montefiore's friendship with Hodgkin can only have intensified these ties.[55]

With the active involvement of Jews, Quakers, and the mainstream banking establishment, it seemed to many that the Alliance Assurance Company could hardly fail. "Nothing could be more respectable or substantial than the security [of the promoters]," wrote one contemporary, "the Bank of England could not be better."[56] The early 1820s saw a boom in the formation of new insurance companies in Britain, with a 20 percent rise in the value of insurance shares.[57] In a sense, Montefiore and Rothschild were simply riding the crest of the wave. Yet the mass of wealth and connections they brought enabled them to go one better.

At £5 million the proposed share capital of the new insurance company was vastly greater than that of rival foundations. More importantly, the political influence of its directors helped to catalyze a dramatic liberalization of the British marine insurance market. When the promoters of the Alliance first met in March 1824, two companies, the Royal Exchange and London Assurance, enjoyed a monopoly on marine underwriting. In 1810 attempts to overturn this situation had come to nothing. But now the backing of M.P.s like Buxton, Irving, and William Thompson enabled the bill to pass within barely a month. Fifteen new insurance companies were founded in its wake. Ironically, the founders of the Alliance were then forced to separate marine insurance from its fire and life insurance concerns, with the creation of a sister company, Alliance Marine Insurance.

A year later Montefiore became involved in the Provincial Bank of Ireland, one of Britain's first joint-stock banks. The Alliance had reinforced Montefiore's links with Gurney and his Quaker connection; involvement with the Provincial Bank brought Montefiore into very different circles. Catholics and Quakers were at opposite ends of the Christian religious spectrum, but in the context of nineteenth-century British politics both were similarly disadvantaged. Catholics were even more stigmatized than Dissenters—especially in Ireland, where the exclusion of the Catholic majority from holding civil office had created a travesty of representative politics. By the mid-1820s, however, the cause of Catholic emancipation had reached crisis point thanks to the charismatic populism of the Irish nationalist leader Daniel O'Connell.[58]

The Provincial Bank of Ireland had clearly political objectives. It was created in opposition to the exclusively Protestant National Bank of Ireland by a group of Irish M.P.s with Catholic inclinations, including the

The hustle and bustle of the City: Cheapside as seen from a rooftop, by T. M. Baynes, 1823. (Courtesy of the Guildhall Library, City of London)

whiggish Thomas Spring-Rice and the secretary of the British Catholic Association, Edward Blount—who later joined the board of the Alliance. O'Connell may even have been one of their number, although his subsequent disgust at the Provincial Bank's "rascality" and involvement in founding the rival National Bank suggest otherwise.[59] But the Provincial Bank also needed to connect with broader business interests. Other founding directors included Montefiore's first cousin Jacob and Ralph Ricardo, a relative of the famous economist and politician. Montefiore himself became involved in February 1825—the very month when Sir Francis Burdett reopened the Catholic question in Parliament. Shortly afterward Montefiore toured Ireland with Blount and another English director, Mr. Medley, to negotiate the opening of individual branches.

In 1824 Montefiore was instrumental in founding a third successful business: the Imperial Continental Gas Association. Gas lighting was still relatively new, and the company was at the cutting edge of contemporary technology. It was the brainchild of Major-General Sir William Congreve, whose contacts as equerry to George IV left him well placed to obtain gasworks concessions on the Continent. For financial backing, Congreve had turned to Montefiore, Isaac Lyon Goldsmid, and Matthias Attwood.

Goldsmid was both a connection and a contemporary of Montefiore's. But the firm Mocatta & Goldsmid was not what it had been, and Isaac Lyon was still rebuilding his family's fortunes after the terrible suicides of both his uncles. Matthias Attwood, a partner in the Birmingham bank of Spooner & Attwood, was yet another leading Quaker businessman. Like Gurney and Buxton, Attwood was an antislavery activist. He also had close family connections with political radicals in his native Birmingham. Attwood was also an associate of Thomas Joplin, a Newcastle banker and author of a series of pamphlets endorsing the idea of joint-stock banking, which had partially inspired the founders of the Provincial Bank of Ireland. Imperial Continental Gas struggled in the first years of its existence, and disputes over management prompted Goldsmid to resign. Attwood's involvement enabled the company to call in Joplin, who acted as executive director from 1829 to 1832. Thanks to Joplin, it soon began to turn a tidy profit.

The early 1820s saw a classic cycle of boom and bust in the British economy. During 1824 and early 1825, the City was seized by almost unprecedented excitement as numerous promising companies were launched on the London Stock Exchange. Most had very unstable foundations. According to the City's chronicler, John Francis, the atmosphere

"Will you let me a loan?"
Isaac Lyon Goldsmid, from
Richard Dighton's City
Characters *(London, 1818).*
(Courtesy of the Guildhall Li-
brary, City of London)

of hysterical speculation enabled dishonest, disreputable—and, in his
view, often Jewish—characters to flourish.

With huge pocket-book containing worthless script; with crafty countenance and cunning eye; with showy jewellery and thread-bare coat; with
well greased locks and unpolished boots; with knavery in every curl of
the lip, and villany in every thought of the heart; the stag, as he was afterwards termed, was a prominent portrait in the foreground. Grouped together in one corner might be seen a knot of boys eagerly buying and
selling at a profit which bore no comparison to the loss of honesty they
each day experienced. Day after day were elderly men with shabby faces
and huge umbrellas witnessed in the same spot, doing business with those
whose characters might be judged from their company . . . In every corner, and in every vacant space might be seen men eagerly discussing the
premium of a new company, the rate of a new loan, the rumoured profit
of some lucky speculator, the rumoured failure of some great financier—
or wrangling with savage eagerness over the fate of a shilling.[60]

Insurance and mining were two fashionable—and usually disastrous—
forms of investment. In 1824 and 1825 speculators invested a nominal
capital of £32,040,700 in new insurance companies, but real capital

amounted to only £2,242,800, and most of the companies collapsed
during the crash of 1825–26.[61] Montefiore's Alliance Assurance—still a
going concern today—was one of only six to survive. A similar rash of
South American mining companies appeared during the closing months
of 1824—thirty in total, all of them enjoying the prestigious backing of
big City names and apparently facing a rosy future. Montefiore was on
the board of two such companies: Imperial Brazilian Mining, and Chil-
ian and Peruvian Mining.[62] In general, the grand claims made for these
companies were not worth the paper on which they were written.[63] Once
again Montefiore was able—quite literally—to distinguish the gold from
the dross. Only eight mining companies survived into 1827, and by the
1850s only two had paid substantial dividends. Montefiore's Imperial
Brazilian was one of them.

In the early years at least, he was a fairly hands-on director. Together
with Sam Gurney, Montefiore effectively ran the Alliance in the late
1820s, and he was sufficiently involved in the management of Imperial
Continental Gas in 1830 to tour the company's gasworks in Holland
and Germany with Wolverly Attwood.[64] He remained on the boards of
all three companies for many decades, and was also a director of the
Irish Manufactory and the British Colonial Silk Company. We know
that he inspected the latter's mulberry plantations when he passed
through Malta in 1827.[65] In other words, Montefiore did more than
pick a sound investment; he also made sure the investment prospered.
He may have worked with Rothschild in founding the Alliance, but the
long success of his other ventures vindicates his abilities as a businessman in his own right.

Montefiore's involvement in these companies reflected a significant
diversification of his business interests. It was standard practice for
successful businessmen to move into safer investments and less labor-
intensive activities as they grew older.[66] This shift into lower-risk activities was, perhaps, a form of retirement, but it by no means represented a
complete withdrawal from business. Montefiore retained a lifelong interest in the companies he founded and continued to function as an active director of Alliance Assurance and Imperial Continental Gas for
years to come. So closely involved was he with the Alliance that he used
its office as his base in the City for decades, writing countless letters on
communal and international Jewish affairs from this address.

Everything indicates that Montefiore's transition from stockbroker to
company director was gradual. We know that he gave up his countinghouse on October 30, 1820, and that his visit to the Stock Exchange on
February 17, 1824, was the first for more than a year. But the fact that
he did not resign from the Stock Exchange altogether until 1845 implies

a residual interest in its affairs. Membership in the General Purposes Committee of the Stock Exchange from 1824 to 1827 suggests an even more active interest in these years.

Most members of the General Purposes Committee were voted in on a near-unanimous basis. For two of the three years in which he stood for election, however, Montefiore received 70 and 115 votes fewer than other members. Such relatively low levels of support indicate resentment and hostility among his fellow brokers. To what extent this reflected wider jealousy of his family and friends is hard to judge. We know that in 1823 his brother Abraham was "publickly attacked & insulted" by a Mr. B. Carr, who claimed to have "suffered very severely by six persons who had been introduced to the Stock Exchange by Mr. Montefiore" and "told Mr. Montefiore that his family had robbed him." The way in which Montefiore replaced his dying brother on the General Purposes Committee reinforces the sense that the family continued to operate as a discrete interest group.[67]

Yet the shocking death of his younger brother Abraham at the age of thirty-six undoubtedly led Montefiore to think more deeply about his own life. Abraham left an estate of roughly £500,000 in 1824—the equivalent of over £35 million today.[68] Montefiore cannot have been significantly less wealthy, and the phrases he copied into his diary in January 1825 suggest he was beginning to feel that enough was enough:

Chi parla semina, chi tace racolta. [The talker sows, the silent reaps: Italian proverb]

A wise man will desire no more than what he may get justly, use soberly, distribute cheerfully and live upon contentedly. [Benjamin Franklin]

He that loveth a book will never want a faithful friend, a wholesome counsellor, a cheerful companion, or an effective comforter. [Isaac Barrow]

The studies afford nourishment to our youth, delight to our old age, adorn prosperity, supply a refuge in adversity, and are a constant source of pleasure at home; they are no impediment while abroad, and attend us in the night season, in our travels, and in our retirement. [Cicero]

He may be well content that need not borrow nor flatter. [English proverb]

Such sentiments were seriously at odds with Montefiore's daily reality. In 1825 he was still on the General Purposes Committee, still very busy setting up the Provincial Bank, still overlooking the affairs of his two South American mining companies. Only his move to the West End of London hints at a change in direction. Comfortably ensconced in a smart, newly built townhouse at 7 Grosvenor Gate, Park Lane, Montefiore and Judith were now a stone's throw from Hyde Park, that favorite resort of the fashionable world. Here they could observe the interminable throng of horses and carriages from their windows or take a turn in Rotten Row, trotting alongside society beauties, dashing officers, and outrageous dandies. Leaving the filthy, cramped, uneven lanes of the City behind them, they could enjoy the elegant squares, broad streets, and grand modern buildings that housed "the chief Nobility and Gentry of the Kingdom."[69] This was a step up in the world and a step away from the cut and thrust of City life. But Rothschild moved to Piccadilly at about the same time without reducing his business activities, and a fragment of Judith's diary surviving from December 1825 appears to show Montefiore also continuing his business life as normal.[70]

Not that business life was normal for anyone in late 1825. As boom finally turned to bust, the mood in the City was grim. In mid-December the *Morning Chronicle* claimed that the country had not seen the like of the current crisis: "'Never were such times,' cried many of the oldest visitors of the 'Change, while others exclaimed, 'If this state of things continues, we must ask not who is gone, but who stands? For unless something is done to relieve the pressure, and to restore confidence, few can resist so overwhelming a torrent of distrust.'"[71] None of this inclined Montefiore to further speculation. Early in 1826 he recorded: "On the same day when the death of an unfortunate speculator caused a general gloom to prevail in the financial world, I was asked by a gentleman if I had the courage to join him in a speculation, my reply was I would see him to-morrow . . . I fear this day's awful lesson is quite lost on him."[72] Montefiore did not experience the trauma of the crash directly, but he knew those who did: his youngest brother, Horatio, failed in 1826, presumably as part of the general crisis.[73] Loewe, who read the original diaries, was in no doubt that Montefiore's decision to scale down his business activities resulted directly from the financial and political upheaval of these years.[74]

But this was hardly the first such crisis of Montefiore's career. Things had also been bad in 1819, a year described by the timber merchant Charles Churchill as "full of successive Shocks on Confidence—with falling Markets in every Branch of Trade—& from Month to Month going from bad to worse."[75] Montefiore responded differently in 1826 because his outlook on life had changed. Judith remained childless, and as she entered her forties there was little chance that she might conceive. With no dynasty to build and no children to inherit his fortune, he saw little reason to follow the example of Abraham, who (it was widely believed) had worked himself to death. Judith had always taken a strong interest in her husband's work and was not above dabbling in financial markets.[76] Now even she advised him: "Thank God, and be content."[77]

As she came to terms with her infertility, Judith, too, may have experienced a personal watershed. Writing in 1825, Montefiore felt the need to reaffirm his love in a letter to be opened on his death: "you were from the first moment I had the happiness of being united to you a blessing & comfort & to you I am endebted for the happiness it has been my good fortune to enjoy, you made me acquainted with the inestimable value of God's Blessing." He signed himself "ever Yours Moses," and added as an afterthought: "Never man had better Wife or one more worthy of her husband's Affections & esteem, she was ever kind virtuous & charitable, pious & by her example stimulated her Partner to follow the precepts of her honored Parent. May God reward her. Witness Moses Montefiore."[78] He felt the need to reaffirm this statement on four occasions, in 1830, 1831, 1833, and 1835.

This oddly legalistic declaration hints at Judith's sense of inadequacy as a barren Jewish woman—and perhaps at Montefiore's difficulties in resisting sexual temptation. Childlessness carries a particular stigma in Judaism: a man can divorce his wife after ten years if their marriage is without issue.[79] The implication is clear: infertility is the woman's fault. Persistent rumors of Montefiore's affairs and illegitimate children in later life suggest that in this case it really was. Whether Judith knew of his infidelities or not, she probably saw her failure as divine retribution. For in Jewish tradition, a childless couple marks a break in the chain of Jewish continuity, and will suffer in the next world without descendants to say prayers for their souls. As she counted the days of her menstrual cycle and hoped against hope that this month there would be no blood, Judith may (like many other Jewish women) have turned to God, reciting special prayers and seeking to atone for her sins in the belief that charity, faith, and religious observance might bring about the miracle of conception. By emphasizing Judith's other virtues and reiterating his belief that "Never man had better Wife," Montefiore wanted Judith to know that he had no regrets.

Chapter 4

The Road to Jerusalem

The trees were loaded with spring blossoms when Montefiore and Judith set out for Jerusalem on May 2, 1827. Preparations had been under way for months, the last few days a whirl of elegant farewell treats. Only the night before, Nathan and Hannah Rothschild had provided an evening of sumptuous hospitality for the whole family, delighting Judith with a succession of brilliant performances by the best continental musicians. After attending synagogue to secure the blessing of divine providence, Montefiore climbed into the carriage full of "those exhilarating feelings which he usually experiences on commencing a journey." It was, he noted, a lovely morning. Judith was rather less sanguine. Torn between a pleasurable sense of expectation and anxieties, "the presence of which we scarcely wish to acknowledge even to ourselves," she prayed that the Almighty would "bless and prosper" their undertaking.[1]

In truth, she had feared making such a journey. Back in 1818, when they visited the family in Livorno, the couple had taken a boat out into the harbor to see two ships bound for Jaffa. Pilgrimage to the Holy Land had become well established among Italian Jews in the eighteenth century, and shiploads of such pilgrims regularly departed from Livorno.[2] That night Judith wrote uneasily of Montefiore's "great inclination to visit Palestine, which enterprise I hope he will not undertake."[3] But the desire remained an *idée fixe* for her husband, one that assumed an increasingly concrete form.[4]

The Torah tells us that the land of Israel is God's gift to his chosen people: a territory covenanted to them in perpetuity if they remain loyal to him and live according to the laws he has given them.[5] The prophets recount how the people of Israel fell into sin, and how in return they were finally forced into exile. Over the centuries, Jewish thinkers elaborated a complex mystical geography in which the land of Israel featured as the center of the world, the heavenly portal of holiness connecting heaven and earth. But this holiness can be realized only in conjunction with God's holy people, and so Jews continued to see the land of Israel as the place where God's people really belonged, the country to which they would one day return. Thus the sense of connectedness to the land of Israel cultivated through Jewish liturgy was intimately linked to the yearning for a messiah, whose coming would deliver Jews from the oppression and persecution of the diaspora. Montefiore prayed for this miraculous event on a daily basis, saying the ritual words: "Return in mercy to Jerusalem your city and dwell in it as you have promised. Rebuild it soon in our days as an eternal structure and speedily install in it the throne of David. Blessed are you the Lord who rebuilds Jerusalem."

Every week after performing the ritual that marks the end of the Sabbath, the Montefiores (like all Sephardim) read a hymn in honor of the prophet Elijah, whose task it is to announce the coming of the messiah. On one such Saturday evening, Montefiore and Judith fell to talking about "the good news of which this prophet's appearance was to be the harbinger for Jerusalem." What fun it would be, they thought, to visit Mount Carmel and see the very spot where Elijah had confounded the priests of Ba'al. Many years later, an elderly Montefiore showed his nephew Leonard a simple gold ring, engraved with the Hebrew words *Koneh hacol*, meaning "possessor of all things." Montefiore told Leonard how that night "I dreamed I saw in front of me a venerable man whom I knew to be Elijah the Prophet: he pointed to Jerusalem which I recognised in the distance, and said only those two words engraved upon my ring . . . I awoke, and then dreamt this a second time and then a third time, each time hearing only the words *Koneh hacol*. And the dream made so strong an impression upon me, that I resolved the very first thing I would do when I had time would be to go to the Holy Land."[6]

The nineteenth century was an age of faith as well as reason. Like many of his Christian contemporaries, Montefiore believed the coming of the messiah was a historical inevitability and that God was an omnipotent and omnipresent being, constantly intervening in human affairs to reward the virtuous and punish the wicked. But the "Providence" of which Montefiore and Judith wrote so frequently took Jewish form in his subconscious. Jews recognized Elijah as God's messenger on earth: a real figure who might appear at any moment bearing good tidings, to restore the sick to health or bring help in an hour of need.[7] Many Jews have seen him in their dreams, like Montefiore; others have met him in a marketplace or on a lonely road. Who better than Elijah to articulate Montefiore's deep-seated ambivalence about his worldly possessions and his sense of unfulfilled yearning?

The Montefiores would travel many times to Palestine, but this first pilgrimage carried a special emotional charge. Judith's travel diaries had always provided a space to stop and think about her experiences; only now did she feel that others might find interest in these reflections. On her return, she reworked her 1827 journal and published it privately, dedicating it to her beloved husband: "A slight Memorial of Pleasures and Dangers Shared Together, in the contemplation of Many Sacred Scenes."[8]

Montefiore's diaries were rather more businesslike: they described who he met, where he went, and what he did with them; only occasionally what he thought and felt. But even Montefiore regarded the diaries from his first trip to the Holy Land as special. The family papers contain a complete transcript of these diaries: page after page of elegant copperplate, carefully written into a blue, leather-bound volume to be treasured as an heirloom when he died.[9] Never previously used by historians, it is the most complete of all his diaries to survive.

At first their progress was unspectacular. By the time Montefiore, Judith, and their manservant, Thomas Armstrong, had boarded the steamboat *Crusader* at Dover, the fog was so thick that the captain could barely find Calais harbor. But the sea was smooth as glass, and when they eventually reached France they were joined by Judith's niece Jeanette and her husband, David Salomons, both in their late twenties.[10] It was not always easy going. Even in May, the snow on the Alpine passes near Mont Cenis was deep enough to cover the wheels of their carriage, forming a wall on each side and making for slow progress. Farther south, when Montefiore fancied walking down a mountain in the Campagna, Judith entertained "a thousand vague fears of *banditti*, and other sources of danger."[11] But they arrived without incident at Rome, which Judith greeted as an old friend. "On this our third visit to the Eternal City," she wrote in her diary, "I found my gratification equal to that which I experienced at the first view of it, and perhaps greater."[12] Here they spent the Sabbath and celebrated their wedding anniversary with "an elegant dinner at the Hotel d'Europe," to which they invited the Salomons and the Mazzaras. "Thanks be to Providence for having preserved us to enjoy this day," wrote Montefiore. "God bless my dear wife."[13]

In Rome Montefiore and Mazzara came to some kind of financial understanding that enabled him to join the party. And so it was that three traveling carriages clattered out of the city bound for Naples, whence they hoped to set sail for Alexandria. By this time it had become clear that Jeanette was in no state to continue. No sooner had the Salomons joined them at Calais than David began to wonder whether such a challenging tour was suitable for ladies. He and Jeanette finally parted company with the Montefiores in Naples. Judith was made of sterner stuff than her niece, and it is to Montefiore's credit that he entertained no doubts about her ability to endure danger and discomfort like a trouper.[14]

Initial inquiries made it clear that direct travel to Alexandria was out of the question, so Montefiore decided to head for Malta. Even this itinerary proved a tall order. The owner of a British brig wrote offering berths for the outrageous sum of £100. Montefiore refused instantly, resolving to "wait with patience" rather than be taken for a ride. Four days later, this patience was wearing thin. When the captain of the *Porcia* asked £50 for the same journey, Montefiore had little choice but to accept—even though the captain warned him that there was no cook, a very bad steward, and no accommodation for passengers. "[I]t is too much," he wrote with resignation, "but we are at his mercy."[15]

The delay left plenty of time for preparations. While Judith packed her jewelry into a small box, which she left with the Rothschilds for safekeeping, Montefiore and Mazzara went shopping. By the time they had finished, the Montefiores' hotel rooms were crammed with portmanteaux, mosquito nets, leather flasks, military saddles, even a portable bedstead—enough, said Judith, "to make anyone believe we were about to travel with the caravensary." Joking apart, she was only too well aware of the challenges that lay ahead of them.[16]

For one thing, the political situation was unstable. The 1821 revolt of Greek Christians against Ottoman rule had destabilized the entire eastern Mediterranean, unleashing an orgy of religious and ethnic violence from Jerusalem to the Peloponnese—a wave of massacres and riots in which Christians and Muslims, Greeks, Turks, and Arabs, took enthusiastic part. At first neither side could force a victory. Then Sultan Mahmud appealed to his overmighty vassal, Mehmed Ali of Egypt, promising land in return for help in quelling the rebellion in Crete. By early 1825, Ottoman forces under Mehmed Ali's son Ibrahim were making rapid progress. As news of Egyptian atrocities reached western Europe, the British foreign secretary found himself under growing pressure to act. But Canning was also wary of the Greeks' Orthodox loyalties. Unwilling to allow Russia a foothold on the Mediterranean and equally unhappy at the prospect of Egypt's emerging as a serious power, he declared himself ready to mediate between the two sides. An Anglo-Russian protocol early in 1826 paved the way for international intervention. Even as the Montefiores packed their bags in Naples, Britain, France, and Russia were negotiating a treaty designed to put an end to hostilities by forcing the sultan to recognize an autonomous Greek state.[17]

Judith and Montefiore must have considered the implications of this situation before they left London. Perhaps as a result, the plan of continuing to Jerusalem remained "extremely doubtful." Now, however, they were on the point of actually embarking for the East. As Judith made ready to depart for what was effectively a war zone, she felt a combination of hope and trepidation, praying "that the Almighty might grant us health, safety, and courage; and render us grateful for all His mercies!"[18]

Her first impressions were hardly reassuring. Judith was always a bad sailor, but her sufferings on board the *Porcia* were worse than anything. Never had she passed so dreadful a night, "in a space scarcely sufficient to sit upright; intense heat, added to that unrelenting sea-malady; the throbbing of my head keeping pace with the violent rolling of the ship; the noise of bottles, decanters, earthenware . . . clashing against each other on the floor, joined to the uproar of the roaring billows and peals of thunder." Feverish and agitated, she was in such a state that the frugal Montefiore thought nothing of paying £20 for a detour to Messina so that they could cross Sicily by land. The lack of decent roads forced them to travel in a glorified sedan chair, known as a *lettiga*. Cooped up in a tiny space, overcome by the heat, they struggled to retain their dignity amidst the dissonant jangles of the mules' bells and the cries of "He!—cattio! cattioo allo!" with which their guides drove the mules forward down the rough, bumpy track. Nor did things improve during the choppy crossing from Sicily on board a primitive *sperenara*, whose captain appeared to lack basic navigational equipment and ability.[19] "Thank God! to be comfortable on land," declared Montefiore with feeling when they finally reached Malta.[20]

Whereas Sicily had provided a taste of the discomforts ahead of them, the British colony of Malta represented a brief return to normality. The capital, Valetta, perched precariously on a hill in the bright sunlight, a maze of steps and winding streets, accessible only to pedestrians and baggage mules. Like London and Livorno, but hotter and more exotic, Valetta was a meeting place for "strangers from every country under heaven."[21] But Malta also contained much that was familiar. As an outpost of the British Empire, it offered wealthy travelers an opportunity to socialize with the great and the good—in this case, Governor and Lady Ponsonby, Sir John and Lady Stoddart, and several British naval officers and their wives. Montefiore and Judith went sightseeing, attended formal dinners, exchanged morning calls, inspected the local free schools and a workhouse. They even hosted a slap-up dinner for nearly 150 employees of the British Colonial Silk Company, of which Montefiore was a director.[22]

The tense international situation continued to render traveling hazardous. Britain, France, and Russia had signed the Treaty of London only days before the Montefiore party arrived in Malta in early July. No one knew how the sultan would respond to the ultimatum of these three great powers. "The reports here today are that war will commence against the Turks," Montefiore wrote glumly. "I sincerely hope not: as in that case, I should not know what to do."[23] He appears to have concealed his doubts from his wife. She noted with fond resignation: "Montefiore seems bent upon going . . . I trust we shall be guided safely by that good Providence which has hitherto preserved us."[24]

Piracy was an added complication. Forced onto the defensive by Ibrahim's army, control of the seas became the Greeks' only advantage. With little infrastructure or taxation, they turned to privateering to finance their campaign, unleashing what the French Admiral de Rigny described as "[t]he most appalling maritime brigandage to which the misuse of words has ever given birth."[25] The situation made it almost impossible for Montefiore, Judith, and Mazzara to obtain a safe passage to Alexandria. Ponsonby had advised them "to go on a ship of war, on account of the Greek pirates."[26] It was two weeks before the Montefiores found a merchant vessel willing to transport them, and another fortnight until a British naval convoy was ready to escort the *Leonidas* to Alexandria.

The voyage to Egypt was disrupted by nothing worse than seasickness and a couple of false alarms; Alexandria proved more of a shock. Judith was repelled by the filth and stench of the place, and the gross sight of pigs and dogs scavenging for food amid piles of ordure and rotting refuse. But she was attracted, too, by the exotic novelty of it all. The "Turks" riding their donkeys through the narrow streets and the loaded camels swaying decorously brought home to her "that we were no longer in Europe or among Europeans." As she began to feel more comfortable in these strange surroundings, she was able to appreciate the antiquity of the city, every quarter of which presented a "reflecting mind" with "some relic of past grandeur."[27]

The Montefiores had arrived in Alexandria at a moment of extreme political uncertainty, and it seemed best to continue almost immediately to Cairo and the Pyramids. Their retinue now included Mazzara, Armstrong, Captain Anderson of the *Leonidas*, two seamen, and their Mal-

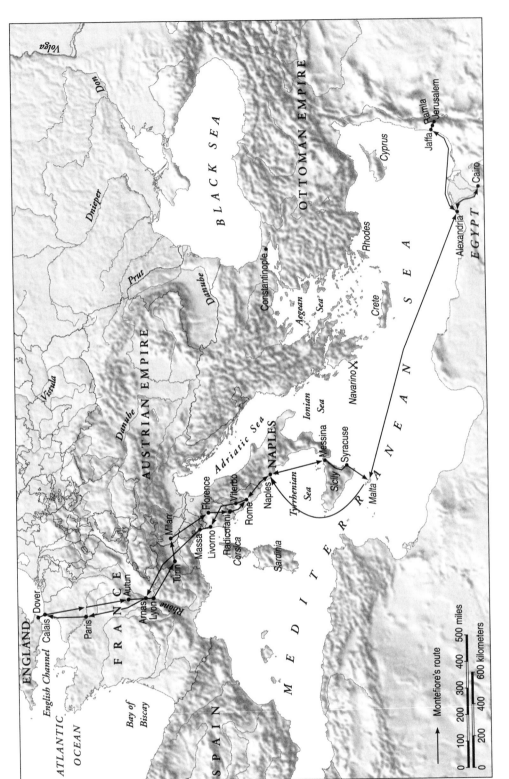

Route taken by the Montefiores on their first visit to Palestine, 1827–28

tese servants, Marguerite and Paulo. Judith complained endlessly of the heat and the intolerable swarms of mosquitoes, but Montefiore was stoic. He enjoyed the moonlit boat trip and the picturesque banks of the Nile: the huts built from reeds, the fields humming with activity, the boats laden with transports of corn and "female Black Slaves ugly as devils, but with fine necklaces and earrings." As for the Pyramids, "they must be seen to be felt," he wrote in a rare display of awe and humility, "a sensation that cannot be described."[28]

On their return to Cairo, Mr. Salt, the ailing British consul, informed Montefiore that as a wealthy and well-connected European he was expected to pay his respects to Mehmed Ali.[29] Born to provincial insignificance in the Macedonian town of Kavala, this illiterate Albanian had, in the words of one British diplomat, "carved his way to power and fame by his own indomitable courage, perseverance and sagacity."[30] From the beginning, Western observers suspected that Mehmed Ali wanted to break free of his Ottoman overlord. He was nothing if not cautious, and wisely began by consolidating his position in Egypt. Surrounding himself with foreign experts, he launched a comprehensive modernization program that aimed to turn Egypt into a heavyweight industrial and military power. But, as one British traveler noted, the cost of maintaining fancy modern equipment in Egypt's new shipyards and armaments factories was out of all proportion to its usefulness: iron rapidly corroded in the humid atmosphere, and the desert sands clogged the machinery until it ground to a halt.[31] Mehmed Ali was, moreover, openly contemptuous of his Egyptian subjects; he spoke only Turkish and refused to learn Arabic. The changes he introduced brought money flooding into his own coffers, but life grew harder for the poor fellahin of the countryside. Irrigation and new systems of land tenure were no compensation for conscription and heavier taxation in the desperate struggle to make ends meet. Meanwhile, behind the facade of bureaucratic and consultative government, Mehmed Ali continued to make all the decisions himself. According to one contemporary, he ran his country from a secretariat "composed of *effendiya* [clerks] who all write in the palms of their hands, crouching on a divan."[32]

By the time he met Montefiore, Mehmed Ali was in his late fifties, a stocky man with a clean-shaven head and a piercingly intelligent expression.[33] But as Montefiore discovered, the pasha of Egypt had lost none of his capacity to impress and charm. Keen to promote his public image as an energetic and visionary ruler, Mehmed Ali spoke of his eagerness to introduce "every new invention" and made a point of informing Montefiore that he "never indulges in more than four hours' sleep."[34] All this had the desired effect: on his return from the meeting, an enthu-

with great devotion; all the tunes new to me. *Paras[h]a[h]* [Torah portion] by a boy under 14. Between 30 & 40 small oil lamps burning, and 3 larger before the *Achal* [Ark] . . . We afterwards attended a small but neat synagogue at 6a0 the property, and kept at the sole expence of Mr. Fua, elegantly lighted with a great number of wax candles, and real glass lamps: about 40 persons present; all, except the Proprietor & his aged uncle (above 90) were Europeans in Frank dresses. The Evening prayers were extremely well read with great devotion and many of the tunes were the same as in our Synagogue in London. The Ladies Gallery was splendidly illuminated with wax candles. One lady in a rich Turkish habit, covered with diamonds and pearls.[42]

Judith accompanied Montefiore to this third synagogue, where she pronounced the congregation to be "numerous and respectable."[43]

Montefiore and Judith certainly considered the exotic dress of the Jews in Alexandria to be worthy of notice. Yet as far as possible, given the obvious differences in wealth, culture, and status, this encounter with their Egyptian brethren was a meeting between equals.[44] Of course, Montefiore was also struck by the poverty he encountered among the Jews of Alexandria, and by the decrepit state of the synagogues in which he prayed. Naturally, he felt most comfortable in the Fua synagogue, where nearly everyone wore European clothes and he knew the tunes well enough to sing along with the rest. As a member of Bevis Marks with relatives of his own in Livorno, Montefiore had much in common with the wealthy Francos of Alexandria.

His wife was equally at ease with them. When Judith visited the Ladies' Gallery in the Fua synagogue on the Day of Atonement, she found it "well attended; among the ladies were many from various parts of Europe, more especially from Leghorn [Livorno] . . . Italian seemed more generally spoken than Arabic; all the children, as well as the Franks, conversing in that language. It was most satisfactory to see so numerous a class of our brethren so highly respectable and well educated as those were whose acquaintance I had so recently formed in this remote and neglected country."[45] Far from experiencing culture shock, Judith found herself very much at home.

Montefiore's diary stresses small differences between the services he attended in Alexandria and those of his own congregation at Bevis Marks. Such notations bring home his fundamental familiarity with the Jewishness of his surroundings. On the second day of the New Year, for instance, Montefiore noted that the Torah scrolls were kept in a wooden case instead of being draped in vestments. He was also interested by the *shofar* they used, "a Ram's horn, not half the length of those used in

London, and extremely crooked, but sounds well." Likewise, when he attended the Great Synagogue for the Day of Atonement, Montefiore remarked that the prayers were "well read and with devotion, but not in so solemn a manner as with us in London."[46]

Judith was far more critical, complaining that the women in the Ladies' Gallery chatted rather too merrily. "The gentlemen tell me, it is not considered essential for ladies to observe that strict piety which is required of themselves," she wrote, "but surely at a place of devotion the mind ought to testify due respect and gratitude towards the Omnipotent." Since Judaism demands relatively little of women in terms of formal religious observance, Judith's emphasis on female piety reflected her assimilation of the religious values and practices of the English middle classes. Yet there is no cultural arrogance in her remark, only a sense that Mrs. Fua and her friends should have been expected to demonstrate the kind of respectful behavior that Judith took for granted. Unlike Christian travelers from Europe, neither she nor her husband saw their coreligionists in Egypt through "orientalist" eyes.[47]

By the time the Montefiores celebrated the Day of Atonement in Alexandria, they had been in Egypt for nearly two months. Their chances of continuing to Palestine appeared virtually nil. Fua advised that "it would be worse than madness to attempt going at this period to Jerusalem; the plague is at Acre; the whole of Syria in a state of revolt. The Christians have fled to the mountains for safety; and besides all this, the undecided question of war and peace between the English and the Turks."[48] Struggling with constipation and the acute discomfort caused by suppurating boils on his neck, Montefiore conceded defeat. Reluctantly, he prepared to set sail for Livorno with the first available convoy.[49]

Then, quite suddenly, news reached Alexandria that Mehmed Ali's son Ibrahim was likely to come to terms with the British and French squadrons in the eastern Mediterranean. This was an unlooked-for window of opportunity, and Judith persuaded Montefiore to seize the moment.[50] "As no convoy will sail for 15 days," Montefiore explained in his diary, "I have determined, at all risks, to proceed to Jaffa and Jerusalem. I find my health and strength failing me so fast in this City, that I deem it more prudent to flee from it, even at the chance of encountering the Greek pirates, for which purpose, I have agreed with Capt. Jones of the Henry Williams, a Brig of 167 tons, to take us to Jaffa & bring us back for £50."[51] Mazzara refused to accompany them. Frankly terrified at the prospect of traveling without an escort, he claimed he was coming down with an attack of boils himself. Instead, the party consisted of Armstrong, Paulo, Captain Anderson, and a local merchant, Thomas Bell.

Bell introduced the Montefiores to a physician from Ireland named Richard Madden. As the pioneering author of a history of the United Irishmen and their republican rebellion of 1798, Madden was destined to become a major figure in Irish historiography. A devout Catholic and proud Irish patriot, he had something in common with Montefiore's collaborators in the Provincial Bank of Ireland. His experience of religious discrimination in Britain placed him in the same category as Thomas Hodgkin and Sam Gurney, with whom as an antislavery activist he shared wider humanitarian concerns. He became a lifelong friend of the Montefiores, dedicating his account of his experiences in Africa and Asia to Montefiore and returning with them to Alexandria in 1840.[52] In both temperament and background, he conformed to the pattern of Montefiore's friendships outside his immediate Jewish circle: religiously disfranchised, socially committed, intellectually engaged.

On this their first encounter, Madden had just returned from Damietta, after being taken captive by Greek pirates while traveling on a ship carrying a cargo of Turkish tobacco.[53] Yet he blithely informed the Montefiores that they would encounter no pirates—although he did advise Turkish dress.[54] Judith promptly purchased a white muslin turban and a blue burnoose, obviously tickled at the romantic prospect of traveling in disguise. As Madden subsequently admitted, "it required more than ordinary courage to think of undertaking the journey at such a moment," but the much-tried Montefiore felt only elation at the prospect.[55] "No one," he declared with uncharacteristic emotion, "will ever say the *Agada* [Passover service] with more true devotion than I shall do when it pleases Providence to restore me to my Country, and redeem me and my dear Judith from this horrid land of misery & plagues, the hand of God being still upon it."[56]

No sooner had they set sail from Alexandria than Montefiore's health began to improve. When they arrived in Jaffa four days later, he had nothing but praise for the beautiful weather and delightful countryside they encountered in the Holy Land. Most English visitors commented on its desolation, but Montefiore was struck by the "large Gardens" they passed on the way to the Greek convent at Ramla, which boasted "Pomegranates the finest we had ever seen; Figs, Pears, Oranges and Lemons." They woke early the next morning with the prospect of a good ten-hour ride ahead of them. Some of the way lay across a sandy, partly cultivated plain, but much of it took them up rocky and difficult mountain passes—prompting Judith to remark cheerfully that the hills of Palestine were nothing compared to the mountains of Sicily.[57]

"Jerusalem from the road leading to Bethany," as rendered by the Scottish artist David Roberts, who visited Palestine and the Middle East in 1838–39; in The Holy Land, Syria, Idomea, Arabia, Egypt & Nubia, *vol. 1 (London, 1855), plate 6. His iconic sketches shaped the image of the Holy Land in Victorian England. (By permission of the Bodleian Library, University of Oxford: Mason HH90)*

After all they had been through, both Judith and Montefiore were profoundly affected when they finally reached their destination. "Our feelings of gratitude were indescribable," wrote Judith of the moment when they finally caught sight of the "long wished for view of Jerusalem."[58] For once, Montefiore's diary is more personal: "With humble thanks to my God, the God of my Fathers, the only True God, we arrived safe, without any accident in the City of our forefathers, the great and long-desired object of our wishes and journey. May God Almighty bless my dear Wife and honoured Mother, make me more deserving of his manifold blessings & mercies, that I may become every day a better man, a more righteous Jew, and more useful to my poorer brethren in general: so that my latter days may be virtuous and peaceable! May my God guard and protect me and my dear Wife to the end of our lives, and then receive our souls to His Almighty Care!"[59]

Their contrasting responses to Jerusalem undermine the assumption that Judith—not Montefiore—was the more religious of the two.[60] Judith certainly saw Jerusalem through Jewish eyes, but her reliance on

Josephus' classic account of Roman Judea and her lengthy historical reflections on Jerusalem's tragic past demonstrate a European sensibility
that sets her apart from other Jewish pilgrims in this period. Deploying
received religious formulas rather than the imaginative style of European travelogues, Montefiore's reaction is more profoundly rooted in
Jewish tradition. He knew intuitively that prayer was the only appropriate response. His style is stilted and formal, but it conveys a sense of
occasion that is entirely fitting. In his heartfelt wish to become a better
man, Montefiore gives voice to the moral commitment that lay behind
his desire to visit Jerusalem. He demonstrates his continued preoccupation with mortality and his instinctive understanding of the connection between charity and righteousness in Judaism—a connection underpinned in Hebrew, where the word used for charity *(tzedakah)* and
the word used to describe a righteous Jew *(tzaddik)* share the same root.
In London, these ideas had been central to Montefiore's personal religiosity; in the holy city, they would acquire still greater force.

Jerusalem in 1827 was a shabby, tumbledown place of crumbling stone
walls and arches, of winding lanes and passageways.[61] From a distance
it looked impressive: a city of domes and fortresses rising out of a rocky,
mountainous landscape, the dry, dusty country relieved only by olive
trees and the ruins of ancient graves. But the majestic city walls concealed a backwater, inhabited by fewer than 15,000 people, moldering
away quietly in a forgotten corner of the Ottoman Empire.[62]

The streets appeared to European visitors to be overflowing with the
rubble of centuries—stones, earth, ashes, bits of pottery, bones, and
wood.[63] The city's inhabitants felt no compunction about burying the
contents of their latrines in the middle of the street. Piles of rubbish were
simply left to rot, while Jerusalemites dragged the carcasses of horses,
donkeys, and camels outside the walls to be devoured by dogs and jack-
als. Not for nothing was Judith moved to reflect on the city's "fallen,
desolate and abject" state. Indeed, it seemed to her that "not a single
relic" was left of "the city that was the joy of the whole earth."[64]

The city was not even a major administrative center. Situated in a part
of Palestine traditionally disputed between the neighboring Pashaliks of
Sidon and Damascus, Jerusalem was reduced to garrisoning a few soldiers and housing a minor provincial governor. Ottoman power in the
surrounding area had been undermined over the centuries. Local chiefs
in the mountains of central Palestine assumed many of the functions of
government, taking responsibility for tax collection and law and order.[65]
The mountain chiefs commanded small armies drawn principally from

their own extended families. These militias defended the inhabitants against the frequent attacks by Bedouin tribesmen, but they found plenty of opportunity to fight among themselves. Palestine was a rough, dangerous, sparsely populated country, where the rule of Ottoman law counted for little outside the towns in a society governed by ties of kinship, honor, and force.

Jerusalem made up in religious authority for what it lacked in administrative clout. Economically moribund, the holy city was relatively isolated from its rural hinterland. Most cities in the Arab world were dominated by an alliance of Muslim clerics, craft guilds, and leading merchants, but in Jerusalem the religious elite, known as the *ulama,* ruled supreme. For Jerusalem was home to the Al Aqsa mosque, revered as the third holiest site in Islam. In practice the city was governed by the Islamic judge or *cadi,* with the help of the guardians of Al Aqsa and other holy men. Yet Jews and a variety of Christian sects made up over half the population.

Jerusalem's approximately 3,000 Jews probably represented about a quarter of the total.[66] Unlike the city's Christians, they lacked powerful protectors abroad—and so the Jewish quarter was widely reviled as the filthiest part of the city, right by the municipal abattoir. European travelers emphasized the contempt with which Jews were treated by men for whom the word "Jew" was "the very lowest of all possible words of abuse."[67] They described how Jews walking through the city streets looked as if they expected to be stoned and insulted, and how Arabs urged their recalcitrant donkeys forward with cries of *"Emshi ya'Ibn -el yahoodi!"*—"On you go, O son of a Jew!" Muslim court records tell a different story.[68] They reveal a city in which Jews were an integral part of the economic system, active not just in finance but as craftsmen, merchants, and physicians; a city in which Jews turned to Islamic law to seek redress not just against their Muslim and Christian neighbors but also within their own community; a city where the *cadi* regularly defended Jewish causes against high-handed local governors and arbitrary provincial rulers. The inferiority of Jews was built into the system, but it affected their daily life in a relatively limited way.

Some Jews in Jerusalem were wealthy, but most relied for their survival on handouts from the Jewish diaspora.[69] Communities all over Europe and the Mediterranean had established funds and organized collections to support Jews in the land of Israel. Italy came to play an important part in this process, with large sums from Germany, North Africa, and other Italian cities passing through Livorno, where communal leaders made an offer to buy Palestine for the Jews.[70] During the eighteenth century much of this money, known as *halukah,* began to be

gathered and sent on to Palestine by two central fund-raising committees, the Istanbul Officials (Pekidei Kushta) and the Amsterdam Officials
(Pekidim ve'Amarkalim be'Amsterdam, or Pekam). In addition, it was
common practice for Jewish communities in the four holy cities—Jerusalem, Safed, Hebron, and Tiberias—to send emissaries on fund-raising
tours throughout the diaspora.

Pilgrimage reinforced this sense of connection. In an era that saw the
birth of tourism, it had become customary for "every Sephardi Jew who
fears God and has the means to go to the Land of Israel once in his lifetime" in order to visit Jerusalem and the graves of Jewish holy men.[71]
The richest came with quite an entourage: a servant to prepare their coffee, a ritual slaughterer, and a scribe to take down descriptions of the
holy places.[72] It was considered virtuous to die in the land of Israel, and
over the centuries many elderly Jews traveled there with this in mind.
This trend led to a relatively aged and disproportionately female population in the Holy Land.[73] In the eighteenth century, these most traditional forms of Jewish migration were bolstered by the activities of the
Istanbul Officials, who drew up annual lists of would-be immigrants and
chartered ships to take them to Jaffa in large groups. They were joined
by growing numbers of Sephardi scholars, who established important
centers of talmudic and cabalistic learning in Jerusalem.[74] During the
same period, the followers of certain Ashkenazi rabbis in eastern Europe
also began to move to Palestine.[75] For all its poverty, Jerusalem retained
its place at the emotional and spiritual heart of the Jewish diaspora.

These connections enabled the Montefiores to arrive bearing intro-
ductions from London's two leading rabbis.[76] Montefiore's origins in the
Western Sephardi diaspora had helped them feel at ease among the Jews
of Alexandria. Now he and Judith were among real friends. They had
made arrangements to stay with a Moroccan Jew from Gibraltar who
had visited London on two extended business trips in 1799 and 1808,
when he would have worshipped with the Montefiores at Bevis Marks.
Joseph Amzalak had apparently started out as a slave-trader, but after
settling briefly in Malta he was persuaded by a distinguished rabbi to
cease trafficking in souls.[77] Upon moving to Palestine, he dedicated the
rest of his life to Torah study, repentance, charity, and good deeds. His
wealth and British citizenship placed him in a different class from the
rest of the community. According to the Protestant missionary Joseph
Wolff, Amzalak "never visited any of the Jews: he was a Prince among
them; they all came to him, but he went nowhere."[78] For wealthy Jewish
visitors from England, he was the obvious host. Yet the Montefiores'
decision to stay with Amzalak set them apart from other European tourists. The governor of Jerusalem, clearly feeling that a convent was more

suited than the Jewish quarter to wealthy Westerners, offered to find them a house elsewhere in the City. Montefiore refused the invitation, noting in his diary: "I hope I shall ever live, and die, in the society of my brethren of Israel."[79]

Even within the Jewish community, the Montefiores' decision caused some resentment. The Ashkenazi Rabbi Mendel had been eagerly awaiting their arrival, and pressed them to stay with members of his own community. Amzalak, however, warned them that to do so "would be offering him the greatest possible affront."[80] When the Montefiores were invited to dine with Mendel, Amzalak did his best to disrupt the occasion by reminding them that he had invited Captain Anderson and Mr. Bell to dinner himself. Showing scant respect for Mendel, Amzalak urged his honored guests "not to prolong our visit beyond what politeness on our part required." The upshot was that Judith and Montefiore found themselves obliged to dine twice.

This wrangling reflected deep-rooted tensions between the Sephardi and Ashkenazi communities.[81] In about 1700 a group of eastern European followers of the false messiah, Shabbatei Zevi, had set out for Jerusalem. In 1720, when they failed to maintain repayments on a loan, frustrated creditors destroyed their synagogue. Remnants of the community and the trickle of new immigrants from Russia and Poland disguised themselves as Sephardim to avoid being taken hostage as security on the outstanding debt. But they kept coming, and by the time of Montefiore's visit in 1827 there were 160 Ashkenazi Jews in Jerusalem—a tiny minority, overshadowed by the well-established Sephardi community, but a growing minority importing new religious trends from eastern Europe.[82]

The Sephardim of Jerusalem dressed in the robes and turbans of the Middle East. They spoke Arabic as well as Ladino (a form of Judeo-Spanish), and some at least made a living as craftsmen and shopkeepers. They understood their place in Ottoman society and knew how to cope in the Muslim world. The Ashkenazim, who now lived openly in Jerusalem, wore fur hats and black silk caftans as if they had never left their cold northern homeland. Since they spoke Yiddish, they struggled to communicate with their Arab neighbors and had to use Hebrew with the Sephardim to make themselves understood. Profoundly religious and desperately poor, all they wanted was to study and pray. The two communities kept to themselves: they inhabited different parts of the Jewish quarter and married only among themselves.

Throughout the diaspora, it was customary for Jewish immigrants to adapt to the religious traditions of the established community, but the Ashkenazim in Jerusalem refused to do so. This obduracy mattered be-

cause religious practices like burial and ritual slaughter were important
sources of income for the Sephardi community, which was responsible
for paying the whole community's taxes. They refused to allow the Ashkenazim to establish their own communal institutions, to supervise kosher butchers, or to bury their dead separately. Ashkenazi resentment
only grew under the existing system, which enabled the Sephardim to
appropriate property left by Ashkenazim who died in Israel. Disputes
over the distribution of *halukah* monies added to the tensions. In the
early 1820s a group of Ashkenazim applied to the Ottoman government
for formal recognition as a distinct community.

It was the particular wish of London's Ashkenazi chief rabbi, Solomon
Hirschell, that Montefiore try to resolve the difficulties between the two
communities.[83] He clearly understood very little about them, identifying
eastern Europeans with the German Jews he knew in London and the
Ottoman Sephardim with his own Spanish and Portuguese congregation. "We called on the *Haham* [chief Sephardi rabbi]," he wrote in his
diary; "I entreated him to act always friendly to the German Jews . . . At
12 with the German Rabbi Mendel: tried to persuade them to unite with
the Portuguese, but found it impossible. They said, when the Messiah
comes there will be two *Minogs* [traditions], and in the days of David it
was so."[84] Throughout his visit he tried to be even-handed, but the fact
that he was staying with Amzalak inevitably shaped Montefiore's experiences. Although he was Sephardi and Judith Ashkenazi, in terms of
dress and culture they belonged to neither camp. As the first European
Jews of wealth and distinction to visit the Holy Land, their arrival was
such an extraordinary event that it seemed "almost like the coming
of the Messiah" to the *Haham Bashi,* as the Sephardi chief rabbi was
called.[85]

On the second day of their visit, Amzalak took Montefiore on a tour
of communal institutions and Jewish holy places.[86] Judith, meanwhile,
set out on a day trip to Bethlehem, stopping at the Tomb of Rachel,
which she visited in the company of a group of Jewish women. This
desolate, solitary, crumbling ruin, its dome half open to the elements,
was a holy site for all Jews.[87] For an infertile woman like Judith it may
have had special significance. The Old Testament contains many tales of
barren women who were finally able to conceive through divine intervention. The matriarch Rachel was one of them. Indeed, Rachel had
been so distressed by her inability to bear children that she went to her
husband Jacob and complained, "Give me a child! And if there will be
no child, I shall die!"[88] Consequently, the Tomb of Rachel has become a
favorite site of religious pilgrimage for infertile Jewish women.[89] It seems
strange to associate such a practice with a well-educated Englishwoman

Judith's amulet asks for an opening of all the gates—those of the holy city of Jerusalem, as well as those of the tombs of the prophet Haggai and the prophetess Huldah. The stairs down to the water used by Aaron the High Priest and the waters of Shiloah are almost certainly a reference to the ritual called *tahara*. Down the right side, a poem for Judith forms an acrostic of her name. *(Courtesy of Robert Sebag-Montefiore; photograph by Lykke Stjernswärd)*

like Judith. Yet she must have been more aware of these superstitions than her published diaries indicate, because Judith was the owner of a fertility amulet—written for her by two Sephardi rabbis, whose family were the hereditary guardians of Rachel's Tomb.[90]

We think of amulets as objects, but in Judaism an amulet is a document containing a blessing or prayer. Judith's is a beautiful symbolic representation of the holy city, and the script calls on the spiritual power of the Holy Temple and the other holy sites in Jerusalem. A Jewish woman will conceive only after she has immersed and purified herself in running water, in a ritual called *tahara;* the depiction of the stairs down to the water used by Aharon the High Priest and the waters of Shiloah is probably a reference to this process. The amulet, which almost certainly dates from this first visit, when Judith was already in her early forties, is the earliest concrete evidence of a fertility cult at Rachel's Tomb. She was clearly moved by the experience. The language in her diary is direct and unselfconscious: there is no mention here of her favorite trope, "the reflecting mind." Instead Judith uses the first person, describing herself as "deeply impressed with a feeling of awe and respect, standing, as I thus did, in the sepulchre of a mother in Israel. The walls of the interior are covered with names and phrases chiefly in Hebrew and other Eastern characters; but some few English are to be found among them, and to these I added the names of Montefiore and myself."[91] What she hoped as she did so, we cannot know. All we can say is that in later life both she and her husband felt an emotional attachment to this holy site. Upon her return ten years later Judith was so distressed by its derelict state that she persuaded Montefiore to have the shrine restored and to arrange the transfer of rights over it to local Jews; when she died, he built her a mausoleum in its image.[92]

Judith's experience at the Tomb of Rachel underlines the religious character of the Montefiores' first trip to Palestine. It was in this spirit that Montefiore woke at half past two on the morning of their departure, to spend the whole night in prayer and study. He left deeply impressed with Jerusalem, declaring: "No city in the whole world can be finer situated than this, nor is there a better climate." That evening at the Greek convent in Ramla, Montefiore wrote in his diary with messianic yearning: "May the Almighty make us worthy to return when our brethren are gathered together! May it be in a short time, Amen."[93]

Two days later he celebrated his forty-third birthday on board the *Henry Williams.* He felt that it marked a new spiritual beginning:

I humbly pray to the God of my forefathers, my God, the one only true God, to grant that I may henceforth become, a more righteous and better

man, as well as better Jew, and that I may daily be more deserving of his
abundant mercies; that I may, to the end of my days, be guarded and directed by His Almighty Providence, and when it pleases Him to take me
from this world, May He graciously receive my soul, pardon & forgive
my iniquities; support and comfort my dear dear wife. This day I begin a
new era. I fully intend to dedicate much more time, towards the welfare
of the poor, and to attend as regularly as possible on Monday, Thursday,
and Saturday Synagogue.[94]

Secular Jews who revert to strict religious observance are known today as *ba'al teshuvah,* those who have done repentance. The term historically referred to those who had transgressed Jewish law and, after a
period of introspection, returned to the straight path. The concept of
returning to the fold makes sense in the modern world, where secularization and assimilation have undermined religious practice. It cannot
have had the same meaning in the early nineteenth century to someone
like Montefiore, whose religious beliefs and practices reflected the customs and traditions of Western Sephardim. Montefiore's emphasis on
the interplay between religious observance and philanthropy and the
reference to his own impending death reflected longstanding concerns.
His resolution on board the *Henry Williams* was no sudden conversion; it was the logical expression of a deep-rooted process of spiritual
growth. But it was also, in a way, a modern moment. Montefiore had
spent the past ten years refashioning himself as an English gentleman; he
now shaped himself consciously as a practicing Jew.

The Montefiores' return from Palestine appeared to their friends in Alexandria as little short of miraculous. It seemed that the *Henry Williams*
was the only ship sailing unprotected in that part of the Mediterranean
to have escaped attack by pirates during the past three months.[95] Within
days of their arrival, the most dramatic reports began to circulate: the
Allied squadrons charged with enforcing the naval blockade against
Mehmed Ali's son Ibrahim had been drawn into battle at Navarino and
destroyed the entire Egyptian and Ottoman navy at a stroke.
    News of the battle at Navarino wrought havoc in Alexandria. Women
filled the streets in a public outpouring of grief. It was rumored that the
sultan had sworn to massacre all his Christian subjects.[96] Panic spread
within the Christian community and among Francos like Fua, who
feared that Mehmed Ali would exact a dreadful revenge. Fortunately, he
took a realistic view of the situation. "I told them what would be the
consequence; did they think they had to deal with the Greeks?" he is

said to have exclaimed in exasperation on receiving the news. Aware that he would gain nothing from retaliation, Mehmed Ali promised to protect the Europeans in Alexandria. Montefiore reported that in public the pasha "spoke light of the loss of his fleet, said he should soon have another."[97] His real feelings were otherwise, and in a private letter he voiced his anger and despair, asking: "Shall I lament my fleet that is destroyed, or lament the fate of those Muslims who will fall victims of starvation?"[98]

Eager to be quit of Alexandria at this troublesome time, the Montefiores finally left Egypt on November 7, accompanied by Mazzara and Madden. The journey proved a nightmare for all of them; the *Leonidas* struggled for three weeks to make it to Malta in appalling weather. Judith and Montefiore kept to their beds, watching in terror as their furniture and boxes rolled from side to side of the state cabin. The *Leonidas* itself was leaky, her pumps constantly at work. "To describe such a storm is out of my power," wrote Montefiore; "the sea was truly running mountains high, and every instant breaking over the ship in a manner almost to swamp her, and sticking against her sides with a violence it appeared a miracle for her to withstand. Indeed, my poor Judith almost gave herself up for lost."[99] Two days later, as gathering clouds promised another dreadful storm, he made a desperate appeal for divine intervention. Shortly before noon on November 26, Montefiore: "threw into the sea, a piece of my Passover Cake, at the same time praying to God to preserve us, as He had, in old time, preserved our forefathers, from the turbulence of the sea, and in his great mercy, to grant us a fair wind, sufficient for our purpose."[100] In so doing, he reached back into Sephardi tradition and demonstrated his faith in an old seafaring charm. The Passover cake Montefiore threw into the Mediterranean was a piece of *Afikoman*—half of one of the three pieces of matza that play a special role in the Passover service. According to some traditions, breaking the middle matza into two halves symbolized the parting and crossing of the Red Sea. The *Afikoman* is the better part of this middle matza, and so, when a piece is thrown into the sea, the sea remembers God's promise of saving those who sail on, from danger.[101] The gesture certainly seemed to work for the Montefiores: that night, for the first time in more than a week, they enjoyed a "[f]ine moonlight Evening, with a smooth sea." "Thanks to the Almighty we are again in security," wrote Judith.[102]

Interestingly in the light of subsequent developments, Montefiore's own diary fails to make this linkage. In any case, the fine weather proved short-lived. Five days later, on a Saturday, Montefiore wrote that the winds "blew almost a hurricane [*sic*]: a frightful sea: the ship rolled and pitched so as to occasion the serious alarm of all on board . . . Our Captain had never in his life experienced a worse night." Only now did Montefiore begin to interpret his experiences in terms of divine protection, vowing: "I shall never forget the night, but, on each Sabbath eve, shall recollect with gratitude God's mercy to us, in saving us from destruction."[103] Retrospectively, he attributed greater significance to his own intervention with the *Afikoman*, and seems to have fused this experience in his memory with their survival of the later storm.

It is still a custom in the Sebag-Montefiore family to end the Passover service by reading a page from Montefiore's diary, dated Monday, November 26, 1827. This passage describes the events of the day in solemn and portentous language explicable only by hindsight. Here Montefiore attributes the miraculous turn of events to divine intervention much more clearly than in the original diary entry. He constructs a coherent narrative opening with a vivid account of their past sufferings, reaching a dramatic climax when "at this awful pause a little before noon" he finally decided to act, and ending with the resounding words of Captain Anderson: "I have not seen a finer night out of the Heavens for many & many a year." Finally, in recognition of "the Almighty's kind interposition in our behalf," Montefiore vows that he will "for ever bear Witness . . . & annually while I live repeat this fact to those I may have the happiness of being surrounded by on the Evening of the *Agada*."[104]

While in Egypt, both Judith and Montefiore had drawn parallels in their diaries between their own experience and the Exodus. For Montefiore, watching his *Afikoman* calm the storm gave these parallels added significance. Reinterpreted in this way, Montefiore's experiences on his return to Malta seemed a fitting end to his pilgrimage and to the process of spiritual rebirth that had accompanied it. They validated his belief in divine providence and enhanced his sense of personal blessedness before God.

Safe return to Malta meant weeks of quiet boredom in quarantine and a welcome return to the mundanities of normal life. When they were finally allowed ashore, Judith and Montefiore became caught up again in the social whirl of colonial life. Montefiore was particularly pleased to meet Admiral Sir Edward Codrington, the victor of Navarino—now under attack for commencing hostilities in very questionable circumstances. Codrington "took much pains" to explain himself to Montefiore, complaining that the ministers at home "did not appear to know or to be aware of all the instructions he had received from Stratford Canning," the British ambassador in Constantinople.[105] When the Montefiores set out for Naples in HMS *Mastiff*, Codrington gave Montefiore a letter addressed to the duke of Clarence—later King William IV—giving his own version of events.

It took the Montefiores three months to reach England, traveling via Rome and Montefiore's Livorno relatives—"Mun desiring to revisit his Native City after having been gratified by seeing the Holy City," as Judith explained.[106] Montefiore's health was near breaking point, and they wondered if it was wise to proceed. But he longed to see his "dear Mother," and so they decided to return home. After an emotional reunion with Rachel, Montefiore headed for the Admiralty, where he delivered Codrington's letters to the future William IV. Navarino is now a forgotten battle, but to Montefiore's contemporaries it really mattered; his role in "carrying despatches of the Battle of Navarino" would eventually form part of the Montefiore myth.

Back in London Montefiore resumed his business activities, but he did not forget his trip to Jerusalem. Two years later he sought to commemorate the experience by requesting the duke of Norfolk, hereditary marshal of England, to grant him "such an addition to his Crest as may perpetuate the remembrance of the said visit to the Holy City and as may be proper to be borne by Your Memorialist and his Descendants and by the other Descendants of his said late Father according to the Laws of Arms."[107] In such a formal document, it is surprising and oddly touching to find mention of the "arduous journey" he undertook "accompanied by his beloved Wife" in pursuit of their "anxious desire to Visit the City of Jerusalem in the Holy Land of their Forefathers." The duke of Norfolk responded by incorporating three banners emblazoned with the Hebrew word "Jerusalem" into the Montefiore coat of arms.

Sometimes we may find it hard to reconcile the two faces of Montefiore: the successful City businessman who cracked open a bottle of champagne at the Pyramids to toast "success to the Alliance and Marine, and Sam Gurney," and the religious Jew who used his *Afikoman* to quiet the troubled waters, and traveled all the way to Jerusalem after a prophetic dream.[108] The Montefiore coat of arms reminds us that for Montefiore, these aspects of his personality were complementary. At a time when most of his Jewish contemporaries aspired to blend unassumingly into the English gentry, Montefiore's proud desire to display his Jewishness in public was socially daring, perhaps even shocking. To say simply that he was not ashamed of his origins does not go nearly far enough.

Chapter 5

Rise, Sir Moses

In January 1828 the duke of Wellington formed a new government. That month the Irish Catholic agitator Daniel O'Connell organized an impressive display of numbers, with simultaneous meetings held in several thousand Irish parishes attracting more than one and a half million supporters. Whigs and Radicals were often instinctive supporters of religious liberty, but no one expected a national hero rejoicing in the sobriquet "Iron Duke" to compromise on traditional "Church and King" Tory values. They failed to appreciate that Wellington was, at bottom, a pragmatic military man. This was an era of weak party loyalties. Catholic emancipation was now a burning political issue, and the survival of Wellington's government depended on his alliance with the remnants of the pro-Catholic Canningite grouping.

The Catholic question was part of a wider debate about religious freedom. Under British law, Catholics, Protestant Dissenters, and Jews experienced differing degrees of discrimination. Catholics suffered most because the papacy was widely believed to pose a fundamental threat to British liberties, but both the Houses of Parliament and the universities of Oxford and Cambridge were closed to all non-Anglicans. O'Connell's mobilization of the Irish masses rendered the Catholic cause most compelling, but giving way could open the floodgates to democratic politics and Irish nationalism. By contrast, emancipating the Dissenters seemed relatively harmless. Here was an open-and-shut question of religious toleration; in terms of parliamentary politics, it stood far greater chances of success. When Montefiore returned from Palestine in late February, pressure to lift the disabilities against Dissenters was building.

In April 1828 Wellington set the parliamentary process in motion. His proposed repeal of the discriminatory Test and Corporation Acts had radical implications. "It is a really gratifying thing," noted the rising Whig politician Lord John Russell, "to force the enemy to give up his first line, that none but churchmen are worthy to serve the state, & I trust we shall soon make him give up the second, that none but Protestants are."[1] Russell did not mention Jews, but it should have been clear to all that the principle that none but Christians were worthy to serve the state would be the enemy's third—and most hard-fought—line of defense.[2]

From a Jewish perspective, the Dissenters' emancipation proved disastrous. Unlike Catholics, Jews as well as Dissenters had benefited from annual indemnity acts in recent decades, although continued civil disabilities still limited the social and professional opportunities open to both groups. The legislation drawn up to replace the old Test Acts introduced a new religious test to be administered on taking parliamentary or municipal office. This left Jews out in the cold. Not only were they stigmatized as a non-Christian minority for the first time; the new wording even threatened to deprive them of privileges they had previously enjoyed, like the right to vote.

In the spring of 1828, it was left to an individual to appreciate the significance of the impending repeal legislation. Alarmed at what he heard, Montefiore's intimate and business associate Isaac Lyon Goldsmid wrote to Wellington, asking him to rephrase the new religious test.[3] Such a move was out of the question, because the home secretary, Sir Robert Peel, had made the test a condition of his support for the bill. Wellington politely informed Goldsmid that he did not think an alteration would be possible.[4]

Anglo-Jewry still lacked a properly elected system of self-government, but it did possess a central coordinating body: the London Committee of Deputies of the British Jews.[5] At Goldsmid's instigation, this semi-moribund institution now held its first meeting in eight years.[6] This meeting marked the beginning of Montefiore's long involvement with the so-called Board of Deputies. Freshly returned from Jerusalem, his interest in Jewish emancipation caught fire. Together with Goldsmid and Nathan Rothschild, Montefiore threw himself into the world of political lobbying. These dynamic City figures, men at the height of their powers, represented a new generation of Anglo-Jewish leadership. Rothschild and Montefiore were a better-known team, but Goldsmid was very much part of Montefiore's extended family. Temperamentally they were very different.[7] Montefiore was profoundly spiritual; Goldsmid found inspiration in the Utilitarian philosophy of Jeremy Bentham. Montefiore's religious sensibility gave him something in common with devout Evangelicals and Quakers; Goldsmid's relatively secular and politicized worldview was more in keeping with the Enlightenment rationalism current among old-school Whigs and Radicals. Goldsmid was the more active of the two at this stage, but then he was a little older than Montefiore, and his activities already had a more political edge.[8]

Goldsmid was a key figure in establishing the nondenominational University College London, which opened its doors in 1829. UCL represented a significant breach in the Anglican establishment, and its founding council contained representatives of all the main constituencies in the battle for civil and religious liberty: the Whig Lord John Russell; the Evangelical abolitionist Zachary Macaulay; the banker Alexander Baring; the Benthamite political philosopher James Mill; George Birkbeck, founder of the Mechanics' Institution; and the Catholic duke of Norfolk. Besides Goldsmid, there were five Jews on this council, including Nathan Rothschild and Montefiore's uncle Moses Mocatta.[9] It is no coincidence that Goldsmid's eldest son, Francis Henry, was one of the first to take advantage of UCL by training as a barrister. The repeal of the Test Acts appeared as a sudden obstacle to his chosen career: Francis now needed to take an oath including the words "Upon the true faith of a Christian" if he wanted to be called to the bar.[10]

His son's predicament was very much on Goldsmid's mind when he wrote asking Wellington for a bill confirming the rights that Jews had exercised until now. This moderate step met with the approval of Lord Holland, nephew and political heir of that arch-Whig, Charles James Fox. Holland argued that whereas the government might support and implement a partial measure, the true friends of religious liberty could not propose anything less than complete emancipation without undermining their position, "and *that*, though reasonable and just and unobjectionable is as yet, I fear, unattainable."[11] Still, he thought that Jews would be fools to reject a partial measure on such grounds, because, after all, "half a loaf is better than no bread."

In the beginning, Jewish emancipation was very much a family affair. An engaging entry in Montefiore's diary from February 1829 recounts:

> Mr Isaac L. Goldsmid paid me a long visit, consulting as to the best mode of procuring general toleration for the Jews. Judith and self took a ride to see Hannah Rothschild and her husband. We had a long conversation on the subject of liberty for the Jews. He said he would shortly go to the Lord Chancellor and consult him on the matter. Hannah said if he did not, she would.

The spirit manifested here by Mrs Rothschild, and the brief but impressive language she used, reminded me most strikingly of her sister, Mrs Montefiore.[12]

The campaign itself was conducted largely behind closed doors—at meetings called in private houses and at political dinner parties, where Montefiore, Goldsmid, and Rothschild (and their wives) hobnobbed with the great and the good. The interlocking worlds of politics, business, and philanthropy ensured that all three men were already well networked in the circles that mattered.

These decades saw an unprecedented boom in British philanthropy. A plethora of voluntary societies embraced causes ranging from missionary activity through penal reform and antislavery to education, provision of medical care, and poor relief. Two complementary forces were at work: the spread of associational activity among the middle classes, and the rise of a dynamic Christianity dedicated to promoting the moral renovation of the world. With the same names cropping up repeatedly on charity boards, a philanthropic nexus emerged out of the close-knit structure of overlapping committees. Quakers and Evangelical Anglicans predominated in this charitable public sphere, but a smattering of political Radicals and Unitarians added an element of enlightened rationalism to the mix.[13]

Many took an interest in London's Jewish community. In a dynamic, rapidly growing metropolis, the Jewish poor represented a shockingly impoverished minority just as much in need of help as the rest of the underclass.[14] But philanthropy was never simply about doing good.[15] Giving enabled businessmen to enhance their social status and to nurture important contacts in the financial world. While the Quaker Matthias Attwood commented on "the liberality of the Jews to Christian institutions," the willingness of Christian businessmen to attend fundraising dinners on behalf of Jewish charities says something about the prominence of Jews in the City.[16] In 1838 Montefiore would preside over one such evening in aid of the Jews' Free School. It was attended by an array of City dignitaries, most of whom were well known to Montefiore: T. A. Curtis, governor of the Bank of England; Matthias Attwood, cofounder of Imperial Continental Gas; George Carroll, a longstanding business associate; Jno. Alteston, master of Montefiore's livery company; and the solicitor David Wire, based just around the corner from Montefiore in New Court, whose Evangelical Christianity suggests more complex religious dynamics at work.[17]

Often early nineteenth-century philanthropists were motivated by deep Christian commitment. In particular, men and women saw the flagship issue of antislavery as a means of purifying society from the sinful trade in souls.[18] The preoccupation with sin and a passionate desire to reform humanity reflected a climate of millenarian expectation. Many Protestants believed that the acceptance of Christianity by Jews was integral to the final process of mankind's redemption. Widespread faith in the imminence of the apocalypse prompted a resurgence of missionary activity focused on Jews.

This phenomenon built on existing tendencies within Anglo-Saxon Protestantism.[19] During the English Civil War, the spread of popular millenarianism had fostered a cultural fixation with Jews so powerful that it contributed to their readmission under Cromwell. That English Protestants identified sympathetically with the biblical Israelites only enhanced their nascent philo-Semitism.[20] As the spiritual heirs of God's chosen people, it behooved the English to show some care for those whom he had now forsaken. From the beginning, converting Jews was part and parcel of the wider religious revival. In 1809 members of the London Missionary Society founded the London Society for Promoting Christianity among the Jews to focus on this task.[21]

Very quickly the London Society became a charity of choice for the Protestant elite. Princess Victoria's father, the duke of Kent, was a patron. Other high-profile supporters included the banker Sir Thomas Baring and the abolitionists Wilberforce, Macaulay, and Lord Bexley. As chancellor of the Exchequer Bexley had worked closely with Nathan Rothschild for more than a decade. In 1826 his preoccupation with converting Jews led him to help found the Philo-Judean Society. Like the London Society, it attracted royal support through the patronage of Victoria's uncle, the duke of Sussex. As an 1830 advertisement coyly put it, the Philo-Judeans aimed "to conciliate Jews to Christians and Christianity by doing them temporal good without reference to their state of mind."[22] None of these men were "friends" of Montefiore, but they moved on the edges of his social world. Some, like Bexley and Baring, he knew personally; others, like Wilberforce and Macaulay, had close links to his Evangelical and Quaker friends Buxton, Hodgkin, and Gurney.

Such connections underpinned the campaign for Jewish emancipation.[23] At a particularly important meeting in June 1828, hosted by the duke of Norfolk, one of Goldsmid's collaborators at UCL, Goldsmid and Montefiore found themselves doing business with—among others—the leading English Catholic Edward Blount, cofounder of the Provincial Bank of Ireland and a board member of the Alliance. Some months later, at a private City dinner held around the corner from Rothschild's offices at New Court, Goldsmid and Montefiore rubbed shoulders with the Irish

Catholic activists O'Connell and the O'Gorman Mahon, alongside their good friends Buxton, Gurney, and Attwood.[24]

But Jewish emancipation was at the top of no one's political agenda. The election of O'Connell as M.P. for County Clare in July 1828 was proving decisive in Ireland. Without Catholic emancipation, he would be unable to take his seat. Faced with the prospect of widespread civil disorder and political chaos, Wellington bowed to the inevitable. By early 1829, affairs had reached a turning point, and once again Jews found themselves at the bottom of the confessional agenda.

If anyone was in a position to squeeze concessions from the government, that man was Nathan Rothschild. In 1828 Rothschild's connections with Wellington were close enough for Thomas Duncombe, M.P., publicly to express the hope "that the Duke of Wellington and the right hon. Secretary for the Home Department [Peel], would not allow the finances of this great country to be controlled any longer by a Jew."[25] When it came to seeking Wellington's support for Jewish emancipation, however, Rothschild drew a blank. In late March and early April 1829, Rothschild and Montefiore tried repeatedly to obtain a meeting with the lord chancellor, Lord Lyndhurst; he put them off again and again. As the famously louche Lyndhurst explained when they finally met, "they were at the time so preoccupied with the Catholic business, they could attend to nothing else."[26]

Montefiore and Rothschild assured Lyndhurst that they "would do nothing for the present." Holland, too, advised caution. Believing the government "to be friendly" to the Jewish cause, he thought "their wishes and convenience should be consulted as to the time and manner of bringing it forward."[27] But when Jewish emancipation eventually came before the House of Lords in 1833, Wellington opposed it in terms that showed him to be a dyed-in-the-wool Tory.[28] Unlike the Catholics, Jews were only a tiny minority in Britain. To men like Wellington their emancipation was, quite simply, a step too far.

If even a seasoned political practitioner like Lord Holland failed to understand the situation, it is hardly surprising that Montefiore, Rothschild, and Goldsmid were caught out. Ignorant of Wellington's real feelings, a meeting of the Board of Deputies held in March 1829 confidently declared "the present Era . . . propitious for the Advancement of the Civil Interests of the Jews of the United Kingdom." They were encouraged by a self-satisfied Goldsmid, who read numerous letters of support from the great and the good, and intimated "that he had reason to calculate on further powerful influence thro' Mr. M. Montefiore & other friends." Rothschild was equally upbeat when the board reconvened a month later, with Catholic emancipation safely passed: "he had consulted with the Duke of Wellington, the Lord Chancellor, & other influential Persons connected with Government" about Jewish disabilities, and recommended that a petition for Jewish relief be prepared for presentation to the House of Lords "whenever it may be thought right." After what Loewe tactfully describes as a "long debate," the board agreed to go ahead.[29]

Montefiore, along with Rothschild and Goldsmid, was a prime mover in the events that followed. In late April 1829 the three men consulted a second time with Lyndhurst, who advised them to test the water by presenting a petition to the House of Lords.[30] He thought "it would make some sensation" if the controversial Holland presented the petition, so the three friends turned instead to Rothschild's onetime collaborator, the Philo-Judean Lord Bexley. Bexley was "doubtful of their obtaining all the privileges that year," but after much discussion the deputies drew up a petition asking for exactly that.[31] It represented the triumph of hope over experience. In the event, wiser counsel prevailed.

Even as the deputies were preparing to sign the petition, Holland was busy advising that precipitate action would do more harm than good.[32] This assessment was only too accurate. Disguising his own antipathy toward the Jewish cause, Wellington explained to Bexley that "having recently carried so important a measure as the Catholic Relief Bill which had excited the feelings of all Classes of Society from one end of the Kingdom to the other and that as such feelings were now subsiding he was averse to the risk of creating any hostile feelings to the Government by lending his support to another bill so similar in its Character during the same session."[33] After consulting with Bexley and the abolitionists Henry Brougham and Stephen Lushington, the deputies decided to hold their fire.

In early 1830 the Board of Deputies adopted the petition for Jewish relief prepared in the previous year and set about legitimizing the initiative by obtaining as many signatures as possible from British-born Jews. Meanwhile Goldsmid and Montefiore pressed Rothschild to use his influence with Wellington. Taking advantage of a meeting about government finances, Rothschild urged the duke: "God has given your grace the power to do good—I would entreat you to do something for the Jews." Wellington was polite but noncommittal. Aware of the duke's political difficulties, Rothschild thought it best to wait. The less emollient Goldsmid talked Montefiore and Rothschild into a second meeting with Wellington. Pushed into a corner, he advised the Jews to delay their petition to Parliament. Montefiore mistook this reticence for neutrality and concluded optimistically that "the Duke would take no part against them."[34]

Acting on this misguided assumption, the board asked the Evangelical M.P. Robert Grant to present their petition in Parliament. Grant readily agreed; as a friend of Wilberforce and an enthusiastic Philo-Judean, he believed that emancipation could only hasten the conversion of the Jews. Still, Grant did wonder if the board was wise to rule out the possibility of partial relief. Goldsmid, however, regarded emancipation as a matter of principle. In no mood for pragmatism, he was outraged at Grant's suggestion, declaring that he would "prefer losing all than to give up Parliament." To Montefiore, such intransigence seemed crazy. "I decidedly differ with him," he wrote with exasperation in his diary, "we should accept all we can get."[35] Yet he agreed to go along with Goldsmid's all-or-nothing approach.

Initially, things went well. To the "infinite surprise" of at least one supporter, the Bill for Jewish Relief passed its first reading with a majority of eighteen.[36] Montefiore watched the debate with bated breath from the gallery of the Commons. He returned home delighted, and called with Judith "to congratulate N. M. Rothschild and Hannah on the result of the last night's debate."[37]

Everyone knew that this triumph could only be a first step. Ashamed of his failure to stop Catholic emancipation, George IV made it clear that he would stand firm in defense of the remnants of England's Protestant constitution. Grant thought the only way forward was popular pressure: the board needed to go beyond Parliament and appeal to the people "out-of-doors." Acting on his advice, a subcommittee met daily to coordinate a national petitioning campaign.[38]

Once again Jewish relief fell victim to the popularity of other progressive causes. By 1830 prominent Whigs were beginning to throw their weight behind a Radical campaign for parliamentary reform that was attracting widespread public support. Disillusioned Ultras, hard-line Tories who believed that Catholic emancipation would never have got past a reformed House of Commons, were inclined to do the same. Wellington knew that the slightest hint of support for Jewish relief could push potential Tory rebels into open revolt. The climate of political uncertainty discouraged M.P.s from supporting such a radical step when there were far more urgent issues at stake. "[T]he Jewish matter is not going through," Rothschild informed his brother James two days before the second reading of the bill.[39] It was defeated by a majority of sixty-three.

To some extent, resistance to Jewish emancipation reflected deep-rooted and instinctive prejudices. The radical populist William Cobbett saw Jews as "descendants of the *murderers of Christ*"—unproductive middlemen, whose swindles and extortions undermined the values of rural England and heralded the death knell for the honest English laborer. "Every nation that has fostered the Jews has become miserable in proportion to their numbers and influence," he thundered. If the English did not assert themselves and expel Jews, along with "Italians and Negroes and Germans and other foreigners," then "the children's children of Englishmen . . . [will] toil like slaves and live on crusts that fall from the table of . . . pampered Israelites or Israelitish Christians."[40]

Cobbett's virulent combination of xenophobia, economic stereotypes, and religious hatred was not taken up by more respectable political figures. The Evangelical Tory Sir Robert Inglis nonetheless perpetuated longstanding stereotypes when he told the House of Commons "that the Jews were aliens, not in the technical and legal sense . . . but in the popular sense of the word: they were aliens because their country and their interests were not merely different, but hostile to our own. The Jews of London had more sympathy with the Jews resident in Berlin or Vienna than with the Christians among whom they resided."[41]

Like Cobbett, Inglis instinctively associated Jews with money, and Jewish money with a threat to Englishness. He argued that Jewish wealth would lead to disproportionate Jewish representation in Parliament because bribery and "the command of capital would enable the Jews to obtain seats." Once in Parliament, Inglis warned, Jews would set about undermining the English constitution and pursuing their own national agenda, for "certain he was, that within seven years after the entrance of the first Jew, Parliamentary Reform would be carried."[42]

Yet for all Inglis' undeniable prejudices, his opposition to emancipation was also principled. He genuinely believed that "the system of Christianity had been protected by the Parliament and approved by the people." Giving Jews seats in the legislature represented a fatal tear in the moral fabric of English society and the Christian character of the English state. Every speaker in the 1833 House of Lords debate on emancipation would present a variant of the Christian state argument.[43] Even some conservative Philo-Judeans, like the Evangelical social reformer Lord Ashley, shared these concerns.

Religious principle is not necessarily identical with religious prejudice, and we should beware of viewing opposition to Jewish emancipation solely through the prism of economic, cultural, and religious anti-Judaism. The relationship between church and state was the defining political issue in Britain during this period.[44] Emancipation for Dissenters and Catholics was only a step on the road toward genuine religious equality. Throughout the 1830s, both groups continued their attack on the Anglican establishment, forcing it into a bitter but relatively successful defense of its prerogatives. Irish Catholics claimed the right to appropriate Church of Ireland tithes, while Dissenters fought for the freedom to marry in their own chapels and for an end to what they saw as the invidious system of church rates, a form of parish tax. At a time when Catholics and Dissenters were still barred from Oxbridge, it is hardly surprising that opposition to Jewish emancipation was so entrenched.

In 1830 these debates lay in the future. For the time being, the July Revolution in Paris had given new impetus to the campaign for parliamentary reform. It was beginning to look as if the Whigs might take power after over fifty years in the political wilderness. If they did, Jews would have real friends in high places. In November three of the board's more radical members called a meeting to urge further action. "After a long & desultory discussion," the board adjourned to allow the deputies time to consult their congregations. The result was far from encouraging. The emancipation campaign had already run up legal costs of £979 1s 1d. All four London synagogues declared themselves firm supporters of the campaign in principle; none would pay a penny more toward it. In the absence of funds, the board concluded that it could not continue. It was a controversial decision, carried only by Moses Mocatta's casting vote.[45]

The timing of this decision was terrible: less than three weeks later, Wellington's government finally fell. Although Lord Grey, the new Whig prime minister, was known to be unenthusiastic about emancipation, other leading Whigs were keen supporters of the Jewish cause. Henry Brougham was now lord chancellor, and Lord John Russell would emerge as a key figure in drafting the Great Reform Act. Goldsmid was hopeful, but the deputies would only reiterate their deep regret that they were "not possessed of any Funds to defray any Expence that may be incurred, nor can they hold themselves liable to any charge whatever."[46]

Feelings ran high, and the president of the board, Montefiore's elderly uncle Moses Mocatta, felt incapable of dealing with the situation. What, he asked querulously, was he to do if "Persons high in Government" wrote to the deputies proposing concrete steps on the Jewish issue? Such a letter would call for "an immediate reply, or even some immediate Act to be done, not allowing Time to call you together." Mocatta begged "leave to state directly that I am determined not to act on my individual responsibility."[47]

Even supporters of emancipation were divided over the best course of action. The government's entire attention was directed to the crucial question of parliamentary reform. With the best will in the world, now might not be the right time to act. In early 1831 Montefiore noted that "Robert Grant, Lord Holland, the Lord Chancellor [Brougham], and others all advise us to put off the 'Jewish Relief Bill' till next session, the

Ministers having so much important business now on hand." Montefiore assured Lushington that the Board of Deputies would "gladly accept anything the Government might offer, however short of the repeal of all their disabilities." Looked at pragmatically, the issue of Jewish representation in Parliament was only the tip of the iceberg. Better, thought Montefiore, to start with the vexed question of Jewish land-ownership and the lesser disabilities, which prevented Jews from holding civil, municipal, or military office, from working as schoolmasters, court ushers, or lawyers, and from voting in parliamentary elections.[48]

Montefiore had in any case always been inclined toward compromise—but then he had no political aspirations, whereas everyone knew that Goldsmid had his eye on a seat in the Commons. Goldsmid was livid at his friend's attitude. In the heat of the moment, he threatened to wash his hands of the whole business, and of the deputies, too: "he did not care about the measure, and would establish a new Synagogue with the assistance of the young men; he would alter the present form of prayer to that in use in the Synagogue at Hamburg."[49] He was referring to the first stirrings of the Jewish Reform movement in Germany, and his words must have stung the religious Montefiore to the quick. Goldsmid seems to have thought better of it—but the idea lingered.

With the emancipation campaign in tatters, Montefiore's mind turned to thoughts of retirement. On his return from Jerusalem in 1828, he had drawn up a list of resolutions. Recognizing its importance, this was among the few papers Sir Joseph chose to keep. Forgotten for over a century, it is worth reproducing in full:

> Make a plan for relieving or affording some Assistance to Poor persons in *Abel* [literally: in mourning; figuratively probably: the poor Jews of Jerusalem mourning the destruction of the Temple].
>
> Attend the *Misvah*'s of the Poor and during the Week at the Houses of their Families.
>
> Endeavour with the Assistance of Dr. Hodgkin to form some plan for the employment of our Poor.
>
> Never refuse to see and hear patiently, every one that applies to me for charity or assistance and to relieve them as far as prudence will permit.
>
> Visit my Farm at least once in six weeks. Go there in the Tonbridge stage.
>
> As soon as I can possibly obtain my dear Juds Consent dispose of our House in Park Lane.

Alter my Will and leave my Farm to Horatio & his Son for their Lives,
then to Louis Cohen & his son or in default of a son to my own
right heir provided it be *not* one of my Brother Abraham's Children,
in that case to Solomon Sebag's son.

Never to speculate in Consols or any English Stock above 90,000 nor
above 10,000 in Foreign.

Get rid of my Shares as soon as I can do so without loss, and never buy
any more.

Between the business of life and day of death a space should intervene.

After disposing of my house in Park Lane, *Rent* one in some Sea Port
Town, where there are Jews.

Get my account Books wrote up, and Balanced without delay.

Settle and Pay all my Bills on the 1st of every month.[50]

The cumulative message is clear: Montefiore wanted to turn his back
on the Stock Exchange, to retire from London, and to put his affairs in
order before he died. Consciously framed in the language of Jewish tradition, the first four of these resolutions are particularly striking. They
reflect Montefiore's desire to give meaning to the rest of his life through
practicing the *mitzvah* of *tzedakah,* or charity: one of the cardinal obligations for a religious Jew.

If resolutions are made to be broken, then Montefiore's were no exception. Rather than signaling the beginning of genteel retirement in
a quiet seaside town (with Jews), Montefiore's return from Palestine
marked the beginning of a new phase as a leading figure in Jewish—and
British—public life. He was, after all, only forty-three. Yet these resolutions did color his behavior. Montefiore had given generously to the
Sephardi community in the past; now he became more actively involved.
In 1831 he served on the congregational board appointed to supervise
the sanitary condition of the community's poor, and contributed personally toward warm clothing and blankets for the harsh winter months. In
1835 he donated a further £900 to the upkeep of the almshouses he had
founded in Cock Court.[51] But of the 20,000 Jews living in the metropolis in 1830, only 2,500 were connected with Bevis Marks.[52]

A diary entry in 1830 contains a fascinating account of Montefiore's
activity on behalf of a Committee appointed to visit "the houses of all
the Jewish poor," Sephardi and Ashkenazi alike.

We were from soon after 10 in the morning till 5 P.M. about Petticoat
Lane and the alleys, courts &c. We there visited the rooms of about 112
persons. To 108 we gave cards [vouchers] to obtain relief from the General Committee on Thursday. We witnessed many very distressing scenes:
parents surrounded by children, frequently six or seven, seldom less than

two or three, with little or no fire or food, and scarcely a rag to cover them; without bed or blanket, but merely a sack or rug for the night, a bed being almost out of the question. Few had more than one room, however large the family. The rent was from 1s 6d to 3s. per week. Of those who had two rooms, the upper one was most miserable, scarcely an article of furniture. In fact, the distress and suffering appeared so great, that although we had agreed, according to a resolution of the General Committee, only to give cards, we could not refrain from giving what money we had in our pockets.[53]

Montefiore's third resolution makes clear that he saw such visits as a traditional Jewish *mitzvah*. They also reflected the latest English thinking about poverty and, very probably, the views of Hodgkin, whom he had resolved to consult about "some plan for the employment of our Poor."[54] Back in 1811, Hodgkin's former employer William Allen had written an influential article "On the Duty and Pleasure of Cultivating Benevolent Dispositions," in which he argued that if only those in "genuine" need received poor relief, the less deserving would be forced to help themselves.[55] Rather than sinking into a dependency culture, the working classes would become thrifty and industrious; both they and society would be better off. Possibly because he lacked the Evangelical preoccupation with saving souls rather than comforting bodies, Montefiore found it difficult to put these ideas into practice. Confronted with the brutal realities of overcrowding, hunger, and deprivation, he was unable to stop himself giving whatever money he had. Even so, by visiting the poor at home and handing out cards that entitled deserving cases to obtain "relief" in due course, Montefiore and his Jewish committee were consciously implementing ideas current within the abolitionist-Evangelical milieu of his Quaker friends.[56]

This blend of Jewishness and a particular kind of Englishness marked Montefiore's life in other ways as well. He and Judith had visited the Kent resort of Ramsgate on their honeymoon. In 1822 they rented East Cliff Lodge, a pretty, precociously neo-Gothic mansion perched on the cliffs above the town. Its extensive gardens boasted wonderful sea views and romantic tunnels cut into the cliff face. Perhaps Montefiore was already thinking in terms of Ramsgate when he wrote in 1828 of his desire to retire to the seaside. In July 1830 he returned to the town with a view to buying East Cliff Lodge at auction. "If, please God, I should be the purchaser, it is my intention to go but seldom to London, and after two or three years to reside entirely at Ramsgate," Montefiore wrote excitedly in his diary. "I would build a small but handsome Synagogue, and engage a good and clever man as Reader." To his great disappoint-

East Cliff Lodge, where Montefiore lived for over fifty years. Home to Admiral Lord Keith, commander-in-chief of the Channel Fleet during the final years of the Napoleonic Wars, it boasted stupendous sea views and proved very convenient to Dover. From the 1890 edition of the Diaries of Sir Moses and Lady Montefiore, *edited by Louis Loewe.*

ment, Montefiore was outbid, but the house came on the market a year later, and he bought it for the handsome sum of £5,500.[57]

Montefiore lost no time in launching his plans to build a synagogue.[58] One Friday evening in August 1831, he and Judith took a happy walk around the field they had purchased in the hamlet of Hereson for the purpose. Almost two years later the stage was set for grand celebrations as the Montefiores proudly prepared to inaugurate their beloved synagogue. Some 200 friends and acquaintances received invitations to what was unquestionably the social event of the year in the Jewish world. Montefiore arranged for fireworks and hot-air balloons, engaged dozens of musicians and singers, installed 4,000 lights to illuminate the gardens, and filled the inner quadrangle at East Cliff Lodge with a grand marquee, complete with chandeliers.

At first it looked as if the event would be a washout. Waking up to a torrential downpour, Montefiore and his younger brother Horatio rushed into Ramsgate and engaged every sedan chair in town. Chief Rabbi Hirschell tried to console a downcast Montefiore with the thought that "all things must not go as we wish, since the destruction of the

Temple." "But," Montefiore wrote in his diary, "thanks to Heaven before three the rain had passed away & the weather on the eveng was
delightful. The Dedication commenced at Tea & finished about 1/4 past
eight oclock. all delighted with the Ceremony as well as with the music
& singing. May Heaven's Blessing attend it."[59]

Eighty-two sat down to dinner at East Cliff Lodge that evening, and
the following day he threw a lavish entertainment for "all our Christian
neighbours as well as our own party." "I glory in the occasion," wrote
an ecstatic Montefiore when all was over. "We can never forget the two
last days." That Saturday, he and Judith had the happiness of attending
services in their very own synagogue morning, afternoon, and evening.
Montefiore thought it "looked like Paradise." This, he told Judith, was
the spot where he wished to be buried when he died.[60]

East Cliff Lodge was not a great country estate, and its architecture
lacked the cachet of classicism.[61] Still, everyone knew that landowner-
ship was the stepping stone to membership in the social elite, the clear-

*Interior of the Montefiore synagogue at Ramsgate, probably early twen-
tieth century. (Courtesy of the Spanish and Portuguese Jews' Congregation, London)*

est determinant of class among the wealthy and the most obvious focus of personal ambition.[62] This was particularly important for Montefiore, since it was widely held that owning land gave a man a genuine interest in the country—and Jews were regularly accused of being permanent aliens. By purchasing such a prestigious property, he was buying into English society and needed to behave appropriately. That meant shouldering all the responsibilities of a local notable, including support for the local parish church and its charities. He threw himself into the role with gusto. All this was part and parcel of the wider struggle for Jewish emancipation. Like most of his contemporaries, Montefiore was so deeply aware of rank and social status that it can be hard to tell where his personal ambition stopped and the political agenda began. Indeed, the personal was inherently political for an outsider like Montefiore in a world in which class and power were so integrally linked.

He had taken his first steps in high society in 1829 under the aegis of the duke of Norfolk, who presented him to the king at a royal levée alongside his fellow religious activist, Edward Blount.[63] After the Commons threw out the Jewish Relief Bill in April 1830, Montefiore and his relatives set about infiltrating the more exclusive corners of the British establishment as the most effective way of justifying their claim to equal political rights. In June both Montefiore and Francis Goldsmid were elected to the Athenaeum club, which, in the words of one contemporary, numbered "a large proportion of the most eminent persons in the land" among its members.[64] The Athenaeum's Whig bias would be an added advantage once Lord Grey's ministry came to power.

The first year or so of the new government was a time of unprecedented political excitement, as election followed election until the House of Lords was left with no choice but to accept the Great Reform Act.[65] With parliamentary reform a *fait accompli*, Jewish leaders hoped that their own cause would return to the political agenda. They were sorely disappointed. When Montefiore made an effort to regain the initiative on Jewish emancipation in 1832, he met with a total blank. "I have made several fruitless attempts to obtain an interview with our friend both at the Treasury as well as at his own house," he wrote to Nathan Rothschild in exasperation. "I was sent from the one place to the other, but I believe he was engaged with some of the Ministers in Downing Street. I exceedingly regret my want of success."[66]

Nevertheless, in 1833 a Jewish Relief Bill made its way through the reformed House of Commons. Once again Montefiore exerted what influence he could in its favor, urging Sir Robert Peel's brother-in-law to persuade the Tory leader to withdraw his opposition.[67] Along with other leading Jews, Montefiore also signed a letter to *The Times*, reiterating

their "warm interest" in the Jewish cause.[68] Isaac Goldsmid was lobbying feverishly behind the scenes, alternately bullying, cajoling, and
pleading with M.P.s. His efforts paid off when the bill passed its third
reading in the Commons with a majority of 137. This was a pyrrhic victory, and probably Goldsmid knew it.

The Great Reform Act had been designed to empower the middle
classes. In practice, this step involved giving significant new rights to
many Protestant nonconformists, who numbered barely 500,000 but
constituted some 20 percent of the electorate after 1832.[69] Aristocratic
Whigs still nominally led the government, but control of the Commons
depended on their forming alliances with Radicals and Dissenters. The
upper house remained a bastion of Tory and High Church opinion. Like
Rothschild before him, Goldsmid was to discover that personal influence counted for little when religious principle was at stake: Jewish relief met with a concerted resistance in the Lords, where it was summarily defeated by a majority of fifty.

The following year, Goldsmid and his friends sought to strengthen
their case through a more aggressive and popular campaign. In the City
of London, 23,398 put their names to a petition calling for the relief of
Jewish disabilities. Even in Edinburgh, which had no Jews to speak of,
6,200 endorsed the Jewish cause. A flood of petitions underlined the
central place of Jewish emancipation within the wider political agenda
of the 1830s, but the Lords remained unimpressed—and they gave
equally short shrift to conversionists like Bexley, the earl of Radnor, and
the marquis of Westminster. In 1834 the upper house threw out the Jewish Disabilities Bill by a resounding majority of nearly 100.[70]

For much of this time, Montefiore was too ill to follow what was happening. The boils from which he suffered so terribly in Egypt had returned in the shape of a massive carbuncle, and nothing seemed to relieve the agony. Eventually his doctors decided they had no option but
surgery.[71] The operation was excruciating, and Judith was beside herself
with anxiety. For months she scarcely moved from her beloved Montefiore's bedside. Faced with the prospect of losing him, she took comfort in the thought that she was doing all she could. As she explained to
Benjamin Gompertz, "I have ever endeavoured to surmount little difficulties in the satisfaction of performing ones duty indeed I could not feel
happy or content in this instance were I to relax, for it is the province of
a wife to attend on her Sick Husband."[72]

By mid-January 1834 the worst appeared to be over. "The medical
men say that they think the cook will soon be required in preference to
the doctor," Judith's brother Solomon reported thankfully to his wife
from Ramsgate's Albion Hotel.[73] Still, Montefiore's convalescence was

slow and painful—so much so that his doctors advised a journey to the south of France to aid his recovery. By the time he and Judith returned to England in August, the emancipation campaign was already over for another year.

Montefiore's illness goes some way toward explaining his low profile during 1833–34. Yet Loewe's edition of his diaries contains remarkably little about the campaign for emancipation, and it is hard to escape the conclusion that Goldsmid made most of the running. In 1835, however, Montefiore returned to public life with a vengeance—seizing control of the Board of Deputies and facilitating one of the critical political initiatives of the day.

Hitherto the board had played a halting and inglorious role in the campaign for Jewish rights. In 1835 Moses Mocatta finally resigned from the presidency, and Montefiore, who had presumably been waiting for this opportunity, grasped it with both hands. His first move as president was to appoint a subcommittee to draw up a constitution that would finally place the Board of Deputies on a formal footing. The draft document approved by the board in May 1835 proposed, first, that the board assume sole responsibility for the political welfare of British Jews; second, that it propagate its views by establishing a system of elected deputies that could potentially extend to the provinces; and third, that the communities actually represented contribute financially to the board. Money had been a major obstacle in 1830, and this was probably the major motivation behind the whole document.[74]

Once the deputies had agreed upon a draft, they distributed it among the four London synagogues, which sat on it for nearly a year. During this period the board was totally inactive. Consequently, it failed to note the passage of Lord Lyndhurst's Marriage Act—a seemingly harmless piece of legislation, which endangered the legitimacy of marriages recognized by Jewish tradition but prohibited by English law on the grounds of consanguinity. Tellingly, the London synagogues imposed only one alteration on the draft constitution—restricting their potential financial contribution to between £50 and £100.[75]

As the new constitution made its slow way toward ratification, Montefiore found time to engage with other pressing concerns. In August 1835, for the first and last time in his life, he contracted for a major government loan. In full partnership with Nathan Rothschild, he underwrote the huge sum of £15 million, taken on relatively unfavorable terms.[76] This was bad business but very good politics, because the money was destined to finance the final abolition of slavery in the British Em-

pire. Montefiore's willingness to take it on at a time when he had nominally retired from business underlines his place at the heart of Britain's
philanthropic and abolitionist nexus.

Middle-class activism in this period is generally associated with the
Great Reform Act, but antislavery was the middle-class cause par excel-
lence—and no one embraced antislavery like Evangelicals and Dissenters.[77] In 1833, one in five adult males signed petitions calling for the abolition of slavery in the West Indies. Three-fifths of the 5,000 petitions
sent to Parliament that year originated with the forces of religious dissent. The Whig government knew better than to resist this unstoppable
political force. That year it finally passed legislation paving the way for
the emancipation of all slaves after a transitional apprenticeship period.
By contracting for the West Indian loan, Montefiore and Rothschild
were associating themselves with the political cause of the moment. The
more unfavorable the terms, the more credit they would accrue with the
people who mattered in abolitionist circles.

The leader of the antislavery lobby in Parliament was none other than
their longstanding associate, Buxton, while the new chancellor of the
Exchequer, Thomas Spring-Rice, was another of Montefiore's abolitionist business partners. But it was Buxton who emerged as the lynchpin in
the alliance between the Whig government and the forces of Evangelical
Dissent.[78] Passionately Christian in his approach to politics, he famously
declared: "It has pleased God to place some duties upon me with regard
to the poor slaves and these duties I must not abandon."[79] This attitude
would have been readily understandable to Montefiore, who took a
"special interest in the abolition of slavery," and whose Jewishness enhanced a sense of empathy with the West Indian slaves as another oppressed people.[80] Loewe tells us that the loan for the abolition of slavery
reminded Montefiore of the words of the prophet Isaiah to Israel (52:3):
"Ye have sold yourselves for nought, and ye shall be redeemed without
money," and as he reflected on the events of the day in his diary he fell
to contemplating "the former glory of Zion and its present state of sorrow."[81]

Contracting the emancipation loan was an act of practical and symbolic importance, but the summer of 1835 marked a political turning
point in other ways too. The Whigs had just returned to office after a
brief spell in opposition. Strengthened by the knowledge that the king
could not manage without them, they continued their efforts to reform
England's notoriously corrupt urban oligarchies. The Municipal Corporations Act of 1835 threw open the governing bodies of English towns
to the forces of electoral politics by obliging all aldermen and council-
lors to run for office. It created a whole new field of political activity for

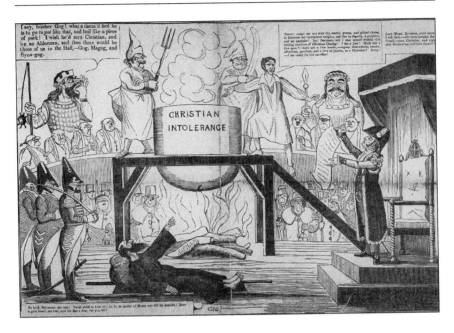

"Immolation of the Jew!" This 1835 cartoon by Charles Jameson Grant shows David Salomons ascending a platform holding a steaming cauldron of "Christian intolerance" and refusing the lord mayor's entreaty to renounce the Jewish faith in order to become an alderman. (Courtesy of the Guildhall Library, City of London)

the middle classes, and the Jewish elite threw themselves immediately into the fray.

In theory, the oath taken "Upon the true faith of a Christian" was also a condition of entry into municipal politics. But the friends of religious liberty were a force to be reckoned with in the Corporation of London, where men like the Philo-Judean glass manufacturer Apsley Pellatt had led the way in admitting Jews to the freedom of the City in 1830.[82] This sympathetic environment enabled Montefiore's former traveling companion, David Salomons, to get himself elected as one of the City's two sheriffs, although Parliament had to pass a special bill before he could take office.[83] To move up through the City hierarchy Salomons needed to become an alderman. In November 1835 he stood for election in Aldgate ward—and won. This time Salomons met with greater resistance from the political establishment. Finding himself unable to take up his new position, he persuaded the largely Jewish electorate to take the matter to court.

Montefiore meanwhile was congratulating himself on becoming the first Jewish member of the Merchant Taylors' Company thanks to the support of his business associate Attwood.[84] Attempts to pull strings outside the confines of the City proved less successful. In November 1835 Montefiore wrote to Spring-Rice asking that he recommend him to Lord Camden as a lieutenant of the County of Kent, a position for which ownership of East Cliff Lodge appeared to qualify him. Rural counties like Kent were almost empty of Jews, so such an appointment would have been a real coup.[85] In the event, Lord Camden refused to cooperate, claiming—perhaps with justification—that there were no vacancies.[86]

This was a setback, but by 1835 Montefiore had firmly established himself as a dominant figure in Ramsgate. In September the little town proudly played host to the young Princess Victoria and her uncle, King Leopold of Belgium. Along with other members of the official welcome committee, Montefiore waited nervously at the parish boundary for Victoria and her mother to arrive. He then accompanied the royal carriage back to the center of town at the head of a large procession, walking "bareheaded all the way." The bunting was out, and the streets were festooned with greenery. Local people had turned up in the thousands to catch sight of England's future queen. Montefiore was one of the lucky ones: he was introduced to Victoria and her mother, the duchess of Kent, as well as to Uncle Leopold and Aunt Louise when they arrived by ship at the pier. These were red-letter days for Ramsgate, and Montefiore was in the thick of it, presenting addresses to the royal visitors and attending a special ball at the Albion Hotel. He noted with pleasure that Sir John Conroy was "particularly polite."[87]

Conroy was widely believed to be the duchess' lover.[88] Like his father and brother before him, King William IV was a fanatical Tory, but the duchess and Conroy were famous Whigs—a fact that may have contributed to the latter's conciliating behavior. Either way, Montefiore welcomed Conroy's overture, eagerly promising to provide the royal party with a key to the grounds of East Cliff Lodge. This offer must have been premeditated, because early the next morning Montefiore came calling with a special golden key "for the use of Her Royal Highness, Sir John Conroy and his family."[89] He later had a gate made exclusively for them.

If Montefiore hoped to see Victoria in his garden, he was probably disappointed. The duchess—not her daughter—seems to have been the main beneficiary of his generosity.[90] Conroy's ill-considered attempt to render Victoria wholly dependent on himself and her mother through an obsessively cloistered upbringing was beginning to backfire badly. By the autumn of 1835, Victoria's household at Kensington Palace had become the scene of draining confrontations. When the royal party arrived in Ramsgate, Victoria was already an emotional and physical wreck. She managed to keep going as long as her beloved Uncle Leopold was with her, but collapsed within hours of bidding him farewell. The illness was a serious one, and she was confined to her room for nearly a month.[91] Once she was safely on the road to recovery, her physician recommended exercise in the open air. Victoria took regular walks in Ramsgate in the winter of 1835–36 and again the following autumn, but her diaries make no reference to the grounds at East Cliff.[92] Despite this, according to at least one of her biographers, a very much older Victoria cherished fond memories of her walks in Montefiore's garden—a garden to which, she said, she still possessed the key.[93]

When Victoria came to the throne, the incident was magnified out of all proportion.[94] Gradually the tale of the young princess and the little gold key acquired a life of its own, receiving pride of place in every account of Montefiore's career.[95] Even before his death unlikely stories began to circulate about the friendship between the great queen and the elderly Jew. In 1879 a German Jewish newspaper proudly credited Montefiore with persuading the duchess of Kent to leave her home at Amorbach and travel back to England when she was pregnant with Victoria, because only a child born on British soil could inherit the throne.[96] Well over a century later, I heard a different version of this story from an elderly Russian Hasid living in England. This time Victoria herself featured as the pregnant mother, worried about the implications of giving birth to her first-born child on a trip to India. Once again, Montefiore saved the day—cannily advising her to give birth on board a Royal Navy ship.[97] Victoria and Montefiore had become permanently linked in the Jewish imagination.

By the time Victoria became queen in June 1837, Montefiore had made further inroads into the Christian establishment and consolidated his position at the helm of Anglo-Jewry. In 1836 he became one of very few Jewish Fellows of the Royal Society as a gentleman "much attached to Science and its practical use." More controversially, he put himself forward as a governor of Christ's Hospital, a historic school for charity children—ostensibly to support the child of a passing acquaintance who had committed suicide.[98] Opponents argued that Montefiore's "admission to such an establishment as Christ's Hospital must be prejudicial, his faith establishing that Jesus Christ was an impostor, and the Christian religion a delusion." One clergyman from Hitchin even avowed "his knowledge of the determination of the Jews to buy Christ's Hospital, and alter the charity altogether!" In the event, Montefiore won by a majority of twelve, but the incident underscores the importance of philanthropy as an area of growing (and much resented) Jewish influence.[99]

A month later Montefiore chaired the first meeting of the new-look Board of Deputies. The board was just beginning to appreciate the impact of Lord Lyndhurst's Marriage Act, and Chief Rabbi Solomon Hirschell was eager to ensure that the proposed Dissenters Marriage Bill did not further undermine Jewish religious law.[100] Together with the Sephardi Haham, Raphael Meldola, Hirschell drew up a petition to Lord John Russell urging that Jews be exempted from the proposed bill. The rabbis wanted the state to stop meddling in their business, but leading secular Jews had a different agenda. They hoped to strengthen the case for emancipation by incorporating Jews in British legislation as just another Dissenting sect. Opinions were divided, and the board voted eight to nine against endorsing the rabbis' petition as "expressive of the wishes of the British Jews." In 1837 Montefiore went against the spirit of this decision when he persuaded the board to back a special Jews' Marriage Bill to resolve the doubts raised by Lord Lyndhurst's Marriage Act.[101] It was in this context that he famously declared in his diary, "I am most firmly resolved not to give up the smallest part of our religious forms and privileges to obtain civil rights."[102]

On the face of it, these disputes centered upon the relatively trivial question of whether or not an uncle could marry his niece or a man his dead brother's wife, as Henry VIII had done so fatally. The real stakes were higher, for the question of Jewish marriage reflected the balance between religious autonomy and the encroaching power of the state. From a Jewish point of view, this was about the relationship between religion and citizenship. In an English context, it had wider implications because the traditional pattern of church-state relations was already under attack. Montefiore's position resonated with the attitudes of High Church Anglicans, who wanted to limit political interference in the internal affairs of the church, and with radical Dissenters campaigning for complete disestablishment. Montefiore's opponents within the Jewish community had more in common with liberal Anglican Whigs, like Russell, who envisaged a union of church and state that could encompass sectarian differences within a broader Christian framework.

As yet, the divide within the Jewish leadership was relatively easy to bridge. When Spring-Rice announced his intention of putting another Relief Bill before Parliament, Montefiore wrote asserting the Board of Deputies' position as "the only official channel of communication" between the British state and its Jews. David Salomons, the Goldsmids, and their emancipationist friends were eager to join forces with Montefiore, who hosted a meeting at his home to facilitate collaboration.[103] Still, tensions remained between uncompromising emancipationists and their religious leadership. In December 1836 Chief Rabbi Hirschell refused to endorse a pamphlet written by Francis Goldsmid on the Jewish question, because he believed public office was incompatible with a truly Jewish life.

Hirschell's fears were not unreasonable. In March 1837 the Corporation of London approached Montefiore informally with a view to appointing him a sheriff. They discovered that he nurtured considerable religious qualms. Montefiore's attitude provoked an outcry among friends and relatives. How could he decline this honor when it would do so much for the Jewish cause? Bowing to the inevitable, Montefiore agreed to go ahead, but he remained deeply concerned: "I shall have the greatest difficulties to contend with in the execution of my duty," he wrote, "difficulties which I shall meet with at the very outset. The day I enter on my office is the commencement of the New Year. I shall therefore have to walk to Westminster instead of going in my state carriage, nor, I fear, shall I be able to dine with my friends at the inaugural dinner which, from time immemorial, is given on the 30th of September. I shall, however, endeavour to persuade my colleague to change the day to the 5th of October."[104] The Corporation was disposed to be accommodating—it had elected Montefiore in order to make a political point. Yet he remained strangely reluctant. In a touching letter to Judith, he wrote: "I would not lose so much of your company again for all the Honors either Queen or People can bestow."[105]

Needless to say, Montefiore rose admirably to the occasion. At his belated inauguration dinner, he applauded the City's lack of religious prejudice and nailed his colors firmly to the mast of 1830s political reform. The shrievalty was not, he believed, a political office,

> and yet . . . it has duties both to the Queen and to the public, I hope, in the execution of those duties, to swerve neither to the right nor the left, but on the one hand to uphold the rightful prerogatives of the Crown, and on the other to support the just liberties of the people. Called upon by the free, intelligent, and wealthy citizens of this great city to fill so important an office, I trust I shall never be found wanting in any efforts to prove that the great privilege of electing their own Sheriffs may be safely entrusted to the people.[106]

This speech is normally cited in the narrow context of Jewish emancipation; it is far more interesting as a rare statement of political faith from a man who preferred to keep his views to himself. His reputation for conservatism in later life may be justified, but in 1837 he shared the predilection of his contemporaries in the City for meaningful—if limited—reform.

Montefiore has gone down in history as the only sheriff to arrive at the Guildhall wearing his robes of office and carrying a kosher chicken.[107] The story may be apocryphal, but his orthodoxy took the City into uncharted territory. He never attended functions on the Sabbath or Jewish Holidays, and on the eve of Passover "caused great inconvenience" by leaving the courts of the Old Bailey early.[108] Montefiore's colleagues found much to amuse them in his religious dedication, and his cold kosher beef became a standing joke. He used to send a dish of it early in the morning when hosting dinners at Newgate with his fellow sheriff, George Carroll. The beef was labeled with a card bearing Montefiore's name, and its appearance on the table prompted uproar as everyone cried out for a "slice of Sir Moses' cold beef." He liked to recall one occasion when the demand was so great "that he was reduced to dining off the wing of a fowl which, luckily for him, had been specially provided for his friend, David Salomons."[109]

Being sheriff was not simply a ceremonial role. It entailed presenting petitions to Parliament, attending sessions of the criminal court in the Old Bailey, and overseeing the City prisons. The first of these duties gave added weight to Montefiore's continued efforts on behalf of emancipation. In December 1837, for instance, he and George Carroll presented a petition from the City urging Parliament to include Jews in the Municipal Declarations Bill introduced on behalf of certain Dissenting sects.[110] Meanwhile Montefiore's legal responsibilities enabled him to indulge his interest in the fashionable cause of penal reform.[111] He gave the issue pride of place in a letter written at the end of his year's service, explaining that he and George Carroll had "endeavoured to mitigate the sufferings of the prisoners, and to open [to] them better and happier courses of life, as far as public justice and the necessary strict rules of a prison would permit."[112]

Montefiore's great-great-niece Hannah Cohen recalls that he had a particular horror of capital punishment and was proud of saving the life of the only prisoner condemned to death during his time in office. The incident brought him into contact with Lord John Russell. Russell, then home secretary, listened without emotion as Montefiore and George Carroll made their case, before dismissing them with "Is that all you have to say, gentlemen?" Montefiore never forgot it, and concluded that Russell "was the most cold-blooded man I ever saw." Forty years later, when an elderly Russell fell ill during a visit to the archbishop of Canterbury, the ninety-four-year-old Montefiore is said to have sent the ailing statesman "six bottles of the very finest port," adding with a dry chuckle—as the thought of Lord John's "coldbloodedness" clapped into his head—"that will warm him—if anything can!"[113]

This was a grudging verdict on a man to whom he owed a very great deal. It was Russell who suggested to Victoria that she mark her accession to the throne by bestowing a baronetcy on the lord mayor and a knighthood on the City's two sheriffs. As a longstanding friend of religious liberty, Russell would have been only too well aware of the implications of this advice. That the Jewish sheriff was called Moses only added to the piquancy of the proposal. Indeed, Montefiore liked to claim that his name had provoked serious debate in the family circle: "They all said *Sir* Moses would sound so very bad. I told them 'Moses' I was and 'Moses' I'd remain. I had lived 'Moses' and I'd die 'Moses.' If I don't hurt the name, the name won't hurt me."[114]

The day of Victoria's first formal visit to the City of London was a dazzling and glittering occasion. "Throughout my progress to the City, I met with the *most gratifying, affectionate, hearty* and *brilliant* reception from the greatest concourse of people I ever witnessed," she wrote in her diary, "the streets being *immensely crowded* as were also the windows, houses, churches, balconies, everywhere."[115] Montefiore was equally excited as he and Judith rode in a carriage to the Guildhall, before he continued on horseback with Carroll and the rest of the City officials. Nothing could have prepared him for the thrill he experienced when the queen "placed a sword on my left shoulder and said 'Rise, Sir Moses.' I cannot express all I felt on this occasion. I had, besides, the pleasure of seeing my banner with 'Jerusalem' floating proudly in the hall."[116] His pride in his Jewishness, so obviously displayed in his coat of arms, made this a particularly special moment. Victoria's uncle, the Philo-Judean duke of Sussex, rushed up to congratulate him, exclaiming gladly, "This is one of the things I have worked for all my life!" Victoria described Montefiore in her diary as "an excellent man," adding: "I was very glad that I was the first to do what *I* think quite right, as it should be."[117]

This honor would have been enough for most men, and it certainly should have been enough for someone like Montefiore, who had "retired" ten years earlier and was to be so publicly vaunted for his selfless generosity in later life. Yet only five months after his knighthood, Montefiore wrote asking Lord John Russell to make him a baronet on the occasion of Victoria's coronation. This hitherto-unknown letter marked both the summation of his social and political achievements in the 1830s, and their ultimate disappointment. In it, Montefiore presumed heavily on his relationship with the young queen, emphasizing particularly their contact at Ramsgate. He then listed the social attributes that in his view qualified him for this honor: "the possession of a considerable Fortune (partly by Inheritance) and a Landed Estate of some extent, in the administration of which I have always kept in view the duties which any man of property owes to the public; I may add that my style of living and association are not such as to disgrace the Baronetage." Finally, Montefiore made it clear where his political loyalties lay, declaring his "supreme attachment to our happy constitution as now reformed, and a decided hostility to any further Organic Changes." He added, somewhat smugly: "I feel the deepest gratitude to that Government by whose Energy the Reform was effected, and by whose prudence it has been consolidated and brought into beneficial operation, and as far as my Influence extends (and it's [sic] sphere is not very contracted) it will be steadily exerted in the support of the existing Ministry, and in maintenance of the Principles held by them."[118]

Montefiore's Jewishness was the unspoken undercurrent in this letter. Aware of the sensitivity of the issue, he stressed both his "Official Situation" as sheriff, which would provide a pretext for his elevation, and his lack of offspring, since "as I am without a Family the Baronetcy if granted will expire with me." There had been only one Jewish knight before Montefiore: Sir Solomon de Medina, who had been knighted by William III in 1700. Nathan Rothschild had refused the honor in 1815, but in 1838 his son Lionel registered with the College of Arms as an Austrian baron.[119] Even so, Montefiore would have been the first properly Anglo-Jewish baronet. Such an honor would have been both a source of personal pride and a symbol of communal advancement. In the event, this distinction would go to Goldsmid.

Montefiore's particular brand of religious fatalism no doubt helped him to come to terms with the rejection. As Montefiore had explained in a letter to Judith a year earlier, "I believe whatever is, is by the permission of Heaven, & that we are not the free agents we appear to be."[120] Writing in the late summer of 1837, he had prayed the Almighty "so to enable me to conduct myself during the Whole business [of the shrievalty] that we may have the gratification of looking back to it with satisfaction after the fatigues and anxieties of the year be passed. that we may then have the happiness of visiting the Holy City & afterwards returning to the enjoyment of peace & content at our own dear fireside." The year in office had surpassed his best hopes and expectations; he was now free to turn his mind to other things.

Chapter 6

The Land of Milk and Honey

No sooner had Montefiore completed the formalities attending his year in office than he and Judith set out again for Palestine. The first part of the road was familiar: from Guillacq's Hotel at Calais through the Low Countries and Lyon, over the Alps, and on past Genoa to Livorno, where a sentimental Montefiore marked the anniversary of his father's death by saying the memorial *kaddish* "in the Synagogue so near to the house in which I was born."[1] After spending a couple of days with his Italian relatives, Montefiore continued with Judith to Rome, arriving just in time for the famously exuberant Carnival. "To be for the fourth time in Rome, after an interval of eleven years, appears indeed like a dream," Judith wrote a little wistfully.[2] As she realized, however, the intervening years had wrought such changes in the Montefiores that any similarities to their earlier journeys were largely superficial.

For one thing, they were more religious. "I am mortified to find that though there are many Jews in this place, there is no Synagogue," wrote Montefiore in his diary when they passed through Avignon. "No meat, prepared according to Jewish law, can be procured. We could manage with fish and vegetables, but I exceedingly regret not being able to join public worship on Sabbath. Tomorrow will be the first time we have omitted so doing since we left London, and [I] shall be happy if it is the last."[3] Religious observance lent a different tenor to their travels, and as they wended their way southward they commented on the variations in Jewishness they encountered. Montefiore's close involvement with the campaign for Jewish emancipation gave these experiences a new, political edge.

Crammed into the tiny, squalid Ghetto, the 3,500 Jews of the Eternal City lived in the shadow of the River Tiber, whose yellow waters regularly lapped around the remains of the ruined Portico d'Ottavia, forcing those in the lower streets to take refuge upstairs, where the rooms became unbearably full and a suffocating atmosphere spread like the plague. Montefiore noted that although Jews were regularly subjected to proselytizing sermons, they could now open warehouses outside the Ghetto, and that the pope "frequently sends them money from his own purse."[4] This poor but ancient community boasted a fine collection of ritual vestments and silver. For legal reasons, all five synagogues were crowded together under one roof. Visitors were enchanted by red and gold tapestries, pillars draped in damask embroidered with Hebrew verses, and the ceiling decorated like a Roman basilica, with reliefs showing the temple of Solomon and the holy objects used there.[5]

It was in this extraordinary building that the Montefiores encountered a friend from England: the budding orientalist Dr. Louis Loewe.[6] Born into a rabbinical family in Prussian Silesia, Loewe had studied the Talmud with the great Hatam Sofer, scourge of the Reform movement and one of the leading rabbis of the age. After finishing his rabbinical studies in Pressburg, Loewe acquired a secular education at the universities of Vienna and Berlin. By the time of his first visit to London in 1835, he had mastered ten languages—a remarkable accomplishment for a man of twenty-six. Loewe had already spent time in Hamburg classifying an important coin collection. Clean-shaven with carefully styled curls (but no sidelocks), he wore a skullcap and dressed like a gentleman. On his arrival, he made contact with leading scholars and their patrons, many of whom—like Hodgkin and the duke of Sussex—were well known to Montefiore.

Loewe's presence inevitably attracted comment in the intellectual backwater that was Anglo-Jewry. The Ashkenazi Chief Rabbi Solomon Hirschell was highly suspicious of the talented young German and wrote to the Hatam Sofer requesting more information. As Hirschell explained, "it is truly a matter for wonder in our eyes to see a young man such as he is, understanding both to speak and to write many tongues and conducting himself with such piety." He feared that Loewe might spread dissent in the Anglo-Jewish community, bringing with him the heresy of religious reform from radical circles in Hamburg and Berlin.[7]

Montefiore, however, lost no time in inviting Loewe to East Cliff Lodge. The aspiring young intellectual was delighted by the refined, cosmopolitan company he met there: "The conversation of the visitors being frequently in French and German, many an hour was spent in reading letters and poems addressed to Mr and Mrs Montefiore in these languages." The Montefiores, in turn, were eager to take advantage of Loewe's talents. Judith wanted to learn a little Turkish and Arabic, and Montefiore asked Loewe to draw up a plan for their next visit to Pales-

*Montefiore's aide and confi-
dant, Louis Loewe. This engraving was made after
1840, but it may be based on
an image of Loewe as a
young man. (Courtesy of Pro-
fessor Raphael Loewe; photograph by Frederic Aranda)*

tine, noting in his diary: "If my dear Judith consents to our again visiting the Holy Land, I should be glad to obtain the company of the Doctor on our pilgrimage."[8]

In the event, Montefiore's energies were diverted to the City, and
Loewe set out for Egypt, Syria, and Palestine on his own. Although he
suffered a brutal attack by Druze tribesmen in Safed, the experience did
not lessen his enthusiasm for the East. When Montefiore suggested that
Loewe return with them to Palestine, he accepted eagerly—even though
Judith had just received a warning that war between Egypt and Turkey
was now imminent.

Tension between the pasha of Egypt and his Ottoman overlord had
been brewing ever since the Greek Revolt. In 1831–32 Mehmed Ali had
conquered Syria and Palestine with the help of his son Ibrahim, a brilliant general who went on to invade mainland Turkey, where he smashed
the Ottoman armies in the battle of Konya. With Russian backing, Sultan Mahmud brokered a compromise that allowed Mehmed Ali to keep
Syria but not the rest of Ibrahim's territorial gains. Mehmed Ali found
Syria harder to control than he had expected: the peasantry resented
conscription and higher taxation, while the traditional elites fought hard
to defend their influence. Still, by May 1838 he felt strong enough to announce his intention of making Syria and Egypt independent, hereditary kingdoms. Mahmud prepared to retake the territories by force. As
the war clouds gathered, Betty de Rothschild wrote begging Judith and

Montefiore to abandon a journey that "might be attended with the greatest danger."[9] Frankly staggered by this news, they decided to ignore her advice.

By the time the Montefiores reached Malta, cholera had become a more serious threat. Political news was confused, but the newspapers reported that in Jerusalem forty or fifty died of the disease every day. An English couple recently returned from the holy city assured the Montefiores that the situation was not so very bad.[10] The Jews of Jerusalem were in a desperate state, Mr. Freemantle added, and "looking most anxiously for the arrival of Sir Moses."[11] Montefiore felt he had no choice but to continue; he was sufficiently concerned to suggest traveling alone. "This I peremptorily resisted," Judith reported in her diary, adding with some pride that "the expressions of Ruth furnished my heart at the moment with the language it most desired to use: 'Entreat me not to leave thee, or to return from following after thee; for whither thou goest I will go, and where thou lodgest, I will lodge.'"[12] At some level, Judith was obviously terrified; by identifying herself with a favorite biblical heroine, she found the courage to go on.

The journey to Alexandria proved uneventful. Judith could not help contrasting the steamer that took them to Malta—replete with piano and music books—with the ramshackle craft they had sailed in some ten years earlier. She found Alexandria to be similarly improved, admiring the spacious square in front of Mehmed Ali's new palace, the grand consular residences, the railways, and the clean, modern quay. Stoically ignoring reports that the war had already started, the Montefiores then continued to Beirut, where they were greeted by a welter of letters welcoming them to the Holy Land. Still, as Montefiore remarked ruefully, "our visit is not the most timely for our comfort, pleasure or safety; the political state of the country is most unsatisfactory and uncertain; a single day may bring about a complete change in the government of Syria and Palestine. The forces of the Sultan have certainly crossed the frontier, and Ibrahim Pasha will positively resist any further advance."[13]

In 1827 the Montefiores had been made aware of the financial difficulties faced by Jews in Jerusalem and their dependence on funds from abroad.[14] Their relations with the diaspora had since become mired in controversy, and the community itself was chronically divided. Political upheavals, economic uncertainties, and religious enthusiasm were prompting Jews in both Europe and North Africa to seek a new life in the Holy Land. The Jewish population there had doubled since 1800, escalating in the 1830s to a peak of nearly 10,000 before the disastrous earthquake of 1837. Even at the best of times, nearly half the community died every ten years. This state of affairs gave immigration real impact. In 1800 only 5 percent of Jews in Palestine were Ashkenazim; by 1839 they represented over 30 percent of the Jewish population. The new arrivals upset the existing ethnic equilibrium, overturning long-standing financial arrangements and introducing new religious antagonisms.[15]

The Sephardi-Ashkenazi divide was only the most obvious of these ethnoreligious fault lines. In fact the internal cohesion of both communities was being undermined from within. Hundreds of North African Jews had settled in the Galilee by 1839—enough for contemporaries to describe Tiberias as "the little Meknes," and for the Judeo-Arabic of Morocco and Algeria to begin to displace the Ladino of the Ottoman Sephardim.[16] Ladino speakers continued to predominate in Jerusalem, but the two groups could not even pray together. The North Africans complained that Jews of Ottoman origin had "quite different customs and ceremonies, yea even their dialect of Hebrew being different from ours."[17] Relatively speaking, however, the Sephardi community was a model of harmony.

The first Ashkenazim to arrive in significant numbers were a group of Hasidic rabbis, who came from Belorussia in 1777 accompanied by a rabble of impoverished hangers-on.[18] Unable as yet to live openly in Jerusalem, the newcomers settled in Safed, an important center of Jewish mysticism in the north. Their style of worship soon began to cause difficulties. According to one Christian observer, the praying Hasidim "appeared as if determined at once to take heaven by storm, springing upon their toes, beating their breasts, and groaning and crying simultaneously at the highest pitch of their voices."[19] The Safed Sephardim, who had generously offered the new arrivals half their own synagogue, could hardly hear themselves think. Eventually the Hasidim founded a separate congregation in nearby Tiberias, a run-down town on the Sea of Galilee, revered as an ancient center of Jewish learning and the site of holy tombs.

Unlike traditional eastern European Judaism, Hasidism prioritized spirituality over book learning. Inspired by the mystical teachings of the Ba'al Shem Tov, popularly known as the founder of Hasidism, Hasidic rabbis stressed the importance of faith and joy in the performance of *mitzvot* (religious obligations). To some, the mysticism that characterized this new religious movement smacked of heresy. Known as *mitnagdim*, opposers, they saw Hasidism as a distraction from the Torah and the miracle-working Hasidic leaders as charlatans who exploited the ignorant.

Resistance to Hasidism was led by the foremost Lithuanian scholar of his generation: Rabbi Elijah, the *Gaon* (genius) of Vilna, who died in 1797.[20] Almost ten years later, a group of the *Gaon*'s disciples set out for Palestine and settled in Safed. Socially and intellectually, they were the antithesis of the mainly poor, uneducated Hasidic immigrants. Called Perushim because they held themselves apart from the world, the followers of the *Gaon* represented a scholarly avant-garde, whose departure for the land of Israel may have reflected a conscious attempt to accelerate the process of redemption.[21] The arrival of the Perushim added a potentially explosive element to the already-volatile mix of Sephardim and Hasidim in the Galilee.

By the late 1820s, all these different groups were at loggerheads. The Perushim had even split into two factions, one remaining in Safed while the other moved to Jerusalem. Meanwhile fifty-six followers of the Hasidic Rabbi Schneur Zalman of Liadi founded their own congregation alongside the small Sephardi community in Hebron, because they could no longer "sit together with the other Hasidim."[22] Religion was central to these disputes, but financial issues could be even more divisive: none of the Jewish communities was self-supporting, and all three congregations were heavily in debt. All—but especially the Hasidim and Perushim—included a large number of people without employment; all (in practice) paid taxes to the Ottoman government, with the Sephardim ostensibly responsible for the collection of those taxes; and all were vulnerable to financial extortion at the hands of their creditors, unscrupulous officials, and local sheikhs. As a result, the issue of how to collect and share out the *halukah* monies sent from the diaspora was hotly contested.

The 1820s saw protracted negotiations between Sephardim, Perushim, and Hasidim over the distribution of *halukah* from Europe. To complicate matters further, Rabbi Zvi Hirsch Lehren, a prominent Dutch banker with cabalistic leanings, wished to ban all Jews living in Palestine from dispatching emissaries in accordance with time-honored custom. Lehren envisioned centralizing the fund-raising process so that all monies from western Europe and the United States passed through Pekam, his own organization in Amsterdam.[23] English Jews tended to agree that the traditional emissaries were a waste of money, but they had no desire for Lehren to monopolize arrangements. In 1830 the synagogue at Bevis Marks had appointed Montefiore one of three deputies with special responsibility for administering donations to Palestine. The new deputies allotted a fixed share of the money to each of the four holy cities: Jerusalem, Safed, Tiberias, and Hebron. They made it plain that they would have no dealings with emissaries, and they repeatedly re-

jected appeals from those who turned up anyway. But the emissaries
kept coming. By 1835, Montefiore and the other two deputies were so
fed up that they resigned *en bloc*. The London communities gave generously to survivors of a catastrophic earthquake two years later, but refused to involve the latest emissary from Palestine—offering a token £5
if only he stayed away.

As one of relatively few Jews to have visited the Holy Land, Montefiore took a strong interest in these debates. His public profile aroused
acute jealousy in Lehren, who claimed that the Englishman was motivated by pride not piety.[24] Lehren was aghast to hear that his rival
planned to make a second visit to Jerusalem—this time, armed with
large donations from London for survivors of the earthquake. Determined to protect his own position, Lehren warned the Perushim that
they would regret becoming involved with an assimilated Jew like Montefiore, who regularly gave "to idolatrous causes" and planned to open
a school in Palestine where young Jewish children would learn subjects
"contrary to the holy Torah."[25] They must be polite, but under no circumstances should they give Montefiore "any kind of function regarding the finances of the Land of Israel."[26]

Arriving with the money at Beirut in May 1839, Montefiore found
himself in something of a quandary. He had counted on a local bank to
transfer it to Palestine, but Mr. Kilbee of Kilbee, Haugh & Co. could
find no one willing to face the attendant risks of violent robbery, civil
disorder, and the plague of cholera.[27] Eventually Montefiore saw no option but to divide the money into eleven small parcels and secrete them
in his own luggage.

The dangerous trek over the mountains was exalting and romantic.
Loewe in particular was excited by the contrast between his present situation and the awful circumstances in which he had left the Holy Land
some months earlier—bruised, penniless, and in Bedouin dress. Judith,
meanwhile, experienced "a strange mingling of feelings" to find herself
"seated like our forefathers, in the land of the patriarchs" and enjoying
a hearty dinner in their tent. Quite a number of Jews had been sent to
greet the Montefiores, and the whole party recited prayers and psalms
as they made their way to the Tomb of Zebulun at Sidon, "rejoicing to
make resound, as best we could, the mild and solitary scenes with the
praises of our God." Only the news that one of their servants had been
attacked dampened this religious enthusiasm. Understandably alarmed,
Loewe spent an anxious night patrolling round the sleeping Montefiores
and brandishing loaded pistols.[28]

Perched on a precipitous mountain slope, Safed had been utterly devastated by the earthquake of 1837, which killed roughly half the Jewish

population and reduced the whole town to rubble.[29] The roofs of the houses lower down the hillside formed part of the streets immediately above, and so the entire town had collapsed in on itself, leaving one gigantic ruin. Jews suffered disproportionately because the Muslim quarter was built on relatively level ground. Two years later Montefiore thought Safed still presented "an awful spectacle of destruction; the few miserable hovels they have erected are for the most part little better than caves, more fit for the beast of the field than for human beings."[30]

This dreadful earthquake was only one of several recent calamities. During the revolt of the Arab peasantry against Mehmed Ali in 1834, villagers from the surrounding area had sacked the Jewish quarter, assaulting and killing the men, raping the women, plundering and destroying their homes.[31] When Loewe first visited in 1838, the much-depleted Jewish community suffered a terrifyingly similar attack at the hands of the rebellious Druze. No wonder, then, that the Jews of Safed greeted Loewe's reappearance with incredulous delight. They had wholly unrealistic expectations of what Montefiore might do for them and rushed out to meet him, "young and old, rich and poor, with dancing and shouting of praise, clapping of hands, sounding of the Darrabuka, and singing."[32]

The Montefiores arrived just in time to celebrate the festival of Shavuot. Too exhausted even to leave the house, Montefiore deputed Judith to go to synagogue in his place, knowing that arrangements had been made to dedicate a particularly venerated Torah scroll. This was an extraordinary experience for a Jewish woman. Judith found herself at the head of a procession, bearing a wax taper, and walking under a special canopy immediately after the Hasidic Rabbi Abraham Dov, who was carrying the scroll itself. Overcome by the responsibility, Judith was petrified that her taper might set fire to the canopy or drip wax onto the white silk of the Torah covering. She could relax only once she was safely sitting down again.[33]

Montefiore meanwhile had time to consider his next step. As Judith wrote in her diary that evening, her husband hoped to provide employment for Jews young enough to work, but either too stupid or too lazy to study Torah all their lives. He thought agriculture might prove "a fit occupation, if protection could be procured for property." In the weeks that followed, he devoted much effort to exploring the ramifications of this plan.[34]

In the past, it had been impossible for non-Muslims to buy real estate in Palestine, but Mehmed Ali's policy of promoting religious equality changed this equation, although Jews who were not Ottoman citizens still faced restrictions on owning land. Growing security and more ef-

fective government made agriculture an increasingly attractive option:
Jews felt safer traveling through the countryside now, and were less fearful that marauding Bedouin would steal their crops.[35] In 1834 Rabbi
Moshe Sachs had set out for Europe to drum up support for Jewish agricultural colonies.[36] This enterprising German represented a new wave
of dynamic immigrants to Palestine, but his plans to revive the Jewish
economy ran directly counter to Lehren's more limited, religious vision.
Undeterred by the latter's efforts to blacken his reputation, Sachs continued to London, where he put his proposals to Montefiore and other
leading English Jews.

Meanwhile a small trickle of Jews in Palestine began to invest in agriculture as a promising commercial opportunity. Montefiore met several
Jews with detailed knowledge of farming and even went on a day trip
to inspect the village of Djermek, which Ibrahim Pasha had granted
in compensation to Rabbi Israel Bak, a printer from Berdichev whose
business had been destroyed during the first sack of Safed.[37] Bak drew
up a list of nearly twenty villages suitable for Jewish agricultural development, expounded on the different kinds of farming that might be
profitable, and advised Montefiore to negotiate a twenty-year lease with
the Egyptians, guaranteeing Mehmed Ali an income and exempting
Arab workers from military service.[38]

Writing in his diary shortly afterward, Montefiore concluded optimistically:

From all information I have been able to gather, the land in this neighbourhood appears to be particularly favourable for agricultural speculation. There are groves of olive trees, I should think, more than five hundred years old, vineyards, much pasture, plenty of wells and abundance
of excellent water; also fig trees, walnuts, almonds, mulberries, &c., and
rich fields of wheat, barley, and lentils; in fact it is a land that would produce almost everything in abundance, with very little skill and labour. I
am sure if the plan I have in contemplation should succeed, it will be the
means of introducing happiness and plenty into the Holy Land. In the
first instance, I shall apply to Mohammad Ali for a grant of land for fifty
years; some one or two hundred villages; giving him an increased rent of
from ten to twenty per cent, and paying the whole in money annually at
Alexandria, but the land and villages to be free, during the whole term,
from every tax or rate . . . and liberty being accorded to dispose of the
produce in any quarter of the globe. This grant obtained, I shall, please
Heaven, on my return to England, form a company for the cultivation of
the land and the encouragement of our brethren in Europe to return to
Palestine. Many Jews now emigrate to New South Wales, Canada &c.;

but in the Holy Land they would find a greater certainty of success; here they will find wells already dug, olives and vines already planted, and a land so rich as to require little manure. By degrees I hope to induce the return of thousands of our brethren to the Land of Israel. I am sure they would be happy in the enjoyment of the observance of our holy religion, in a manner which is impossible in Europe.[39]

This famously prophetic diary entry has led later generations of Zionists to claim Montefiore as their own.[40] Yet the language of nationalism is strikingly absent from a text in which Montefiore repeatedly refers to Jews as his "brethren"—a Christian term in English, with strong religious connotations. Tellingly, Montefiore only once used the word "nation" to describe Jews in his most complete surviving diary, and he did so in the traditional Sephardi sense of the word.[41] Instead, Montefiore's grand vision was the product of his dual identity as a religious Jew and a successful London businessman.

In 1831 Elliott Cresson, a Philadelphia Quaker, had arrived in England as an agent of the American Colonization Society (ACS). Founded in Washington some fifteen years earlier, the ACS promoted the emigration of free African Americans to colonies in Liberia as a solution for the intractable racial tensions caused by slavery in the United States. Hodgkin was an early English convert to the cause.[42] He published a pamphlet on the subject and soon became a leading member of the British African Colonization Society. There is an obvious resonance between Hodgkin's enthusiasm for the return of African Americans to farm their historic homeland and his friend Montefiore's dream that European Jews could leave "countries where persecution prevents their living in peace" to found agricultural settlements in Palestine.[43]

Most in the British antislavery movement were skeptical about African colonization, but the belief that agriculture could solve Africa's problems proved surprisingly compelling. In 1839 Thomas Fowell Buxton published a manifesto calling for the civilization of Africa through a judicious combination of the Bible and the plow. In *The African Slave Trade and Its Remedy*, Buxton argued that agriculture was the only viable alternative to slavery. He proposed obtaining land "by treaty" from African rulers and farming it in accordance with the latest European techniques; an "agricultural company" would take care of the actual settlements while a "Benevolent Society" lobbied for money and government support. Buxton's missionary agenda made it unthinkable for Montefiore to add his name to those of Hodgkin and the Gurneys in the list of supporters published at the beginning of this book. Nevertheless, Montefiore did own a copy—and must have known all about the project when he left for Jerusalem in 1838. Montefiore's belief that agriculture not commerce was the way forward, his approach to Mehmed Ali, and his intention to form an agricultural company in England demonstrate a striking similarity of method between the two schemes. Consciously or otherwise, Montefiore's vision was very much a product of his humanitarian milieu.[44]

Yet there were limits to this influence. Pamphlets calling for Britain to hasten the process of redemption by facilitating the return of Jews to Palestine were a staple of Evangelical literature, but Montefiore's library contained no such tracts.[45] He conspicuously failed to make the usual argument about the strategic importance of Jewish settlement in Palestine for British interests, and nothing in his diary indicates that Christian Zionism had any impact on his ideas.

Many European Jews were committed to occupational restructuring, and Montefiore's plans have usually been seen as part of a wider movement for Jewish productivization. Accepting strictures about the dignity of manual labor at face value, self-consciously "enlightened" Jewish thinkers elevated working the soil above other forms of economic activity.[46] This was a response to the age-old complaint that Jews were economic parasites: if only Jews would abandon finance for the "real" work of farming or learning a trade, they could hope to become like the rest of society. In 1838 Germany's leading Jewish newspaper even published a series of articles idealizing the biblical Israelites, in which the editor, Ludwig Philippson, claimed that only an agrarian society could be fit to receive divine truths.

As a successful businessman, Montefiore cannot have shared this disdain for commerce. Tellingly, he said nothing in his diary about the inherent value of working the land; instead, by describing the project as a "speculation" he indicated that his interest was purely practical. He would have had no ideological objections to Arab peasants working in the fields under Jewish overseers. Indeed, it is clear from the minutes of his conversation with Israel Bak that Montefiore knew perfectly well that this arrangement was what the Jews of Palestine had in mind.[47] Given the limitations of the local economy, he simply saw agriculture as the best way for the Jewish community to generate a stable income. In keeping with Enlightenment ideas about the division of labor, he also recognized that Torah study was not for everyone, and hoped that agriculture could provide a living for those "unable to do justice to a Holy profession."[48]

Of course, this vision had wider religious significance. Many Jews regarded the year 5600 (1840) as especially favorable for the coming of the messiah.[49] In the climate of Jewish messianic speculation that characterized the 1830s, Montefiore's wealth created particular expectations. On receiving news of Montefiore's first visit to Jerusalem, Rabbi Simhah Bunam of Przysucha apparently expressed surprise that he did not try to purchase land from the Turks.[50] When a disciple asked him what Jews would do with the land of Israel, "seeing that the Almighty has not yet ordered us to return there," the pragmatic Polish Hasid replied: "Let the Jews take over. The Messiah will soon follow." In 1836 an unknown rabbi from Thorn (Toruń), in east Prussia, took this idea one step further when he wrote to Frankfurt asking Amschel Rothschild to buy the land of Israel—or at least Jerusalem—in order to reinstitute the biblical cult of sacrifice on the Temple Mount.[51]

Decades later Zvi Hirsch Kalischer would emerge as a founding father of religious Zionism. Had he written a month earlier, this famous letter would have arrived when Montefiore himself was in town.[52] In the event, Montefiore probably knew nothing about it; the Rothschilds received so many cranky begging letters that Kalischer's visionary proposal is unlikely to have stood out. In any case, the whole family was still coming to terms with the unexpected death of Nathan Rothschild, who had collapsed with septicemia on his son's wedding day.[53] The catalogue of Montefiore's library indicates that he had no direct access to traditional Jewish scholarship of any kind.[54] In 1839 he was sufficiently ignorant of the theology underpinning Jewish messianism for Loewe to give him a personal introduction to the subject, explaining "the different predominating opinions respecting rewards and punishments in the future world, the Messiah, and the opinions generally entertained relative to our holy religion, and the origin of the Mishna and Talmud."[55] But as an observant Jew, even Montefiore would surely have been aware of the particular virtue attached to "settling" the land of Israel—although the rabbis were divided as to whether this *mitzvah* was best fulfilled before or after the coming of the messiah.[56] His talk of the "return" of his brethren hints at a messianic subtext even at this stage, but the very concrete considerations outlined elsewhere reflect different priorities.

For the time being, the whole question of almsgiving in Palestine was so controversial that Montefiore needed to tread carefully. Wherever he went in the Holy Land, Montefiore was plagued with complaints about financial malpractice. Sometimes there were genuine improprieties. More often there was simply resentment that wealthy communal leaders took too much of the money, leaving the poor to starve. From a European perspective such complaints seemed justified, but Jewish el-

Distributing alms in Safed, 1839, from The Graphic, August 1885. *Face-to-face giving became a hallmark of Montefiore's philanthropy and seems to have given him great pleasure.* (By permission of the Bodleian Library, University of Oxford: N.2288.b.7)

ders were acting in accordance with established practice. The problem was rather that a system established primarily to support a few scholars now had to finance a larger, more diverse community—and one that had undergone a series of cataclysmic shocks. What, then, should Montefiore do with the donations he had brought from England, to which he added a good deal of his own money?

Eventually he decided to hand it out personally: a Spanish dollar to everyone over thirteen, two dollars to the blind, and half a dollar to every child. This exhausting procedure—which was repeated in each of the four holy cities and on several subsequent visits—enabled Montefiore to conduct a comprehensive survey of the Jewish population. Proper statistics would, he hoped, make it easier to plan for the future. Knowing that Jews were superstitious about being counted, he guessed correctly that the promise of a shiny dollar would overcome their fears.

Crowds of people soon gathered outside Montefiore's house. As his servants struggled to keep order, communal officials made sure that everyone came and all got more than their due. The atmosphere must have been stifling, but Montefiore sat from dawn till dusk distributing the money, with Loewe beside him asking questions and taking notes. Only the occasional sprinkling of vinegar and water served to relieve the intense heat and the press of dirty, sweaty humanity. But in later life, individual almsgiving would become one of the hallmarks of Montefiore's charity; he probably found the process deeply fulfilling.

This philanthropic marathon gave Montefiore the chance to meet most of the Jews in Palestine face to face. Some could communicate in a mixture of French, German, and Portuguese; if not, Loewe was always there to translate. Often they brought gifts—cake, sweet wine, a dish of potatoes. Personal contact was important because so many wrote to Montefiore individually. These letters, frequently written on scraps of paper, provide a rare window on to Jewish society—a litany of endeavor, disappointment, and loss.

Almost all the petitioners had lost close relatives in the earthquake, but they had plenty of other problems too: Yossef Shlomo Haim Sefardi needed a dowry for his daughter; Haya Raphael wanted a divorce; Zvi from Leitenwitz could no longer work after being robbed on the way to Palestine; Said Ben Yossef Halevy Elkavats was crippled by debt; Pinchas the ritual slaughterer could not live upon his meager earnings; Zvi Shlomo from Istanbul had stopped receiving money from his rich London relatives; and the requirement for Muslim witnesses meant that Dov Beer the bookbinder was afraid to turn to the Islamic courts to resolve a business dispute.[57]

Recent events in Safed and Tiberias added a new layer of misery. Zevi Hirsch ben Sander, Shalom Tordjemann, and Shmuel Rachamim, the son of Abraham Dov, typified the *nouveaux pauvres* applying to Montefiore for compensation or help with new enterprises.[58] The former had lost a large house and assets worth 15,000 gerush in the earthquake; the latter had built up a successful business printing religious books, only to see it ruined when the Druze attacked Safed.

News of Montefiore's generosity created an atmosphere of hysterical expectation. "[T]he light of his holy face has shone upon and lit up the good mountain of the Upper Galilee," wrote the leaders of the Sephardi community in a typical letter from Tiberias. Their intensely religious worldview and the traditional Jewish association between philanthropy and redemption caused them—like the rest of Palestine's Jews—to see Montefiore as God's instrument on earth, both the author of their immediate salvation and one whose generous practice of *tzedakah* would hasten the coming of the messiah:

. . . and, as the Talmud said, the land was lit up from his grace, and all the congregation as one sang and rejoiced and danced since they hope for G-d's redemption, since G-d delivers his redemption through his [Montefiore's] hand to do good for all the House of Israel . . . and not for nothing did G-d awaken his pure and holy spirit, but . . . in order for him [Montefiore] to be able to see the poverty of your people, the House of Israel, the poor and the miserable and the beaten, and those tortured with troubles of many, many kinds. And He [God] will awaken his [Montefiore's] mercy and benevolence and pity to do good in the way that he sees fit.[59]

In some ways, Judith's presence intensified these tendencies. The Jews of Palestine consistently treated Judith as an equal partner in her husband's philanthropy, making her director of a Talmud Torah in Hebron and several women's charities, and glorifying them both in official correspondence. Everyone sympathized with their childless state, and the Sephardim of Tiberias spoke for many when they undertook to bless Montefiore "so that it will be more pleasant to him that G-d will be with him than it is to have children." Others were less realistic, holding out the hope that he might yet be rewarded for his charity with "male sons" to "raise . . . in the light of the Torah."[60] The realities of the situation gave customary formulas of this kind a deliberately poignant edge.

It goes without saying that Montefiore and Judith never read any of these elaborate Hebrew letters. Nor did Loewe's terse, businesslike summaries—"*The Portuguese Congregation stating their great happiness at Sir Moses arrival*"—capture the flavor of the originals. Yet the couple understood enough to be profoundly touched. It was quite something for a retired English gentleman and his wife to be greeted on their arrival in Tiberias by thousands of voices, shouting: "Live the protector! Long live the protector!"[61] Travelers sometimes found Tiberias a gloomy place despite its lakeside setting, for its walls had been reduced to rubble by the earthquake, and those buildings left standing were constructed from an unremitting black stone.[62] But to the Montefiores, Tiberias was positively magical—every house illuminated in their honor, the streets crowded with people, and the rooftops covered with women in colorful dress.

That Muslims as well as Jews seemed eager to welcome the Montefiores only added to the general excitement. By now the whole population had heard of their unprecedented generosity and their tactful determination to give as much to poor Muslims and Christians as to Jews.[63] The governor of Tiberias overwhelmed the couple with kind attentions.[64] Undoubtedly aware of Montefiore's social status, he hoped that this distinguished foreigner could persuade Mehmed Ali to rebuild the town's defensive walls.[65]

The Montefiores spent six days in Tiberias discussing agriculture, distributing alms, and praying at holy sites. Meanwhile they agonized over whether they should proceed to Jerusalem. Finally, Montefiore received word from the British consul urging them to disregard the cholera now rampant in the holy city.[66] Still, it seemed wise to keep their distance, and they resolved to camp on the Mount of Olives rather than enter the city itself. With fourteen or fifteen deaths reported daily, Montefiore gave orders for a rope to be set up around their encampment and for all documents to be handled with pincers and stored in the open air. Hundreds of people made their way up the mountain from Jerusalem. At any one time a cluster of twenty or thirty Jews could be seen laying out their petitions outside the *cordon sanitaire*.

Looking down at the city from the safety of their encampment, the Montefiores could not fail to notice how things had changed. Previously, they could hardly have spent a night outside its walls without the protection of a large private army. Now, as the governor of Jerusalem declared proudly, "you may walk with a bag of gold in your hand. Not a soul would molest you."[67] Other differences were less glaring, but equally profound: the European great powers were engaged in a fierce competition for influence in the Ottoman Empire, and Jerusalem was an obvious target for their ambitions.

Russia and France enjoyed certain advantages in this struggle—the former as protector of Orthodox Christians and the latter as defender of Catholic interests. Lacking such historic status, the British were inclined to adopt Jews as their own client group. In 1829 Lord Holland had suggested that Anglo-Jewish emancipation might encourage the economically influential Jews of the Middle East to support British interests.[68] Just under ten years later, Holland's old friend Palmerston opened a British consulate in Jerusalem as part of a wider policy to expand diplomatic representation in the area.[69] Palmerston's motivations were entirely pragmatic, but, like many British Evangelicals, his son-in-law, Lord Ashley, regarded this development as a world-historical event that would pave the way for the coming of the messiah.[70] "The ancient city of the people of God is about to resume a place among the nations," Ashley enthused in his diary, "and England is the first of the Gentile Kingdoms that 'ceases to trod her down.' I shall always remember that God put it into my head to conceive the plan for His honor, gave me the influence to prevail with Palmerston and provided a man for the situation; who can remake Jerusalem in her glory."[71] The reality was more prosaic. Palmerston did instruct the new vice-consul, William Young, to "afford Protection to the Jews generally," but Young's Evangelical zeal only alienated both the Egyptian authorities and his diplomatic superior in Cairo.[72] Even so, the Montefiores were impressed.[73]

As the days passed, Montefiore and Judith felt tempted to break their self-imposed quarantine and go down into the city. And so, less than a week after their arrival, Montefiore, Judith, and Loewe found themselves entering Jerusalem in grand style at the invitation of the very courteous Egyptian governor, with an array of Egyptian troops lining the route and special guards to protect them from contact with the potentially contagious crowds. Every inch of the city was thronged with people, cheering the visitors from afar as they made their way to pray at the different Jewish synagogues and the Western Wall. Montefiore was delighted by their reception. "The Lord God of Israel be praised and thanked for permitting our feet to stand a second time within thy gates, O Jerusalem," he wrote in his diary that evening; "may the city soon be rebuilt in our days. Amen. I believe the whole population was looking at us, and bestowing blessings upon us."[74]

This sensational experience confirmed everything Montefiore had heard about the improved situation of the Jews in Palestine under Egyptian rule. Yet the new religious harmony was precarious and superficial. Many people resented Mehmed Ali's disregard for traditional religious hierarchies and envied the emergent merchant class, whose members were drawn largely from previously despised minority groups. The Montefiores had tested the limits of this new toleration on several occasions by visiting sites holy to both Jews and Muslims in defiance of established custom. Near Safed they had prayed at the place where Jacob was said to have mourned Joseph.[75] In Jerusalem they had persuaded the governor to allow them to see the tomb of David.[76] But in Hebron they discovered that such behavior could provoke a vicious backlash, when their insistence on trying to visit the tombs of the biblical patriarchs fatally undermined the fragile religious balance in this notoriously volatile area. If the Montefiores had succeeded, they would have been the first non-Muslims for generations to visit the Cave of Machpelah. Instead, they were nearly lynched.

The Muslims of Hebron found the sight of these wealthy European unbelievers parading through the streets on their way to the mosque intolerable. The Montefiores were followed by large numbers of the town's downtrodden Jews, eager to make the most of a unique opportunity. When they arrived at the main gate, accompanied by the governor and the *cadi,* the Montefiores found to their horror that a huge crowd had gathered, waving sticks and hurling abuse. Disregarding the uproar, they managed to enter the building, but the Jews behind were unable to fight their way through. Inside the mosque, Montefiore, Judith, and Loewe ran the gauntlet of angry shouts and threatening fists in their efforts to reach the cave itself. Had they continued, they would have been lucky to escape with their lives.[77]

Montefiore was beside himself with anger that the governor had exposed them to such an insult. In fact he had advised against the expedition. It was the complacent, obstinate Montefiore who refused to listen, and now the Jews of Hebron paid the price. Infuriated Arabs had already fallen upon a number of Jews hurrying back to their quarter, and the whole community was terrified of what might come. Only the arrival of twenty-one cavalrymen from Jerusalem prevented the Montefiores from fleeing the holy city of Hebron in a state of alarm.

They traveled back to Beirut through a countryside in crisis. Ibrahim Pasha had taken every available soldier for his army, leaving the towns unprotected and the Druze on the rampage. There was an atmosphere of total panic. Many Jews fled in terror from Safed and Tiberias to the relative safety of Haifa, while the wives of the governor of Acre took refuge with Carmelite nuns. As always, the Montefiores were lucky. They feared the worst when they heard the rumble of cannon fire in the distance, but the cannons were only firing in celebration: Ibrahim had won a famous victory near Nessib, annihilating the Turkish army at a stroke.

Setting sail for Alexandria, Montefiore carried the hopes of the Jews of Palestine with him. His personal presence, fabled generosity, and triumphal reception had established his status in the Holy Land—even if, in practice, the money Montefiore gave counted for little compared with the traditional flow of *halukah*. The breakaway faction of Perushim in Jerusalem even appointed Montefiore British and American director of their campaign to raise money to rebuild Jerusalem's oldest Ashkenazi synagogue, a ruined compound known as the Hurva.[78] Less controversial charities of all kinds rapidly followed suit. Like the Perushim of Jerusalem, they authorized Montefiore to "establish new and old *shofarot* [forms of publicity], *kupot* [funds], and [financial] dedications for this *mitzvah*, and to appoint officials as he wishes with his pure hand."[79] No doubt the administrators of these charities hoped to encourage a sense of financial obligation in Montefiore; they also realized that their wealthy patron represented a new kind of diaspora support.

As a first step, Montefiore made the most of his forty-eight-hour stopover in Egypt by securing an interview with Mehmed Ali. He now had a host of pressing issues to raise with the pasha. Landing late on Thursday evening, Montefiore learned to his frustration that religious scruples would prevent Mehmed Ali from meeting him the next day. Saturday was the Sabbath, but Montefiore was too old and unwell to contemplate walking through Alexandria himself. Eventually he managed to secure a kind of sedan chair, in which he sat sweltering in full-dress costume, wearing a military hat and feather and his massive sheriff's chain. This naive attempt to convey an impression of his social consequence back-fired seriously; no one in Alexandria had ever seen anything like it be-fore, and Montefiore's sedan chair soon attracted a large and curious following, mystified by the sight of "a dressed image in a glass box, [be-ing] carried into the palace, sent from the English idolators."[80]

All in all, the interview was only a qualified success.[81] Glowing with confidence at the news of Ibrahim's stunning victory, Mehmed Ali prom-ised to give immediate orders regarding the protection of Jews in Pal-estine, reconstruction of the walls of Tiberias, and the admission of evidence by Jewish witnesses in Muslim courts. He enthusiastically wel-comed Montefiore's proposals for a chain of joint-stock banks from Al-exandria and Cairo through Beirut and Damascus to Jaffa and Jerusa-lem, with a combined capital of one million pounds. But he was unwilling to commit to Montefiore's plans for Jewish agriculture. Even-tually he agreed to cooperate if and when Montefiore could demonstrate that there was government land in Palestine that could serve as a basis for colonies along the lines Montefiore outlined. In the last hours before their departure from Alexandria, Loewe called repeatedly at the palace in a vain attempt to obtain something more substantial. Mehmed Ali remained evasive, promising only that he would write to confirm every-thing in due course.

Yet Montefiore's reception and Mehmed Ali's promise did not go un-noticed in Europe. In early August the *Allgemeine Zeitung des Juden-tums* carried a report from London's *Morning Chronicle* claiming that Montefiore had "already rented a large stretch of land in Palestine for a period of fifty years" and was eager for his coreligionists to farm the soil of their forefathers once his plans to establish a bank in the area had been realized.[82] Torn between skepticism and grudging admiration, the *Chronicle* ridiculed Montefiore for his vanity in appearing before the pasha in a uniform to which he was no longer entitled, but hinted none-theless that his rash plan might prove the seed of something truly re-markable: the long-awaited restoration of the Jews. The article in the *Morning Chronicle* reflected a growing sense of millenarian expectation among Evangelicals. Many were inclined to dismiss these sentiments as the ravings of a restorationist fringe; but with events in Turkey and Egypt escalating so rapidly, for a moment it almost looked as if anything might be possible.

Sultan Mahmud of Turkey died on June 30, 1839, leaving the Ottoman Empire in the care of a sixteen-year-old boy. Within days the new ruler

"Interview with the viceroy of Egypt [Mehmed Ali], at his palace, Alex-andria," as rendered by David Roberts, in The Holy Land, Syria, Idomea, Arabia, Egypt & Nubia, *vol. 6 (London, 1856), plate 213. Montefiore's encounters with the pasha of Egypt would have been much like this one. (By permission of the Bodleian Library, University of Oxford: Mason HH91B)*

learned that the Ottoman army had been annihilated by Ibrahim Pasha, an event that prompted the entire Ottoman navy to defect to Mehmed Ali. Hearing of these dramatic developments at Malta, Montefiore feared for his dream of establishing Jewish agricultural settlements in Palestine.[83] But he did not forget the plan altogether. In December Montefiore wrote reminding the pasha of his undertakings; weeks and months passed, but Montefiore waited in vain for a reply.[84]

Mehmed Ali's silence was understandable. For different reasons, the great powers of Europe seemed determined to deny him the fruits of Ibrahim's victory, and in a collective note issued on July 27 they forbade direct negotiations between the sultan and his rebellious vassal.[85] It was Palmerston, the flamboyant British foreign secretary, who took the lead in international efforts to cut the viceroy of Egypt down to size.

Palmerston believed that the rise of Mehmed Ali posed a threat to the balance of power in Europe, and that British interests in India rendered the future of Syria and Egypt a matter of vital concern. Under no circumstances should Turkey be allowed to cede Syria to Mehmed Ali: "To

frame a system of future policy in the East upon the accidental position
of a man turned seventy would be to build on sand." Many thought the
Ottoman Empire was falling apart; Palmerston begged to differ. In the
first place, he took the view that "no empire is likely to fall to pieces if
left to itself." In the second place, he was "disposed to think that . . . the
daily increasing intercourse between Turkey and the other countries of
Europe must in a few years, if peace can be preserved, throw much light
upon the defects and weaknesses of the Turkish system, and lead to various improvements therein."[86]

For most of the 1830s, France and Britain had cooperated over the
Eastern Question. Now France's longstanding support of Mehmed Ali's
ambitions threatened to undermine the alliance between these two self-
consciously liberal states. Neither the French government, nor the
French public, nor the influential coterie of Frenchmen with vested interests in Egypt shared Palmerston's skepticism about the pasha. Instead,
they saw both him and Egypt as a vehicle for French resurgence in the
Middle East.

The crisis of 1839 had quite the opposite effect on Anglo-Russian relations. Russian expansion into Central Asia posed a threat to British
India, and British policy in relation to the Ottoman Empire had long
been motivated by the need to contain the tsarist menace. Like Palmerston, Nicholas of Russia preferred a weak Ottoman Empire to the chaos
that was likely to attend its collapse. He was eager, too, to tempt Britain
away from her alliance with postrevolutionary France. In September
1839 Nicholas sent his confidant Baron Brunnow to London offering
Palmerston full cooperation on the Eastern Question. Russian control of
the Bosporus proved a critical sticking point, but by the end of 1839
Nicholas declared himself ready to share defense of the straits. Montefiore's interest in Palestine led him to follow these developments closely,
but the events of early 1840 would soon create a new synergy between
Jewish preoccupations and the crisis in the Middle East.

Chapter 7

The Damascus Affair

In the spring of 1840 the Board of Deputies held an emergency meeting at Montefiore's house in Park Lane. Such gatherings were normally relaxed and intimate occasions.[1] With just twenty-two members representing the four London congregations, these were men who knew one another well. They did business together; they socialized together; indeed, many were related. But on April 21 the atmosphere must have been electric. For the first time in the board's history, these successful London businessmen found themselves addressing a matter of life and death with implications for the whole Jewish world.[2] In an unprecedented display of cross-Channel solidarity, they were joined by a Frenchman: Adolphe Crémieux.[3]

Barely six weeks earlier, on March 13, the *Sémaphore de Marseille* had reported the suspected involvement of "a number of Jewish families" in the mysterious disappearance of an Italian friar from Damascus. Torture was standard practice in Ottoman investigations of this kind, and the *Sémaphore* noted in passing that the Jews were "subjected nonstop to torture in order to force them to name the authors of a crime which revolts everybody."[4] Leading newspapers like the *Journal des Débats, The Times,* and the *Leipziger Allgemeine Zeitung* reprinted the article without further comment.

The belief that Jews used Christian blood to bake their Passover bread was a medieval fantasy that resonated powerfully in the popular imagination. Allegations of this practice, which became known as the "blood libel," had been a regular feature of Jewish life in Europe since the thirteenth century.[5] In the 1820s and 1830s they erupted with growing frequency among the large Christian communities of the Middle East. Reports soon began to reach Europe that the leading Jews of Damascus had been convicted by the Egyptian government of ritual murder on evi-

133

dence produced by the French consul, the comte de Ratti-Menton, and that similar barbarities had been perpetrated by the Jews of Rhodes. In early April the *Sémaphore de Marseille* carried a more elaborate and gruesome description of the alleged murder of Father Tommaso, explicitly presenting this shocking episode as part of a wider Jewish cult of human sacrifice. The damning article reappeared in newspapers all over Europe—not one of which chose to cast doubt on the official version of events.

Four days later, on April 8, the *Journal des Débats* published a devastating critique of the Damascus allegations. Its author was Adolphe Crémieux, vice-president of the Consistoire Central des Israélites de France, the governing body of French Jewry. For centuries, Jewish businessmen had preferred to exercise power behind closed doors. This was the traditional role of the *shtadlan,* the Jew whose wealth and position enabled him to "stand before kings" and speak out in defense of his people. Now Crémieux broke with this tradition in a revolutionary step apparently taken with the full approval of James de Rothschild.[6] His article marked the beginning of a new Jewish politics, one that combined the influence that Jewish financiers wielded behind the scenes with a vocal campaign for Jewish rights.

Still in his early forties, Crémieux was a brilliant, ambitious lawyer, whose courtroom skills had done much to remove the last vestiges of Jewish inequality in France. An ardent secularist, he rapidly established himself after 1830 as a leading defender of liberal ideas in the law courts and the press. Writing in the *Débats*, Crémieux portrayed Ratti-Menton's willingness to embrace the ritual-murder allegations in Damascus as a betrayal of the universal values championed by France since 1789. He contrasted the readiness with which even progressive French newspapers had accepted and disseminated "this miserable calumny born of the infamous prejudices of medieval Christianity" with "the ideas of progress and liberalism" they professed to support. Referring to France's role as a pioneer of Jewish emancipation during the Revolution, Crémieux concluded with a stirring appeal to his Christian fellow citizens: "you have set the world an example of the gentlest and purest toleration. Serve as our shield having served as our support!"[7]

The blood libel was centuries old, but the Damascus Affair because a cause célèbre because the involvement of the French consul lent the accusation credibility—and because a British consul took the lead in pressing charges against the Jews of Rhodes. The initial publicity surrounding these events reflected improved communications, the spread of missionary networks, and the growth of European political influence in the Middle East. But the long-term impact of the Damascus Affair lay in

French lawyer, politician, and Jewish leader Adolphe Crémieux. (By permission of Alliance Israélite Universelle, Paris, Collection Renée Neuer No. 1950)

demonstrating the interconnectedness of the Jewish world in an age of incipient globalization. Throughout the United States and continental Europe, Crémieux's article provoked an unprecedented wave of protest meetings, petitions, and deputations in defense of the Jewish prisoners in Damascus, as newspapers all over the "civilized" world debated the truth of the allegations. With Jewish emancipation a live issue in Britain and most of continental Europe, Western Jews could not afford to be found guilty by association. This was the momentous issue the deputies had gathered with Crémieux to discuss.

The meeting began with a solemn refutation of the allegations of ritual murder and a public reading of the desperate appeals that Montefiore and the Rothschilds had received from Damascus and Rhodes.[8] The letters made grim hearing. Writing from Damascus, Abram Conorte and Aron Coen recounted how suspicion had fallen on the Jews after claims that Father Tommaso and his servant were last seen in the Jewish quarter. Investigations led to the arrest of a Jewish barber, who was dragged before the Egyptian governor, where the authorities "accused him, and gave him 500 Stripes inflicting other cruelties." The barber eventually broke down and, "seeking by that means to relieve himself, accused

Messrs. David Arari, Isaac Arari, Aron Arari, Joseph Legnado, Moses Abolafia, Moses Benar Juda and Joseph Arari, as instigating accomplices, who had offered him P[ias]tres 300 to murder the above mentioned [Father Tommaso], in as much as the Passover Holidays approaching they required [Christian] blood for their [Passover] cakes; that he did not however give ear to their instigations, while at the same time he knew not what might have happened to the Priest and his servant."

Two of the men he named were rabbis, and the rest belonged to a leading merchant family; the governor lost no time in arresting all of them.

These prisoners suffered "the most severe beatings and cruelties," while the 5,000 Jews of Damascus ran the gauntlet of threats, intimidation, and extortion. Several butchers were "beaten to such an extreme that their flesh hung in pieces upon them," and all the children at one primary school were chained and incarcerated in the expectation "that the fathers for the sake of liberating their children would confess the truth of the matter." When a Jew came forward to say that he had seen Father Tommaso and his servant leaving town on the night in question, he was flogged to death. After an energetic series of house searches, the governor reverted to torturing the prisoners with "further castigations and torments, the most cruel of which was the tying one end of a cord to the member of virility by the other end of which they were dragged through the Governor's Palace to a Water Closet into which they were thrown. Incapable of bearing further torments they prepared to die and confessed that the Calumny was true!!!"

More Jews were implicated, and more arrests followed. One prisoner claimed to have secreted the blood in a bottle, which he delivered to Rabbi Moses Abulafia. The rabbi was beaten so savagely for his failure to produce the bottle that he eventually converted to Islam—lending his authority to the ritual-murder calumny.

This account of the Jews' sufferings failed to do justice to the shifting balance of power in an area where European penetration was exacerbating the economic rivalry between Jews and Christians.[9] The Ottoman authorities had always acted quickly to suppress blood libels, but Damascus was now under Egyptian rule. In most of Syria and Egypt, Mehmed Ali's policy of enhancing the status of local Christians had forced Jews onto the defensive. Yet the collective wealth of the Jewish elite in Damascus was nearly four times as great as that of their Christian rivals.[10] Few thought it a coincidence that the very richest Jews in the city were the targets of the blood libel. Father Tommaso enjoyed French protection, and local Christians had been the first to implicate the Jews. Ratti-Menton and Jean-Baptiste Beaudin, his Machiavellian subordinate, who was seen as the real instigator of the agitation against the Jews, took the lead in moving the case forward.[11] Of course, they had relied on the active support of the Egyptian authorities to pursue the investigation. But Sherif Pasha's willingness to endorse the blood libel was dictated by his desire to curry favor with French officials at a time when France was Mehmed Ali's best hope of survival.

The letter smuggled out by the Jews of Rhodes revealed similar undercurrents. A ten-year-old Christian had gone missing there shortly after the disappearance of Father Tommaso. The boy was an Ottoman citizen, but once again European consuls took it upon themselves to interfere in the case. After two Greek women claimed to have seen him leaving the city in the care of a Jew, they had the Jew brought in for questioning. This time it was the British vice-consul, J. G. Wilkinson, who refused to believe Eliakim Stambouli's protestations of innocence. With the exception of the Austrian consul, the entire diplomatic corps appears to have watched as

> having been loaded with chains many stripes were inflicted on him [Stambouli], red hot iron wires were run through his nose, burning bones were applied to his head, and a very heavy stone was laid upon his breast; in so much that he was reduced to the point of death, all the while they were accusing him, saying *"You have stolen the Greek boy to deliver himself to the Rabbin; confess it at once if you wish to save yourself."* There [sic] object was to calumniate our Rabbin, and to take vengeance on all the Community, and they stated openly that this was done for the purpose of exterminating the Jews from Rhodes or compel them to change their religion, so that they might be able to boast in Europe of having caused an entire community to change their religion.

As in Damascus, the confession of the tortured prisoner paved the way for a wider persecution of the town's Jews.

Although the content of these letters cannot have been news to the men gathered in Park Lane, they were still appalled by what they heard. Taking their cue from Crémieux and the French Rothschilds, the deputies resolved to combine political lobbying with a press campaign—deputing a selection of the most influential to call on Palmerston, and taking out advertisements in the *Times, Morning Chronicle, Morning Herald, Morning Post, Standard, Globe, Sun, Courier, Examiner, Spectator, Observer, Sunday Times, John Bull, Literary Gazette, Liverpool Mercury, Manchester Guardian, Birmingham Gazette, Birmingham Journal, Edinburgh Scotsman, Edinburgh Weekly, Dublin Warden, Dublin Register, Bristol Journal, Bristol Mercury, Plymouth Herald,*

West of England Conservative, Exeter Post, Exeter Times, and *Brighton Guardian.*[12]

Montefiore, of course, was a member of this deputation. Having twice met (and admired) Mehmed Ali, he must have felt a strong personal interest in the case. Like the rest of the delegates, he was delighted with their reception. Palmerston sent at once to the British consul in Alexandria, instructing him to "represent to Mehemet Ali the extreme disgrace which the Barbarous enormities perpetrated at that place [Damascus], reflect upon his administration." Writing on the same day to the ambassador in Constantinople, Palmerston expressed the hope that the Ottoman government would immediately launch an inquiry into the blood libel allegations at Rhodes. Shocked by the suggestion that the British consul was partly responsible for instigating the allegations, he demanded that Wilkinson provide a full report of the affair, for "H.M.'s Govt cannot possibly believe it to be true . . . that a British Vice-Consul should be a Party to an act so directly in opposition to the Principles & Sentiments which ought to distinguish a British Agent."[13]

These letters marked the first formal intervention by a British government in the cause of international Jewish relief.[14] Parliament had yet to grant British Jews full equality, but Palmerston's support for the Jews of Damascus and Rhodes was entirely consistent with his zeal in eradicating slavery and his belief in the fundamental morality of Britain's imperial mission. Only a year later he would finally secure the cooperation of every Christian state except the United States in his war on the international slave trade; for, as he famously remarked, "Our duty—our vocation—is not to enslave, but to set free; and I may say without any vain glorious boast, or without great offence to anyone, that we stand at the head of moral, social and political civilization."[15] Like many of his fellow countrymen, Palmerston believed that British foreign policy had a moral dimension. He did not hesitate to apply this dimension to Jews.

By contrast, the French government continued to prevaricate. Adrien-Louis Cochelet, the French consul in Alexandria, steadfastly defended Ratti-Menton and refused to cooperate with the efforts of Anton von Laurin, the Austrian consul in Alexandria, to reopen the case. Thanks to the intervention of Salomon Rothschild, Laurin soon had the full backing of the influential Austrian chancellor, Prince Klemens von Metternich, but, as Cochelet explained to Prime Minister Adolphe Thiers, "it was not for the agent of a foreign power to constitute himself the defender of the murderers of a monk under French protection."[16] Privately, Thiers was unconvinced by the ritual-murder allegations. But Thiers was not the biographer of Napoleon for nothing. He was attracted by the glamor of an aggressive foreign policy, hoping to strengthen both his own government and the Orléanist regime through nationalist agitation.

As support for Mehmed Ali led to France's growing diplomatic isolation, Thiers chose to link the accusations against Ratti-Menton to the wider international situation. When the only Jewish deputy raised the issue in the French Parliament on June 2, Thiers took refuge in an attack on Jewish power: "At this very moment they [the Jews] are putting forward their claims in every foreign chancellory. And they are doing so with an extraordinary vigor and with an ardor which can scarcely be imagined. It requires courage for a minister to protect his agent under attack . . . and our consul has no support except in the French ministry of foreign affairs."[17]

This speech inflamed an already sensitive situation. Taking its cue from the prime minister, the ultramontane Catholic *Univers* concluded that the Damascus Affair had revealed the existence of a Jewish national interest and given the lie to the platitudes of liberals who wished to grant Jews equal rights. In Britain, only *The Times* was willing to contemplate the possibility of ritual murder; in France, the Catholic press proclaimed its belief in the blood libel in uncompromising terms.[18]

Writing to his family in London, Nathaniel Rothschild admitted that Crémieux had perhaps erred in making so much of the affair. But, he continued, "upon this occasion when the prime minister of France declared in the Chambers that he thought the Jews committed murder for the sake of Christian blood to be used in a Hebrew religious ceremony, it strikes me that such a calumny upon all those who have Jewish blood in their veins ought not only to be contradicted but proved to be false. The only practicable way of so doing in my opinion is to send Crémieux accompanied by some sober steady Englishman, who would moderate his zeal, to Damascus . . . and find out the guilty parties and the motives."[19]

There was, in his opinion, only one possible candidate: he hoped his uncle Montefiore would set sail for Egypt as a matter of urgency.

Two weeks later, Jewish speakers at a public meeting in London's Great Synagogue underlined the critical importance of sending such a mission to Damascus. As David Salomons explained, the blood libel allegations affected "every portion of that [Jewish] community, not only those who are resident here, but those in every part of the globe." Amid loud applause, Montefiore then proclaimed his readiness to join Crémieux on his mission of mercy. "We go," he declared, to "unravel, if possible, the dark mazes of this diabolical transaction . . . to remove from our brethren in the East the foul stain attempted to be cast on our nation by the bigotry and intolerance, the fraud and rapacity of unprincipled persecutors. We go to attempt more than this—to infuse into the Governments of the East more enlightened principles of legislation and judicial procedure, and in particular to prevail on those Governments to abolish the use of torture, and to establish the supremacy of law over undefined and arbitrary power." Entrusting himself to the protection of the Almighty, Montefiore concluded with "a prayer for the peace of Jerusalem—in ardent supplication that the blessing of the HOLY ONE of ISRAEL may rest upon her."[20]

His devoutly religious tone was out of keeping with the secular approach of earlier speakers, but it would have resonated powerfully with the Evangelicals and Dissenters who read reports of the meeting in the press the next day. These circles set the tone for much of the British middle classes. The speech underlined their spiritual affinity with Montefiore and his instinctive grasp of their concerns. Montefiore's emphasis on the universal implications of the mission, his talk of "the claims of humanity, outraged in the persons of our persecuted and suffering brethren," and his reference to the conflict between law and "arbitrary power" represented a conscious attempt to reach out beyond the Jewish community by playing on the sensitivities of this humanitarian milieu.[21]

Ten days later these themes took center stage at a "Grand Public Meeting" in the Mansion House, official home of the lord mayor of London, where Evangelicals, Quakers, Radicals, and antislavery activists declared their support for the Jewish cause. Jews like Montefiore still lacked the right to sit in Parliament, but this unprecedented meeting confirmed their place at the heart of a wider political alliance, united in its commitment to "civil and religious liberty" at home and abroad. Prominent figures in the Damascus agitation included the Irish nationalist Daniel O'Connell; Montefiore's business associates Sam Gurney, Wolverly Attwood, and Edward Blount; and his fellow sheriff, Sir George Carroll.[22] The movement helped to construct a new political paradigm, in which Jewish activists could situate the cause of Jewish relief within the wider framework of British (and international) humanitarian campaigns. But perhaps the most striking aspect of the Mansion House meeting was the way speaker after speaker used the language of imperialism and English domestic politics to defend the Jewish cause.

The triumph of the antislavery movement lent British imperialism a strong moral flavor in the 1830s, and no one felt any reservations about identifying Montefiore's expedition to Damascus with this wider sense of mission. All England, according to the politician and businessman Sir George Larpent, "was determined to raise its voice against oppression and against the infamous use of torture," and all England would support "that champion and apostle Sir Moses Montefiore" in his efforts "to stay the arm of the oppressor and the bigot, and to establish the character of Asian nations for toleration; and to place England with Europe at the head of those communities in this world which enforced religious toleration and civil liberty." British identification with the biblical Israelites and the sympathetic climate created by Evangelical philo-Semitism facilitated the use of such patriotic rhetoric—although not all those who supported Jewish relief abroad necessarily endorsed emancipation at home.[23]

Montefiore left London on July 10, confident that he enjoyed the full backing of the British government. An international campaign had been launched to finance and publicize the mission, and money was flooding in—nearly £7,000, of which Montefiore contributed roughly a third.[24] Besides Judith, his entourage included Loewe and the Evangelical solicitor David Wire, a longtime City friend. Touched by the many "kind and good people" who left "their beds at unseasonable hour" to bid him Godspeed, he was optimistic. A few days in Paris allowed the realities of the situation to sink in.[25] French influence was likely to predominate in Egypt, and, unlike the British contingent, Adolphe Crémieux and the Paris-based orientalist Salomon Munk had no official support.[26] Even so, Montefiore feared that they would insist on forming a separate delegation, but he was pleasantly surprised by the "cordial and frank behaviour of the French Committee," reporting to the Board of Deputies that since Crémieux did not represent his government, it had been agreed "that he should act as my Counsel in conjunction with Mr. Wire."[27]

The reality was rather different. Crémieux's article in the *Journal des Débats* was largely responsible for the entire Damascus agitation, and he never forgave Montefiore's arrogant assumption of authority. Many weeks later he declared bitterly: "the day when you, Sir, wanted to become head of a mission which belonged in the beginning to myself alone, and which I had asked you to share with me, [on] that day . . . you lost every right to my confidence . . . you ensured that every avenue was closed to you, when you wanted to be master, because you were rich."[28]

Even at the time, Crémieux made clear that he was unhappy with the situation, and he certainly never accepted to be placed on a par with Wire. But, as Anselme de Rothschild pointed out, the mission needed a leader, and since Thiers had refused his backing, Montefiore was the obvious choice. The Rothschilds saw their rich relative as a steadying influence; having offered Crémieux 40,000 francs for making the journey, Anselme regarded him as a glorified employee.

Relations between the two men deteriorated during the three-week

An Englishman among the Eastern peoples: Montefiore arriving in Alex-andria in 1840, from The Graphic, *August 1885. (By permission of the Bodleian Library, University of Oxford: N.2288.b.7)*

journey to Alexandria as the Montefiores repeatedly asserted their rights to the best cabins and subjected Crémieux to a series of social slights. Crémieux soon concluded that it would be impossible to do business with them. Sir Moses and his wife were "good people, but the arrogance born of money, and the English vanity of these two individuals surpasses anything that can be imagined."[29] Nor did he warm to Montefiore's entourage, which now included his old friend Dr. Madden, who added medical expertise and Catholic connections to the linguistic and legal skills of Loewe and Wire.

The Jewish mission arrived in Alexandria just as Britain, Russia, Austria, and Prussia reached agreement about the future of the Middle East. It would take time for news of the Quadruple Alliance to reach Egypt, but everyone could sense which way the wind was blowing. Mehmed Ali recognized that Thiers's nationalist government was now his only hope. Palmerston's support for the Ottoman sultan made it easy for the British to obtain justice in the Rhodes blood-libel episode, but in Egypt French influence remained paramount.

Trusting as he did in God and Palmerston, Montefiore appeared sublimely indifferent to these realities—an attitude that Crémieux found

profoundly irritating. It was clear to him that the mission needed to focus on winning over Cochelet, but he had trouble persuading Montefiore even to call on the French consul. Cochelet himself proved so hostile that he refused to introduce his compatriot to the pasha, leaving
Crémieux to watch in frustration as the British consul, Colonel John
Lloyd Hodges, presented his rival to Mehmed Ali.

Montefiore intended to request a *firman* (decree) authorizing his party
to proceed to Damascus and conduct a thorough, impartial investigation of the murder of Father Tommaso. Complacently, he assured
Crémieux that the pasha would "not let me leave the palace without acceding to my demands."[30] Dressed in his uniform, and flanked by Wire
and Madden, Montefiore hoped to read his petition to Mehmed Ali in
English—and indeed he subsequently circulated the text to the European press, where it made quite a splash.[31] But, as Crémieux noted, the
pasha's receptions were too informal to allow for grand speeches.[32] Saying only, "It is long, it is long; shall be translated!" Mehmed Ali refused
to be drawn out on the Damascus Affair.[33] He was delighted when Madden came forward to present a congratulatory address from the Anti-
Slavery Convention. Montefiore's subsequent efforts to change the subject fell on resolutely deaf ears.

Montefiore spent the next weeks in an agony of uncertainty. Within
days of their arrival, Mehmed Ali received formal notification of the ultimatum by the Four Powers: if he submitted to the sultan immediately,
he would be rewarded with hereditary rule in Egypt and control of
southern Syria for his lifetime; if he waited longer than ten days, he
would lose Syria; if he waited more than twenty, the offer would be
withdrawn. Hodges informed Montefiore that "the door of negotia-
tion was now not only shut, but locked," and advised him to be ready
to leave at any time. Meanwhile Count Alexandre Walewski had arrived from Paris, apparently armed with offers of "Ships, Money and
Men."[34]

Continual disagreements between Crémieux and Montefiore added to
their problems. Both men identified strongly with their countries; each
tended to overestimate the influence of his own consul and to dismiss
that of his rival. Crémieux initially formed the more accurate judgment,
but he failed to change his opinion when the power advantage shifted
away from France. According to Madden, "it was impossible for any
person of common intelligence not to perceive that the appearance of
a British squadron off these shores, and the non-appearance of any
French force, had operated very beneficially on the moral views of his
Highness." Yet Crémieux maintained that "the Pasha should not be
pressed with further applications during his present difficulties," and

that Mehmed Ali's understandable aversion to the British made it advisable to "trust solely to French influence."[35]

Buoyed by his faith, Montefiore took a categorical view of their situation. He had no doubt that similar blood libel allegations would resurface "both in the East and in Europe" unless the charge was "boldly met."[36] Crémieux, with a subtler cast of mind than his rival, tended to see shades of gray. He was inclined to endorse a proposal that would have liberated the prisoners and defused the ritual-murder accusations, leaving himself and Montefiore free to pursue their inquiries in Damascus should Syria revert to the sultan. This difference of opinion led to a "violent dispute" between the French and British delegations.[37] By the end of August even Montefiore had been brought to recognize that an unconditional discharge was the best they were likely to get. War between Britain and Egypt now seemed certain, with Mehmed Ali busy repairing fortifications, erecting new batteries, and calling in his troops. In a somewhat shamefaced letter to the Board of Deputies, Montefiore explained that the "critical state of affairs" made it necessary to demand "less than we ought." Even at this juncture, however, Montefiore continued to believe "in the justice of Him, who is the Judge of all the Earth, and who assuredly will in his own time . . . make clear the innocence of our brethren."[38]

Suddenly Mehmed Ali bowed to the inevitable and accepted the ultimatum. The long months of crisis had undermined him physically, and that very morning he underwent an unpleasant operation on a boil on his backside. Crémieux had found the time to befriend Mehmed Ali's physicians, and the two medical men took it upon themselves to push the Jewish cause. Referring pointedly to the international crisis, they argued that "in the current circumstances the voices of six million Jews raised in your favor will not be without great importance. You must grant them their request."[39] Mehmed Ali had presumably reached this conclusion independently: he undertook to free the prisoners without further ado.

Crémieux intended leaving that morning for a ten-day sightseeing trip to Cairo. Beside himself with excitement on hearing of the breakthrough, he felt it necessary to set out anyway, returning that evening on account of his wife's supposed ill health. He sent Montefiore a mysterious letter announcing his departure, bragging of his triumph in veiled terms and exhorting him to "absolute secrecy," warning: *"do not go to the Vice Roy, without being summoned, you will spoil it all."*[40] Understandably mystified by this communication—and probably suspecting something underhand—Montefiore immediately set out for the palace, where, sure enough, he received news of the prisoners' release.

Bitter recriminations followed. Crémieux demanded to know why his

letter had been ignored. When Montefiore blamed Crémieux for trying to keep him from the pasha, the latter exploded: "Your only interest
in our magnificent mission is pride and vanity."[41] "You are wrong sir,"
Montefiore retorted. "It is all down to the English and the Pasha's
change of policy. Neither you nor your friends have anything to do with
it." For Crémieux this was the last straw. "Oh! That's a good one! . . .
All this national vanity, which shows me how wrong I was to come and
fetch you from London . . . Everything I propose is rejected, everything
you propose, I have to accept. My friends can do nothing; yours will do
everything . . . and yet every day shows the error of our ways and justi-
fies my approach . . . Write to Europe!" he urged Montefiore; "say, if
you will, that you and the English have done everything, and . . . I will
write for my part, and I will say everything that has happened, and Europe will judge between you and me!"[42] His threat brought all the players to their senses. It was left to Madden to placate Crémieux, who after
considerable self-justification agreed to dine with Judith, Montefiore,
and the rest.

The squabbles continued when Crémieux acted unilaterally to have
the word "Pardon" removed from the order liberating the Jewish prisoners. Montefiore could hardly disguise his irritation. He blamed Loewe
for the episode—and began to scold him as soon as Crémieux's back
was turned. "What Sir? you didn't understand the word. You said nothing to me [about it]!" But he soon had his revenge: after promising
Crémieux that they would write to Damascus together, he proceeded to
send the good news without a word to his rival. Thanks to Mehmed
Ali's physicians, Crémieux still managed to get a letter in his own name
there first.[43]

The prisoners' release was received with joy in Damascus, but the triumph of the Jewish mission fell short of total vindication. With Syria in
revolt and Damascus likely to return to direct Ottoman rule, Montefiore
concluded that his best bet was to sit out the crisis in Constantinople,
where he would be well placed to influence events. He realized, however, that without further investigation at Damascus, the release of the
prisoners would look like a whitewash. Demonstrating a natural talent
for political theater, Montefiore told Crémieux that they should "publicize everywhere that we wish to go to Damascus, and resist all those
who urge us not to expose ourselves [to danger]. In this way, we will be
able to say that we were not allowed to go. But in fact, we should make
arrangements either to go as quickly as possible to Constantinople, or to
return home."[44] He also did his best to turn partial success into outright
victory by persuading Mehmed Ali to issue a statement publicly refuting
the blood libel.

Crémieux was disinclined to cooperate, but Madden persuaded him

that it was the only way to end their mission with dignity. When Crémieux began to voice his frustration at Montefiore's vanity and pride,
the Irishman responded with unexpected sympathy: "*Eh! Mon Dieu,
Monsieur,* you tell me nothing new. I am leaving tomorrow, do not imagine that I was sent here just as his doctor; Lord John Russell sent me
with him: but, believe me, you must take this initiative [together], then
all will be over between you. It is impossible that you will ever reach an
understanding with Sir Moses."[45]

Madden also urged Crémieux to go along with Montefiore's wishes
by including a line or two requesting the abolition of torture. This was
essentially a piece of political positioning that would allow the Jewish
activists to emphasize the universal implications of the Damascus Affair by highlighting the connection with other human rights issues.[46]
Crémieux thought torture was such a big question that it deserved to be
dealt with separately: a second petition would attract more attention
and stand greater chances of success. Wire and the Austrian consul
agreed with him, but Montefiore refused to decouple the Jewish mission
from the torture initiative, obstinately repeating: "It is better, I assure
you, to put everything together."[47] Crémieux eventually yielded. While
the French half of the delegation finally headed for Cairo, Montefiore
and his entourage continued to Constantinople as planned.

For once, their timing was excellent. Britain had played the central role
in forcing Mehmed Ali to give way to the sultan, and Palmerston was
happy to exert his newfound influence on behalf of Jews. During the
1830s the prolonged crisis over the Eastern Question and the growing
influence of Evangelicals in British society had given renewed impetus
to Protestant millenarianism. Now, the interplay between international
and domestic politics brought restorationism into the mainstream for
the first time.

In January 1839 Lord Ashley published a long article in the influential
Quarterly Review, in which he claimed that there was a burgeoning desire among European Jewry to return to Palestine. That same month, a
memorandum addressed to the "Protestant Powers of the North of Europe and America" called upon their rulers to follow in the footsteps of
Cyrus and restore the people of Israel to their native land. Forwarding
this petition to Queen Victoria, Palmerston expressed every confidence
that her "pious feelings" would "be excited to give the Scriptural hopes
and expectations therein set forth your earnest attention, considering
the high station it hath pleased Almighty God to call this Protestant land
to, as the great seat of the church."[48]

This was not just rhetoric. Palmerston had been discussing the Eastern Question with his son-in-law for well over a year now; by the summer of 1840 Ashley's efforts were beginning to bear fruit. In late July and early August, two leading British newspapers suggested that Jews could play an important part in the reconfiguration of Syria.[49] Both *The Times* and *The Globe* deliberately distanced themselves from theological speculation, arguing that Jewish settlement in Palestine would free Jews from persecution in Europe and enable them to fulfill their historic role as agents of civilization in the Middle East.

These articles reflected an important shift in government policy. On August 11, 1840, Palmerston wrote to the British ambassador in Constantinople, describing the desire of European Jews to return to Palestine and asking him to raise the matter with the Porte (as the Ottoman government was called).[50] Such a scheme would be "of manifest importance to the Sultan": the presence of Jewish settlers would serve as a check upon Egyptian ambitions, while the wealth they brought with them would "increase the Resources" of the Ottoman Empire as a whole. Recognizing that the lack of security was a crucial impediment, Palmerston hoped to resolve the problem by authorizing British consulates to refer Jewish grievances directly to Constantinople. The idea behind this proposal came from Ashley, but Palmerston's initiative can only be understood in terms of his wider political strategy.

Preserving the Ottoman Empire had become a central aim of British foreign policy, and Palmerston believed that this was possible only through comprehensive reform.[51] Hitherto, powerful vested interests had blocked the Ottoman reform agenda, but the crisis of 1839 brought a clique of modernizers to the fore. In November Abdul Mecid, the new sultan, declared his commitment to radical change by issuing a decree known as the *Hatt-i Sherif* of Gülhane. Addressing an assembled audience of Ottoman notables and European diplomats in a square outside Topkapi palace, Reshid Pasha, the reform-minded foreign minister, made a bid for European support by announcing plans for a new legal and political framework that would guarantee security of life, honor, and property for all. The projected reforms would strengthen the state both internally and externally, while the explicit commitment to religious equality and the language of reciprocal rights and obligations spoke to European (specifically British) concerns. Conservatives inevitably resented European attempts to impose changes that bore no relationship to traditional Ottoman policies. Reading between the lines, Palmerston perceived that the reformers needed allies at every level if they wanted to realize their modernizing ambitions; he saw Jews as a potential engine for change.[52]

This background made it hard for the sultan to refuse Palmerston's suggestion; yet his advisers had no choice. Jews were indeed "wealthy men," and their "transfer to the Imperial and Protected Dominions" might well "create a new cause and means for the flourishing of the country."[53] But it would cause the empire "many problems in the future" if the new Jewish arrivals were not treated as full Ottoman subjects—and this was what Palmerston's proposal implied.[54] By undercutting Ottoman authority, the proposal threatened to undermine the real aim of Ottoman modernizers, which was to minimize foreign intervention in domestic politics by enabling the state to meet the European challenge head-on. There is no evidence that Montefiore knew anything about these developments, but he could hardly have chosen a better moment to arrive in Constantinople.

His reception by Reshid Pasha was certainly all that he could have wished. As ambassador to France in the 1830s, Reshid had been the toast of smart Parisian society. In a Turk, his witty repartee and smooth good manners caused a sensation: he gave excellent parties and attended every social event that mattered, cultivating government ministers, diplomats, writers, and journalists. Now the Anglophile foreign minister turned his charm on Montefiore and promised him an interview with the sultan.[55] Montefiore and Loewe had already prepared a document for the sultan to sign, formally refuting the blood libel and guaranteeing the right of Jews to follow the dictates of their religion, in accordance with the *Hatt-i Sherif* of Gülhane.[56] Such a declaration would add credibility to the formal denial published by Haham Meldola and Chief Rabbi Hirschell, which Montefiore was planning to translate into Turkish, Arabic, Greek, and Armenian, and circulate en masse.[57]

A subsequent report to the sultan combined a clear understanding of Montefiore's status with sensitivity to European public opinion.[58] On the one hand, Montefiore was one of "the esteemed people of the Jewish *millet* [nation]" and "a relative of the famous banker Rothschild"—an important consideration given efforts to involve both him and the Rothschilds in Ottoman finances.[59] On the other, Montefiore possessed "a special document . . . given to him by the state of England," and Ambassador John Ponsonby had intimated that Britain expected the sultan to comply with his request. All in all, Montefiore's visit represented a significant propaganda opportunity. The "severe treatment" of the Jews in Damascus by Mehmed Ali "had caused grave effects in Europe," with even the government of the United States expressing its concern for the Jews. By contrast, "the compassion stirring measures taken by the Great

"Port Constantinople," by William Bartlett, in Julia Pardoe, The Beauties of the Bosphorus, *vol. 3 (London, 1874), facing p. 200. Montefiore
visited the Ottoman capital three times, in 1840, 1855, and 1863; on
each occasion he was granted an interview with the sultan. (By permission
of the Bodleian Library, University of Oxford: 246.h.348)*

State [Ottoman Empire] regarding the Jews of the island of Rhodes had
been received with great pleasure." If the sultan granted Montefiore the
firman he had requested, Reshid Pasha believed "the praiseworthy displays of his Imperial Exalted Personage would spread all over Europe,"
with "even further great beneficial effects."[60]

On October 28 Lord Ponsonby presented the sultan with a sacred
standard taken from Ibrahim Pasha by Ottoman troops in Syria—a vic-
tory they owed to the active support of British forces at sea and on land.
In response, the sultan expressed his hope that this fruitful collaboration
might lead "to still more intimate friendship between Himself and Her
Majesty"; in other words, he wanted a formal alliance.[61] That evening
Montefiore and his entourage were conducted through the streets of
Constantinople with all due ceremony.

Visitors to the city were invariably struck by the stunning panorama
of hills rising out of the water: the sea alive with ships, and the land a
sprawling mass of gaily painted houses and fantastic palaces, domes,
minarets, and towers. At close quarters, however, the Ottoman capital
was a ramshackle maze of narrow, dirty streets—every major thorough-

fare thronged to capacity with horses, donkeys, camels, and oxen, wagons and pedestrians, slow-moving pack-carriers and vociferous street traders. Montefiore and his party rode in two carriages preceded by six soldiers and six torchbearers. Even so, they made such slow progress that they were running a quarter of an hour late by the time they reached the palace.[62]

The content of the interview was a foregone conclusion. Speaking before an audience of Ottoman courtiers and officials in a grand Western-style drawing room, Montefiore thanked the sultan for the "wisdom, justice and love of truth" he had shown in delivering the Jews of Rhodes. Dwelling characteristically on the patriotism and industry of the Jewish people, he assured Abdul Mecid that they looked "with love and veneration" toward the Ottoman province of Palestine and prayed to the Almighty to strengthen his benevolent rule.[63] In return, the sultan undertook to grant the desired *firman* and promised Jews the "same protection, and . . . the same advantage, as all other subjects in my Empire"—by which he meant primarily other non-Muslims, although the projected reforms envisaged treating all Ottoman subjects equally in due course.[64]

The final text of the *firman* more than lived up to Montefiore's expectations. Opening with a categorical denial of the blood libel, the sultan repeated his promise that Jews would "enjoy the same privileges" as other peoples living under his authority. Indeed, the document went far beyond the draft version drawn up by Montefiore and Loewe; for the sultan announced that he had "given the most positive orders that the Jewish nation [*millet*], dwelling in all parts of our Empire, shall be perfectly protected, as well as all other subjects of the sublime Porte, and that no person shall molest them in any matter whatever (except for a just cause), neither in the free exercise of their religion, nor in that which concerns their safety and tranquillity."[65]

The first part was essentially a reiteration of the *Hatt-i Sherif* of Gülhane, but the second part was more significant. Probably its authors calculated that a clear commitment to Jewish rights at this stage would make it easier for the sultan later to reject Palmerston's more substantial request.

Montefiore was delighted. With such an outcome, the Damascus mission could honorably claim to have "acted in the name of enlightened Europe" and "diffused a more liberal spirit" in the East.[66] Comparing the *firman* to Catholic emancipation and the repeal of the Test and Corporation Acts in England, he pronounced it the "Magna Charta for the

Jews in the Turkish Dominions."[67] In private, however, he appreciated the irony of European moral superiority. Placing the *firman* firmly in the context of Anglo-Jewish politics, Montefiore sent a copy to his "dear Friend" Isaac Lyon Goldsmid, in the hope that it might "teach a lesson to other governments . . . and lead to the realization to [*sic*] your wishes in the repeal of those obnoxious laws which exclude us from office and power at home."[68]

Montefiore's travels had exposed him to the reality of Jewish life in Egypt and Syria. He knew that Jews in the Ottoman Empire were expected to pay an extra tax, the *djizya,* and that they could not expect to be treated as equals in an Islamic court. Even so, the contractual relationship between Muslim rulers and their non-Muslim subjects, known as *dhimma,* gave Jews greater liberties under Islamic law than they enjoyed in many European states; hence Montefiore's proposal that European Jews might find a haven from persecution in Palestine. Yet the shocking events in Rhodes and Damascus boded ill for the future: he concluded the *firman* could be only a "first step."[69]

Unlike Montefiore, Crémieux had neither knowledge nor experience of Jews in the Middle East; both he and Salomon Munk were appalled by what they saw. Where Judith had found her brethren in Alexandria "highly respectable and well educated," Munk bemoaned their "very low level of intellectual development," blaming the "oppression and suspicion that weigh upon our co-religionists in the Orient."[70] This was the typical verdict of a European orientalist. It echoed the patronizing stereotypes perpetuated by Christian travelers in a way that emphasized Munk's cultural and social distance from the local community. But unlike European Christians, Munk felt a particular responsibility toward the Jews of the Middle East. Eager to raise their cultural level (as he saw it), Munk suggested that Crémieux establish two model schools.[71] Crémieux was very taken with the idea, which fitted neatly within the broader contours of informal French cultural and political influence in Egypt. French was to have pride of place in the curriculum that Munk subsequently outlined, alongside Hebrew, Arabic, and Italian—the language of the mercantile Jewish elite. Crémieux planned to fund the initiative with money from Betty de Rothschild, and he suggested that Montefiore could found a Jewish hospital as well.[72]

His rival was not inclined to be forthcoming. "It is the Jews of the Holy Land, who need help," Montefiore informed Crémieux by way of explanation. "They are in a state of profound distress there . . . but we have so much to do in London, that it is not possible even to think of something else for the time being. I have asked influential people in London to give to the poor Jews of Jerusalem . . . and Tiberias, who lack bread, but they all reply that we have enough to do here as it is." This view reflected the traditional philanthropic hierarchy, in which only the Jews of the land of Israel might take precedence over the members of one's own community—and even then, not necessarily so. Crémieux, with his secular education and lack of respect for rabbinical Judaism, had no appreciation of this value system. He concluded that Montefiore's lack of vision was all of a piece with his mean-spirited attitude toward the Jews of Alexandria.

In his diary, Crémieux made much of Montefiore's failure to give to local charities. Yet the Englishman had in fact paid considerable attention to communal affairs. Not only did he convene a meeting with a view to drafting a written constitution; he also commissioned a comprehensive survey of the Jewish population.[73] This census left Montefiore well placed to assess the community's needs. He was certainly better able than Crémieux to distinguish between the destitution caused by the earthquake in Palestine and living conditions in a cosmopolitan port city like Alexandria, where the community was dominated by wealthy Levantine merchants. Perhaps he also realized that Crémieux was imposing French priorities on local Jewish leaders, commenting that "if the congregation here should really wish any assistance" they should have applied to him first.[74]

Crémieux had been horrified by the Jewish schools in Alexandria, where he saw children squatting on mats or bare earth, rocking forward and backward as they repeated verses from the Torah in Hebrew and translated them into Arabic.[75] Montefiore's impressions in Constantinople were more positive, possibly because he saw no harm in a traditional religious education. He "found the schools in good order—the children well acquainted with the knowledge of our law and the commentaries thereon." What worried him was that most remained "ignorant of the language of the people amongst whom they lived." Not only did this exclude "them from employment and situations they were well calculated to fill"; it also "tended to engender and foster prejudice."[76] While the former restricted Jews to relatively low-prestige occupations—most were shopkeepers or artisans—the latter made it easier for calumnies like the blood libel to take root.

This view owed something to personal experience. English had long been the language spoken by British Jews, and as a governor of the Jews' Free School in London Montefiore would have understood the importance of education in preparing immigrants for British life. Probably he was also influenced by his non-Jewish companions. Ignoring the separation of institutions maintained under the *millet* system, Madden in particular bemoaned "intolerance" toward Jews and "the great evils that arise to the people of the Jewish persuasion in the East . . . from their rigid separation from the society of their fellow-men of any other creed."[77] Montefiore, too, was in no doubt of the pernicious effects of social and cultural isolation, and he concluded that teaching Jews the vernacular of the places where they lived was the best way to proceed.[78]

Montefiore's plan represented an attempt to export the European emancipation paradigm.[79] In most of western Europe emancipation was conceived as a two-way process, in which Jews adopted the culture and values of the host society in return for social integration and greater civil and political rights. By teaching Ottoman Jewry to read and write the extraordinarily complex mixture of Turkish, Persian, and Arabic that was the language of government in the Ottoman Empire, Montefiore hoped to kick-start a similar process in Ottoman lands. This was a very different agenda from what Crémieux intended. Ottoman was also the language of government in Egypt, but Crémieux had been primarily concerned with spreading European civilization in the form of French culture—something that might make Jews more acceptable to visiting Europeans, but was unlikely to promote their integration in the Otto-man world. The schools he founded in Cairo and Alexandria smacked of cultural imperialism; Montefiore's proposal to teach Ottoman through the existing school system was more attuned to the needs of the Jews he sought to help.

It may even have reflected the influence of his host in Constantinople, the prominent financier and communal leader Abraham Camondo. For centuries the city had been home to the empire's richest and most pow-erful Jewish bankers, men like Camondo whose financial clout gave the community a certain influence with the Porte. More recently, Armenians had ousted Jews from their dominance of state finances. Like Greek Christians, they owed their ability to edge out Jewish rivals in part to their greater familiarity with Ottoman and to the fact that Armeno-Turkish used the same Arabic script. While Montefiore's proposal that Ottoman Jews should learn the language of government amounted to an educational revolution, it was one that a modernizing minority almost certainly welcomed.

Such a plan could succeed only if it received the backing of rabbis and Jewish elders. For weeks, Montefiore entertained between fifty and sixty visitors daily in his efforts to win over local Jewish opinion, and he ar-ranged for Loewe to deliver a three-hour sermon in four different lan-guages on the festival of Simchat Torah. His assiduous generosity to communal charities must surely have helped his cause.[80]

The execution of the Ottoman Empire's leading Jewish bankers after the revolt of the Janissaries in 1826 had left the 40,000 Jews of Constantinople without protection, and in 1835 they successfully petitioned Mahmud to reinstitute the ancient position of *Haham Bashi*.[81] As the primary channel of communication between Ottoman Jews and their government, the *Haham Bashi* in Constantinople was both public official and religious leader, grand rabbi of the Ottoman Empire and head of the Jewish *millet*—a largely autonomous, religiously defined community, subject to Ottoman and Islamic jurisdiction when dealing with the government or members of other religious faiths.[82] Yet this sweeping authority was to some extent a fiction: far from the capital, the widespread fact of communal autonomy and the sheer size of the Ottoman state made it almost impossible for the *Haham Bashi* to exert meaningful control.[83]

It was, nonetheless, a real coup for Montefiore that the *Haham Bashi* agreed to issue a decree to all the Jewish communities of the empire. Preempting attacks from traditionalists, he asserted that it was "proper for men to use all diligence in acquiring knowledge and learning," before exhorting "the children of our nation [to] learn to read and write the Turkish language [Ottoman], whereby, it cannot be doubted, they will obtain many precious advantages."[84] The decree was read aloud in every synagogue in Constantinople, but in practice it remained a dead letter. There were no Jewish teachers qualified to teach Ottoman, and the community was too poor to support the extra costs.[85] In the long run, Jews would play a disproportionate role in the Ottoman bureaucracy, but this development was by no means a result of Montefiore's intervention, which, at best, created a slightly more sympathetic environment for future educational change.[86]

European opinion took no account of these realities, and Montefiore's initiative won him glowing praise from both Christians and Jews.[87] Such accolades testified to Montefiore's success in publicizing his activities. Writing from Marseilles while en route to Egypt, he had urged the Board of Deputies to circulate his letters.[88] Noting that *The Times* and the *Morning Chronicle* were sending special correspondents to Alexandria, Montefiore appreciated that Jews would need to give the public their own version of events if they wanted to ensure the mission a good press. This talent for publicity had been a major cause of friction with Crémieux, who was determined to use the Damascus mission to raise his own profile. Crémieux was outraged when an article appeared in a Smyrna newspaper full of praise for Montefiore's achievements in Alexandria, and wrote a furious letter warning his rival that he would not let him "steal my share [of the glory]."[89] Montefiore, conversely, was distressed to see Crémieux's version of events reported in one of the Smyrna newspapers.[90]

Reading Crémieux's diary in all its self-righteous indignation, it is impossible not to conclude that the personal ambition, vanity, and national pride he so disliked in Montefiore were qualities the Frenchman shared. Montefiore may have lacked Crémieux's flagrant careerism, but he still had his eye on a baronetcy. This personal ambition was mediated by a religious self-belief that led him to see himself as God's instrument. Used to working either with paid subordinates or with men whose wealth and position more than matched his own, he was incapable of accepting Crémieux as an equal and failed to appreciate his standing in France. His behavior toward the thrusting, successful lawyer was tactless and ill-judged.

Montefiore was also a British patriot. Anglo-French rivalry in the Middle East—coupled with genuine outrage at French behavior in Damascus—left him determined that the Board of Deputies would "not let the French run away with honor due to our country and fellow Citizens."[91] His triumphant visit to Constantinople put an end to any such fears, inducing paroxysms of rage in Crémieux when he read a report of Montefiore's reception by the sultan in the *Journal de Smyrne*. But, as Anselme de Rothschild remarked pointedly, the Damascus mission had set out not to free the prisoners but to rehabilitate the Jewish religion.[92] In neglecting to accompany Montefiore to Constantinople, Crémieux had only himself to blame. His concerns were, in any case, exaggerated. The Jews of Europe welcomed Crémieux as a conquering hero, and he thoroughly enjoyed his triumphant return journey, during which he and his wife were fêted and flattered every step of the way.

While Crémieux made the most of this ecstatic reception, Montefiore and Judith went to Malta. The failure of the mission to proceed to Damascus was already attracting unfavorable comment, and on his arrival Montefiore heard that *The Times* had accused him of a gross breach of public confidence; he was so alarmed that he seriously contemplated turning back. Malta had been a hive of activity during the recent crisis, and with so many frigates returning from the Middle East there were plenty of naval officers to turn to for advice. All, "without a *single exception*," agreed that "it would be madness" to set out for Syria in such an unstable situation.[93] Montefiore was taking no chances and persuaded several to give their opinion in writing. These letters would prove a vital weapon in his efforts to "convince all that from the hour I left England" he had done everything "that prudence and energy could accomplish" to discover the truth of the Damascus affair.[94]

As if to prove this point to both himself and his countrymen, Montefiore made one final effort to clear the name of the Jewish people. He learned at Malta that the tomb in Damascus containing a cache of bones unearthed during Ratti-Menton's investigations carried a deeply disturbing inscription: "Here rest the bones of Father Tommaso of Sardinia, a Capuchin missionary, murdered by the Hebrews on the 5th of February 1840."[95] Concerned about the long-term implications of this epitaph, Montefiore resolved to travel back to London via Rome, where he hoped to persuade the Catholic authorities to have it removed.

In the months before the departure of the Jewish mission, the ultra-Catholic *Univers* had played the role of chief prosecutor. The newspaper greeted reports of the prisoners' unconditional discharge with incredulous outrage.[96] Indeed, its editors concluded that the Jewish mission and Mehmed Ali's change of heart merely provided proof of the disturbing reach of Jewish "money and intrigues." Judaism had "reappeared as a power, as a nationality . . . and as such, it has held all of Christianity in check."[97] Who could say how far Jewish ambitions would reach? Already semiofficial articles were appearing in the English press in favor of restoring Jews to Palestine. Indeed, *L'Univers* concluded that Jewish money was very probably behind the failure of French foreign policy in the East—a view shared by newspapers like the *Constitutionnel*.

Fortunately for Montefiore, the papacy had never endorsed the line taken by *L'Univers*. Yet the Roman clergy had taken umbrage at Crémieux's vigorous defense of the Jewish prisoners, issuing a refutation in the *Diario di Roma* and allowing the publication of a viciously anti-Jewish pamphlet.[98] Both Hirsch Lehren and Montefiore's nephew Louis Cohen believed the Damascus Affair to be part of a wider Catholic conspiracy against Jews. Montefiore was inclined to think they might be right. This was fantasy, but there was no doubting the hostile attitude at the Vatican. As Mr. Aubin, the British agent in Rome, warned Montefiore: "all the people about the Pope were persuaded that the Jews had murdered Father Tommaso and if even all the witnesses in the world were brought before the Pope [neither] he nor his people would be convinced."[99]

Under these circumstances, Montefiore needed to tread carefully. Mindful that few as yet knew of the incriminating epitaph, he was "extremely anxious to avoid doing mischief" and feared that his progress would be "slow."[100] On his last visit to Rome he had socialized with liberal-minded clerics.[101] This time he reported despondently that "neither the Austrian Minister nor Baron de Binder [an Austrian attaché] will do anything. The Hanoverian Minister has not returned my card, and has expressed to Baron de Binder his total inability to assist me with an audience with His Holiness. Mr. Aubin has done, at least he says so, all he can but most ineffectually, Cappaccini [under-secretary of state] entreats I may not insist upon seeing him. The Cardinal Tosti has taken no notice of my letter or card." Failing in his efforts to make contact with the Vatican, Montefiore decided to "work my way from the bottom up to the top." If he could not meet His Holiness, he would try to persuade Cardinal Rivarola, the head of the Capuchin order, to comply with his request.[102]

All the Catholic officials he encountered took it for granted that Montefiore had paid for the *firman* in Constantinople, and several intimated that if he made "some presents of money" he stood a good chance of having the inscription removed. He was outraged when Cardinal Rivarola suggested that "the *Firman* might have been obtained by Rothschild's fortune," and promptly retorted that he had "not given a Dollar in the East for the *Firman*, nor would I have been the agent to obtain Justice by Bribery."[103] Rivarola agreed to advise the removal of the epitaph, although he made it plain that he continued to believe in the Jews' guilt.

Montefiore's belief in the guiding hand of providence would have led him to see either success or failure as an expression of the divine will. In the event, he concluded that the cardinal's promise was an "additional mark of [the Almighty's] Protection and goodness towards us and our Brethren at Damascus."[104] His faith had sustained him during the difficult weeks in Alexandria, and subsequent events only reinforced his belief that God was watching over him. As he prepared to set out for Paris and London, where he hoped to see his aging mother one last time, Montefiore entertained no doubts that the cardinal would keep his word.

Chapter 8

Unity and Dissent

For weeks the Jews of London talked of nothing but the returning hero.[1] The poor met in cheap taverns and took out penny subscriptions in his honor; the rich debated whether a banquet, a school, or a piece of silverware would make the most appropriate testimonial. When Montefiore made his way through the City on March 15, 1841, to attend the special service of thanksgiving in his honor, large crowds gathered outside the gates of Bevis Marks. Heavily built now, and tall enough to stand well above the multitude, he must have cut an impressive figure—proud of his achievements and a hard man to cross.[2]

The synagogue yard was packed with children and pensioners, although only a lucky few had tickets: members, their wives, the elite of the Ashkenazi community, Montefiore's Jewish relatives, and his Christian friends. Hundreds of candles illuminated the beautiful Queen Anne building, and all the people who mattered were there: the Rothschilds, Sheriff David Salomons, Isaac Lyon Goldsmid, even the renegade Disraeli family, which had converted to Christianity two decades before. Prayers were read in Hebrew, but specially printed booklets carried a full English translation. The sermon, too, was calculated to appeal to both British and Jewish sensibilities.

To the learned cantor of Bevis Marks, the Damascus Affair was an instance of divine providence in action—a providence that manifested itself not merely through divine intervention but also through adversity. News of the persecutions in Syria and Rhodes had called forth "heroic acts of piety, zeal, public spirit and self-devotion" in Montefiore and Crémieux, awakening the sympathies of "the whole civilised world." Indeed, David de Sola noted proudly, "a degree of interest in our welfare superior to any previously shown was exhibited on this occasion by the enlightened Government of this mighty country, by the wealthy in-

158

tellect and influence of this great metropolis, by the sympathy of the free and generous British and by other civilised nations."[3]

Jewish leaders all over Europe drew similar lessons from the success of the Montefiore-Crémieux mission. Hidden among the superlatives, those who listened carefully in Bevis Marks would also have found a warning; for de Sola related how the increasingly comfortable conditions in which European Jews now lived had sapped their moral fiber so "that energy and devotion and attachment to the observance of the law diminished visibly in every generation. The bonds of fraternity and reunion . . . became daily more relaxed and apathy . . . and stagnation introduced itself gradually and insidiously among us . . . sapping the foundations of our holy faith and nationality . . . But the unexpected news of the Damascene atrocities aroused our dormant energies. At the call of our distressed brethren in remote countries, at the call of outraged humanity, all Israel rose as one man . . . May this teach us the advantages of unity of purpose and to avoid by peevish discontent to endanger our nationality by directing and dispersing those forces so necessary, so indispensably necessary to our defence and well being."[4]

Few can have doubted that de Sola was referring to the rise of the Reform movement—and to the pressures for religious change within the Sephardi community that were tearing it apart. By March 1841, the grand display of unity was only a facade.

This traumatic situation reflected a deeper crisis of identity among western European Jews.[5] Many were quite simply embarrassed by the chaotic nature of their services: the raucous practice of auctioning *mitzvot* to the highest bidder; the informal hubbub that reigned in synagogues; and the lack of a generally accepted starting time, which led to a steady stream of late arrivals, all of whom stopped to greet fellow worshipers before reciting the prayers at their own pace. The general atmosphere of disorder was exacerbated by customs attached to particular festivals, like dancing around the synagogue on Simchat Torah, or the stamping of feet and waving of rattles on Purim. Such practices were hard to explain to Christian observers, accustomed to the silence and decorum of church services. They appeared increasingly alien to those Jews who had (in most other respects) embraced the culture of the countries in which they lived.

Nor was the willingness to internalize Christian criticism of Jewish practices restricted to external forms. Protestants placed great emphasis on faith and on establishing a personal relationship with God through prayer. Judaism, by contrast, takes as its starting point a complex web of religious obligations that give pattern and meaning to every aspect of life. Christians had always accused Judaism of excessive formalism.

Now some Jews began to experience their own rituals as meaningless, regretting the lack of inspirational preaching and the seemingly endless Hebrew prayers that many could neither follow nor understand. Religious skepticism, rational theology, the Protestant preoccupation with the Bible, and the scientific approach to biblical criticism all encouraged those Jews who had acquired a Western education to refocus their attention on the Torah—and to question the centrality of the Talmud in both rabbinical Judaism and their own daily lives.

These tendencies began to make themselves felt in England during the 1820s through low levels of synagogal attendance. The consequence was a trickle of superficial reforms designed to increase decorum and to reduce the more embarrassing elements of the service. Montefiore was at the forefront of this activity. In 1828 the Spanish and Portuguese Jews had established a Committee for the Promotion and Improvement of Religious Worship. It eventually recommended that members of the Mahamad remain in synagogue until the end of the service, that the singing of psalms be abridged, and that public announcements be made in English not Portuguese. Even such moderate changes were controversial. The elders accepted the switch to English only after a six-hour debate in which Montefiore played a prominent role—just as he did a year later, when he spoke strongly in favor of introducing regular English sermons on alternate Saturdays.[6]

Everything we know about Montefiore's religiosity during the 1820s and 1830s suggests a surprising degree of common ground with the innovators. Services at his own synagogue in Ramsgate were conducted in exemplary fashion: Montefiore was always in place before they started, a choir of six Jewish schoolboys lent dignity to the occasion, and a ban on public offerings to charity and the sale of *mitzvot* ensured a suitably reverent atmosphere. Having given her pretty flowered silk wedding dress to make a Torah mantle and matching cover for the reading desk, Judith viewed their little synagogue as a joint project. A common spiritual commitment lay at the heart of the Montefiore marriage, and Judith seems to have shared her husband's attitudes to public worship as well as his devotion to God. Exceptionally for a Jewish woman, she accompanied him not just on Saturday mornings, but for afternoon and evening services, and on some weekdays, too.[7]

It is striking that the only serious Jewish scholarship in the Montefiores' personal library at this stage was a complete edition of Moses Mendelssohn, widely respected as the father of the Jewish Enlightenment *(Haskalah)*.[8] Notwithstanding his patronage of traditional Jewish learning, Montefiore was consistently supportive of self-consciously enlightened scholars. In keeping with Mendelssohn's emphasis on breaking down linguistic barriers through use of the vernacular, Montefiore encouraged his friend de Sola to publish new editions of Sephardi prayers in English translation.[9] In 1830 Montefiore had even attended a meeting of the Society for the Cultivation of the Hebrew Language and Its Literature to demonstrate his enthusiasm for this central plank of the *Haskalah*.[10] That Montefiore's protégé Louis Loewe was himself the very model of a Mendelssohnian Jew—combining secular scholarship with religious observance and traditional learning—only served to underline Montefiore's own commitment to these twin ideals. But Mendelssohn's original enlightenment vision had long since been overtaken by events.

In Germany, the acculturated Jewish elites of Berlin and Hamburg were beginning to experiment with dramatic changes in religious practice: minimizing the separation between the sexes, cutting back the liturgy, reciting some prayers in German, introducing regular sermons, and using an organ despite the strict halakhic prohibition against instrumental music on the Sabbath. In Hamburg, they succeeded in establishing a permanent congregation and publishing the first comprehensive Reform liturgy. As part of this process the more radical heirs of the *Haskalah* and the first generation of university-trained rabbis started to develop a new theology designed to revitalize Judaism and to justify its existence in the modern world. By the late 1830s, pressure for religious change had thrown German Jewry into ideological ferment and communal turmoil.[11]

Watching from across the Channel, Montefiore was alarmed by this development. As Judith's sister-in-law put it, Montefiore "is so much troubled with what is happening abroad that he does not want us to start quarrelling at home."[12] His concern was hardly surprising. Montefiore's immediate circle included many of the wealthiest, most socially integrated English Jews—precisely the constituency that had embraced religious reform abroad. Some, like Isaac Lyon Goldsmid, David Salomons, and his own brother Horatio were enthusiastic supporters of change; others, like Judith's brother Joseph, remained staunch defenders of the status quo. The new ideas from the Continent threatened to destroy forever their cosy family life.

In 1836 Montefiore's uncle Moses Mocatta approached the elders of Bevis Marks with a set of proposed religious changes. Montefiore seems to have kept his distance, noting briefly in his diary: "Horatio informed me that the Elders yesterday threw out the proposal for a Committee to enquire of the *Be*[*th*]*din* [religious court] the possibility of abolishing

Return of the Jewish Volunteer (From the Wars of Liberation to His
Family Still Living in Accordance to Old Rites), *by Moritz David Oppenheim, c. 1868. This painting exemplifies the clash of generations and cultures that divided mid-nineteenth-century German Jewry. (By permission of
the Jewish Museum, New York / Art Resource, New York)*

the 2nd day of the Holidays. 16 against 13 for." This relatively close
outcome reflected the religious sympathies of the elite, not those of the
wider community: a day later the elders received a countermemorial
with over 150 signatures. When the reformers refused to give up so easily, the atmosphere at Bevis Marks became increasingly charged.[13]

Montefiore's second trip to Palestine prevented him from becoming
embroiled in this bitter communal conflict, but thanks to his brother he
had a good idea of what was going on. In November 1838 Horatio reported that an overwhelming majority had voted in favor of a choir.[14]
A month later he was concerned that the most recent meeting had
passed "without anything being done in the way of enquiry [into possible change] and a meeting was convened at Mr. Abecassis to prevent any
alteration. The Elders last Sunday passed a resolution strongly deprecating such proceedings they considering that it was calculated to create

dissentions amongst the Congregation." Horatio declared himself unable to understand why "all our laws [should not] be translated in English as well as the sacred writings of the five books of Moses," and found the widespread "unwillingness to investigate" traditional practices absurd.[15]

Back in London, proselytizing tracts containing excerpts from the Talmud and the Mishnah were circulating widely in the Jewish community. Horatio regretted that the lack of an authentic Jewish translation had forced him to turn "to the insidious writing of persons professing another religion."[16] Still, he was deeply disturbed to see passages that "no man in his senses would for an instant subscribe to," which seemed to show the oral law of the Talmud directly contradicting the Torah. He could only hope that they were a fabrication, "because if they cannot be contradicted with truth it is high time that this subject should be taken up by conscientious men professing the religious and sacred laws of Moses."[17] Horatio's ignorance of the Talmud illuminates the limits of Montefiore's own religious education: like so many Victorian Jews, his spirituality was firmly rooted in the Old Testament and he rarely—if ever —cited a rabbinic source. Horatio consequently made no attempt to disguise his own support for the reformers' agenda; throughout this correspondence he assumed that his brother shared these enlightened ideas.

By early 1840 the hard core of Sephardi reformers—including three Mocattas and three Montefiores—had been joined by a smattering of Ashkenazim, led by three members of the allied Goldsmid clan. In April they met at the Bedford Hotel to sign a declaration attributing the lack of religious observance among the current generation "to the distance of the existing Synagogues from the place of our residence, to the length and imperfections of the order of the service, to the inconvenient hours at which it is appointed, and to the absence of religious instruction."[18] Together, they would establish a new congregation in the West End where they could worship as they saw fit. Montefiore and Judith may have been happy to walk the four and a half miles to Bevis Marks whatever the weather; the less high-minded were understandably reluctant to do the same.[19]

Founding a Reform synagogue was bound to be controversial, but the stakes for the Sephardim were particularly high. One of the oldest regulations of the Spanish and Portuguese Jews' Congregation (known as *Ascama* No. 1) prohibited members from establishing a rival community on pain of excommunication—and Rabbi David Meldola refused to waive this draconian law. This had been the situation when Montefiore set out for Alexandria in July 1840. He preferred to exert influence in the Sephardi community informally, but he always intervened directly when it really mattered. On his return from the East, for the first time in over a decade, Montefiore was elected to the Mahamad.[20]

Barely a month after the grand celebrations at Bevis Marks, the Mahamad received a letter from the Ashkenazi Great Synagogue proposing to exclude the Reformers from the Board of Deputies. Neither Montefiore nor the rest of the Mahamad had any qualms about endorsing this suggestion. They advised the Sephardi elders that it was the duty of every congregation "to unite as one Body in order to oppose and denounce" any attempt "to alter, modify, or change, any of the Laws, Ordinances, or Institutions which have been handed down to us & it is our duty as Jews to support and maintain." The elders voted in favor of the exclusion by just one vote—whereupon Hananel de Castro, the outgoing president of the Board of Deputies, put forward a rival motion to rescind *Ascama* No. 1.[21]

Some twenty-four hours later, de Castro encountered Montefiore in a very different capacity, when he called to announce his opponent's reelection as president of the Board of Deputies.[22] This appointment came at a moment of crisis for Anglo-Jewry. The elderly Chief Rabbi Hirschell had been house-bound for over a year, while the Spanish and Portuguese Jews were effectively leaderless, having failed to replace Haham Meldola after his death in 1828.[23] With Hirschell on his last legs and Meldola's quarrelsome son David exercising only limited authority, Montefiore's views as lay leader of Anglo-Jewry were likely to prove decisive.

By this stage it was almost too late to reach a compromise. In May 1841 the Mahamad agreed to consider establishing a Sephardi branch synagogue in West London, but on August 24 the elders of Bevis Marks received a letter from sixteen leading members of the Sephardi congregation outlining the principles on which their synagogue was to be conducted.[24] The seceders included two of Montefiore's paternal cousins, his uncle Moses Mocatta, and another eleven relations on his mother's side.

Compared with the radical proposals current in Germany, the religious changes introduced at the "West London Synagogue of British Jews" were conservative.[25] Essentially, they were designed to make Judaism as convenient, respectable, and English as possible, with a view to fusing more completely with Christian society and hastening the pace of emancipation. In one respect, however, the West London Synagogue broke new ground. By eliminating the practice of celebrating festivals for two days, as laid down in the Talmud, its members acknowledged the primacy of the mutually acceptable Old Testament over the exclusively Jewish Talmud, thus prioritizing the written over the oral law.[26]

Two weeks later, on September 10, Chief Rabbi Hirschell drafted a formal statement, countersigned by David Meldola, announcing that "any person or persons declaring that he or they reject and do not believe in the authority of the Oral Law, cannot be permitted to have any communion with us Israelites in any religious rite or sacred act."[27] The "British Jews" faced formal excommunication if they did not repent their newfangled ways. It would be five months before Hirschell decided to promulgate this forbidding declaration, but the elders of Bevis Marks lost no time in outlawing their own members for deliberate breach of *Ascama* No. 1.[28] Almost certainly, they adopted this ruthless course of action thanks to Montefiore's energetic leadership as president of the Mahamad.

Montefiore (and Loewe) always maintained that he left this decision to the rabbis and obeyed their injunctions "at whatever cost to himself."[29] It was a convenient fiction that placed responsibility for excommunicating the Reformers firmly with Hirschell and Meldola. Yet the Anglo-Jewish historian James Picciotto, a boy of eleven at the time of the crisis, claimed to have been "informed by unimpeachable authorities" that Hirschell and Meldola signed the excommunication "with the greatest reluctance, knowing that it would cause much exasperation, that it would sow dissension . . . and that it would tend to convert a temporary difference into an irreconcilable enmity. But the reverend gentlemen yielded to the powerful influences put to bear on them."[30] Other contemporaries blamed Montefiore explicitly for the rabbis' hardline stance.[31]

Undoubtedly, it coincided with his own inclinations. Montefiore believed that "the religious tenets of Israel, as revealed in the Code of Sinai, would invariably stand the test of reason." Presumably regarding both the Torah and the Talmud as part of the same divine revelation, he "did not consider that he would be acting in accordance with the dictates of truth and justice if he were to accept laymen . . . as authorities on religious subjects."[32] And Montefiore can have been under no illusions as to the disastrous consequences for both his brother and communal unity if he endorsed the orthodox position so categorically.

The strength of his feelings was very much in evidence six months later, when Francis Henry Goldsmid wrote asking him as president of the Board of Deputies to empower the newly consecrated West London Synagogue to conduct marriages in accordance with British law. Both Montefiore and Hirschell regarded this concession as unthinkable, and Montefiore lost no time in informing Goldsmid as much. Dashing off a second (quite unnecessary) note a day later, he elaborated: "I think it right to add that I do not consider the Place of Worship in Burton Street referred to by you to be a Synagogue."[33]

It was hardly surprising that Montefiore took the matter so personally. The recent death of his mother, Rachel, had left him vulnerable. It must have been painful indeed to see her brother—the uncle responsible for his Jewish education—leave Bevis Marks to found a Reform congregation, taking the bulk of his Mocatta family with him. Now it looked as if Montefiore's own surviving brother intended to do the same.

Very much the baby of the family, Horatio lacked the drive of Moses and Abraham, as well as their sound judgment in worldly affairs. Shortly after his marriage, their mother confided in Montefiore that she "never saw a young man go to housekeeping with so little courage, I hope they will do well I am certain they will both be very careful."[34] Care was not enough to ensure success on the Stock Exchange, and Horatio failed repeatedly—in 1823, 1826, 1827, 1828, and 1832.[35] Throughout this shaky career, his oldest brother was a tower of support: Montefiore employed Horatio as a clerk when he started out in 1815, transferred his expensive broker's medal to him in 1831, arranged for him to become a director of Imperial Continental Gas in 1832, gave him use of the farm at Tinley Lodge in 1837, and promised to have him made an auditor of Alliance Assurance in 1839.[36] Almost certainly, Judith's childless state encouraged Horatio to hope that he and his children would inherit Montefiore's fabulous fortune and perpetuate the family name.[37] With such a history (and such prospects) it must have taken something very powerful indeed for Horatio to risk cutting his ties with his brother by withdrawing from Bevis Marks and joining the new Reform synagogue. He delayed for six months before making this decision. Then, in February 1842, he did exactly that.[38]

Montefiore never forgave his brother's act of conscience: he had showered kindness on Horatio and been repaid with public betrayal; in return, he cut his brother dead. His stubbornness went beyond religious principle. In 1839 Judith's niece Hannah Rothschild had renounced Judaism to marry a Christian, but by 1845 neither Judith nor Montefiore felt much compunction about inquiring after the renegade Mrs. Fitzroy's health.[39] Horatio, of course, still considered himself Jewish, but Montefiore's attitude was infinitely less forgiving. He consistently refused his brother's efforts at reconciliation, turned the cold shoulder at family functions, and informed their sister Sally in 1861 "that it rested with himself as he was fully aware, on the terms, those only on which I would consent, he knew them years ago, they are to leave the Reform & become a Member of our ancient Spanish & Portuguese Congregation."[40] Since Horatio later married Charlotte (daughter of his late brother

Abraham and Henrietta Rothschild), we can only guess at the tensions that Montefiore's hard-line attitude continued to provoke within their extended family.

Only once did Montefiore let down his guard enough to reveal a glimmer of fraternal feeling. In 1867, with Horatio on his deathbed, Montefiore wrote to ask after him. Even now he was unable to bury the hatchet. When Horatio replied gratefully that he was feeling much better, Montefiore stiffly expressed the hope "that this new life given you by the mercy of the God of Israel may lead you to seek his Divine help to bring you back to the ancient faith of our Fathers and to the love and union of family ties."[41]

The great schism in Anglo-Jewry did not detract much from Montefiore's status as a symbol of Jewish unity. His triumphant return from the East prompted a stream of ecstatic journalism and a series of very public celebrations. Reports from British and German newspapers in 1841 and 1842 reveal the participatory nature of such initiatives—and the complex interplay between the fledgling Jewish press and an emerging civil society. While the Jews of Frankfurt clubbed together to present Montefiore and Crémieux with identical silver goblets, the Jews of Hamburg struck a gold medal in honor of Montefiore and Judith, offering cheaper bronze and silver copies for sale to the general public.[42] The influential *Allgemeine Zeitung des Judentums* even coordinated an impressive commemorative album, replete with the signatures of 1,490 subscribers, an elaborately decorated text, and an original oil painting by Moritz David Oppenheim, the doyen of contemporary Jewish art. An accompanying address praised Montefiore for breaking with the tradition of passive suffering and for renewing the ties that united the Jewish world. His journey from England to Alexandria and Constantinople had demonstrated once and for all that "a community lying beyond the mountains of Lebanon is as much a part of Israel, as those [situated] in the valleys of free lands."[43]

The Damascus mission had created a climate of anticipation among Jews in the Middle East and North Africa, who saw Montefiore as the man sent by God to relieve their suffering. The first of many appeals came in September 1841, when Montefiore heard from Isaac Pincherle, an old acquaintance from London now living in Smyrna, a Turkish port on the Aegean that Montefiore himself had visited in 1840, which had now been devastated by a terrible fire.[44] Pincherle painted a grim picture of the situation: "The whole of the Hebrew Quarter is reduced to ashes: the Jews have lost their houses, their property and their clothes. The

Turks suffered much, but not so much as our poor brethren." In the name of the God of Israel, Pincherle begged Montefiore "to render further assistance for your account, on account of your friends, and in behalf of every sympathising individual in your capital, to this stricken community."[45] Suitably moved, Montefiore forwarded this letter to the *Voice of Jacob,* which noted proudly that nearly £500 had already been raised in London and Manchester alone.

Jewish communities had always collected money on behalf of the Jews of Palestine and for the redemption of Jewish prisoners. The diversification of these practices began in the sixteenth century, when Doña Gracia Nasi, a Portuguese *converso* and international banker, established an escape network that saved thousands of Jews from the Inquisition.[46] Two centuries later, in 1745, Maria Teresa's expulsion of Jews from Prague had sparked a campaign throughout Europe to overturn the initiative. Such interventions inevitably drew upon transnational Jewish networks: not just the commercial and family ties that underpinned the Atlantic and Levantine diasporas, but also the individual, dynastic, and intercommunal connections created by itinerant rabbis, scholars, and religious ministrants that characterized (and to some extent bridged) both the Ashkenazi and Sephardi spheres. Such interventions were also extremely rare.[47]

Montefiore's campaign for Jewish victims in Smyrna was a very different proposition, reflecting a fundamental transformation in the structures of international Jewish solidarity that was both cause and product of the Damascus crisis. Admittedly, he was still dependent on personal connections for information. Once alerted to the disaster, however, Montefiore deployed modern communications to rally the forces of civil society through a subscription-based fund-raising campaign. Such an approach would have been unthinkable before the launch of the *Allgemeine Zeitung des Judentums* in 1837.[48] Now a handful of publications catering to the Jewish reading public made it easy to disseminate specifically Jewish disaster news and to coordinate an organized response. This phenomenon served to liberate Jewish philanthropy from the straitjacket of communal institutions—but it also underlined the place of religion in an emerging civil society, promoting the confessionalization of the public sphere.

Interestingly, Montefiore chose to play down the sectarian nature of the Smyrna campaign. In October 1841 the *Voice of Jacob* announced that "the Jewish subscriptions, though raised specially, will be thrown into the general collection from all nations and creeds."[49] As part of this process, Montefiore and his nephew Lionel de Rothschild joined the General Committee established in London to bring aid to the people of

Smyrna. Their decision to merge Jewish funds with those intended for the rest of the population symbolized the fusion of Jewish and non-Jewish society that was the bedrock of emancipation (and Reform). It was a logical extension of Montefiore's efforts to link the Damascus crisis with wider humanitarian concerns.

The reality was less appealing. Within two months, reports began to reach London that "the daily bread of the starving Jews, supplied by the general fund to which their European brethren have so liberally contributed, is . . . doled out through the medium of apostate Jews (missionaries of the English Conversion Society) who abuse the opportunity, to influence the poor creatures to recognise Christianity."[50] This disappointing outcome revealed the fragility of Montefiore's universalist aspirations and the ambivalence at the heart of British concern for Jews.

Still, there was no denying the genuine goodwill displayed by many British officials, from the foreign secretary down to the humblest vice-consul. As an outlying province of the Ottoman Empire, Iraq was notoriously difficult to control, but the distance from Constantinople did not stop the Jews of Baghdad from putting their faith in the new Jewish hero and his government. After the British consul saved the life of a Jew falsely accused of attacking a Muslim, Baghdadi Jews called a general meeting, "saying to each other 'Why do we remain silent to all that befalls us, have we not all one father Moses the shepherd of Israel? have we not heard of him who rescued our brethren of Damascus, from the hands of the tormentors, are we not aware of his personal appearance at Constantinople?'"[51] Taking their courage in both hands, they wrote to Montefiore begging him to obtain formal British protection for them, too.

Such a step was out of the question, but the Baghdad appeal reflected a broader sense that the Damascus Affair was a triumph for British values. Palmerston, of course, had given the Jews his full backing. On his return from the East, Montefiore had presented a copy of his *firman* to Queen Victoria. She rewarded him with the grant of heraldic supporters for his coat of arms "in commemoration of these his unceasing exertions on behalf of his injured and persecuted brethren in the East, and the Jewish nation at large." And so, when the grand "testimonial of respect and gratitude" prepared for him by the Jews of the British Empire was finally ready, the artist gave equal weight to the twin themes of Jewish liberation and British civilization.[52]

This extraordinary creation combined biblical symbolism and contemporary reportage in three and a half feet of elaborate silverwork. Figures of Moses and Ezra implicitly likened Montefiore to Israel's biblical liberators, while bas-reliefs of Montefiore landing in Alexandria, the liberation of the Damascus prisoners, and his audience with the sultan portrayed him in his City uniform surrounded by exotic "orientals": the proud bearer of British civilization in the East. Some viewers were even left with the impression that Montefiore had "worn his uniform . . . during the whole of the mission"—a deliberate piece of artistic license designed to heighten the dramatic effect of the Montefiore Centerpiece.[53] Events two years later seemed to confirm the sense that British and Jewish sympathies were marching in step.

In the autumn of 1844 an elderly Moroccan Jew received a letter from William Willshire, the British vice-consul in Mogador (now Essaouira).[54] The news was certainly shocking: Muslim inhabitants had fled to the countryside when French warships attacked the port, leaving the Jews and a handful of Europeans alone in the deserted town. Forbidden by Muslim law from carrying guns, the Jews were unable to defend themselves when successive hordes of Kabyle tribesmen swept down from the hills to pillage, rape, and loot. Writing to his brother in London, one survivor recounted: "They all rushed in, some ransacking the house, and others stripping us of our clothes and leaving us naked as we were born, without regard to age or sex, even taking away our very shoes. Thus naked and desolate, not one of these savages had the least pity." That evening he and the rest of his party fled into the countryside, where they "overtook many Jews, only covered with rough rash mats," and slept "on the bare sands, naked and destitute of everything . . . the poor children, about fifty in number, shrieking for water, of which there was not a drop at hand."[55] Nobody blamed the government for these developments; indeed, the sultan of Morocco immediately dispatched 10,000 ducats to assist the Jews. But this sum would hardly meet the needs of 4,000 refugees.

The recipient of Willshire's letter was Judah Guedalla, whose son Haim had married a daughter of Montefiore's favorite sister, Sally. Guedalla was a dominant figure in Anglo-Moroccan relations, the son of the richest man in Morocco, who retained considerable property in the country of his birth. Arriving in England in 1798 to manage the family firm, he had married a cousin of Montefiore's and soon began to play a leading role in Moroccan diplomacy.[56] But for all his worldly success, Guedalla remained a deeply spiritual man, praying for four hours daily and devoting his retirement to Maimonides and the Cabala.[57] His status was such that he had little difficulty persuading Montefiore and others in the London Jewish community to take action on behalf of the Jews of Mogador—his hometown.[58]

Montefiore launched the Mogador relief fund through the pages of the *Voice of Jacob*. Once again he deliberately underplayed the Jewish-

The Montefiore Centerpiece, presented to Montefiore by the Board of Deputies on his return from the East; designed by Sir George Hayter and sculpted by Edward Baillie. The Damascus mission is depicted on the panels around the stand, and the imagery is symbolic of relief from oppression. The sphinxes stand for the captivity of Israel in Egypt; the four figures are Moses; Ezra, the great deliverer of the people; a Jew of Damascus in chains; and one released. On the top is David rescuing the lamb from the lion. The base is chased with images of the passage of the Dead Sea, Lawless Violence (shown as wolves devouring flocks), and the Millennium as described by the prophet Isaiah. Bearing the mark of Mortimer and Hunt, the Montefiore testimonial weighs 37.4 kilograms and was displayed with its specially made case at the Great Exhibition of 1851. (By permission of the Montefiore Endowment / Victoria and Albert Museum)

ness of the appeal by suggesting that the handful of Christians in Mogador might look to him for support. It would never do for Jews to seem selfishly particularistic—and they would raise a great deal more money if they could target Christians, too. With this motive, the *Voice of Jacob* described the plight of the Jews of Mogador in sectarian, religious, and universal terms, as a cause that would appeal to "the Israelite . . . in aid of his suffering kindred," to the "friend of Israel, on behalf of a race to whose ancestors so much is due," and to "the philanthropist, in that wide sense which regards every suffering man as *therefore* a creditor, be his creed or clime what it may."[59]

That under half of the original subscribers to the relief fund were Jewish lent such claims a certain credibility. Yet the prevalence of Evangelicals and Montefiore's City associates among the list of Christian donors suggests that conversionist ambition and personal connections were a more powerful motivation than humanitarian principle.[60] For Montefiore, however, the Mogador relief fund was an unmitigated triumph. As he proudly informed *The Times* in January 1845, the committee had correctly estimated the number of sufferers; consignments of money, food, and clothing were already on their way to Morocco; and all in all they had raised over £2,500.[61] The Rothschilds launched a similar campaign abroad.[62]

Montefiore's letter to *The Times* was a deliberate attempt to keep the fate of the Jews of Morocco in the public eye. A couple of months earlier he had received a visit from a British merchant of Mogador suggesting that "if he [Montefiore] were to appeal to the Emperor of Morocco for a *firman,* to place the Jews in the same position as his other subjects," he stood an excellent chance of success.[63] In January 1845 Loewe drew up an elaborately decorated address to the sultan of Morocco, which Montefiore forwarded to the Foreign Office. Underlining the importance of his Ottoman *firman* as a precedent, Montefiore explained that although the sultan meant well by his Jewish subjects, they continued to be "subjected to the dangers of popular fanaticism" and suffered "distinctions and exclusions often fatal to their welfare and security, greatly injurious to their mental improvement, and tending to keep alive the prejudices of their fellow countrymen."[64] Whether he really expected a *firman* to change the situation is another story. Montefiore was too well-connected in Morocco to be in any doubt about the limitations on the sultan's authority, and it may well be that his concern was with public relations rather than with political reality. In any event, the grand vizier of Morocco informed Montefiore categorically that his concern was misplaced: "The Hebrew Nation enjoy throughout the whole of His Empire all that particular protection which can be obtained under the

Shadow of Justice and Truth [Islam]. They have all the privileges and advantages and are defended exactly as the *Mosslimin* [*sic*] and other subjects in his dominion. The most noble Law entertains the greatest consideration towards them, and for this reason, protects their property and their affairs."[65]

Not only did this reply fail to address the gap between the theory and practice of government in Morocco; it also focused on security of person and property at the expense of the subtler forms of discrimination Montefiore had in mind. Jews benefited from clearly defined rights under Islamic law, but these rights by no means amounted to civil equality, and it was stretching the truth for Montefiore to inform the general public that the Jews of Morocco already enjoyed "in every respect the same advantages as the Mahomedan population."[66] The *Voice of Jacob*, which conveyed this misleading information, suggested that copies of the correspondence might usefully be disseminated in Morocco and concluded optimistically that the sultan only needed the power to enforce his authority "to put an end to those anomalies of which his Jewish subjects complain"—a view that both the *Allgemeine Zeitung des Judentums* and the *Occident and American Jewish Advocate* appeared to share.[67]

Yet who could blame the press for ignoring the transparent failure of Montefiore's intervention? Jewish financiers had always used their influence in royal courts on behalf of their brethren, but it was quite something for a European Jew like Montefiore to be exchanging diplomatic courtesies with the sultan of Morocco, a ruler with whom he had no previous connection. If this was failure, what would be success?

Chapter 9

Winds of Change in Russia

Properly maintained highways made travel relatively easy in western Europe, but—as Montefiore, Judith, and their companion Loewe discovered—things were very different in Russia. There were reportedly only two decent roads in the entire country, and on the great *chaussées* it was still "better to travel day and night and remain in the carriage, for he must be a bold man who would be willing to face the vermin of all kinds, even for a single night, in a way-side hotel." Throughout the winter the great rivers of northern Russia were covered with ice so thick that it was easy to cross in a coach and four. When spring came, the sight of melting rivers was both euphoric and terrifying. Immense blocks of ice rushed toward the ocean, crashing into one another and assuming beautiful, grotesque shapes under the heat of a suddenly radiant blue sky. Flocks of wild swans accompanied these spring torrents, which dragged anything and everything in their wake: not just uprooted pines and fir trees, but ships and sailors driven helplessly by the current toward the open sea.[1]

The ice had not yet melted when the Montefiores reached the Western Dvina late in March 1846, but it was already so thin that they could cross only at their own risk. The whole party watched anxiously as first the carriages, then their wheels, and finally all the luggage were hauled over the ice on sledges drawn across from the other side.[2] Just ahead of them, a man lost his footing, slid into the freezing water, and died, but after twenty agonizing minutes Montefiore and his companions finally reached land. Pausing only to dry their clothes at Riga, they continued on their journey, nearly losing the carriages when they crossed the river Lugu, and finding the road so thick with snow that they had to get out and walk some of the way. What a relief to reach the shabby wooden houses and gloomy barracks on the outskirts of the capital, not to mention the imposing city center, so grand but so devoid of life that it prompted one traveler to remark, "I count fewer men than columns on the squares of St. Petersburg."[3]

Business not pleasure had brought Montefiore to the capital of the Russian Empire—home, since the late eighteenth century, to the largest concentration of Jews in the world. They lived in Lithuania, the Ukraine, Belorussia, and the Kingdom of Poland: territories that became part of Russia only with the partitions of Poland. The population here was extraordinarily diverse. Besides Poles, Lithuanians, Belorussians, Ukrainians, and Jews, there were Tatars, Romany, Germans, Italians, Scots, Armenians, and Greeks. Economically at least, Jews were an integral part of this wider society. Socially and culturally they remained a world apart. Communal autonomy had been a hallmark of the Jewish experience in Poland-Lithuania, and the local Jewish community *(kahal)* continued to define most aspects of daily life. Only a few individuals ever crossed the resulting ethnoreligious divide.[4]

Particularly in the eastern regions of these provinces, Jewish merchants, craftsmen, and small shopkeepers were the mainstay of the urban economy. Many actually lived in towns with a Jewish majority. Elsewhere, bearded Jews in traditional silk kaftans and sidelocks still dominated the urban landscape because so many Christian townspeople continued to work the land. Even Jews living in villages and rural market towns tended to own shops, market stalls, and taverns, to work as moneylenders, peddlers, and land-agents rather than tilling the soil.

Ever since the reign of Catherine the Great, the Russian state had struggled to fit its Jewish subjects into the wider social system of the empire. No one moved freely in imperial Russia, and in 1804 Jewish residence had been formally restricted to the Kingdom of Poland and the western provinces known collectively as the Pale of Settlement. Here legislative measures promoted the gradual erosion of communal autonomy and the parallel integration of Jews into the Russian estate structure. This process went far enough for some Jews to acquire the municipal voting rights to which their economic status entitled them. But although Catherine and Alexander I disliked the idea of the *kahal,* they were unable to manage without it, preferring to reinforce its authority with a view to maintaining order and collecting taxes. As with so many aspects of Russian life, it proved impossible to override local differences and to standardize legislation across the various territories under tsarist rule.[5]

The accession of Nicholas I in 1825 injected a note of urgency into this situation.[6] In the first years of his reign, Nicholas had extended conscription to many groups living in the western borderlands. In 1827 it was the turn of Jews in the Pale.[7] Nicholas undoubtedly hoped that conscription would prove a stepping stone to conversion; to this end the statute made special provision for drafting Jewish children aged twelve to eighteen. But other religious minorities found themselves the targets of his missionary agenda as well, and the conversion of Jewish soldiers never rose above 1 percent. Except for a ban on promotion, they enjoyed equal rights with the Russian Orthodox population, and their freedom of conscience was explicitly protected once they reached adulthood. Psychologically, however, the 1827 statute was a watershed. Soldiers served at least twenty-five years in the Russian army, and the need to fill the quota created bitter divisions within Jewish communities. Christians also hated the draft, but the cultural gulf between Jews and their neighbors intensified its traumatic impact. Fear of conversion added an extra dimension to the heartbreak that every parent felt at losing a son to the army.

Conscription marked the beginning of a new kind of relationship between the Russian government and its Jews. In 1840 Count Pavel Kiselev, minister of state domains and the driving force behind efforts to emancipate the peasantry, established a Committee for the Determination of Measures toward the Fundamental Transformation of the Jews in Russia. It concluded that the Jewish problem was the product of an invidious religious separatism, rooted in the Talmud but perpetuated by communal autonomy, cultural difference, and the shoddy education dispensed by superstitious, ill-trained Jewish teachers. Persecution only exacerbated the situation. Instead, the Kiselev committee proposed a comprehensive reeducation program to promote social unity. Measures included abolishing the *kahal* and reforming Jewish communal taxes, outlawing traditional dress, creating a network of state-sponsored Jewish schools, supervising the appointment of official rabbis, reclassifying Jews socially according to their economic usefulness, and settling the "useless" as farmers on state lands.[8]

Rather than attacking Jewish schools, Kiselev could have contrasted high levels of literacy among Jews with the complete absence of education available to the rest of the population.[9] Rather than stigmatizing Jews as exploitative and unproductive, he could have acknowledged their crucial role in the economy and the ways in which economic, geographical, and social restrictions limited Jewish options. But Kiselev's approach was shaped by endemic prejudice and the attitudes of local officials, who blamed unscrupulous Jewish middlemen for corrupting the peasantry and saw Jews themselves as dishonest, superstitious, and unclean.[10] Equality was a meaningless concept in a state in which the overwhelming majority remained serfs tied to the land. To western European

Jews, however, the Kiselev report suggested that Russia had embraced the German model of emancipation, whereby Jews would become more like their Christian neighbors in exchange for steady progress toward equal rights.

One person who interpreted it this way was twenty-three-year-old Max Lilienthal, who left Munich in 1839 to run the new Jewish school in Riga.[11] In January 1841 Count Sergei Uvarov, the minister of national enlightenment, summoned Lilienthal to collaborate in the reeducation of Russia's Jews. Uvarov was the government's chief ideologue. In a landmark report written after the failure of the Polish revolution in 1830–31, Uvarov had coined the slogan "Orthodoxy, Autocracy, Nationality" to promote a uniquely Russian path to modernity.[12] The Russification of minorities was a central feature of this program, so it was natural for Uvarov to play a key role in the Kiselev reforms. As a first step, he instructed Lilienthal to find suitably enlightened teachers for some 200 Jewish schools.[13] The German Jewish newspaper editors Isaac Jost and Ludwig Philippson were soon busy assembling a list of possible candidates. In the event, both Lilienthal and Uvarov got cold feet; but their defection did not derail educational reform, and in June 1842 the tsar placed Jewish primary schools *(hadarim)* and rabbinical academies *(yeshivot)* under Uvarov's direct control. In a bid to win over the Jews themselves, Nicholas also summoned a commission of Jewish leaders to advise on "swift implementation" of the reforms.[14] That July Lilienthal invited both Montefiore and Adolphe Crémieux to join the deliberations in St. Petersburg.

In his letter to Montefiore, Lilienthal contrasted the degraded state of Russian Jewry with the tsar's enlightened intentions, conveying something of the culture shock he himself had experienced during his visits to the Pale.

> Synagogues and Schoolhouses are overspred [*sic*] with filth, Divine worship and ceremonies are practised in wild disorder of which no Jew reared in the western part of Europe can form an idea . . . and the aspect of recklessness pervading the whole is disgraceful to the Jew in every relation of life. Intolerance is one result of such a spiritual condition and the evil effects of these exhibit themselves in every part of their social structure. The desire to preserve in their system that element in which these rank weeds germinate, prejudices from entering their mind any idea of Emancipation and the dignity of man and prompts them to view every thing beyond the sphere of their comprehension with dislike.

Lilienthal maintained that both Uvarov and Kiselev were inclined toward emancipation but insisted that Russian Jews acquire "useful knowledge and loyal principles" first. He could not answer for the consequences if the Jews proved recalcitrant. Montefiore's presence in St. Petersburg at this critical juncture might just tip the balance.[15]

Montefiore was of two minds about this invitation: several enclaves of Russian Jewish modernizers urged him to accept, but his contact with Hasidic leaders and the important community in Vilna probably led him to suspect that Uvarov's education reforms were a cover for the government's proselytizing agenda.[16] There was some justification for this view, although traditionalist concerns also reflected a deep-rooted fear of the *Haskalah;* for, as the Vilna authorities noted, "in Germany, where they have neglected the study of the Talmud these past thirty years and have indulged in the study of all kinds of profane sciences, our Jewish religion has been sadly wronged, the ties of the heavenly yoke have been loosened; the old-respect for our sacred ordinances is gone, and many of our brethren have embraced Christianity."[17] With Anglo-Jewry bitterly divided, such concerns must have troubled Montefiore too.

Still, he was worried by the prospect of extending conscription to Jews in the Kingdom of Poland, confiding to his nephew Louis Cohen: "the Governor of Warsaw has issued the most odious orders against the Jews of Poland, the Jews write but in the greatest confidence that . . . they have no choice between a continual life of martyrdom and leaving their Religion."[18] In this context, Lilienthal's letter presented an opportune moment to intervene.

On December 16 Loewe finally replied in the affirmative, stipulating only that Montefiore receive a formal invitation. Last-minute opposition from Kiselev's Jewish Committee ensured that this never arrived. The governor-general of Vilna feared bad publicity, and education officials concluded that western European Jews were unlikely to provide meaningful financial or moral support. The rest of the Jewish world was not party to these delicate negotiations, and there was widespread disappointment at Montefiore's failure to set out.[19]

Crémieux, now a member of the French Chamber of Deputies, was particularly harsh. He was constrained by political commitments, but (as he cattily put it) "Sir Moses, whose fortune is immense, is withheld neither by public functions, by professional duties, nor by family; he enjoys therefore, all the freedom which I lack."[20] This critique revealed a difference in style rather than substance. Like Montefiore, Crémieux declared that he would set out only after he received an official invitation; the difference was that Crémieux issued the condition publicly, whereas Montefiore chose to operate behind closed doors. This fundamental disagreement about how best to handle the Russian question would resurface with greater clarity in the months to come.

The faith of Western Jews in the tsar's good intentions collapsed in April 1843, when Nicholas issued a decree *(ukase)* announcing the imminent expulsion of all Jews from within fifty versts of the Prussian and Austrian borders. Many Jews were active in cross-border smuggling, but the proposed expulsions seemed draconian. In fact this was by no means the first such piece of legislation. Ever since 1825, Jewish residence in the border zone had been restricted to urban areas, and the practice of forcibly resettling Russian Jews dated back to 1804.[21] Now, however, Lilienthal had thrown the spotlight of the new Jewish press on Russia, while the Jews of neighboring Prussia felt sufficiently confident to lobby on behalf of their brethren. Not content with drawing up a memorandum for Nicholas, they issued a circular to Jews in sixteen prominent western European communities and sent copies of the *ukase* directly to Crémieux and Montefiore. A covering letter warned: "These measures threaten to drive half a million of people from their homes and to give them up to the most dreadful misery if the voice of the public does not succeed in changing the mind of the Emperor."[22] Montefiore went at once to call on the Russian ambassador, Baron Brunnow. He listened sympathetically but stressed that "no public steps should be taken in the way of petition to the Emperor, as there were two years still before the Ukase would take effect."[23] Yet the expulsion order was soon the talk of the town.

The Tory *Morning Post* described the *ukase* as a "truly benevolent and humane measure," reiterating the archetypal Russian accusation that Jews were "designedly intoxicating the Christian population, in order to incite them to commit crimes!"[24] By March 1844, however, English conversionists were holding meetings and drawing up protest resolutions. The *Journal des Débats* proclaimed that Russia had "declared war against the civilization as well as the generous and philosophic spirit of our age ... Every day the German journals bring us accounts of persecutions exercised by order of the Emperor against the Jews."[25]

In the light of all this publicity, Montefiore's silence seemed inexplicable. In fact he was hoping that the Rothschilds' diplomacy would pay off: in Frankfurt, Amschel had discussed the expulsions with the Russian finance minister and the grand duke of Hesse-Darmstadt; in Vienna, Salomon had mentioned the matter to Metternich, the Russian ambassador, and Count Orlov; and in Paris, James and Betty had approached Prime Minister Guizot on the Jews' behalf. Only in London did Foreign Secretary Aberdeen agree to take action—although he warned Lionel de Rothschild not to raise the question in the Commons as he had planned.[26]

These behind-the-scenes negotiations reflected the limited impact of public opinion in autocratic Russia. Such low-profile tactics did not play well with the Jewish press. In an effort to contain the mounting criticism, the *Voice of Jacob* urged the Deputies to give "a frank assurance . . . that something is being done, but that there exists special reasons for all this reserve."[27] Montefiore felt torn. In January 1844 he wrote assuring Jacob Franklin, editor of the *Voice*: "I believe everything has been done *privately* that was possible and I find no disposition on the part of those best acquainted with the most likely remedy for the evil if there be any remedy, to promote an public measure, believing that more harm than good might arise from it." But he clearly had misgivings about this approach, adding: "for myself, I think the Public Press must have beneficial influence and I hope it will continue to advocate the cause of humanity and of our oppressed Coreligionists."[28]

If Montefiore felt frustrated by the tactics of the Board of Deputies, then he must have been delighted to hear that Nicholas was visiting England in June. "I will do everything I possibly can to approach the Emperor, and pray for our brethren in his dominions," he wrote in his diary; "it engrosses all my thoughts." Aberdeen thought there would be no harm in forwarding an address from the deputies, although he warned that Nicholas "was very firm when he had once made up his mind on a subject." Meanwhile the situation in the Pale grew worse. The formal abolition of the *kahal* in 1844 turned out to have limited impact in practice. Reports that the expulsions were under way aroused more immediate concerns.[29]

Montefiore had just finished a term as commissioner of the peace for Kent and for the Cinque Ports, but his new role as sheriff of Kent made travel to Russia impossible for a while. Shortly before the end of this second period in office, he received a visit from Israel Binenfeld of Kraków, who urged him to try to overturn proposals to ban traditional Jewish dress. Binenfeld was the emissary of five distinguished Polish Hasidim, who had applied to Montefiore on the initiative of the great Hasidic leader Rabbi Israel Friedmann of Sadgora, in Bukovina.[30] Montefiore was sympathetic but requested more information, pointing out that modernizing dress and education were not necessarily bad things. In response, Rabbi Israel (who famously dressed like a Christian nobleman) agreed that "some of them are decrees, which, as His Excellency says, seem to be for the good, such as the decree relating to the schools. But I, observing from afar, am sure that the decrees are specifically intended to damage and violate our holy Torah, to cause desertion of the Jewish faith."[31]

Montefiore finally decided to go in early 1846 amid a climate of anti-Russian hysteria. While *The Times* warned that Nicholas wanted to convert *all* his subjects to Orthodoxy, the *Jewish Chronicle* declared melodramatically that by the time Montefiore actually left England "half a million of Jews may have fallen as martyrs to their faith, and another half a million may have gone over to the Russian church."[32] The Jewish press was united in supporting the Montefiore mission—although quite what he or they thought to achieve is unclear. Brunnow had already advised Montefiore that there was "very little hope of the object of his journey being accomplished," adding that if he must go, he should keep it "as quiet as possible."[33] The *Allgemeine Zeitung des Judentums* urged Montefiore to promote mass Jewish emigration to the New World, and only the *Voice of Jacob* expressed any real optimism.[34]

Arriving in St. Petersburg after a frankly terrifying journey, Montefiore began his ascent up the official ladder. He and Loewe were disconcerted to find that the brilliant but unscrupulous Uvarov made no effort to conceal his contempt for Russia's Jews. They were "different from the Jews in other parts of the world" because "they were orthodox, and believe in the Talmud"; they were, moreover, so "ignorant of their own religion" that "he was obliged to force them to study Hebrew, their own language." Neither Montefiore nor Loewe could let such statements go unchallenged, but Uvarov simply reiterated that there could be no question of emancipation before reeducation, hinting darkly that he expected the process to take "a long time . . . perhaps a century." Still, he did persuade the tsar to meet for the first time with a Jew face to face.[35]

Everyone who encountered Nicholas I commented on his height, his majestic bearing, his exceptional good looks, and his military air. Less flatteringly, they noted the rigid personality that prevented him from smiling with his eyes as well as his mouth. By 1846, however, the ruler of all the Russias was past his prime: he lost his hair early, was subject to depression, and became incapable of controlling his temper. Yet his impeccable manners prompted the marquis de Custine to comment: "one immediately recognised a man obliged, and accustomed to consider the amour propre of others."[36] Montefiore was so charmed that he preserved the gloves he wore on this occasion for the rest of his life.[37]

From the moment Nicholas drew Montefiore aside with the informal words "À présent causons," the tsar behaved with consummate diplomacy.[38] He had arranged for the guard in front of the Winter Palace to be composed entirely of Jewish soldiers and spoke of them warmly: "they were always brave 'the Maccabees.'" When his guest asserted that all Russian Jews "were faithful, loyal subjects, industrious and honourable citizens," Nicholas replied cryptically, "S'ils vous ressemblent" (if

His Majesty, Nicholas I, Emperor of all the Russias, at Vosuesensk, September 6, 1837. (Lithograph by Denis Auguste Marie Raffet; by permission of the Science and Society Picture Library, London)

they are like you). The tone of his remarks led Montefiore to warn his nephew Louis Cohen that they would cause "a mixture of pain and pleasure." In later life, he insisted that the tsar's attitude "was not radically hostile," although he admitted to hearing "some details concerning and against the Jews which made every hair of my head stand on an end."[39] He concluded that Nicholas had been infected by the prejudices of his entourage.

Everyone assured Montefiore that the mere fact of a reception by His Imperial Majesty would be of "the utmost importance," and Russian Jews certainly never forgot the meeting between the Iron Tsar and the devout British Jew.[40] By the turn of the century, the story had acquired such fantastic proportions that one folktale transposed the entire encounter to Montefiore's palatial residence in Ramsgate, where Nicholas was startled to find the floor and walls decorated with gold, silver, and precious stones, and the furniture made from a crystal so fine that it was invisible to the naked eye.[41]

As for Nicholas, all we know is that he later described Montefiore as "a kind and honest man, yet he is a Jew and a lawyer—and for this reason it is forgivable for him to wish many things." He added, "We must remain cautious, and offer and explain only the possible, without being enticed into excessive philanthropism." Blithely ignorant of this assessment, Montefiore believed "that as soon as our Brethren can overcome the prejudice of their fellow subjects there will remain but little difficulty of their being placed by the Government on an equal footing."[42] Given their shocking attitudes toward the Talmud, he surely included Nicholas and his ministers in the category of those in need of persuasion. But when the tsar invited him to tour the Jewish parts of the country, Montefiore concluded that there were real grounds for hope.

Leaving St. Petersburg for Poland and the Pale of Settlement was far from straightforward. While Montefiore waited for the necessary permissions, he was able to discuss matters with Kiselev himself. Like Uvarov and Count Nesselrode, the foreign minister, Kiselev regarded Jews as "great fanatics" and "complained of the Talmud being the cause of their degraded position." But Kiselev's hostility seemed to go further than that of his colleagues when he announced that the Jews "might go out or in as they pleased, that 5 or 6 hundred thousand might go, I might take ten thousand to Palestine, or anywhere else, he would give them passports."[43] If necessary, Kiselev would force Jews to become economically useful; he produced a draft *ukase,* requiring them to register in four economically useful categories: as members of one of the three merchant guilds, as townspeople who owned a residence, as members of an artisan guild for which they were suitably qualified, or as agriculturalists.[44] Those who failed to comply before the deadline of 1850 would face punitive measures.

Like so many of Kiselev's reforms, this *ukase* built on previously unsuccessful initiatives. Polish Jews had long been forbidden to own land or to settle as farmers, but the *ukase* declared that they were now free to do so. These claims were exaggerated. Only nine of the most prominent Jewish businessmen were authorized to buy land in the Kingdom of Poland under special conditions, and attempts to encourage agricultural settlement elsewhere were similarly halfhearted.[45] Many Jews had set out when they were promised land in Kherson, but government officials refused to subsidize the journey, and the majority died of starvation on the way.[46]

Montefiore was ignorant of these precedents. Already enthusiastic about Jewish agricultural settlement in Palestine—and probably flattered by Kiselev's request to "suggest any changes which he might think advantageous"—he informed the British ambassador that he was entirely satisfied with the sorting decree.[47] In his correspondence he elaborated on his motivation: "I fear there is the greatest poverty among them

[the Jews]. [T]he most likely remedy for this evil would be their employment in the cultivation of land, and the establishment of manufacto-
ries; these pursuits require capital, which I apprehend it will be difficult to raise in this country."[48] Kiselev hoped that "the rich Jews of
London Paris Berlin etc would be willing to form Companies for this
purpose."[49] Montefiore warned the minister that they could not count
on such support.

During the weekend, Montefiore and Loewe were invited to pray with
the small community of Jews in St. Petersburg.[50] It was a cold, rainy day,
and the walk of two miles through the mud, sleet, and rain to the barracks exhausted the sixty-year-old philanthropist. The synagogue itself
was a large room with three glass chandeliers, and Montefiore found
200 soldiers assembled there—some with wives and children, all dressed
in full uniform with their helmets by their sides and their prayer shawls
over their heads. Despite the gentlemanly distaste he felt at hearing the
soldiers pray in their chaotic "Polish manner," Montefiore was delighted
to witness "in so distant a part of the World, in such a place, and a
whole Congregation of Soldiers, the same Ritual, the same *Parasha*[*h*]
[Torah portion], the same *Hallel* [psalms of celebration], the same *Kadiz*
[*kaddish*] as I have been accustomed to see in the several Congregations
I have visited in the three quarters of the Globe." Both the soldiers and
the handful of nonmilitary Jews present found the experience similarly
unforgettable; twenty years later they would put up a plaque to commemorate the event.[51]

The Third Department was by no means enamored of these developments. An intelligence report drawn up during Montefiore's stay in the
capital complained: "The Polish Jews who reside here under various
pretexts drag themselves daily to the house of the English Messiah, who
. . . conveys to them his wish—to occupy himself with bettering the lot
of Jews in Egypt, Turkey, and Russia (what an indecent comparison)—
tells of the kindness with which he has been treated here by the Sovereign Emperor, and makes it out that His Majesty, shaking his hand, has
promised to agree to everything that he, Montefiore, should find useful
for Jews in Russia." Nor did the police spy think much of the Jewish
emissaries sent to visit Montefiore, who apparently included "some pair
of deputies from Shklov, and also a certain Minkin from Bobruysk, a
contractor, a great talker and a most unreliable man."[52]

To Montefiore, their combination of long beards, modern dress, and
uncovered heads was proof of their desire to obey the government.[53] To
the spy, they were subversives, who talked endlessly about their sufferings: "Does it become his [Montefiore's] stature to heed the musings of
greedy Yids about their imaginary oppression? He ought at once to put
a stop to such talk and to remind them that he came "'not for condemn-

ing the decrees of the Government,' but solely in order to occupy himself with the Jews in the sense of their morals, for the correction of their deplorable condition."[54]

But Montefiore, who was known as a leading opponent of "enlightened" Judaism in London, could hardly be a "true leader" to his coreligionists: "He adopts European customs only for show, but in his heart of hearts is a true Jew, who fanatically supports all things strictly Jewish and is concerned above all else with the preservation of the Jewish national identity." To spread such ideas among the Jews of Poland was tantamount to "pouring oil into a fire"; it would be necessary to "institute the closest surveillance" during his tour of the Pale.

Like the rest of Montefiore's journals, the diaries he kept during his trip to Russia were burnt at Ramsgate. Hermann Shandel saw something special in the visit to Vilna and rescued these pages from the flames. The first impression we have of how Montefiore responded to his encounter with Russian Jewry comes from a diary entry written in the Lithuanian town of Vilkomir (Ukmergé). He was struck by the sheer number of devout Jews in this backwater, noting: "I was delighted to see in every house on our way to the Synagogue several candles burning." He was shocked, too, by what he saw:

> this little town is pleasantly situated but its inhabitants are in dreadful distress in consequence of the high prices . . . the two last years there has been no harvest, all the crops entirely failed, many die of hunger every week we were assured, the Government do all in their power to assist they have sent money & . . . bread to each family . . . the Jews as well as the Christians, and have not collected any Taxes the Jews appear sick & miserably destitute may the Almighty help them. I gave the Elders 100 Rubles to distribute among the Jews & 30 among the Christians of the town . . . yesterday 57 Jewish recruits entered this town on their way to St. Petersburg they had 8 women & 2 Children with them, they were to proceed this afternoon, but in consequence of an application they made to the Commandant of the town they were allowed to remain till Sunday Morng on condition of their going a double distance that day.[55]

While Montefiore, Judith, and Loewe were traveling from St. Petersburg, the 30,000 Jews of Vilna were busy preparing for their arrival. Ideas had always traveled in the Yiddish-speaking world of Ashkenaz, and the fusion of Jewish and European culture promoted by the German Jewish enlightenment had also spread to eastern Europe. By the 1830s the Russian *Haskalah* was beginning to acquire critical mass, particularly in Vilna and Odessa, where there were soon enough "enlight-

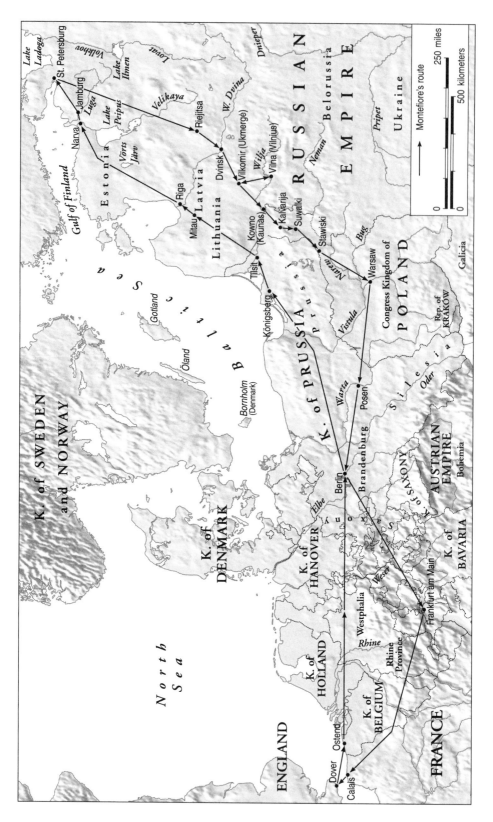

Route taken by the Montefiores on their visit to St. Petersburg, the Pale of Settlement, and the Kingdom of Poland, 1846

ened" Jews *(maskilim)* to sustain a progressive synagogue and a modern school.[56] Vilna—the "Jerusalem of Lithuania"—had long been a center of intellectual and cultural ferment. Support by indigenous *maskilim* for Uvarov's educational agenda meant that in 1846 the community was in a state of cultural civil war.[57] When Lilienthal had addressed a public meeting a couple of years earlier, opponents of secular education had actually threatened him with violence while the whole crowd chanted: "We don't want, we don't want!"

As a beardless Jew who dressed like an English gentleman, Montefiore's appearance in such a culturally charged environment was potentially explosive. But Montefiore was known for his religious observance—and revered as the hero of Damascus and the patron of Jews living in Palestine. Both *maskilim* and traditionalists were determined to welcome him, and they agreed a truce for the duration of his visit. Traditionalists represented the overwhelming majority, but they agreed to equal representation at every meeting.[58] When the time came to dispatch a welcome delegation, the two groups fell to quarreling over who would greet him first.[59] The wealthy *maskil* Nisan Rosenthal eventually seized control by driving to meet the visitors on his own.

It was touching to see the elderly Englishman and his secretary descend from the carriage amid the cheering crowd. The scene became even more emotional as Judith emerged and burst into tears when the *magid* (preacher) of Vilna "blessed her for offspring," even though they all knew she had already passed this stage.[60] Her husband was eager that they do Judith honor, modestly asserting through Loewe: "Every expression of thanks belongs exclusively to Lady Montefiore, as it was she who originally persuaded me to undertake my journey to Egypt and also thither."[61] She was still struggling to shake off a severe chill caught in St. Petersburg, but the hope their mission might prove successful gave her the strength to carry on.[62]

By the time they reached Vilna, the whole town was in uproar. The Russian police attributed this enthusiasm to greed, explaining that Montefiore had distributed 4,000 silver rubles in Vilkomir, and "Vilna's Jews are likewise expecting a significant allowance."[63] Yet they laid on extra security when they heard that Jews were planning to drag his carriage through the streets themselves. "The windows of even the highest stories—nay, the roofs of the houses" were overflowing with Jews and Christians—the former moved to tears by the Hebrew word "Jerusalem" incorporated in the coat of arms on the side of Montefiore's carriage, the latter torn between admiration and envy at the fabulous progress of the "Zydowsky Krol" (King of the Jews).[64]

The evening after this momentous reception, Montefiore summoned all the Jewish notables of Vilna. Knowing that the government would receive reports of his activities, he expressed his sorrow on hearing from the tsar that Jews were "sluggards and inveterate idiots, dreading all work, and loath to cultivate the land."[65] To some extent, he was playing devil's advocate. But Loewe expressed his own *maskilic* beliefs when he attacked the Jews of Vilna for their opposition to secular learning—just as Montefiore spoke from the heart when he urged them to abandon their distinctive dress.

Vernacular education became a recurrent theme of Montefiore's stay in Vilna as he and Loewe visited Jewish schools, distributing alms and offering hefty bribes to pupils and teachers if they would "learn the Russian language" too.[66] On one occasion, they went to a yeshiva in Zarzceze presided over by the intellectually brilliant founder of the Mussar movement, Rabbi Israel Salanter.[67] When Montefiore and Loewe berated him for his inability to speak Russian, Salanter did not hesitate to answer back. The argument lasted a good half-hour, and Montefiore left the yeshiva visibly displeased.[68]

He was rather happier with the "enlightened" school funded by Rosenthal and Hirsch Klatschko—although his diary expressed surprise that the boys in the Asylum for Destitute Children "could translate into German but knew nothing of Russian."[69] The high-minded Vilna *maskilim* looked to Germany for intellectual leadership; Montefiore had more practical priorities. In Russia as in Turkey he wanted Jews to learn the language of the state in which they lived. It was soon common knowledge that Loewe had repeatedly urged Russian Jews to embrace western European education, arguing: "When the Messiah comes and the Jewish kingdom is restored, then the Jews cannot be allowed to fall behind other peoples."[70] This news was music to the ears of the isolated, despised *maskilim* in surrounding areas, who adopted Loewe and Montefiore as standardbearers for their cause. "We have sinned and we have done evil because we have eyes like a bat that do not look towards the rays of the sun of the wisdom," wrote one, "and therefore you the almighty Messiah should . . . rebuild the hearts of the people of Israel to devote their time also to the Haskalah."[71]

The official Jewish leadership in Vilna was at a loss to interpret this development. Salanter subsequently recalled a chance meeting with the spiritual leader of the Lithuanian *mitnagdim*, Rabbi Isaac (Itzele) of Volozhin, who was rushing through the streets to meet the Montefiores. "Rabbi of Volozhin, where are you going and why are you hurrying so?" he asked, meaning: how is that you, the head of our community, are not holding these meetings in your house? Rabbi Itzele replied diplomatically: "Does the evil-doer in *Geihinom* [hell] know where they are taking him? I do not know where they are leading me." This lack of control must have been a worry for many traditionalists, since (as the Orthodox activist Jacob Halevi Lifshitz later remarked) "when there appears an advocate of his people, a righteous man, who is nevertheless beardless, the free-thinkers may argue that it is possible to be a good Jew and yet be clean-shaven."[72]

But Montefiore's profoundly Jewish spirituality meant that he had less in common with the modernizers than it seemed. Not only did he and Judith refuse an invitation to a public dinner for fear it would not be kosher; they famously ate "nothing except tea and fruit" when they attended a ball at the governor-general's house.[73] Montefiore made a point of wearing his "little black Cap" indoors and manifested a touching attachment to Jewish tradition.[74] The Vilna correspondent of a Birmingham businessman recounted how Montefiore had visited the graves of pious men and how "[o]n the tomb of the Gaon, of blessed memory, both Sir Moses and Lady Montefiore prayed and wept with much fervour, and distributed a large sum of charity."[75]

The complex religious stance of Louis Loewe compounded these mixed messages. On their second Sabbath, Loewe gave a sermon in German in the Great Synagogue. This was nothing short of a cultural revolution in a town in which the religious establishment regarded the language of Moses Mendelssohn with suspicious loathing. Yet far from bolstering the *maskilim*, Loewe's sermon seems to have reinforced the traditionalists. One observer gloated: "He has caused the new-fashioned Jews that were styled 'Berlinskys,' to repent and become religious. During many years these men had no Phylacteries, and never attended divine service; but now they have procured Phylacteries, and regularly go to prayers in the synagogue."[76]

The devout and progressive aspects of Montefiore's public persona were reflected in the many engravings sold during his visit, in which he was either "devoutly wrapped in his *talit* [prayer shawl], or dressed in his [City] uniform." This outfit, which Montefiore had worn to the governor-general's ball, was a thing of wonder to the Jews of Vilna. The *maskil* Isaac Meir Dick described their amazement at the sight of the pious Englishman with his bushy side-whiskers, dressed in royal red with gold buttons, white-gold gloves, a sword on his thigh, and a hat with an ostrich plume on his head: "his face changed and he was like a warrior, and the people feared to approach him."[77] Christian notables had caviled at the prospect of socializing with this rich foreign Jew. They soon changed their tune once they saw the English visitors—Montefiore resplendent in his uniform and Judith adorned with diamonds, sapphires, and gold bracelets worth at least half a million rubles.[78]

The Great Synagogue, in the heart of the medieval Jewish quarter at Vilna, early twentieth century. Begun in 1630, the synagogue developed into a complex of fourteen structures around a courtyard and included prayer halls, communal building, ritual bath, and rabbinical library. (Photograph by Jan Bulhak; from the Archives of the YIVO Institute for Jewish Research, New York)

Throughout his stay in Vilna, Montefiore devoted considerable time and money to the town's charitable foundations.[79] News of his benevolence traveled fast. The *maskil* Mordecai Aaron Ginzburg recounted that Montefiore "accumulated more than three thousand letters of request, and even after the police doubled the guard it did not help for the people crowded and waited like wolves." Every time he opened his carriage door, the poor would throw their letters at him. One missive nearly took his eyes out, and Loewe lost his hat amid the general kerfuffle as people started to shout: "Give us money!"[80] After this he became more careful; but the flood of begging letters from Jews and Christians continued unabated.[81]

"[M]y Visit has cost me altogether £850," Montefiore commented ruefully at the end of it, "but thank God the Poor have received it."[82] Not everyone thought the expense worthwhile. One Lubavich Hasid told Montefiore that he would have done better to stay at home and use the costs of the trip to bribe the Russian government.[83] Montefiore was outraged: his whole approach to Jewish politics was to eschew this kind of corruption by defending Jews on moral and humanitarian grounds.

On the evening of their last Sabbath, the leading Jews of Vilna gathered in Montefiore's rooms alongside emissaries from towns like Minsk and Vitebsk, and the border communities threatened with expulsion.[84] By now Montefiore had established that there was a vast difference between what the government told him and the reality on the ground. One evening, a Hebrew teacher called Rabbi Ya'akov Ha'cohen Wallak had asked Montefiore why the government banished Jews from rural areas.[85] When Montefiore asserted that on the contrary the authorities were eager to encourage Jewish agricultural settlement, Wallak burst into tears. Their embarrassed host explained apologetically that Wallak was one of the many rural Jews forced to quit their homes. The reports now presented by the communal leaders in response to the government's accusations reinforced the impression left by such encounters. Loewe "repeatedly noticed tears rolling down the cheeks of the venerable elders of the community" as they defended Russian Jewry, while "Sir Moses and Lady Montefiore themselves could hardly suppress their emotion." It was two in the morning before the conference broke up, Montefiore drinking a toast to "better times, and to the health and prosperity of his brethren in Russia."[86]

The emotional connection forged between the English visitors and the Jews of Vilna was equally apparent when it came to a final parting. The endless crowds had been a nuisance, but Montefiore and Judith must have been overwhelmed by their encounter with such a large and observant Jewish community. The hustle and bustle of a Friday afternoon as thousands upon thousands prepared for the Sabbath, the extraordinary quiet of the streets when night fell, the unique sensation of descending the colossal staircase into the interior of the Great Synagogue, filled to capacity with some 5,000 or 6,000 Jews—all this was without parallel in their experience of the Sephardi and western European Jewish worlds.[87] When he climbed once more into his traveling carriage, Montefiore was so choked that he could hardly speak. "I leave you," he told his hosts, "but my heart will ever remain with you. When my brethren suffer, I feel it painfully; when they have reason to weep, my eyes shed tears."[88]

The contrast between Vilna and Montefiore's second major destination could hardly have been more striking. Warsaw, capital of the Kingdom of Poland, was a rapidly expanding city in the throes of industrialization, grimy, bustling, and lacking in charm. Like many Polish towns, Warsaw had traditionally been closed to Jewish settlement, and the burgeoning Jewish community there had existed for many years in defiance of the law. By 1840, 36,934 Jews made up over a quarter of the city's population. Many were first-generation migrants, most had to pay a special tax for the privilege of living there, and barely 130 families were allowed to reside outside the Jewish quarter.[89]

Jews in the Kingdom of Poland operated in a different legal framework from their brethren in the Pale: the Jewish Statute of 1835 had confirmed the status of Russian Jews as citizens of the Russian Empire, but in Poland Jews enjoyed neither state nor municipal citizenship. Yet the continued importance of the local Jewish community rendered these distinctions less significant. Despite laboring under greater legal disadvantages, Jews in Warsaw were actually better integrated in Polish society than their counterparts in the Pale. Merchants who visited Saxony and Prussia, and young men who had studied at German universities, had been among the first Jews to settle the city. As early as 1800, Henrik Rzewuski observed that their dress and custom did not differ markedly from that of other Poles, and that "[o]ne could quite frequently meet among them really enlightened learned men."[90] Precisely because the Warsaw rabbinate lacked the authority conveyed by centuries of tradition, these wealthy Jewish businessmen exercised decisive influence within the community, dominating both its charities and the consultative Jewish Committee established in 1825. The emergent bourgeoisie was closely allied to the small Jewish intelligentsia; both groups pursued communal reform and modernization in tandem with the prolonged struggle for civil and political rights. While some rich Jews remained attached to their traditional lifestyle, others dressed like Poles and sent their children to mainstream schools.[91]

Montefiore arrived in Warsaw on May 13 at a moment of crisis. The recent uprising in Austrian Poland had alarmed the tsarist authorities. When the revolutionary government in Kraków issued an appeal "To the Polish nation," the Russians placed their own Polish territories under martial law. Only those with passports could enter or leave the capital, while travel restrictions elsewhere caused galloping inflation and serious food shortages.[92] Nevertheless, the British consul Colonel Gustave Du Plat reported that "Montefiore's hotel was literally besieged from morning to night: the small square in its front is filled with persons of all ages: Police Agents are obliged to guard the door of the House, and even the doors of his apartments: and he cannot stir beyond their threshold, no matter whether on foot or in a carriage, without being followed by a dense crowd that increases as it moves along, and fills whole streets."[93]

Given the strict prohibitions on all forms of political assembly, Du Plat viewed the indulgence with which the police treated this menace to public order as proof of the government's good intentions. Montefiore behaved with obsessive discretion but was still subjected to constant supervision. The eyes of a large portrait in his hotel room had round holes instead of pupils, and (as Montefiore and Loewe soon discovered) it was possible to "hear every word spoken within" from the corridor outside.[94]

Official newspaper accounts give the impression that Montefiore spent his time with wealthy businessmen and intellectuals, most of whom were hand in glove with the government.[95] They included the philanthropic banker Jozef Epstejn, the first Polish Jew to obtain honorary citizenship; the entrepreneur Mathias Rosen, widely regarded as the most influential Jewish leader in 1840s Warsaw; the government censor Jacob Tugendhold; and the radical Antoni Eisenbaum, deputy director of the Warsaw Rabbinical School. All were important figures in the community; all were also prominent sponsors or exponents of the Warsaw *Haskalah*. On one level, it was perfectly natural for Montefiore to visit the Rabbinical School and the German synagogue on Danielewiczowski Street, as well as Epstejn's Jewish Hospital and Rosen's Aged Needy Asylum. But whereas the latter were relatively uncontroversial, the former occupied a central place in the life of the city's *maskilim*. Nor was Montefiore insensitive to their contested status. The *Kurjer Warszawski* made much of his praise for the "superbly advanced students" at the Rabbinical School, but he later protested—inaccurately—to Uvarov that the establishment tolerated apostates as teachers of Jewish youth.[96]

The complaint is suggestive, although sadly we know almost nothing about Montefiore's interaction with Poland's religious leadership. Most of what we do know is based on Hasidic legend rather than hard fact.[97] One such story describes Montefiore's encounter with Rabbi Itsche (Isaac) Meir and other Hasidic leaders in Warsaw. Loewe tried to persuade them that there was "a good case to be made in favor of the Enlightenment" by arguing that if Mordechai had not understood the dialect of Bigtan and Teresh then he would have been unable to uncover the plot against King Ahasuerus, and so his linguistic ability had saved the Jewish people. Rabbi Itsche responded that the book of Esther proved quite the contrary. Had it been generally known that Jews understood the native language, then Bigtan and Teresh would never have been so indiscreet; Mordechai was a member of the Sanhedrin and therefore a linguist, but the same did not apply to the masses.[98]

Unwilling to enter into such high-flown talmudic disputation, Montefiore intervened pragmatically. "If you oppose the study of secular subjects, who will be qualified to protect your rights before the Government?" Rabbi Itsche smiled politely. "We are praying for the advent of the Messiah, but until then we are well satisfied with you, honored Sir."[99]

These Hasidic tales are so resonant with the concerns voiced during

Montefiore's better-documented visit to Vilna that they probably contain a kernel of truth. They also leave much unsaid. Loewe also refers to this encounter in his edition of Montefiore's diaries, but the outcome is rather different, and the Hasidim appear in a more enterprising light: "a deputation of that pre-eminently conservative class of the Hebrew community, known by the appellation of *Khasseedim* [*sic*] paid us a visit . . . They were headed by Mr. Posener, a gentleman who had done much for the promotion of industry in Poland, and his son; and he informed Sir Moses that he would, though an old man, comply with the desire of the Government and change the Polish for the German costume. Being a man held in high esteem by the Jews, and well spoken of by the Prince [Viceroy], his example would have a most favourable effect upon others."[100]

Almost certainly this was the same delegation, since the entrepreneurial Solomon Marcus Posener had earlier collaborated with Rabbi Isaac of Warka, Rabbi Itsche Meir, and Rabbi Haim Davidsohn of Warsaw in signing a manifesto urging Polish Jews to settle the land.[101] That this was a project dear to the hearts of the *maskilim* and the government, and that Posener himself was not a Hasid but an "enlightened" *mitnaged* underlines the complex interaction between these different factions in Polish Jewish society and the extent to which they defy easy categorization.

Neither Montefiore nor Loewe was alive to these subtleties. Arguably, the inner life of the Jewish community was no longer their prime concern. Warsaw was a seat of government, not an administrative hub like Vilna, and Montefiore's dealings with the Russian authorities took center stage. When the viceroy embarked on the usual litany of complaints about how "the Jews would not cultivate the land, though the law allowed them to purchase it," his English guest knew enough to answer back, informing Prince Paskevich that "hundreds of Jews had expressed to me their ardent desire to obtain land, and that I feared there existed some difficulty in the requisite formalities."[102] Armed with his new knowledge, Montefiore hoped to take advantage of the tsar's imminent arrival in Warsaw, but his efforts to obtain a second interview proved unavailing.

Passing through Berlin on their return journey, Montefiore was treated like Jewish royalty.[103] Within no time, prints of the Anglo-Jewish hero praying in Berlin or negotiating with Mehmed Ali and the tsar were available for purchase in the Prussian capital.[104] In Warsaw, meanwhile, they cast a commemorative medal with images of Montefiore and Judith that was to be treasured in Jewish homes for half a century or more.[105] Others were more skeptical. Writing from Posen (now Poznań) in East Prussia, one correspondent of the *Allgemeine Zeitung des Judentums* complained that it was naive of Montefiore to equate the complex situation of Russian Jewry with a miscarriage of justice in Damascus. The only sure result of his mission was its disastrous impact on Jewish civil society. The cause of their oppressed coreligionists had begun to arouse lively interest among European and American Jews—"an interest that emanated from a concentrated unity of action and that promised to achieve great things through the power that lies in every significant association, but never with an individual who lacks the authority of the collective." Now Montefiore had taken executive action, the rest had fallen silent, and "the holy flame had flickered out."[106]

The *Voice of Jacob* disagreed profoundly: Montefiore's action had lent dignity to the whole Jewish people. Regardless of the actual outcome, widespread and sympathetic news coverage testified to the progress being made in the battle for emancipation, now "that the humanity and intelligence of Europe are ready to cast their weight into our scale." The presence in St. Petersburg of "a gentleman, with a *personnel* like Sir Moses Montefiore . . . universally known, and as universally respected," could transform Russian attitudes to the Jewish question.[107]

Montefiore was certainly eager to exploit the situation. On his return, he sent Prime Minister Peel an account of his travels and respectfully solicited to be made a baronet. Ten years earlier, a similar honor had been refused. Now Sir Robert was happy to oblige in "the Hope that it may aid your truly benevolent efforts to improve the social condition of the Jews in other Countries by temperate appeals to the Justice & Humanity of their Ruler." The *Jewish Chronicle* was in ecstasies: by rewarding a Jew for services to his coreligionists, Queen Victoria had placed herself firmly "at the head of religious freedom, of genuine liberality."[108]

Having returned with sackloads of letters, petitions, and reports, Montefiore drew up a set of recommendations that demonstrated how much he had learned during his travels. In the first of two letters to Kiselev, Montefiore contrasted the assertion that Russian Jews could participate in municipal elections, join merchant corporations, settle at will, and acquire immovable property anywhere inside the Pale with the plethora of exceptions and legal exemptions.[109] In a second letter, Montefiore contrasted the civil, geographical, social, and economic exclusion experienced by Jews in the Kingdom of Poland with the Organic Statute of 1832, which explicitly declared that "protection of the law equally extends to all the inhabitants of the Kingdom without any distinction of rank and social condition." On reading these reports, Nicholas himself commented: "the letter is written in a gracious manner and there are just remarks regarding contradictions in the laws and where these must be corrected and supplemented."[110]

With regard to the Russian Jews, Montefiore stressed the difficulties faced by merchants who were unable to travel into the interior, and the impact of abolishing the *kahal* on their ability to provide poor relief. Far from being parasitic middlemen, most Jews were "either mechanics or common labourers, they do not appear to be of idle disposition; on the contrary, they seek work as far as they are permitted to extend their movements." Far from refusing to engage in agriculture, the obstructionism of local officials simply prevented Jews from doing as they were asked. Montefiore was concerned that Kiselev's sorting decree would result in "more than four-fifths of the Hebrew population" being designated as "useless." He proposed two further economic classifications: one for laborers and white-collar workers; the other for rabbis, scholars, and religious officials.[111]

In conclusion, Montefiore stated categorically that the complete emancipation of Jews under tsarist rule would be the best solution to the Jewish question. Failing this, the government should allow complete freedom of residence within the Pale; suspend all decrees preventing Jews from selling alcohol in the villages; admit Jewish merchants, artisans, and tradesmen into Christian corporations; grant them freedom of travel in the interior; reestablish the *kahal*; permit Jews to employ Christian servants, to live as agriculturalists, and to keep distilleries; and promote Jews in the army on the same basis as others. As for the Jews of Poland, equalizing their status with that of their Russian brethren would be a just and very beneficial step.[112]

In a third and final letter to Uvarov, Montefiore outlined the pleasing state of Jewish education.[113] The failure to teach Russian was simply a question of money: no sooner had he provided the funds than suitable masters were promptly engaged. The low numbers attending public schools were equally explicable: most Jews could not afford proper clothes or textbooks, and they questioned the use of higher learning when their choice of careers was so circumscribed. Yet Montefiore stressed the Jewish fear of apostasy. If the government wished to show good faith, it should stop appointing converts as Jewish teachers, allow rabbis to retain control of yeshivot, and put an end to the unjustified confiscation of Hebrew books.

Tsarist officials subjected all three of these letters to detailed scrutiny. The minister responsible for investigating Montefiore's complaints in Poland demonstrated a striking sympathy for Jews. In his report, Turkul' confirmed Montefiore's claims about the specific disadvantages faced by Jews in the Kingdom of Poland. He agreed that residence restrictions were counterproductive; saw no reason to oppose Jews joining guilds or acquiring real estate; regarded allowing Jews to attend university but not to enter state service or the learned professions as illogical; and concluded that the ban on Jews' giving evidence against Christians was out of keeping with "the spirit of the times."[114]

These recommendations may have reflected deeper frustrations with Jewish legislation. Kiselev, too, proved unexpectedly receptive to Montefiore's comments. In a memorandum to Nicholas prepared in May 1847, he explained that "the Jews, not tolerated in the Great Russian provinces and faced with constraints in places of their permanent settlement, of necessity had to turn to various illegal means of making a living, thus provoking new restrictions against them. This condition of the Jews is a repetition of all that was happening to them everywhere in Europe, until the Governments there altered the pre existing system and, by means of improvements, gradually made them into useful members of the State." Such restrictions ran directly counter to the thrust of government policy, which aimed at "uniting them [the Jews] with the general population and directing them toward labor that is useful to the State." It was time to reconsider, and "to grant the Jews within the boundaries of their current Pale of Settlement the rights of commerce, trade, manufacture, and farming, in a measure that is as equal as possible to that of the native inhabitants."[115]

Ultimately, Russia was an autocracy—and a very inefficient one.[116] Even when the tsar did issue instructions, they often took years to implement, and vested interests could prevent their enforcement. Sometimes this state of affairs carried advantages for Jews. The infamous ex-upulsion *ukase* was never implemented not because of Montefiore's visit (although he took the credit for it), but rather because local officials protested against its devastating effects. Sometimes, however, this inefficiency worked against Jews. Montefiore's plea to raise Polish Jewry to the same status as their brethren in the Pale was so consistent with the tsar's policy of Russification and centralization that he had approved the idea even before 1846. In practice, Nicholas' clearly expressed wish to standardize Jewish legislation was discussed by numerous Polish committees before being buried in paperwork. But the real problem for Montefiore was the tsar himself.

Nicholas's approach to the Jewish question was inherently contradictory. In the very same sentence, he instructed Kiselev both to promote the equalization of Jewish economic rights "without fail" and to "keep in mind that, until the desired transformation in their morals and civic daily life takes place, the Jews may not have rights that are equal *in all respects* to those of the Christians." In much the same way, the tsar's desire for rationalization ran counter to an intuitive respect for custom, which led him to authorize Kiselev to reconsider all Jewish legislation except in "those provinces that possess their native privileges."[117] The truth was that Nicholas never overcame the instinctive aversion that led him to see the conscription of Jewish children as a tool for mass conversion. In a separate letter to Kiselev he declared categorically: "when Montefiore speaks of the full equalization of the rights of Jews with those of Christians, in work and other matters—to permit this is impossible, and in my lifetime I will not allow it."[118]

In a sense, this attitude rendered the entire Montefiore mission pointless—and yet there is no doubt that the government took Montefiore's proposals seriously. They generated hundreds upon hundreds of pages of paperwork, listing endless points of agreement between him and the government and many recommendations to improve the law. Some— like the relaxation of residence requirements in Poland—were even implemented. If most other recommendations remained a dead letter, then neither Montefiore nor the officials in question were really responsible. When it came to action, both he and they were helpless in the face of the intractable nature of the tsarist regime.

Chapter 10

Trial and Error

Montefiore's mission to the East in 1840 had launched him as a figure on the world stage; the journey to Russia consolidated his prestige as an international troubleshooter for the Jewish people. Even before then, his mailbag was voluminous. The most complete record of incoming correspondence dates from 1844–45, during which Montefiore apparently received 295 letters, of which 144 came from Palestine and just 8 from England. The rest were a colorful mix from Holland, Portugal, Germany, the Habsburg lands, Malta, North Africa, and various parts of the Ottoman Empire. They included interminable correspondence about the Jews of Palestine, requests to dedicate scholarly works, appeals on behalf of communal charities, petitions for intervention with the Ottoman government, reports of persecution, and—inevitably—begging letters. Montefiore's linguistic skills were no match for such a varied correspondence. He turned, quite naturally, to the invaluable Dr. Loewe.[1]

As early as 1840, Adolphe Crémieux had remarked on Loewe's intimacy with the Montefiores. He dismissed the orientalist as "a veritable servant, with neither will, nor opinions, who only ever mentioned Sir Moses and Lady Montefiore with a kind of pride."[2] No doubt Loewe did take pleasure in his friendship with the noble couple, peppering his speech with "Sir Moses" this and "Lady Montefiore" that. For the rest, Crémieux's assessment was wide of the mark.

Loewe was sufficiently well regarded to be a very serious candidate for the chair of Hebrew at University College London. He was also a modest man, who responded to the wreck of his academic ambitions by setting up as a private schoolmaster in Brighton. There he devoted much of his time to dealing with Montefiore's mail. The task proved so exacting that Montefiore wrote apologetically, "I have long thought that I am to have no rest in this World and I believe you must begin to think that I do not intend you to have any either."[3] Yet he never paid Loewe properly for his time. Indeed, oral tradition has it that whenever one of the Loewe children became engaged, Montefiore would send a monetary present—leaving their father to remark that the check effectively represented his salary.

In practice, Loewe's role entailed more than producing brief summaries of foreign correspondence and drafting suitable replies. There was no point in translating routine receipts, begging letters, or requests from Jews in the New World to forward money to their relatives. Instead, Loewe scribbled a couple of lines on the back—enough to give Montefiore the gist, but no more. The sheer quantity involved and the flowery language favored by so many rendered anything else out of the question. His own correspondence with his employer combined mundane practicalities and thoughtful advice: "be careful with respect to *sealed* letters which you may be requested to transmit, the reason thereof I shall communicate to you verbally," he warned on one occasion, before launching into a detailed analysis of letters recently arrived from Palestine and enclosing a couple of documents to sign.[4] By acting as a gatekeeper, Loewe served as a filter between Montefiore and his correspondents: it was the "Dear Doctor" who emerged with the clearest understanding of the letter-writers and their world.

Loewe habitually downplayed this influence, but observers were unconvinced. Yehiel Mendelssohn from Lublin wrote to Loewe in 1846, explaining: "I knew that his honor took part in every deed of *tzedakah* and benevolence that this dear man [Montefiore] . . . did, and by his [Loewe's] command everything will happen . . . therefore I chose to send this letter to the hands of his grace with the hope that he will swiftly give them to the hand of my lord Montefiore."[5] It was said in the Loewe family that whenever Montefiore wished to refuse a request without embarrassment, he would remark forbiddingly, "I will first ask Dr. Loewe."[6] His charitable activities were a collaborative venture, in which the intellectual and the wealthy businessman each played a part.

Both Montefiore and Loewe returned from Russia to a mountain of correspondence. Easter 1847 saw a spate of ritual-murder allegations in Syria and Palestine. The first was so ridiculous that it hardly amounted to anything. A squabble between a Jewish and a Greek Orthodox boy in Jerusalem left the latter with an injured foot. When Christians accused the Jewish boy of stabbing an innocent, a Muslim court endorsed the blood libel. Jewish protests were unavailing; reference to the *firman* granted to Montefiore in Istanbul was not. The pasha of Jerusalem asked to see a copy. On reading Abdul Mecid's ringing condemnation of the blood libel, he asked Muslim religious leaders "if they meant to fly in the face of that document." And that—for the moment—was that.[7]

Barely two weeks later a four-year-old boy went missing in the predominantly Christian town of Dayr al-Qamar, already a focus of sectarian tension because of its strategic location in the heart of Druze Lebanon.[8] Asserting that the child's mutilated body had been found three days after his disappearance from the Jewish quarter, locals appealed to the French consul for "justice" and protection against the bloodthirsty Jews. He subsequently reported that the inhabitants of Dayr al-Qamar had failed to prove the Jews' guilt, adding: "in any case the Jews presented a *firman* obtained in Constantinople in 1841, which enjoined the Pashas in the Provinces to protect them against persecutions that might arise in similar circumstances."[9] The alleged plight of Maronite Christians in the aftermath of Lebanon's recent civil war was a central focus of French public opinion and foreign policy. It was hardly surprising that the Dayr al-Qamar blood libel found its way into the French press, where the Catholic *Union Monarchique* published a damning account of the "atrocious crime."[10] Worse still, *The Times* republished the report without a word of commentary or explanation. A letter from Montefiore informed the editor that the missing child had been found in a nearby vineyard—cold, tired, and hungry, but very far from dead.[11] Although the Montefiore *firman* prevented both episodes from escalating, the hostility of the Catholic press remained cause for concern.

The Damascus Affair had created bad blood between Jews and Catholics, and nowhere more so than in Damascus itself. The French consul, Ratti-Menton, was now in China, but his manipulative subordinate Jean-Baptiste Beaudin remained. In April 1847 a twelve-year-old boy who worked for one of the protégés of the French consulate was sent out on an errand and failed to return. Two days later, Beaudin requested that the governor institute a formal search, reminding him "that according to the faithful tradition, the wicked Jews are in the practice of decoying children in their power during this period of this festival for which reason, the master of the boy strongly suspects that he is in the Jewish quarter."[12] The governor dismissed the allegations, but the rumor was enough to revive the hysteria of 1840.

The leading Jews of Damascus reported to Montefiore that "the Christians, in particular, endeavoured to persuade the Mohamedans that the Jews were actually murderers," and that a mob of both denominations had gathered outside the Jewish quarter, threatening violence and attacking those Jews still on the streets "till the ground was drenched with their blood as though it were water." They begged Montefiore to intervene with the French government on their behalf.[13]

Montefiore had been thoroughly disgusted by the attitude of the French authorities during the Damascus Affair.[14] These new letters from Damascus confirmed his sense of unfinished business. Palmerston was now back in the Foreign Office; when Montefiore met him in early July, he proved sympathetic and well informed.[15] He did not hesitate to endorse Montefiore's trip to Paris, where he intended to meet Louis-Philippe and procure a formal refutation of the blood libel.

The king of the French had led an eventful life before coming to the throne during the revolution of 1830.[16] A war hero whose father had voted to execute his cousin Louis XVI, Louis-Philippe worked as a Swiss schoolmaster and toured the United States before spending the Napoleonic era in retirement in Twickenham. He never overcame his fear of exile and for many years steered a skillful path through the internecine politics of the July Monarchy. By 1847 he had become set in his ways. "The King has reached an age when he no longer accepts other people's observations," wrote his son François de Joinville. "We are confronting the Chambers with a detestable internal situation; and foreign affairs are no better. All this is the work of a King who wishes to govern but who lacks the strength to take a firm resolution."[17]

Nowhere was this tendency more marked than in foreign policy. Valuing peace above everything, Louis-Philippe had embraced the politics of nonintervention, placing an alliance with liberal Britain at the heart of his struggle for European recognition of his regime. Unlike France, Britain had other choices. Harmony alternated with periods of tension until Thiers's belief that war was a crucible for domestic stability precipitated a major international crisis in 1840. Palmerston's failure to keep the French informed of his negotiations with the Holy Alliance of Austria, Prussia, and Russia at this time reinforced suspicions of perfidious Albion—not just in Thiers, but in Louis-Philippe and his ambassador in London. That ambassador was Guizot, now the dominant force in the French government. He, too, supported the British alliance, but this policy sat uneasily with an Anglophobic public. Tensions reached a climax over the need to find marriage partners for Queen Isabella of Spain and her sister. The crisis confirmed Louis-Philippe's jaundiced view of Palmerston as "the enemy of my house."[18]

When Montefiore reached Paris a year later, the British ambassador "could only regret Sir Moses' inopportune arrival. The King was somewhat annoyed at the differences with England, and although Sir Moses might go direct and obtain an interview, still it might be difficult . . . to move the King . . . sufficiently to induce him to get Monsieur Guizot to take the matter up."[19] Guizot did not think much of Lord Normanby's blundering diplomacy, noting caustically, "he's a good fellow, but he doesn't understand our language."[20] Nor, presumably, did Montefiore, who was imperiously summoned to see him on the Sabbath—and walked there in the blistering midday sun only to be told: "His Lordship . . . had read over all my papers in respect of the declaration I wished the King to make; he believed it would be impossible to obtain it, and thought I must give up the idea."[21]

The British ambassador was not Montefiore's only contact in Paris; he found James de Rothschild infinitely more amenable. The Rothschilds had recently resumed their dominance of French finance, issuing major government loans in 1841, 1842, and 1844. James declared proudly that he saw all the ministers daily, complained directly to Louis-Philippe if he disliked their policies, and, "since he [the king] knows that *I have much to lose* and only desire peace, he has every confidence in me and pays attention to everything I tell him."[22] Within three days of Normanby's brush-off, Montefiore found himself face to face with Guizot.

Montefiore later recalled that the cerebral French prime minister maintained a thoroughgoing dislike for all Jews, and that he liked the Rothschilds least of all.[23] Guizot still welcomed Montefiore as an old London acquaintance and promised to take firm action in the East. Then, on August 9, James showed Montefiore a handwritten letter from the king promising to see him personally. Portly and amiable, Louis-Philippe listened attentively to Montefiore's address refuting the blood libel and stressing the duty of every European to spread civilization in the East.[24] His Majesty agreed graciously with everything, leaving Montefiore sublimely confident "that the great object he had at heart had been blessed with success."[25]

Even before the interview Guizot had written to the new consul in Damascus, demanding an explanation. Deploying a markedly different rhetoric from Palmerston, Guizot stated that the French government placed no faith in accusations that were clearly rooted in religious and ethnic rivalry—and expected its agents to toe the line. They should "refrain from the public manifestation of contrary opinions, and above all from inciting the Muslim authorities to persecute a whole people . . . on the basis of vague suspicions and without proof of any kind." When the consul suggested that Beaudin's actions were influenced by "a presentiment sadly only too well founded since the regrettable episode of Father Thomas," Guizot gave him short shrift. Stiffly stating that his earlier observations remained valid, he advised Vettier de Bourville to abide by these guidelines.[26]

Montefiore's jaunt across the Channel attracted the usual superlatives from the Board of Deputies, but he left at a critical moment in the struggle for Jewish rights.[27] Emancipation had made frustratingly slow progress since 1835, when David Salomons had been elected alderman of the City but remained unable to take his seat. After four years of litigation, Salomons begged the deputies to take his case to the House of Lords.[28] They refused, claiming that "it would be more expedient that relief should be sought by Legislative Enactment than by any further [legal] Appeal." Yet when Edward Dickett introduced a bill in the Commons to relieve Jews of their disabilities in municipal government, the deputies conspicuously failed to petition Parliament. Opponents like the archbishop of Canterbury felt able to state categorically: "the greater portion of Jews are perfectly indifferent about the Bill."[29]

Salomons returned to the fray in late 1843, when he dispatched two eloquent letters to the Tory prime minister, Sir Robert Peel. A long list of Jews had already filled distinguished offices, but until Parliament took action not one was eligible for election in even the humblest county town. When Peel procrastinated, Salomons returned to the hustings. This time the board was with him. Noting "the advancement of liberal feelings in all classes of the community," it deemed "the present period fitting to take measures for the removal of the civil disabilities of the Jews."[30] In February 1845 Montefiore and Goldsmid led rival deputations to confer with Peel over Salomons' reelection as alderman.[31] That July an Act for the Relief of Persons of the Jewish Religion elected to Municipal Offices passed into law.

Salomons' successful tactics were inspired by the campaign for Catholic emancipation. What had worked twice might work a third time. Motivated by a combination of familial pressure, communal rivalry, and *noblesse oblige*, Montefiore's nephew Lionel de Rothschild took the next obvious step: he was formally adopted as a Liberal candidate in the general election at the London Tavern on June 29, 1847. Six days later Montefiore convened a meeting to discuss what role the deputies should play.[32]

The upshot was curiously noncommittal. The board highly approved the efforts of Rothschild and other Jewish gentlemen to get elected, but saw no need for communal action. Seven deputies then volunteered to join Rothschild's electoral committee, and Montefiore set out almost immediately for France. It was a strange decision for the president of the board and the candidate's uncle. He returned from Paris to find Rothschild M.P. for the City of London and the country on tenterhooks about what would happen next.

In December 1847 the Whig prime minister, Lord John Russell, introduced a bill to remove parliamentary disabilities. The balance of public opinion had now shifted. Former opponents like Gladstone were willing to endorse emancipation, and some of the country's most influential newspapers did so too. But whereas the *Times, Morning Advertiser, Morning Chronicle,* and *Manchester Guardian* were all in favor, the *Standard, Morning Post,* and *Morning Herald* were still against. As in the 1830s, Jews turned to petitions and public agitation to influence the forthcoming vote. They had little difficulty getting the bill through the Commons. Even Sir Robert Peel announced his conversion to emancipation, noting among other things that Foreign Office backing for Montefiore's missions to Russia and Damascus would have been far more persuasive if it was generally known "that every ancient prejudice against the Jews had been extinguished" in Britain.[33]

The Lords were a different matter. On May 25, 1848, the Montefiores made their way to the Upper House with some trepidation. Judith took a seat in the gallery alongside her sister Hannah Rothschild; Montefiore watched the whole debate from a place near the throne. Lord Malmesbury later recalled that he had never seen the House so full as on this occasion, but the numbers did not bode well for the Jewish cause. Bishop after bishop rose to speak against the measure. The hostile atmosphere was epitomized by Sam Wilberforce, bishop of Oxford, who dwelt on the traditional Jewish hatred of Christianity before reminding their lordships that the Jews had killed Christ. Charlotte de Rothschild reported that Anthony and Mayer returned home "crimson in the face . . . they said the speeches were scandalous and I was advised not to read a word of them . . . Apparently, when the result of the vote was declared, a loud, enthusiastic roar of approval resounded."[34] Montefiore, too, found the debate "a painful excitement. The majority against us was thirty-five, much greater than was expected."[35] With emancipation still a distant dream, his mind turned once more to the East.

Montefiore's second trip to Palestine, in 1839, had consolidated his prestige among the Jews of the Holy Land, while his plans for Jewish agriculture attracted the attention of Christians and Jews. The events of 1840 had given renewed impetus to hopes for an imminent restoration to Palestine. The quickest to take up the challenge was Colonel Charles Henry Churchill. Dashing, religious, and more than a touch eccentric,

Churchill first encountered Montefiore at Malta in November 1840 when he called to offer his services as a courier to Damascus.[36] Montefiore entrusted him with copies of the sultan's *firman* and a box of letters and newspapers. In February 1841 Churchill entered the city with the rest of the Allied army.

Raphael Farhi, head of the Jewish community in Damascus and one of the liberated prisoners, saw Churchill's arrival as an opportunity to cement their recent triumph. On March 1 he held a grandiose reception in Churchill's honor, inviting Allied officers, the leading merchants of Damascus, and, of course, his fellow prisoners. It was a glittering occasion that enabled Farhi to show off his wealth and newfound influence. But Churchill saw greater potential.

Standing in the grand reception hall replete with mosaics, carpets, and immense chandeliers, he recalled that in their hour of need England had proved the Jews' truest friend. "May this happy meeting be looked upon as . . . a forecast of such a connection and alliance between the English and the Jewish nation as shall be honourable and advantageous to both," he continued. "May the hour of Israel's deliverance be at hand. May the approximation of Western civilization to this interesting land be the dawn of her regeneration, and of her political existence; may the Jewish nation once more claim her rank among the powers of the world!" His audience applauded with cries of "*Inshallah! Inshallah!* God grant it! In England will we place our trust!"[37]

In June 1841 Churchill wrote to Montefiore as president of the Board of Deputies. He believed it possible for Jews to regain sovereignty of Palestine if they could persuade the European powers to support their views: "Let the principal persons of their community place themselves at the head of the movement. Let them meet, concert and petition. In fact the agitation must be simultaneous throughout Europe . . . you would conjure a new element in Eastern diplomacy—an element which under such auspices as those of the wealthy and influential members of the Jewish community could not fail not only in attracting great attention and exciting extraordinary interest, but also of producing great events."[38]

His vision of a Jewish nation reborn in Palestine differed little from that of other restorationists. Inspired by the Damascus mobilization, however, his emphasis on collective Jewish action broke new ground.

Two months later Churchill left Damascus for England, where he presented Montefiore with a less ambitious plan. Noting the insecurity of life and property in Syria, Churchill speculated that if the country were safer, "Hundreds and thousands [of Jews] . . . would strain every effort to accomplish the means of living amongst those scenes rendered sacred by ancient recollections."[39] As an interim solution, he suggested that the British government could send a special representative to protect them. Montefiore eventually put these proposals to the deputies, who fell back on the well-worn excuse that the matter lay beyond their remit.

Nevertheless, Montefiore thought well enough of Churchill to entrust him with a small capital sum intended to provide low-interest loans of 500 or 1,000 piastres to Jews already living in the Holy Land.[40] Once Churchill reached Syria, his enthusiasm for Montefiore's microfinance initiative proved lackluster. His own views extended far beyond "the mere improvement of the condition of the Jews actually in this country."[41] He informed Montefiore that until the Jews of Europe took collective action to effect their restoration, spending money in Palestine was a waste of time. Churchill then purchased a Lebanese village, married a Syrian, and established a prosperous farm. When he suggested that Montefiore might invest in Lebanese agriculture, the latter observed: "[he] only writes when he wants anything."[42] Loewe was equally dismissive, adding: "I am afraid it will take him a long time to distribute your benevolent gift among the poor."[43]

Churchill's grandiose plans proved unappealing to the Anglo-Jewish establishment, but they did not go unremarked. Several German Jewish newspapers reported his speech in Damascus, and a precocious group of Jewish activists ensured that *Der Orient* took up the matter at greater length.[44] Back in 1836 the future editor of the *Jewish Chronicle*, Abraham Benisch, had joined with Moritz Steinschneider to form a secret student society in Prague.[45] Its goal was to propagate the return of Jews to Palestine. Two years later the two friends transferred their activities to Vienna, where they joined forces with Albert Löwy and Wilhelm Oesterreicher. Steinschneider even persuaded the editor of *Der Orient* to embrace the idea.

When Crémieux passed through Vienna on his way back from Alexandria in 1840, Benisch and Oesterreicher hastened to approach him. Crémieux was enthusiastic about their proposals and suggested that Montefiore was the man to take them up. Moving to London enabled Benisch and Löwy to provide *Der Orient* with a stream of articles promoting "the Restoration and Nationalisation of the Jewish People."[46] Thanks to Crémieux, Benisch also made contact with Montefiore, who presented him to William Young, the British consul in Jerusalem. At Young's request Benisch then prepared a memorandum on his plans for a Jewish colony in Palestine.

Like Christian restorationists, Benisch recognized that British financial and political support was essential for the success of his project; like them, he was confident it would be forthcoming. The colony would provide Britain with new markets and contacts thanks to Jewish commercial flair, promote the modernization of the Ottoman Empire in line with British foreign policy objectives, facilitate the propagation of European civilization, and reflect Britain's historic role as the "country where Protestantism has taken the deepest root." In short, the British imperial mission to spread Commerce, Civilization, and Christianity was tailor-made for Jews.[47]

Waiting in vain for a reply to his proposals, Benisch concluded despondently that nothing was to be expected in Britain unless German Jews did their bit. "I still see Montefiore fairly often," he wrote. "His predilection for the East continues unabated and with powerful incitement it would still be possible to arouse this inactive man . . . [But t]he phlegmatic Englishman needs much time to recover from his efforts during the Damascus Affair so that he is capable of exerting himself once more."[48]

Montefiore may have been halfhearted in his support for Benisch, but he remained deeply committed to Palestine. When John Ponsonby and his wife visited the Montefiores after returning from their posting in Constantinople, the two couples discussed the need to promote industry in the Ottoman Empire. Recalling his promise to replace the equipment that Israel Bak had lost in the sack of Safed, Montefiore dispatched a top-of-the-range printing press to the Holy Land.[49] In July 1842 the *Voice of Jacob* announced that a Hebrew book had recently been published in Jerusalem.[50] "Printing has, at all times, been the forerunner of improvement," it crowed. "Where printing is, there is an encouragement for reading: where there is reading, there are new ideas excited, there is life, there is progress."[51]

Arguably, this enthusiasm reflected the editor's *maskilic* agenda, not Montefiore's aims. By sending a beautiful Torah scroll along with the printing press, he made clear that he expected it to be used for religious publications. A correspondent of the *Voice* soon complained that "the Hebrew books lately printed in the East . . . are . . . not adapted for the instruction or social improvement of our brethren." It would make more sense to print books in Europe and send them to Jerusalem, "as in that case, we might be sure that necessary information would be circulated." Only after perusing an almanac produced in Jerusalem in 1843 did the *Voice* conclude with relief: "there is a safe influence at work there, and certainly not exhibiting those superstitious and one-sided views, with which our eastern brethren are so frequently reproached."[52]

These rumblings reflected wider concerns about the willingness of Jerusalem's Jews to embrace modernity.

In September 1842 Ludwig Philippson, editor of the *Allgemeine Zeitung des Judentums,* launched a dramatic appeal to establish a Jewish hospital in Jerusalem: the need for medical care was acute, and the insidious activities of conversionists could no longer be ignored.[53] Missionaries had been a growing presence in the city since the mid-1820s, although they did not make their first conversion until 1835. Until the early 1840s their relations with Jews remained ambiguous. Then the establishment of the Anglo-Prussian bishopric and a Protestant church, plans for a Jewish hospital, and the arrival of the well-qualified Dr. Edward Macgowan began to tip the balance.

Philippson's idea was timely, but as a well-known exponent of moderate religious reform he was not best placed to pursue it. The Rothschilds promised 100,000 francs if the hospital was built together with an industrial school, but Hirsch Lehren of Pekam refused to have anything to do with the proposals.[54] Fear of modernity lay at the heart of his opposition, which reflected a narrowly religious vision of Jewish settlement in the Holy Land as the vocation of a pious elite.

Montefiore took the missionary challenge more seriously. After promising money to Philippson's Jewish hospital, he dispatched a Jewish doctor and medical dispensary to Jerusalem.[55] This dispensary was the first modern Jewish charitable institution established in Jerusalem, and Dr. Simon Fränkel of Zülz was the first Western Jew to be formally employed in such an enterprise; his involvement represented a turning point in the transformation of the diaspora's traditional engagement with Palestine. By August 1843 Fränkel had already set to work. "He is very active and attentive, and has much to do," Macgowan reported. "His practice, however, has not relieved me of any portion of my own labours among the Jews."[56] With plans for the Christian hospital reaching fruition, a decent Jewish alternative seemed more essential than ever.

Yet most of those living in Jerusalem were no more enthusiastic about Philippson than Lehren. The Ashkenazim in the holy city retained close contact with their communities of origin in eastern Europe. All had chosen to live there for religious reasons, and some saw themselves quite consciously as refugees from the *Haskalah.* At a time when Russian Jews were fighting a bitter campaign against secular education, plans for an industrial school were inevitably controversial. Rather than tolerate such a monstrosity, the Perushim and Hasidim of Jerusalem began to explore alternatives. While the former hoped to expand their own society for visiting the sick, Israel Bak initiated a joint Hasidic-Sephardic venture.[57]

In July 1844 Montefiore received a letter signed by rabbis from both communities. "In consequence of an article printed in the *'Allgemeine Zeitung des Judenthums'* Sept. 11. 1842 the writers declined having anything to do with the Hospital, as an establishment conducted upon principles such as advanced by the author of the German Article, would be misleading them in the performance of religious duties." They urged Montefiore to "annihilate" Philippson's plans—and announced an alternative of their own.[58]

The alliance between Hasidim and Sephardim in Jerusalem solidified over the summer. In September 1844 Montefiore received a letter from Haim Abraham Gagin, the *Haham Bashi,* "stating the peace which now prevails at Jerusalem, the hospital which the Congregation will build is to be under the superintendance of Dr. Frankel, and Israel Drucker [Bak] made the architectural plan."[59] A copy of the regulations of the new hospital arrived by separate cover, along with a document signed by Israel Bak and Moshe Hazan appointing Montefiore and Judith "the patrons of the Hospital."[60]

Early in 1845 the first Jewish hospital in Jerusalem was up and running: windows and doors painted green, kitchen and washing facilities on the ground floor, four large wards opening off the terrace, and the whole in perfect repair.[61] Proudly, Israel Bak told the missionary Johann Nicolayson that "they now had no need of our hospital. And no excuse for going there." Nicolayson responded complacently that "there were sick Jews enough to fill both, and others besides." The *Voice of Jacob* was soon lamenting that although, "thanks to Sir Moses Montefiore," Jews had their own hospital and risked excommunication if they resorted to its rival, "Jews *will* go to that hospital, and *will* go to Dr. Macgowan, the Conversionists' physician." This rather overstated Montefiore's role in the initiative. Although he did form a fund-raising committee in December 1845, he remained a semidetached figure and did not move his own dispensary there until 1847.[62]

By this time, European ideas about the need to render at least some of the Jews in Palestine economically self-sufficient were beginning to find support. In May 1844 Judith had published the diaries she kept during their 1839 visit to Palestine. Her book became a central reference point in debates about productivization and was serialized in the *Univers Israélite.*[63] The main body of the text referred repeatedly to the desire of Jews to work and their ability to do so—but the *pièce de résistance* was undoubtedly the appendix, for which Loewe translated some of the let-

ters Montefiore had received at the time. Taking care to remove anything offensive to an educated European audience, Loewe deliberately
obscured Jewish proposals to employ Arab labor rather than work the
fields themselves.[64] His emphasis on Jewish agricultural work as a cure
for poverty in Palestine reflected wider debates about Jewish emancipation in Europe but undermined the spiritual logic behind *halukah*.

Lehren viewed the productivization agenda as blasphemous, but not
all devoutly observant Jews took this line. In late 1844 the visionary religious Zionist Rabbi Zvi Hirsch Kalischer wrote Montefiore "[o]n the
subject of Israel's return to the Holy Land" and subsequently requested
a copy of Judith's journal.[65] Even in Palestine, some Jews were open to
the idea of promoting industry. In the summer of 1844 Montefiore received several letters regarding the potential for cotton manufacturing.
Some went so far as to express limited support for Philippson. Mordechai Zoref, for instance, who asked Montefiore to forward a circular
outlining the need for both a hospital and a cotton factory, added that
"a school of trade . . . was also a great desideratum . . . but they do not
require the aid of a European teacher."[66]

Gradually these ideas made their way into the Jewish press. In February 1845 the *Voice of Jacob* reported that Rosenthal, a Prussian Jew
living in Jerusalem, had argued in *Der Orient* that some things were
"still more urgent than an hospital, and those are food, and the opportunities of earning it."[67] Like Montefiore's correspondents, he believed
that wool and cotton manufacturing was most likely to meet the community's needs.

To what extent this idea originated with Montefiore is an open question. When he brought three Jerusalem Jews to England to learn the art
of weaving, the men he chose were Rosenthal, Zoref, and Nisan, son of
Israel Bak. The three Jerusalemites spent much of 1845 in Preston and
Cotteral, where, Zoref claimed, they acquired a "thorough knowledge"
of the weaving trade.[68] Proudly, Montefiore announced his intention of
establishing a cotton factory in Jerusalem.[69] He was frustrated to discover that his protégés had delusions of grandeur and minds of their
own. "[I]t has given me much pain to find our Eastern people have been
corresponding with people in Manchester asking advice of them," he
complained to Loewe in early June. "I shall send for them back if I find
they are not attentive and so most certainly shall give them no introduction to anyone at Manchester. As to spinning machines and Power
looms, they will get none from me."[70]

The *Jewish Chronicle* thought the whole idea quixotic. In June 1846 it
reproduced a letter published in a German newspaper pointing out that
weaving was unlikely to prove profitable in Jerusalem given "the quan-

tity of goods made by that art imported here from England, Austria, and other states."[71] Indeed, the *Chronicle* claimed that "[t]he men who were sent to Preston . . . returned to London after three months' absence, were discarded, and went about begging from door to door. The owner of the manufactory at Preston himself ridiculed the idea, that men of that age and of such habits should be able to carry on a factory at Jerusalem!"[72]

In other respects, the visit was a success. Taking advantage of his presence in Europe, Nisan Bak visited his spiritual leader, Rabbi Israel of Sadgora, and persuaded him to appoint Montefiore *gabbai* (trustee) of the Volhynian Hasidim living in the Holy Land.[73] The breakaway faction of Perushim in Jerusalem had been the first to take such a step in 1839; Nisan Bak's initiative reflected a growing trend.

German Jewish newspapers first began casting doubt on Lehren's financial integrity in 1840.[74] Obdurately, the Dutchman refused to publish his accounts; he claimed disingenuously that "it might damage the Jewish interest, if it were known how much we donate annually to our brothers in Palestine." This stance failed to quell rumors of favoritism and mismanagement, prompting congregations in Britain, France, and Germany to seek an alternative to the traditional routes of *halukah*. Montefiore was the obvious choice.[75] At first, his role as financial intermediary was restricted to Western Jewish communities, but the mission to Russia expanded his sphere of influence and contacts. Shortly after Montefiore's return, the Jerusalem authorities wrote to him for what was probably the first time, acknowledging "the receipt of £1220 from the Holy Land Committee of Wilna."[76] The Perushim were the group most closely associated with Lehren, and the Vilna community had always been their major source of revenue. For Montefiore to act as their intermediary was a major coup. When even the chief rabbi of Warsaw decided to send the city's contributions via Montefiore, his position was assured.[77]

By 1847 suspicion of Lehren had reached the United States. In January a relative of Loewe in New York informed Montefiore that an elderly gentleman was sending him £60 by the latest steamer: "in consequence of complaints from the people of the Holy Land concerning his [Lehren's] unequally distributing the money there, they came here to a conclusion to send it to you."[78] The gentleman in question was Isaac Baer Kursheedt, president of the Hebra Terumot Hakodesh, a society dedicated to raising money for the Jews of Palestine. His decision to switch from Lehren to Montefiore received considerable publicity in the American Jewish press.[79]

Of course, Lehren remained an important figure. Yet the collapse of his fund-raising monopoly testified to the scale of the revolution shaking the Jewish world. Jewish newspapers had shattered the stranglehold of communal authorities, and nowhere was this phenomenon more apparent than in international affairs. The old networks still existed, but they were rapidly being superseded by the emergent public sphere. Through newspapers like the *Allgemeine Zeitung des Judentums* and the *Occident and American Jewish Advocate*, Jews all over the world could communicate with one another directly. The word of Lehren and his associates was no longer law, and those who depended on their bounty were no longer bound by their dictates. When Lehren wrote to Kursheedt in New York discrediting an emissary from Hebron, Kursheedt forwarded the letter to the editor of the *Occident*, who published it with a caveat. Without "throwing any doubt upon the pious labours of the Great philanthropist, Rabbi H. Lehren," the editor maintained "that the poor of Hebron had a right to call upon distant Israelites for voluntary aid, and we do not see any good policy in preventing their receiving it."[80] The readership of the Jewish press represented a new clientele for the Jews of Palestine, beyond the reach of established fund-raisers and wealthy beyond their wildest dreams. This was a public that Montefiore—not Lehren—was best placed to exploit.

Late in 1848 cholera swept Palestine. When the Anglo-Jewish authorities refused to take action, Montefiore launched an emergency appeal.[81] Regular lists of donors soon appeared in the *Jewish Chronicle*, but together they gave barely £200.[82] Meanwhile the crisis in the Holy Land grew worse. "We have no strength to nurse them," wrote the elders of the German congregation in Jerusalem despairingly; "many who have been stretched on a sick bed without support, without nursing, without care, without bread, and without water, have fallen victims to their disease."[83]

The missionary hospital added an extra dimension to this catastrophe. The religious authorities did what they could to stop Jews from going there, but the needs of the poor were simply too great. All the communities begged Montefiore to "devise a proper plan for a new JEWISH HOSPITAL" and to advertise their need as only he could: "Oh that you may publish our distress in every province and country, and appeal in that spirit of piety which distinguishes your character on behalf of a charity which is above every other . . . We . . . beseech you, the prince of the Land [of Israel], the man of Jerusalem, to plead our cause in the hearing of your friends, the wealthy inhabitants of England, the 'merchant princes' of the house of Rothschild, and to all the leading men of the Jewish captivity [diaspora]."[84] Even Judith, who gave regularly to the Jews of Palestine in her own name, was called upon to do her bit "among the women of Judah and Israel."[85]

In February 1849 Montefiore entertained the leading lights of London's Jewish community at dinner, along with several of his Evangelical friends. The sensation of the evening was Colonel George Gawler. He was delighted that the Montefiores would be setting out once more for Palestine and excited to add that he would be traveling with them.[86]

Ten years younger than Montefiore, Gawler had distinguished himself in the Peninsular War (1808–1814) and the Battle of Waterloo before he got religion and began "making a great cake [fool] of himself converting the men."[87] For the next twenty years Gawler served variously in Derbyshire, Ireland, and North America; made a name for himself as a military author; and was appointed second governor of South Australia in 1838. As a colonial administrator he proved effective but spendthrift: the population of the new colony tripled during his two years in office, but he ran an unauthorized deficit of £155,000. When the Board of Commissioners realized what he was up to, it sacked him without further ado.

Humiliated, Gawler found a new outlet for his religious and colonial enthusiasms. In 1845 he published a restorationist tract purportedly designed as a memorandum to the foreign secretary and boldly titled *Tranquillization of Syria and the East: Practical Suggestions in Furtherance of the Establishment of Jewish Colonies in Palestine, the Most Sober and Sensible Remedy for the Miseries of Asiatic Turkey.*[88] The central ideas were not particularly original, but Gawler's experience in South Australia gave him a firm grasp of practicalities. His "memorandum" elaborated on how to avoid "exciting the prejudices of the native population," the best arrangements for transporting Jewish emigrants and their baggage from England, and the need to time the settlers' arrival so they would be able to plant crops. Like Churchill before him, Gawler made contact with Montefiore, urging Jews to use their influence in the City and stressing *the real urgency of the case.*"[89]

Montefiore was intrigued by the proposal and the man behind it. Despite his frank loathing for the missionaries in Jerusalem, he nurtured close contacts with restorationist and Evangelical circles—even archconservatives, like Lord Ashley, who opposed emancipation. That very summer, Montefiore and Judith went out of their way to make friends with a similarly conservative figure: Charlotte Elizabeth Tonna, editor of the *Christian Ladies' Magazine* and the author of a conversionist novel. Tonna's views on Jews were well known, but she had raised more money on behalf of the Jews of Mogador in 1844 than anyone else, and she had

Colonel George Gawler,
c. 1843. (Photograph courtesy
of the State Library of South Aus-
tralia, SSLA B14428)

taken the lead in coordinating the protest against Nicholas I's Jewish policy. When Tonna arrived in Ramsgate to take the sea air the Montefiores paid a courtesy call. They invited their new acquaintance to East Cliff Lodge, where Montefiore delighted her by pointing across the sea from his library window in the direction of Jerusalem as they both repeated Isaiah's "glorious promises of Israel's future."[90]

As Tonna's health deteriorated rapidly, the Montefiores become devoted friends. When she set out on her final journey to Ramsgate from London, it was Montefiore who bade her farewell at the train station and handed her a basket of grapes. The Christian lady and the Jewish gentleman shared a love of the Old Testament and a faith in the return of the Jews to Israel. Yet Tonna never abandoned her conversionist instincts, and her last words were directed at the Montefiores. "Tell them that Jesus is the Messiah," she gasped before expiring.[91] Gawler had publicly disavowed any such agenda.[92] Montefiore's decision to travel with him to Palestine still implied a surprising sympathy with his ideas.

Gawler and the Montefiores arrived in Beirut on June 16, 1849, accompanied by Loewe and (for the first time) the Ramsgate ritual slaughterer. Judith's health had never really recovered from the trip to Russia, and a renewed bout of sickness delayed their departure by three weeks.[93] In

Beirut she suffered a relapse and was confined to her apartment for several days.[94] The heat was stifling, and the graves of several travelers who had died during quarantine did nothing to lift her spirits. Montefiore was equally gloomy. Gawler confided to his family that "[p]oor Sir Moses . . . was . . . very unwell last night and would not take even a cup of tea this morning. He is evidently very apprehensive of his own bodily condition . . . [his] strength has failed greatly."[95] But it would have been out of character not to continue, and the Montefiores did just that. Their first stop was Damascus, where Montefiore hoped to lay to rest the ghost of the blood libel.

As the largest and oldest town in Syria, Damascus was famed as a station on the pilgrims' road to Mecca and a cradle of Islam. Ten years earlier, the *Hatt-i Sherif* of Gülhane had proclaimed the transformation of the Ottoman Empire. Believing Ottoman renewal to be the best guarantee of British interests, Palmerston threw his weight behind the Tanzimat reforms. Like most Victorian diplomats, Consul Richard Wood in Damascus saw himself as an agent of progress (and British influence).[96] In February 1849 he had written to the British ambassador in Istanbul denouncing the exclusion of Jews and Christians from the provincial council of Damascus. Both groups had been represented on the council under Egyptian occupation, but "by dint of ill-treatment, the transfer of their salaries to Mahometan Members and the use of opprobrious language and epithets applied to them personally, they were compelled to withdraw." This development had deprived Jews and Christians of "the essential political privilege granted by the Sultan to his *Rayah* subjects" and left them "in total ignorance of the mass of Instructions transmitted by the Porte in their behalf."[97]

Wood's complaint did not go unnoticed, and in July he reported with satisfaction that the injustice had been overturned.[98] But this kind of British intervention was appreciated neither by the French seeking to retain their traditional influence in Syria, nor by officials concerned to protect Ottoman sovereignty and the Muslim population at large. When Montefiore arrived in Damascus two weeks later, he found the delicate pattern of relations between Muslims, Christians, and Jews in a state of flux.

He came with the aim of removing the epitaph that still adorned the supposed tomb of Father Tommaso, asserting that he had been killed by the Jews. The visit evoked painful memories and did nothing to ease the religious tensions. While the principal of the Capuchins regretted he could do nothing to help Montefiore, the French consul proclaimed a grand mass in Father Tommaso's honor. This calculated insult was aimed not just at Montefiore but also at Wood, a key player in the strug-

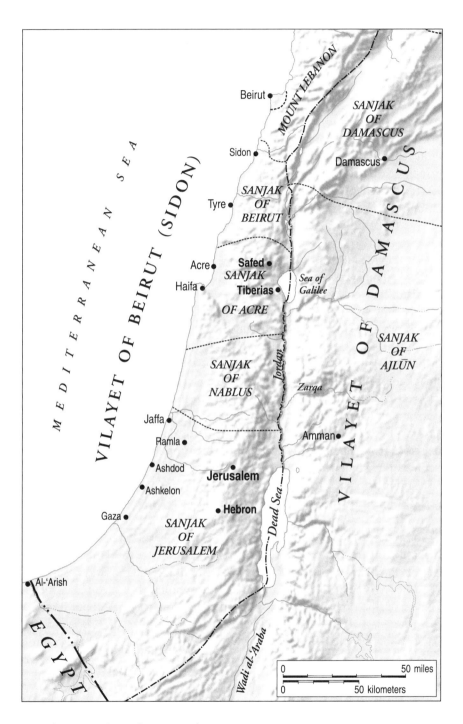

MEDITERRANEAN SEA

Beirut

MOUNT LEBANON

SANJAK
OF
DAMASCUS

Sidon

Damascus

SANJAK
OF
BEIRUT

Tyre

VILAYET OF BEIRUT (SIDON)

Acre

Safed

SANJAK

Tiberias

Sea of
Galilee

Haifa

OF ACRE

VILAYET OF DAMASCUS

Jordan

SANJAK
OF
NABLUS

SANJAK
OF
AJLŪN

Jaffa

Zarqa

Ramla

Amman

Ashdod

Jerusalem

VILAYET OF DAMASCUS

Ashkelon

Gaza

Hebron

Dead Sea

SANJAK
OF
JERUSALEM

Al-'Arish

EGYPT

Wadi al-'Araba

0   50 miles

0   50 kilometers

Palestine in the mid-nineteenth century

gle for influence in Syria.[99] Only the joyful prospect of his third pilgrimage to Jerusalem could compensate Montefiore for this crushing lack of
success.

If the British consul was to be believed, he was doomed to disappointment. Writing to Palmerston after Montefiore had left Jerusalem, James
Finn reported that the Englishman had "announced everywhere that his
principal object was to ameliorate the condition of his people by the
establishment of schools and trades, and by affording medical relief,
among themselves and by themselves." But the Jews had resisted his attempts to conduct a second population census, and their opposition to
the proposed schools was even more entrenched. Indeed, it had been
Finn's "painful lot to overhear and to hear repeated numerous jests . . .
applied to Sir Moses' own European costume and infringements of Tal-
mudism."[100]

This view of the situation was not entirely accurate. Montefiore's desire to promote industry and modern education in Palestine was undercut by the fact that he continued to give alms to the poor in the traditional fashion.[101] Conversely, Jewish opposition to anything that
smacked of the *Haskalah* did not necessarily extend to productivization.
Thus a long letter from the leaders of the Ashkenazi communities did
not oppose Montefiore's efforts to promote greater economic activity.
The Ashkenazi authorities simply suggested that cotton factories would
be more promising than agriculture or vocational training, given the difficulties Jewish craftsmen faced finding work and the deteriorating security situation. Plans for modern education were a different matter altogether. "We know he means well for his people," they wrote,

> but . . . it is common knowledge that people who left their country and
> family and occupation in order to study Torah in the Holy Land and
> work in it naturally wish to bring up their children in the ways of Torah,
> and in particular the Russian immigrants among us . . . who . . . still re-
> member the time when the command came from the Tsar about learning
> the language of the land . . . How many cries and fasts our brothers made
> in response to this decree, and how many people smuggled their children
> to other countries and in particular to the Holy Land, and . . . how can
> we and our children bring ourselves to agree to establish schools, which
> in our opinion and experience are a pitfall to the house of Israel, which
> G-d forbids, removing one from the way of eternal life and carrying him
> after the pleasures and nonsense of this world . . . we . . . saw with our
> own eyes the evil that the children of Israel found in the large cities of the

land of Russia, and if we too will accept such schools here, we will be jeered at by our brothers in the diaspora.[102]

This self-conscious, programmatic language demonstrated the impact of the culture war in the Ashkenazi heartlands of eastern Europe. It pointed away from a world in which religious observance could be taken for granted, toward a future in which those who clung to the old ways were forced to mobilize behind an increasingly inflexible and radical fundamentalism. It was in striking contrast to the more open-minded approach taken by the relatively Westernized German and Dutch Congregation in Jerusalem, who showed a certain sympathy for Montefiore's educational ideas.[103]

Despite their differences, however, almost every Jewish organization in the Holy Land recognized Montefiore's potential as a fund-raiser. The Sephardim and the Ashkenazim, the Perushim, and the Hasidim of the four holy cities all entrusted either Montefiore or Judith with the formal authority to act in Europe and America on their behalf.[104] This flood of letters of authorization was instigated by Mordechai Zoref. Having promised Montefiore in London "to try hard regarding this issue with all the congregations," he realized that it was now the moment to act.[105]

If Consul Finn knew of these developments, he chose to keep silent. His own relations with the Jews of Jerusalem were embroiled in controversy, and it was in his interest to present them as fanatics to his superiors. Finn was a devout Evangelical restorationist, deeply committed to the project of converting Jews in Palestine. His beautiful and assertive young wife, Elizabeth, daughter of the prominent missionary Alexander McCaul, was just the same. Both were genuinely committed to Jewish welfare, and since both could communicate in a multitude of European and oriental languages they were in a position to put this concern to good use. But Finn was a quarrelsome man with an independent streak. His stocky figure and dashing moustache disguised a rash, domineering character that made him many enemies during the seventeen years he spent in Palestine.[106]

In 1840 Sultan Abdul Mecid had rejected Palmerston's proposal to promote Jewish settlement in Palestine and the rest of the Ottoman Empire. But Palmerston did not abandon his vision of Jews as an engine for progress, and in April 1841 he issued a general circular to British agents in the Ottoman Empire. Noting that they were "not authorized to interfere officially with the Local Authorities, except in favor of those Jews

who might be [legally] entitled to British protection," Palmerston nevertheless urged that "upon any suitable occasion" they "make known to
the Local Authorities that the British Government feels an interest in the
welfare of the Jews in general, and is anxious that they should be protected from oppression; and that the Porte has promised to afford them
protection, and will certainly attend to any representations which Her
Majesty's Ambassador at Constantinople may make to it on these matters."[107] Aberdeen, who succeeded Palmerston as foreign secretary in
1841, substantially qualified this statement.[108] But Palmerston's guidelines remained operative, and when he returned to the Foreign Office,
Finn took up the matter.

In March 1847 Finn sent Palmerston a copy of his original instructions and asked if the principles outlined would permit him to extend
official British protection to Russian and Austrian Jews, who were often
disowned by their consuls once their temporary passports expired. It
transpired that whereas the Austrian consul-general was happy to act
on behalf of all Austrian Jews in Palestine irrespective of their legal status, his Russian counterpart, Konstantin Basily, believed that the tsar
would be delighted to lose his shiftless Jewish population. Cautiously,
Palmerston suggested that if Consul Basily actually volunteered the
transfer of Russian Jews to British protection, Finn could go ahead. Basily was soon on the point of surrendering roughly 800 Russian Jewish
protégés to the British—a decision that flew in the face of longstanding
political rivalry over the protection of religious minorities in the Middle
East. In June 1849, however, Basily began to voice unease about the
proposals, claiming that Jews were horrified at the prospect of finding
themselves at the mercy of the Evangelical Finn.[109]

The British consul was indignant.[110] But he knew perfectly well what
all the fuss was about. Earlier that year Mendel Diness, an Austrian Jew
intending to convert to Christianity, had applied to Finn for British protection—which the latter was happy to grant.[111] When Finn used his
authority to sequester Diness' Jewish wife and son in the British consulate at Jaffa, the result was mayhem. Ashkenazi Jews mobbed the consulate, while their leaders applied to anyone and everyone for help. Finn
argued speciously that Diness was no different from any other British
Jew under his protection; in reality, he was hoping to convert Mrs. Diness and her child as well. She, meanwhile, faced an agonizing dilemma:
if she chose to stay with her husband, she would be ostracized by the
Jewish community forever; if she chose to divorce him, she would lose
her son for good.

The crisis dragged on for months, and Montefiore's imminent arrival
added to the tension. After a particularly grueling episode, one Jew

"Jaffa, looking North," by David Roberts, in The Holy Land, Syria, Idomea, Arabia, Egypt & Nubia, *vol. 2 (London, 1855), plate 62. (By permission of the Bodleian Library, University of Oxford: Mason HH90)*

warned Finn darkly: "Now . . . we know what is in your heart, and [we] will take care that Sir Moses Montefiore, and Sheriff Solomons shall know it, that they may tell the Queen and Parliament." Niven Moore, the acting consul-general in Beirut, was himself a committed Protestant with a record of supporting missionary activity. When Montefiore appeared in July 1849, Moore did his best to smooth things over by presenting the proposed transfer of Russian Jews in the best possible light.[112]

Montefiore was a patriotic Englishman. He had received endless appeals from Jews in other parts of the Ottoman Empire for British protection, and his encounter with the harsh realities of Jewish life in Russia and Poland hardly predisposed him to see the tsar's agents as fit custodians of his brethren in the Holy Land. Moore reported that he was "delighted" to hear of the new situation, "[b]ut should his suspicion once be roused that there is an intention of making the arrangement subservient to conversion, I am persuaded that he would be the first to encourage the Jews to accept it."[113] Personally, Montefiore was horrified by the tragedy that had engulfed the Diness family, but he still endorsed the transfer plan.

By the end of 1849 the British consulate in Jerusalem had assumed responsibility for roughly 1,000 Russian and Austrian Jews. Even before the transfer was completed, Moore had resolved a nine-year dispute in their favor, reducing the tax burden of the Jews in Safed by some 30,000 piastres a year.[114] News of this welcome development no doubt consoled Montefiore for what was on balance a very mixed trip.

But Montefiore was tenacious. His name was forever linked to the refutation of the blood libel, and he refused to let sleeping dogs lie. He and Judith barely had time to recover from the expedition to Palestine before they set off again to Frankfurt to consult Amschel Rothschild about the Damascus epitaph.[115] Two months later, Montefiore wrote to Amschel's brother James in Paris, urging him to persuade the French government to have the incriminating epitaph removed.[116] Writing effusively on her husband's behalf, Betty de Rothschild explained that James could hardly approach the pope on a matter of minor importance when he had just obtained important concessions "regarding the civil liberty of our brothers in the Papal States."[117] And so, with Palmerston's backing, a disheartened Montefiore sent a personal appeal to Louis-Napoleon Bonaparte, president of the Second French Republic. Louis-Napoleon eventually granted him a discreet but sympathetic interview.[118] But the Damascus Affair was no longer news, and the future Napoleon III had other things on his mind. If Catholics in Europe and the Middle East continued to believe that Father Tommaso had been "murdered by the Jews of Damascus," then Montefiore and Judith were the only ones who really cared. Nor was Betty wrong in thinking that their preoccupation with the damning epitaph was primarily "a question of amour propre."[119]

Failure is always disheartening. By the spring of 1850, an uncharacteristically querulous note had begun to enter Montefiore's correspondence with Loewe. "[T]he accompanying letters have reached me and no doubt some of them require answers," he wrote in March; "pray do the needful for me I am almost worn out, and find the fatigue too great to continue much longer, so numerous a correspondence while you were near me it was done without anxiety on my part it is different now. If I could get a Committee to believe me I should be happy."[120]

This claim was disingenuous: at sixty-five Montefiore showed no signs of retiring. David Salomons and Lionel de Rothschild were both well placed to replace him at the Board of Deputies, but "the Pride of Israel" had no intention of standing down for his younger (and more liberal) relatives. Personal prestige gave him a peculiarly firm grip on the machinery of communal power. Even so, he found his authority undercut by broader social trends.

Anglo-Jewry was beginning to outgrow its immigrant origins: most Jews were native born and proud of it.[121] Nearly half the Jews in London lived on the breadline, but their grinding poverty disguised a certain change of status. Where once they had been peddlers, now they scraped a living by making and selling the items their fathers had hawked: slippers and caps, watches, shoes and umbrellas, recycled glass and patched old clothes. For some this change of status brought prosperity. In the 1820s, Montefiore and the Rothschilds moved to the West End as a badge of gentility; by the 1850s, several thousand Jews had joined them. A smattering had always made a living from supplying the navy, and many of the old port congregations were still flourishing. Something other than profit brought the new Jewish middle classes to the seaside. As they strolled along the pier at Brighton or took the waters in genteel resorts like Bath and Cheltenham, a whole generation of synagogues followed in their wake.

Elsewhere the rise and fall of Jewish communities reflected the changing patterns of commerce. Jews deserted county towns as they subsided into rural tranquility and settled instead in the great provincial cities of Victorian England; by the 1850s Birmingham, Liverpool, and Manchester all boasted communities of well over 500. Just as the English middle classes had chafed at the dominance of the landed elite and the archaic political geography of the House of Commons, so the rising Jewish middle classes began to question the authority exercised by a few wealthy City families through their own Board of Deputies.[122]

No one symbolized the rule of this traditional elite like Montefiore.[123] By 1850 there were perhaps 35,000 Jews living in Britain and some forty-three provincial congregations. Yet roughly a third of the twenty-nine deputies elected that year were members of Montefiore's extended family, no less than seven belonged to the small but wealthy Sephardi community, and only two represented synagogues outside London.[124] When he first became president in the mid-1830s, Montefiore had signaled the emergence of a dynamic new generation of communal leadership. Nathan Rothschild was dead now, and Isaac Goldsmid had thrown in his lot with the hated Reformers. Only Montefiore remained at the helm: an aging but childless patriarch, so set in his ways that he still wore the huge white neckcloth, high-collared coat, and frilled shirt-fronts fashionable twenty years earlier.[125] A glance was enough to suggest that he no longer represented change but stability—or stagnation.

In the immediate aftermath of the first emancipation campaign, Isaac Lyon Goldsmid had famously indicted the Board of Deputies as undemocratic, unrepresentative, and inactive.[126] Fifteen years later, anglicization, gentrification, and the rise of provincial Jewry gave this critique greater force. So far, Montefiore had successfully defended his power base. He refused to open meetings of the board to the press; rejected proposals for proper communal statistics as the basis for a more interventionist social agenda; and resisted calls from the self-consciously antiestablishment Manchester New Hebrew Congregation to make the board more efficient, transparent, and democratic by timing meetings to facilitate provincial involvement and establishing an executive committee to take charge of urgent affairs.[127]

This position was increasingly untenable. In 1852 the influential journalist William Rathbone Greg commented perceptively that public meetings and the press were fast encroaching on Parliament as the central arena for political debate in the country: "Every man has become a politician . . . [and] the country often takes precedence of the Legislature, both in the discussion and decision of public affairs."[128] Middle-class Jews were beginning to flex their political muscles in a national context. They were hardly likely to accept exclusion from communal politics indefinitely. Pressure from below was already forcing synagogues up and down the country to revise their oligarchic constitutions; disgruntled elements in Liverpool and Manchester had even founded rival congregations.[129] The language of reform current in British domestic politics was being transposed into an Anglo-Jewish key.

In many ways, Montefiore had lost touch with the priorities of the younger generation. While his nephews David Salomons and Lionel de Rothschild continued chipping away at British resistance to Jewish emancipation, he was happy to let progress take its course. If Judaism itself was under attack, Montefiore was always the first to take action—deluging the Board of Health with correspondence when it looked as if legislation designed to reduce cholera would stop Jews' being buried according to religious law.[130] Otherwise he seemed more concerned with suppressing Reform than with the battle for Jewish political rights.[131]

In 1851, for instance, the Board of Deputies had backed an appeal from the Manchester Jews' School to lobby for state funds to be directed toward Jewish primary education. Even Catholics now had access to government education funds, and Rothschild's election to Parliament transformed the political climate. At first it looked as if the issue would be resolved with a minimum of fuss.[132] But Montefiore could not resist exploiting the situation for his own purposes. He unilaterally took steps to ensure that only schools recognizing the religious authority of the chief rabbi and the Board of Deputies would be eligible for funds.[133] The aim was—flagrantly—to exclude the Reformers and reinforce his own authority. This was a step too far for Salomons and Rothschild, who used their influence with the Jewish Free School and the Jews' Hospital Committee to force Montefiore to back down.

At least one former deputy saw the episode as part of a wider conspiracy to subvert Jewish "liberties and independence." Many others thought the proceedings of the board "a matter of notoriety." News that Montefiore had threatened his resignation prompted even the *Allgemeine Zeitung des Judentums* to take notice. To those already dissatisfied with the board and its leadership, the controversy was like a red rag before a bull. One correspondent of the *Jewish Chronicle* put the matter in a nutshell when he asked: "does the Board as at present constituted, *truly* represent the entire Jewish body? . . . We must demand a reform to *our* Parliament—viz. the Board of Deputies—so that it may act in accordance with those liberal and enlightened principles which ought to guide all men in the nineteenth century." It so happened that the board's triennial elections were due shortly. When four provincial Jewish communities elected members of the Reform synagogue as their representatives, over a decade of smoldering resentment finally burst into flames.[134]

Montefiore's unbending attitude to the Reformers had always provoked criticism. There had been numerous attempts at Bevis Marks to repeal the *herem* (excommunication), but the shifting loyalties of the Jewish press reflected a wider change of heart.[135] In 1845 Benjamin Elkin, a leading member of London's Reform synagogue, declared complacently that the initial "acerbity of feeling" was now behind them.[136] The Reformers were simply too wealthy and influential to be ignored indefinitely. Before the decade was out, even Judith and Montefiore were working alongside them for the same charities.[137] Marriages had taken place between the two parties, and, as David Salomons commented dryly, when one of Montefiore's nephews married the daughter of a Reformer both "Baron de Goldsmid and Sir Moses had attended at the wedding ceremony, and had acted as godfathers."[138] Nor were the religious differences as glaring as they had been. With the exception of the Reformers' refusal to celebrate two days of festivals, the *Laws and Regulations* issued by the new chief rabbi in 1847 brought the practices of the two communities broadly into line.[139]

None of these developments made the election of four Reform deputies any more palatable. Montefiore was used to controlling the board through sheer force of personality, but in 1853 he faced an unprecedented situation: twenty-nine provincial communities had elected their own representatives, most for the very first time.[140] Emboldened by their victory over Jewish education, Salomons and the Rothschilds resolved to challenge their uncle's might. Arguably, they had little choice. They could hardly continue to claim seats in the House of Commons when hard-liners in their own community refused elected religious dissidents the very same right.

Like the opponents of Anglo-Jewish emancipation, Montefiore put religious conviction (and personal bitterness) before democratic principle. When three of the freshly elected Reform deputies arrived to attend their first board meeting, he responded in the most insulting terms.[141] "I observe that certain strangers have entered this room," Montefiore declared loudly to the cheers of the orthodox party, "and during their presence no business can be proceeded with. I do not know these strangers, but I call upon them to leave the room; and I rely on those around supporting me, and I am fully prepared to take upon myself the responsibility of sending for the police."

Pandemonium followed as deputies on both sides clamored to express themselves; the noise was so deafening that none could be heard. An element of farce entered the proceedings when a precipitate deputy summoned a policeman, and Montefiore eventually saw no option but to vacate the chair. His withdrawal did not stop more progressive deputies from trying to address the meeting, but whenever one of the Rothschilds rose to speak the hard-liners shouted him down with cries of "No Chairman!" When David Hesse from Manchester proposed Salomons as an alternative, Montefiore declared the meeting over and promptly fled the room.

These scenes of undignified chaos brought everyone to his senses: thereafter nothing could have exceeded the courtesy displayed by all sides. The board met again three months later to reconsider the matter. Twenty-three voted in favor of admitting the Reform deputies and twenty-three against. Speaking for the progressives, Salomons argued that the 1841 constitution had intended "to separate the Board from the religious part of the question. Had not the Board long since mixed itself up with these religious quarrels, the peace question would ere this have been settled." Louis Cohen put the case for the hard-liners, declaring: "He was ready too eat, drink, and trade with these gentlemen [the Reform deputies], and with the members of their congregation; but he would not join with them in any religious act; and therefore, considering them disqualified, he could not vote for their admission." The deciding vote lay with Montefiore as president; he used it to keep the Reformers out.[142]

A very public spat between Montefiore and Salomons followed this showdown.[143] Ostensibly, the two friends quarreled over arcane questions of procedure. The subtext was that Montefiore and the other Sephardi deputies had carried their private feud into Anglo-Jewish public

Sir David Salomons, the first Jewish sheriff, alderman, and lord mayor of the City of London; ceremonial portrait by S. A. Hart, c. 1856. (Courtesy of the Guildhall Art Gallery, City of London)

life. Other criticisms were more personal. Montefiore's fellow deputy Lazarus Simon Magnus described his conduct at the meeting as "such a decided act of partizanship, that it is nearly equivalent to a resignation of your chair as president."[144] David Jonassohn, one of the excluded Reformers, referred obliquely to Montefiore's treatment of his brother Horatio as proof of his "vindictive spirit" and "the littleness of Sir Moses Montefiore's mind."[145] The *Allgemeine Zeitung des Judentums* was even more damning, declaring that in outlawing freedom of conscience Montefiore had placed himself on a level with the persecutors of the Jews.[146] The hard-liners were jubilant, of course, but the whole experience had been utterly draining.[147] In February 1854 Montefiore collapsed while on holiday in the bleak and chilly beach resort of Scarborough.[148] He was confined to his bed for forty-three days. The crisis was over by the time he returned in late April; its legacy would last for years.[149]

Chapter 11

The Crimean War and After

Some two years earlier—at ten minutes to eight on the morning of June 21, 1852—Montefiore had arrived punctually at a London railway station to greet His Highness Mohammed Said Pasha, crown prince of Egypt. Ten years younger than his nephew Abbas, who had succeeded Mehmed Ali in 1848, the colossally fat and indolent Said had made a place for himself in Egyptian politics as a magnet for the opposition.[1] Montefiore had cultivated Said during his visit to Alexandria in 1840, when the prince was just a plump, unprepossessing teenager. He now found himself playing host to a leading member of the Egyptian royal family and his vast personal entourage: Said's political adviser, the British railway engineer Mr. Galloway, two physicians, a secretary, four Mamelukes, and a quantity of servants.

The next two weeks passed in a daze of activity.[2] When he was not busy with the Turkish ambassador, exchanging courtesies with the queen and Prince Albert, or indulging his penchant for military reviews, the thirty-year-old prince lounged about chatting with his hosts, drinking coffee, and smoking his beloved water pipe. Montefiore must have been quite worn out by all this frivolity: running down the Thames to Gravesend in a luxurious screw steamer, touring the Royal Observatory, and accompanying his guest to watch the troops at Hyde Park, Woolwich, and Wormwood Scrubs. Judith, meanwhile, played the gracious society hostess. Said repeatedly assured the Montefiores that their "dinners were better than any he had eaten" and "that he was more comfortable with us than he had been anywhere else since his arrival in England." Montefiore found him "very kind, good tempered and affable" but also "somewhat of a spoiled child."[3]

Visiting oriental dignitaries were a perennial excitement in Victorian London, and an endless stream of ambassadors and politicians left cards in Park Lane. The pasha must have added considerably to Montefiore's consequence—but we cannot begin to guess why this Muslim prince chose to stay with the country's leading Jew rather than with a more mainstream member of the British establishment with interests in the East. Said's visit created a special relationship between Montefiore and the Egyptian royal house, but it suggests that this relationship was already longstanding. Montefiore, at least, had a clear agenda. He hoped that Said would "be a friend to our co-religionists in Egypt and the Holy Land when he becomes Viceroy of Egypt," that he would "remember the kindness and attention shown to him by the British Government as well as by individuals, and that he may, whenever in his power, serve the British interest, and befriend my brethren in the East."⁴ He must have been delighted when his troublesome houseguest acceded to the throne only two years later at a time of renewed international interest in the Eastern Question and the plight of Eastern Jews.

The Crimean War (1853–1856) demonstrated the symbiosis between politics and religion in the Eastern Question.⁵ This was a war fought over the rights of Catholics in the Christian holy places of Jerusalem and Bethlehem and the rights of Orthodox Christians living under the sultan; but the issues at stake had very little to do with Christianity, and both sects served as proxies in the struggle for mastery of the Middle East. What began as rivalry between Orthodox Russia and Catholic France over influence in the Holy Land quickly escalated into a full-fledged great-power conflict when the Tsar Nicholas I occupied the Danubian Principalities of Moldavia and Walachia. Unable to contemplate the dismemberment of the Ottoman Empire by the Russians, Britain and France sent a fleet to defend Constantinople in January 1854. On March 28 they formally entered the fray.

The day before this momentous development, Ludwig Philippson published the first in a major series of articles about Jews in the East. They had once been renowned for their wealth and culture, but the "terrible, stultifying, unlimited, dishonest rule of the Rabbis" had created the conditions for tragic decline. The war rendered Christian emancipation inevitable; the future of Jews was less secure. Since the rabbis were bigoted and obstructive, it was for their rich brethren in Europe to intervene.⁶

Jewish leaders in Britain and France needed no persuasion. The Damascus Affair had been the first instance of diplomatic intervention in the Jewish question in the name of "humanity" and "civilized" values; it set a precedent that encouraged Eastern Jewish communities to turn to Britain for support. What this meant in practice varied from consul to consul. Even with Palmerston's explicit support for Jewish relief in the Ottoman Empire, formal diplomatic intervention remained the privilege of those Jews legally recognized as British protégés. In the 1840s, Montefiore and British Evangelicals lobbied their government on a case-by-case basis. By 1853 the habit of intervention had become ingrained in Britain and was beginning to make headway in France.

The nexus between French consuls and local Christians in Syria ensured that throughout the 1840s French representatives in Syria lent a sympathetic ear to the blood libel. Since France traditionally saw itself as the protector of Eastern Catholics, defending Jewish rights became an important site for strengthening alliances between French liberals and acculturated Jewish leaders.[7] In Britain, the imperial ideology of commerce, Christianity, and civilization was underpinned by a broad consensus in favor of exporting civil and religious liberty. In France, foreign policy became a battleground in the struggle between ultramontane Catholics and anticlericals. It was in this context that conservative Catholic writers portrayed the Crimean War as a "holy crusade," while secularists sought to reframe it as a struggle between barbarism and civilization. Grasping the implications of this polemic for the status of Jews as French citizens, the Consistoire Central des Israélites de France appealed to Emperor Napoleon III, recalling France's historic commitment to Jewish rights and urging him to promote Jewish emancipation in Constantinople.[8] It received no reply.

Anglo-Jewish lobbyists were more successful. Like Palmerston before him, Foreign Secretary Clarendon believed that Jewish emancipation would reinforce British efforts to prop up the Ottoman Empire. He was happy to oblige when the Rothschilds (and later the Board of Deputies) pressed for formal assurances on behalf of Jews in the East.[9] Underlining the implicit connection between Jewish rights and British foreign policy, Clarendon instructed Stratford "to use your best endeavours to promote the objects stated in the Jewish Memorial [regarding Ottoman Jewish emancipation], and in the letter from Sir M. Montefiore [regarding the right of Jews to own land], as I conceive that the attainment of those objects would equally conduce to the interests of the Porte and of the Jews in the East."[10] In practice, of course, this was something of a red herring, since Islamic law made no distinction between Christians and Jews, only between Muslims and other peoples of the Book. But the publicity given these initiatives suggests that they were conducted with at least one eye to European public opinion. Both Montefiore and Philippson had greater things in mind.

Montefiore's plans for the Jews of Palestine had made little progress during his recent visit to Jerusalem, but his companion, George Gawler, returned filled with visionary zeal. At first glance, Gawler's lectures were merely a continuation of his earlier activities.[11] He and Montefiore remained in close touch. "I have so much to say to you respecting the Affairs of the East, the Jewish Hospital & Colonel Gawler's intended publication that I am most anxious to pay you a visit," Montefiore wrote Loewe in December 1849.[12] The two men were so close that when the guests at the annual dinner of the Portsmouth and Portsea Hebrew Benevolent Institution rose to drink Montefiore's health, Gawler took it upon himself to reply. He praised his friend's efforts to improve Jewish-Christian relations and commended to the meeting "an object of which he knew Sir Moses Montefiore took a very great interest. He alluded to the rendering of assistance to their destitute brethren in Palestine (hear, hear)."[13]

This emphasis on transdenominational harmony underpinned their collaboration. In his 1853 pamphlet, *Syria and Its Near Prospects,* Gawler produced four proofs to support his assertion that the return of the Jews to Palestine was already under way: first, the current explosion in human knowledge; second, the "almost complete inversion of the state of feelings which so long subsisted between Christians and Jews"; third, the depopulated and war-torn state of Syria; and fourth, the Jews themselves, who had finally begun to be "wisely, practically, and scripturally willing" to return to their own land. In all this he attributed a critical role to "that expansive-minded, and large-hearted man, Sir Moses Montefiore."[14] Gawler held Montefiore largely responsible for the emergence of three rival groups dedicated to renewing the Jewish presence in the Holy Land—and declared his firm belief that only if Jews and Christians worked together would this ever come to pass. A maverick handful of messianic Jews nurtured similar ideas.

In June 1852 Yehudah Alkalai, an Ottoman Jew from Sarajevo who had studied in Jerusalem before being nominated rabbi in the Hungarian town of Semlin (Zemun), wrote to the *Jewish Chronicle* refuting rumors that he was "a clandestine Mohamedan missionary." "How such trash is directed at me, I am at a loss to guess," he protested angrily, before elaborating his view that the rulers of the earth were destined to bring about the redemption. Convinced that Abdul Mecid, the present ruler of Palestine, was "one of the shepherds, a principal man, mentioned by the Prophet Micah," Alkalai announced that he had come to London to urge "the influential men of Israel" to take action. God would incline the hearts of the nations of the earth toward them, and with their support an appeal to the sultan would surely meet with success.[15]

As aspiring English gentlemen, the members of the Mahamad at Bevis

Marks were embarrassed by Alkalai's prophetic enthusiasm and advised the Beth Din to ignore him. Rabbi David Meldola even inserted a midrash into the *Jewish Chronicle* reminding the house of Israel to maintain the traditionally passive stance of Jews in the diaspora and to expect redemption through God not man. Montefiore kept quiet, but his fellow deputy Solomon Sequerra was enthused by Alkalai. Together with the journalist Abraham Benisch, he proceeded to establish an Association for Promoting Jewish Settlement in Palestine. War in the East made this a timely initiative. Sequerra and a group of like-minded Christians founded the Palestine Land Company as soon as Britain entered the conflict. Its remit was to settle some 100,000 Jews in Palestine, and its shares were priced reasonably to attract the "working man."[16]

Indeed, to many it seemed that the war resurrected the possibilities that had hovered so tantalizingly during the crisis of 1840. In June 1854 Lord Ashley, now earl of Shaftesbury, renewed his own efforts to hasten the return of Jews to Palestine. "All the East is stirred," Shaftesbury confided in his diary in terms reminiscent of the future Zionist slogan; "the Turkish Empire is in rapid decay . . . [and] Syria is 'wasted without any inhabitant' . . . There is a country *without a nation,* and God now, in his wisdom and mercy, directs us to *a nation without a country.*"[17] Eager to seize the moment, Shaftesbury urged Clarendon to use Britain's newfound influence to promote Jewish landholding in Syria and other parts of the Ottoman Empire. He had no idea that Montefiore was thinking along the same lines and wrote asking him how Jews would respond. But while Shaftesbury dreamed of the fulfillment of prophecy, Montefiore's plans were focused on the here and now.

The Crimean War wrought havoc in Palestine. With no soldiers to keep order, the countryside was in uproar. Trade was at a standstill, the flow of Christian pilgrims had shrunk to a trickle, and the fighting prevented peasants from cultivating their crops. The harsh winter would have made 1854 a difficult year in any circumstances, but hoarding created famine prices as corn merchants kept back their stock to sell to the troops. Snow covered the streets of Jerusalem, where the poor could afford neither fuel nor clothing to protect themselves from the icy winds. No one suffered more than Jews in this time of hardship. Suddenly cut off from the flow of Russian *halukah,* they had little choice but to starve.[18]

For Consul Finn and his redoubtable wife, Elizabeth, this was both a human tragedy and a heaven-sent opportunity. Distressed to see people of all faiths reduced to eating bread mixed with grit and tares, Finn decided to buy wheat and sell it at cost price. When five camel loads of corn arrived from Hebron, he and his missionary friends opened a subscription. Thereafter they baked and distributed loaves twice a week. Finn later recalled the heartrending sight of blind, lame, ragged, old, and widowed Jews queuing up for their handouts in a babble of Hebrew, German, Spanish, and Turkish. Many could hardly walk for fever; some carried babes in their arms.

Like all good Victorians, Elizabeth and James Finn saw hard work as a panacea for poverty, in Jerusalem as elsewhere. Caroline Cooper, an old friend of Elizabeth's, already devoted her small income to a sewing charity for Jewish women. She found many willing to brave the threat of excommunication from the rabbis by slaving from sunrise till noon for the sake of a few piastres. In later life, Elizabeth would become known as the founder of the Distressed Gentlefolks' Aid Association. In 1854 she established the Sarah Society, a group of Christian ladies who paid regular visits to the Jewish quarter and did what they could for the poor.[19]

Four years earlier, Finn had purchased a small plot of land at Talbieh.[20] He wanted a summer house outside the city and began by using Jewish workers to build walls around the estate. Finn was not wealthy, and his finances soon became hopelessly entangled, but this did not stop him from taking a further £250 loan to buy a second estate on the desolate, rocky hill he called Kerem Avraham. The famine of 1854 injected a note of urgency into these activities. Soon money began to trickle in from Christians in Britain, India, and the United States—enough for the Finns' Industrial Plantation to hire nearly 100 poor Jews. The Finns genuinely wanted to help, and with uncharacteristic tact they forbade London Society missionaries access to Kerem Avraham. Even so, the Jewish authorities declared the work unlawful. Montefiore, too, was unhappy with the situation. Rather than allow Evangelicals to head the relief effort, he decided to launch one of his own. In May 1854 Chief Rabbi Nathan Adler issued a pastoral letter to the Jews of the British Empire and North America. The condition of Jews in the four holy cities of Palestine was, he said, "absolutely heartrending."[21] Montefiore had urged him in the name of Zion and Jerusalem to take steps so that they did not starve.

Adler had arrived in London from Hanover ten years earlier: a competent but undistinguished German in his early forties, whose friendship with Victoria's uncle, the duke of Cambridge, proved to be his lucky break.[22] University-educated rabbis were commonplace in Germany, but in Britain the new chief rabbi was the first of his kind. As a Sephardi, Montefiore had no formal role in Adler's appointment. Informally, he was delighted. They needed someone to heal the wounds in the Jew-ish community, and he thought Adler "the most likely of the three candidates to obtain the confidence of all parties."[23] Their interests proved complementary: Adler sought to impose his religious leadership throughout the British Empire, while Montefiore wanted the Board of Deputies to monopolize the defense of Jewish interests in the public sphere. Each threw his weight behind the other, and before long they were collaborating over Adler's pet project, an establishment known as Jews' College intended to provide preliminary training for English rab-bis and a suitably religious education for the sons of the Jewish middle class.[24]

The two men also shared a global vision. Three years before his ap-pointment, Adler had sent Montefiore £20 on behalf of the Jews of Smyrna.[25] Once in office, he happily lent his authority to Montefiore's charitable schemes. When the Jews of Palestine empowered Montefiore to raise money for them in the United States and throughout the British Empire, several authorized Adler to do so too.[26] And when news of fam-ine in the Holy Land began to reach England in 1854, the two men acted as one.

From the first, they were on the defensive. Montefiore's plans for Jew-ish agriculture and cotton manufacturing had seemed revolutionary in the 1840s. Ten years later, with little to show for the enterprise, it was hard to escape the conclusion that he had failed. As Lazarus Magnus noted scathingly in the *Jewish Chronicle*, Montefiore had spent a for-tune on the Jews of Palestine to no very good effect. He persisted in act-ing unilaterally when he would have done better to join forces with the rest of the Jewish community by establishing a series of local and gen-eral committees and systematically implementing their ideas. Arbitrary, dictatorial, amateurish: many applied these adjectives as readily to the Board of Deputies as to the Holy Land Relief Fund. In the past, such critics had rarely attacked Montefiore personally, and his foreign activi-ties had remained sacrosanct. The crisis of 1853 changed everything. Now the gloves were off, and even those who supported Montefiore domestically threw their hats into the ring.[27]

Attacks on the relief fund focused on three issues: first, the need for consultation and collaboration; second, the need for long-term solu-tions; and third, the spiritual and intellectual poverty of the Jewish com-munity in Palestine.[28] Some, like Sequerra, wanted a piece of the action. The rest shared the prejudices of their host society—in favor of work-fare and against traditional Jewish religiosity. Most were hopelessly un-realistic. It was absurd to think that a couple of thousand pounds could reeducate the entire Jewish population and assist those who refused to cooperate in emigrating to Australia. Montefiore could be infuriating, and some of his ideas were deeply old-fashioned, but there was much in the relief fund that was genuinely new.

For a Jewish charity, its success was unprecedented. Committees formed up and down the country; Christian associations got up weekly penny subscriptions; ministers appealed to their flocks on a Sunday morning. Everyone from countesses to railway workers added their names to the lists. Nor was support restricted to the usual suspects. Alongside Gawler, Attwood, et al. were Welsh Methodists, Jersey Freemasons, and Evangelicals of every hue. In 1855 Montefiore and Adler declared proudly that their appeal had been answered "by all classes of different creeds in all parts of the world."[29]

This was in some sense a tribute to Montefiore and other leading Jewish figures. Years of giving to non-Jewish charities had finally brought their reward. As the *Hampshire Independent* put it, "When the famine was sore in the land—when the poor Irish were perishing with want, the Rothschilds and the Montefiores sent princely subscriptions in their assistance. We trust, then, that Christians will show they are not to be surpassed in the works of charity and benevolence by their Jewish fellowsubjects."[30] Such reasoning appealed to a domestic audience, but there was nothing parochial about the relief fund, which found its most lavish donors overseas. Although many lived in France, Germany, and Italy, the appeal of the relief fund was not restricted to Europe.[31]

Like the Damascus Affair, the famine in Palestine combined religion with the exotic East and disinterested humanitarianism in a way that was peculiarly attuned to British imperial sensibilities. Nothing symbolized this convergence more clearly than the words of a black Canadian minister, who urged the cause of the Jews in Jerusalem "not only on the score of common humanity, but also on the benevolence of Christianity, which . . . inculcates kindness to every human being, independent of creed or colour."[32] Roughly a third of the money was raised in distant Australia, where the universal nature of these concerns enabled the radical politician Dr. John Dunmore Lang, the governor of South Australia, the Anglican bishop of Tasmania, and the Catholic archdeacon of Sydney to find common ground.

The Holy Land Relief Fund changed the face of international Jewish philanthropy forever. It was the first successful attempt to use the press and modern subscription-based fund-raising to help the Jews of Palestine, and it was pioneering in targeting Christians as well as Jews. Ludwig Philippson's campaign for a hospital and industrial school had been similarly groundbreaking—except that Philippson never attained his object, while Montefiore raised nearly £20,000. Up to a point this success

was due to timing. The Damascus Affair had raised the profile of Ottoman Jewry in the West, but the Crimean War focused the attention of
both Jews and gentiles on Palestine. Yet Philippson would always have
struggled to compete with Montefiore. German Jews were more embattled than their British counterparts. Philippson lacked Montefiore's celebrity, his ability to connect with Jews and Christians of all kinds, and
his familiarity with the global networks of the English-speaking world.

In the past, the system of collecting alms for Palestine had followed
ethnic and cultural fault lines, with one committee in Constantinople
and another in Amsterdam. By the mid-nineteenth century this echo of
the traditional geography of the Jewish world was beginning to break
down. The great rabbis of eastern Europe took responsibility for their
own disciples, while the horizons of western European Jewry included
North America and the rest of the British Empire—from Canada and
the West Indies to India, Australia, and Hong Kong.[33]

The United States was no longer a British colony, but historical ties
with the rest of the English-speaking world made it part of the emerging Anglosphere. When Jewish organizations in Palestine invested Montefiore (and later Adler) with the authority to raise money in the British
Empire, they naturally included the United States as well.[34] Only Pekam
failed to accept the logic of this situation. Yet even before Lehren's death
in 1853, Montefiore had emerged as the primary channel for money
from North America to the Holy Land. Old Isaac Baer Kursheedt of the
Hebra Terumot Hakodesh was among the first of Montefiore's American correspondents, but by the early 1850s his contacts stretched from
Baltimore, New York, and Cincinnati to Charleston, Savannah, and
New Orleans.[35]

Montefiore saw this activity as a central feature of international Jewish unity. As he explained in a letter thanking American Jews for their
generous donations to the Holy Land Relief Fund, "It is a comforting
fact to observe that, whether the Jew dwell under the say of an aristoc-
racy, the rule of a monarchy, or the shadow of a commonwealth, the
'Jew is a Jew for a' that' . . . And surely our due maintenance of Jerusalem must be considered as one of the inseparable links that unite the
broad Atlantic with the waters of the mighty ocean, and it again with
the waters of the middle sea; which kiss the shore of that land from
which floweth the waters of salvation and of life everlasting."[36]

There were perhaps 50,000 Jews living in the United States in 1850,
when Montefiore heard of some 30 or 40 grubbing for gold in San Francisco. No one else took much interest in this handful of individuals on
the edge of the known world, but he sent them a Torah scroll "in order
that when you are assembled together you may hear and fear the Lord

our God and observe to do all the words of his Law.[37] Writing the opening or closing words of a Torah scroll was one of Montefiore's favorite *mitzvot,* and he regularly employed scribes in Vilna and Palestine to complete the remainder.[38] In outposts like San Francisco and the Australian gold town of Ballarat, Montefiore's Torah scrolls were arguably the most tangible link with the global Jewish community.[39] They created an environment peculiarly receptive to his ideas. When seventy-eight-year-old Judah Touro of New Orleans needed someone to administer a bequest to the Jews of Palestine, he saw Montefiore as the obvious choice.

Touro was a childless bachelor who had rediscovered religion in later life through his friendship with Gershom Kursheedt, a man half his age. Judaism became his passion. He was a difficult character, but he kept kosher, kept the Sabbath, and, when he died, gave most of his fabulous fortune to charity.[40] Kursheedt's father had been president of the Hebra Terumot Hakodesh, and Gershom himself took an interest in the Jews of Palestine, so it was only natural for Touro to leave money there, too. He hoped that Montefiore would use it "to ameliorate the condition of our unfortunate Jewish Brethren in the Holy Land and to secure to them the inestimable privilege of worshipping the Almighty according to our religion, without molestation."[41]

Montefiore knew what to do with Touro's $50,000. He had long been concerned about the missionary hospital and believed that Jews needed one of their own—not just a small, improvised affair, but a building grand enough to defeat the missionaries once and for all. He had already commissioned plans for a monumental neoclassical foundation with a synagogue attached. Now, he could finally afford to build it. That summer Gershom Kursheedt traveled to England as Judah Touro's executor. He made no difficulties about going along with Montefiore's plans for the hospital—until he discovered that the Rothschilds had got there first.[42]

Ludwig Philippson had been the first to appreciate that the Crimean War represented a cultural and political opportunity. His articles in the *Allgemeine Zeitung des Judentums* made much of the "mental and physical debasement" of Eastern Jews, portraying emancipation as meaningless without internal reform. Whereas Montefiore had sought to integrate these communities more effectively into the Ottoman Empire, Philippson's solution (like his analysis of the problem) reflected a European orientalist's disdain for Eastern culture. He proposed to kick-start the process of cultural transfer by training young Ottoman Jews in Europe, where they could experience Western civilization for themselves.[43]

Philippson and Montefiore had worked together against the expulsion of Jews from the Russian borderlands, and Montefiore had stopped to see Philippson on his way to St. Petersburg in 1846.[44] Before the crisis of 1853, the German might still have looked to the Englishman to implement his vision. Now, Philippson turned to the Consistoire Central des Israélites de France instead.[45]

Unlike the Board of Deputies, the Consistoire was a religious body. The runaway success of the Holy Land Relief Fund left its members uneasy about an initiative in which Jerusalem took second place.[46] In principle, they were happy to assume leadership of Philippson's civilizing mission. In practice, they refused to commit themselves before the talented Hungarian orientalist, Albert Cohn, returned from his mission to Palestine. Cohn had prepared the Rothschild boys for their bar mitzvahs. He was a leading light in the world of Parisian Jewish charity and traveled to Jerusalem on the Rothschilds' behalf.

Three years earlier, Montefiore had been delighted when James de Rothschild's son Gustave set out for the Holy Land. "You see the prophecy of the ancient Rabbis confirmed in our days," he wrote to Loewe with messianic enthusiasm. "Israel or the Holy Land will never be left in widowhood. The most powerful family of the Jews of the whole Globe has sent a Son to relieve the distress of the People."[47] Nothing much came of Gustave's expedition before the war rekindled Rothschild interest in the East. The family earmarked 100,000 francs for the Jews of Palestine and dispatched Cohn to make sure it was well spent. In the summer of 1854 he spent three weeks in Jerusalem—long enough to establish not only the small Rothschild Hospital but also a lying-in charity sponsored by Betty, a loan society named after Anselme, a girls' school supported by Mrs. Nathaniel, and an industrial school for boys under the auspices of James's two sons.[48] After inaugurating the hospital with due pomp and ceremony, Cohn traveled back via Constantinople and returned boasting about his achievements. Philippson, for one, was unimpressed. "We must stress again and again, that the affairs of Jerusalem and the Oriental Jewish question are two completely separate things," he insisted in the *Allgemeine Zeitung des Judentums;* "the former concerns a poor community whose members come from every possible country, the latter concerns raising many thousands from a state of religious, moral and material degradation. But does Mr. Albert Cohn really think that the eight days he spent in Constantinople are even enough to assess the situation, let alone take significant steps?"[49]

Montefiore, meanwhile, took offense at Cohn's deliberate denigration of his own medical efforts.[50] There was more at stake here than philanthropic rivalry. As in 1840, the Crimean War had focused the attention of Western Jewry on their Eastern brethren. Once again, the national loyalties of Jewish leaders threatened to undermine Jewish unity. Britain and France may have been allies against the Russians, but they remained political, cultural, and imperial rivals. Much like their governments, French and British Jews vied with each other to lead the Jewish world in the battle against cultural backwardness and political oppression. The former were fully emancipated, and the latter were not, yet the global reach and humanitarian ideology of the British Empire meant that Britain—not France—proved more committed to defending the cause of the Jews of the Middle East.[51]

The British advantage had infuriated Crémieux, and it also rankled with Cohn, who used his visit to Jerusalem to proclaim "the ascendancy of French influence [in Palestine] with the decline of that of England."[52] When Montefiore arrived a year later, he told Finn roundly that "no other object than that of contradicting by facts that unfounded assertion, could have brought him here at so advanced an age, and in so enfeebled a state of health." This last was no exaggeration. Early in 1855 Montefiore had consulted an eminent London doctor, who "informed him that his heart was feeble, there was poison in his blood, and his digestive organs were not perfect."[53] Suffering as he did from a morbid frame of mind, rheumatism, and a touch of lumbago, he must surely have been inclined to fear the worst.[54]

Montefiore's aims in Jerusalem were threefold. First, he wanted to inspect the various charities already established by the Holy Land Relief Fund; second, he needed something constructive to do with the rest of the money; and third, he still hoped to found a grand Jewish hospital with the Touro legacy. In a bid to contain missionary activities, the Ottoman government had banned foreigners from purchasing land in Syria.[55] Accompanied not just by Kursheedt, Judith, and Loewe but also by his niece Jemima and her husband Haim Guedalla, Montefiore consequently set out for Constantinople. On arrival they were welcomed once again by Abraham Camondo.[56]

Like Montefiore, the legendary Levantine banker was now in his early seventies, his thin, determined face framed by a fez and a white beard; a forceful figure still, with a shrewd, calculating expression. Both were products of the Italian Jewish diaspora: energetic, elderly businessmen, who dominated their home communities, combining piety and support for secular education with respect for traditional learning. In London, these traits made Montefiore a reactionary; in Constantinople, Camondo was on the cutting edge of change. Only six months earlier he had

thrown his weight behind Albert Cohn's efforts to found a modern Jewish school—persevering after the latter's departure in the face of hysterical communal protest.[57] In other contexts Camondo remained at the
height of his powers. Jews had given a million piastres toward the war
effort, and Camondo was the lynchpin of Ottoman finance, so closely
allied to the reformist ministers Ali and Fuad Pasha that he was showered with honors in his lifetime and would eventually receive something
approximating a state funeral. Like the city in which he lived, he was
caught between two worlds. To Jemima, his children seemed European,
while his ancient mother still dressed *à la Turcque*—in slippers, satin
trousers, a tunic, and an elaborate bejeweled headdress.[58] The support
of such a man was unquestionably an asset, but with British troops
propping up the sultan, the influence of the British ambassador may
have counted for more.

Utterly contemptuous of the society in which he lived, Lord Stratford
de Redcliffe had made a point of never learning Turkish. His arrogance
was galling, his temper atrocious, and his endless meddling in Ottoman
politics did little to bolster the sovereignty of the sultan. Yet at this moment of crisis Stratford was arguably the best friend the Ottoman government had. He threw his weight behind it in the struggle with Russia
and embraced the Tanzimat with genuine zeal. Like Palmerston, who
was now prime minister, Stratford believed that Christians and Jews
were the most dynamic elements in the Ottoman Empire. He was delighted to endorse Montefiore's requests to build a hospital outside Jerusalem and to allow the Jews of Palestine to own land.[59]

Always on the lookout for the guiding hand of providence, Montefiore
found it "rather singular" that he had met every one of the sultan's ministers on his last visit, "when they were in much less responsible positions in the Government."[60] In reality, the government had considerable
reservations about his plan. Ali Pasha, the brilliant young grand vizier,
acknowledged that Montefiore's "arrival here is solely for the desire to
make a service to humanity, and [that] since the hospital that he has requested a license for will be dedicated to the poor, it will be considered
as charity, [so] there does not seem to be any harm in it."[61] But Ali feared
that it might prove the thin end of the wedge. Philanthropy was still a
means for the British to exert influence in Palestine, and it was Ottoman policy to restrict both European religious activity and the numbers
claiming consular protection in Syria as a result. He therefore advised
the sultan to grant permission to build a hospital only if the location
was "free from objections" and if the management was "in the hands of
the subjects of the Great State [Ottoman Empire]." As for Jewish landholding, Montefiore merely requested permission to "visit the Holy

Land, to carry out the necessary assistance [so] that the poor of the [Jewish] *millet* will be occupied with agriculture and other crafts, and thus they will be free from begging."[62] This motive seemed uncontroversial to Ali, who was more preoccupied by European encroachment than by the rights of indigenous religious minorities—a battle that had, in any case, already been lost.

On June 28, 1855, Montefiore and Loewe made their way to the new palace: a grandiose baroque fantasy on the banks of the Bosphorus, all glass and delicate stonework.[63] This was the public face of the Tanzimat, designed to proclaim the sultan's power to a new, European audience. Here, in a splendid but only partially furnished room, Abdul Mecid promised Montefiore the necessary authorizations and—as a conciliatory gesture—finally granted the Perushim permission to rebuild the Hurva of Judah Hehasid as the first modern Ashkenazi synagogue in Jerusalem. Islamic law forbade the construction of new places of worship for non-Muslims, and for fifteen years the Ottoman authorities had blocked the redevelopment of this ruined Ashkenazi compound.[64] Their change of heart probably had more to do with Finn and Stratford than with Montefiore.[65] In Jerusalem, however, his success in obtaining a *firman* to rebuild the Hurva seemed something of a coup

News of Montefiore's impending arrival created great excitement in the Holy City, where he was said to be bringing some £30,000. Even the poorest Jews supposedly began to walk tall, spending what money they had "in certain anticipation that they would receive it back from Sir Moses in manifold proportion." Exactly what he planned was a matter for speculation. Some thought he should invest in agriculture, others put their hopes in manufacturing, and yet others exclaimed energetically, "Oh Torah, wilt thou be forgotten, shall Sir Moses not provide for the disciples of the wise?" None had any understanding of the real nature of his mission.[66]

Obstinate and opinionated though he was, Montefiore had been unable to ignore criticism of the Holy Land Relief Fund. In February 1855 he and Adler took the novel decision to publish its accounts.[67] The accompanying report stressed their long-term perspective—and that they intended to stem the hardship at its source. Montefiore would be traveling to Palestine to buy land and found institutions, not doling out alms as before.

At first everything went swimmingly. The track from Jaffa to Jerusalem was as precipitous as ever, but all the local governors came out to pay their respects, and the horsemen of the mountains entertained the travelers with dazzling displays, pirouetting on their steeds and firing off their guns in all directions. Had the Montefiores been younger and stronger, they might have enjoyed it. As it was, Montefiore felt he had "never suffered so much fatigue, and I may add fright in any journey in my life . . . God only knows how we reached the end of our journey in safety." Exhausted but deeply moved, the party set up camp outside the Jaffa Gate. Jemima soon thought them "in fine order; we have a nice washing stand and its appurtenances of pewter, a good deal table, nice pieces of matting, fine leather armchair, also a foot bath . . . and camp stools." After the stifling, insect-ridden heat of Constantinople in high summer and the rat-infested steamer to Jaffa, this was paradise.[68]

On July 23 Montefiore set out in his sedan chair to pay a ceremonial visit to the governor of Jerusalem. Kiamil Pasha offered his guest every facility, summoned the (rather elderly) city council to discuss the Hurva and the hospital, and ordered the guards to present arms when he finally left.[69] In excellent spirits, Montefiore then made his way to the Western Wall, where he prayed for his friends and family individually, and for the congregations that had given so generously to the Holy Land. He returned to visit the Temple Mount by special invitation on the day after Tisha Be'av.

This holiest of religious places had been forbidden territory to non-Muslims for centuries. But the Crimean War upset longstanding religious certainties, and when the duke and duchess of Brabant asked to see the Temple enclosure the sultan felt unable to refuse.[70] Thanks to Kiamil Pasha's careful management, the breaking of this ancient taboo in March 1855 had passed without incident: Christian pilgrims charged the Turkish soldiers stationed around the Temple enclosure, but the Muslim crowds that lined the city's streets did not explode into violence as he feared. The relaxed atmosphere that marked Montefiore's visit to the Temple Mount contrasted starkly with this drama.[71] Four months earlier, the nerves of the visitors had been on a knife-edge, and the screams of a frustrated dervish had prompted the pasha to hurry them on as fast as he could. He posted 100 soldiers to guard the enclosure during the Montefiore visit, but this time the tour was far more extensive; they even spread carpets under the Dome of the Chain so that the Montefiore party could look about at their ease.

The next day Louis Loewe called on an old friend, the renowned Russian Talmudist Samuel Salant.[72] The two men had spent several weeks together in Constantinople in 1840, when Salant was a sickly young scholar on his way to build a new life in the sun. Presuming on this long-standing connection, he castigated Loewe for allowing Montefiore to

"The Mosque of Omar, on the ancient site of the Temple," by David Roberts, in The Holy Land, Syria, Idomea, Arabia, Egypt & Nubia, *vol. 1 (London, 1855), plate 8. Montefiore was the first Jew in modern times to set foot on the Temple Mount. (By permission of the Bodleian Library, University of Oxford: Mason HH90)*

visit the Temple enclosure when there was a binding talmudic injunction against anyone except the high priest entering the Holy of Holies, which—since no one knew its exact location—had been expanded to encompass the entire Temple Mount. The whole rabbinical establishment was equally horrified, but only Salant dared call Loewe to account.

"You are wrong again," Salant insisted after some debate; "they both, Rambam [Rabbi Moses Maimonides] and Rabad [Rabbi Abraham ben David], agree that there is an absolute prohibition of entry to the Holy of Holies, and this is binding for all times. Where their opinions differ is only in the definition as to the class of transgression it fits into."

"I am sorry, I made a mistake," Loewe finally admitted. "However, Sir Moses would not have accepted my advice not to enter."

"Sir Moses would never have entered," Salant declared with conviction, "had his attention been drawn to the gravity of such a step."

Probably Loewe knew his employer best. Far from agonizing over the situation, the pragmatic Englishman had paid £3 for the stones on which

Abraham and the angels had reputedly stood.[73] Indeed, Montefiore's ignorance is hard to credit at a time when the prohibition was common knowledge among the Jews of Jerusalem.

Rabbi Haim Hirschensohn later recounted that Rabbi Moses Joseph Lissa had grabbed a *shofar* and excommunicated Montefiore, prompting the rest of the city's rabbis to leap to their guest's defense. The father of modern Hebrew, Eliezer Ben-Yehuda, claimed that "when Sir Moses got to know [about the excommunication] . . . he asked for the names of those who pronounced the *Herem* upon him. Next morning when he was called to the *Sefer* [Torah], he asked to have a *Mi sheberach* [prayer] read for them . . . in recognition of their honest action." Both men were mistaken, but the combination of piety and ignorance Montefiore displayed in the second story enabled him to retain his lustre as a *tzaddik*, or righteous Jew. The most popular tradition absolved him completely: for it is said even today that Montefiore stayed in his sedan chair throughout the visit, so his feet did not touch the holy soil at all.[74]

This episode set the tone for a sadly acrimonious encounter between Montefiore and the majority of the city's Jews. Up to a point it was a straightforward drama of disappointed expectations. When they realized that Montefiore had not come to give them immediate support, poor Jews laid siege to his camp: hundreds of men, women, and children, threatening violence, shouting that they were starving, and clamoring for work. Kind words and a few piastres were not enough for the ringleader, who was dragged away kicking and screaming by no less than twelve guards. "Really," Jemima commented when another man began haranguing them a day later, "if this annoyance continues we shall scarcely be safe in our tents."[75]

The response of the communal authorities was more complex. Montefiore's behavior was shocking, but his piety seemed genuine; despite his eccentricities they could still relate to him as a God-fearing Jew. Unlike Philippson and the Rothschilds, Montefiore was, moreover, a known quantity—and the charities he had established granted considerable autonomy to Jerusalem's Jews. This readiness to work with rather than against the grain of traditional Jewish society was both a weakness and a strength.[76]

Of course, Montefiore could not ignore the concerns of enlightened Western Jewry altogether. When he sent £1,000 in emergency aid to the four holy cities, he insisted on appointing special committees "with strict instructions to distribute this amount among all the poor of the different congregations, without any distinction, in equal amounts to each individual; to require a receipt from each head of a family, with his name in full and the number of his children, and to form a list of the recipients, certified by the several European Consuls of the different localities."[77]

More permanent initiatives needed to be managed locally, although they could perhaps be regulated from afar. The benevolent loan societies that Montefiore established in the four holy cities were a classic example. Each was governed by "a code of laws authorising small loans from 100 to 1000 Turkish piastres to be advanced, without interest, to the industrious or who can produce security, and have probable means of weekly or monthly repayment."[78] These constitutions ensured a degree of conformity, but the day-to-day decisions remained in local hands.

Only the weaving institution in Jerusalem deviated from this model. Montefiore had long dreamed of establishing a cotton factory, and the relief fund enabled him to send half a dozen handlooms to Palestine— along with Mr. Bradshaw, an Irish Christian whose task it was to teach ten Jewish boys the work. But importing British expertise proved easier said than done. Bradshaw could not communicate with his students and refused to cooperate with the Jews placed in charge.[79] Montefiore was left to pick up the pieces. After consulting with the management committee, he warned Bradshaw "that he must submit to the directions of the Com. to admit 10 persons they may send him to teach, and to teach no others in the house. They have the only power to admit and discharge pupils. Mr. Bradshaw said we paid the lads too little ps., that Mrs. Finn gave 4p. with eggs and bread; but I find 3 is the usual rate of wage, and we have a great number of persons anxious to be employed. The Com. in my opinion have acted prudently and with great good judgment."[80] Bradshaw would have none of it. Montefiore concluded that there was no alternative but to let him go.[81]

This kind of culture clash was best avoided: the most successful of Montefiore's initiatives was entirely managed by local Jews. Surprisingly, perhaps, they were women. "Not an individual is seen but has shared in the benefit," Rabbi Moshe Sachs reported to the *Jewish Chronicle:* "Sir Moses sends from London linen, flannel, and all other materials for making up clothes. There are several women appointed to take charge of the materials. These are then given out to four females to work them up, of course for wages, and they are afterwards distributed among the poor." Two hundred women set to work in Jerusalem, and similar charities were founded in the other holy cities.[82]

These women inhabited a patriarchal world, but their deeply religious priorities lent it a distinctive flavor. Both Sephardim and Ashkenazim dressed with extreme modesty, covering or shaving off their hair and draping themselves from head to toe in white sheets. They were usually married young to complete strangers, lived for years with their in-laws, and rarely had time to communicate with their husbands, who spent all day studying outside the home. "If she would only let me talk with my husband," one woman complained sadly. "When his mother is asleep . . . he tells me stories from the Talmud and sometimes reads them to me aloud. I enjoy those hours immensely."[83]

The flip side of this was that women were often left to support the entire family unit. Shouldering this economic burden was both easier and more usual for Ashkenazim than for their Sephardi sisters. The former could open shops and small businesses, but the latter followed Islamic custom and stayed as much as possible indoors. Where Caroline Cooper brought Jewish women to her charitable workshop, the Institution for the Encouragement of Needlewomen and Laundresses empowered Jewish women by giving them oversight of the project and allowing them to work in the privacy of their homes.

Judith had always taken a particular interest in the women of Jerusalem. The Hevrat Bikur Holim ve'Hakhnassat Kalah, of which she was a patroness, was probably the oldest women's organization in the city, and sister societies had now been established in the other holy cities.[84] Childbirth and marriage were traditional causes, but in 1855 Judith demonstrated her desire to introduce more radical change into the female sphere. Roughly a week after their arrival in Jerusalem, she accompanied her husband and Loewe to pay a formal visit on Haim Nissim Abulafia, the *Haham Bashi*. "He wishes me to buy houses and land that they may pay their debts," Montefiore reported in his diary, "and he consented to send his young daughter to a school if my dear Jud established one for teaching Hebrew and sewing."[85]

To a European, there could be nothing controversial about such an establishment. But there was no tradition of organized female education in Jerusalem, and the decision of the missionaries to branch out in this direction hardly rendered the idea attractive to the city's Jewish inhabitants. The attitude was so hostile that the Rothschilds were forced to pay for the privilege of teaching Jewish girls in Mrs. Nathaniel's new school.[86] Montefiore knew that Judith's school would get nowhere without the *Haham Bashi*'s backing and had no intention of allowing him to back down. "The *Haham Bashi* didn't give the notice this morning at the Synagogue regarding the Girls' school," he noted tersely. "I said to him if it was not done this afternoon I would have nothing more to do with the Sephardi Congregation."[87] Sure enough, all eighty-four of the girls who finally enrolled were Sephardim. Jemima speculated that the Ashkenazim had been prevented from attending by their religious authorities, and she was quite right.[88]

It was for this—not for trespassing in the Holy of Holies—that Montefiore was excommunicated in 1855.[89] His foray into educational modernization made him so unpopular that boys threw stones at his sedan chair while their parents shouted abuse from the rooftops, and the *shofar* was ritually sounded in the synagogue of the Hurva courtyard that he had helped to build. Yet Montefiore remained sublimely indifferent to these developments: his diary makes no mention of the *herem*, although it devotes considerable space to the machinations of the *Haham Bashi*.[90]

What really irritated him, however, was the impossibility of buying land at a reasonable price, and where possible he chose to rent rather than buy.[91] Such expedients were out of the question when it came to the Touro hospital, and Montefiore found his protracted land-purchase negotiations with Ahmed Aga Dizdar trying beyond belief. Loewe—who liked to tell a good story—later claimed that whenever he tried to broach the subject, Achmed Aga replied: "You are my friend, my brother, the apple of my eye, take possession of it [the land] at once. This land I hold as an heirloom from my ancestors. I would not sell it to any person for thousands of pounds, but to you I give it without any money: it is yours, take possession of it."[92] Montefiore had sent the former governor of Jerusalem £10 when he fell on hard times in 1844.[93] "No one can possibly express the vexation I feel here," Montefiore wrote after a day or two of this treatment. "Achmet Aga sent an excuse. He could not go to measure the land, he must first send to Ali Aga for his consent to sell it. This is an excuse. Have patience."[94] "So much for friendly professions," he commented bitterly when he ended up paying the Aga £1,000.[95] As the first land purchase by a Western Jew in modern Jerusalem, the transaction had considerable symbolic value. One hundred Muslim schoolboys came out of the city to congratulate Montefiore, and in his memoirs Finn described with quiet satisfaction how "a Hebrew possession [was] once more appropriated in the Land of Promise after an interval of many ages."[96]

With their business in Jerusalem satisfactorily completed, Montefiore and the rest of his party returned to Jaffa via Hebron. Still convinced that agriculture was the best hope for the future, he had given £360 to delegations from Safed and Tiberias—enough to assist nearly 100 Jewish families "in purchasing Oxen, and to enable them to cultivate the Land which, whether as owners or renters, they already possessed."[97] But Montefiore really wanted to establish new farms, and there was no land to be had. No sooner had he agreed on the price of a field in Hebron than its value increased tenfold overnight.[98]

Roughly a year earlier, the locally based Rabbi Moshe Sachs had pub-

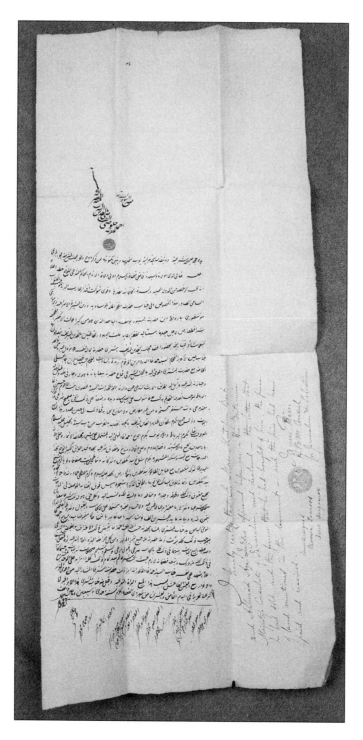

Title deeds of the land Montefiore purchased near Jerusalem in 1855.
(Courtesy of Robert Sebag-Montefiore; photograph by Lykke Stjernswärd)

lished an appeal to his American brethren in the *Occident* describing the Jaffa region as ideally suited to Jewish agriculture.[99] By 1854 it had become the focus for a trio of eccentric individuals, all of whom nurtured visionary agricultural plans. The first was a Christian farmer from Danzig called Peter Classen, who bought an estate near Jaffa "to do good for Israel."[100] In May 1853 he began leasing this land to Mrs. Clorinda Minor, a disappointed Millerite from Philadelphia, who had first traveled to Jerusalem in 1849 impelled by the conviction that she was the prophetess Esther, summoned by God to go to Mount Zion and "make ready the land of Israel for the King's return."[101] There she met the converted Jew John Meshullam. She returned in 1851 with a small troop of Seventh Day Baptists to help farm the fertile valley of Artas, where Meshullam hoped to establish a "Manual Labour School of Agriculture for the Jews of the Holy Land."[102] The project collapsed in acrimony, causing Mrs. Minor to relocate to Jaffa with her fellow American colonists. But while Classen changed his name to David and began converting to Judaism, Mrs. Minor became associated with the missionary American Society for Ameliorating the Condition of the Jews.

One of those present at Classen's circumcision was Warder Cresson, a farmer from Pennyslvania, who soon replaced Mrs. Minor as Classen's tenant. Born and bred a Quaker, in his search for religious truth Cresson became first a Shaker, then a Mormon, then a Seventh-Day Adventist, then a Campbellite, and—finally—a Jew. His conversion created a major scandal in Philadelphia, where his wife attempted to declare him legally insane. More than 100 witnesses were called in a trial that lasted four years, during which Cresson published a plan "for the Promotion of Agricultural Pursuits [and] for the Establishment of a Soup-House for the Destitute Jews in Jerusalem."[103] Enthusiasm for such ideas clearly ran in the family: his brother Elliott had won over Thomas Hodgkin to the cause of African colonization some twenty years before.

Warder, however, proved an ineffectual colonist. When his attempt to establish a model farm in the Refaim valley foundered, he transferred his attentions to Jaffa, where he linked up with Moshe Sachs and his Committee for Agriculture in Palestine. Impressed by the effective support offered Mrs. Minor by the American navy, Cresson wrote to yet another Philadelphian enthusiast for Jewish agriculture, appealing for the protection of the U.S. government on behalf of the putative Jewish colonists. The recipient of this letter was his old friend Rabbi Isaac Leeser, editor of the *Occident*.[104]

During 1853 and 1854 Leeser's newspaper published letters from almost all the major players in Jaffa. These included Mrs. Minor, now happily farming her own land. She disavowed any conversionist intentions, stressing instead her halcyon relations with Raphael Judah Men-achem Ha-Levi, the leader of Jaffa's small Jewish community. As the owner of a large orchard situated in a plain of lush cornfields and flow-ering fruit trees, the seventy-five-year-old rabbi from Dubrovnik was himself something of an agricultural pioneer. He had now reached the end of his resources and asked Mrs. Minor to take over. Then Mon-tefiore made arrangements to buy Ha-Levi's orchard himself.

In his diary, Montefiore described with barely contained fury how

> [a]fter a great number of hours and days passed at Jerusalem and the great expense incurred to complete my purchase of Rabbi Levi Judah's land at Jaffa I find at the last moment when I am here, pay the purchase money and take possession of the land, that the person in possession claims to hold a lease of the property, now refuses to give it up, although she declared to Dr. Loewe in the presence of Rabbi Levi her anxiety that I should purchase the property, and that she would leave the land, house, etc. instantly, having purchased another place more suitable to her pur-pose. Mr. Kayat [the British vice-consul in Jaffa] says the American Con-sul told him she claims 7,000 piestas for improvements before she will give me possession. I have sent Dr. L. to see her before I pay the purchase money. I shall take possession by placing a man there.[105]

Loewe eventually managed to broker a compromise, and Montefiore set sail leaving Mrs. Minor in charge for another three months.[106] As a final irony, David Classen was one of the two Jewish men who ended up working the land.

"I am dreadfully cheated and imposed upon," Montefiore wrote as he prepared for his departure, "but tho' I know it well, I am obliged to sub-mit . . . thank God, a few weeks will now bring it to an end." At the age of seventy, he surely realized that he was unlikely to return. "May all my sins be forgiven," he prayed; "may my want of temper be pardoned, and may my weak and feeble efforts for the support of our Holy Religion and the happiness of our brethren in the Holy Land be accepted for all my weakness and sins! Amen."[107]

The Montefiore party traveled back to Britain via Alexandria, where they were eagerly awaited by Said Pasha, their erstwhile guest. "On our arrival here the Vice Roy of Egypt, Said Pasha, sent his barges to bring us & our luggage from the steamer," Gershom Kursheedt wrote excit-edly to his family in the United States, "and *now* your humble brother is occupying the quarters of the Prince or rather King of Egypt, at what is called the ambrosia villa, where of course everything is done up in royal style . . . I feel quite like a nobleman myself now, although I am not the less wedded to republican institutions."[108] The Montefiores were greeted by no less a person than the chief lord of the Treasury, driven through the streets in two royal carriages, and provided with a French chef and an army of personal attendants to cater for their every whim. Every now and then, Said sent an officer to ask if they needed anything. Someone asked for a toothbrush, and before long a whole box arrived—enough, Loewe thought, to open a small shop. It was too good a joke not to be repeated, and of course their request for a clothes brush had the same effect.

Nor was the pasha alone in making a fuss of the Montefiores. Over the years they had acquired a disparate acquaintance here. Besides Jewish leaders, they were apparently on close terms with English merchants like Thomas Bell, who had accompanied them to Palestine in 1827. Family gossip has it that Montefiore had an affair with Bell's first wife, Hester, whose son, the future manager of *The Times,* was said to be Montefiore's illegitimate child. With his high forehead and cheekbones, Charles Moberley Bell certainly looked the part, and rumors of his Jewish origins were sufficiently widespread for his daughter Enid to deny them in her biography. The timing of Moberley Bell's birth makes the story unlikely: he was born in Alexandria and conceived in the late summer of 1846, when Montefiore had been nowhere near the Middle East. Hester was dead now, but Thomas and his new wife remained in Alexandria, where the Montefiores' return in 1855 may have revived an old scandal.[109]

Even so, the couple received a warm welcome. While Judith and Jemima visited the pasha's wife in the palace harem, the men hobnobbed with businessmen and philanthropists. Among them was the middle-aged Frenchman Ferdinand de Lesseps, who had just obtained exclusive rights to form an international company to build and operate a canal between the Mediterranean and the Red Sea.[110] Everyone knew that a Suez canal would dramatically cut the journey time to India, but British concerns about protecting the overland route led Palmerston to oppose the plan. Montefiore's wealth, reputation, and well-known interest in the East made it inevitable that de Lesseps would seek to interest him in the project. Surprisingly perhaps, he thought the undertaking was likely to fail "from the financial point of view."[111] But Montefiore was no stranger to the politics of the situation, having become involved in plans to build a rival railway across the Middle East.[112]

The British had long toyed with developing an alternative route to India, crossing the desert from the Mediterranean to Aleppo and continuing down the Euphrates valley to the Persian Gulf. Back in the early

1830s, the soldier-explorer Captain Francis Chesney had mapped the river secretly before leading a disastrous official expedition, which entailed transporting two steamers overland from Antioch and reassembling them in Mesopotamia piece by piece.[113] Neither vessel survived, and the British government abandoned the idea, but twenty years later Chesney took up the scheme again. This time he proposed a railway in the Euphrates valley, to be linked by road to Damascus and thence to the Holy Land. The project captured Montefiore's imagination, and he began lobbying for financial support. As de Lesseps' plans for a Suez canal became increasingly concrete, hopes for a Jerusalem-Jaffa railway began to materialize as part of the larger rail network Chesney envisaged between the Mediterranean and the Persian Gulf.[114]

Montefiore saw in this project the finger of God. "With proper arrangements Jerusalem might be reached in eight days with ease from London," he wrote enthusiastically to Gershom Kursheedt in April 1856,

> and who shall say how many more thousands will go up to Jerusalem and perhaps the Jews in crowds three times a year as the Prophet says "Comfort ye comfort ye my people saith your God, Speak ye comfortably to Jerusalem and cry unto her, that her warfare is accomplished &c &c. Prepare ye the way of the Lord, make straight in the desert a highway for our God. Every valley shall be exalted and every mountain and hill shall be made straight and the rough places plain. And the glory of the Lord shall be revealed and all flesh shall see it together for the mouth of the Lord hath spoken it."
>
>   Now my dear friend have I not good reason to hope and expect that there will be a railway to Jerusalem indeed I feel with you that the appointed time is fast approaching for the happiness of Israel may it be in our day Amen. It must I am sure be a happiness to you to know, that by your kind influence with the late Mr. Touro Peace to his Soul, you have been the means of directing the eyes and hearts of many of our Brethren towards the Holy Land and contributing to the Welfare of our coreligionists now dwelling in that land of our Fathers, may every succeeding year tend more and more to the complete fulfilment of the Prophecies.[115]

This passage is the most unapologetically messianic sentiment that we know Montefiore voiced. None of his surviving journals contains anything like it. The theme of redemption is even absent from the spiritual jottings at the back of his personal Bible, although by 1856 it was clearly central to his religious beliefs.[116] But whatever Montefiore said privately to his intimates, in public he kept his views to himself. Having served briefly as a director of the South Eastern Railway Company, he knew that practical considerations would determine the success of the Jerusalem-Jaffa plan.[117]

A memorandum written in 1856 gives some indication of what he had in mind. The railway was to be a limited-liability company, with the Porte guaranteeing interest of 5 or 6 percent; a British government agent would receive custom duties at Jaffa; and the land itself would be free from all tax.[118] First, they needed financial and political backing. For the former, Montefiore looked to his immediate circle of business and religious connections: shareholders in companies like Alliance Insurance and the Provincial Bank of Ireland, his fellow Sephardim Joseph de Castro (son of the former president of the Board of Deputies) and Francis Cavalho, and the president of the Evangelical Alliance, Sir Culling Eardley. Devout, dark-haired, and coarse-featured, Eardley soon emerged as a key partner. His mother was a convert from Judaism, and on his father's side he was descended from the legendary Jewish banker Sir Sampson Gideon, all of which added a personal edge to his proselytizing philo-Semitism.

Eardley's missionary agenda made for a tense working relationship. On the morning of an especially critical interview with Palmerston, Montefiore warned his Evangelical friend to be under no illusion "with regard to the object he (Sir Moses) had in view respecting the railway to Jerusalem, it was his opinion that, when finished, it would not induce fifty Jews to return to the Holy Land, but he had no doubt it would greatly conduce to the improvement of their situation; that he would have nothing whatever to do with it if the undertaking was to be regarded as a sectarian measure."[119] Eardley took these comments in good part, and they found the prime minister receptive.

Palmerston had no intention of committing the government financially, but he thought the scheme a sound one, which would open new opportunities for British business and strengthen the Ottoman Empire, too. Grand Vizier Ali Pasha was in Paris anyway, attending the peace conference that marked the end of the Crimean War. Having formally established the Ottoman Empire's place in the concert of European powers, he continued to London, where at Palmerston's suggestion he met with Montefiore and other backers of the Jerusalem-Jaffa railway—not just Eardley and Chesney, but Count Pavel Edmund Strzelecki, Laurence Oliphant, and the Honorable Mr. Ashley, one of Lord Shaftesbury's younger sons.

If Ashley and Eardley represented wealth, Christianity, and social position, their colleagues were more in Colonel Chesney's line. Strzelecki was a friend of Florence Nightingale's, a Polish scientist and explorer, who had surveyed great swathes of Australia on foot. As for Oliphant, in later life he would leave the House of Commons to join a bizarre American sect, spend several years living in Palestine as a Christian Zionist, and found a new religion based on "pure" sexual love. In 1856, however, he was known primarily for his dashing exploits on the fringes of the Crimean War.

This collection of strong-minded, somewhat eccentric individuals was characteristic of the men who made British imperial policy on the ground. From Montefiore's perspective, they were far from ideal. "The men we should have for directors," he told Eardley, "must be those whose names are well known for wealth and connected with other railways, but on no account with religious societies." Yet Montefiore was the only serious City figure—and he had been in semiretirement for a great many years. So shaky was the economic rationale behind the project that the engineer appointed to survey the route advised against it. His verdict did not discourage Montefiore and Eardley from beginning negotiations with the sultan over a railway concession.[120] But early in 1857, Eardley made a fatal error. Overcome by enthusiasm toward the end of a meeting at Strzelecki's, he voiced the hope that the railway would encourage more Jews to convert. Montefiore supposedly paid his debts, took his hat, and abandoned the whole affair.[121]

It therefore comes as a surprise to find him in Jerusalem just four months later, accompanied by Mr. Galloway, the celebrated Egyptian railway engineer. They attracted considerable attention. Montefiore told the new governor of Jerusalem that he only wanted to break even, but Count Pizzamano, the Austrian consul, remained unconvinced. Hinting darkly at machinations in Constantinople, Pizzamano warned Finn that Montefiore's railroad was a financial impossibility. After raising the specter of French plans for a carriage road, Pizzamano proposed instead "a Joint stock speculation of all Europeans," which he expected would be dominated by Austrian finance. When Finn suggested that Montefiore was essentially disinterested, Pizzamano brusquely disagreed: "Do not you believe it, a Jew is a Jew still—and the Turks cannot give a guarantee of 7 per cent."[122]

Montefiore laughed off the episode. He did not care who built the road, he told Finn; "let it be done by French or Austrians, and let all try who can do it first—but the latter said long ago that they were able to do it, have they moved a stone yet?" His lighthearted approach may have stemmed from a realization that Pizzamano was probably right. There was no money to be made in a railway between Jaffa and Jerusalem, and nothing came of it in 1857 or in 1861, when Montefiore and Chesney resurrected the plan.[123] But of course the railway was not Montefiore's main reason for coming to Jerusalem. He was there to wrap up the unfinished business of 1855.

When Montefiore had left the Holy Land two years earlier, his various charitable initiatives were still in a precarious state. The weaving institution needed a new instructor, the girls' school remained deeply unpopular, and Mrs. Minor—to whom he had entrusted the Jaffa orchard—had died by the end of 1855. Contradictory reports in the Jewish press made it hard to gauge what was happening. In the absence of concrete information, European and North American Jews continued to debate the merits of industry versus prayer. Meanwhile, conditions in the holy city remained desperate. Faced with this onslaught of criticism, Montefiore and Adler sought to steer a middle course.[124]

The *Second Report* of the Holy Land Relief Fund, published in 1856, was both a vindication and a call for further action. The self-appointed trustees reiterated their belief that industry and agriculture provided the best hope of a sustainable future, but expressed solidarity with the pious and elderly scholars who devoted their lives to studying Torah "in the very place whence the Law and the Word went forth." The relief fund was only a beginning. All Montefiore and Adler could do was to produce detailed accounts of their expenditure and appeal to their brethren to continue the good work. "If the desire be earnest to rescue our brethren in Zion," they concluded, "all must endeavour to consolidate the institutions already established, to wait patiently for their development, and to slacken no exertion until adequate funds be raised."[125]

Meanwhile the Crimean War drew to a successful conclusion. In 1856 the sultan promulgated a *firman* declaring that "[e]very distinction or designation tending to make any class whatever of the subjects of the Empire inferior to another class on account of their religion, language, or race, shall be forever effaced from the laws and regulations of the Empire."[126] The *Hatt-i Hümayun* of 1856 was the most tangible sign yet of the willingness of European powers to intervene in the internal affairs of the Ottoman Empire in the name of religious and civil equality. Motivated above all by concern for Eastern Christians, it still transformed the context in which international Jewish activists operated and the legal framework in which Eastern Jews lived their lives. In theory, of course, the *Hatt-i Hümayun* symbolized the sultan's acceptance of European standards in the treatment of religious minorities and created an important precedent in the Muslim world. In practice, it would also raise the stakes in Christian Europe, where most Jews still lacked full political rights.

Writing in *The Israelite,* one American Jew saw the emancipation of Ottoman Jewry as the first of several positive developments. Alongside the "munificent institutions" established by Western Jewish philanthropists, he stressed the importance of steam, "the absolute civilizer of our age." Once the holy city of Jerusalem had been so distant that most Jews could not even contemplate going there. Now it was near enough for schools to be established and land purchased, so that "[i]nstead of receiving messengers from Jerusalem for the purpose of collecting alms, messengers are sent thither, to see, what beneficial results the charity of the European Jews is producing."[127]

This was no less than the truth. The Crimean War marked a sea change in diaspora engagement with Palestine, heralding the dawn of a more intensive and interventionist Western Jewish philanthropy that would ultimately affect the whole Middle East.[128] It is no coincidence that in 1855 the French scholar and journalist Isidore Cahen looked with admiration to the Universal Evangelical Alliance and wrote of the need for Jews to create an alliance of their own.[129] The *Jewish Chronicle* spoke in similar terms, calling for an organized fund-raising infrastructure and a central guiding hand.[130]

For the time being, there was a nagging sense of duplication. Too many of the charities funded by the Holy Land Relief Fund were nearly identical with those founded by Albert Cohn. On his way back from the holy city, Alphonse de Rothschild spoke regretfully of this lack of focus. "What has my honoured friend Sir Moses Montefiore done for Jerusalem?" he asked the militant *maskil* Ludwig Frankl, en route to found yet another school for girls with money from the Viennese widow Elisa Herz. "With bottomless generosity he has given more and more money . . . But you will not find a permanent establishment to his name. When he dies, he will be forgotten, like a cloud showering blessings once it has passed by."[131] This verdict anticipated that of future historians, but Montefiore fully appreciated the fragility of what he had begun. Setting out for the Holy Land in 1857 with Kursheedt, Hodgkin, and an ailing Judith, his mood was correspondingly bleak. "I am sorry to say I take but a gloomy vista regarding the result of my Journey to the Holy Land Weaving, School &c &c," he wrote Loewe. "Where will friends be found to support them after next year?"[132]

This was a serious issue, but the problem of the Touro legacy was in some ways more pressing. Montefiore's original intention had been to build a hospital, and it was for this that the sultan had authorized him to buy land. Since the plot allowed scope for further development, he had decided in 1855 to add a windmill as well. A letter from a Ramsgate builder written in January 1856 mentions drawings for both a hospital and almshouses, and the builder himself suggested a flexible, multipurpose design that would enable Montefiore to combine the two. Cost, however, was clearly a consideration. As Montefiore traveled to Jerusalem in 1857 he agonized over what to do with the Touro legacy, suspecting (quite rightly) that "the amount in question will not accomplish the object I had in view." Even on his return he was clearly undecided. As late as December 1858 he was writing a little wistfully about when he might visit "our Mill & Hospital."[133]

But at least the Touro legacy had a budget and a future. The same was hardly the case for Montefiore's other foundations. His orchard in Jaffa was already struggling, running an annual deficit of £40 despite its 1,400 trees. Nor were the farmers in the north doing much better. Most had lost their cattle, and the whole area around Safed and Tiberias had been ravaged by cholera and drought. Only the weaving institution and the girls' school were flourishing. The former enabled eight men to make a good living, while the latter was becoming a real success.[134]

It is true that Ludwig Frankl wrote disparagingly of its soporific atmosphere, but the English missionary Mary Eliza Rogers described the courtyard as a rare oasis of greenery and the pupils as a crowd of happy, industrious girls.[135] When Montefiore visited in 1857 he found 125 schoolgirls, of whom two-thirds were "German children, and very clever indeed."[136] This modest growth in numbers was partly due to rationalization, for Albert Cohn had recently closed the rival Rothschild foundation. The presence of so many Ashkenazim hints at a more fundamental transformation. As a Jewish teacher from Trieste told readers of the *Educatore Israelita,* attitudes were changing in the holy city, and there was now "a strong wish among many families to have their daughters taught some European languages."[137]

This was precisely the outcome toward which—in their different ways—Montefiore, Philippson, the Rothschilds, and Elisa Herz had been working. Yet just as the relief fund initiatives began to make headway in Jerusalem, diaspora interest in the Holy Land was waning. The weaving institution and the girls' school cost £600 a year to keep going.[138] Barely twelve months after Montefiore's return from Palestine, both institutions were forced to close down.

Chapter 12

The Mortara Affair

Crossing the Alps at Mont Cenis was one of the wonders of European travel. The road from the Italian side led upward across a succession of rough bridges, each precipice steeper than the last, the views increasingly wild and majestic, the sheer drop to the raging torrent below both terrifying and awe-inspiring. From the barren summit you could see the still, clear blue of the lake and its extended plain surrounded by broken cliffs. In the summer, once the snow had melted, Piedmontese shepherds led their flocks up to pasture among the rocks and Alpine flowers. Montefiore had always loved dramatic scenery, and his travels took him many times to Mont Cenis.[1] It was a magical place, where the presence of the Almighty seemed near.

By 1857 Judith had been ill for a long time. Passing through France on their latest trip to Jerusalem, she found "six or eight hours a day travelling in a Railway Carriage . . . as much as she could bear."[2] The warmer weather of Palestine did little to ease her condition; back home she remained so poorly that they saw no option but to head for the sun.[3] But traveling to Italy with Judith's brother and his wife early in 1858 proved no panacea: Judith became seriously ill in Florence, and Montefiore was bedridden for seventeen days. Acting on the advice of their Ramsgate physician, they began a slow, painful journey home.

Montefiore was filled with foreboding. Here, on the roof of the world, he had often sought spiritual sustenance. Writing in his Bible in this most private of places, he felt able to express his deepest fears:

Monday the 12 Tammuz 5618
the 14th June 58 On the summit of Mount Cenis With my dear Jud
Heal her O God of my salvation
I beseach [*sic*] thee. Heal her [*illegible*] I beseech

258

thee   Think and Thank
The Salvation of the [*illegible*] is from the Lord
for he is their strength in the time of
Affliction. The Lord shall help & deliver them
and save them because they confide in him.

He added horizontally on the next page: "And I will offer my prayer unto thee O Lord! in an acceptable time: in thine abundant mercy, O God! answer me in the truth of thy salvation lead me O Lord in thy righteousness because of my enemies."[4]

From the summit, the road descended through black mountains and stony valleys to the pretty French village of Lanslebourg. Continuing on to Paris, Judith remained poorly and weak, with Montefiore increasingly worried about his own health and the return of a dangerous illness. The news that summer can have done nothing to lift their spirits.

Early that July the British press began to carry reports of a shocking episode in the northern Italian town of Bologna, a thriving commercial center with a strong revolutionary tradition.[5] Here, on June 23, 1858, the city inquisitor had ordered a detachment of papal carabinieri to seize a six-year-old Jewish boy named Edgardo Mortara who (it was claimed) had been secretly baptized some years earlier by the family's Catholic housemaid, Anna Morisi.[6]

Little Edgardo's parents were totally unprepared for this disaster. His mother, Marianna, collapsed on the sofa, his father began tearing his hair out, and six of the remaining seven children fell to their knees begging the policemen to relent. For the next twenty-four hours, two policemen stood guard over the traumatized child while his relatives sought desperately to intercede with the papal authorities. Marianna became so hysterical that Momolo, the boy's father, decided to send her elsewhere. As she was driven away in a closed carriage, prostrate with grief, her piercing cries brought the entire neighborhood to their windows. Edgardo was calmer by the time the caribinieri returned for him, but his guards were in tears, and Momolo fainted when the child was taken from his arms.

Before the revolutions of 1848, this incident might have passed unnoticed. Now, it confronted enlightened opinion with the persistence of religious persecution in the heartlands of European civilization. The peculiar place of Jews in Catholic theology had preserved a continuous Jewish presence in Rome since the fall of the Second Temple. The restrictions faced by Jews in the Papal States were probably harsher than anywhere else in western Europe. In a state run by the church, Jews were inevitably denied access to education and public charity. They also

suffered important vocational and legal disabilities: excluded from the
civil service and most prestigious trades and professions, unable to testify against a Christian in civil law. In fact there had always been a difference between dogma and practice. That a growing minority owned
real estate testified to improvements in Jewish status, but all Jews remained subject to the Holy Office of the Inquisition, which ran a network of refuges for converts known as the Houses of the Catechumens.
Most chose to go, tempted by the prospect of a cash payment of 100
scudi and a less trammeled existence. Once brought inside, a Jew could
be kept there for up to forty days. A law still in force in 1858 prescribed
three lashes and a heavy fine to any Jew who passed within sixty yards
of the building. And so it was that after taking him from his parents, the
Inquisition conveyed little Edgardo Mortara to the House of the Catechumens in Rome.[7]

Forced baptism had been a hazard of Jewish life in Italy for centuries.[8]
In theory, the Catholic church condemned those who baptized children
against the wishes of their parents unless the child was in mortal danger.
In practice, the church regarded baptism as an irreversible act of grace—
and claimed such children as its own. Only seven years earlier, the Jews
of Reggio and Modena had petitioned Duke Francesco V to put an end
to this inhuman practice.[9] Shortly before Edgardo's abduction, a Jewish
family fled Modena after a young servant claimed to have baptized their
daughter. They sought refuge in Turin, capital of Piedmont: the only
Italian state with a constitution, and the only state in Italy to have emancipated its Jews. Here the role of anticlericalism in forging a political
consensus between right and left ensured them a sympathetic hearing.[10]
A liberal deputy even raised the issue in the Piedmontese parliament.
His intervention highlighted the uneven experience of Jewish communities in pre-Unification Italy, where pockets of liberty like Piedmont and
Montefiore's native Livorno existed alongside autocracies like Modena
and the theocratic regime of the Papal States.

There was in fact some doubt about the validity of Edgardo's baptism, because such acts were controversial in canon law. The Mortaras
claimed that Morisi had been too ignorant to perform the sacrament correctly (and was in any case too disreputable to be taken at her word).[11]
More important, they asserted that even if Edgardo were Christian, he
remained their son and it was their right to bring him home. As the case
became an international cause célèbre, debate centered on two issues:
Edgardo's own feelings about what had happened, and the wider implications of the episode. Both raised fundamental questions about freedom of conscience and parental rights

The Catholic press abounded with stories of little Edgardo's Christian vocation. A long article in the Piedmontese *L'Armonia della Religione colla Civiltà* was typical of such accounts. Among other things, it described the first meeting between Edgardo and Momolo at the House of the Catechumens in Rome. The loving child had hoped to convert his father, and wept bitterly when he refused to see the light. Momolo, in turn, urged his son to come with him, reminding Edgardo of the commandment to honor his father and his mother. But Edgardo replied thoughtfully, "The Pope knows the commandments better than you or I, I shall do what the Pope says." *L'Armonia* concluded by turning the arguments of the Mortaras' supporters on their head: "And they want a child of such quick faith to be delivered up to the Jews! That would be a cruelty without name, and the most open violation of that principle of liberty of conscience which the Liberals have ever in their mouths."[12]

Marianna, however, gave a very different account of her own reunion with Edgardo: "Trembling with emotion, I embraced him repeatedly, and he in turn embraced and kissed me. He was evidently struggling between fear of the people with whom he lived and his love for his parents; but the latter at length prevailed, and he declared that he would return home with us. I told him that he was born a Jew, and that like us he ought to persist in his faith. 'Dear mother,' he answered. 'I repeat the *Sceman* [*shema* prayer] every day!'"[13]

Variants of both accounts and other similar anecdotes were extensively reproduced in the European press.

Heartbreakingly for the Mortaras, Edgardo's devotion to Christianity became genuine—although precisely when, it is hard to say. Many people are successfully brainwashed by religious cults, and Edgardo's conversion was a testament to the intensive indoctrination methods deployed by the Inquisition. Decades later, as a Catholic missionary, he recalled that his parents "adopted every means to recover me, caresses, tears, prayers, and promises. In spite of this I showed not the slightest desire to return to my family, which I still cannot explain rationally, unless it showed the supernatural force of Grace."[14]

The Mortara Affair came at a bad time for the Vatican. French troops had been propping up papal government ever since 1849, when the overthrow of the radical Roman Republic enabled Napoleon III to curry favor with Catholic opinion back home. With time, the competing interests of the church and the French state in fields such as education started to reassert themselves—as did the inherent tensions between Gallican Paris and ultramontane Rome.[15] By 1858 the marriage of convenience between throne and altar was beginning to come apart.

These developments had profound implications for Italy. Napoleon III's success in the Crimean War encouraged his natural inclination toward an opportunistic and revisionist foreign policy. Napoleon had once been a *carbonaro,* sworn to strive for Italian unity. His narrow escape from assassination at the hands of the revolutionary nationalist Felice Orsini in January 1858 reminded him that the penalty for forsaking his oath was death and restored his commitment to the Italian cause. Besides Austria, the papacy was the biggest obstacle to Italian unity. The three largest French newspapers all had more or less distant ties with the government.[16] When *Le Siècle, La Presse,* and *Le Constitutionnel* took up Edgardo's cause, it was hard to avoid the conclusion that the Mortara Affair was about more than the fate of a small Jewish boy.

Ever since their brief emancipation under the first Napoleon, the fate of Italian Jewry had been intertwined with that of the nationalist movement.[17] Jewish rights and liberal reforms tended to go together. While nationalists like Giuseppe Mazzini, Carlo Cattaneo, and Massimo d'Azeglio wrote in support of emancipation, their Jewish compatriots threw themselves into the Risorgimento with disproportionate zeal. Some, like Mazzini's companion Angelo Usiglio, became political exiles. Others remained in Italy, distributing nationalist literature and joining secret societies like the Florentine Antologia, the Corriere Livornese, and Giovine Italia.[18] One of Montefiore's relatives was arrested for his involvement with I Veri Italiani, an allied society based in Livorno.

Emancipating Piedmontese Jews in March 1848 was part and parcel of this symbiosis. As editor of *Il Risorgimento,* the future leader of the Piedmontese government Count Camillo di Cavour had criticized the new constitution for failing to guarantee religious freedom; twenty days later the government granted Jews full civil and political rights.[19] During the revolution that followed, Piedmont briefly led a war of liberation against the Austrians, but the triumph of Italian liberal nationalism proved short-lived. As governments all over Italy reverted (more or less) to the status quo ante, nationalists came to recognize that constitutional Piedmont was their best hope. By 1858 Cavour had already been in power for nearly a decade, and *L'Opinione* had replaced *Risorgimento* as the official government mouthpiece. Its Jewish editor and proprietor, Giacomo Dina, worked so intimately with the prime minister that he never took a major editorial decision without consulting him. In the hands of Dina and the Jews of Piedmont, the case of Edgardo Mortara became yet another stick with which to beat the papacy and Italy's unrepentantly reactionary regimes.

On July 21, 1858, a week after the first article about Edgardo appeared in the French press, Napoleon III met Cavour at Plombières-les-Bains. It was here, in this quiet spa town, that the emperor secretly agreed to back Piedmont militarily in a war against Austria. The two men planned to redraw the map of Italy by expanding Piedmont and Tuscany at the expense of the Papal States and the other central Italian duchies. Cavour later reported that Napoleon was "delighted with the Mortara Affair, as with everything which could compromise the Pope in the eyes of Europe and of moderate Catholics. The more complaints there are against him, the easier it will be to impose on him the sacrifices demanded by the reorganisation of Italy."[20]

With the triumphant conclusion to the long-running emancipation campaign in Britain, the countries in which Jews had achieved full political rights now formed a solid core in western Europe, stretching down through France and the Netherlands to northern Italy, although the situation in German-speaking lands was more ambiguous. In an appeal issued by the president of Turin's Jewish community on behalf of every synagogue in Piedmont, Italy's emancipated Jews explained pointedly that it was natural for the initiative to "emanate from this State of Italy, where complete religious liberty is sanctioned by the law, and earnestly and uniformly enforced by the Government." The abduction of Edgardo Mortara might once have gone unremarked, but "times have changed and the civil and political conditions of several European States permit us now at least to express our abhorrence of those deeds of cruelty which are still committed in some parts of the civilized world, in the name of religion, by ignorant and fanatical ministers. It becomes therefore, an obvious duty . . . that we should avail ourselves of the universal Press to appeal to all mankind against acts which violate the most sacred rights of paternity . . . and that we should endeavour by all possible means not only to obtain redress for the outrage in question, but to prevent the re-enactment of such an event."[21]

Talk of "civilization," "humanity," "barbarous practices," and "fanatical ministers" echoed the rhetoric of 1840 and the opposition between West and East invoked during the Damascus Affair. But the "deeds of cruelty" decried by the Jews of Piedmont had been perpetrated in western Europe—and Catholics, not Jews, were in the dock.

Contemporaries understood this. In the words of the liberal Catholic *Journal de Bruxelles*, the plight of Edgardo Mortara had been taken up by "the revolutionary or antireligious newspapers in Piedmont and other countries, and it serves as a text for their protestations against the Holy See." This lumping together of political and spiritual enemies reflected the growing tension between secularizing liberalism and a revitalized Catholicism. Like the new Jewish public, both operated in an increasingly global public sphere.[22]

Before 1848 the church had accommodated both liberal and ultramontane Catholicism, but the radical turn taken by the revolution in

Rome led Pius IX to embrace political reaction.[23] Many Catholics now saw liberalism as the enemy of papal authority. Liberals, in turn, identified Catholicism with superstition, backwardness, and tyranny. They found in unreformed papal government a soft target for their critique. In Britain, the crusade against papal tyranny was led by no less a politician than William Gladstone. In France, 1858 saw the serialization of a devastating attack on the papal regime in the official *Moniteur*. Edmond About presented Rome as a weeping sore, sapping the lifeblood from Italy's potentially vibrant society and economy; the pope's subjects wanted laws and railways, not the arbitrary government of priests.[24] That a poor Roman was likely to be wealthier and better educated than his London or Paris counterparts was irrelevant.[25] Spiraling debt, a lack of productive labor, and the unhealthy relationship between Rome and the provinces had left the papacy hostage to the temporal power that was supposed to guarantee its freedom, paralyzing it politically and undermining its moral stature.

Devout Catholics were well aware of this agenda. Writing in the ultramontane *Univers*, Louis Veuillot asserted: "In the past Christians would have accepted the Papal decision: now the same people criticize his action. A revolution in values and beliefs has shaken modern society and pagan prejudices have taken precedence over eternal verities." Veuillot also made other unpleasant accusations, claiming that the agents of Mazzini, so determined to wound the pope, were financed by the Jews. "Everywhere that eastern race rules supreme. They have purchased the copyright of all the important newspapers in Europe: the *Times, Constitutionnel, Débats*, etc."[26] These allegations were echoed by a long article in the Jesuit journal, *Civiltà Cattolica*, which was the papacy's only public response to the episode.[27] Here the Mortara polemic pointed toward a more modern anti-Semitism, deploying the language of race not religion, and reflecting the association between Jews and the forces of revolution made by many on the religious right.[28]

Militancy of this kind failed to contain the public-relations disaster faced by the Vatican. In October 1858 the French police reported that popular indignation was unparalleled.[29] Moderate Catholics could only look on in despair.[30] It was this clash between liberal and Catholic worldviews at a moment of critical international tension that gave the Mortara Affair global significance—and rendered it a transformative episode in the Jewish world as well.

In a sense, the Mortara Affair was merely the latest humanitarian outrage to transfix an international Jewish public. Montefiore certainly knew how to respond to the appeal from Piedmont. First, apply for co-operation from Jewish communities overseas; second, publicize the issue as widely as possible and stress the universal aspects of the case; third, reach out to other religious and political constituencies in Britain that were likely to prove sympathetic; fourth, persuade the Foreign Office it ought to intervene; and fifth (if necessary), send a deputation to the pope.

To launch his campaign, he sent a copy of the Mortara appeal to *The Times*, which published it in full—alongside a short report of the Board of Deputies' response.[31] A letter addressed to Jewish communities in Germany, the United States, and elsewhere indicated clearly the line Montefiore thought they should take. "You cannot fail to perceive," he wrote, "that this is a matter affecting not the Jews alone, but also every other denomination of Faith, except the Roman Catholic, further that it cannot be regarded exclusively under a Religious aspect, but as placing in peril, personal liberty, social relations and the peace of families."[32]

In an effort to encourage interfaith protest, Montefiore arranged for the piece in *The Times* to be sent to every Catholic clergyman in Britain, around 1,800 in all. Only one was willing to come out publicly against the papacy; some of the rest were apparently so outraged that they returned Montefiore's letter defaced or half-burnt.[33]

By this stage he had already approached the Conservative foreign secretary, Lord Malmesbury, enclosing copies of everything the board had received from Piedmont. Malmesbury sent to France and Italy the next day requesting further details.[34] Replying from Paris, Lord Cowley was able to provide him with a blow-by-blow account of the dramatic encounter that had taken place between Pius IX and the French ambassador, who described in a letter to his superior, Count Alexandre Walewski, how

[t]ears flowed gently from his [the pope's] eyes and I must admit that even I could not but feel a certain anguish on assisting at this solemn combat . . . between the absolutely rigorous duties of the Holy Pontiff and the voice of nature, which the crown has not wholly silenced in Pius IX. It is hard to describe the bitterness of his regrets and the sadness of his words . . . He sympathised painfully with the suffering of the parents, every day he was further saddened by the attacks on religion for which this unfortunate incident was cause or pretext; he understood all that was painful and contrary to nature in this hidden baptism and its harsh consequences; the law of the church condemned it, religion forbade it and those guilty of it were liable to excommunication . . . but . . . in his eyes, in his soul, in his conscience, the child which he had examined was sufficiently

mature to know what he wanted, and his voice could not be misunderstood . . . It was impossible for the head of this Church, as representative of Jesus Christ on earth, to refuse this child the benefit of Our Saviour's blood, shed for his redemption, which he pleaded for with an almost supernatural faith . . . His resolution was unshakable. The child would remain Christian.[35]

Yet Antoine Alfred Agénor, the duc de Gramont, refused to take no for an answer, raising the matter with Pius and the Vatican's secretary of state, Cardinal Giacomo Antonelli, at every available opportunity. He was so disgusted by the Mortara Affair that he even contemplated kidnapping Edgardo himself.[36]

News that French efforts were getting nowhere dictated the response of the British government. Recognizing a dead end when he saw one, Malmesbury telegraphed to Italy, canceling his previous instructions to apply a little unofficial pressure to the papal government. His decision left the government in an awkward position domestically, where the Mortara Affair was fanning the flames of anti-Catholic prejudice.[37]

"No Popery" in Britain dated back to the Reformation, but had been crucially reinforced by the Civil War and the Glorious Revolution. Politically, Catholicism was associated with the absolutist monarchies of the Continent; theologically, it was associated with the spiritual pretensions of the church hierarchy, whereby priests mediated between God and man, and the pope's word transcended the moral law. Both were anathema to the self-image of the British as a free and Protestant nation. Catholic emancipation, the mass immigration of poor Irish workers, and the ensuing revival of English Catholicism exacerbated popular anxiety about the perceived papal threat.

In this atmosphere of growing sectarian tension, the restoration of the Catholic church hierarchy in 1850 prompted mass hysteria.[38] Traditional bonfire-night celebrations turned to mob violence, nearly 32,000 signed the petition organized by the Protestant Defence League, and in Parliament Lord John Russell felt no qualms about playing the anti-Catholic card. The influx of Italian political refugees and a string of scandalous court cases during the decade that followed ensured that papal abuses remained in the public eye. Inevitably the abduction of Edgardo Mortara prompted a further spate of scare stories.[39] The *Morning Post* concurred with the Republican *Siècle* that "never in modern times has the Church of Rome, as represented by the Government of the Pope, shown as much courage in endeavouring to impose its laws, its tyranny, on mankind."[40]

Such attitudes rendered Montefiore's efforts to present the Mortaras'

Pope Pius IX. (By permission of Adoc-photos/Art Resource, New York)

cause in universal terms relatively straightforward. It appealed most to influential Protestant organizations with a strong tradition of anti-Catholic agitation. Chief among them was Sir Culling Eardley's Evangelical Alliance, which invited two Jews to attend its annual meeting in Liverpool and speak about the merits of the case. Montefiore refused politely, noting that "an independent movement on the part of that influential body, would have far greater moral weight, than would result from direct solicitations from the Jewish community."[41] The decision proved sound, since Eardley's support at the Liverpool conference was framed in highly controversial terms.

After stressing the natural sympathy that every intelligent Christian was bound to feel for the Jews, Eardley proceeded to elaborate the obvious, namely that the Mortara Affair affected "the Papacy—that grand impediment to the conversion of the world—and he included in that description the grand impediment to the conversion of the Jews." Amid loud cheers, he then demanded the return of Edgardo not in the name of liberty, but rather because it impugned the "honour of Jesus Christ . . . to take away, in the name of Christianity, a child whose parents are opposed to it and who, because they have seen nothing of Christianity except Popery . . . are unwilling that their child shall be made a Christian."[42] The *Jewish Chronicle* could only decry his proselytism and the lack of a more humanitarian perspective, showing equal respect for Catholics, Protestants, and Jews.[43]

But there was no denying the potency of Evangelical protest. By December 1858 Malmesbury had received petitions from the Protestant Association, the Scottish Reformation Society, and Lord Shaftesbury's Protestant Alliance demanding British intervention in the Mortara Affair.[44] In reply, Malmesbury reiterated his (well-founded) conviction "that the intervention of a Protestant State in such a case would do more harm than good."[45] Eardley then persuaded the lord mayor of London and the lord provost of Edinburgh to accompany a Protestant deputation to Paris, where they would join forces with their brethren from France, Germany, and the United States to present Napoleon III with a memorial focusing on the Mortara Affair, but addressing the plight of French Protestants as well.[46]

Evangelicals and Dissenters opposed to the state-church connection on principle saw the proposed expedition as a unique opportunity to make an international and interfaith stand in defense of religious freedom—and to prove that their commitment amounted to more than self-interest. Not only did Eardley invite Montefiore to participate; he also planned to remind the emperor of the energetic campaign recently waged by Protestants in Turkey, Hungary, Switzerland, Piedmont, France, Holland, and the United States on behalf of a handful of Swedish converts to Catholicism. Montefiore declined the invitation. The decision undermined a lifetime of interfaith activism, but even the Board of Deputies reluctantly concluded that lobbying the emperor was unlikely to work. For Eardley and his Protestants, the Mortara Affair was both a matter of principle and a propaganda opportunity. For Montefiore and the Jewish public, it was a wrong that required immediate restitution: an abuse related to the specific environment of the Papal States, which could be rectified only in Rome.

Efforts to coordinate an international Jewish response were uneven. In September 1858, just three months after Lionel de Rothschild finally took his seat in the House of Commons, the *Jewish Chronicle* maintained smugly "that neither the French institutions, nor the religion of the majority of the nation, nor the influences for the present in the ascendant beyond the Channel afford the same scope for actions to the Consistoire Central des Israélites de France as enjoyed by the English

Board of Deputies." French Jews took precisely the opposite view. Writing in the *Archives Israélites*, Isidore Cahen concluded that the time had come to found an international defense committee, based in Paris, charged with promoting Jewish rights.[47]

If anything this was a comment on the fragmented response of the Jewish world to news of Mortara's abduction. Rothschild loans kept the papacy afloat, and both James and Lionel de Rothschild had written personally to the secretary of state, Cardinal Giacomo Antonelli. Jewish authorities in Britain, France, Holland, Piedmont, Prussia, and the United States had lobbied their respective governments.[48] Inspired by Ludwig Philippson, forty-five distinguished German rabbis had appealed directly to the papacy.[49] Yet only the Jews of New York proved willing to dance to the tune of the Board of Deputies.

This response was testimony to the institutional immaturity of American Jewry. The Mortara Affair aroused powerful emotions across the Atlantic, where Montefiore's appeal provided a critical element of leadership. In 1840 the United States had intervened on behalf of the Jewish prisoners in Damascus; with civil war looming, President Buchanan was in no position to take the moral high ground. He refused to interfere in the Mortara Affair, stating a concern for "the principle of nonintervention on the part of the United States between foreign sovereigns and their own subjects." As the Chicago-based *Daily Democrat* commented, "an Administration which defended slavery . . . could not protest against the gross injustice of tearing a child from its parents. Does not slavery daily tear children from their parents and parents from their children?" Unwilling to take no for an answer, the Board of Representatives of the United Congregations of Israelites of the City of New York deputed Gershom Kursheedt in London to cooperate with European Jewry on their behalf.[50]

Montefiore had already agreed to present a memorial to the pope in person. His colleagues concluded that it would "be inexpedient to associate any delegate to act in conjunction with the Board [of Deputies]."[51] Kursheedt resolved to accompany his friend in an informal role. Likening the Mortara Affair to an electric shock administered to the whole Jewish community, the *Jewish Chronicle* described Montefiore's mission to Rome as "the visible effect of this intensified feeling of Jewish oneness, bringing it clearly and distinctly to the consciousness of all members."[52] The *Archives Israélites* was more skeptical, regretting Montefiore's refusal to collaborate with Eardley's Evangelicals in lobbying Napoleon III.[53] Cahen would later criticize the deputies more explicitly for sending Montefiore "in the name of English Israelitism, rather than of Judaism in general . . . an Englishman likes to overcome obstacles alone, so that he alone can enjoy the profit or the glory."[54] Such criticism reflected the limits of individual activism in a world increasingly willing to embrace liberal ideas and representative structures. As civil society broadened and deepened, Montefiore's political repertoire seemed increasingly out of touch.

Like Russia, the Vatican had yet to adapt to these emerging political realities. In a situation in which one man could still decide everything, Montefiore's face-to-face approach remained the best option. It had proved impossible to sway the tsar, whose empire was too important to be subjected to the patronizing moral imperialism that Britain imposed on the Ottoman sultan. The pope was far more vulnerable to the interplay between public opinion and great-power politics. His position as the moral arbiter of the Catholic world still gave Pius the status to disregard arguments made by Jews, Protestants, and secularists in the name of European civilization.

The urbane and cosmopolitan British attaché in Rome remembered Montefiore perfectly. A nephew of the former Whig prime minister, Odo Russell was freshly arrived from Constantinople, where he had served as an aide to Stratford de Redcliffe. As the representative of Protestant Britain, Russell lacked proper diplomatic status and had yet to make his mark. He informed Montefiore frankly that an interview with the pope was the best he could do. "What can a poor Attaché expect, when the French Ambassador with a French army with him has failed after making every endeavour?" he added gloomily. This view was echoed by Joseph Barclay Pentland, author of *Murray's Handbook to Rome,* who urged Montefiore to call on Gramont. Montefiore refused to listen. "I am," he said, "so much of an Englishman that I prefer the English representation, and would only act in accordance with the advice of Mr. Russell."[55]

His patriotic bluster hardly mattered—but only because Edgardo's fate had been sealed some six months earlier. If anything, the pope's attitude had hardened in the interim. Pius was furious at the outcry, which threatened to overturn the Vatican's efforts to keep a grip on its lands in central Italy, and subsequently told Edgardo that he paid a high price for the boy's soul.[56] In a dramatic confrontation with the leaders of Rome's Jewish community in January 1859, the pope had turned on Sabatino Scazzochio, the communal secretary, shouting: "You, yes you have thrown oil on the flames, you have blown into the fire . . . you have even taken yourself to newspaper offices, you visited the editors of *Civiltà Cattolica,* always with a view to opposing and distorting . . . But the newspapers can write what they choose—I laugh at the whole world!"[57] His outburst so terrified Scazzochio that he promptly burst into tears.

None of this boded well for Montefiore's mission. In fact, he cannot have expected to succeed. The Jews of Piedmont had always recognized that public protest would cast only "a momentary disgrace" over the Vatican.[58] By appealing to the Board of Deputies and the Consistoire Central des Israélites de France to influence their respective governments, Piedmontese Jewish leaders hoped only "to secure some guarantee that at Rome, as elsewhere, nobody shall be permitted to disturb the happiness and order of Jewish families."[59] Implicit here was the acceptance that the Mortara campaign was essentially a preventative measure. Montefiore had never persuaded the Vatican to remove the incriminating inscription from the tomb of Father Tommaso in Damascus. His firsthand experience of the obstruction and prejudice of Roman officialdom gave him a good idea of what lay ahead. Arriving in Rome on April 5 in the company of Kursheedt, Hodgkin, and a long-suffering Judith, he must also have realized that his timing was appalling.

In the first place, it was Easter: Rome was filled with pilgrims, and the pope and his court were busy with time-consuming rituals and services. Montefiore had seen it all before and was, in any case, in no mood for sight-seeing. Second, Judith remained in poor health; all he wanted was to complete his mission and go home. Finally, and most important, political events in Italy were reaching a head. On New Year's Day 1859 Napoleon III had made a casual remark to the Austrian ambassador, deprecating the poor relations between their two countries. War had been in the cards ever since. Official Piedmontese rhetoric was increasingly bellicose, while the publication of a quasi-official pamphlet titled *L'Empéreur Napoléon III et l'Italie* left no doubt about where the latter's sympathies lay.

Britain now emerged as a key player. Politicians on all sides were united in execrating the abuses of papal government. Whereas Liberal leaders like Gladstone, Palmerston, and Russell were sympathetic both to Piedmont and to Italian nationalism, Conservatives like Malmesbury and Disraeli feared that the overthrow of papal rule would give republicans and revolutionaries free rein. Malmesbury's preferred option was to see both France and Austria withdraw their troops from the Papal States while all the European powers pressed Pius to reform. He devoted the early months of 1859 to a last-ditch effort at mediation.[60]

Malmesbury's efforts made Protestant Britain a force to be conciliated: avoiding war was unquestionably in the pope's interest, although he found the rest of Malmesbury's agenda less palatable. Antonelli even undertook to evacuate French and Austrian troops from papal soil. The problem for Malmesbury was that neither France nor Austria wanted to do business. Negotiations dragged on into early April, but there was no persuading the papacy to accept the legitimacy of a conference on Italian affairs at which its role would be purely consultative. On April 9, the day after his first meeting with Montefiore, Russell attempted at length to persuade Antonelli that—short of war—a congress was his only option. The secretary of state refused to cooperate, noting pointedly that if the powers wished to avoid war, they should turn their attention to Piedmont instead.[61]

Montefiore was not privy to these developments, but he appreciated enough to realize that the outlook was gloomy. On April 11 he wrote in his diary: "Everything I hear and see unfortunately confirms the opinion given me before my arrival. I have not heard from any person since I left London that there was the slightest hope of success for my mission, and now fear that I may even be denied the opportunity of presenting the address of the Board to the Sovereign Pontiff." Shortly afterward Russell confirmed that Antonelli had refused even to discuss Edgardo Mortara. The papal chamberlain, Monsignor Gilbert Talbot, assured Russell that Pius would probably see Montefiore, but Talbot—like Antonelli—"considered the question closed." Less than ten days later, Austria issued an ultimatum to Piedmont. War was suddenly a certainty—and Montefiore was still waiting despairingly for his interview with the pope.[62]

The atmosphere in Rome reflected this tense international situation. In late April, angry crowds gathered outside the residence of the French military commander, shouting: "Long live France! Long live the General! Long live the Emperor! Long live Italy! Long live Independence!"[63] Montefiore, meanwhile, found himself caught between two very different worlds: on the one hand, the carefree society of well-to-do British tourists; on the other, the oppressive drudgery of the Ghetto.

Rome had always been a popular destination for Montefiore's compatriots, offering an unsurpassed combination of classical ruins, baroque art, and the inevitable frisson Protestants felt at being within a stone's throw of the Vatican. Shops in the English quarter sold everything from Crosse and Blackwell's pickles to Mappin's razors, Atkinson's perfumery, Guinness' stout, and Allsopp's pale ale.[64] An Englishman could live just as he did in London, giving teas and champagne suppers for his fellow tourists, catching up on the latest news in Piale's Reading Room, and discussing parliamentary affairs in the English club. Yet the overpowering presence of Catholicism gave the city a sinister exoticism. "[Y]ou see priests on every side," wrote the journalist Edward Dicey;

"Franciscan friars, and Dominicans, Carmelites and Capuchins, priests in brown cloth and priests in serge, priests in red and white and grey, priests in purple and priests in rags, standing on the church-steps, stopping at the doorways, coming down the bye-streets, looking out of the windows—you see priests everywhere and always."[65]

In 1859 Rome was more than usually thronged with tourists: 1,500 Britons, and another 1,000 or so from elsewhere. These included foreign royals like the king and queen of Prussia, Montefiore's old acquaintance Lord Stratford de Redcliffe, and Edward, Prince of Wales. The last was traveling with his mentor, Colonel Charles Andrew Bruce, who administered a harsh diet of private study, sightseeing, and improving dinner parties—to one of which Montefiore was invited. The evening seems to have been typical of these sober, rather stuffy occasions. "Conversation was on general topics," Bruce's wife was the only woman present, and the party broke up early, at about nine. Montefiore could not have had a more gratifying evening, and he rounded it off by attending a "most lively and agreeable party" held by the royal physician for 150 guests. His mission made him something of a celebrity. Everyone "expressed an ardent desire for my success," Montefiore wrote that night in his diary, "but not one among them thought that there was a hope of it . . . having left my dear wife weak and poorly, I got away as soon as I well could."[66]

The contrast between this glittering social occasion and the reality of life in the Ghetto could not have been starker. English visitors to Rome stayed in the grander part of the city. Even so, they were not complimentary: the shops lacked window fronts; the streets were narrow and gloomy, with ragged washing hanging from window sills; the prevalence of footpaths, absence of pavements, and reckless driving rendered the city unsafe for pedestrians; the buildings themselves were monuments of decaying grandeur, with holes where scaffolding had once been fixed, large blotches of peeling plaster, and great lumps of stonework lying unused in the mud.[67] Yet all agreed that the squalor of the Ghetto was in a class of its own. "[N]either rain nor wind nor sun can clean the Ghetto," wrote Edmond About; "it would take a flood or a fire to purify it."[68]

With 4,000 Jews forced to live in a few streets, large families were often reduced to a single room; the houses were tall, narrow, and ramshackle, the streets a warren of shabby yards and lanes, uneven cobblestones, and crumbling walls. They were also—perhaps inevitably—alive with people. In a famous passage, the German historian Ferdinand Gregorovius, who lived in Rome during the 1850s, described how the Jews of Rome sat

in the doorways, or out in the alleys, which give little more light than the
damp and moldy rooms, and waste away in plundered junk . . . Bits of
rag lie before the doors in great heaps, and there is every kind and color,
golden fringes, pieces of silk brocade, pieces of velvet, red rags, blue
shreds, orange, yellow, black, white, old, torn, ripped, worn bits and
pieces . . . The Jews . . . sit before them and burrow in the sea of fragments, as they look for treasures, at least a little buried piece of Gold
brocade . . .

The daughters of Zion sit on these rags and sew what can be sewn . . .
It was sad to see them, pale and down-at-heel, bent double and working
busily with the needle—men and women alike, girls and children.[69]

These great heaps of cloth, this endless sewing represented the traditional occupation of Roman Jews, who worked in what was quite literally the rag trade. Economic and educational restrictions left this as one
of the few ways in which they could earn a living. Only about 100 of the
Ghetto's inhabitants were wealthy enough to pay taxes; more than half
depended on communal charity. In a petition to the pope, the community complained that it could do nothing to improve its lot.[70] But such
complaints were rare. Centuries of ritualized humiliation and the recent
outbreaks of anti-Jewish violence during the revolution had left a psychological scar. In his popular attack on the papal regime, About described how even "the bravest [Jews] urged me to write nothing in their
favor if I did not wish to aggravate the evils that overwhelmed them."[71]

On April 15, the night after Montefiore's gratifying evening with the
prince of Wales, all hell broke loose in the Jewish quarter. Three young
boys had gone missing a couple of days earlier. Their parents consulted
a local barber, well known for his psychic powers. Then the young
woman he used as a medium supposedly revealed in a trance that Jews
had decapitated the eldest boy, kept his head, thrown the body into a
cellar, and stored the blood in a copper vessel for use in baking matza
for the forthcoming festival of Passover; the other two boys were still
alive, but destined for the same treatment. That night a police brigade
entered the Ghetto, occupied the main square, and searched the house
next to the synagogue. The authorities soon imprisoned the barber and
his assistant, but the brigade was instructed to stay in the Ghetto.[72]

In the streets, the atmosphere remained threatening. Bystanders threw
stones at passing Jews; women and children shouted, "Take care of your
children, or the Jew will murder them." So alarming was the situation
that Jewish guests invited to dine with the Montefiores were afraid to
return to the Ghetto alone. There were several attempts to hide missing
children in the synagogues in order to foment a new accusation; on one

"The Ghetto, Rome," by Louis Haghe from a painting by S. V. Hunt, in Picturesque Europe, *vol. 3 (London, 1878), facing p. 209. (By permission of the Bodleian Library, University of Oxford: Hist.d.125–129)*

such occasion, the *shamash* (beadle) found a child hidden under a seat, apparently asleep. An angry crowd gathered half an hour later, accusing the Jews of ritual murder, and the hysterical mother led the police to the very spot where the child had been hidden. It was, Montefiore thought, only "by the mercy of heaven" that "these plans were frustrated, and in each case the lost child was found." As a gesture of support, he offered to sleep in the Ghetto, but the offer simply underlined the gulf between him and the rest of Rome's Jews.[73]

Montefiore was no stranger to such fabrications. Just ten years earlier, when he and Judith were encamped at Nazareth, a local woman had begun screaming near their tent, shouting that they had murdered her missing child.[74] Yet he took the events in Rome decidedly personally. The day after the first incident, an article appeared in *Il Vero Amico del Popolo,* the least respectable of Rome's three newspapers, recounting a separate blood libel accusation and recalling the murder of Father Tommaso in Damascus.[75] Strict censorship in the Papal States meant that the article had been tolerated by the papal authorities. Montefiore seems to have suspected that both it and the disturbances in the Ghetto were deliberately instigated to frustrate his efforts.[76]

In a narrow sense he was wrong: the police spared no efforts to find the missing children, who eventually turned up 100 miles away in Spoleto.[77] But the Mortara Affair did see a revival of the blood libel in Catholic newspapers following ritual-murder allegations in Romania. *Il Cattolico* drew a clear link between the two episodes, commenting that the liberal press had made a huge commotion when the pope arranged for a Jewish boy to be "brought up . . . in a Catholic boarding school," but "[a] Jew kills a Christian boy, in the most horrible way, and the liberals, we are certain, will not have a single word to say about it."[78]

With such accusations surfacing in Rome for the first time, in addition to Judith's illness and the continuing political crisis, Montefiore felt increasingly anxious at hearing nothing from the Vatican. "Suspense and perplexity still prevent me from writing," he telegraphed to the deputies on April 17. Ten days later Russell finally informed Montefiore that "it was not usual . . . to answer such applications when the favor solicited could not be granted."[79] This outcome was hardly surprising. Yet it was widely rumored that the worldlier secretary of state disagreed with his master over Edgardo, recognizing the need to put politics before principle.

One of a dying breed—an unordained cardinal promoted for his brilliance as an administrator—Antonelli was widely reviled as a cynical opportunist and political manipulator.[80] A womanizer, who enjoyed the good things in life, he had ruthlessly set about making his fortune at the church's expense. Now this canny operator did his pragmatic best to minimize the affront to Montefiore, authorizing Russell to tell him that "he would receive the Memorial, of which you are the bearer, from your own hands, and present it himself to the Pope." This was a significant concession at a time when international events must have demanded Antonelli's complete attention. Even so, the *Jewish Chronicle* saw the pope's refusal as a "gratuitous insult to a man everywhere respected for his universal philanthropy"—a man whose past encounters with royalty entitled him to expect that he might "be received in person by a potentate of a third-rate power, sitting on a tottering throne."[81] The interview with the secretary of state was better than nothing: a face-saving exercise on both sides.[82]

After climbing the 190 steps to the Vatican's secretarial apartments—which according to the historian de Cesare were "hung in blue and furnished in a style more suitable to a gay lady than . . . an ecclesiastic" —Montefiore found himself confronted with an implacable courtesy.[83] Contemporaries who remarked the cardinal's sprightly, attractive manners also noted his "sallow, intensely Italian face; those great black eyes, never at rest; those parted lips, that show the glittering teeth; the jet-black hair; the worn yet defiant look so full of intelligence, power and pride, can belong to none but Antonelli."[84] After listening politely to

Montefiore, the cardinal explained that "as the child . . . had been baptized, it would be contrary to the Law of the Holy See to allow it to return to its parents without that religious education, to which it was entitled as a member of the Roman Catholic Church." Antonelli refused to discuss the validity of the baptism, reiterating that the matter "was now closed."[85]

Yet he did try to pour oil on troubled waters by suggesting that when Edgardo was old enough he could make up his own mind, and by stressing that the pope did not wish to take undue advantage in cases of conversion. Indeed, the cardinal emphasized his own goodwill toward the pope's Jewish subjects and his "readiness to improve their condition, so long as it could be done without interfering with the established laws of the Holy See." In his report to the Board of Deputies, Montefiore commented merely: "Most ardently do I hope that these assurances may ere long be fulfilled. I regret however to say that the actual present condition of the Jews of Rome is most deplorable." But in later life he liked nothing better than to recount how a passing reference to the *firman* of 1840 prompted Antonelli to ask how much of Rothschild's gold he had paid for it—a slur to which Montefiore famously (but perhaps apocryphally) replied: "Not so much as I gave your lackey for hanging up my coat in your hall."[86]

Even after this meeting, Montefiore undertook to wait twelve days before abandoning all hope of a papal interview. The political situation was heating up alarmingly. "The English are all taking their departure," Montefiore wrote in his diary just two days after his encounter with Antonelli. "It is reported that hostilities have actually commenced between Piedmont and Austria; also that 14,000 Tuscan troops have gone over to Piedmont, and the Grand Duke fled to Bologna." Twenty-four hours later, things looked even blacker: "Unpleasant reports are in circulation to-day regarding the state of the political world," Montefiore commented. "Some feeling, it is said, has been evinced in several Colleges. It is expected that the greatest part of the French troops will leave Rome. My companions are all very anxious that we should return to England."[87] Finally, on May 5, he capitulated and bought tickets home at double the normal price.[88]

By now the city was in turmoil, and Jews in the Ghetto were living on a knife-edge. Montefiore himself witnessed an unpleasant incident, when a papal recruit burst into the synagogue during evening prayers, intent on making trouble. Nothing came of it, but Montefiore was "quite knocked up"—and devoutly grateful when they finally set sail a few days later. "It is some satisfaction that all whom I had consulted in the Mortara case agreed in opinion that I could do nothing more, and that, in the present state of things, my remaining at Rome would in no way be useful or desirable," he wrote despondently on the day of his departure. "This journey and mission has been, on many accounts, a painful and sad trial of penitence, and, I may truly add, of perseverance but our God is in Heaven, and no doubt He has permitted that which will prove a disappointment to our friends, &c., and is a grief to us, for the best and wisest purposes. Blessed be His name!"[89]

Returning to England, his religious fatalism and a typically liberal faith in the grand march of history helped Montefiore to come to terms with his first public defeat. The mission had failed, he admitted to the Board of Deputies, yet none could doubt

> but that under the blessing of the Almighty good will result therefrom.
>
> At all times it is a difficult task to attempt to penetrate the veil that hides the future from our view, but we may feel assured that the cause of civilization, however rude the shocks it may occasionally sustain, must progress, that the time cannot be very far distant when men of every creed will denounce all laws (if any such there be) that are in contravention of the Law of Nature, and when the rights of Conscience will be universally acknowledged and respected, if so, however melancholy the immediate effects of the Mortara case, may this not be a link in the Chain of events which under the directing eye of an all-wise God are tending to mitigate individual suffering and to promote the moral, social and political condition of the human race.[90]

Superficially, indeed, the Mortara agitation achieved little. Yet the *Jewish Chronicle* portrayed Montefiore's mission as "an epoch in the history of general progress": he had dared to beard the Roman lion in his den at a time "when Catholicism displays its grasping encroaching character with a daring such as not exhibited since the middle ages." This approach resonated with Jewish and Christian readers, several of whom suggested that the time had come for a more permanent testimonial to Montefiore—a hospital or almshouses, perhaps?[91]

Montefiore was unenthusiastic.[92] On his return from Jerusalem in 1857, he had resumed his post as president of the Board of Deputies with manifest reluctance; two years on, he noted that "increasing years and other circumstances of a more or less disqualifying tendency may ere long impair such efficiency as I may be able at present to exhibit in the performance of my duties."[93] In practice, however, he and his fellow deputies were swept up once more by the ongoing Mortara campaign.

On May 13, only two days after Montefiore and Judith had left Rome, the Evangelical Alliance Committee of Council met to discuss the failure of the Jewish mission. Contingency plans were already in place, and a meeting was planned with the Baptist railway contractor and radical Liberal M.P. Sir Morton Peto, the lord mayor, "and other friends" to consider what to do next. Two months later, the second great public meeting held at the Mansion House in the cause of Jewish relief approved a "Protest on behalf of British Christians." It was eventually signed by more than 2,000 leading citizens, including 79 mayors and provosts, 27 dukes and peers, 22 bishops and archbishops, and 36 M.P.s. Under the circumstances, the Board of Deputies could not do less than follow suit—drafting a second address to the pope on July 14, the day after the Mansion House event.[94]

The phrasing of the "Protest" was combative, declaring the abduction of Edgardo "repulsive to the instincts of humanity, in violation of parental rights and authority as recognised in the laws and usages of all civilised nations, and, above all, in direct opposition to the spirit and precepts of the Christian religion." A petition drawn up in parallel by the deputies took entirely the opposite tack: recalling a memorial sent in 1847 to thank Pius for his benevolent treatment of Jews living in the Papal States; reiterating the possibility that Edgardo had never really been baptized; and suggesting that by restoring the boy to his parents, His Holiness would "be upholding the sanctity of parental rights, maintaining the claims of justice, restoring peace to an afflicted family, and securing the approbation of the good and wise of every creed."[95] The contrast between the vigorous political posturing of British Protestants and the invariably respectful—not to say cautious—approach of British Jews under Montefiore's leadership could hardly have been starker. At this stage, however, neither Christians nor Jews can have expected to have much influence on events.

Four months later, things looked rather different. War between Austria and a Franco-Piedmontese alliance in the spring of 1859 saw the rapid defeat of Austria followed by the collapse of existing governments in central and northern Italy, including Edgardo Mortara's hometown of Bologna. By early July, Napoleon III was sufficiently disconcerted by the scale of the upheaval to conclude a separate peace with Austria, prompting a disagreement between Cavour and Victor Emmanuel II of Piedmont, which led to Cavour's resignation as prime minister. The timid cabinet that replaced him was no substitute, so the political initiative shifted to Britain and the new provisional governments of northern and central Italy. It was in this context that plans for an international conference to resolve the Italian question began to take center stage once more. To Momolo Mortara, this turn of events appeared to offer an opportunity to revisit his son's case.[96]

In November 1859 Eardley headed a deputation of British Christians entrusted with presenting the Mortara "Protest" to Lord John Russell, the new foreign secretary. Russell was well known for his defense of religious liberty, and Eardley did not hesitate to express the hope that Britain would raise the question of Jews living under papal rule at a putative conference on Italian affairs. Eardley argued that since Edgardo Mortara was no longer a papal subject, it was possible to address the issue without violating the principle of nonintervention in the affairs of a foreign country. Instead, it would be enough for Britain to "demand of the congress of nations, the freedom of Bologna concurrently with the freedom of Mortara."[97]

As Russell pointed out, the restrictions on Jewish rights in Austria, Prussia, and Russia rendered such a suggestion eminently impractical. The *Jewish Chronicle* suggested that Russell might square this circle by establishing a wholly new kind of international framework, in which such interference was justified in terms of generally accepted moral principles: "the only means we see for preventing the recurrence of any such crime is to memorialise the foreign Secretary to press upon the attention of the approaching Congress the expediency of establishing liberty of conscience . . . as an international law of the civilised world." Responding to the promptings of Momolo, the *Chronicle,* and several Anglo-Jewish communities, the Board of Deputies eventually endorsed this strategy.[98]

On December 26, 1859, Montefiore chaired a meeting of the Board of Deputies which resolved unanimously "that a Memorial be presented to the approaching Congress urging upon its consideration the Mortara case, with the view to obtain the restoration of the child Edgar Mortara to his family & to prevent the recurrence of a similar outrage & with the object of placing the Jews throughout Europe upon an equal footing with their fellow countrymen."[99] In the event, there was no congress, and Edgardo remained in Rome. Plebiscites not power politics led to the incorporation of the central Italian duchies and papal legations into Piedmont during the spring of 1860, while the revolution led by Garibaldi in Sicily paved the way for the formation of an Italian "nation-state." The moment was, nonetheless, significant. Here, for the first time, we see the faint stirrings of an awareness of the role of international action in dealing with the problems of religious or ethnic minorities, and imposing what we would now see as universal standards of human rights.

Edgardo Mortara may have remained in Rome, but the collapse of temporal power and the triumph of liberal Piedmont left many with a sense that the forces of progress and civilization (with which the Jews so emphatically identified) were winning the argument. Both the blood libel and forced conversion had long histories on the European continent. In 1840, Thiers had endorsed the ritual-murder fantasy; but in 1858, after the kidnapping of Edgardo Mortara, Napoleon III withdrew support decisively from the Papal States. The role of Jewish relief as a litmus test in the contentious process of redefining European civilization in terms of liberal values and humanitarian politics appeared to be gaining ground. By situating international Jewish relief within this universal framework, Jewish activists helped to constitute this broader humanitarian agenda.[100]

Chapter 13

Grief and Sore Troubles

Judith's failing health rendered the ongoing Mortara crisis the least of Montefiore's troubles; the thought of losing his life companion was almost too much to bear. "I have been very anxious regarding Lady Montefiore," he confided to Loewe in February 1860; "she has been so long suffering her complaint not yielding to any Medical Treatment."[1]

Montefiore may not always have been faithful to Judith, but they continued to find great joy in each other. Writing on their wedding anniversary in 1844—only two years before his rumored dalliance with Hester Bell—Montefiore described Judith as "the great cause of my happiness through life . . . A better and kinder wife never existed, one whose whole study has been to render her husband good and happy."[2] She voiced identical sentiments in a poem dated July 10, 1850:

With thankful heart
and glowing thoughts
How can I thee express
Who grants to me the greatest boon
Affection could dictate
The Husband of my Choice!
For Life's succeeding years we pass
In happiness and bliss.
May gratitude never cease to guide
and all my deeds dictate
That we on Earth fulfil the Aim
Which so much bounty claims.[3]

To the younger generation, the Montefiores' marriage may have seemed incongruous. Charlotte de Rothschild had only guarded praise for "the pompous Sir Moses" but thought "there is probably no wiser

woman in the whole world than this good Lady Judith." But the younger generation had not known Montefiore during the carefree travels of
the early days of their marriage. Charlotte was familiar only with the
aging communal leader, stiff and formal in his mannerisms, so self-
righteous and blinkered in his faith that he still refused to speak to his
brother after all these years. Jewish more through social obligation than
through personal inclination, Charlotte sympathized with Horatio. She
could not relate to the shared religiosity and sense of common purpose
that bound the elderly couple: they traveled together, they prayed together, and they gave together.[4]

The mythology surrounding them made much of this dual vision.
When Montefiore undertook to sponsor the orphaned son of a leading
Sephardi rabbi in 1845, it was Judith who provided the boy with comfortable clothing. When Montefiore paid his annual visit to the Bevis
Marks school prizegiving—where he gave anything from a florin to a
crown to all 300 pupils—it was Judith who petted the younger ones as
they toddled up to the platform. In the gendered societies in which they
moved, this philanthropic engagement was an essential counterpart to
Montefiore's own, better-publicized activities.[5]

Journeying through the Holy Land and Egypt, Judith repeatedly
proved invaluable. Her status as the European Lady Montefiore allowed
her greater latitude than the women she encountered, but her sex enabled her to enter the harems, pray in the ladies' galleries of the synagogues they visited, and meet the wives and mothers of the men who
mattered to her beloved "Mun." Better educated and more self-
consciously cultivated than Montefiore, it was Judith whose account of
their adventures served to propagate Montefiore's vision of Jewish agriculture to an international public.

In Britain, she served on the ladies' committees of countless charities
alongside members of her immediate Jewish circle, women like Florence
Nightingale and the wives of aristocratic philanthropists and diplomats.[6] In Palestine, she fulfilled a similar role from afar. Recognizing her
distinctively feminine influence, even Jerusalem's rigidly orthodox Perushim empowered Judith to act as *gabbait* (female trustee) in the hope
that she would "command the holy guard that scatters the spring of our
benevolence and advocacy of the tribes of Israel to all the tranquil ladies
to capture them with the love of Zion and Jerusalem."[7]

These were lofty vistas, but Judith never forgot her primary responsibilities in the Montefiore household. As editor of the first Jewish cook-
book published in English, she saw herself as a role model in the domestic sphere. Her main aim in *The Jewish Manual* was to demonstrate the
compatibility of keeping kosher with gentility, proving to the aspira-

*Detail from a portrait of
Lady Judith Montefiore in
later life. Montefiore was
later depicted seated in front
of this very picture, holding
the* dahir *he had received
from the sultan of Morocco
in 1864. (Courtesy of Robert
Sebag-Montefiore; photograph by
Lykke Stjernswärd)*

tional housewife that she could make an elegant meat sauce without butter. The book was a vehicle for preserving—even advertising—the rich culinary heritage of "the Jewish nation." It also enabled Judith to disseminate her own vision of womanhood. Here, she elaborated her belief that feminine accomplishment went hand in hand with domesticity, that it was "the unfailing attribute of a superior mind to turn its attention occasionally to the lesser objects of life," and that true refinement was to be found not in à la modality but rather in simple elegance and an "air of graceful originality."[8]

At the heart of Judith's home there was—unavoidably—an absence. Cuddling the children of the Sephardi poor was no substitute for motherhood. Nor could Montefiore's habit of inviting boys from local Jewish schools to Friday night dinner in Ramsgate fill the gap where their own offspring should have been.[9] Of course, Judith and Montefiore took an interest in their nieces and nephews.[10] Ironically, the child they came to know best was little Tousson Pasha, only son of the viceroy of Egypt, who visited for the first time in 1857 and remained for several months.

Forced into *locum parentis* in their early seventies, the Montefiores

found the willful three-year-old something of a handful. Like most tod-
dlers, he refused to obey his doctor, and it "required all the tact of Lady
Montefiore, and sometimes all the firmness of Sir Moses, to make the
young Pasha submit."[11] The experience was not without its compensa-
tions. In August Montefiore and Judith accompanied their charge to Os-
borne, where, dressed in a green and silver uniform with epaulettes, full
white trousers, high boots, and a diamond-encrusted sword, the little
prince was presented to Queen Victoria.[12] They enjoyed another royal
audience when Tousson returned to England a year later, although Montefiore's "dear Judith" was too ill to attend.[13] But by the end of Tousson's third visit, the Montefiores felt unable to cope with his demands.
"[T]he young Prince is thank God well," Montefiore wrote to Loewe in
September 1859, "but the Lady who attends him becomes every day
more troublesome and as Lady Montefiore's health is very far from satisfactory we both of us find the responsibility we have incurred more
and more painful."[14]

He was in no doubt, however, about where his duty lay. It was obviously in Jewish interests for Montefiore to host the prince of Egypt;
Montefiore liked to think it was in British interests, too. He never sent a
letter to the viceroy without showing it to the Foreign Office, and he did
everything he could to ensure Tousson's visits were a success.[15] "I am
very anxious that the young Pasha, should do that which will best prove
his happy Remembrance and bright appreciation of Her Majesty's con-
descension, to him, on his former sojourn in England," Montefiore
wrote to Sir Charles Beaumont Phipps, keeper of the Privy Purse, before
requesting the honor of a second royal audience.[16] He even had Tousson's likeness taken by Solomon Alexander Hart, R.A., with a view to
publication in the *Pictorial Times* or the *Illustrated London News*.[17]

Barely six weeks later disturbing reports began to reach Montefiore
from Gibraltar. The Spanish enclaves of Ceuta and Mellila on the Moroccan coast were a perennial flash point. For centuries, the specter of
Christian expansion in North Africa had fostered the emergence of *jihad* as a legitimating ideology at the heart of the Moroccan state, which
experienced Christian rule on Muslim soil as a permanent affront.[18] In
1859 domestic instability led Spain to provoke Morocco into a conflict
that would enable the premier, General Leopoldo O'Donnell, to woo
public opinion by relaunching the Iberian war of conquest in North Africa. The death of Sultan Moulay Abd-er-Rahman seemed opportune.
Spain had already manufactured a casus belli out of a series of naval and
territorial disputes. Now the Spanish ratcheted up the pressure as Morocco descended into political turmoil, revising their ultimatum until the

new sultan could not afford to back down. Remembering the catastrophe that befell the community in Mogador during the French bombardment of 1844, Jews living in Tétouan, Tangier, and other coastal towns fled en masse. A minority with French connections set sail for Algeria; a handful ended up in Algeciras; nearly 6,000 took refuge on Gibraltar.

"It is heartrending to see how they have come," wrote one eyewitness; "the best accommodated see their ruin before their eyes, accustomed to a cheap comfortable living, and having now to provide for the wants of their families at very high prices, and with their means of support lost. They are, indeed, much to be pitied, but still far more than they are the poorer classes, which are, unfortunately by far the greatest portion."[19] These had nothing to live on and nowhere to go. The governor, Sir William Codrington, provided tents and blankets, but the refugees could hardly spend the winter on the Rock.

Concerned locals and an emergency committee formed by Jews in Gibraltar wrote at once to Montefiore, David Salomons, and the Board of Deputies. London already housed a substantial and well-connected Moroccan community, including Montefiore's nephews Joseph Sebag and Haim Guedalla. Joining forces with members of the Mogador elite fleeing the troubles, they founded a committee under Montefiore's leadership and launched an international fund-raising campaign.

Trauma and displacement were inevitable by-products of war, but the existence of newspapers and the telegraph ensured that the Moroccan refugee crisis was played out before world opinion. To contemporaries it seemed an unheard-of disaster. One speaker at a fund-raising meeting in Toronto declared the case "almost unprecedented, where so numerous a body had to fly from their homes for life, leaving all their earthly goods behind them."[20] Montefiore had already tapped a global humanitarian public with his Holy Land Relief Fund. He found it relatively easy to set the wheels in motion once more. As some £40,000 poured in, the *Jewish Chronicle* could hardly contain its delight: "In former years there was a sharp line of demarcation drawn between Jew and Gentile . . . even on the neutral ground of charity . . . How different now, when we see the Jew in the hour of need confidently appealing to his Christian neighbour, and this neighbour nobly justifying this confidence by substantial proofs of sympathy. A strong tie, binding together Jew and Gentile, thus springs up between the two."[21]

Once again, there was no denying the particular resonance of the Morocco Relief Fund in the English-speaking world. In the United States, Gershom Kursheedt persuaded the newly formed Board of Delegates of American Israelites to spearhead a campaign that collected $20,000.

"Encampment at Gibraltar of Fugitive Jews from Morocco," Illustrated
London News, *February 11, 1860, p. 129. (By permission of the Bodleian Library, University of Oxford: N.2288.b.6)*

From Dublin to Cape Town, from Toronto to the West Indies, Jews and
Christians alike embraced the Moroccan cause. In Kingston, Jamaica,
£44 was raised after the Reverend A. B. Davis so moved his audience
that they "almost forgot where they were—every heart beat high as the
Reverend Gentleman eloquently dwelt on the freedom and glory of England, under whose banner the poor and persecuted of every faith find
protection."[22] There seemed something peculiarly British about the welcome that Governor Codrington had provided the refugees on Gibraltar; it embodied a spirit of generosity in which white settlers far from
the homeland were determined to share.[23]

Writing in the *Archives Israélites,* its future editor Isidore Cahen was
full of admiration for this demonstration of humanitarian unity in the
Anglosphere. He could only regret "that nothing of the kind has taken
place in France."[24] This was a bitter disappointment to the man who, on
receiving news of the refugee crisis, confidently declared Paris and London the "two metropoles of civilization . . . the twin tribunal where the
universal conscience sits in judgment, the twin home of international

charity."[25] It would take the outbreak of civil war in Mount Lebanon to demonstrate the truth of this assertion—and the very different face of Jewish humanitarian philanthropy on either side of the Channel.

The Ottomans had never really governed Mount Lebanon, delegating authority to powerful locally based emirs and a network of feudal lords that bridged the sectarian divide. Egyptian rule in the 1830s unsettled this situation. Religious identities gradually became politicized in new ways as Maronite (Christian) peasants rejected the rule of their Druze overlords and members of both elites looked to Britain and France for support. For ten years after the civil war of 1845 these tensions simmered under the surface. Then the *Hatt-i Hümayun* of 1856, announcing the "emancipation" of Ottoman Jews and Christians, blew the whole edifice apart. In 1858–59 political, social, and religious pressures combined to pit peasants and feudal lords, Maronite and Druze elites against one another in a struggle for control of the mountain. The result was catastrophe. Outnumbered, outgunned, and underprepared, the Druze emerged as victors after a campaign of brutality on both sides, which saw the razing of Christian villages, mass killings in the mixed districts, and the destruction of longstanding bastions of Lebanese Christianity such as Zahlé and Dayr al-Qamar.[26]

Violence was nothing new in Lebanon, but the Muslim masses of nearby Damascus saw the failure of Ottoman authorities to prevent it as a signal to follow suit. Ever since the 1830s, European patronage had set the increasingly prosperous Christian community against its Muslim fellow citizens, who denounced reforms like the *Hatt* as alien impositions. On July 9, 1860, Muslim mobs ransacked the Christian quarter in Damascus. Peasants, Bedouins, and other tribesmen flooded in from the surrounding countryside to join in the mayhem. It lasted days. Churches, convents, and patriarchates, six foreign consulates, and 6,000 homes were razed to the ground, and more than 3,000 Christians lost their lives.

News of these events reached Montefiore in Ramsgate on July 11. Judith was weaker than usual that day, her husband exhausted from traveling back and forth on City and Jewish business. Both were appalled by what they read in the papers, in particular Stratford de Redcliffe's claim that 20,000 Christian refugees were wandering starving through the Lebanon. After talking the matter over with Judith, Montefiore drew up a letter calling for charitable intervention and drove immediately to London. He arrived after midnight in time to catch the next day's *Times*. "I have done all in my power to prevent any loss of time in affording assistance to the unfortunate and destitute fugitives in Syria," he wrote in his diary with a complacent sense of sacrifice. "I left my dear Judith with great reluctance. I was poorly, my legs swollen, and I had travelled five hundred miles, and this night's journey added a hundred miles to it. I have not spared any exertions this week to fulfil my duty."[27]

This is the story as Loewe tells it. But there was more to Montefiore's initiative than sympathy with the sufferings of his fellow man. That day in Paris, Adolphe Crémieux issued an appeal to French Jewry in support of the Syrian cause. Both men had realized the potential of the catastrophe to situate the politics of Jewish relief within a broader, less partisan agenda. On the one hand, the plight of the Syrian Christians drew attention to the consequences of persecution and religious intolerance. On the other hand, ostentatious generosity underlined Jewish commitment to the universal humanitarian values invoked by Montefiore and Crémieux during the Damascus and Mortara Affairs. That the riots in Damascus had devastated the very community behind the blood libels of 1840 was a fortuitous irony. The terms in which the two men framed their response to news of the Syrian massacres said much about the contrasting traditions of humanitarian politics in Britain and France, and the place of Jewish activists within them.

Montefiore's letter to *The Times* was a private expression of sympathy. "Being intimately acquainted with the nature of that country and the condition of its people," he appreciated "but too painfully the vast amount of misery that must have been endured." Knowing "from experience, the philanthropy of my fellow countrymen," he was confident the public would give generously to relieve "the distress of the unhappy multitude now defenceless, homeless, and destitute." He called for the formation of "a small, active and influential committee . . . with the view of raising subscriptions" and enclosed a check for £200 toward the proposed Syrian Relief Fund. Parallels with the Holy Land Relief Fund and the Morocco refugee crisis were implicit in this formulation, although Montefiore shied away from making aggressive sectarian capital. His aim was rather to develop the British culture of interfaith humanitarian philanthropy, of which Jewish causes (and Jewish leaders) were a constituent part.

Crémieux took a very different tack. In an emotive address to his coreligionists, he recalled the unique role of "Christian France" in initiating the emancipation of European Jewry. "French Israelites, let us be the first to come to the help of our Christian brethren," he declared. "Let the signal for a vast succor proceed from the midst of a Jewish body, formed in the capital of civilization. This signal will meet with a response from our brethren in England, Germany, Belgium, Holland, and all Europe, both in the countries which acknowledge them as citizens, and in those which still withhold from them this noble title."[28]

His patriotic language reflected the traditional hold of Lebanese Christians on the French imagination, but Crémieux's real agenda lay elsewhere. Echoing the suggestion made by the *Jewish Chronicle* in the aftermath of the Mortara Affair, Crémieux speculated that "God who governs all things has perhaps permitted this awful catastrophe, in order to afford the followers of all religions a solemn opportunity to assist each other, to defend themselves against those furious animosities, daughters of superstition and barbarism. A permanent committee in every country, carefully watching all attacks made on the liberty of conscience, a general fund for the support of the victims of fanaticism, without distinction of creed."[29]

Wishful thinking of this kind struck a powerful chord in the Jewish world. In Russia, the elite Jewish merchants of St. Petersburg and a handful of students in Moscow forwarded their contributions to the Foreign Ministry, while less privileged Jews in towns like Odessa, Zhitomir, and Simferopol' publicized their contributions through the newspaper *Aurora*. Italian Jews—both the emancipated citizens of Florence and Livorno and their unemancipated brethren under papal rule in Rome—gave with similar generosity. Even the tiny community of Corfu played its part in the campaign.[30]

Little if any of this generosity was disinterested. Instead, the politics of Jewish gesture were inflected differently from place to place. In Florence and Paris, giving to the Syrian Christians was an act of gratitude; in Russia and Rome it was a challenge to the intolerant status quo. Those communities whose donations received greatest publicity were precisely those most recently in the news. Regular readers of the Jewish press would have had no difficulty relating the Corfu contribution to the continuing controversy over the status of Jews in the Ionian Islands, or the participation of Jews like David Hatchwell in the Gibraltar Syrian Relief Committee in the welcome accorded Moroccan refugees six months earlier.[31]

The popularity of Crémieux's tactics outside western Europe and North America is particularly striking. It was one thing for the *Jewish Chronicle* to comment that the calamity afforded Western Jews an opportunity to forget past persecution and to show their Christian fellow citizens "how completely we identify ourselves with their sorrows, and how anxious we are to reciprocate the kind feelings with which they responded to the cry of distress lately raised by some of our distant brethren."[32] It was more surprising to learn that Romanian Jews empathized with the Syrian Christians, praying that the Lord might "purify the hearts of all people, to remove all religious hatred from the world, and then we too, could live peacefully."[33] The geographic focus of Crémieux's original appeal reflected French assumptions about the limits of a civilized Jewish public. Its impact in eastern Europe and the eastern Mediterranean revealed that even the most traditional communities were active participants in an increasingly global public sphere.

As politics, Crémieux's campaign was a failure; it merely hardened attitudes toward Jews in Catholic Europe across the secular-clerical divide. In Italy, *Il Contemporaneo* was outraged to see Livornese Jews engaged in fund-raising before the Papal Curia had taken action.[34] In France, the legitimist *Union* decried the Jews' temerity in seeking "to take sole responsibility for the defense of civilization and humanity."[35] Ludwig Philippson was furious at Crémieux's misdirected approach. "Why did Crémieux not call for a general collection?" he thundered; "an appeal from Jews to Jews alone for non-Jewish purposes is a new form of separation, which merely serves to keep the old ones alive!" Complaints in the *Archives Israélites* that Parisian Jews were being pressured into making donations confirmed this view of Crémieux's heavy-handedness.[36] Montefiore's decision to avoid sectarian grandstanding attracted less attention. From Philippson's perspective, it was far better judged.

Whereas Crémieux chose to head an international but narrowly Jewish movement, Montefiore chaired the Executive Committee of the Syrian Relief Fund. Apart from himself, Lionel de Rothschild, and David Salomons, this was an exclusively Christian—and deeply British—affair. Presided over by none other than Stratford de Redcliffe, it drew on virtually every important political strain in high-Victorian society: old-fashioned Whigs, Evangelicals, Quakers, Tories, veterans of Eastern politics and the Crimea, Manchester Liberals, and City bankers. Within a year they raised over £28,000.[37]

This coalition reflected the central place of humanitarian universalism in British imperial culture. Indeed, the eclecticism of the Syrian Relief Fund was deliberate. In its first printed appeal to the general public, the executive committee expressed the hope that "Ministers of Religion of every denomination—the Anglican clergy, the Roman Catholic priesthood, the ministers of the Hebrew Community, and of every persuasion of Dissenters, will heartily co-operate in this great work of philanthropy by private and Congregational Collections, and thus afford to the jarring and mutually exasperated sects of the East and to the world at large the most convincing evidence of the humanizing and harmonizing influence of the religion of the Bible."[38] The honorary secretary, Sir Culling Eardley, wrote to the Syrian subcommittee, advising explicitly that the British public attached great importance "to our contributions not being used so as to throw weight into the scale of any race, or creed, or party," and requesting the Beirut relief committee to co-opt "resident gentlemen of character and respectability belonging to the Jewish, Roman Catholic, and Greek persuasions, and connected with other than the British and American nations."[39]

It is hard to escape the conclusion that the appeal of the Syrian cause to both Eardley and Montefiore lay precisely in its potential for this kind of religious politics. To the former, it was a continuation of the philo-Semitic ecumenism he had embraced during the Mortara Affair. To the latter, it represented the high-water mark of the alliance constructed in the 1830s around the rallying cry of "civil and religious liberty" and cemented by the Damascus Affair.

Speaking in Plymouth, Eardley made a point of describing Montefiore as "the most valuable and zealous coadjutor he had ever had to do with."[40] He added that he had removed New Testaments from the relief packages sent to Syria because it "would not be dealing fairly with the Jews to allow the mode of transit which had been placed at the joint disposal of the committee of Christians and Jews to be the means of throwing the weight of one side." Conversely, when Swedish donors stipulated that their contributions fund Evangelical asylums, Montefiore declared that the money "was a trust to be used for Christianity, and he hoped that it would be used for the purpose of Christianity." Some, at least, suspected hidden undercurrents. The Anglo-Catholic Reverend William Palgrave dismissed the whole episode as "nothing else but a mere Protestant-Israelitish job."[41]

Montefiore's much-vaunted sympathy with the Syrian Christians was certainly less than wholehearted. Shortly before the massacres, the Jews of Damascus had been the target of yet another blood libel.[42] Their safety remained his prime concern.[43] As Ottomans and Europeans took steps to pacify the province, the balance in Damascus shifted in the Christians' favor. They soon began accusing Jews of complicity in the riots, causing several to be thrown into prison, where one died.[44] Montefiore remained embroiled for months in the affair, plugging away at the Foreign Office until the remaining prisoners regained their freedom. Eager to remove all taint of guilt from the Jewish community, he urged that they be exempted from the general tax levied on Ottoman citizens to compensate Christians for their losses. Finally, in September 1861 the wealthiest Jews in the city agreed to contribute 150,000 piastres as a goodwill gesture; in exchange, Fuad Pasha promised to issue an official declaration of their innocence to the European press.

Montefiore's attention lay elsewhere. By October 1860 Judith could hardly leave her bedchamber, let alone accompany him to synagogue.[45] Despite medical advice to the contrary he hesitated to spend the winter in sunnier climes. In November Judith's doctor informed him roundly that "they were making no progress, and he must determine at once to leave England within ten days, or make arrangements at Park Lane for the Winter." Montefiore continued to dither: "I cannot make up my mind to leave England and from day to day postpone positively fixing the time for our departure. At any rate, it now cannot be before the end of the month. May the God of Israel in his mercy direct us!"[46]

Things persisted in this vein for months as the couple alternated between Ramsgate and London. Shortly after their wedding anniversary in June 1861, Judith felt well enough to accompany her husband to Smithembottom. This nostalgic trip to the weekend retreat of their early married life moved Montefiore deeply. The village appeared much "the same quiet place" it had been half a century ago, when, as he fondly recalled, "the quietness of the place, which afforded us the opportunity of keeping the Sabbaths undisturbed by the fluctuations which were at that period daily taking place in London from the vicissitudes of the war, endeared Smithem Bottom to my dear Judith and myself far beyond every other place we have ever seen, excepting Jerusalem and East Cliff." But if Smithembottom was unchanged, the same could not be said for its inhabitants. Montefiore was bound to "reflect on the withdrawal from this world of so many dear friends, who had partaken with me of the happiness of its old host and hostess!" He was bound, too, to wonder whether he and Judith would come again.[47]

Struggling with depression through the winter of 1861–62, Montefiore tried to keep busy.[48] Judith urged her husband "not to discontinue attending to his usual pursuits on her account," but he seems to have had little stomach for them. On July 2, 1862, he finally refused reelection as president of the Board of Deputies, pleading advancing years and medical advice.[49]

Four days earlier, he and Judith had celebrated their golden wedding anniversary in Ramsgate. The little port was unequivocally jubilant. Church bells rang out, flags flew from the rooftops proclaiming "Long live Sir Moses and Lady Montefiore" and "Peace to Jerusalem," schoolchildren marched through the streets, and there was a celebratory service in St. George's church. To crown it all, local residents presented a formal address paying tribute to Montefiore's support of local charities and his role as Ramsgate's premier grandee.[50]

But at East Cliff all was not well. Judith could not attend the special service in their beloved synagogue, nor could she leave her bedroom to assist at the little ceremony held in their home. "The absence of my dear Judith was a severe drawback to the happiness I had in being permitted, by the mercy of God, to write the concluding words of the Pentateuch scroll," Montefiore wrote in his diary that evening. "May He, in His merciful goodness, allow me to have the happiness to complete the next sacred scroll which is being written for me at Wilna, in my dear wife's presence."[51]

By the end of the summer Judith was showing signs of improvement. In September she traveled up to London, where she drove about in their brougham, accompanied Montefiore to inspect some new carpets for Ramsgate, and bought a silk dress in Ludgate Hill. Then she took a sudden turn for the worse. Overcome, Montefiore gathered his family around him, distributed alms among the Jewish poor, and attended synagogue both morning and evening. On the evening of September 23, 1862, he completed yet another Torah scroll from Vilna. The ceremony took place in a room adjoining their bedchamber, enabling Judith to listen through the open door as her husband, friends, and relatives prayed to the Lord to restore her health.[52]

The next day was the eve of the Jewish New Year. Judith lay silently, barely able to incline her head in greeting to the steady stream of well-wishers come to pay their last respects. As dusk fell, she gestured to Montefiore to go and join the evening service. On his return, he placed his hand on her forehead and recited a blessing over her. Shortly after he had gone down to dinner, Hodgkin called him back upstairs. Then—or so Loewe tells us—"[a]ll present immediately followed Sir Moses, the solemn prayers for the dying were recited, and the pure spirit of Judith, the noble, the good, and the truly pious, took flight Heavenwards."[53]

Judith was buried that Sunday in Ramsgate. The *Jewish Chronicle* reported that besides "several personal Christian friends" and the inevitable crowd of Jewish dignitaries, "hundreds of the inhabitants of Ramsgate" gathered silently around the synagogue and burial place.[54] The shops would have closed anyway, but it was in Judith's honor that ships in the harbor flew their flags at half-mast. Her death saw the birth of a legend: "Good Lady Montefiore," "a perfect daughter of Israel." As a barren wife, Judith was far from the Jewish ideal, but her infertility enabled the public to invest her with special significance. Had she been a mother, her loyalties would have been to her children; childless, she belonged to them all. Chief Rabbi Nathan Adler praised her as "a mother in Israel" and drew parallels with the matriarch most closely identified with the Jewish people, describing how Judith "shed tears for the poor of Jerusalem, like Rachel weeping bitterly for her children."[55]

There was also widespread agreement that Judith had been the real impetus behind her husband's achievements. The *Chronicle* declared her Montefiore's "beneficent genius," and Montefiore subsequently endorsed this view.[56] "I am no great man. The little good that I have accomplished, or rather that I intended to accomplish, I am indebted for it to my never-to-be-forgotten wife, whose enthusiasm for everything that is noble, and whose religiousness sustained me in my career."[57]

This interpretation has been accepted by historians and—more recently—embraced by feminists. It was, of course, a cliché. In fact the couple's diaries reveal Montefiore to have been the more religious of the two. His willingness to ascribe his successes to Judith reflected a lifetime of love for her. "The crown of my head has fallen, my glory hath departed," he wrote in his Bible on a visit to Smithembottom in December 1862. "Thou which hast shewed me grief and sore troubles shall quicken me again and bring me up again from the depths of the Earth."[58]

In some ways Montefiore never recovered. East Cliff Lodge became a museum to Judith's memory: her portraits were everywhere, the old-fashioned furniture and faded damask curtains remained just as she had left them, and every scrap of linen in the house was marked with a memorial inscription in Hebrew.[59] "Oh my dear dear Jud," Montefiore wrote on their wedding anniversary seventeen years later. "Alas Alas how what a Change Happy 10 June 1812 But the God of our Fathers granted me the happiness of blessed Wife for 50 short very short years the Companion & guide to me of every good action O God [*illegible*] forgive me repining."[60]

Montefiore's probable infidelity suggests that these expressions of adoration for his wife may have been colored by guilt and a sense of his own unworthiness. Family gossip has it that he fathered several illegitimate children besides Charles Moberley Bell.[61] One particularly well-established paper trail links Montefiore to the son of Louisa Thoroughgood Walden (née Sherrin), born in April 1863, when his mother was in her late teens. Despite being married to a farm laborer, Louisa did not name her husband as her son Joseph's father.[62] All eight of his children apparently regarded Montefiore as their grandfather instead. From the somewhat confused account given by his descendants, it appears that Joseph was raised in a Brentwood orphanage but retained contact with his mother and stepbrothers in Leeds, one of whom went regularly to

London to collect money. The 1871 census records suggest, however, that he was boarding with a family elsewhere in Essex.[63] Be that as it may, in 1983 Joseph's daughter-in-law recalled that her husband, George, had overheard his stepuncle say: "You are not my brother. Your father is Sir Moses Montefiore."[64]

In 1909 or 1910 Joseph is said to have responded to an advertisement in one of the national newspapers. This move prompted a visit from a solicitor, who stood him a drink in the local pub and told him, "If you are the boy, half of Shoreditch is yours." Family legend has it that Joseph was a respectable man and could not face the stigma of illegitimacy. More to the point, perhaps, the investigation seems to have petered out.[65] Either way, Joseph claimed that the family could all be well off if he cared to "put himself out." He spoke often of an old man visiting him on horseback at the orphanage, but only in old age did he reveal his origins to his son. When George began to make inquiries after his father's death in 1922, none of his siblings could remember much about the solicitor. Unsurprisingly, Edmund Sebag-Montefiore was "unable to give any information" either.[66]

In the Sephardi world it is customary to call a first-born son after his grandfather. Joseph's name and his training as a gas fitter lend credence to the claim that he was Montefiore's child. Yet the 1861 census—produced just over a year before Joseph was conceived—provides no evidence of his mother either living with the Montefiores or working as a servant in London.[67] At that time, Louisa Sherrin was still living with her uncle many miles away in Somerset. Whatever the truth of the matter, persistent and relatively well-documented rumors of Montefiore's infidelity hint at a more troubled side to his famously blissful marriage —and, indeed, his personality. At least as the couple grew older, it seems likely that Montefiore had sexual needs that his wife could not meet.[68] From a strictly religious standpoint there would have been no objection, since in Jewish law adultery is forbidden only to women. Whether Montefiore, with his Evangelical connections, would have seen matters in this light remains open to doubt. If the Walden claim is accurate, there was something fundamentally exploitative about the affair between an old man and a girl sixty years his junior, who worked as a maid in his house.[69] That this liaison took place while his wife was on her deathbed and resulted in the birth of a son would have complicated his response to Judith's loss immeasurably.

No sooner had the seven days of mourning expired than Montefiore began putting his affairs in order. On a railway journey—presumably be-

tween London and Ramsgate—he appointed his nephew Joseph Sebag
his heir; other relatives were not best pleased.[70] The weeks immediately
following this decision saw a flood of condolence letters from Jewish organizations in Britain, the Continent, and the New World, friends and
relatives in the Anglo-Jewish community, business associates, and members of Montefiore's wider Christian circle. "I called at your house, and
found what had happened," wrote Eardley in a letter that illuminates
the unique nature of their friendship; "you have long expected it, but (I
know) that will not make the blow less heavy. God himself comfort you,
I wish I could convey to you all the comfort that I had, at a similar moment, but I do not like to seem a proselyter. God bless you."[71] Such gestures did not go unappreciated. "Though there is only one source of real
and enduring consolation in our sore trials and afflictions," Montefiore
told Hodgkin, "yet are the kind words of a pious and good Friend most
surely contributory to our present comfort and solace in our great
grief."[72]

None of this sympathy, however, roused Montefiore from depression,
and his health went from bad to worse. Recognizing that his old friend
would find comfort only in activity, Hodgkin accompanied him to the
Continent for the winter with the vague intention of continuing to Constantinople and Jerusalem on Holy Land business. They had a sorry time
of it. Montefiore suffered repeatedly from bad colds and related exhaustion. With nothing to gain from traveling anywhere in particular, they
meandered slowly through France and Italy constantly changing their
plans.

Montefiore's spirits lifted when they were joined by his sister Sally,
only to plummet when she left for home. "I cannot tell you how greatly
I miss your Mother's society," he wrote to Joseph Sebag. "I have been
like a fish out of water, the Hotel appeared quite a desert, she made our
sojourn at Pisa as well as the whole of our journey to that place of
greater satisfaction and I should say gratification than I could have possibly anticipated"[73] A letter to little Tousson Pasha written on the death
of his father Said captures Montefiore's despondent state. "You have
heard that I had the affliction to lose Lady Montefiore who loved you so
much," he wrote in February 1863. "We all lose our friends one after
another & as you have my best wishes for your true happiness I must
remind you that we have one Father above whom we cannot lose, who
sees & knows all things & should you fear him & endeavour to keep a
good conscience he will be your sole protector & great reward."[74]

By April Montefiore and Hodgkin had abandoned all intention of visiting Jerusalem; they did not reach Constantinople until mid-May.[75]
Here Montefiore distributed alms, visited Jewish charities, and enjoyed

an interview with the new Sultan Abdul Aziz, who confirmed the rights accorded to Ottoman Jews in the *Hatt-i Hümayun* and those granted to Montefiore in 1855. Having achieved the ostensible object of his journey—and utterly exhausted by it—he set out for home. In Ramsgate he drove immediately to Judith's grave, where he prayed for the strength to bear her loss with resignation. That evening he noted in his diary: "I have returned home in safety, and somewhat better in health, after a long journey and an absence of more than six months, but am still very depressed in mind."[76]

Outsiders were more upbeat about this latest undertaking. Both the *Jewish Chronicle* and the pioneering Hebrew-language newspaper *Hamagid* noted that Montefiore had been "rapturously hailed" by Orthodox and Reform Jews alike, receiving deputations and touring public institutions in every community he visited en route. "Why is this man more respected than other Jews who might be more wealthy, more wise, more politically involved, and better able to communicate with the highest authorities?" asked *Hamagid*. "Because of the national feeling ever-burning in his pure heart with love for his religion, for his people and for the land of Israel."[77] The *Chronicle* provided a more sophisticated analysis that deserves to be quoted at length. After describing Montefiore's journey as "one long ovation," the *Chronicle* dared to hope that this homage might have soothed Montefiore's wounded feelings by demonstrating the vitality of the Jewish people, not least

> since it may have suggested to him the idea that it was his labours in the cause of his people which contributed towards rousing and strengthening this sentiment of oneness, and calling up that consciousness of fellowship which before his missions seemed to be but faint and rudimentary.
>
> In this respect Sir Moses' last journey has a significancy which constitutes it an event . . . We have now seen that, however widely scattered the sections of Israel, however differing in their religious views, yet there is a broader, more comprehensive basis, on which they are all one, and there are connective links which in a wider bond hold them together. For let it be known that in this homage to Israel's illustrious champion . . . the organs of ultra-reform as well as ultra orthodoxy, sinking all their differences, joined in doing honour to the man whose rare merits they were all ready to acknowledge . . . But even as the muscles of the animal organism become more strengthened and better fitted for new exertions by frequent exercise, so do feelings, habits, and virtues of the mind become more confirmed and more easily evokable the more frequently they are called into activity. This new service has Sir Moses' recent journey rendered to us. It has brought to light the existence of unanimity and strength of Jewish

feeling amidst jarring differences, for which few were prepared, and has, by rousing, marvellously intensified it.[78]

Hyperbole aside, the *Chronicle* had identified a genuine phenomenon. Montefiore's extensive travels, his political missions, and his fund-raising campaigns provided a critical focus for the emerging Jewish public—although their impact depended above all on coverage in the Jewish press. Without newspapers like the *Chronicle,* Montefiore's ecstatic reception in 1863 would have mattered only to the inhabitants of the communities through which he passed. Ultimately, it was the journalism not the journey that constituted an "event."

Chapter 14

Mission to Marrakesh

By the 1860s, Jewish activism was beginning to come of age. In 1860, three years before Montefiore set out for Constantinople, a small group of influential and acculturated French Jews had launched an international organization dedicated to the struggle for Jewish rights: the Alliance Israélite Universelle.[1] The Moroccan refugee crisis, the Syrian Relief Fund, and Montefiore's triumphant progress through Europe reflected different facets of this emerging Jewish solidarity: the unifying response to news about international disasters, the emphasis on humanitarian universalism, the complex interplay between the Jewish press and Jewish leaders on the one hand and international politics and communal realities on the other. All these factors would come into play as the attention of the Jewish world reverted to Morocco.

Montefiore's Morocco Relief Fund had been conceived as an ad-hoc response to an emergency situation. By the summer of 1860 it had a surplus of £6,500—enough to set a new agenda for Morocco's 100,000 Jews.[2] Events had already prompted a rapid expansion of the fund's initial terms of operation. First, the Spanish occupation of Tétouan led Montefiore to grant £600 to the Jews left behind there. Then an energetic British vice-consul persuaded the committee to clean up Rabat's Jewish quarter and commit £100 a year to proper medical care. These proposals proved contentious. When Moses Picciotto, a Sephardi deputy of Syrian origin, was sent to investigate, he returned recommending that the surplus be spent on education and sanitation.[3]

Earlier that year Haim Guedalla had publicly criticized the lack of interest in Morocco shown by French Jews, contrasting the vibrant voluntarism and transparency of Anglo-Jewry with the sterile top-down structures of the French Jewish community. Albert Cohn responded that the French relief effort had focused instead on the reception of Jewish refugees in Algeria. As Picciotto toured Algeciras, Gibraltar, and Morocco in the summer of 1861, the Consistoire Central des Israélites de France sent Cohn on a mission of mercy to Tétouan.[4]

For centuries the 6,000 Jews of Tétouan had shared the trauma of expulsion from Spain with their Muslim neighbors. Nostalgia for this common past was reflected in a love of Andalusian melodies, in the elaborately bejeweled outfits of wealthy Jewish and Muslim women, and in the keys to long-lost homes treasured by families of both faiths. The events of 1859–60 left this culture of coexistence in tatters. Tétouanese Jews abandoned their hatred for the butchers of the Inquisition and embraced Spanish rule, collaborating with the occupier and profiteering as Spanish troops and officials pillaged Muslim homes. Anti-Jewish violence was a well-established outlet for political frustration in Morocco. As Spain prepared to evacuate the city, Tétouan's Jewish inhabitants dreaded the prospect of Muslim retribution.[5]

From this perspective Cohn's mission was a triumph: with British and Spanish backing he met the sultan's brother to ensure that the handover passed without incident and persuaded General O'Donnell to insert in the treaty a clause protecting Jewish interests. Cohn also used his time in Tétouan to spread the gospel of modern education. In a community famed for its piety and learning, he persuaded the chief rabbi to go along with his ideas. This was something of a breakthrough. Cohn had learned from his experience in Jerusalem: he exploited the presence of educational missionaries in the Jewish quarter and granted the communal authorities supervisory rights.

Even so, uncertainties about funding remained. Cohn and Montefiore had been at loggerheads in Jerusalem; they found it easier to collaborate over Tétouan. In 1861 the Morocco Relief Fund had agreed to annual contributions of £100 toward the proposed Jewish school, £80 for medical relief, and another £70 for a second school in Mogador.[6] The communal authorities here knew nothing of "secular education," but the Spanish occupation had exposed Tétouan to the full force of European culture, and the new school could have filled its places three times over when it opened in December 1862.[7] Funded by Montefiore's Morocco Relief Fund, the Consistoire Central, and the Alliance Israélite, it represented the first concerted attempt to realize Ludwig Philippson's dream of "civilizing" oriental Jewry through Western education. This was the moment when Moroccan Judaism moved decisively into a European orbit. For the Alliance Israélite, it marked the beginning of an educational network that would span fourteen countries and change the face of Jewish life in North Africa and the Middle East.[8]

Throughout Morocco the Spanish war was a decisive caesura. Ever since the French occupation of Algeria, Morocco had been confronted by a revitalized European imperialism and the economic uncertainties resulting from integration into the global capitalist system. The government faced an impossible situation. In a polity stretching from the Mediterranean to the Sahara, crisscrossed by mountain ranges, home to urban civilizations and nomadic tribal cultures, the sultan's power rested on his religious authority as a descendent of the Prophet and the attendant obligation of waging *jihad*. Such a strategy had worked well for his predecessors, but the military challenge posed by the industrializing powers of nineteenth-century Europe was of a different order. The sultan faced defeat if he chose to fight the foreign enemy, internal disorder if he neglected his duties as religious and political leader of the Maghrebi *umma* (nation of Islam). Morocco's strategic importance proved its greatest asset. Commanding the gateway to the Mediterranean and the sea routes to Africa, India, Australia, and the Far East, an independent Morocco was a cornerstone of British foreign policy. Both Spain and France nurtured imperial ambitions in North Africa, but neither could follow through so long as Britain endorsed the sultan's regime.[9]

Before 1859, British economic and political influence had been paramount, thanks to the Anglo-Moroccan commercial treaty of 1856 and the efforts of its author, Sir John Drummond Hay, who dominated Moroccan politics for over forty years.[10] Briefly, the war tipped the balance. It left the sultan disillusioned with Hay's counsel, provided Spain with its own commercial treaty, and further undermined Moroccan social and cultural isolation by introducing a network of Spanish customs officials along the coast to monitor payment of the Moroccan war debt. An enthusiastic believer in his country's imperial mission in North Africa, the Spanish representative Don Francisco Merry y Colom was eager to press home this advantage. He overstepped the mark in August 1863, when the unexpected death of one of these new officials, a Colonel Mantilla, became an international cause célèbre.[11]

Under pressure to provide an explanation for Mantilla's death, the Moroccan authorities arrested his fourteen-year-old Jewish servant on suspicion of poisoning his master. Jacob Benyuda was flogged until he confessed to the murder, naming three other Jews as accomplices. They, too, were imprisoned and tortured, prompting a further wave of arrests. One, Elias Beneluz—a Turkish subject with some claim on British protection—was trussed upside down and beaten, then crushed inside a wooden box until he was ready to speak.[12]

For political reasons Merry wanted to make an example of the "murderers." He insisted that the Jews be summarily tried and executed—although Beneluz had already retracted his confession and Benyuda's evidence was increasingly contradictory. Still reeling from military defeat, the Moroccan authorities proved compliant. As the sultan explained to his foreign minister, since "the [Spanish] Ambassador demanded that our *sharia* [law] be applied, we have applied what is stipulated by the *sharia*."[13] He chose to ignore the fact that Muslim legal experts were divided, some maintaining that a confession extracted under duress was meaningless, others that any admission of guilt qualified as proof under Muslim law. But even death was not good enough for Merry. He had the body of Jacob Benyuda publicly mutilated in Safi before transporting Beneluz on a Spanish warship for execution in Tangier. So effectively did this move broadcast Spanish influence that Merry wanted to repeat the procedure for the remaining prisoners to drive his message home.

The Tangerine Jewish community reacted with horror. Like Jews all over the Muslim world, Moroccan Jews lived as *dhimmis* under the Pact of Umar.[14] This offered protection but not equality, guaranteeing life, property, and communal autonomy in exchange for the *djizya* tax, limited rights under Muslim law, and a range of ritualized humiliations. Here as elsewhere, European travelers decried what they saw as second-class status: the distinctive dark robes, black slippers, and skullcap; the gratuitous insults from Muslim children; the requirement in many places that Jews walk barefoot; and enforced residence within the *mellah*, or Jewish quarter, which (like the ghettos of Italy) was firmly locked at night.[15] There was truth in these observations, but they obscured a more ambiguous reality, in which Muslims and Jews honored each other's saints and coexisted within a web of mutual obligation bridging the confessional divide.[16]

Europeans viewed relations in the tribal hinterland between Jews and their Muslim "masters" as akin to slavery. In fact such patronage was a prerequisite of survival for the Berber Jews of the mountains and the men of the *mellahs* who earned their living as traveling salesmen far from home. Life was uncertain and wretched for the Jewish masses; for all Moroccans it could be nasty, brutish, and short. Jews resented the everyday humiliations and inequalities, but their ambiguous position led many to welcome the walls of the *mellah* as a source of security and a way of keeping to themselves. Moreover, as Drummond Hay reported in 1861, conditions were improving; in Tangier at least the Jews were "as free from oppression as the most favoured subjects of any country. The annual taxes levied on the whole Jewish population of Tangier, do not amount to one hundred Pounds, there is no forced government service, they elect their own Rabbis and Sheikhs, and the corporal punishment of a Jew is hardly known, and even the imprisonment of any person of that sect is a very rare occurrence."[17]

Such improvements reflected the role of Jewish merchants in European commerce and their increasing recourse to consular jurisdiction.[18] Up to a point, this was an extension of the Jews' traditional function as financial pillars of the sultan's government. With time, however, the Jewish elite found that by dressing in top hats, drinking tea at five o'clock, and acquiring foreign protection they could put themselves beyond the reach of the Moroccan authorities and the restrictions imposed by Muslim law. To such men the public execution of Elias Beneluz at the behest of the Spanish set a dangerous precedent. This was not what they had come to expect in Tangier, and his claim to British protection only made matters worse.

Montefiore received the news from Morocco on a Saturday, when letters that might otherwise have been forwarded to the Board of Deputies were opened for him as a matter of course.[19] Recognizing that time was of the essence, he left at once to persuade the Foreign Office to take up the case of the Safi Jews.[20] Merry's confrontational attitude had so far deterred British diplomats from intervening. Now, on receipt of a telegram from London, Acting Consul Thomas Reade began exerting himself on behalf of the remaining prisoners.[21] As Montefiore continued to plague the Foreign Office about the British failure to protect Beneluz, Lord John Russell informed his subordinates: "Every thing we can properly do, without undue interference with Moorish Authority, shall be done."[22]

It soon emerged that *Naib* Mohammed Bargash, the Moroccan foreign minister, was unwilling to provoke the Spanish unnecessarily. He would, of course, do whatever the British asked, provided that they in turn would support the sultan "in any fresh difficulty or complication that might arrive consequent upon the ill will or demands of the Spanish Minister."[23] Bargash knew that Britain had failed to stand by Morocco during the war of 1859, and that Hay himself had devoted much of the past four years to keeping the peace with Spain. Hay had no intention of imperiling this fragile modus vivendi, advising Lord John Russell that he had done as much as he reasonably could.

Montefiore knew nothing of these developments. Convinced that the British had done everything possible to secure the prisoners a fair trial, he suggested to Loewe that the time had come to intervene.[24] On November 6 Joseph Mayer Montefiore sensationally announced to the Board of Deputies that his venerable uncle "considered a general persecution of the Jews of Morocco . . . as imminent" and proposed to travel to Morocco and investigate the case.[25] Montefiore's entourage would reflect the needs of the moment in Safi, but he hinted from the beginning that he also had something else in mind.[26] Russell therefore instructed Hay to provide him with letters of support "if he should desire to visit other places in the Moorish dominions [apart from Safi] in the hope of improving the condition of the Jews residing there."[27]

Montefiore left London on November 16, accompanied by Hodgkin, Haim Guedalla, and Sampson Samuel, a solicitor and secretary of the Board of Deputies. Their immediate destination was Madrid. Anticlerical elements in Britain and France had been quick to blame Spain for the Safi incident, overturning assumptions of Christian cultural superiority and emphasizing instead the legacy of the Inquisition. The *Jewish Chronicle* was less hasty, suggesting that Merry might well be acting on his own. Only four years earlier Spain had provided a haven for some of the Moroccan Jewish refugees; now, in response to an appeal from James de Rothschild, the government had already postponed execution of the Safi Jews.[28]

Tensions in Morocco, however, were escalating. In late October a squabble between a Spanish protégé and two Tangerine Jews prompted a minor diplomatic incident, after Merry had them severely whipped opposite the home of a British (Jewish) subject, who made a formal complaint. When Hay raised the matter with the Moroccan authorities, Bargash indicated that "the extreme severity demanded [by Merry] with regard to these Jews had, perhaps, been occasioned by his [Merry's] knowledge of the late remonstrance made to the Moorish Government through Mr. Reade." Hay responded that Merry would be "playing a dangerous game" if he sought to express his antagonism toward the British by mistreating Moroccan subjects. News of a similar episode in Tétouan and Merry's peremptory dismissal of another complaint brought by a British (Jewish) subject revealed that he was determined to pick a fight. In breach of protocol, Merry refused even to call on his British colleague—an insult that Russell took up in Madrid.[29]

All this set the stage for Montefiore's appearance in the Spanish capital, where he had little difficulty securing a string of high-profile meetings with government ministers and members of the royal family.[30] Rothschild loans bankrolled the Spanish government, and Montefiore's access was facilitated by his great-nephew the Rothschild agent Daniel Weisweiller, who—in a country where Jews were still forbidden to worship in public—was "certainly the most influential person in Madrid."[31] But although Montefiore played up the graciousness of his reception by a heavily pregnant Queen Isabella, the reality was that the government refused to admit responsibility.[32] Instead the prime minister, Manuel Pardo Fernández de Pinedo, marquis of Miraflores, struck a delicate bal-

ance between conciliating Britain and national amour-propre. He told
Montefiore that he would happily release the remaining Jewish captives
but continued to assert their guilt, assuring Merry by letter of his full
backing: "Here I am to defend you & support you, whatever charges be
brought against you."[33] For once these vague promises were enough for
Montefiore, who seems to have seen the Safi Affair as a pretext rather
than an end in itself. Putting the grand boulevards of the capital behind
him, he continued his journey south—by rail and public diligence—to
Cádiz.

The steamer to Tangier arrived at five in the morning. Landing facilities
were primitive, so Montefiore was carried ashore on a sofa made from
mattresses and rope, with a vast crowd of porters and poor Jews wading
alongside.[34] The town itself was a monotonous mass of low, whitewashed houses stretching up the sleep slopes of the bay, remarkable only
for its pretty glazed minaret and the ruins of a fortress destroyed by the
French in 1844.[35] Tangier's 2,500 Jews had turned out in force to greet
the English visitors. Hoisting an elaborate handmade banner before
them, the men chanted blessings of welcome while the women ululated
in Moroccan fashion.[36] They accompanied Montefiore up the poorly
paved road into town, forming a public procession that pushed at the
boundaries imposed on Jewish behavior by the Pact of Umar.

Tangier, however, had long since digressed from such norms. As a former British colony, Moroccans regarded the town as polluted. Until the
1850s it was the only part of the country to tolerate Europeans, serving
as residence of the *naib* and senior members of the diplomatic corps.
Hay recalled that once "an Englishman cd. hardly pass through Tangier
without being stoned or insulted."[37] Now foreign influence was so per-
vasive that men of both creeds were adopting Western dress.[38] This cos-
mopolitanism was especially pronounced in the Jewish community. Regular traffic between Tangier and Gibraltar created a network of business
and family ties across the straits, reinforcing the spread of European
citizenship and protection among the Jewish elite. Such an environment
bred a particular kind of coexistence. Without a *mellah*, Jews and Muslims lived "intermingled" even if in practice they kept to their own
streets.[39]

Montefiore had intended to stay at a Scottish hotel; instead he found
himself staying in the well-appointed home of Moses Pariente, a wealthy
merchant who doubled as interpreter at the U.S. consulate. Here Montefiore wasted little time making peace between the British and Spanish

representatives thanks to an admonitory letter from Miraflores and another from Merry's own father.[40] His visit unleashed a new kind of Anglo-Spanish rivalry as Merry instructed his consuls to adopt a proactive approach to Jewish rights in a bid to prevent the spread of British influence. Montefiore, meanwhile, had come to Tangier to free the prisoners, and with Merry's backing he did just that, preferring to drop a veil over the Spaniard's conduct and the rash of unpleasant incidents that had followed the Safi Affair.

Hay agreed with this strategy, but it was with trepidation that he endorsed Montefiore's next step: a proposal to visit the royal court in Marrakesh.[41] Like Fez and Meknes, the other great cities of the interior, Marrakesh remained closed to Europeans. Popular hostility toward Christians was such that those who disregarded the prohibition tended to disguise themselves as Jews.[42] Only the desire to placate Britain and to quell any lingering concerns about Moroccan justice led Bargash to recommend that the sultan deviate so dramatically from normal practice. Under the circumstances, he advised his master to make an exception for the well-connected English *dhimmi*.

Waiting in Tangier for the necessary permission, Montefiore had time to engage with his surroundings. He gave £300 toward a school for Jewish girls in Judith's memory; interceded on behalf of a Moroccan tribesman imprisoned without trial on suspicion of murdering two Jews; and held an evening party enlivened by Hodgkin, who performed a series of chemical experiments culminating in an attempt to generate electricity from a machine constructed out of a wine bottle.[43] Hay, meanwhile, authorized Reade to accompany the Montefiore mission—although he stressed that the consul would be traveling in a strictly personal capacity.[44] The distinction was a fine one, and most observers concluded that Montefiore had his government's official blessing. As the French consul reported from Mogador, Reade's involvement and the provision of a Royal Navy frigate for the first leg of Montefiore's journey via Gibraltar to Mogador promoted a widespread belief that he "would be discussing other questions in Morocco [Marrakesh] than those relating to the fate of the [Safi] Israelites."[45]

This, indeed, was Hay's biggest worry. Suspecting that Montefiore had more in mind than a simple visit of thanks, the British representative warned "good old Sir Moses" that "though he would find the Sultan & his Chief Minister far more advanced in liberal views than the generality of Moors, he (Sir M.) shd. be careful not to ask for concessions, which might raise the fanatical feelings of the Mohammedan population & place not only in jeopardy the safety of the Jews but even the throne of

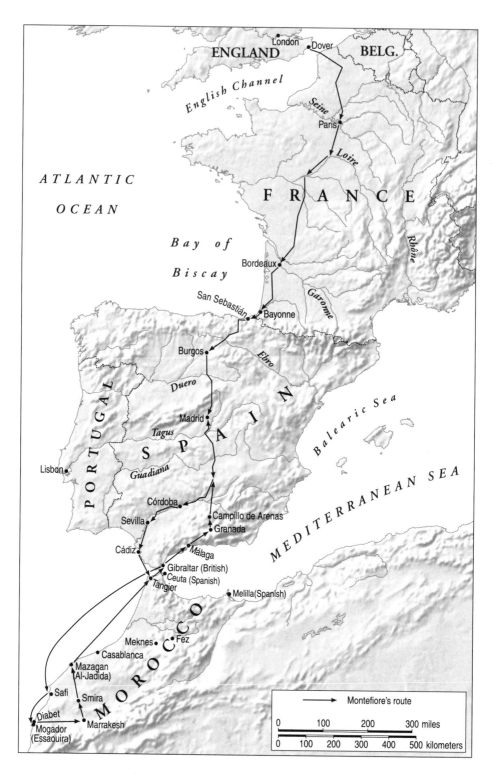

Route taken by Montefiore on his visit to Morocco, 1864

the Sultan. Edicts & laws become too often dead letters, when men are not sufficiently civilized to appreciate them."[46]

Jews made up one in ten of the population on Gibraltar, where Montefiore's role in the Moroccan refugee crisis assured a warm reception. But it was here, as they awaited the arrival of HMS *Magicienne,* that he received awful news. Barely six months earlier, Montefiore had enjoyed the company of his beloved sister Sally in Pisa; now he learned that she had died of bronchitis. It was, Hodgkin thought, "a heavy blow to him, & altogether unlooked for."[47] Worse still, it meant losing the company of Sally's son-in-law, Haim Guedalla, whose contacts and knowledge of Morocco would have rendered him invaluable.

Grief-stricken, Montefiore turned his attention to packing. Tents, bedsteads, mattresses, blankets, lanterns, towels and napkins, food and cooking utensils, all had to be loaded on the *Magicienne,* where Montefiore lodged in the captain's cabin while his entourage slung their hammocks on the gun deck.[48] The weather, in early January, was filthy. Along the rocky Atlantic coast, the surf ran so high that Montefiore abandoned all thought of landing in Safi, signaling to the shore to ascertain whether the prisoners had indeed been set free.

Mogador itself was a gleaming white gem: a small, walled city perched on the rocks and virtually cut off from its hinterland at high tide. A royal port founded barely a century earlier as a means of controlling trade and limiting foreign interactions, it served instead as a bridgehead for Western penetration.[49] Here, as in Tangier, the wealthier Moroccan Jews had abandoned their loyalties as merchants of the sultan and set up as brokers for European firms in exchange for consular protection. Wearing frock coats and living in the Casbah alongside more bona fide foreigners, they wielded their power in the Jewish quarter from afar. This was widely viewed as the worst part of the city. One English visitor described it as "a very dunghill" of filth and chicken feathers; less biased observers saw little to distinguish its narrow, dirty alleys from the working-class slums of Whitechapel.[50]

As the hometown of leading families like the Sebags and Guedallas, this isolated commercial outpost loomed large in Anglo-Moroccan trade and Anglo-Jewish consciousness. For Montefiore, however, Mogador was just a launching pad for his trek to Marrakesh. It was here that he made contact with Abraham Corcos, a wealthy Jewish merchant whose family exerted considerable influence at the royal court.[51] But it was Reade's presence that mattered to the sultan, who gave instructions for both the consul and the London *dhimmi* to be treated as official visitors.[52] Montefiore consequently found himself greeted by a guard of honor and invited to a splendid official dinner, before being sent on his way accompanied by Corcos and an escort of nearly 100 horsemen, muleteers, camel drivers, and servants.

Once fitted up, this sprawling caravan proceeded in stages of fifteen miles across the Moroccan steppe. Shaken and jolted in a *chaise à porteurs* belonging to the Portuguese consul, Montefiore could hardly have covered the distance on horseback but found even "this mode of transit . . . very trying and exhausting." The countryside was barren, rocky, and largely desolate—a dry brown wasteland stretching from horizon to horizon, interrupted every so often by signs of human habitation: a caravan in the process of breaking up its encampment, a handful of half-ruined villages, a bustling farmers' market near a local saint's tomb.[53]

The great red city of Marrakesh lay in the center of a vast plain, covered with olive and date trees and bounded to the south by the snowy peaks of the Atlas Mountains. Lodging in the *mellah* was unthinkable for a British consul, so the sultan put them up in one of his minor royal palaces—a musty, isolated two-story building that had been hurriedly carpeted and decorated, and was still distinctly underfurnished. For once the inner courtyard was not open to the elements, but the windows lacked glass, and their shutters failed to keep out the bitter wind from the mountains. Restricted to a large and neglected orchard by day, huddling around kitchen braziers for warmth by night, they had little to do but make plans until the sultan was ready to receive them. Jews made up perhaps a third of the population and lived in close and meaningful commercial and cultural proximity with Muslim *Marrākshīs*, as the city's inhabitants were called. Despite the intensive comings and goings between the Jewish *mellah* and the Muslim *medina*, contemporaries experienced Montefiore's presence in the Muslim part of the city as an affront. On his departure, the building was sealed up because "a house in which Jews or Christians had lived was regarded as unclean and unfit for the dwelling of a true believer."[54]

Before he reached Marrakesh, Montefiore had assured Hay that "the sole object of his visit was to thank the Sultan for liberating the Saffee prisoners & to recommend his co-religionists."[55] Now Consul Reade was appalled to discover that Montefiore intended to submit a petition asking the sultan to grant legal equality to both Jews and Christians— a formulation shamelessly designed to court European public opinion, since the latter already benefited from consular protection.[56] Reade realized, however, that he had limited room for maneuver. The British had given Montefiore too much public backing; they would lose face badly if he was seen to fail.

It was a longstanding convention of international relations that Europeans and their dependents living in Muslim lands received justice in consular courts rather than under *sharia*. Recently France and Spain had begun aggressively recruiting protégés as part of the wider contest for hegemony. From a Moroccan perspective this tendency was deeply corrosive. Protection encouraged foreign protégés to break the law by placing them beyond the reach of the local authorities, absolving a small but very wealthy minority from paying any taxes.[57] In practice, moreover, commercial and diplomatic realities ensured that most such individuals were Jewish. The privileges accorded these erstwhile *dhimmis* outraged the Muslim population and divided the Jewish community along new class lines.

All this was of grave concern to the Moroccan government, and Reade presented Montefiore's petition as a potential remedy. By improving the status of Moroccan Jews, the sultan could cement his ties with European countries and "remove the principal, if not only cause that is, or can be, assigned in justification of the abuses that are from time to time perpetrated by some of the Foreign Representatives, with regard to the protection they accord to Subjects of these Dominions." In the Ottoman Empire the spread of religious toleration had contributed to the support provided by Britain and France during the Crimean War—and Sultan Abdul Mecid had given "a singular manifestation of this [tolerant] spirit . . . in 1840, when he acceded to a petition of a similar nature to the one we are now treating—which was, as on the present occasion, submitted to His Imperial Majesty by the distinguished Baronet, Sir Moses Montefiore."[58]

In short, Reade had prepared the ground well for Montefiore when he finally set out to meet the sultan, accompanied by the grand vizier, the imperial chamberlain, and a mounted guard. Europeans were not welcome in Marrakesh itself, so the route of the Montefiore party skirted the city between two high, mud-baked walls. These were lined with a motley array of infantry, most lacking shoes or stockings, their legs only partly covered by shabby trousers and their jackets indiscriminately red, blue, or green. Finally, the Montefiore party arrived at a vast parade ground lined with thousands more cavalry and foot soldiers where the sultan rode out to welcome them on a superb white horse. Sidi Mohammed himself hardly lived up to the splendor of this imposing reception: a middle-aged man of mixed race, he suffered from a pock-marked face and a profound speech impediment.[59]

On the face of it, Montefiore got everything he wanted. Sidi Mohammed issued a *dahir* (edict) commanding his subjects "to treat all the Jews residing in our dominions in the manner God Almighty prescribes, equally with the same balanced scales of justice and perfect equality in the courts of law as all other subjects, so that none of them be a victim

"The Quadrangle of the Palace in Marrakesh Where the Sultan Received Sir Moses Montefiore," as drawn by Dr. Thomas Hodgkin, who accompanied him there. Published posthumously in Hodgkin, Narrative of a Journey to Morocco, with Geological Annotations *(London, 1866).*

of the slightest imaginable portion of injustice nor of any kind of malicious nor humiliating measures." To mollify domestic opinion, however, the sultan stressed that he was not altering the fundamental condition of Jews in Morocco. "This edict we issue, was already made known. It was established and explained, but we repeat it to reinforce it, so that it may be more clearly understood and carried more effectively." He was merely strengthening the protection accorded Jews by *sharia* and had no intention of adopting a more European understanding of religious toleration.[60]

How far Montefiore appreciated this is open to question. In the account he sent to the Board of Deputies, he hailed the *dahir* as an "important document securing the future well-being of upwards of half a million of persons."[61] Yet he felt sufficiently uncertain of this outcome to urge Russell privately to instruct British representatives to "support the Sultan in his benevolent and earnest desire to give full effect of the provisions of the Imperial Edict."[62] With men like Corcos to advise him, Montefiore can have nurtured no illusions about the limits of the sultan's authority or the opposition that a fundamental change of Jewish status was likely to encounter. He knew, too, that it had taken sixteen years in the Ottoman Empire for the egalitarian language of his 1840 *firman* to find fulfillment in the *Hatt-i Hümayun.* In Europe at least,

The dahir *granted Montefiore in 1864 by the sultan of Morocco. (Courtesy of Robert Sebag-Montefiore; photograph by Lykke Stjernswärd)*

Montefiore was a gradualist. The declared "enemy of all sudden transitions," he believed the Jew should "in his claims and wishes not outstrip his age. Let him advance slowly but steadily . . . and what is now not attainable even by an arduous struggle, will after a certain time fall into his lap like a ripe fruit."[63] But emancipation was now spreading across western Europe, and, in the wake of the *Hatt-i Hümayun,* Montefiore hoped to kick-start a similar process in the Muslim world.

For Montefiore, then, the *dahir* was both a beginning and a propaganda coup; to inflate the latter, he needed to play up the former—and to disguise any private reservations. Presenting the *dahir* to Queen Isabella of Spain and Napoleon III on his return journey was a step in this direction. It soon became clear that the romance of Montefiore's latest mission was enough to secure endless press coverage. As the *Daily Telegraph* put it, "Old, silver haired as he is, the Jewish baronet heard of the sufferings of his brethren and took ship for Mogador. The rugged roads of Morocco in winter are no slight obstacle to the wayfarer; but Sir Moses was resolved to see the Sultan, and ask justice in the name of God and man."[64]

In the Jewish world, Montefiore's mission to Morocco reinforced a burgeoning sense of international solidarity fostered by the dynamic relationship between civil society and the press. The nature of this response varied from country to country and from community to community; what was striking was its ubiquity. All in all, Montefiore received some 2,000 letters of congratulation.[65] From Prussia to the West Indies, Australia to Czernowitz, Jews held special services to mark his achievement—and passed details of their activities to the Jewish press.[66] The trend was epitomized by Rabbi Avner Katvan of Ibrail in Romania, who later recalled arranging for his congregation "to pray to G-d in every synagogue in my town for your success in the Holy [mission] to redeem our brothers [in Morocco], and for your safe return, and this was announced in the journal *Hamagid.*"[67]

This kind of vicarious participation enabled Jews like Katvan to demonstrate the growing sense of connectedness and an awareness of what was happening to Jews elsewhere that were a by-product of early globalization. For religious reasons, eastern European Jews had always maintained contact with their brethren in Palestine, but this connectedness had rarely extended in a meaningful way to other parts of the Middle East or North Africa. Thanks in part to Montefiore's mission, the 1860s saw the strengthening of ties between the Jews of East and West. This was a two-way process. When the news from Morocco eventually reached Persia, Jews in Hamadan sent addresses congratulating Montefiore, Adler, Crémieux, and the Alliance Israélite on their efforts—and imploring their aid.[68] A subsequent report in *Hamagid* did not fail to draw attention to the condition of Persian Jews as a suitable focus for public concern. Writing in *Hamagid,* Nehemiah Zvi Czernowitz of Warsaw underlined Montefiore's place at the heart of this evolving dynamic: impressed by the Englishman's outstanding deeds in Morocco, he resolved to send an annual contribution in his honor through *Hamagid* to the Alliance Israélite.[69] The interplay between Montefiore, press, and civil society in the globalization of Jewish consciousness could hardly be more apparent.

Nearer home, Jewish enthusiasm for the mission to Morocco carried a different subtext, testifying to the gradual transformation of Jewish society and the modernization (or otherwise) of associational life. In New York City, a public meeting called to discuss the provision of free education endorsed proposals for a Montefiore college. In Trieste, plans for a marble monument were shelved in favor of another charitable foundation, while the tide of popular enthusiasm created an atmosphere in which the Jewish owner of the Café National could rename his establishment Café Montefiore. Farther east, the Association for the Promotion of Handicrafts and Agriculture among the Jews of Hungary set aside £25 to create a Moses and Judith Montefiore Endowment. But a group of Lithuanian Jews living in the more observant world of Kovno

(Kaunas) chose to express their thanks differently—through prayers in Judith's memory and annual donations to the poor.[70]

The Jewish press gave such activities a greater impact: the Odessa-based *Hamelitz* reprinted addresses to Montefiore from towns like Mohilev and Berdichev, while the editor of its Yiddish counterpart, *Kol Hamevaser,* planned to raise money for Jerusalem with a commemorative album.[71] *Hamagid* itself was in the vanguard of this popular movement, gathering signatories from numerous communities for a collective expression of gratitude.[72]

As always, such calls for unity were undermined by concurrent processes of nationalization and fragmentation among the Jews of Europe. In Hungary and the Netherlands, these trends led Jewish leaders to initiate centralized responses to the Montefiore mission with varying degrees of success.[73] Elsewhere Anglo-French rivalry led the Jewish (and non-Jewish) public to react in dramatically different ways. In Britain, the *Jewish Chronicle* exulted to see Montefiore the object of veneration and gratitude among his "fellow-countrymen and co-religionists."[74] In France, the *Archives Israélites* was dismayed by the deafening silence of Parisian Jewry—contrasting their meanness of spirit with the warm welcome Montefiore received from gentiles on the other side of the Channel.[75]

Anglo-Jewish leaders had not missed the significance of the misleading reference to Christians in Montefiore's petition to the sultan. Sensitive to the universalist currents in Victorian culture, they appreciated the need to present international Jewish relief as part of Britain's wider civilizing mission. Politically the time was ripe. Taken together, the interfaith give-and-take of the Morocco and Syrian Relief Funds and the semiofficial status accorded Montefiore's mission to Marrakesh underlined the community of interest between Jewish activism and British aspirations to moral hegemony.

Even before Montefiore's return David Salomons—now a member of Parliament—had asked in the Commons for information about his progress. As expected, the under-secretary of state for foreign affairs responded with official news of the *dahir,* stressing both the support given Montefiore by the British government and the "noble and generous spirit of humanity and philanthropy which actuated him, without reference to any sect or creed, and which extended to the people of every nation who were suffering wrong or injustice."[76]

Montefiore's fellow deputy Alderman Benjamin Phillips returned to this theme two weeks later when he brought a motion to the Court of Common Council mandating the Corporation of London to tender its thanks to Montefiore for his services in "the cause of humanity." After a long speech interweaving the language of local and national patriotism, freedom and humanitarianism, Phillips concluded by urging his colleagues to add Montefiore's name to the roll call of those the City had previously chosen to honor:

> Remember, he is one of your own fellow-citizens—he is a true type of an Englishman (Applause.) I hope the court will agree to the proposition—(Hear, hear)—for it will once again demonstrate that this land is the home and this great city the cradle of civil and religious liberty—(hear, hear)—it will moderate the tyranny of despots, and give hope to those who live under their sway—it will win the respect and applause of all good men, and the great and everlasting gratitude of the oppressed—and it will also add honour and happiness to the declining years of this great public benefactor, and give consolation to his broken-spirited, down-trodden race in other countries.[77]

The proposal was carried by acclamation—and popular enthusiasm did not stop there. Roughly four weeks later, the great and good of the Jewish community came together with a motley collection of Liberals, Radicals, Evangelicals, and Quakers at the London Tavern in a grand public demonstration of gratitude to Montefiore, the sultan, and the British government.[78]

It was too much for Montefiore. Exhausted by a long return journey, all he wanted was "to be allowed to remain four & twenty hours in quietness at Ramsgate."[79] He was soon struggling to cope with the demands of his newfound celebrity. "I am quite worn out & almost too weak to write," he complained to Loewe shortly after his arrival;

> As the increase of my labours has injured my health I can get no exercise by day & little sleep by night, both friends and strangers overwhelm me with their kind congratulations . . . I am obliged to receive as early as I can the addresses sorted at the Town Hall Ramsgate—the address of the Meeting at the London Tavern, the address of the Corporation of the City of London,—the address of the Board of Deputies of the London Court & addresses from several of our Country Congregations who desire to send me deputations with their addresses—you may see how much I am pressed . . . May God help us both, with strength & nerve to get through the business.[80]

By the time of the meeting in the London Tavern, however, the accolades pouring in to Montefiore had lost all basis in Moroccan reality. Far from presenting Montefiore as disinterested, the contemporary Moroccan historian Ahmed Naciri understood his mission as a variant of traditional Maghrebi Jewish politics. The Jews of Morocco had appealed to Rothschild, "the most considerable Jewish merchant in London," to improve their situation; the latter was notorious for the "immense loans" he granted the British government and his resulting political influence; consequently Rothschild had "designated one of his in-laws to visit the sultan (may God have mercy on him) and to deal with this matter and other matters. He gave him magnificent presents [to bring to the sultan] and requested the English government to intercede with the sultan and to write to him [in order to help] satisfy his request." Moreover, Naciri stressed that although the *dahir* contained nothing substantial, the Jews had used it to foment disorder:

> they made copies of it, which they sent to all the Jews of the Maghreb. They started then to perpetrate acts of transgression and rebellious deeds, for they wanted to administer themselves in an autonomous way. Those who lived in seaports, in particular, swore oaths and [concluded] pacts between themselves [on these grounds]. But God canceled their tricks and disappointed them. For when the sultan (may God have mercy on him) saw that it was his *dahir* which made the Jews go astray, he wrote another edict stating explicitly his idea and declared that his recommendations were only in favor of virtuous Jews and the needy [who were] striving to earn their living, but the bad subjects known for their unfairness, their greed, and their shady occupations, would get the punishment they deserve.[81]

This was in fact a fairly accurate assessment of the situation. Montefiore had barely left Marrakesh before the sultan issued letters of instruction to his subordinates, clarifying the scope of the *dahir* along these very lines.[82] Sidi Mohammed's conservative understanding of the *dahir* counted for little when influential Jewish leaders like Abraham Corcos—who as foreign protégés were themselves immune from retribution—sent copies of the document to the most far-flung and isolated *mellahs*. Encouraged by the pomp and ceremony accompanying Montefiore's mission, Jews all over Morocco began interpreting the *dahir*'s contents far more radically. As Bargash reported, "it appears they supposed they were no longer under the control and Government of the Sultan's Authorities. Words and deeds proceeded from them which were most disorderly and which produced great irritation amongst the Mohamedan population and Authorities."[83]

In effect, Moroccan Jews ceased to accept the treatment they had once taken for granted. This change manifested itself both through concerted acts of defiance—the expulsion of a Muslim guard and the appointment

of a self-governing junta in Tétouan—and more random gestures of insubordination: a man who refused to take off his shoes when passing a
mosque, a tailor who insisted on being given a good price before making
a suit of clothes for the provincial governor.[84] Local officials clamped
down hard on such behavior, but the resulting floggings prompted
wealthy Jewish merchants to complain to their respective consuls.

Hay could hardly remain aloof from this situation. He had opposed
Montefiore's action in Marrakesh but now felt compelled to prevent
"the step which the Sultan has voluntarily made, in favour of religious
tolerance" from being retracted.[85] The upshot was a circular issued to
British consuls throughout Morocco, instructing them not merely to
speak up against "any persecution or cruel treatment of the Jews, in
contravention of the orders in the Sultan's Edict" but also, if necessary,
to take such individuals temporarily under British protection.[86] His Italian counterpart had issued a similar declaration, but the French consul
warned his subordinates to treat Jewish complaints with the greatest reserve "and only take them up with the governor of your province once
you are scrupulously assured of their exactitude."[87]

Hay's circular marked a fundamental break with British policy.[88] The
British had always attempted to limit foreign protection—most recently
through the Béclard Convention of 1863, which allocated a strict quota
of protégés to European firms doing business there. Now Hay suddenly
announced his willingness to extend irregular protection to any Jew in
need of it. This move did not merely outrage diplomatic convention; it
went further than Palmerston's much-vaunted policy of protecting Jews
in Ottoman lands. The result was chaos.

As news of clashes between Jews and Muslims in Salé, Casablanca,
Azemmour, Mogador, Fez, Meknes, the Gharb, and parts of the Atlas
Mountains filtered through to Europe—via the Jews of Tangier—Montefiore felt compelled to write reminding the grand vizier of the "worldwide celebrity" attained by his mission and urging the sultan to make
sure the *dahir* was strictly enforced.[89] The sultan, meanwhile, told Bargash to raise the issue with Hay, whose circular had exacerbated an already dangerous situation.[90] Chastened, Hay asked British consuls to
read the riot act to local Jewish elders, emphasizing the risks they ran
"by exasperating their Mohamedan fellow-subjects" and disassociating
the British government as far as possible from the Montefiore mission.[91]
When Hay's account of these developments reached London in early
September, Montefiore was summoned to the Foreign Office to read the
dispatches for himself.

He found them deeply alarming. Of course, Montefiore was inclined
to think that "Jews throughout the World are especially characterised as

loyal obedient and peaceful subjects and [that] . . . if any of the Jews of Morocco have been represented to Sir John [Hay] as exceptions to this universally admitted truth there is really no solid foundation for the charge."[92] But he also had to take Hay's complaints seriously. His response was to issue a circular of his own to the Jewish communities of Morocco—a kind of manifesto for the gradualist approach to emancipation that he had adopted in his own country.

Referring (though not in so many words) to the halakhic injunction *dina demalkhuta dina*—the law of the kingdom is the law—Montefiore stressed the Jewish tradition of political obedience to secular authority, the benevolent intentions of the sultan of Morocco, and the need for his Jewish subjects to behave in exemplary fashion regardless of the treatment to which they were subjected. He concluded: "It is by conduct such as this, we may hope, that, under the Almighty's blessing, the hearts of those who would molest or injure you will be softened; or that, should injustice be done it will be speedily and surely punished."[93] Both this circular and Hay's *volte-face* seem to have quelled the immediate crisis provoked by Montefiore's mission. Protection, however, remained a running sore, and complaints from Jews in places like Tétouan rumbled on for years.

In the long run, Montefiore's mission and European intervention encouraged Moroccan Jews to see themselves as the victims of a despotic government and "fanatical" population—and Muslims to condemn them for collaborating with foreign powers. From Montefiore's perspective, this state of affairs may not have mattered. The point was rather that—in principle if not in practice—Muslim countries were increasingly expected to apply British standards of civil and religious liberty to the treatment of their religious minorities. This trend marked a fundamental break with tradition in Muslim lands even if, back on the European continent, many countries continued to discriminate against their Jewish subjects.

Chapter 15

Building Jerusalem

In June 1863 Leo Holländer—the leading Hungarian campaigner for Jewish emancipation and onetime quartermaster-general in Lajos Kossuth's revolutionary army—published an account of two days he had spent with Montefiore in Budapest. Holländer found his English visitor to be "a fine stately, tall man of nearly eighty . . . in indifferent health and frequently obliged to keep his bed." But it was exciting to meet a living legend, and the Hungarian enjoyed Montefiore's engaging reminiscences. Holländer was touched, too, by the great man's simple dignity and a certain plain-speaking "eloquence of the heart—which always knows how to find the suitable words, and for this reason strikes home into the hearts of his audience." Amid acres of press coverage, the article stands out as a record of Montefiore's personal style and what Holländer termed his "inward mental life."[1]

Tears came to Montefiore's eyes when he spoke of Judith; he pulled himself together with a thought of the world to come. Only his relentless campaigning seemed to give the old man something to live for. Holländer described how Montefiore's eyes glistened when he spoke of improving the condition of his fellow Jews, how "his voice becomes firm and clear, and the infirm octogenarian becomes a vigorous man, who is inspired by enthusiasm to a remarkable degree." Such passion testified to the "profound, sincere—I should almost say glorifying—religiousness" that seemed to Holländer "the most striking feature in Sir Moses' character." Living as he did in the hotbed of competing nationalities that was mid-nineteenth-century Hungary, Holländer conveyed Montefiore's Jewish commitment in strikingly contemporary terms:

Next to the religious it is the national idea which never leaves him . . . The answer which he gave to my question, whether he really entertained any hope of a future national restoration of the Israelites in the Holy Land characterises the man. With a smile which lighted up his countenance, he replied, "Of this I am quite certain; it was my constant dream, and I hope will be realised one day when I shall be no more." And to the objection how it would be possible to gather in the Israelites scattered in all corners of the globe, he replied: "I do not expect that all Israelites will quit their abodes in these territories in which they feel happy, even as there are Englishmen in Hungary, Germany, America, or Japan; but Palestine must belong to the Jews, and Jerusalem is destined to become the seat of a Jewish empire."[2]

Two decades before the birth of Zionism, these sentiments appear to foreshadow the emergence of secular Jewish nationalism. But a Jewish empire centered on Jerusalem was the goal of every messianic visionary—and Montefiore was not alone in nurturing this dream.

One such man was Rabbi Zvi Hirsch Kalischer, who had first made contact with Montefiore nearly twenty years earlier.[3] Committed as he was to a realistic messianism that discerned in current affairs the hidden miracles of God, the rabbi of Thorn (Toruń) had little difficulty interpreting the Crimean War and the flurry of Jewish interest in Palestine as steps on the path to redemption. Twenty years earlier, Kalischer's efforts to reinstitute the cult of sacrifice in Jerusalem had ended in failure, after his former teacher deliberately excised the more favorable sections of a ruling from the Hatam Sofer, the leading halakhic authority of his time. Not until the mid-1850s did Kalischer read this ruling in full. Galvanized by the sage's view that sacrifice was a real possibility, Kalischer rekindled his campaign. In England, Montefiore's friend Nathan Adler was cautiously encouraging. But when Kalischer wrote in 1858 asking to be appointed overseer of the Jaffa orchard, Montefiore and Adler refused.[4] The letter marked the beginning of Kalischer's turn to agricultural activism. Sacrifices remained his priority; he now recognized settling the land of Israel as a necessary first step.

In March 1859 *Hamagid* published an appeal from two Sephardi rabbis in Jerusalem describing the way immigration was pushing up rents in the Jewish quarter, leading to overcrowding, poverty, and congestion.[5] Their plea heralded the arrival of Rabbi Azriel Selig Hausdorf in Europe on a high-profile fund-raising tour. As a member of the small but wealthy Germano-Dutch community, Hausdorf was not a typical emissary to the diaspora. His mission to collect money to house the Jewish poor broke the mold of *halukah*. "Everything is done properly and in the light of day," asserted the accompanying editorial in *Hamagid* in an implicit reference to attacks on Pekam and the widespread accusations of corruption. "Nothing is concealed from the eyes of the public."[6]

The whole structure of the accompanying campaign betrayed the hallmarks of Montefiore's modern approach to fund-raising: committees established in major European cities like Berlin, Paris, Brussels, and Amsterdam; subscription lists reproduced faithfully in *Hamagid*; and endorsements from relatively acculturated Jewish leaders—not just Montefiore himself, but Adler, the Russian plutocrat Baron Ginzburg, and the French orientalist Salomon Munk. Like Montefiore, Hausdorf trumpeted the support of restorationists and sympathetic Christians. Like Montefiore, he looked beyond the continent of Europe, setting sail for North America in June 1859. But unlike the Holy Land Relief Fund, Hausdorf's mission sprang from the heart of Jewish Jerusalem. And with Ashkenazi innovators like Moshe Sachs and Zvi Haim Sneersohn embarking on similar missions, it was far more than a one-man show.[7]

Kalischer was among the many enthused by these plans; his East Prussian hometown became a pivot of Hausdorf's fund-raising drive.[8] Then, in 1860, Kalischer learned that a schoolmaster in Frankfurt an der Oder had launched a society to promote Jewish settlement in Palestine. Over the next five years Haim Luria's Hevrat Yishuv Eretz Yisrael (or Kolonisationsverein, as it was known in German) would become a hub for pragmatic messianists like Kalischer, his friend the cabalist and *tzaddik* Rabbi Elijah Guttmacher of Graetz, and Yehudah Alkalai of Semlin (Zemun), whose visit to London had created such a stir in 1852. It would also act as a magnet for the handful of individuals hovering on the verge of a precocious Jewish nationalism, such as the maverick Hungarian reform Rabbi Josef Natonek and the disillusioned socialist Moses Hess, sometime comrade of Karl Marx.[9]

With only a few hundred members at best, the influence of the Kolonisationsverein was inevitably limited—even if Luria did number the chief rabbis of Britain, France, Adrianople, and Jerusalem among his supporters.[10] Indeed, the importance of the Kolonisationsverein lay precisely in its potential to bridge the gulf between the Jewish heartlands of central and eastern Europe and the more acculturated—and powerful—Jews of the West. This pluralism became apparent in 1862 when the publication of two very different books transformed the public debate about restoring Jews to Palestine.

Moses Hess's Zionist classic *Rome and Jerusalem: The Last National Question* put a radically secular view of the problem. His explicitly political nationalism led Hess to reject emancipation as a chimera because of the radical (and increasingly ethnic) nature of anti-Jewish prejudice in

Europe. Kalischer's *Seeking Zion,* a seminal religious Zionist text, took a very different tack. Kalischer saw the hand of God in the upheavals of his time: "with the help of the blessed Redeemer of Israel, great philanthropists from the Jewish nation have been raised high and seen success, rulers and nobles, honourable princes whose like we have not seen since the time of the destruction [of the Temple]. They hold the rulers' staff, the golden sceptre of those who desire wealth. They are the noble houses of Rothschild, Montefiore, Fould, Albert Cohn and the like . . . They will seek to establish a society for settled land, and along with them many rich Jews, the leaders of the people."[11]

Kalischer proceeded to explain that the emancipation that had brought these Jews to power was the product of divine influence; that "the rays of light" would spread from France to Britain, from Britain to Germany, and from Germany to Russia and Poland; and that emancipation would eventually bring about the return of the Jews to Palestine. "For He has given me freedom among the nations, not as in past years, when Jacob was very wretched and did not raise his head . . . God has made us free in most countries, and we can also possess fields and vineyards in the Holy Land, just like the great Sir Moses Montefiore has done."[12]

These views provoked enormous controversy—not for the reasons that have entranced later historians, but rather because Kalischer's radical messianic activism aroused the indignation of orthodox leaders like Rabbi Meir Auerbach. David Gordon, editor of *Hamagid,* found them inspirational.[13] In a famous series of articles he endorsed the arguments of both Kalischer and Hess, using national language that drew explicitly on the evolution of Jewish civil society—and on Montefiore's place at its heart:

The precondition for our return to the land of our fathers is to achieve national unity across our diasporas . . . The first diaspora to take that step was the British with the establishment of the Board of Deputies in London, headed by the great and pious *sar* [prince], Moses Montefiore. This institution stands by oppressed Jews wherever they are. Following it, the French Kol Israel Haverim [Alliance Israélite] was founded . . . No doubt similar associations will be founded in other countries, together providing the pillar upon which the house of Israel will rest its hopes . . . Another necessary step is to establish a foothold in the land of our fathers: buy land, build houses, and work the land. We rejoiced at the news of our brothers in Jerusalem buying land to build houses. Three years ago, Rabbi Luria founded the Hevrat Yishuv Eretz Yisrael with similar goals, and its membership is growing. Yet many obstacles stand in the way of establishing agricultural settlements for our brothers in the Holy

Land. Who can guarantee their safety from attacks by their savage neighbors, who live off looting? It is critical for the success of this association's
mission that it be headed by those of our brothers who can stand before
kings and rulers, people like the Rothschilds, Montefiore, Albert Cohn,
and the other leaders of the Board of Deputies and the Alliance Israélite.
They are the ones who can convince European rulers to ask Turkey to
safeguard the dwelling of Jews on the land of Israel . . . To those who say:
"The time has not come yet to rebuild the House of the Lord," reply
"Nonsense! The time is very right provided we take actions. What do we
ask of you? To leave your country and all your possessions? No! Just that
you support those who wish to go to Israel and rebuild on the remains
that bear out our honor of the ancient times, as our brothers do now on
Mount Zion . . . Hurry to support [financially] the works of the Hevrat
Yishuv Eretz Yisrael . . . And you, great leaders of Israel who have the ear
of kings and rulers, stand up to lead the people toward achieving this
goal; only with your help can we win back the Land of our fathers."[14]

Montefiore, the target of so much rhetoric, wisely kept silent. Kalischer knew nothing of it, but Montefiore had briefly entered into negotiations with the Ottoman government in 1859, when the Turkish ambassador let it be known "that if the Jews were inclined to return to the
Holy Land, and could advance money to the Turkish Government to effect the withdrawal of the existing coinage, they should have every liberty and land, with all possible protection." Montefiore went through
the motions but doubted that "there was a single Jew in England who
wished to return at present, nor did he believe that a loan for that purpose would be raised." This skepticism—understandably highlighted by
Loewe—disguised a heartfelt zeal.[15]

In his 1856 letter to Kursheedt, Montefiore had voiced a belief in the
fulfillment of the biblical prophecies that was not very different from the
kind of realistic messianism trumpeted by Kalischer. Yet in 1865 he confessed "frankly" to Sir Macdonald Stephenson: "I believe it is to Divine
Agency and not to human means that my Co-religionists must look for
the restoration to them of the Land of their Fathers." This statement
was either politic or disingenuous. Rabbis like Auerbach who settled in
Jerusalem could reasonably claim to be living a life of prayer with no
intention of hastening the advent of the messiah. Montefiore had negoti-
ated with Mehmed Ali and the sultan to promote the return of Jews to
the Holy Land, and this fact put him in a different league. He had great
respect for men like Auerbach, but Montefiore's proposals for Jewish
agriculture, cotton manufacturing, and education threatened to overturn the accepted pattern of Jewish life in Palestine. It beggars belief that

he saw no connection between these activities and his own messianic faith.[16]

Two years later cholera ravaged the eastern Mediterranean. In June 1865 Montefiore sent £50 to relieve Jewish sufferers in Smyrna.[17] Reporting back in early August, the British consul explained that after launching the Jewish subscription the local authorities had turned it into a general fund. Rather than placing Montefiore's £50 in the hands of the sanitary committee, Hyde Clarke proposed entrusting it to those Jews responsible for administering general relief.[18] "It has always been my maxim in the administration of any Funds for the alleviation of distress to see that the relief was applied irrespective of creed or opinion," Montefiore replied with satisfaction, "and I do not doubt but that the same will be done in the present case."[19] He elaborated on this maxim in a less high-minded letter to Joseph Sebag, explaining in a different context that he "thought it only prudent to send the Lord Mayor a Donation, to prevent any person that might have been present saying the Jews only thought of their own people."[20]

It soon became clear that the situation in Smyrna was only part of the problem caused by the cholera outbreak. Yet when Nathan Adler forwarded a desperate plea from the Sephardim of Jerusalem, the Board of Deputies insisted on first taking advice.[21] "This Board, since the departure of Montefiore [from the presidency], only writes letters to the government, and sometimes it does not even do that," declared a disgusted *Hamagid* in late August. "They do not feel for the suffering of the starving Jews, but rather meet, dispute, and then do not do anything."[22] Fortunately, the board was not the only port of call for the Jews of Jerusalem. Two weeks earlier, *Hamagid* itself had launched an appeal on their behalf.[23] By the time a slightly shamefaced board responded to the promptings of Adler and Montefiore, fund-raising in France and Prussia was already under way.[24]

The Holy Land Relief Fund of 1865 was a shabbier affair than its spectacularly successful predecessor. Without the cachet of novelty—or the impetus provided by the Crimean War—it proved harder to sustain public interest. There were still Christian donors in provincial England, but in North America the *Occident and American Jewish Advocate* did not believe that a penny had been contributed by "non-Israelites."[25] More importantly, Montefiore's efforts were no longer the fulcrum of international Jewish activity. With committees in Prussia, France, Amsterdam, and eastern Europe all plowing their own furrow, the amount of money donated via Britain was just £5,000, barely a quarter of the

sum raised ten years earlier.[26] Reporting from Jerusalem in December
1865, Haim Sneersohn complained that barely £400 had been forwarded from England, in contrast to the 60,000 francs already transmitted through Amsterdam.[27]

The money was sorely needed; cholera had brought Jerusalem to a
standstill.[28] The streets and bazaars of the holy city were deserted, its
shops closed, and its wealthier inhabitants nowhere to be seen. Turkish
officials and foreign consuls had decamped to the countryside, leaving
the hard-pressed poor to fend for themselves. By December nearly 3,000
people were dead: 1,500 Muslims, 800 Christians, and more than 900
Jews.[29] Survivors found life in Jerusalem unbearable. There had been no
rain for nearly a year, and on some days the sun burned almost as hot as
in the summer. A plague of locusts in the northern Galilee only compounded the effects of drought. For once, Sneersohn had nothing but
praise for the Jewish religious leadership. Haim David Hazan, the elderly *Haham Bashi*, returned daily to the plague-infested city to comfort
the sick and distribute poor relief, while men like Israel Bak and Selig
Hausdorf traipsed from house to house, gathering lists of the needy and
doing what they could to help.[30]

Back in Europe this selfless behavior seemed barely credible. In 1858,
two years after his return from Palestine, Ludwig Frankl had published
an excoriating (and widely read) account of Jewish life in Jerusalem.[31]
The Viennese philanthropist highlighted the bigoted, self-seeking behavior of religious leaders and the endemic corruption perpetuated by
the flow of *halukah*. *Jeshurun*, the voice of German neo-orthodoxy, attacked Frankl's veracity, but his arguments added grist to the mill of
those who had been urging the cause of change for years. Abraham Benisch was a prime example. Now editor of the *Jewish Chronicle*, he
maintained that although the embittered Frankl was certainly a biased
witness, "the broad outlines" of his account were only too accurate.[32]
By 1865 even the pages of the Parisian *Halevanon*, an ultra-Orthodox
newspaper founded to defend the way of life in the Holy Land, were
riddled with complaints about the unfair distribution of money in Jerusalem.[33] Meanwhile in England one of her majesty's chaplains published
an attack on what he saw as the iniquitous and tyrannical rule of the
rabbis in Safed. There was nothing particularly new in what the Reverend Norman Macleod had to say. What mattered was that his attack
appeared in *Good Words,* which boasted a circulation of over 100,000
British Christians.

The potential damage to the Jewish cause was incalculable. While
Montefiore wrote to Macleod in person, his nephew Haim Guedalla
published a lengthy riposte in the *Jewish Chronicle*.[34] After putting paid

to the myth that the poor starving recipients of European Jewish bounty were idle, lazy, immoral, and suspicious of Western intentions, Guedalla proceeded to explain that the rabbis of Jerusalem were not so very different from their counterparts in Poland, Russia, and Germany. In the lively debate that followed, the Anglo-Moroccan Guedalla repeatedly drew parallels with life in Britain, comparing the electoral and administrative practices of the Jerusalem rabbinate to municipal corporations like the City of London and declaring on one occasion: "There is, no doubt, a great want of organisation at Jerusalem, but not much worse than is to be found in London, where the state of the streets on the 11th inst. [January 1866] would have disgraced any village in Europe, and the sleeping dormitories in workhouses . . . are infinitely worse than any hovel in the Holy Land."[35]

Of course, Guedalla saw room for improvement—but he took issue with those like "S." who decried "[t]he little rivalries" of the Montefiores, the Rothschilds, and the Lehrens, and he called for a "concentrated" international effort.[36] In an age of individualistic voluntarism it was, Guedalla thought, "idle to speak to the Jews of London, Paris, Vienna, and Amsterdam in 1866 of common action in dealing with the affairs of the Holy Land or any other matter."[37] Here Abraham Benisch disagreed with him. The formula for binding together the scattered forces of international Jewry had yet to be found, but he did not doubt "that the name of Montefiore would prove this magic spell, were only authority given to utter it."[38] Readers who detected a certain frustration in this statement were not wrong; only a week earlier, "S." had deplored the inactivity of the trustees of Montefiore's original Holy Land Relief Fund, who purportedly met "about once in seven years to discharge the important but pleasing duty of dining with their noble president."[39]

Montefiore, of course, had not forgotten Jerusalem: he continued, in his own way, to pursue the dream of productivization. Coming from Kent, where windmills and hophouses dotted the gently rolling landscape, he hoped that modern wind technology could bring down the price of bread and help address the subsistence crises that so regularly struck Palestine. In 1858 the *Illustrated London News* proudly displayed a picture of "The First Windmill in Jerusalem."[40] Funded through the Touro legacy and built by Holman of Canterbury on Montefiore's instructions, the windmill was a simple stone structure with an automatic fantail that directed the cap into the eye of the wind and powered four revolving sails. It had taken forty men to carry every piece of machinery over the mountains from Jaffa. Construction lasted four months.

*The Montefiore windmill at Jerusalem in 1859, shortly after completion,
with the Judah Touro almshouses still under construction. (Courtesy of
Mishkenot Sha'ananim, Jerusalem)*

Building the mill was one thing; keeping it going proved quite another.
Only a year later, news of Gershom Kursheedt's imminent arrival jolted
the mill's half-hearted manager into frenetic activity, prompting one English visitor to comment wryly: "The poor neglected old mill must wonder what all the cleaning and oiling means, and I dare say curses his
masters for arousing him from his accustomed lethargy."[41] But the manager was not the only problem. This was a classic example of first-world
technology catapulted into a society ill equipped to receive it. Poorly
sited on a relatively sheltered slope, the sophisticated European windmill proved difficult and expensive to repair—and struggled to generate
enough power to grind the hard local wheat effectively. It had cost a little under a fifth of Touro's $50,000.[42]

The mill was only part of Montefiore's vision. In 1858 he abandoned
his dreams of a grand European hospital and contracted with J. William
Smith of Ramsgate to build almshouses instead.[43] Smith already knew
that it would not be an easy project. A preliminary visit to Jerusalem
had acquainted him with the peculiarities of doing business in Palestine:
wild fluctuations in prices, tedious haggling over every purchase, the difficulty of holding Arab contractors to their agreements, the need to factor *baksheesh* into the cost of any transaction, and the expectation that

workers would be provided with coffee and allowed to take regular to-bacco breaks.[44] The one thing he did not anticipate was that the Otto-man authorities would refuse to let him go ahead.

In February 1859, Mustafa Sureyya, the Ottoman governor of Jerusa-lem, reported to Constantinople that the Touro almshouses contravened military regulations, which forbade building of any kind within a given distance from the city. Montefiore's plans breached the conditions of the *firman* granted in 1855. They would, moreover, transform the nature of Jerusalem, for "the houses that he is going to construct seem like a small quarter, and if they are built without a special permit, there will be noth-ing left to say to those who want to build houses outside the walls."[45]

As James Finn explained to Sir Henry Bulwer in Constantinople, no one could have expected Montefiore to adhere to the letter of the sul-tan's *firman* by situating his hospital a mile and a half from Jerusalem—and it was not as if there were no other buildings within the proscribed area. Finn himself now had two houses outside the city, and even the Anglican mission had built a school outside the walls. When Finn asked Sureyya Pasha why he had not enforced the regulations against the windmill, the latter replied that "on his arrival it was nearly completed, and it was well known that his predecessor had been too lax in such matters."[46] That the Ottoman authorities had allowed the Russians a large former parade ground to the northwest of the city to accommo-date Orthodox pilgrims only confirmed Finn's sense of outrage.[47] Even-tually the Porte caved in, instructing Sureyya that if he persisted in ob-structing Montefiore, "because this man is from among persons whose influence on the state of England are considerable, it will have a bad in-fluence."[48] Finn had already advised Smith to continue regardless of any restrictions; by the time Sureyya received his orders, construction was well under way.[49]

As early as 1856, however, the *Jewish Chronicle* had reported that no Jew would be brave enough to live beyond the security of the city walls.[50] But instead of seeking tenants young and strong enough to de-fend themselves, Montefiore hoped that they would be "persons of ex-cellent character, men well learned in our Law, who devote much of their time to study, and by whom a nice house, free of rent, in a pleasant situation would be considered a boon."[51] The twenty or so Touro Alms-houses were solidly (not to say defensively) built in a simple Gothic style, and equally divided between Sephardi and Ashkenazim. Besides cisterns, kitchens, gardens, and a communal bakery, the first Jewish neighbor-hood outside the walls of Jerusalem boasted a synagogue, a schoolroom, a clinic, and two ritual baths. Yet the situation was so precarious that

Montefiore reportedly paid his tenants 10 Napoléons a year for the privilege of housing them, and even then they preferred to sleep safely in the Old City at night.[52]

In the long run, however, Mishkenot Sha'ananim—as the Touro Almshouses are usually called—became the seed of a modern Jewish city in Jerusalem. "The situation is excellent, although for the moment somewhat unsafe," commented one visitor as early as 1861. "There is, however, room for 200 dwellings, and the site will no doubt gain greatly in every respect when the buildings of the Russian Mission . . . [are] completed."[53] For all the fear of murder and banditry, life even within the walls of Jerusalem was becoming unsustainable. In seeking to address the housing problem, Montefiore was just a little ahead of the game.

Writing wistfully to his nephew Joseph Sebag, Montefiore described how "[r]eading this morning the portion of the Prophets of *Lech Lecha* [in which God tells Abraham to leave for the Promised Land] gave me fresh and enraged desire to revisit the Holy Land." He was "most anxious to have more houses built in Jerusalem" at his own expense, adding jokingly: "Why not persuade me to go? What will [your wife] Adelaide say . . ." In late 1865 Montefiore finally announced that he would be leaving for Palestine in March. The decision proved convenient for the subcommittee of the Board of Deputies responsible for the new relief fund; its members entrusted him with what money they had left and asked him to distribute it to the best of his judgment.[54]

In Britain, news of Montefiore's latest journey attracted the usual accolades. Once again the most striking piece appeared in the *Daily Telegraph,* which described with inimitably imperialistic idealism how Jews had come to Palestine from north, south, east, and west,

and many of them have only not died there because of the open hand of the Englishman who shared their faith. As far north as Damascus the Mussulmans will speak of this Yahoodi as one that "allah has intrusted in mercy." Druses and Maronites know him and his deeds all along Lebanon, and the Bekaa and the bare sides of Hermon. At Nazareth and Nablous you hear good of him, the lepers sitting in the sun under the wall . . . are the better for Sir Moses Montefiore, and even Aghile Agha's Bedouins, who eat the land up along the Jordan like locusts, and take a man's life as lightly as they would cut a goat's throat—even these ragamuffins of the Houran would probably let the caravan of Sir Moses go untouched past their black tents.

There are, then, few of our countrymen of any persuasion who are not proud that the Catholicity of Sir Moses Montefiore—his courage, his cheerful loving nature, and his "good deeds that he had done" are written down in the long list of English beneficencies. It is as an Englishman that he has gone about among the Eastern peoples, using his great wealth for the fellow creatures that he could specially help. It is in English that he has bidden the widow dry her eyes, and the sick take heart, and clothed the naked and fed the hungry. As an English baronet he is starting on one more journey . . .[55]

For Isaac Leeser, editor of the *Occident*, this was precisely the problem. The Jews of the United States had contributed more than most to the second Holy Land Relief Fund. But, Leeser complained, no one had consulted the American Board of Delegates or the B'nai B'rith lodges about what to do with the remaining money. And no one, he thought, could "deem it proper to appoint what is called a committee of one, let this one be who he may, to distribute at his option so considerable sum as was sent from here, which it now appears had not been employed for the object it was sent for as late as January 5th."[56] Leeser had long been skeptical about the ability of British and French Jews to deploy their charity in Palestine effectively. He hoped this would be the last time that American Jews allowed themselves to play second fiddle rather than establishing their own initiatives. As he had pointed out to Adler and Montefiore in the face of a similar insult four years earlier, "It should not be forgotten that our population exceeds that of England, France, or Holland separately, and may possibly be equal to all of them combined; and therefore our influence ought not to be overlooked in the scale of Jewish affairs, whenever our assistance can be rendered available."[57]

Thanks to steam technology, the trip to Palestine from Ramsgate was easy: once it had taken months; now the distance could be comfortably covered in two to three weeks. Besides his old traveling companions Loewe and Hodgkin, Montefiore was accompanied by Joseph and a reluctant Adelaide Sebag. Invalidish and homesick, she derived little enjoyment from the journey—although by the time they reached Jaffa, it was Hodgkin who had fallen seriously ill.

Jaffa itself was changing. Steamships and the telegraph left Palestine less isolated; with the Suez canal nearing completion, integration with world markets was only a matter of time. The port still lacked landing facilities, but the town was constantly growing thanks to flourishing trade and the drip, drip, drip of Jewish immigration. Unlike Jerusalem, it was also an industrious place. Both Ludwig Frankl and Yehiel Bril, editor of *Halevanon*, commented that all Jaffa's Jews made their own living.[58] Yet the atmosphere in the streets was grim. Hoping in vain for his friend's recovery, Montefiore was awakened every morning by the rattling of a drum that summoned the town's inhabitants to collect their daily quota of young, green locusts in a desperate effort to keep the plague under control. His own property nearby had been utterly ruined. The locusts had eaten everything in sight: leaves, fruit, bark, green shoots, vegetables, and experimental cotton plantings.[59]

Back in Jerusalem, Montefiore's impending arrival exacerbated tensions within the Jewish community. While the religious establishment dispatched messengers to greet him, their critics accused them of acting out of self-interest, and malcontents pasted slanderous attacks on Montefiore to the walls of the Jewish quarter.[60] He himself seems to have known something of these developments. As he reluctantly decided to leave poor Hodgkin in Jaffa, Montefiore viewed the task ahead of him with trepidation. "May the Lord direct and guide me!" he prayed.[61]

In the event, his fears proved unfounded. As the party approached the holy city, they found the hills covered with people of all denominations. Hundreds of children lined the roadside singing specially composed Hebrew hymns, and the *Haham Bashi* welcomed the visitors with prayer and refreshment in a tent outside the Jaffa Gate. Adelaide and Montefiore were "quite done up" after a day of shaking and jolting in their litters, but his exhaustion only added to the impression produced on the waiting throng as Montefiore caught sight of the holy city and, "as is customary, rent his garment, and with his companions offered up a prayer for mercy at the sigh of the temple wall! His tears flowed copiously, and every one heard his sobbing."[62]

This was, then, an emotional reunion—although Jerusalem in 1866 was very different from the tumbledown place Montefiore had first known. The windmill and almshouses reflected a wider renewal of the physical fabric of city, as (mostly foreign) Jews and Christians of all denominations vied to construct new centers and places of worship: the Russian Compound outside the walls of the city, the Anglican Cathedral and missionary schools, the Sephardi synagogues restored so splendidly in the 1830s, the Hausdorf housing project, the half-built synagogues of the Hasidim and Perushim, and the Hurva with its soaring dome.

Underpinning these developments was a new demographic reality. Whereas once Jews had numbered a quarter of the city's inhabitants, now they formed a simple majority. Thanks to Montefiore, the "stinking and detestable" slaughterhouse had been removed from the Jewish quarter, and the streets were cleaner, but with twice the number of people crammed into the same area the overcrowding was worse than ever.[63] Rents were dear and house prices even higher than in England.

As always, Montefiore began by paying his respects to the governor. He was, Adelaide thought, "dreadfully nervous but looked remarkably well" in his deputy lieutenant's uniform.[64] The meeting itself proved unusually fruitful. Overcrowding had rendered water very scarce in the Jewish quarter, where Muslim landlords habitually allowed the cisterns to fall into disrepair.[65] In dry years water was either fetid or prohibitively expensive—and disease inevitably rife. Montefiore had long been aware of this issue.[66] Sanitation projects—water and sewage—were the latest fad in European town planning, and he would have known all about the recently established connection between bad water and cholera. Just as Montefiore saw plans for a carriage road between Jaffa and Jerusalem as the literal fulfillment of biblical prophecy, so he believed that "the predictions of another Prophet with regard to the living waters to come out from Jerusalem" would soon be fulfilled.[67] When the governor, Izzet Pasha, intimated that efforts to bring water to the city had run into financial difficulty, Montefiore donated £200 from the relief fund and an additional £100 from his own pocket.[68] In return, the governor authorized him to erect an awning to protect Jews worshipping at the Wailing Wall from the weather—and from the garbage regularly hurled down from the occupants of nearby homes.[69]

By now there was a clear pattern to Montefiore's activities in Jerusalem: besides receiving deputations and exchanging courtesies with local dignitaries, he habitually prayed, collected statistical information, received petitioners, and distributed alms. The major development on this, his sixth visit, was a public meeting attended by 300 of the most prominent Jewish figures in the city.[70] Immigration had only intensified the fragmentation within the Jewish community, and relations among the dozen congregations were inevitably fraught. But for once, it seemed, they were in agreement: rabbi after rabbi rose to give his opinion, and rabbi after rabbi expressed the view that the most urgent need in the holy city was to build new homes for the poor. This was exactly what Montefiore wanted; he probably realized that the unanimity was a put-up job.

With customary chutzpah, Sneersohn did not hesitate to tell the great man after the meeting that if he wanted to build houses he should consult with "practical men" rather than rabbis who understood nothing about it; he added that "the chiefs convened could not be considered as the real representatives of the communal sentiments since they were not elected by the members . . . [and] that the wishes of the multitude are at variance with those of the chiefs."[71] The rabbis wanted charity, honors and money; the masses needed work. He did not doubt that "if . . . liberty were given to every Hebrew to state his views, there would . . . be found hundreds, both Ashkenazim and Sephardim, who would wish for agriculture . . . [or] to be enabled to trade throughout the country." The arrival of a deputation from Safed representing sixty would-be farmers certainly lent weight to such views.[72]

Montefiore was in no state to confront these issues. Three days earlier he had been "dreadfully agitated" by a "most alarming telegram" from Jaffa.[73] It seemed that his dear Friend Hodgkin was sinking fast. In a final letter to his wife in England, Hodgkin wrote that he had been "in almost ceaseless agony" since their stopover in Alexandria. He was conscious almost to the last but found comfort in God. "Difference in religious persuasion need not separate us," he told the Italian doctor looking after him. "We are brethren in Christ, and Christ is not divided."[74]

News of Hodgkin's death reached Jerusalem next evening. Adelaide and Joseph chose not to wake their uncle; they found him the next morning "very depressed and agitated." "We are most anxious to induce him to return with us to Europe," Adelaide wrote two days later; "he is really so weak that we do not like to leave him & we cannot get him to fix the day for departure." It was a week before he could be persuaded to go. By his last day in the city, Adelaide thought Montefiore "scarcely fit to move" and trembled for their departure.[75]

Setting out on the long trek to Jaffa in a state of deep depression, the exhausted Montefiore felt "more deeply than ever impressed with the sacred reminiscences [of Jerusalem] and its perennial beauty, and more fervently than ever offering prayers for its future welfare. 'As a seal I set thee on my heart, as a seal on my arm, if ever I forget thee, Oh Jerusalem, may my right hand forget her cunning.'"[76] In Jaffa he stopped only to visit "poor Hodgkin's grave" before boarding the *Rosetta,* an English merchant ship on which Joseph had rashly booked berths to avoid further delay.

As Adelaide commented tartly, it soon became clear that he "had committed a very grave mistake in taking passage in such a vessel."[77] The *Rosetta* was a ship trading in cattle, with 50 pilgrims, 1,500 sheep, 20 horses, and many other animals on board. There was neither a steward nor any other first-class passengers, and the stench from the animal droppings was indescribable. Montefiore was too frail to get down into his cabin and had to spend the night out on deck.[78] The sea was rough, and the ship rolled terribly. Towering waves periodically crashed over the ship, and with no railing to protect them, sheep, horses, and oxen were swept overboard. Montefiore endured this ghastly experience with his customary stoicism—perhaps reflecting on the terrifying storms he

Dr. Thomas Hodgkin, Montefiore's lifelong friend. This portrait appeared in his posthumously published Narrative of a Journey to Morocco, with Geological Annotations *(London, 1866).*

had survived on his way back from the Holy Land some forty years earlier.

Back in London, Montefiore broke the habit of a lifetime by intervening directly in the Palestine debate. In the past he had left publicity to Loewe and Judith, whose 1839 travel journal remained a central point of reference for enthusiasts of agricultural colonization. Now, Montefiore announced that the lively interest manifested by subscribers to the relief fund had emboldened him "not to restrict myself to a dry Report of my proceedings, and of the conclusions at which I have arrived; but . . . to present a faithful picture of what I myself saw and heard, and . . . put my observations in a somewhat journalistic form."[79] His account stressed the hardworking and pious attitudes he had encountered in Jerusalem—and the good that had been achieved through western European philanthropy.

This leitmotif was apparent from the very beginning, where Montefiore "particularly noticed" forty boys from the school founded by Ludwig Frankl, whose "healthy and neat appearance, and beautifully harmonious voices . . . convinced me that a sincere interest in the welfare of the Holy Land does not, and will not fail to arouse in the breasts of its inhabitants, an enthusiastic acknowledgement." His verdict on Mishkenot Sha'ananim was equally positive. Montefiore pronounced the inmates both scholarly and industrious, "fully deserving of the advantages they were enjoying" and happy to undertake "the hardest work with the object of earning a sum, however small, towards their maintenance." Nor was there truth in the report that the Jews of Jerusalem were too frightened to live there. Even lumber rooms, it seemed, had been turned into family homes.[80]

But the most touching sections of Montefiore's report were those describing his personal experience of almsgiving. After stressing the scrupulous observance of charitable formalities—"each case being carefully investigated, and the particulars noted down"—he portrayed in the most pathetic terms the pious and openhanded behavior of the poor to one another: the father of seven who had adopted two children rendered parentless by the cholera; the near-destitute widow who had taken two more such orphans into her home.[81] This was playing to the gallery; the reality had been far otherwise.

Adelaide, whose diary has been handed down through the Sebag-Montefiore family, felt both disillusioned and disgusted by what she encountered in Jerusalem. She, too, had witnessed Montefiore's encounter with the families of cholera victims, and she had nothing but contempt for what she saw: "About ten oclock Sir M received or rather attempted to do so all the widows and orphans rendered so by the late visitation of cholera the greatest confusion prevailed Sir M. gave each person foreseated to him a piece of money & no doubt expended a large sum but I fear the amount of good done was very small. Many presented themselves whose claims could not be authenticated & nothing could altogether be more unsatisfactory than the whole concern." "Never before had I seen our religion in so unattractive a light," she wrote later, "and I was greatly disappointed to discover where I thought to see the greatest devotion & attention to religion in its place the greatest greediness & attention to individual interests. As in our country the poor are very good to the poor but are less assisted by the rich and I think strict people in England are far more so than the strict in Jerusalem."[82]

Montefiore's glowing report was, then, a deliberate misrepresentation: wishful thinking that added substance to his view that the vast bulk of the relief fund should be kept back to promote Jewish agriculture and build new homes. "Let it not be assumed for a moment that the poor of our community there no longer need the help of their more opulent Coreligionists in other countries," he concluded in rallying tones. "On the contrary, without such help, promptly, liberally, judiciously, and continuously rendered, their position would soon become most pernicious and I feel satisfied that some such measures as those I have suggested are imperatively called for, in order to mitigate, if they cannot entirely remove, the evils of pauperism."[83]

Inevitably, different voices in the Jewish world read different things into Montefiore's latest mission. The ultra-Orthodox *Halevanon* embraced his report as a validation of the line it had taken previously—endorsing Montefiore's call for subsidized housing and taking a further swipe at Ludwig Frankl. The Austrian had invented "stories, dreams, and evil contemplations, and put them in his book to disgrace Zion," but Montefiore had "demanded and listened and inquired after every slander brought on Zion to know its source, and purified the ears so no evil is heard."[84]

Abraham Benisch felt vindicated for quite different reasons. He had been pressing the cause of productivization for years; now his dream seemed immeasurably closer to reality. The views expressed by Jewish leaders during their momentous meeting with Montefiore reflected a transformation in "the institutions of the land" and "the sentiments of the community." Benisch concluded ecstatically that "[t]o hear the representatives of an Eastern community—associated in European minds with ideas of stagnation, sloth, and ignorance—in their deliberation on the interests of their constituencies advocating loan and building societies, expatiating on the evils of insufficient house accommodation, and asking for the means of tilling the ground, is to hear the language of ripened civilization."[85]

Back in the borderlands of central and eastern Europe, the nationally inclined editor of *Hamagid* was similarly enthusiastic. Inspired by the eagerness to embrace Jewish agriculture shown by families in Safed and some of the rabbis in Jerusalem, David Gordon urged Montefiore and the Board of Deputies to join hands with the Alliance Israélite in promoting this cause. "And if the *sar* calls upon his brethren worldwide to unite and support the aspirations of their co-religionists who wish to work the soil of the Holy Land, how can we resist his call?"[86]

Still smarting from Montefiore's high-handed attitude to American Jewry, Isaac Leeser for one remained skeptical. How, he wondered in the *Occident*, could Montefiore enquire seriously into the situation in Palestine, "being beset, on his arrival at Jerusalem, by men who fairly profess to worship him, and prefer all claims to relief and immediate aid,—his health enfeebled by age, and having just suffered the additional grief in the loss of the physician, Dr. Thomas Hodgkin . . ? And if he did what could he do in this short stay, under the unfavorable circumstances just alluded to?" It was time, Leeser concluded, for the eighty-two-year-old Montefiore to retire so that "healthy and younger men" could complete his good work.[87]

Chapter 16

Crisis in Romania

Retirement was the last thing on Montefiore's mind when he returned from Palestine. Within days of arrival he was on the road again, first to Loewe's home in Brighton; thence to Hodgkin's brother in Lewes; and on to London, where he conducted a little business at the Alliance Assurance offices before calling on the Russian ambassador and Lord Clarendon, to whom he described the construction boom in Jerusalem in glowing terms. Not until June did Montefiore allow himself the luxury of a few hours' quiet reflection in Smithembottom. The newspapers that summer were filled with disturbing accounts from Bucharest, but Montefiore was initially more concerned by the trickle of atrocity stories from Persia. "Alas, I am not yet finished with one effort when a new misfortune occurs," he lamented to Loewe. This sense that the troubles of the Jewish world rested exclusively on his shoulders was now central to Montefiore's self-image. As he entered his eighties, the friends and associates of his youth were dying around him. The passing of Judith's brother Benjamin only added to his gloom; and the plight of Romanian Jewry was growing steadily worse.[1]

Had Moldavia and Walachia remained under proper Ottoman control, their Jews would already have been enjoying full civil equality under article 23 of the Treaty of Paris. The Danubian Principalities were still nominally subject to the sultan, but Romanian autonomy was now guaranteed by the European great powers as part of the Crimean settlement.[2] Yet the latter were reluctant to accept the principle of Romanian unity, which undermined British attempts to shore up Ottoman authority and the ambitions of Russia and Austria in the Balkans. The simultaneous election of Alexandru Ioan Cuza as prince in both Moldavia and Walachia enabled Romanians to square this circle. As the principalities moved toward a new political framework, their Jewish inhabitants be-

gan to lobby their brethren in Britain and France for the explicit ac-
knowledgment of Jewish rights.[3]

The upshot was curiously open-ended. Article 46 of the 1858 Convention of Paris had tacitly recognized the existence of Jewish Romanians
by guaranteeing all Moldavians and Walachians equality "before the
law, in taxation, and . . . access to public office in each principality," but
it explicitly restricted political rights to the adherents of "all Christian
confessions."[4] Defenders of Romanian Jewry like the British foreign secretary Lord Clarendon would later claim that article 46 granted Jews
in the principalities "full equality as regards legal and fiscal rights . . .
personal freedom and security for property."[5] Romanians increasingly
maintained that Jews were aliens and consequently denied them civil
and political rights. This claim was both true and false.

Romania had sustained a small community of Sephardi Jews for centuries, but the eighteenth century saw a gradual influx of Ashkenazim
from Galicia and southwestern Russia. In the nineteenth century this influx became a flood. The number of Jews in sparsely populated Moldavia doubled from 30,000 to 60,000 between 1803 and 1848; it doubled
again in the next ten years. By 1859 there were nearly 120,000 Jews in
Moldavia, compared with just over 9,000 in Walachia. While some had
deep roots in the country, most were first-, second-, or third-generation
immigrants. A wealthy minority benefited from the status accorded foreign protégés under international law; in the decades after 1866, the deteriorating situation would lead some 100,000 to claim Austrian protection.[6]

Religious prejudice remained widespread under Cuza, whose reign
opened badly when a blood libel accusation in Galatz (Galaţi) prompted
riots and mass arrests. The real issues were demographic and economic.
The small community of Jews in Walachia was relatively acculturated
and competed for business with Greek, Armenian, and Bulgarian traders. In Moldavia, by contrast, Jews dominated a narrow economic niche
as merchants, craftsmen, moneylenders, and rural innkeepers—alongside the desperate legions of Jewish poor.

Visitors to the capital, Jassy (Iaşi), were amazed to discover that half
its inhabitants were Jews. "[W]ithout Jews nothing, in the full sense of
the word, can be done in Moldavia," commented one German traveler,
who while staying in a hotel discovered that the porter and all the wait-
ers were Jews. In smaller towns the situation was not much different:
the main thoroughfare bustling with Jewish shops and their owners in
shabby gabardine and traditional fur hats, the side streets a promiscu-
ous mixture of whitewashed churches, peasant huts, and sturdy boyar
homes.[7]

The government's response to this situation was contradictory. The idea that all Romanian Jews were foreigners—a separate nation with fewer rights—dated back to the Organic Statutes of 1831, which had been drawn up by Count Pavel Kiselev, the future architect of Tsar Nicholas I's Jewish policy.[8] Anti-Jewish legislation long predated Russian influence, but the pattern of Jews lending money and selling alcohol to Moldavia's impoverished, brutalized peasants echoed conditions in the Pale. Moldavian legislators in the 1830s and 1840s reached for similar solutions. Toothless measures designed to inhibit Jewish economic activity and (if necessary) expel Jews from rural areas created dangerous precedents. They were revived in 1849 and again under Cuza, when the threat of mass expulsions prompted the *Jewish Chronicle* to call for intervention by the guarantor powers.[9]

As in Russia, the stick of Romanian persecution alternated with the carrot of integration. In 1860 Cuza's old friend the liberal reformer and cultural polymath Mihail Kogălniceanu issued an edict urging Jews to take Romania as their fatherland.[10] Our schools are open, proclaimed Kogălniceanu; we ask you only to enroll your children, join the army, and put aside your outlandish clothing. The *Allgemeine Zeitung des Judentums* saw such proposals as heralding a "new era for Romanian Israelites."[11] As in Russia, however, the Romanian government combined pressure to assimilate with the withdrawal of official support from Jewish administrative organs, undermining communal provision of social welfare.[12] In Romania, too, such policies led to cultural civil war.[13] This time the modernizers had more tangible reasons to believe in the government's good faith than their brethren in Russia ever did.

In 1862 Cuza promised to place all Jews "on an equal footing with other inhabitants of the country."[14] The Community Law of 1864 officially recognized the category of native Jews, allowing them to participate in municipal elections—provided that they had reached the rank of noncommissioned officer, studied at an institution of higher education, or established a factory employing at least fifty workers. These restrictive provisions seemed to represent the first faltering steps toward political emancipation. A Jew was actually appointed inspector of finances, and the new civil code made limited arrangements for the naturalization of foreign Jews. Then it all began to fall apart.[15]

Romanian politics had traditionally been dominated by the landowning boyar class, and the antagonism between greater and lesser boyars underpinned the conservative-liberal divide. Cuza managed to alienate both constituencies. Conservatives resented his comprehensive reforms, liberals his dictatorial style. He was finally overthrown in 1866 by a "Monstrous Coalition" of left and right. This was a high-risk strategy, since great-power recognition of Romanian unity had been limited to Cuza's period in office. To preserve international legitimacy and domestic stability, the radical Liberal Ion C. Brătianu orchestrated the election of a cousin of King Wilhelm of Prussia—and escorted young Karl (soon to be known as Carol) von Hohenzollern to his future kingdom incognito.[16]

The resounding approval accorded Carol's election through a rapidly held plebiscite obscured a more halfhearted reality. In Moldavia some saw Cuza's fall as part of a Walachian plot to dominate the principalities, drawing on popular resentment at the rise of Bucharest. The separatist movement soon became a magnet for political and economic malcontents, who blamed Moldavia's relative backwardness on the Jews. Such accusations chimed so neatly with the self-interest of the fledgling Christian bourgeoisie that boyars eager to regain their grip on political power were soon fanning the flames of anti-Jewish sentiment in the hope of overturning political union.[17]

Back in Bucharest the parliament had begun debating article 6 of the draft constitution, which asserted: "The status of Romanian is acquired, retained and lost according to the rules established by civil law. Religion cannot be an obstacle to citizenship."[18] In May 1866 a group of professors at the University of Jassy began to collect signatures opposing Jewish emancipation. When the government attempted to stop them, they had copies of the petition plastered all over the city under the ominous heading: "Out with the Jews! Death to the Jews!" Terrified, Jews in Jassy turned to the Austrian consulate for protection; most were, after all, Austrian citizens. Two weeks later riots erupted in the nearby town of Bacău, causing Jewish men, women, and children to flee for their lives. This was a very precocious outbreak of modern, politically organized anti-Semitism, antedating the emergence of more formal structures in Germany and Austria-Hungary: a toxic fusion of xenophobia, religious prejudice, and mass politics at a time of socioeconomic upheaval.[19]

To those familiar with developments in the Balkans, the Romanian combination of anti-Jewish agitation and Orthodox nationalism did not seem so very novel. In 1856 a petition to Montefiore from the Jews of Belgrade had recounted how for more than two centuries of Ottoman rule they had enjoyed "every right of citizenship," only to see their freedom to live and work in Serbia restricted by the new national government, "urged on by the intolerant spirit of the populace." Montefiore had immediately appealed to Lord Clarendon. In 1859 *Hamagid* reported the presence of three Jews in the Serbian parliament, although it noted the worrying distinction some made between native Serbs and those (like Jews) who had become citizens through naturalization. The pressure on the small Jewish community was such that when the sultan offered free land and housing in Bosnia to all Serbian citizens, many felt they had no choice but to go. Some even asked Montefiore if they could farm his orchard in Jaffa instead.[20]

All this no doubt encouraged the Alliance Israélite to keep an eye on Romania. By June 1866 Crémieux was sufficiently worried to stop off on his way back from Istanbul. The Romanian elite had mostly been educated in France, and Romanian politics were dominated by the men of 1848, who had spent years in Parisian exile. For all his Jewishness, the president of the Alliance Israélite was widely admired as a former member of the French revolutionary government. In Bucharest he carried real clout.

Fêted by the whole political class, Crémieux gave a legendary speech to the Romanian constituent assembly demanding complete Jewish emancipation. "Negroes are free in the United States," he declared "and what the negroes have obtained . . . You refuse to the Jews! *Attendez, Messieurs!* In France, in our beloved *patrie,* our great revolution of 1848 proclaimed equality between white and black . . . Here is a thought to pull at your heartstrings: a French Jew signed and proclaimed the decree that made black [men] the equals, the brothers, of whites. A French Jew emancipated the blacks; this Jew, member of the provisional Government, is talking to you now."[21] But, as Crémieux subsequently explained, the assurances of prince, president, and deputies counted for nothing in an atmosphere of hysterical uncertainty.

Scarcely had the aging democrat left the capital than events took an ugly turn. As Moldavian deputies railed against the emancipation proposals, crowds of anti-Jewish protesters mobbed the parliament building. Brătianu was the dominant force in the provisional government, but his assurances that they would do nothing to harm the Romanian nation failed to placate the rioters. They sacked the Jewish quarter and razed its beautiful new synagogue to the ground. Bowing to "popular" pressure, the ministry then rewrote the draft constitution to include a stipulation that "[o]nly foreigners of Christian religion may become Romanians."[22] Since the authorities maintained that all Jews were foreigners (and many were in fact immigrants), this move stopped the process of emancipation in its tracks.

In 1848, before the mass influx of Jews from Galicia, Brătianu had actively endorsed Jewish emancipation. He now told the national assembly that Jews were

> a social plague, not because they are more backward than us, for we have [in the Gypsies] a class which is more backward than them . . . and we have given them rights without hearing anyone object. Nor shall I raise

against the Jews the consideration that they are less civilized, but simply that of their large number which everyone says is a threat to our nationality, and when the nation is threatened she defends herself and becomes not intolerant but provident. It is only by administrative regulation that we can save ourselves from this disease and prevent the foreign proletariat from invading our country.[23]

Behind all this lay the brutal logic of electoral politics. The largely Walachian ministry needed the support of Moldavian deputies to govern, and the electoral law bestowed disproportionate influence on the urban and professional middle classes, who represented 3.5 percent of voters but made up over a third of the new parliament. Conservatives could count on the support of the overrepresented boyar class, but radicals like Brătianu saw no option but to court the "people." They cynically played the anti-Jewish card as the best way of staying in power.[24]

As always in such situations, both Crémieux and Montefiore appealed to their respective governments—the former in person and the latter through the Board of Deputies, now under the nominal leadership of his nephew Joseph Mayer Montefiore. The Treaty of Paris promised real scope for intervention. As one correspondent of the *Allgemeine Zeitung des Judentums* put it, the riots compromised not just the Romanians but their Ottoman suzerain and the powers overseeing the regeneration of the Romanian state. And if Jews called on the guarantor powers to intervene, they did so not just out of a self-interested humanitarianism, but rather as "the tools of a general need for law and order, [and for] Prince, government and representative assembly to be respected in a European state." This authoritarian discourse reflected a dim awareness of the distinctive threat posed by the democratic populism of Romanian anti-Jewish politics.[25]

Three months after adopting the exclusionary new constitution, Interior Minister Ion Ghica began to revive the moribund anti-Jewish legislation of the 1830s and 1840s. Brătianu replaced Ghica as interior minister in March 1867 and picked up where his predecessor had left off. An energetic series of circulars reminded local prefects that Jews were forbidden to live in the countryside, to keep hotels or public houses, and to lease properties. Brătianu also instructed local authorities to expel (Jewish) "vagabonds" from the districts under their control. News of arbitrary expulsions, mass arrests, extortion, and police brutality in the Danubian Principalities soon transfixed the "civilized" world. The flavor of these reports is captured by a telegram from Jassy to Nathan Adler:

"SENT several despatches. We are in Jassy to the number of upwards of 20,000 families in the greatest danger of our lives; men are pursued in the streets, thrown in chains, hunted we know not whither; about 300 families have already been ruined. Every moment threatens to annihilate all. For Heaven's sake, at once use every endeavour that a despatch be sent from English Government to the consulate in Jassy to take us under their protection."[26]

Appeals sent to Montefiore and to the M.P.s Lionel de Rothschild and Sir Francis Henry Goldsmid elaborated on the expulsion of Jews from villages in rural Moldavia and the outrages that had accompanied Brătianu's recent visit to Jassy. All three Anglo-Jewish dignitaries contacted Foreign Secretary Edward Stanley (later Lord Derby), who instructed Consul-General Green in Bucharest to urge Prince Carol "in the strongest terms" to put a stop to these outrages. "[U]nless this is done," Stanley warned, "the Wallachian Government must not be surprised by any diminution of the interest which is now felt by Her Majesty's Government in the prosperity of the provinces under their present system of administration."[27]

This pointed reminder of the shaky diplomatic status of the principalities—and their dependence on the goodwill of the guarantor powers—had little impact. In a chilling harbinger of the bureaucratic euphemisms deployed by twentieth-century politicians as a cover for human rights abuses, the Romanian government issued an official disclaimer describing the anti-Jewish measures as "simple hygienic and policing measures."[28] Carol himself emphasized the threat of cholera and the squalor of Jewish living conditions in Jassy. But in Jassy itself, officials recognized the importance of international public opinion to a country struggling for recognition. The prefect of Jassy district would eventually warn the population against further anti-Jewish outbursts "[t]oday, when the eyes of Europe are upon us, and we must demonstrate that we are a civilized nation."[29]

The political and cultural aspirations of Romanian nationalism accorded French influence pride of place in the principalities, while Crémieux's trip to Bucharest had reinforced the status of the Alliance Israélite.[30] Carol was in some sense a protégé of Napoleon III and could ill afford to ignore his criticism. Under pressure from both James de Rothschild and Crémieux, the emperor telegraphed to Bucharest warning Carol "how much public opinion here is outraged by the persecutions of which the Jews are said to be victims in Moldavia. I cannot believe that Your Highness' enlightened government authorizes measures so contrary to humanity and civilization."[31] But Crémieux advised Napoleon that Carol was effectively powerless, arguing that it was for the great powers to take action, since the Convention of 1858 had guaranteed Moldavians and Walachians of all creeds the same civil rights.[32]

International responses to Crémieux's appeal reflected different political cultures. While Ludwig Philippson in Germany urged Prince Karl Anton von Hohenzollern to exert informal influence on his son Carol, British liberals expected the pressure of public opinion to obviate the need for more formal humanitarian intervention.[33] Outlining the limits of morality in mid-Victorian foreign policy, the *Manchester Daily Examiner* argued:

> Although we are adverse [*sic*] to meddlesome interference in the affairs of foreign countries . . . there are cases in which it becomes the duty of all who have any share in guiding or expressing public opinion to raise their voice against the perpetration of wrongs which are an outrage upon humanity and a disgrace to the civilisation of the age. There is all the more reason to do this when those who are the subjects of persecution are powerless to resist, and are utterly destitute of any hope of relief except such as they may derive from the righteousness of their cause and from an appeal to the enlightened and just sentiments of the European community at large . . .
>
> . . . We do not, however, desire to appeal to a diplomatic document in a case which can be much more effectually met by a general and earnest expression of public opinion.[34]

In London, meanwhile, the Alliance Israélite found an impassioned representative in Sir Francis Henry Goldsmid. His wealth and standing as one of a handful of Jewish M.P.s naturally fitted Goldsmid for a leadership position within the Anglo-Jewish community, but until the foundation of the Alliance his membership in the pariah West London Synagogue meant that his remained a minority voice. Goldsmid had already established his credentials as a defender of Balkan Jewry by raising the plight of Serbian Jews in the Commons.[35] He bluntly informed the Foreign Office that the "probable result of the kind exertions of Lord Stanley" did not strike him as satisfactory.[36] While Goldsmid and Rothschild refused to take no for an answer, Montefiore was considering a far more drastic step.[37]

As early as June 4, 1867, Joseph Mayer Montefiore had informed the Board of Deputies of his uncle's willingness to set out for Moldavia.[38] "The eyes of all Israel in the province of Moldavian Jewry are directed to you for salvation," the chief rabbi of Jassy had written in desperation. "Surely the man Moses will rouse himself as a lion for the rescue of his people, as he has done in days of old, and in former years, to deliver his brethren, the House of Israel, from their sorrow and distress."[39]

Montefiore was not the man to withstand such exhortations. The memorials he received solicited "so frequently and so urgently my personal presence" that he considered it "an imperative duty, at whatever personal risk and sacrifice, to respond to the appeal thus piteously made."[40] Faced with the failure of diplomatic efforts and Montefiore's track record of spectacular interventions, on July 3 the deputies gave his mission their blessing.[41]

Two days earlier, Lord Stratford de Redcliffe had attacked the government's record on Romania in the Lords. Speaking as one whose name was synonymous with the defense of Ottoman Christians, he emphasized the bitter ironies of a situation in which Britain undertook to guarantee liberal institutions to the (Christian) principalities "and to secure them from what they considered oppression at the hands of the Turkish Government," only to see the Romanians "turning round upon a people of a different religious persuasion" and subjecting them to vicious persecution.[42] By way of reply Lord Malmesbury could only equivocate that "this question was entirely one of internal government." Nor was Foreign Secretary Stanley more forthcoming when Goldsmid returned to the fray in the Commons two weeks later.[43] Time and the pressure of civilized opinion would bring change in the long run; for the time being, Britain and France would do what they could.

But time was not on the side of Moldavian Jewry. Within days of Lord Stanley's liberal platitudes, news reached London and Paris of further expulsions and a horrific incident in Galatz, where several Jewish "vagabonds" had drowned after a bungled attempt by the local authorities to dump them across the Danube in Ottoman territory. Recriminations flew thick and fast when foreign consuls in the town issued a formal protest, prompting a further barrage of diplomatic pressure led by Britain, France, and Austria. "I cannot subscribe to the doctrine that the treatment of the Jews in the Principalities is not a subject for foreign interference," wrote Consul-General Green to the Romanian foreign minister. "The peculiar position of the Jews places them under the protection of the civilized world."[44]

Even before the drownings in Galatz, the politically astute Karl Anton had warned his son that Brătianu would have to go: France was Romania's only supporter, and the Jewish question had galvanized Paris; with the press in the pocket of wealthy Jews, nothing could be published that showed the matter in a more favorable light.[45] Carol, however, was beholden to Brătianu for his throne and had too much faith in the radical's abilities to wish to get rid of him. Instead, he sent his private secretary, Emile Picot, to negotiate with the Alliance Israélite. Picot proved sufficiently persuasive for Crémieux to abandon his usual grandstanding in the hope of exerting more discreet influence.[46] Where he had tried and failed, he cannot have expected Montefiore to succeed.

In Bucharest the wealthy Jewish leaders of the Alliance Israélite were appalled at the prospect of Montefiore's mission. They feared that his presence "would awaken and irritate the excessive susceptibility of the Romanians," leading to a repetition of the previous year's riots.[47] Apparently impressed by the success of Crémieux's press campaign, they urged him (and Montefiore) to leave it at that. But Montefiore had been warned to expect nothing more from the rich, who would inevitably pretend that all was quiet "because they have estates and are obliged to flatter the Government and . . . for fear that their credit in England France and Germany shall not be checked."[48]

In Jassy itself, Jews were torn between bitter realism and a hope born of desperation. "[T]he house of Montefiore stands firm among nations. At old age, Moses renews his youth like an eagle, and blooms like a flower . . . May God help him as he did in Morocco," wrote Carpel Lippe in *Halevanon*. Yet, he continued, "We have but little hope, for Romania is not like Morocco. The Moroccan king has unlimited power . . . He and his advisers did not know what was done to the Jews in the country, but when he found out . . . he stopped the evil . . . Not so in Romania, for there, government leaders are evildoers, and the Prince cannot protest against their actions. And if they promise the *sar* [Montefiore] to better the condition of his brothers, will they follow up on their words?"[49]

This proved a realistic assessment of Romanian politics, but failed to account for the role of international relations in shaping domestic norms. Barely a decade after Anglo-Jewish emancipation, the association between Jewish rights and European "civilization" could hardly be taken for granted. Yet the language used by the prefect of Jassy, Consul Green, Lord Stanley, and Napoleon III demonstrated the success of activists like Montefiore and Crémieux in universalizing the Jewish cause. Indeed, the ability of British and French Jewish leaders to persuade their governments to intervene in the Jewish question testified to the importance of liberal and humanitarian groups within the wider body politic. For the civilizing mission was inevitably framed in terms of domestic political traditions.

Jews remained a contentious feature of the political landscape, but Jewish rights carried a particular symbolic charge on both sides of the Channel. In Britain, they represented the twin causes of humanitarianism and civil and religious liberty; in France, the revolutionary tradition of state secularism and the universalism of the Rights of Man. The spread of emancipation through Italy, the German states, and Austria-

Hungary enabled other countries to appropriate the rhetoric of "humanity" and "civilization" as well. As Jewish relief became a benchmark of European civilization, so the treatment of ethnic and religious minorities became a precondition of acceptance for an emerging nation-state like Romania into an international state system that was increasingly governed by Western norms.

Bucharest was a city of contrasts. It boasted, according to one contemporary, "a prince without a palace, a clergy without morals, an academy without members, immense streets without homes, a library without readers, splendid dwellings and vile cottages, magnificent promenades and filthy dumps." To some it was a cesspit of vice and degradation that encompassed both the louche high society of Romanian boyars and the half-naked Gypsies roaming the streets. To others it was a romantic city, peopled by dark-eyed beauties, grave boyars, bearded abbots, and stately Turks. There were indeed churches with dazzling tin spires, imposing modern buildings, and lovely gardens, but the ubiquitous white plaster was unsuited to the climate while the soft subsoil undermined the city streets. The resulting impression was one of dilapidation, of shoddy plaster and pavements so uneven that even the poor traveled in open carriages rather than risk themselves on foot.[50]

Yet Bucharest was also a metropolis in the throes of a dramatic transformation. With a population of well over 120,000—increasing at a rate of some 30 percent a year—Bucharest dwarfed other cities between Vienna and Istanbul, attracting migrants from all over central and eastern Europe.[51] Thirty years later foreigners would make up nearly half the population. Even in 1867 the seething, vital, ethnically diverse mass of humanity made for an atmosphere of social and political turmoil.

Montefiore arrived armed with the formal backing of all five great powers. This rare unanimity reflected realpolitik rather than humanitarian principles. France and Austria were inclined to support the new regime in the principalities, Russia wanted to strengthen her position in Moldavia, Prussia to stabilize Carol's situation, and Britain to maintain Ottoman suzerainty. Yet all were concerned by the direction of Brătianu's radical nationalist government—and the threat posed by dreams of national independence for a Greater Romania. In Britain and France, humanitarian concerns undoubtedly weighed with the liberal public, while the presence of so many Austrian Jews in Moldavia was a particular consideration in Vienna. But for all the great powers, the Jewish question provided an opportune excuse for interfering in internal Romanian internal affairs.

Brătianu's cabinet had already fallen by the time Montefiore reached Bucharest. Intrigue, factionalism, and populist politics were the order of the day. There were, according to Picot, perhaps 20,000 Romanians capable of reading and understanding the contents of a newspaper. Picot thought them "concerned neither with principles, nor patriotism, nor social economics nor any other major issue . . . everything is reduced to personal rivalries. Everyone wants to be a Minister, Senator, Deputy . . . The authorities have to keep strictly within the constitution . . . But the Press, which stretches its freedom to the limits, constantly reawakens base passions. Ministers are dragged continually through the mud, foreigners and Jews overwhelmed by the grossest insults from those who call themselves liberals."[52]

Montefiore's nephew the barrister Arthur Cohen had already turned back after receiving an anxious telegram from his wife. As for Montefiore, Consul-General Green reported with some relief that he had "with sound judgement" resolved "to avoid giving the slightest umbrage to the Roumanian Government by allusions to the immediate events which led him to undertake his journey. His object is to restore confidence among his co-religionists here, and to be able to assure those in England and elsewhere that the Jews in the Principalities will in future be treated with justice and toleration."[53] To this end, Montefiore hoped to obtain a declaration from Prince Carol along the same lines as the *dahir* granted him in Morocco.

Even Crémieux now recognized that full emancipation was not on the agenda.[54] Montefiore merely entreated Carol and his government "to warn all evil-disposed persons not to molest the Jews in any manner, and to give positive orders that the Jews, dwelling in all parts of the United Principalities, shall enjoy perfect protection in all which concerns the safety of their persons and their property." Green, who presented him to Prince Carol and the new prime minister, Stefan Golescu, was delighted at the "irresistible impression" produced by Montefiore's "dignified and modest language"; he had "no doubt that both the Prince and his Minister had brought themselves to expect words of a very different import." Whether Montefiore's nonconfrontational approach would bear fruit remained an open question.[55]

The young prince of Romania was known for his quiet, earnest manner and the measured punctiliousness that disguised a certain lack of self-confidence.[56] He came across as being easy to influence, but in practice he kept his own counsel. Karl Anton had served briefly as Prussian prime minister and remained a key political confidant. His letters left his son in no doubt of the urgent need to resolve the Jewish question, although Karl Anton's references to Jewish money and the Jewish press indicated a fair amount of sympathy with the agitators.[57] If Carol shared his father's prejudices, he disguised them appropriately, inviting Montefiore to dine at the Cotroceni, the former monastery that he preferred as a summer residence to the royal palace, with its outlook over the pigs and dungheaps of a Gypsy encampment. Here Carol seated his Jewish guest at his right hand, made conversation about his own visit to Morocco, entertained him with military music, and took Montefiore to the garden for coffee, cigars, and liqueur.

This dinner was a gracious interlude in what rapidly became a nightmare situation. Radical nationalist elements in the Romanian press had not taken kindly to Montefiore's intervention. Even before his arrival, the *Naţiunea Română* hinted darkly that the visit of a man who possessed "an immense fortune of 80 million pounds" had been deliberately timed to coincide with the fall of Brătianu's ministry, when "everything is turning in favor of the Jews."[58] Now the same newspaper issued a passionate call to arms:

> Awake, ye Romanians! Let us awake and assemble on that field upon which the sentiment of all political, social, national, and patriotic duty calls, the duty not to allow the naturalization of the Hebrews, of these outcasts, whom even our Redeemer Jesus Christ cursed, that they should possess no country, no home; were we to allow their naturalization, then all Crown domains now exposed to sale, to the ruination of the country, this sacred treasure of our fathers would fall into the hands of the Hebrew bankers! . . . and then! . . . Romania would become a Palestine, and the free Romanian, the Christian Romanian would become the slave of those outcasts! . . . and Romania will be the land of the Hebrews and not the Romanian.[59]

The hyperbole was accompanied by a petition calling for the expulsion of recent Jewish immigrants, an end to further immigration, the refusal of political emancipation, and a restriction on the sale of state domains lest they fall into Jewish hands.

For the past two weeks Montefiore's spirits had been undermined by death threats and reports of intended outbreaks against Jews.[60] Rumor had it that the government itself was behind these sinister whisperings, perceiving in his presence the "renewed collective pressure of the Foreign powers."[61] Shortly after his evening at the Cotroceni Montefiore found his temporary residence, the Hotel Otettaliano, besieged by an angry mob, as thousands pressed forward to sign the petition issued by the faction behind the *Naţiunea* article in defiance of the municipal authorities. The hotel staff were terrified, but the octogenarian was in his element. Buoyed by his invincible faith in the Lord, Montefiore threw

"Sir Moses addressing the threatening populace from his Hotel at Bucha-rest," from the 1890 edition of the Diaries of Sir Moses and Lady Mon-tefiore, *edited by Louis Loewe.*

open a window and stood in full view of the crowd. "Fire away if you like," he declared. "I came here in the name of justice and humanity to plead the cause of innocent sufferers." At first the crowd was non-plussed; then the shouts grew louder; eventually the protesters grew tired of shouting and dispersed.[62]

That night Montefiore received a visit from the Rothschild agent in Bucharest. "We shall all be massacred," cried M. Halfon with tears in his eyes. "Are you afraid?" Montefiore replied cuttingly, well aware that his visitor had urged him not to come to Romania. "I have no fear what-ever, and will at once order an open carriage, take a drive through the principal streets and thoroughfares, go even outside the town and drive near some public garden. Every one shall see me; it is a holy cause; that of justice and humanity. I trust in God; He will protect me."[63]

Ten minutes later he and Loewe set out. Their departure drew crowds of voyeurs, thrilled at the prospect of some extraordinary dénouement; in the event, their only pursuer was an enterprising businessman. They eventually returned to the hotel to find a woman and a soldier awaiting them. Both refused to give their names but insisted on speaking to Mon-tefiore privately on a political matter. He would see neither. "I am," he wrote, "most anxious, weak, out of health, and vexed to the heart. No one can imagine the extreme pain of my situation. Political factions strive to create confusion by my presence in this place."[64]

Loewe was, if anything, still more concerned. Familiar as he was with his employer's obstinate streak, he paid a discreet visit to the British consulate. Mr. Green read the threatening letters, listened closely to the account of the previous night's alarming developments, and saw no prospect of the agitation's dying down. "As for Sir Moses going to Jassy . . . that was quite out of the question."[65]

Fortunately, Carol's reply to Montefiore's petition enabled him to abandon the trip to Jassy with good grace; for the prince declared Jews to be "the object of all my solicitude and all that of my Government." He was delighted that Montefiore had come to see for himself that there was no religious persecution in Romania; he had no intention of taking responsibility for "isolated incidents," but he promised on his honor "always to see freedom of religion respected, and I will exercise constant supervision to ensure the enforcement of laws protecting the Jews like all other Romanians, both their persons and their goods."[66]

Under the circumstances, Carol's promise to protect Jewish lives and property rang hollow. No one visiting the principalities can have nurtured illusions about the stability of the new state or its monarch's authority. There was, moreover, nothing to stop the government from dismissing new outbreaks of anti-Jewish violence as further "isolated incidents." The most important gain was probably Carol's passing reference to "other Romanians," which implicitly contradicted those who maintained that all Jews in the principalities were foreigners.

Having narrowly escaped the clutches of the mob outside the Hotel Otettaliano, Montefiore must have been fully alive to the realities of this situation; he would certainly have realized that Brătianu remained the dominant influence in Romanian politics. Yet he did not wish to present his mission as a failure. Presumably he hoped that Carol's vague written promises would serve as a point of reference if the government resumed its policy of exclusionary legislation and officially sanctioned violence. He therefore gave out that he considered the object of his mission "happily accomplished," regretting only "that my state of health, with other considerations, prevents my going to see my co-religionists at Jassy."[67] And with that he beat a hasty retreat from Bucharest.

Even this face-saving maneuver was enough to provide the city's anti-Jewish agitators with ammunition. How could Mr. Montefiore claim to have "succeeded in all [his actions]," the *Naţiunea Română* wondered, when there was no religious intolerance in Romania?[68] There must have been more to his visit than met the eye. Picking up on these insinuations, the *Sentinella Română* reminded its readers that the *Naţiunea* was a tool of interfering foreign governments, "which lacks only that it is not written in Russian or a Viennese dialect for the form to accord with the substance."[69] Golescu, the new prime minister, had pioneered many of Brătianu's anti-Jewish measures, and those who accused the "government, in other words, the Liberal party," of selling political and landowning rights to Montefiore and the Jews were hardly acting in the national interest.

Three days later the *Sentinella* turned the tables on its opponents when it noted that "since Montefiore's visit in Bucharest, the editor-in-chief of [the vigorously anti-Jewish] *Trompetta Carpaţilor* is not combatting the Jews, as he used to do before." While Brătianu and other leaders of the Liberal party remained "the fear and terror of the *Jewish cause*," it was "impossible for any impartial and intelligent person, not to realize that a hidden and perfidious agreement was reached between Mr. Cezar Bolliac's newspaper and the Jewish organizations in Bucharest, under Montefiore's auspices, having as a goal the attack of the Liberal party."[70] Thus the internecine passions of Romanian politics raged on unabating with the Jewish question at their heart.

Outside Romania the wheels of the Montefiore publicity machine moved swiftly into motion but failed to silence alternative voices.[71] From the beginning, Montefiore's confident assertions of victory were hedged about by doubt. The tone of one article in *Halevanon* quickly lapsed from the biblically jubilant—"Moses raised his hand and Israel has triumphed"—to guarded optimism: "Though evil has not yet vanished from the hearts of the gentiles, and the editor of one newspaper even launched a personal attack on Moses, and one can assume he was not a lone writer, who wishes to demolish the honor of the House of Israel and harm the Jews, today such local voices are insignificant compared to the many who listen to the words of the *sar*, and we greatly hope for a better future for our brothers in Walachia and Moldavia following the *sar*'s visit."[72] *Hamagid* went further, suggesting that Montefiore should have visited Jassy and Galatz before going to see the prince in Bucharest—where Jews were neither drowned, deported, nor forcibly shaved. Even the *Jewish Chronicle* was reticent, declaring Carol's "frank avowal of respect for freedom of conscience" an "important declaration," but voicing "a slight feeling of uneasiness" about some aspects of his letter.[73]

Barely two weeks passed before the *Chronicle* reported "with unspeakable grief . . . that further wholesale expulsions of Jews, by the verbal order of under prefects, have taken place."[74] Isaac Leeser commented with world-weary resignation in the *Occident* that it was curious that "all assurances given by the leaders in the East and Africa fail to procure immunity from prosecution for Israelites. The governments are probably in earnest, but those who are entrusted with the execution of the laws and the common people are often very inimical to us, and therefore persecution not rarely takes place despite . . . the laws framed for the amelioration of the condition of our oppressed brethren . . . But we must be thankful for any favors, and hope that the exertions of Sir Moses Montefiore may be crowned hereafter with more success than they appear to have been just now."[75]

Leeser's assessment revealed the limits of Montefiore's approach to humanitarian intervention. Ever since his interview with the sultan in 1840, he had adopted a very personal style of diplomacy. It depended, above all, on his ability to influence foreign rulers through a combination of British backing, Rothschild connections, the moral support of the "civilized" public and his own considerable address. This approach was all very well in authoritarian states like Russia, the Ottoman Empire, and Morocco—although even here, as Leeser noted, the power of the monarch to shape events on the ground was surprisingly limited. Once politics ceased to be the preserve of a tiny elite, it was a different story. Men like Palmerston and Montefiore believed that by spreading liberal political institutions they would inevitably spread liberal values. Romania revealed the fallacy of this assumption. Democratic politics could promote persecution just as easily as toleration—and Montefiore's brand of face-to-face diplomacy was no solution to modern political anti-Semitism.

The next six months only confirmed this harsh reality, as pogroms in Bêrlad and Călăraşi followed the expulsion of several hundred Jews from the Covurlui district. Disillusioned by the failure of Montefiore's mission, Jews no longer took their complaints to foreign consuls for fear of attracting reprisals. Unsurprisingly, the wealthy Halfon chose to fabricate consular business when presenting a telegram to Mr. Green from the chief rabbi of Bêrlad.[76]

Once the news of homeless families, sacked synagogues, desecrated holy books, and women stripped naked began to reach Western Jewish leaders, Goldsmid, Crémieux, Montefiore, and the Rothschilds leaped into action. This time even Bismarck instructed his representative in Romania to "use all his influence to guarantee the Jews the protection which is due to them in all countries, whose laws are based on the principles of humanity and civilization."[77] But the Jewish public was becoming increasingly cynical. In the words of *Halevanon*:

Undoubtedly, also the other Jewish saviors who received the appeal will rush to help our brothers through the enlightened governments, which are merciful to our brothers . . . Probably the Romanian government (which promises much) will promise that henceforth such incidents will not recur, or will perhaps claim (as the Prince said to Moses Montefiore) that this case, too, is exceptional, and hence his government cannot be held accountable for it. The Prince will use this incident as evidence to show (as Brătianu said to Crémieux when he was here) that government officials are fair to the Jews . . . and there was not a single official among those who attacked the Jews; indeed during the five hours that the mob attacked Jews the government officials in Bêrlad were at the theater . . . We will also hear that the Romanian officials do not wish to distress the Jews of enlightened countries . . . and this is why they stopped the wretched [Jews] of Bêrlad from telegraphing them their sorrows. In conclusion, we must believe that no official has sinned. However, had this happened in Turkey rather than in Romania, and to Christians rather than to Jews, no one would have listened to pretexts, and only war could have atoned for it.[78]

Since Prime Minister Golescu continued to assure Montefiore of the Romanian government's commitment to religious toleration even while blaming the Jews of Bêrlad for the disturbances, such cynicism seemed more than justified.[79]

In March thirty-one radical Moldavian deputies proposed legislation to "Regularise the Situation of the Jews in Romania" by dissolving Jewish communities and committees, excluding Jews from most kinds of economic activity, making it impossible for them to live in the countryside, and giving municipal authorities the right to expel them at will. Recognizing the draft law as a bid to expel the Jewish population from Romania, the *Jewish Chronicle* argued that the question was "not national, but international; not Jewish, but cosmopolitan." It urged "the Great Powers of Europe [to] interfere for their own sake" lest events in Romania "endanger the safety of surrounding countries."[80]

As *Halevanon* had predicted, British and French Jewish leaders immediately began to lobby their respective governments. Once again, Goldsmid raised the matter in the Commons, and Montefiore offered to set out for Bucharest.[81] Once again, Carol declared himself outraged, promising never "to sanction this law or any law of a similar nature." Once again, his promises proved worthless when hundreds of Jews were expelled from Bacău and Movileni even though the proposed legislation never became law.[82] And once again, foreign diplomatic pressure stopped short of formal intervention under the terms of the Treaty and Convention of Paris.

The closest any of the powers came to such intervention was probably a strongly worded dispatch, in which Stanley outlined clearly the risks Romania faced as a result of its anti-Jewish policies. Here he stated categorically that the powers of Europe held "the Prince and his Government generally" responsible for the outrages "and for conduct in direct provisions of the Treaty of 1858, the XLVIth Article of which provides for equal treatment of all classes of the inhabitants of the country, irrespective of race or creed." Denials were useless, for Stanley had documents in his possession that clearly demonstrated "the little respect shown by [the ruling authorities in the principalities] . . . for the engagement of the Powers, from which, in fact, the existence of the present form of government in the Principalities, as regards the Porte, is derived, and on which it alone depends." If the Romanians disregarded their obligations, the powers might do likewise. Carol and his government "should ask themselves whether it is wise or safe for them to incur the odium which a perseverance in their present line of conduct towards the Jews will infallibly bring down on them."[83]

Such considerations were enough to persuade Brătianu to speak against the draft legislation in the Romanian parliament; but they did not bring the cycle of persecution and international protest to an end. Increasingly, there was a sense that those involved were simply going through the motions. Following news of further atrocities in Galatz, the British ambassador in Vienna commented in October 1868 that he

> was not surprised at what had taken place; nothing which could possibly occur in that country could any longer surprise him. He feared that, from the perfect impunity which attended them, these lamentable and disgraceful acts of violence against the unfortunate and helpless Jews would only increase in frequence as in atrocity, whilst it had become long since evident that mere remonstrances would be completely unavailing.
>
> Where all despatches and representation had so signally failed to produce effect, his hope was that Sir M. Montefiore would by this new outrage be again called into the field, and perhaps induce Her Majesty's Government to a more energetic and availing course in behalf of his co-religionists.[84]

In practical terms, Montefiore's involvement with the ongoing Romanian crisis was no longer pivotal. It appears from the Foreign Office correspondence presented to Parliament that Goldsmid and Lionel de Rothschild made most of the running. Montefiore himself seems to have recognized as much. In May 1868 he had (as usual) refused a request from the Board of Deputies to serve as president—this time with some ambivalence. "I feel rather better; have more energy, and very anxious to be, if possible, useful to my co-religionists," he wrote in his diary. "Therefore am reluctant to refuse the proffered appointment . . . as perhaps it may be the means of promoting the general unity of all the Jews in England." He added: "I think our Members of Parliament should be *ex officio* members of the Board, as the best medium of expressing the sentiments of the Board to the Commons."[85]

Since Goldsmid was arguably the most prominent Jewish M.P., this seemingly anodyne proposal was in fact a creative solution to the schism that had divided Anglo-Jewry for twenty-five years. In 1853 Montefiore had used his casting vote as president to block the election of Reform Jews to the Board of Deputies. In 1868 he finally agreed to take on the presidency with a view to effectively overturning this decision on Goldsmid's behalf—perhaps recognizing in the son of his old friend and rival the man best suited to take his place in the battle for international Jewish rights.

The initiative failed, but for Montefiore it marked a personal milestone. His change of heart may have been prompted in part by the recent death of his brother Horatio. "He was a very charitable man, a good husband and father," Montefiore had written stiffly on hearing the news in Vienna. "We entertained the most affectionate regard for each other."[86] Yet there is no evidence that the rift between them ever healed. Horatio's death rendered his grudge against the West London Synagogue less personal. Time was passing. It was time to move on.

Chapter 17

Fading Glory

Five months after resuming his presidency of the Board of Deputies, Montefiore was the center of a charming ceremony in Ramsgate. The town council had commissioned a massive portrait of its most famous citizen. Adorned by a frame quite as grand as the painting, this full-length likeness of Montefiore surveying Jerusalem in his lord lieutenant's uniform hung opposite a picture of Queen Victoria. As the deputy mayor remarked at the unveiling, it had been forty years since Montefiore first came among them, and

> [t]hese 40 years had been marked by many acts of public and private be-
> nevolence. There had not been one society among them to which Sir Mo-
> ses had not subscribed, even to assisting them in building their church.
> Who was it that had supplied the young hearts on occasions of rejoicing
> with good cheer, and taken such an interest in them? The young folks
> would all tell them it was Sir Moses Montefiore. He remembered that . . .
> [on the marriage of the prince and princess of Wales] more than 1,300
> children had a holiday and a treat at the expense of the kind-hearted bar-
> onet . . . The poor had never been forgotten by Sir Moses. It was no little
> difficulty for the worthy baronet to travel to the [Isle of Thanet] Union
> loaded with little articles for the comfort that the inmates might require;
> and he gave them himself to the poor people, thereby doubly enhancing
> their value.[1]

Such occasions were the bread and butter of Montefiore's philanthropy in his hometown; as he grew older he spent increasing stretches
of time there.

In the first flush of mourning Montefiore had contemplated sending
Judith's body to Jerusalem. But he had long ago marked out the spot in
Ramsgate where he wished to be buried, and rather than burying Judith

"Sir Moses Montefiore with the Children." This image appeared in the Christian newspaper The Quiver *in 1883 alongside an article titled "Hymns with a History." The author recounted how the wife of the archbishop of Canterbury once encountered the elderly Montefiore visiting an orphanage in Thanet, where he listened to the children singing a hymn by Dr. Watts, "which he said his mother had taught him as a child." (Photograph © Mary Evans Picture Library, London)*

in the Holy Land he erected a replica of the Tomb of Rachel over her grave. Prayers and psalms adorned the walls of this mausoleum, a lamp was suspended from the dome, and a seat was placed in the corner so that Montefiore could spend time there. For Judith's grieving husband it was still not enough.[2]

Plans to build a convalescent home in Judith's memory had emerged in the weeks after her death, but the fund-raising target of £10,000 proved impossible to meet. Four years later the Lady Judith Memorial Fund was becoming an embarrassment—much to Montefiore's distress.[3] "He is anxious for a public testimonial to the virtues and heroic devotion of his wife," wrote an exasperated Charlotte de Rothschild, "yet he deprecates a further appeal to the public. The charity is to be deemed the spontaneous expression of grateful admiration. Every one is to collect funds—and when the subject is mentioned to the Baronet he grows irate."[4] By the time the fund had raised enough to buy two semidetached villas in South Norwood, Montefiore had other plans.[5]

Back in 1827, he had been impressed by the famous Etz Haim Yeshiva in Jerusalem, where he found "about 15 persons reading, surrounded by shelves of books, the name of Franco [the founder], and [the year] 5498 engraved on them in letters of gold."[6] As the first anniversary of Judith's

The Montefiore Mausoleum and Synagogue, Ramsgate, probably early twentieth century. (Courtesy of the Spanish and Portuguese Jews' Congregation, London)

death approached, Montefiore "resolved on establishing in the Holy Land, in memory of my ever lamented and blessed wife, a College *(Beth Hamedrash)* with ten members, to erect ten houses with gardens for their dwellings, with a certain yearly allowance to them, and to purchase and send them a good Hebrew library for their use."[7] The college that he eventually built in Ramsgate was a variant of this vision, consisting of a library, reading room, and lecture hall, with homes for the scholars and their families all built in Tudor-style brick. Montefiore intended it both as "a Memorial of his sincere devotion to the law of God, as revealed on Sinai" and as "a token of his love and pure affection to his departed consort."[8] Jewish values formed the moral core of Montefiore's philanthropy. This—his sole charitable foundation—was a declaration of love and faith: the summation of a lifetime of *mitzvot*.

In Jewish tradition, *tzedakah*, prayer, and study of the Torah are the three pillars on which the world rests. Montefiore had devoted much of his life to the first of these, but the Lady Judith Theological College revealed the supreme worth he accorded the others as well. Yet if Torah is an absolute value in Judaism, it was one with little place in nineteenth-century European society. Contemporary debates about *halukah* were in many ways a barometer for the declining worth that European Jews attached to Torah study and their readiness to embrace a utilitarian model of charity and social welfare instead.[9]

Montefiore never questioned the vocation of those who chose to pray and study Torah in the land of Israel. Having long practiced the *mitzvah* to spread Torah through his habit of commissioning and distributing Torah scrolls, he now wished to "fulfil also the Commandment of God . . . to teach the Holy Law among the Children of Israel and put it in their mouths."[10] This objective would have been uncontroversial in Jerusalem or Vilna. In Britain, it represented a very public commitment to his own religious tradition—one that played better with Christian visitors like the archbishop of Canterbury and the Oxford theologian Max Müller than it did with many British Jews.[11]

The Judith College was more than an act of loving piety. Resident scholars followed a strict program of study, but they were also enjoined to pray for Montefiore and Judith—and to gather in the library four times a year to read "an abstract of certain occurrences . . . in which the Founder of the Institution and his wife were by the blessing of God, enabled to render a service to the cause of religion and humanity in general." The turn of phrase reflected the balance between the particular and the universal in Montefiore's worldview, while the dates recalled the high points of his career: the triumph over the blood libel, the purchase of land in Jerusalem, and his meetings with the rulers of Russia and Morocco. In keeping with this mixture of piety and personal propaganda, Montefiore entrusted the college librarian with "all the addresses, testimonials, poems and other objects of interest" he had received over the years, instructing him to arrange them "in proper order, so as to afford every facility to the visitors to inspect or read them." Thus Montefiore tacitly recognized the role of the new foundation in projecting his sense of divine mission and his personal religious vision.[12]

With his eyes firmly fixed on the pillars of eastern European Orthodoxy, Loewe had sent a copy of the Judith College regulations to the editor of *Halevanon,* stressing that "the *sar*'s purpose is to increase the Torah and magnify it and support *Talmidei Hakhamim* [rabbinic scholars]."[13] The regulations themselves underlined Montefiore's international perspective, encouraging applicants "from whatever part of the globe they may happen to come." Well aware of the low level of Anglo-Jewish scholarship, Loewe then advertised the positions in *Hamagid.* The responses that survive suggest that it captured the imagination of disheartened, middle-aged men, defeated by the daily grind of rabbinical duties and the struggle to support their families.

To such men the promise of "a chair, a desk, a lamp, and all their needs" seemed a very heaven.[14] "I have tired of carrying the burden myself," wrote one Romanian rabbi, "and therefore my lord the *sar,* after I called to G-d my hope lies with you . . . you founded the Ohel Moshe ve Yehudit [Judith College] to be an *ohel* [house of study] . . . and placed in it people who are learned in the Torah and G-dfearing . . . G-d knows that I did a lot in my congregation for G-d and his Torah, and to lift the honor of the House of Israel . . . but now my strength has failed, and what hope do I have after the bread has vanished from the house and there is not a penny in my pocket?"[15]

In the event, Loewe deemed only three applicants suitable.[16] This small beginning did not deter Montefiore from inaugurating and consecrating his "dear Judith College" in 1869. Freshly arrived from his position as principal rabbi of Czyżew, near Warsaw, Eliezer Saul was overwhelmed. "On my journey hither, I witnessed, to my great regret, the religious apathy that prevailed among the wealthy and aristocratic Jews of Berlin," he reported back to *Hamagid.* "But here, I am gratified by seeing a gentleman who occupies a high rank among the nobility of the land; one who has often stood before powerful rulers, emperors, sultans, kings, and viceroys; worshipping in the house of God with such fervor, that I imagined myself to be in a synagogue at Jerusalem, Vilna, Warsaw, or Voloseyn [Volozhin]." Both he and his colleague Ascher Amschejewitz were soon co-opted into Loewe's publicity machine, translating Judith's journals for an eastern European audience and sending articles (like this one) to the Hebrew-language press.[17]

As for Montefiore, the rabbis enriched his sometimes lonely existence in Ramsgate. They provided company if he wanted it and stimulation in the form of weekly public lectures. Sometimes he was well enough to resume his business interests, traveling up to London for board meetings and even embarking on a tour of Imperial Continental Gas stations in Belgium. Often he was too weak to leave his room.[18] Long visits from his widowed sister Abby Gompertz enlivened the late 1860s; in 1871 she, too, passed away.[19] Not that Montefiore was likely to find himself at a loose end. As Charlotte de Rothschild reported, "Sir Moses . . . dines much, sleeps more, and prays most of all—but never spends one moment of his existence in idleness. How could he? He is overwhelmed with thousands of letters from the religious and the begging communities in all parts of the civilized and not civilized world!"[20]

Letters from Persia had formed part of Montefiore's mail ever since the 1840s, when the forced conversion of the Jews of Mashhad and the ar-

The Lady Judith Theological College, Ramsgate, probably early twentieth century. (Courtesy of the Spanish and Portuguese Jews' Congregation, London)

rival in London of a Jewish emissary from Hamadān drew his attention to their plight.[21] *Dhimma* provided a legal framework common to all Islamic countries, but religious and political rivalry with the Ottoman Empire had combined with the harsh legacy of the Zoroastrian caste system to create a situation of unique intolerance in Persia. The twelve-*imam* Shi'ites, who considered even Sunnis to be ritually impure, treated Jews as the lowest of the low. Their abject position owed something to Catholic spies from Spain and Portugal, whose own brand of anti-Jewish prejudice and racial purity had inspired a draconian set of regulations designed to prevent Jews from transmitting their impurity through touch. The low status of Persian Jews was reflected in their economic profile, with its bias toward "impure" professions such as trade, peddling, alcohol production, dyeing, street-cleaning, and the performing arts. The result was a community living in almost complete isolation, forbidden to touch goods in Muslim shops, use Muslim baths, drink from a public well, or walk in the street on a rainy day. This situation had persisted for nearly two centuries by the time Nissim Bar Selomah set out from Hamadān in 1847. His journey to London and Montreal was just one manifestation of increasing contact with the West.[22]

Persia had long been nervous of Russian ambitions in the Caucasus and the Caspian. The expansion of British India both intensified and relieved these pressures—allowing the shah to play his European neighbors off against each other as Persia became caught up in the Great Game. Underpinned by global processes of economic, technological, political, and cultural change, the struggle for influence in Persia was as much about spreading rival European models of modernity as it was about the North-West Frontier. Here, too, British diplomats sought to promote the rights of religious minorities as part of the imperial nexus of commerce, Christianity, and civilization. Just as they had in the Ottoman Empire and Morocco, they came to embrace the cause of Persian Jewry in its name.[23]

So integral did these values seem to British interests that the first high-profile intervention on behalf of Persian Jews was the inspiration not of Montefiore but of Charles Murray, the cultivated and well-traveled aristocrat representing her majesty in Tehran. In the aftermath of the Anglo-Persian war of 1856–57, Murray wrote to Foreign Secretary Clarendon pleading the cause of nearly 1,000 Jewish families who, having fled Mashhad after the forced conversion of 1839, were now brutally repatriated from Herāt by the retreating Persian army. Comparing their behavior with the hypothetical abduction to Portsmouth of Russian shopkeepers from Sebastopol, Murray asserted that the question was "solely one of humanity on our side, and of avarice on that of the Persian authorities."[24] The issue subsequently formed a major sticking point between the two countries, prompting one Persian minister to wonder "what advantage British Agents expect to derive from the British Ministers constituting themselves arbiters, and granting protection to individuals who are opposed to this government, and are moreover low and miserable Jews."[25]

The following decade saw a steady flow of news from Persia in the Jewish press—and a steady trickle of appeals to Montefiore. In March 1865 yet another desperate missive from Hamadān proved too much for him to bear. "I could not sleep last night for thinking of our poor suffering brethren in Persia," he wrote in his diary. Still basking in the glory of his trip to Morocco, he resolved to obtain a *firman* from the shah himself. "But could not some plan be found to save you from so long and dangerous a journey?" asked Sir Austen Layard when Montefiore announced his intentions. The Foreign Office would be more than happy to forward a petition informing the shah of the concessions granted to Montefiore in Morocco and the Ottoman Empire, and begging him to issue a similar edict in Persia.[26]

At first Montefiore's petition to the shah met with silence. Eventually

Charles Alison, the new British consul, felt compelled to press his case. This overture, too, might have remained unanswered had not a dispute over the seats accorded diplomats at the Tehran races prompted Alison to threaten to suspend all social intercourse with the prime minister.[27] Alison blustered to such good effect that the shah gave formal assurances that "after you have renewed your relations with the Minister for Foreign Affairs, every question of yours which may have remained settled, be it Telegraphic, be it commercial, or otherwise, will be one and all satisfactorily arranged by Us, so that there will be no outstanding claims in your Mission."[28] Barely one month later the shah issued an autograph letter ordering his prime minister to treat the Jews with justice and kindness.[29] As in Morocco, this concession was formulated to reflect local political traditions, which held that the protection of *dhimmis* was a particular responsibility of the shah, whose ability to protect all his subjects against violent excesses was central to the stability of the state. In the early 1860s, moreover, Nasr-ed-Din Shah had introduced a raft of measures intended to help him fulfill this role. Yet Montefiore was only too happy to take the credit. He informed the Board of Deputies that his efforts had (once again) been crowned with success.[30]

Given Alison's strictures about "the reckless inveracity of Persian Ministers," the consul can hardly have been surprised that this document remained a dead letter.[31] In June 1866 news began to reach Tehran of a frightful pogrom in Barfurush (later Bābol) after a Jew was held responsible for the sudden death of a Muslim woman.[32] Recalling the shah's recent promise, Alison demanded that the prime minister investigate. Back in England, Edmund Hammond, permanent under-secretary of the Foreign Office, proposed "to anticipate any representation and at once inform Sir M. Montefiore and Sir F. Goldsmid" of these developments. "Heaven protect the poor Jews," exclaimed a distraught Montefiore when he heard the news. But Hammond advised that Montefiore "could do no good" by setting out for Persia and "must wait with patience" for further dispatches.[33] The Foreign Office had instructed Alison "to express to the Shah the full assurance felt by HM's Govt that the Persons who committed the outrage referred to in your Telegram of the 7th Instant will be severely punished, and that the Jews at that place and elsewhere throughout Persia will be protected from ill-treatment and persecution."[34]

This well-meaning intervention overturned the already delicate religious balance in Barfurush and its surroundings, where official support for the Jews inflamed existing tensions just as it had in Morocco. After a spate of forced conversions in Māzandarān and a fresh outbreak of anti-Jewish violence, the first monshee reported in August that "when recently they [the Jewish community] had killed a Seyed woman, His Majesty, out of consideration for the British Minister, had not given orders for the execution of the murderer but had ordered blood money to be paid. Then Meerza Mehdi Khan, by orders from His Majesty, had been appointed from the Foreign Office to proceed to Barforoosh to investigate matters and effectually to protect the Jews and he went and acted in this spirit. Another reason was that Mr. W. Abbott had been sent by the British Mission to Barforoosh. This also gave a kind of support to them and the agents of the Russian Government also protected them. In consequence of this the Jewish Community began to be insubordinate and struck the Mussulmans and the people of Mazanderan who are inhabitants of a jungle, not being able to tolerate this, had acted in the manner reported."[35]

Skeptical though he was of this interpretation, Alison concluded that "friendly advice and exhortation are not only useless and undignified, but may turn out to be pernicious to the Jews themselves and serve as an instrument in the hands of their enemies."[36] His view was in keeping with the advice of the Persian foreign minister, who warned that the shah had to deal with

> an ignorant and fanatical nation, who have for centuries been accustomed to look lightly upon the ill treatment of a people whom they despise. They would be astounded to see a Mahomedan punished for having injured a Jew, and were the Persian Govt. to take prompt and severe measures to this effect, it might lead fanatics to think that the Shah and His Ministers were false to their own religion and be attended with dangerous consequences.
>
> The remedy can only therefore be introduced cautiously and gradually, by the issue at first of *Fermans* throughout the country prohibiting any further persecution of the Shah's Jewish subjects, and later by more energetic steps.[37]

The shah felt compelled to reassert his authority in the surrounding province, well aware that attacks on Jews were an established form of insubordination. But *Hamagid*—which received regular news via an Alliance Israélite circle in Baghdad—reported that religious leaders exiled to Tehran had carried the bad feeling from Barfurush to the capital, whose inhabitants were now "conspiring to massacre all the Jews."[38] Such repercussions did not deter the Jews of Persia from seeking to improve their situation: their desperate appeals to Montefiore and Crémieux continued as before.[39] When starvation devastated the entire region, Montefiore was the obvious port of call.

The Great Famine of 1871 was a disaster of epic proportions. Many areas had not seen a drop of rain for the best part of two years. Traveling from Büshehr to Tehran at the height of the catastrophe, the director of the new Persian telegraph found some towns empty of inhabitants while others were crowded with the starving and destitute, "most of whom had flocked in from the surrounding country" seeking work and food and many of whom "seemed in a dying state." Whole villages subsisted entirely on grass, cholera was rampant, even the healthiest men looked "cadaverous," and in Isfahan he hardly ever left the house "without seeing one or more corpses in the street."[40]

Informing Montefiore of the unfolding tragedy, Consul-General Henry Jones of Tabrīz warned that the entire Jewish population could be annihilated at a stroke. Montefiore's response was typically nonsectarian: he sent £25 to the Muslims, £25 to the Christians, and £50 to the Jews of Shīrāz—but he also persuaded the Board of Deputies to endorse plans for his Persian Famine Relief Fund. Contributions began to reach Persia two weeks later, telegraphed directly to Tehran with the help of the Foreign Office.[41]

Support for the new relief fund was initially confined to *Hamagid*, in a reflection of the newspaper's pioneering role in contact with Persia. Russian and Polish Jews were used to being a focus of Western Jewish philanthropy; now it was their turn to show they cared. The subscription lists that began to appear in *Hamagid* included the names of some 40,000 Jews living in the Pale of Settlement.[42] Many donations were tiny, but for the hard-up a few kopecks could be a real sacrifice: a tangible connection with the great family of Israel and proof that international subscription fund-raising was not just the prerogative of a social and intellectual elite. After a shaky start, the appeal eventually caught fire in Germany and North America, raising a total of £18,000—embarrassingly little of which came from Montefiore's own community in London.[43] Persia lost nearly a quarter of its population. In Isfahan alone, more than 1,000 Jews were saved.[44]

Writing in February 1872, Ludwig Philippson saw this wave of public enthusiasm as one more manifestation of a distinctively modern phenomenon. "In recent times a feeling of solidarity has developed among the Jews, a united interest in the best and noblest sense of the word," he stated.

> We do not need to recall the bloody events of Damascus in the early 1840s and all that has since occurred, but need only point to recent times, when from the West Coast of America throughout the rest of the world

attempts were made to intervene after a medieval lust for persecution re-appeared in Romania . . . When famine raged in western Russia a few years ago . . . then money flowed in from all over the world as we debated how best to put an end to the distress of the poor Jewish population, transporting a significant number of orphaned children to Germany and France in order to raise them as practical people. When war broke out in Alsace and Lorraine and hit the Jews hard in many places, their German coreligionists readily made sacrifices to come to their aid. Just now came an appeal from Persia on behalf of the starving Jews there, and at once committees formed in our cities to make collections, and the Jewish press fostered this charitable instinct.[45]

As so often, Philippson had his finger on the pulse of developments. The years since 1840 had seen the birth of an international Jewish lobby, rooted in civil society but dependent on European economic and po-litical expansion, the communications revolution engendered by rail-ways, steamships, and the telegraph, new patterns of migration, and the development of a global public sphere.[46] In the 1840s and 1850s this was still an intermittent phenomenon, requiring leaders like Montefiore, Crémieux, and Philippson to spur it into action. With time, more per-manent clusters of philanthropic, political, and journalistic activity arose—not just in London, Paris, Berlin, and Vienna, but in Philadel-phia, New York, Budapest, St. Petersburg, Odessa, Warsaw, and Con-stantinople. As the Jewish press spread from the acculturated communi-ties of the West to the Orthodox heartlands of eastern Europe, so the connections forged between these clusters in times of crisis acquired deeper roots, finding their first institutional expression in the Alliance Israélite. In the early 1860s, Montefiore's activities had provided a cen-tral focus for this global Jewish public; by the end of that decade, they were merely one facet of the increasingly confident, diverse, and autono-mous body that was world Jewry.

Once, the eyes of the Jewish world had been directed toward a succes-sion of individual crises; now such disasters seemed to flow thick and fast. Yet the political and economic transformations that fostered both the rise of anti-Semitism in Romania and the horrific famine in western Russia also enabled Jews to cope in new ways. Thus the global forces of civil society empowered obscure individuals to follow in the footsteps of Montefiore, Crémieux, and Philippson. In 1868 Isaac Rülf, a provincial rabbi from East Prussia, had raised 630,000 marks for the starving Jews of Lithuania. Three years later, a Jewish journalist from Cleveland could muster enough money and political connections to defend the cause of Jews in Romania while serving as U.S. consul in Bucharest.[47] The high

concentration of donors to the Persian Famine Relief Fund in parts of
Russia that had benefited from Rabbi Rülf's philanthropy highlights the
interlocking nature of such initiatives.[48] These were formative years in
which international Jewish activism assumed critical mass.

Integration into this wider Jewish public threatened to overturn Montefiore's dominance of Anglo-Jewry. Men like Francis Goldsmid and Lionel de Rothschild chafed at Montefiore's stifling presence on the Board
of Deputies, which had long basked in his reflected glory. "From an obscure local organisation, it became under his presidency, the leading
body in Israel," the *Jewish Chronicle* had commented in 1862—at about
the time Montefiore began to step back from the everyday running of
affairs.[49] His nephew Joseph Mayer Montefiore had been elected vice-
president in 1858 and served as president during Montefiore's absences.
He was known as a modest and retiring man, who rarely spoke and
"preferred to keep his personality in the background to an almost excessive extent."[50] An ineffectual chair of the deputies' meetings, Joseph was
no match for his overbearing uncle. His unassuming presence at the
helm ensured that the board remained a vehicle for Montefiore's autocratic communal politics: it lent legitimacy both to his diplomatic interventions and to his opposition to religious reform.

Only Goldsmid had both the status and the motive to challenge this
style of leadership. The House of Commons provided him with a platform; association with the Alliance Israélite gave his advocacy of Balkan
Jewry additional clout. Montefiore's proposal to offer all Jewish M.P.s
ex-officio membership failed to meet Reform aspirations for full religious equality. Rather than join the board on Montefiore's terms, Goldsmid took the lead in founding the Anglo-Jewish Association, an alternative organization dedicated to the international struggle for Jewish
rights.

In April 1871 Montefiore had received news of an outbreak of anti-
Jewish violence in Odessa. Orthodox Easter was a recurrent flash point,
and he seems to have thought little of it. "I should like," he wrote, "to
go to St. Petersburg to thank the Emperor for the prompt measure that
had been taken by the Government at Odessa to put an end to the outbreak [of violence] against the Jews." This sanguine assessment owed
much to that government's attempts to cover up the incident. It did not
take long for the truth to seep out.[51]

The *Neue Freie Presse* of Vienna reported that three days of pillage
had left 4,000 Jewish families destitute; "sixteen persons have been murdered; sixty seriously wounded; females have been brutally violated; a
mother, who was trying to prevent her daughter being outraged, had
her ears cut off and died from loss of blood. Jewish synagogues have
been pillaged; the Books of the Law torn and trodden upon . . . and in

the face of such outrages to humanity, the authorities remain silent and public opinion appears indifferent."[52] Goldsmid and others promptly founded an Odessa Relief Fund, but Montefiore's board refused them its backing, claiming it possessed "no funds" to forward the appeal to member congregations.[53] Just two weeks before the board threw its weight behind the Persian Famine Relief Fund, this excuse rang more than a little hollow.

The Anglo-Jewish Association was born three days later. Strictly speaking, its international remit posed no threat to the Board of Deputies, which lacked any constitutional authority to act in foreign affairs—and frequently used this as an excuse for inactivity. Montefiore had always ignored this fact when it suited him; now his supporters and the board rejected all talk of cooperation.[54] "We want no new political Associations in England," wrote Haim Guedalla in the *Jewish Chronicle*, "or branches of a Parisian Quixotic Club celebrated for its meddling energetically when it suited the views of certain influential people . . . The Board of Deputies, backed by the support of the Foreign Office, has been of the greatest service to the Jews in all parts of the world, and, being a representative body, is sure to be recognised by the British and all Foreign Governments as the only official organ."[55]

These arguments cut little ice in some quarters. There had been talk for several years about establishing such an organization, and the upheavals of the Franco-Prussian War made an English complement to the Parisian Alliance Israélite seem suddenly more urgent. For many Odessa was the final straw. As one irate correspondent of the *Jewish Chronicle* noted, "When Sir Moses was written to by the starving population of Shiraz, the Board acted . . . When Sir Moses . . . was not written to, as in the instances of the outrages at Odessa, the Board waited . . . till it was ashamed and did nothing; and its waiting and its silence should for ever stand to its shame."[56]

Other figures in the Jewish world certainly grasped the importance of Odessa. The multicultural port city had once been a magnet for Jewish modernizers and a model of integration in Russian society. Now the Russian government and the press sought to excuse the anti-Jewish violence by pointing the finger at Jewish economic exploitation. Both at home and abroad Jews began to doubt they would ever be accepted in Russia on equal terms.[57] With the fate of one-third of the world's Jews hanging in the balance, Ludwig Philippson concluded that there was "no more important question for the Jewish condition in our time than the situation of our coreligionists in Russia."[58] Montefiore's continued silence is hard to explain.

The spring of 1872 saw yet another crisis in Romania. Montefiore fell back on the well-worn expedient of writing to the foreign secretary.

Goldsmid and other members of the Anglo-Jewish Association founded a Romanian Committee and held a grand public meeting in the Mansion House. With speakers like Edward Baines, Lord Shaftesbury, and the bishop of Gloucester deploying the rhetoric of English liberty and Christian civilization in the name of Romanian Jewry, the meeting drew heavily on the humanitarian nexus Montefiore had nurtured so carefully. The *Jewish Chronicle* thought it a "red-letter day in the annals of the Anglo-Jewish community"—an event evoking the spirit and tradition of City opposition to the Damascus Affair.[59]

The great man's absence was all the more striking. It was all very well for the lord mayor to declare (amid loud cheers) that Montefiore would surely have "taken a foremost part in the movement, had his physical powers enabled him." That very week, the *Jewish Chronicle* had reported "the joyful circumstance that on Sunday last for the first time in some years, Sir MOSES MONTEFIORE appeared in a public Jewish meeting" in buoyant spirits and excellent health.[60] Professional jealousy, not ill health, dictated Montefiore's absence from the Mansion House. It was almost certainly a factor in his surprising decision to set out for St. Petersburg once more.

To contemporaries the projected trip to Russia seemed inexplicable. "Am I demented?" asked one correspondent of the *Jewish Chronicle,* on learning that Montefiore went not to protest the outrages in Odessa but to congratulate Tsar Alexander II on the bicentenary of the birth of Peter the Great. "It is only but yesterday that an indignation meeting was held to protest in the name of our common humanity against outrages [in Romania] indirectly fostered by barbarous [Russian] influences; and to day, lost to every feeling of self-respect, we are about beflattering a dynasty founded and nurtured on monster vices."[61]

Others imposed a more benign interpretation on the Montefiore mission. Foreign Secretary Granville had implied that Russia was behind the recent violence in Romania, and even Philippson was inclined to hope that congratulating the tsar was merely a pretext for Montefiore to address the question of Romanian Jewry.[62] Yet there is no evidence to suggest that the mission disguised a hidden agenda, Romanian or otherwise. Montefiore himself subsequently informed the British ambassador that he had "no request of any kind to make to His Majesty with reference to the Jews in Russia."[63] His journey was just a magnificent *coup de théâtre.*

Montefiore had long enjoyed a love-hate relationship with the Russian authorities. So influential did he appear in the aftermath of his first visit that the Russian ambassador actively sought his support during the tense days of the 1848 revolution. "I believe such a letter from me [to Solomon Posener in Warsaw] may do some good & prevent some of the more ignorant of our Brethren from being entrapped by wicked & designing men in these unhappy times," Montefiore had written to Loewe. "I have no fear of the loyalty of the Jews and know of the desperate hatred of the Poles to them, they would gladly make fools of them & destroy them afterwards . . . and I believe the day is not distant when the Emperor Nicholas will grant them all the privileges they require."[64]

These hopes proved misplaced, and barely two years later Montefiore found himself intervening in a ritual-murder allegation in the Caucasus.[65] By 1854 the Russian government had concluded that his influence was more pernicious than otherwise, banning the distribution of his portrait in Poland during the Crimean War.[66] This move did not deter Montefiore from congratulating Alexander II on his coronation in 1863, or from remaining on excellent terms with the Russian ambassador in London, who took to signing his letters "your very devoted old friend Brunnow."[67] As Montefiore later explained to the German banker Gerson von Bleichröder, "the best way to obtain the cooperation of the Emperor of Russia and his ministers is to show our confidence in their desire to ameliorate the condition of the Jews . . . history . . . teaches us, that the social and political condition of a large community can only be gradually raised."[68] The mission of 1872 reflected his stubborn commitment to this policy—and his stated view that "Religion commands us to be loyal and Faithful Subjects and nothing but disgrace and misery will attend those who are not faithful subjects."[69]

Had Montefiore returned to Vilna in 1872, his impressions of Jewish life under Alexander II would have been different.[70] Neither the draft nor state education had done more than scratch the surface of Jewish society in the Pale of Settlement. Conscription had not led to the mass conversion of Jewish soldiers, while barely 4,000 Jewish boys had passed through Uvarov's much-vaunted modern schools. The graduates and employees of these schools may have formed the vanguard of the Russian Jewish intelligentsia. Compared to the 70,000 educated in the traditional system they remained an embattled minority. When change came, it was unpredictable and unplanned.

The emancipation of the serfs under Alexander II ushered in a period of severe social instability. The Great Reforms created rising tensions between peasants and nobility, land hunger, and social rivalry in the villages, intense economic pressure in the towns. Jews were the victims of this process, not its beneficiaries. Overly concentrated as middlemen in the decrepit semifeudal economy, they were ousted from their traditional role in land management by the return of the nobility to the provinces, while steam and rail destroyed existing trade routes, bringing unwelcome competition and putting both Jewish traders and tavernkeepers out of business. Thus the immediate effect of emancipation was the pauperization of large numbers of rural Jews and a dramatic deterioration of conditions in the towns, where the Jewish population rose exponentially. With the organs of Jewish self-government in freefall and the Jewish elites engaged in bitter cultural warfare, internal divisions exacerbated the crisis of modernization facing Russian Jews.

Montefiore must have known something of this from the Jewish press, the rabbis he had imported to Ramsgate, and his extensive correspondence. But in St. Petersburg he could only be struck by a remarkable flowering of Jewish life. The changes that wrought disaster for the Jewish masses had brought untold prosperity to a handful of Jewish tax farmers and military contractors, who now lived comfortably (and openly) outside the Pale. In the mid-1850s they began to lobby cautiously for the extension of Jewish rights. Confronted by the failure of Jewish policy under Nicholas, the government began—equally cautiously—to lift residence restrictions on certain categories of Jews. First merchants, then students, then soldiers and artisans were allowed to settle in the Russian interior. By the 1870s, St. Petersburg was replacing Odessa as a magnet for Jewish intellectuals and their battle for integration into Russian society.[71]

Not all Jews in St. Petersburg were wealthy or educated. Alongside bankers like the Ginzburgs who rubbed shoulders with Russian officials and nobility, there were aspiring literati who obtained fraudulent residence permits as craftsmen or servants, and traditionally dressed provincials who crowded into the guesthouses and apartment blocks of the down-at-heel Pod'iacheskii district. So alluring did the capital seem that many settled there illegally, lurking in the shadows if they spotted a policeman who might demand their identity card. Comparing his experience under Nicholas with the city in the 1870s, one retired soldier remarked: "What was Petersburg then—a desert! But now—it's like Berdichev."[72]

Montefiore saw only the official face of this emerging community. In his subsequent report, he claimed to have "conversed with Jewish merchants, literary men, editors of Russian periodicals, artisans, and persons who had formerly served in the Imperial army, all of whom alluded to their present position in the most satisfactory terms . . . The Jews now dress like any gentlemen in England, France, or Germany; their schools are well attended, and they are foremost in every honourable enterprise designed to promote their community and the country at large . . . Nothing can surpass the decorum which prevails in all the Synagogues during the divine service."[73]

The reality was less rosy. As the Russian Jewish *Raszvet* commented after the visit of another western European Jewish dignitary, his impression might have been less favorable if, instead of modern synagogues with their well-ordered services, "they had had to show him our dark, dirty, stinking kennels, ruled by noise and uproar and other similar attributes of our quasi-orthodox prayer houses."[74] Montefiore would certainly have been shocked by the experience of Pauline Wengeroff, a banker's wife descended from a long line of Lithuanian rabbis whose move to the capital was the first step on her family's road to conversion. "It was here in St. Petersburg . . . that I had to take off my *scheitel* [wig]," she recalled bitterly at the age of ninety-eight. "It was here, in the face of violent opposition, that I was forced to dismantle my kosher kitchen . . . and gradually banished one beautiful old custom after another from my household."[75] Yet it was common knowledge that Jews arriving in St. Petersburg underwent "a complete metamorphosis": "The tax farmer was transformed into a banker, the contractor into a high-flying entrepreneur, and their employees into Petersburg dandies . . . Big-shots from Balta and Konotop quickly came to consider themselves 'aristocrats' and would laugh at the 'provincials.'"[76] Montefiore's failure to realize the implications of this transformation is unsurprising. If the great Hebrew poet Judah Leib Gordon is to be believed, he showed remarkably little interest in St. Petersburg Jewish life.

A native of Vilna who vividly recalled Montefiore's visit in 1846, Gordon had spent the past twenty years eking out a living as a government teacher in Lithuania.[77] His passionate journalistic advocacy of Jewish integration into Russian society eventually brought him to the attention of Evzel Ginzburg, Russia's leading Jewish banker. Ten years earlier, Ginzburg and other members of the St. Petersburg merchant elite had founded the Society for the Spread of Enlightenment among the Jews of Russia (OPE). As a vehicle for promoting their gradualist approach to the Jewish question it proved lackluster. In 1870 Gordon declared he had "lost all confidence in the capabilities of the committee [OPE board] and its endeavours; experience has taught me two or three times that we should not entertain very great expectations of it."[78] Like Gordon, however, OPE was committed to the idea of a Russian-Jewish symbiosis. It sought to defend Jewish interests and to mediate between the Russian state and Jewish society while raising the cultural level of Russian Jewry to render them more deserving of civil rights. When the organization needed a new secretary in 1872, Gordon moved to St. Petersburg to take up the job.

He had been in town barely a month before he found himself orchestrating the official response to Montefiore's visit. To his disappointment Montefiore took no steps to make contact with the local community and refused to meet anyone before his interview with the tsar. Gordon took umbrage at the "patronising and peremptory" attitude with which Loewe delivered this message. Nor was he pleased to learn that a conceited tailor whose wife had fallen into conversation with Montefiore's housekeeper on the train to St. Petersburg was among the select group Loewe invited to make up a *minyan* that Sabbath. After waiting patiently until Montefiore's reception at the Winter Palace, Gordon was shocked to learn that Montefiore planned to leave the city that night. Even Ginzburg only succeeded in snatching a few words with the distinguished visitor. Gordon would have got nowhere had he not presented himself as the author of an article about Montefiore that had appeared in the *Allgemeine Zeitung des Judentums*.

As a precocious teenager, Gordon had caught a glimpse of Montefiore descending from his coach resplendent in his City uniform. The tall and stately figure of his youth was now a bent and shrunken old man, walking unsteadily with Loewe's help as he came to greet his visitor. He declared himself delighted by the spread of secular education and the continued attachment he thought many Russian Jews showed to "their people, their homeland and the language of the forefathers"; but Gordon realized to his discomfort that these impressions owed much to Montefiore's encounter with a notorious charlatan. Complaints of Montefiore's parsimony, his vanity, his disrespect for communal leaders, and his ungracious attitude to the Jewish crowds that cheered his passing all suggest that Gordon was not alone in discovering that his idol had feet of clay.[79]

From Montefiore's perspective, however, the trip was a triumph. No one could have been more gracious than Tsar Alexander, who had returned to St. Petersburg expressly to save Montefiore the fatigue of traveling to meet him. Both this and the very different public face of the community confirmed Montefiore's faith in the long-term prospects for Jewish emancipation.[80] The truth, in 1872, was far otherwise. Public responses to the Odessa pogrom had revealed an increasingly virulent streak of Judeophobia in Russian society. Disquiet over the Jewish question was not merely a product of economic change and social turmoil. It also fed on the sinister fantasies peddled by Iakov Brafman, a convert to Russian Orthodoxy whose *Book of the Kahal* (based on an authentic Jewish source) became the most influential work of Judeophobia in Russian history. In the words of Ginzburg's secretary Emanuel Levin, Brafman wove truth and lies "so skilfully together not every Jew would be able to disentangle them."[81]

Writing in the late 1860s, Brafman claimed that Jews maintained their separatism through a secret internal organization known as the Kahal. This unsavory organization had long oppressed the Jewish masses through its abuse of talmudic authority, but in recent years it had acquired national and international significance through the creation of five international brotherhoods. Superficially committed to enlightenment, modernization, and integration, the real aim of societies like OPE and the Alliance Israélite was to prepare Jews for citizenship of a future Jewish kingdom. Thus Brafman built on the realities of globalization, Jewish associational life, and the longstanding tradition of Jewish self-government to present a definitively hostile interpretation of international Jewish activism. In the ensuing climate of Kahalophobia, Montefiore's visit was bound to compound popular prejudice. How could it be otherwise when even the supposedly liberal newspaper *Golos* believed he was regarded "as the president of all Europe" by the Jews?[82]

Those looking for evidence of subversive international brotherhoods did not need to look far. When the shah of Persia traveled to Europe in 1873, he was confronted by an apparently united Jewish front. From Berlin, Wiesbaden, and London to Paris, Vienna, and Constantinople, Jews sent deputations to wait upon him and draw the plight of their brethren to his attention. Their generosity during the recent famine made them hard to ignore. In Wiesbaden, the grand vizier protested that "his Majesty had already at Berlin received and answered a similar application." The editor of the *Israelit,* who headed the Jewish delegation, replied that "their object was to attest that everywhere the Jews take the liveliest interest in the welfare of their brethren in Persia, and that the interest had been practically demonstrated during the Persian famine by the bountiful collections that had been set on foot." Whereupon he flourished a copy of Montefiore's relief fund report and was indeed granted an interview, arriving to find the shah eating a lavish breakfast while his vizier inspected the wares of a Wiesbaden jeweler.[83]

Montefiore—needless to say—intervened a little more spectacularly. Only a year earlier, his desire to visit Persia had been so burning that his nephew Joseph Mayer Montefiore joked "it was evident [he] wished to be buried there."[84] But the Foreign Office had forbidden him to contemplate such a dangerous journey—and the shah had come to England instead. Montefiore duly headed a delegation from the Board of Deputies and presented him with a beautifully emblazoned address of welcome, referring at length to the shah's earlier commitment to protect Persian Jewry and eliciting a suitably gracious response.[85] Eager for news of the encounter to reach a Persian public, he had the shah's reply translated into both Persian and Hebrew, composed an obsequious covering letter, and reprinted the whole on one large scroll, which he then forwarded "to hundreds of Hebrew communities in Persia, with instructions to have the scroll affixed to the principal entrance of their Synagogues."[86]

The shah's promises to Montefiore had secured official royal protection for Persian Jews, opposing the European ideal of equality to the subordinate position accorded religious minorities in Islamic law and the deeply held Shi'ite belief in the impurity of non-Muslims. The *Jewish Chronicle* naturally liked to think that "London, England, and Englishmen have had a more satisfactory and telling effect on the SHAH than any town, country or people hitherto visited by him on his European tour."[87] Yet it was arguably Crémieux who exacted the more meaningful concession when he obtained the shah's permission to establish a network of Persian Jewish schools.[88] Nasr-ed-Din himself was much struck by this evidence of international Jewish unity—and by the wealth and influence of the Jews he had met. "I have heard that you, brothers, possess 1,000 Kurur of money," he joked to one of the French Rothschilds. "I think the best thing would be to give 80 Kurur to some state, large or small, in exchange for a province in which to gather the Jews of the whole world. You yourself would become their chief and rule them all peacefully, so that they would no longer be scattered and driven about."[89]

Had the shah looked a little deeper, he might have realized that this show of Jewish unity was a facade. Emancipation, secularization, and acculturation had created new fault lines in Jewish society and replaced traditional communal authority with a more disparate voluntarism. The Jews of London might be united in seeking to improve the condition of Persian Jews, but they still sent two deputations to meet the ruler of Persia: one from the Board of Deputies and the other from the Anglo-Jewish Association.[90]

To some this duplication seemed increasingly untenable—and Montefiore's "policy of exclusion" a nonsense that should not be perpetuated. Mixed marriages, the ceremonial exchange of compliments, the indiscriminate support of Jewish charities, and the role of Reform Jews in both the Commons and the Anglo-Jewish Association all suggested that it was high time to welcome them back into the fold.[91] But it was one thing to accept Reform M.P.s as deputies ex officio, quite another to acknowledge the Reformers' right to elect their own representatives.

When proposals to allow the West London Synagogue two deputies came up for discussion, Montefiore did not hesitate to declare himself "of the same opinion . . . as he was thirty years ago."[92] Yet he also urged Nathan Adler to instruct the board "whether the injunction of the late Revd. Dr. Herschell and his Beth din was still in force or not."[93] No longer quite the towering figure he had been, Montefiore may even have hoped it was not.

Chapter 18

The Final Pilgrimage

Death continued to diminish Montefiore's circle of intimates. He spent much of the autumn of 1873 at the bedside of his widowed sister, Justina. In October she finally died. "Oh, may my end be like hers!" Montefiore wrote wistfully in his diary. "She was the youngest of nine children. I, the oldest, by the mercy of God, still remain, I hope for the purpose of doing some good." Justina was buried in a cap and gown he had given her, but her brother was too frail to follow the coffin to the grave. Weak in body and low in spirits, he observed the seven days of ritual mourning. His hands now shook so badly that his handwriting was becoming illegible; he noted thankfully that at least his head was clear. When the *Kent Coast Times* reported his death a month later, Montefiore did not fail to see the joke: "Thank God to have been able to hear of the rumour, and to read an account of the same with my own eyes, without using spectacles."[1] He was sufficiently recovered by the following spring to resume business as usual—presenting reports from famine-stricken Palestine to the Board of Deputies and launching yet another Holy Land Relief Fund.[2]

Responses to Montefiore's 1874 campaign were decidedly ambivalent. Ludwig Philippson found it hard to justify these endless appeals to Jewish generosity when Christians and Muslims who were similarly affected did not think to ask for help.[3] Official persecution may have contributed to the sufferings of Jews in Lithuania and Iran, but in Palestine they now enjoyed every civil liberty. Yet they still refused to work or to embrace modern education. The failure was theirs and theirs alone. Even the Board of Deputies supported Montefiore's new appeal with reluctance, while Abraham Benisch's *Jewish Chronicle* renewed its call for a committee of practical men to consider "the feasibility of adopting means by

which industrial resources may be encouraged and the periodical inci-
dence of distress may be avoided."[4]

This willingness to impose European solutions arbitrarily on Palestine
was alien to Montefiore. Instead, he wrote formally to the heads of all
the Jewish congregations there, reiterating his longstanding desire "to
ameliorate your condition and cause salvation to spring forth in the
Holy Land by means of industrial pursuits, such as agriculture, mechanical work, or some suitable business, so as to enable both the man who
is not qualified for study, but fully able (by his physical strength) to work
as well as the student, who, prompted by a desire to maintain himself by
the labour of his hands, may be willing to devote the day to the work
necessary for the support of his family, and part of the night to the study
of the Law of God, to find the means of an honourable living." Recognizing that his proposals in 1839 and 1866 had made little impact in the
Jewish world, Montefiore wished to try to "ascertain whether any of
your suggestions regarding the best mode of ameliorating your condition . . . if clearly and distinctly set forth to our brethren [abroad], might
not, under present circumstances, be more favourably received."[5] The
attempt to modernize diaspora commitment to Palestine in collaboration with the Jews who lived there bore all the hallmarks of long experience. But it was precisely Montefiore's track record that gave his critics
cause for concern.

May and June saw a heated debate in the *Jewish Chronicle* about the
merits of Montefiore's earlier initiatives. Haim Guedalla's late father had
founded a yeshiva in Jerusalem. Drawing on his extensive local knowledge, Haim took it upon himself to defend his uncle's achievements.[6]
Guedalla pooh-poohed claims that the Montefiore windmill was a "useless object," that only six of Montefiore's almshouses had deserving tenants, and that one had even been put up for sale. The source of these allegations was an English Jew recently returned from Jerusalem.[7] Henry
Lumley was only too credible a witness. When the deputies met in late
June, they felt obliged to declare "unabated confidence in the wisdom
and alacrity evinced by its venerable President in aid of our poor and
suffering brethren in the Holy Land."[8]

The resolution was timely because the meeting was scheduled to discuss a letter that Montefiore had received from the son of his old traveling companion George Gawler. Now keeper of the crown jewels, John
Gawler was a military man and a Christian who had not forgotten his
father's millenarian vision. Montefiore was enthused by his ambitious
plans. "I feel a deep interest in the question now under consideration of
the London Committee of British Jews, for assisting our brethren to cul-

tivate land in Palestine," he wrote in his diary. "I am confident if capital could be raised for the purpose, the people, the country, and the contributors would all be greatly benefited by the work. I should suggest that a million sterling should be obtained by 1,000,000 of £1 subscriptions, and I believe I could obtain, within one year, that sum for the purpose from the Jews in the four quarters of the globe."[9] He gave Gawler such strong backing that the board was forced to take the proposals seriously.[10]

Jews already living in Palestine remained ambivalent. *Habazeleth* was the organ of the minority Hasidic community in Jerusalem. Unlike the *mitnagdim*, they warmly endorsed productivization and expected the younger generation of Jews there to embrace Gawler's plan. But even the supposedly radical *Habazeleth* wondered how Jewish colonies would survive "the large taxes that those working the land have to pay in our country" and the losses inevitably incurred by observant Jews, since "we cannot work the land all the days of the week, for we rest on the seventh day and in the seventh year we rest the land"—a problem only exacerbated by the many additional *mitzvot* incumbent on those dwelling in the land of Israel [*mitzvot hateluyot be'aretz*].[11]

Such doubts were seldom voiced by those in Palestine who responded to Montefiore's formal inquiries. Their replies included many collective petitions signed by large numbers of poor Jews, apparently overjoyed at his initiative and eager to engage in agriculture or "mechanical pursuits." They also included several letters from individual enthusiasts, all of whom noted the widespread availability of government land for sale and many of whom had their eye on a particular property. Some offered their services as local agents, others as mediators with the Ottoman authorities in Istanbul. A disciple of the hard-line Hungarian Rabbi Akiva Joseph Schlesinger also sent Montefiore a copy of the pamphlet *Kollel Ha'Ivrim*, in which Schlesinger outlined his vision for a Hebrew-speaking ultra-Orthodox utopia in the land of Israel. In the light of rumors that British Christians wished to restore Palestine to the Jews, this correspondent suggested that "[a]rrangements could easily be made for the payment of a fixed annual sum of money to the Ottoman Government for the possession of such a right, in the same way as has been done amongst other nations; this would, if carried out, be a stepping stone to the promised redemption of the Jews."[12]

Longtime residents of Jerusalem were more skeptical. Referring to the Society for the Promotion of the Return of the Crown [Torah] to Its Former Position, which Schlesinger had founded in Palestine, and to other, similar associations, one of Montefiore's most established contacts warned him that many leading figures would be eager to further

Montefiore in old age. *(Reproduced with the permission of The Rothschild Archive, London)*

his agricultural projects, "as they say it bespeaks the restoration and salvation of 'Judah and Jerusalem,' yet, according to my humble opinion, this is not the course that will prove successful with our community." For if the Jews were to work the land themselves and lodge in the villages he doubted "whether they would remain firm in their religion. Nor am I quite certain they could stand the amount of labour which would be imposed, and what would be their end?"[13]

Montefiore's definitive retirement as president of the Board of Deputies further complicated the situation. For years he had been hovering on the brink of this decision, repeatedly acceding to the board's earnest representations in a ritual of communal deference to his charismatic authority. Now he refused to reconsider. At least one deputy attributed Montefiore's resignation to "the unpleasant controversy in reference to the Holy Land."[14] Others rejected the imputation, but there was general agreement that it would be harder to move forward with the Holy Land scheme without him. Montefiore, meanwhile, continued to lobby for Gawler's proposals. This was his last chance to realize the dream of 1839; he intended to take it.

For the past thirty-five years the Holy Land had been central to Montefiore's preoccupations. His comfortable four-poster bed at Ramsgate was adorned with a perpetual reminder of his love for Zion: *Im eshkachekh Yerushalayim tishkah Yemini* (If I forget thee, O Jerusalem, let my right hand forget her cunning; Psalms 137:5). Back in 1839, Montefiore's desire to renew Jewish life in the Holy Land had coincided with the escalation of great-power rivalry in the Middle East under Palmerston, the birth of the Jewish press, and the faltering beginnings of a new wave of Jewish immigration to Palestine. Palmerston's death in 1865 and the explosion of international Jewish activism in the late 1860s had transformed the context in which Montefiore now operated.

Ever since the Damascus Affair, Jews in Palestine, Syria, and the rest of the Ottoman Empire had looked to Britain as a natural protector. Their instincts were justified so long as men like James Finn and Richard Wood saw the defense of Jewish rights as part of Britain's wider mission to spread Commerce, Christianity, and Civilization. The *Hatt-i Hümayun* of 1856 subtly changed this equation. With civil and religious liberty guaranteed under Ottoman law, why should the Jews of Palestine and Syria continue to demand (and receive) extraordinary British support?

It took time for the implications of the *Hatt* to become apparent. Consul James Finn had been an ardent philo-Semite: he did not need to be told that it was his duty to protect the Jews. Three years after Finn's dismissal in 1862, Montefiore received complaints that the system of extraordinary British protection for Russian Jews in Palestine was beginning to break down.[15] When the only genuinely British Jew in the country asked the government to extend this support to Russian Jewish protégés traveling on business in Syria, an unsympathetic Foreign Office questioned "whether Foreign Governments might not have a right to object to Persons, not in any sense being British subjects, being provided with British passports."[16] Montefiore wrote again in 1867, urging the government to reconsider the closure of its consulate in Haifa, which had left Russian Jews in Safed and Tiberias "in a worse position than if they were not under British protection at all." Lord Stanley, then foreign secretary, refused to comply. "[T]here were no British interests to protect & no British Trade to be defended" in Haifa; the British could hardly maintain the consulate for the Jews' benefit alone.[17]

Developments in Damascus further unsettled the situation. Ten years after the massacre of the Syrian Christians, *The Times* carried allegations that the city's Jews had attempted to foment another bloodbath.[18] Montefiore was sufficiently disturbed to publish an official denial. Capitalizing on his longstanding involvement with the Syrian Relief Fund, he hinted darkly at the behavior of "certain persons whose conduct has been hostile to my co-religionists in Damascus."[19] He was referring to the famous explorer and orientalist Richard Burton, best known for his classic translation of the *Arabian Nights*.

Burton had begun his professional life in the Indian Army, where he mastered local cultures and languages with such proficiency that he could pass among native peoples in disguise. After a decade of exploration in Africa and Arabia, he married and joined the diplomatic service. Damascus was the couple's dream post, and on his arrival in 1869 Burton soon resumed his old habit of disguise. Many of the Jewish elite had acquired British consular protection in the aftermath of the Damascus Affair. Burton's facility with Arab culture made him less sympathetic to their demands. When he publicly dissociated himself from their debt-collection practices, a few rich Jewish moneylenders wrote to Montefiore and Sir Francis Goldsmid accusing the new British consul of prejudice. The ensuing Foreign Office investigation found in favor of Burton, whose well-documented Judeophobia in later life inevitably casts doubt on this verdict.[20]

Barely two weeks after completing his report, the British official charged with the Damascus investigation raised the wider question of Britain's continued protection of foreign Jews. When Burton visited Tiberias and Safed to look into the matter further, he "found everything as

might be expected in a state of confusion, and the want of system . . .
complete." It soon transpired that only 670 of the 776 individuals in
Palestine claiming British protection were Russian Jews, of whom some
300 were descendants of those originally transferred to the British consulate under James Finn. With numbers growing all the time, Foreign
Secretary Granville considered the situation unsustainable. In the current political climate it also seemed unnecessary. The British ambassador in Constantinople was unconcerned to hear that many Jews were
too old to seek alternative protection, commenting dryly: "if I believed
such protection to be at all necessary to save them from persecution or
oppression, I should not recommend the withdrawal from them of that
of Her Majesty's Government."[21]

Protest from an alarmed Montefiore caused a slight delay in these proceedings. By this time the Porte had begun to voice concern about continued British protection for the wealthy Jews of Damascus. Times had
changed since the death of Father Tommaso, and "there was no further
necessity for the Jews of Damascus to appeal to the British Consul to
support them on every occasion that they get into trouble." Eager to be
rid of such a troublesome charge, and recognizing the transformation
wrought by the *Hatt-i Hümayun,* the British soon agreed to a mixed
commission investigating those claiming foreign nationality in Syria.
British protection for Russian Jews would be gradually phased out. To
the individuals concerned, this decision was an unqualified disaster; for
the community at large, it scarcely mattered.[22]

When Montefiore returned from the Holy Land in 1866, his calls for
a "general collection" to build homes in and near Jerusalem and to
sponsor Jewish agriculturalists near Safed had fallen on deaf ears. The
Board of Deputies lacked the funds to undertake anything ambitious
and feared "that a fresh call on public benevolence would not meet with
success so many claims having of late been urged on communal consideration."[23]

As the *Jewish Chronicle* commented, however, Montefiore's interest in
the Holy Land had been the catalyst for a more profound change in
diaspora attitudes. These feelings had assumed tangible form in northern Germany, where Kalischer and other members of the Kolonisationsverein were now promoting their own scheme for agricultural settlements—one already attracting the attention of both the Alliance Israélite
and Berlin readers of the Orthodox *Israelit.* When even the Geneva Protestant Henri Dunant, founder of the Red Cross, was lobbying for a
Jewish Palestine, it hardly behooved Anglo-Jewry to look on with in-

difference. Yet despite his longstanding commitment to Palestine, the *Chronicle*'s Abraham Benisch had little faith in these outside agencies: "If Jewish colonies are to be formed in the Holy Land, let them spring up spontaneously . . . Let us by all means encourage agriculture among the Jews in the Holy Land; let us offer them for the purpose every assistance in our power. But let us not waste our strength in the futile attempt to establish, under existing circumstances, Jewish colonies in the Holy Land, and thus draw thither emigrants whom we should neither have the means to support nor the power to protect."[24]

The years immediately following Montefiore's visit testified both to the vitality of the existing Jewish community in Palestine and to its evolving relationship with the diaspora. Early in 1867, for instance, a Parisian charity helped to establish a school in Jerusalem that taught Arabic and Torah studies to children orphaned by the cholera. It soon ran into difficulties with the ultra-Orthodox Ashkenazim, who put up defamatory posters, attacked its (non-Ashkenazi) students, and mobbed the house of the principal, shouting and sounding the *shofar* in excommunication.[25] A second school founded by the Alliance Israélite proved equally controversial. Indeed, events in Safed highlighted the way external organizations like the Alliance could exacerbate internal tensions, when a frustrated group of young men founded a branch and requested the central office in Paris to send them books banned by their own rabbinical authorities.[26]

Talk of Jewish agriculture aroused similar passions. The pages of the Hebrew-language press were filled with vitriolic debate about the merits of active messianism, the proposals of agricultural lobbyists based in Palestine, and the desperate pleas of would-be farmers. Then, in 1868, Charles Netter, the secretary-general of the Alliance Israélite, set out to see things for himself. He returned blaming the iniquitous distribution of *halukah* for social norms like early marriage and the high value accorded Talmud study, which impeded the community's economic and moral progress.[27] Attributing the failure of Montefiore's weaving initiative to the prevailing tariff regime, Netter considered agriculture more promising. Attributing the failure of Montefiore's orchard in Jaffa to the inexperience of the men put to work there, he advocated founding a modern agricultural school to train a new generation of farmers. Orthodox hard-liners and the circle around Montefiore kept their distance from Netter's initiative.[28] The Alliance—and much of the Jewish world—took up the idea with enthusiasm.[29]

At first the Frenchman went out of his way to deal respectfully with Montefiore; but as Netter's plans for an agricultural school at Jaffa gathered momentum, their relationship became increasingly acrimonious.

Contemporaries attempted to give credit to both parties by stressing Montefiore's role as a catalyst for the reawakening of Jewish interest in Palestine. "The *sar* Moses has sown countless seeds of charity in God's land . . . can he be blamed if a few of the grains he has sown failed to germinate?" asked *Habazeleth*. Others might have done more for Jerusalem in practical terms, but Montefiore "laid the cornerstone to all these great deeds in his own works when the country was still barren."[30]

The man who had done so much to redefine the idea of a world Jewish community and to place the land of Israel at its heart proved strangely unable to engage with this increasingly assertive—and global—Jewish public. Montefiore's political worldview had been forged in the voluntarism and extraparliamentary activism of the 1830s. It was rooted in the culture of antislavery and religious dissent that characterized middle-class British politics during the reform era. He was too old to adapt as the forces of democratization and popular politics gathered pace in the decades that followed. Montefiore successfully resisted these pressures at home, but in the wider Jewish world his prestige failed to compensate for his refusal to work with others once international Jewish activism came of age.

The universal rhetoric and flexible, inclusive politics of the Alliance were better suited to this era. No longer able to dictate the agenda, Montefiore risked becoming an irrelevance. His appeals on behalf of the Jews of Palestine continued to resonate with British Christians; elsewhere they met with short shrift.[31] "Once more a great famine in Jerusalem, appeals by the Haham Bashi, Sir Moses Montefiore and the chief rabbi, alarm in the newspapers, pious souls touched, charitable hearts moved, the same drama re-enacted, the same tears wept, the same grand finale as usual," the American *Israelite* had reported scathingly when Montefiore launched yet another fund-raising campaign in 1870. "We do not want saints in Jerusalem to pray or read the Talmud for our souls; we do not believe in it. We do not wish to support persons anywhere who do nothing, and think those persons are spoiled and ruined by our charity. We want the whole thing changed, radically changed."[32]

Such responses naturally fed into debate about the Alliance agricultural school in Jaffa, now up and running, and reportedly doing well. While Akiva Lehren of Pekam continued to rail against those who wished to work the land of Israel, Haim Guedalla accused Netter of stealing Montefiore's idea.[33] Netter responded smugly that "Sir Moses Montefiore, convinced that the Jews of Palestine are industrious, capable, skilful, and honest workers, [had] appealed in vain to the Jewish world to construct outside Jerusalem dwellings for the poor; and to purchase land near Safed in order to erect homes for sixty families, for whom cattle, agricultural implements, and grain would have been procured. The Alliance, convinced that the present generation did not have the above named qualifications, resolved on, and succeeded in, establishing a school of agriculture for the young."[34]

In this context the events of late 1874 were explosive. When the Board of Deputies resolved to establish a memorial fund to commemorate Montefiore's retirement as president, it took the unusual step of asking him what to do with the money. His answer was predictable. Needled by the successes of the Alliance, inspired by Gawler's ambitious proposals, and emboldened by the replies he had recently received from Palestine, Montefiore urged the board to devise a scheme to promote industry, build model houses, and acquire land on a moderate scale "in strict accordance as far as possible with their own suggestion in the letters they have earnestly addressed to me."[35]

Anglo-Jewry did not take kindly to this development. "Sir Moses Montefiore is as proud of being an Englishman as of being a Jew," wrote one correspondent of the *Jewish Chronicle,* "and the memorial—*as perennius*—of his many virtues should be established here rather than wasted abroad."[36] Forced to defend its support for the Sir Moses Montefiore Testimonial Fund, the *Chronicle* appealed to the "cosmopolitan" nature of the Jewish people, arguing that the focus on Palestine would "probably lead to the uniting of other nations with England in this testimonial. This should be so, especially as Sir MOSES MONTEFIORE's services belong as much to other countries as to ours." English Jews could not be blamed for their lack of enthusiasm, but since the Testimonial Fund was to be spent in the Holy Land they ought "to look at the matter in the best possible light and to regard it as a religious movement, one likely to be pleasing to him whom the Jews justly delight to honour."[37]

There was some truth in the claim that the universal significance of Jerusalem would appeal to multiple audiences. The *Sunday Telegraph* saw no reason why the Testimonial Fund would not attract "many Englishmen proud of the enthusiasm for freedom and justice which Sir Moses learned in our air, and glad of the lesson of universal charity which his life has taught." Montefiore's achievements in the East owed much to "the free land of his birth and abode," and nothing could be more fitting than this appeal on behalf of a city, which belonged "by undying and sacred associations to Christendom."[38] But the rhetoric of Christian imperialism and English liberty held no attractions for the Jews of eastern Europe, who saw the Testimonial Fund as a different kind of national enterprise. *Hamagid* did not wish to prevent Christians from contributing, but it stressed that the fund was a matter for the Jewish people, for Montefiore, and for the people on whose behalf the money was being collected. The fund was "not just the duty of English Jews but of Jews in the entire diaspora!"[39]

The reality failed to live up to such expectations. By May 1875 the committee had collected barely £7,000. It did not seem to matter that the Testimonial Fund was endorsed by religious and communal leaders in Britain, France, Germany, and America, or that the Orthodox *Halevanon,* the more progressive, Hasidic *Habazeleth,* and the nationally minded *Hamagid* all gave it their backing. Many Western Jews were disillusioned by Montefiore's failures and inclined to endorse Netter's agricultural school. Meanwhile, traditionalists in eastern Europe feared that Jewish agriculture would undermine the primary commitment to Torah study in the Holy Land. These suspicions were not unfounded. The Testimonial Fund committee was strikingly slow to tap this particular constituency—precisely because its members wished to investigate the situation for themselves.

Early in 1875 two pillars of the Anglo-Jewish community left for Palestine. Samuel Montagu was a successful banker in his early forties: rich, deeply religious, well known for his charitable work. His companion, Dr. Asher Asher, was secretary of the United Synagogue. Neither was an obvious troublemaker, and both could be expected to sympathize with the spiritual values of Jews living in the Holy Land. They returned from an intensive two-week tour appalled by what they had seen. Echoing the verdict of more secular visitors like Ludwig Frankl, Netter, and the German-Jewish historian Heinrich Graetz, Montagu and Asher deplored the lack of hygiene, the resistance to modern education, and the immoral practice of *halukah,* which inhibited perfectly capable men from earning their own living and cemented the hold of reactionary religious authorities over the whole community. The Sephardim were largely exempt from these criticisms, but the Ashkenazim had perpetuated a system of organized beggary that gave Jews all over the world a bad name.[40]

This was where Montagu and Asher differed from Montefiore. They did not rule out the prospects for Jewish agriculture; they explored the possibilities for industry and the need for handicraft education; they were enthusiastic about cheap credit, building societies, almshouses, and medical infrastructure. But they concluded that "[n]othing whatever of a permanent character can be effected for the good of the Jews of Jerusalem unless through a European Agency established in Jerusalem by the committee."[41]

Rumors of the report's content were widespread even before Montagu had completed it. By way of damage limitation Montefiore could only announce another mission to Palestine.[42] He followed the announcement with a rare visit to Bevis Marks and a well-publicized appearance at the Stepney Jewish Schools' prizegiving. Introducing his uncle, the aspiring liberal politician Arthur Cohen did not hesitate to address the controversy du jour.

[Y]ou have now before you a man who has done more to raise the name of Jew than any man during the last hundred years; and I do hope that if Sir Moses Montefiore does leave the shores of England in six or seven days, he will be accompanied by the unanimous and fervent prayers of all the Jewish community (Applause.) . . . because I tell you this: he goes not only to Tiberias, but he goes for reasons which, perhaps, in a few days you may learn, to vindicate the name of the Jews of Jerusalem—to show that the Jews of Jerusalem are worthy of your charity and worthy of your respect. And now let me warn you that in these days of modern civilization when we are trying to do some good, we are apt to fall into grievous mistakes. Some benevolent individuals would be anxious to transplant our modern civilization right off to Jerusalem, to set up shops at every corner, to drive away those pious men who think that there is something which their religion binds them to do when they pass the last days of a pious life in that sacred city. Now, I warn you this. If you wish to succour the Jews of Jerusalem you must enter into their spirit. You must not force upon them institutions which are perhaps suited neither to the climate nor to the genius of the inhabitants; but like a loving father who watches the capabilities and tendencies of his children, you must . . . study carefully the habits, the institutions and the customs of the Jews of Jerusalem and then do that which wisdom and experience may point out. If ever you hear people say that the Jews of Jerusalem are beggars and ignorant, tell them that the chief Rabbi, Sir Moses Montefiore, and Arthur Cohen . . . believe them to be otherwise. They point [sic] over their commentaries and over their Bible. They know the Arabic language; and if they do not know English and French, do we know Arabic and Mahometan languages? (Applause and laughter.)[43]

Cohen's speech may have been admirably free of cultural imperialism, but his nonjudgmental attitude was unlikely to appeal to men like Montagu and Netter, who believed that the European way of doing things was inevitably superior. Cohen himself probably agreed with them; but he owed his place at Cambridge to his uncle's intervention with its non-Jewish authorities, and his status in the Jewish community was too closely bound up with Montefiore for him to contemplate deserting the latter now. More genuinely sympathetic to the religious priorities of Jerusalem's Jews, Montefiore was, quite simply, moved. "He could not speak of all he felt on that occasion—he wished he could; but he would act . . . He hoped by God's blessing to bring soon his own report of the condition of the Jews of Jerusalem. He would like that all present could go with him to Jerusalem and see for themselves (Cheers.)"[44]

Montefiore's departure for Palestine was attended by all his usual rituals; the journey itself was remarkable for little other than the providentially fine weather. News of cholera was unsettling, but Montefiore believed that he had "a certain duty to perform—a duty owing to our Religion, to our beloved Brethren in the Holy Land." It is a *mitzvah* to die in the Holy Land, and the ninety-one-year-old Montefiore presumably felt little alarm at the prospect. He was overcome with elation when they finally steamed out of Alexandria. "God granted me his special blessing to find myself again on the road to Jerusalem; the sea was calm as a lake, not a ripple to be seen on its glowing mirror; the accommodation on board the ship, the readiness of the Austrian Captain and his officers to make every arrangement for our comfort, all contributed to make me utter heartfelt thanks to Him, who thus guided me."[45]

Awestruck by the sight of two massive steamers passing each other at the mouth of the (British-owned) Suez Canal, Montefiore was inevitably captivated by the new commercial opportunities it presented. But his first thought on disembarking was a more personal one. After doing his duty by the Jewish crowds that gathered in Jaffa to greet him, he paid his respects at Hodgkin's tomb before continuing to the country house of the British vice-consul, Haim Amzalak, where dinner was served "in the best European style." On his first visit to Jerusalem Montefiore had stayed with the consul's father, Joseph. He now rejoiced to see the son of his old acquaintance so honorably established. Too frail to venture out much in person, he held court from four large tents in Amzalak's garden. Montefiore was relieved to find that reports of the ruin of his orchard in Jaffa had been much exaggerated. With 900 of the original 1,407 trees still flourishing, he concluded that all the estate needed was considerably more investment. Confined to his tent by a knee injury, he found time to conduct a small experiment designed to refute claims that the Jews of Palestine were idle beggars.[46]

In Jerusalem, meanwhile, Montefiore's impending visit was compounding communal tensions. The deputies had suppressed the Montagu report in England, but *Habazeleth* began serializing a Hebrew translation to coincide with Montefiore's arrival in Jaffa.[47] Montefiore preferred to dwell on the signs of communal unity and entrepreneurial activity he encountered: the letter of welcome signed by representatives of all the different congregations; the thriving Jewish guesthouse serving travelers on the new carriage road between Jaffa and Jerusalem; the rabbis dressed as Bedouin who rode gaily out to greet him; and the sturdy Jewish porters communicating in a babel of European and oriental languages.

There was naïveté here, and a desire to report only the best to a skeptical British public. Montefiore's impressions were inevitably shaped by religious feeling and by his affection for key communal leaders, some of whom he had known for over thirty years. Writing in *Halevanon*, Benjamin Ze'ev Halevi Sapir described how the old man and his companion Loewe rent their clothes and burst into prayer when they caught sight of the domes of Jerusalem, and how Montefiore embraced and kissed his old friend Rabbi Samuel Salant when he finally reached Jerusalem. Yet Montefiore was genuinely amazed by the scale and pace of Jewish construction work outside the city walls: here was a house in Jewish hands, there a plot of land belonging to another member of the community; here were the fifty houses of the new settlement of Nahalat Shiva; there was an area designated for sixty more.[48] Only a few years earlier not a single Jewish family had lived outside the gates, "and now I beheld almost a new Jerusalem springing up, with buildings, some of them as fine as any in Europe. 'Surely,' I exclaimed, 'we are approaching the time to witness the realization of God's hallowed promises unto Zion!'"[49]

This exodus reflected the Jewish community's ability to move with the times—though not necessarily in a way that acknowledged the superiority of European civilization.[50] Jews in Britain, France, Germany, and America often lamented the fragmentation of the Jerusalem community into a multiplicity of congregations, but the habits of self-determination and communal autonomy acquired in the diaspora were also a strength. Taking their cue from Montefiore and Hausdorf, the much-maligned Ashkenazim led the way in the rush to build neighborhoods like Beit Ya'acov, Eben Israel, and Meah Shearim, where Montefiore was too ill to lay the foundation stone for a new row of houses.[51] Like most of the new quarters, it eventually became a byword for hard-line Jewish orthodoxy.

The building societies that financed these initiatives were entirely in keeping with the corporative voluntarism that was such a feature of the traditional Jewish world. Montefiore soon discovered that Jerusalem was home to well over thirty charitable societies, including a soup kitchen run entirely by women, loan societies, hostels for Jewish pilgrims, burial societies, associations for visiting the sick, and dowry funds for impoverished men and women.[52] Western visitors tended to disregard this rich diversity of associational life because it was dominated by

The almshouses built by Montefiore in Jerusalem, with some inhabitants.
(Courtesy of Mishkenot Sha'ananim, Jerusalem)

the religious leadership, which they perceived as reactionary and self-seeking. Their instinctive dislike of the *halukah* system also blinded them to the brutal realities of life in Palestine. As *Halevanon* put it, "If our brothers who care for Jerusalem know how barren the land is, and who destroys and ruins it, they will understand why those who love Zion see the very barren ways of Zion when they come to Jerusalem, but also the good in the cherished children of Zion. But those whose ways are different from ours see an inverted world"[53]

Montefiore had set out to vindicate the Jews who lived in Palestine.

His recommendations for the future were the same as ever; he returned still convinced that "[t]he Jews in Jerusalem, in every part of the Holy Land . . . do work; are more industrious even than many men in Europe, otherwise none of them would remain alive."[54] This consistency in outlook was only to be expected. The views of Dr. Bernhard Neumann, who managed the Rothschild hospital for twenty years, carry greater weight. In his 1877 memoirs, Neumann condemned the false reports circulated by European visitors, whose fleeting visits and inability to communicate with the Jewish inhabitants led them to set too much store by the black propaganda emanating from the Protestant mission to the Jews. Far from living in idleness on the generosity of others, most Jews in Jerusalem were businessmen and artisans, "well known as the most reliable and hard working in the town." Like Montefiore, Neumann sympathized with their spiritual values. No one moved to the holy city for economic reasons. Men who had sacrificed everything to lead religious lives would naturally "strive to pass on the traditional religious ways of their fathers undiminished to their children and consequently fear an invasion of new religious ideas."[55]

As ever, Montefiore's return to Britain prompted general acclamation. His appearance at a thanksgiving service in the Great Synagogue occasioned scenes of "the wildest excitement" as throngs of worshippers inside the building—and crowds of enthusiasts outside—eagerly sought the opportunity to clasp him by the hand. Two policemen and a volunteer managed to clear a passage, enabling Montefiore to make his way through the streets amid prolonged and intense cheering. This continued even after Montefiore had vanished into No. 14 Bevis Marks. He eventually reappeared at the window and took off his hat, saying, "God bless you, pray for Jerusalem." Hats were taken off, caps thrown into the air, and handkerchiefs waved until the crowd finally began to disperse.[56]

Enthusiasm for the man did not extend to his pet project. "The name of Sir Moses is reverenced and affectionately remembered by the continental Jews, and yet little money comparatively reaches England from them in aid of the Fund," noted the *Jewish Chronicle*. "What *can* be the reason? It is said that while it was first expected that the fund would reach over £100,000, the committee will be glad now if £10,000 be received. This sum would be almost useless for carrying out the objects for which the fund is being raised."[57]

In Jerusalem, meanwhile, the editor of *Habazeleth* expressed his concern about Montefiore's collusion with those in power.[58] Instead of conducting meaningful enquiries or speaking to the disfranchised, he had left the house only three times and had allowed the leaders of the Perushim community to dictate his report. *Hamagid* reported similar grumblings among eastern European supporters of the Testimonial Fund. Its editor counseled patience: Montefiore might conceal the sins of the few out of concern for the reputation of the many, but the money was not his to spend as he chose. "The heads of the London community have made a public appeal to the Jews of the whole world, and they surely will not lend themselves to an injustice. If they have done Sir Moses the honour to consult him as to the form which the Testimonial shall take, they have not handed over to his management the whole affair."[59]

This, indeed, was the nub of the problem. With £375,000 to his name and no children to inherit it, Montefiore did not need to appeal to a global Jewish public in order to build houses, buy land, or establish agricultural colonies.[60] Yet his earlier initiatives had failed for the lack of paltry sums. Contemporaries never addressed this question outright, but Montefiore's reluctance to invest much of his own money was hardly a vote of confidence. Just £1,200 a year would have kept both the weaving institution and the girls' school running. Since he could easily have afforded to support both institutions personally, we have to ask why he did not—and why he failed to use his great wealth to fund more permanent change in Palestine as Baron Edmond de Rothschild did in a later generation.[61]

The answer is perhaps that Montefiore believed such initiatives were valueless without public backing—and that he was always more interested in the process of giving than in the end result. But it is fair to say that Montefiore lacked the clarity of vision that motivated both traditionalist hard-liners like Zvi Hirsch Lehren and aggressive modernizers like Ludwig Frankl. Torn between a Victorian belief in self-sufficiency, the Jewish commitment to prayer and Torah study in the Holy Land, and an activist messianic vision, he was unable to commit to any one line of action or to formulate anything approaching a coherent plan. His 1839 plans for agricultural colonization were radical but unrealistic. This was the only time he really set the agenda. The older he grew, the more he found himself the prisoner of others' proposals—reacting to humanitarian crises, fielding public criticism, and struggling to maintain his primacy once wealthy Jewish leaders like the Rothschilds and Baron Hirsch began to invest serious money in their own, better-thought-through schemes.

Obsessive about detail, absurdly careful in his paperwork, obstinate and dictatorial in his dealings with others, Montefiore may also have lacked faith in the ability of future generations to remain true to his preoccupations. As he once remarked in a different context, "trusts connected with charitable or strictly religious institutions are more liable than others to be, if not strictly misappropriated, at least misdirected, though it may probably be unintentional, more especially when the religious views of the trustees differ form those of the testator."[62]

Given the nature of Montefiore's views about the Holy Land, such an outcome would have been almost inevitable. The report of this, his seventh and final pilgrimage to Palestine, was published in early 1876, along with "An Open Letter" from Rabbis Auerbach and Salant—personal friends perhaps, but also the main targets of the anti-*halukah* party. This combination, as the *Jewish Chronicle* admitted, did not make a good impression. *Habazeleth* blamed Loewe for allowing Montefiore to be manipulated by the Perushim—and likened him to a misguided father who loves his son so much that he listens to the advice of those who do not actually understand his needs. The old man meant well, but he was now the tool of his entourage.[63]

Rhetoric aside, Montefiore's call to build houses and found agricultural colonies differed from the Montagu report only over the desirability or otherwise of secular education. The Testimonial Fund Committee therefore had little difficulty agreeing to spend its (rather limited) resources on buying land, building houses, providing cheap credit, and helping the able-bodied inhabitants to make a living through trade and agriculture.[64] But who would administer the money? The *Jewish Chronicle* was adamant that it must be "entrusted to European agents, one of whom should take up his residence in the Holy Land, and be responsible to the Executive for the management."[65] This had been Montagu's original proposal. When he persuaded the other committee members to support it, Haim Guedalla resigned in disgust.[66] The fund still carried Montefiore's name, but it now represented the defeat of everything he stood for.

No sooner had the committee appointed its agent than it found itself overtaken by events.[67] The Ottoman Empire had been in crisis since 1874, when the outbreak of a peasant revolt in Herzegovina sparked rebellion in the Balkans. Austria, Germany, and Russia failed to impose a settlement, leaving the sultan little alternative but to send troops. Thousands of Christian refugees then began to flee to Serbia, Montenegro, and Austria. Britain remained aloof until 1876, when the crisis began to spread to Bulgaria. Here the outbreak of a nationalist uprising saw waves of massacre and countermassacre between Muslim and Christian villagers. One thousand Muslims and anything between 3,000 and 12,000 Christians died during this first round of atrocities; in the long run, the Muslim dead would greatly outnumber Christian victims. For the time being, however, vastly inflated claims that fanatical Muslims had slaughtered between 30,000 and 100,000 Christian villagers soon transfixed the European public. In Britain, outrage over the "Bulgarian atrocities" became one of the great semireligious, semipolitical agitations of the age. More than 500 public meetings were held within six weeks. When Gladstone wrote a pamphlet on the subject, he sold 200,000 copies in less than a month.[68]

Such movements had been a staple of British politics since the abolition of the slave trade. Operating on Parliament and the public from outside the ordinary party system, they provided an outlet for classes that had inherited little traditional political power and whose political sensibilities were shaped by the Evangelical revival. Richard Cobden had drawn on this moral and religious spirit in the Corn Laws agitation of the 1840s, and Montefiore repeatedly appealed to the same constituency when he deployed the language of civil and religious liberty in the name of international Jewish relief. His success reflected the hegemony of Palmerstonian foreign policy, which combined defense of the Ottoman Empire with gunboat diplomacy and the rhetoric of British liberty. Now the liberal gloss applied to British realpolitik was beginning to wear thin. Russian influence in the Balkans no longer seemed such a threat to European liberties, while periodic outbreaks of violence against Ottoman Christians reinforced perceptions of "Turkish barbarism."

The Bulgarian agitation of 1876 culminated in the great National Conference on the Eastern Question held in Piccadilly, which attracted a glittering array of religious, intellectual, and political figures—men like the son of Sir Thomas Fowell Buxton, Montefiore's old friend and business associate, who only three years earlier had appeared on a similar platform to express solidarity with Romanian Jews. The readiness of Buxton and Gladstone to invoke parallels with slavery highlighted continuities between the two movements. This new political constellation threatened to unpick the political alliance Montefiore had assembled over the years. In theory, there was no contradiction between Jewish and Christian calls upon the humanitarian conscience. In reality, Jews and Christians had conflicting interests in the East, and their brethren in Britain took opposite sides.

As war raged in the Balkans many Jews held aloof from the agitation, but in January 1877 Montefiore contributed £100 to the Stafford House Relief Fund in aid of wounded Turkish soldiers. In a covering letter to the Ottoman ambassador, he welcomed "the opportunity now presented to me to evince my gratitude to the Turkish Government for the kind and effective protection they have at all times extended to my coreligionists." The Turcophile *Daily Telegraph* was second to none in its longstanding admiration for Montefiore. Even now it unquestioningly deferred to his judgment, noting that Montefiore had devoted much of his life to the condition of Jews in the East and their persecution at the hands of Eastern Christians. "What then becomes of the charges made against Ottoman intolerance, and of the allegations that solemn decrees are mere waste paper? Here is a case where the charter of religious liberty granted by the Sultan is vouched for, by one who is as well qualified as any man to speak of the facts, to have been amply, efficaciously and righteously observed."[69]

Benjamin Disraeli had inherited the mantle of Palmerston in foreign policy. His presence at the helm of the Conservative government was an added irritant to Gladstone and his supporters, who portrayed Disraeli's pragmatic view of the Eastern Question as contrary to the national interest and un-Christian. The premier was, of course, an Anglican; yet he had cultivated the mystique of his Jewish origins through novels like *Tancred*, and his opponents readily attributed his stance on the Eastern Question to racial sympathies. "[A]s long as Lord Beaconsfield is Prime Minister we are not safe," warned the Anglo-Catholic canon of St. Paul's Cathedral, Henry Liddon. "His one positive passion is that of upholding Asiatics against Europeans—non-Christian Asiatics against Christian Europeans." The radical historian and liberal Edward Augustus Freeman went further in his 1877 pamphlet on the Eastern Question. Noting that the pro-Ottoman press was almost invariably in Jewish hands, he stated categorically that "everywhere, with the smallest class of exceptions . . . the Jew is the friend of the Turk and the enemy of the Christian." Disraeli's sympathy with the Jews was perfectly understandable. "But we cannot sacrifice our own people, the people of Aryan and Christian Europe, to the most genuine belief in Asian mystery. We cannot have England or Europe governed by a Hebrew policy."[70]

The presence of prominent Jews like Montefiore, Goldsmid, Baron Henry de Worms, and Sir Albert Sassoon on the committee of the Turkish soldiers' relief fund reinforced such prejudices. But the poisonous atmosphere also reflected more deep-rooted changes in British society: resentment at the rise of a well-connected Jewish plutocracy; the reaction against Evangelicalism and the emergence of a more liberal theology that dissociated Christianity from its Old Testament origins; a tendency to look to the Greeks rather than the Jews for the origins of Victorian civilization; and the emergence of race as a powerful new mode of social analysis.[71] These were gradual processes, for which the

Bulgarian agitation acted as something of a turning point. They did not displace existing pockets of restorationism and philo-Semitism overnight.

After the disappointment of the Montefiore Testimonial Fund, John Gawler and other enthusiasts for Jewish agriculture had founded their own society to "promote the colonization of Syria and Palestine by persons of good character (more especially Jews)." The warm reception allegedly accorded them by the Ottoman ambassador in December 1875 encouraged Montefiore to hope that "notwithstanding the present disinclination of the Testimonial Committee to encourage agriculture, the time might yet arrive when they would gladly avail themselves of a favourable opportunity to promote his long cherished scheme."[72]

Mobilization by the holders of devalued Turkish bonds lent weight to such initiatives. Once again, it seemed that crisis in the Ottoman Empire might play to the restorationists' advantage. In January 1876 the *Jewish Chronicle* published a letter from Jerusalem floating the possibility that uncultivated government land in Palestine could be exchanged for defaulted government bonds worth 10 million francs nominal value.[73] In April the English committee of Turkish bondholders took up the idea under Guedalla's leadership, and the *Chronicle* intimated that the matter was under consideration by the Ottoman grand vizier.[74] Rumors were soon widespread that Guedalla had offered eight million pounds sterling for Syria "on behalf of the Jews of England, France and Austria." That July—at the height of the Bulgarian agitation—he wrote into the *Jewish Chronicle,* suggesting that the convergence of the Testimonial Fund with the bondholders' proposal represented "the finger of God." George Eliot's publication of *Daniel Deronda* that very month had drawn public attention to this vision of "a new Judea, poised between East and West." Guedalla raised the question at this time of crisis so "that a plan may be elaborated by the heads of the Jews of various countries at a congress of their body."[75]

There was nothing really new about these proposals. As in 1840 and 1856, the eccentric hopes of restorationists and Jewish activists like Montefiore, Guedalla, and Benisch came to nothing. The latter were, in any case, a tiny minority. "If Palestine should be purchased, who is to go there?" asked the Cincinnati *Israelite* in the aftermath of the crisis. "The American Jew is an American to all intents and purposes. So is the English Jew an Englishman, the French Jew a Frenchman, and the same is the case in Germany, Hungary, Italy, and also in Russia . . . If one believes that the Jews would go to Palestine if that country was purchased by Jewish capitalists and made a quasi Jewish country, he is gravely mistaken. The Jew's nationality is not endemic; it is not conditioned by space, land or water."[76] By this time, the window of opportunity had closed.

Sultan Abdul Aziz had been deposed in June 1876 and a constitutional monarchy instituted, but Russian intervention in the ongoing Balkan crisis led to military defeat and unconditional surrender for the new Ottoman regime. The Treaty of San Stefano of 1878 allowed Russia uninhibited access to the Dardanelles and paved the way for Russian domination of the Orthodox Balkans as Romania, Serbia, and Montenegro all achieved independence while a vastly expanded Bulgaria gained full autonomy. These gains were unacceptable to the other great powers. With European war an inevitability if the Russians refused to reconsider this settlement, Bismarck maneuvered for a comprehensive renegotiation in Berlin. As a result of the Treaty of Berlin of 1878, the Ottoman Empire still lost two-fifths of its territory and one-fifth of its population, but British interests were protected by Austrian expansion, the fragmentation of Bulgaria, and limitations on the Russian military presence. It was Disraeli's finest hour.

This outcome was relevant to the Jews—though not in the way that Guedalla expected. Of the many causes that preoccupied Jewish activists in the 1860s and 1870s, the long-running drama of Romanian Jewry had come closest to generating united action. It provided a focus for two pioneering conferences in 1872 and 1876, bringing together first thirty, then sixty-five Jewish delegates from nine countries. One thing on which they could all agree was that the great-power guarantee of Romanian autonomy provided a vehicle for linking existing international treaties with the defense of the country's Jews. In the aftermath of the Romanian declaration of independence the Congress of Berlin presented a last-ditch opportunity for Jewish activists to persuade the powers to enforce respect for Jewish rights. From this perspective, it was a triumph. Formally guaranteeing the religious, civil, and political rights of Jews and other minorities in the Balkans under international law, article 44 of the Treaty of Berlin marked a caesura in the history of human rights.[77] The challenge of enforcing its provisions in the teeth of Romanian resistance would open a new (and disappointing) chapter in the evolution of humanitarian intervention.

This landmark development owed more to the old-fashioned influence of the Court Jew than it did to the activities of a modern Jewish lobby. The key figure behind the scenes was Bismarck's banker, Gerson von Bleichröder, who had written proudly to Montefiore, "in my modest way I am following in your footsteps and likewise concern myself with a warm heart for our poor coreligionists on the Danube. I have succeeded in gaining the weighty support of Prince Bismarck for our troubled coreligionists in Rumania, and in accord with his humane outlook he has promised to put his whole weight behind the demand for the equality of all religions at the Congress which we hope will meet soon." Montefiore assured him that the British government "had expressed its earnest desire to see the principles of justice and religious toleration applied in all their integrity to the Jews of Rumania, and its intention to use its best endeavors to effect this object." As always, he was willing to come to Berlin in person; in the event, his services were not required.[78]

Bleichröder was right to see the connection between this initiative and Montefiore's own activities. If the Treaty of Berlin provided an entirely new legal framework for addressing the issues of minority rights internationally, this framework was still a product of international Jewish activism: it had been formulated, above all, for the Jews. That Montefiore was no longer a central player should not detract from his pivotal role in creating the preconditions that enabled Bleichröder to act. Montefiore remained in many ways the embodiment of international Jewish activism even if, in practice, his contribution had been no more (and no less) pioneering than that of men like Philippson and Crémieux.

On Tuesday, July 16, 1878, Disraeli returned to London from Berlin. A crimson viewing gallery had been set up against one wall of the railway station, and the whole platform was festooned with flowers. The *Daily Telegraph*, which had so steadfastly supported his Eastern policy, retailed in gushing tones how a heaving mass of men and women mobbed the prime minister and followed his carriage out under the archway until their cheers were drowned out by the those of crowds lining the route to Downing Street as "voices from north, south, east, and west converged in a national and Trafalgar Square chorus." The ninety-five-year-old Montefiore was also present, and the *Telegraph* described how Disraeli "grasped him warmly by the hand, and seemed delighted with the kindly veteran's welcome."[79]

Opponents of Disraeli interpreted the incident in a more sinister light. For the radical journalist T. P. O'Connor, it revealed "the meaning of the apotheosis of Lord Beaconsfield by a Christian people . . . That day represented the triumph not of England, not of an English policy, not of an Englishman. It was the triumph of Judea, a Jewish policy, a Jew. The Hebrew, who drove through those crowds to Downing Street, was dragging the whole of Christendom behind the Juggernaut car over the rights of the Turkish Christendom, of which he was the charioteer."[80] By sharing so publicly in Disraeli's triumph, Montefiore made himself a target for the new British anti-Semitism—and added fuel to the fire.

Chapter 19

End of an Era

Ramsgate. 1883. A foggy morning. The sun was just beginning to break through the clouds at nine o'clock, when sixty church singers and schoolchildren gathered on the lawn at East Cliff Lodge to serenade Montefiore on entering his hundredth year. They began with Hebrew hymns and moved on to "God Save the Queen" and "Rule, Britannia." The old man sat by the great bay window looking out to sea and listened as an endless stream of telegrams arrived at his door. The good wishes of Queen Victoria mattered most to him, but postal clerks struggled more with the barrage of congratulations from abroad, often in foreign languages and sometimes containing hundreds of words—so many that the vast bulk had to be left unopened. Whole vans of boxes came up to the house from the station, containing works of art, floral tributes, and exotic fruit. Special trains from London and elsewhere began to disgorge day-trippers; the post office and railway companies had taken on extra staff to cope with the workload, while 100 additional police constables patrolled the town.[1]

Bunting waved gaily upon the craft in the Royal Harbour. The little Kentish port was festooned with flags, banners, and ambitious triumphal arches emblazoned with the mottoes "All nations honour him, all honour to Israel's patriot," "All honour to Sir Moses, the mariner's friend," and "Honour to the wedded life of Sir Moses and Lady Judith." The streets were soon filled with people, the fields between East Cliff Lodge and the synagogue so crowded that guests could hardly make their way to the special thanksgiving service. But the central event of the day was a 5,000-strong procession. Aldermen, military bands, policemen, Freemasons, coast guards, lifeboatmen, Oddfellows, firemen, sailors and operators of fishing smacks, temperance campaigners, schoolchildren, Sunday School children, and a few Jewish delegations all

403

presented themselves in turn before Montefiore's window, lowering their
flags and cheering loudly. No one could remember the last time a private
individual had attracted such an overwhelming display of affection.
Standing on the balcony, the hero of the day lifted his black velvet skullcap and waved repeatedly. He tried several times to address a few words
to the crowd, but found himself too overcome to speak.

The house itself was jam-packed with visitors. Montefiore received
deputation after deputation in his bedroom, finding a good word for
them all. To the directors of the South-Eastern and Metropolitan Railway Companies, he spoke of the railways' contribution to humanity and
his own (considerable) traveling experiences, assuring them that "he felt
himself to be a young man of certainly not more than 60." To the delegation from the Isle of Thanet Union, a workhouse, he declared that
he "loved the inmates of the Union as much as if they were his richest
neighbours, and he prayed God Almighty might bless them." To the life-
boat representatives, he promised that he "always thinks of them &
prays for their safety." To the Jew come especially from Poland, he said
he "was sure that the present Czar wished to do all he could on the right
side, 'Why shouldn't he, haven't we sixty thousand brave boys in his
army?'" And to the head of the Spanish and Portuguese Jews' Board
of Guardians he said: "Do you think I could forget you and your dear
wife? Your wife is a good woman, and you are a good fellow. God bless
you." His doctor worried about the exhaustion of it all, but Montefiore
was exhilarated.

Reflecting on his employer's life and work in a public lecture at Judith
College that evening, Loewe highlighted his visionary commitment to
Jewish agriculture in Palestine, his efforts to promote the vernacular and
"[e]ducation based on sound principles of religion," his encouragement
of industry in Palestine, and his concern for medical care there. In an
age of increasing racial hatred, those who sought to honor Montefiore
should follow in his footsteps "because Sir Moses is a man who has
shown all his life no difference between one race of human beings and
another in all his acts of benevolence." Many in America had already
founded schools, hospitals, or asylums for the poor in his name; such
institutions should aim "to implant brotherly love in the heart of every
inmate, patient, pupil or fellow-worshipper." And because Montefiore
had extended his benevolence to other parts of the world—especially
the Holy Land—"everyone of his friends" should think particularly of
those who had fled the pogroms in Russia for Palestine to build a new
life cultivating the land. "So many thousands of pounds have been devoted to the sending of hundreds of sufferers from persecution to America, and why should not those who steadfastly adhere to their religion,

Punch's *Fancy Portraits, No. 161 (1883):* "Sir Moses Montefiore, a 'Hebrew of the Hebrews,' Who, on the 8th day of Chesvan (i.e., Nov. 8, "very Old Style"), enters on the Hundredth Year of his blameless, brave, and universally beneficent Life." (Courtesy of St. Catherine's College, University of Oxford)

for which reason they preferred the Holy Land to the New World, receive a similar amount of support?"[2]

This was the terrible irony of 8 *Heshvan* 1883. Ramsgate and the Isle of Thanet had done their duty by Montefiore's ninety-ninth birthday; in the words of the *Jewish Chronicle,* they spoke "not for themselves only, but for the nation generally; and not for the nation alone, but for *civilised humanity in all parts of the world.*"[3] But Montefiore's life could no longer be taken to symbolize the triumph of "civilised humanity" over prejudice and intolerance. He had been five years old at the outbreak of the French Revolution, came of age in the year of Trafalgar, was thirty-one at Waterloo; he had seen the coming of railways and the telegraph, the extension of the franchise, the unification of Germany and Italy, the Crimean, Austro-Prussian, and Franco-German Wars. These changes found their echo in the condition of his own people when nation after nation granted civil and political rights to their Jews. As the *Chronicle* itself noted, however, Montefiore had also lived to see "a reaction from these emancipatory movements." But even "present day Jew-haters" were "careful to exclude Sir MOSES from the catalogue of crimes with which they charge our race. And, thank God, he is still among us, the best refutation of Anti-Semitism."[4]

The Times, which had published an admiring biography of Montefiore

and devoted a leading article to his ninety-ninth birthday, was more ambivalent about recent developments. It saw German anti-Semitism as
testimony to the Jews' disproportionate success: "their power in Europe
is very great and far-reaching. Much of the Continental Press is in their
hands. They control the Bourses. National financial operations are regarded by them as to a great extent their own affair."⁵ This exaggerated
misconception of alien influence lay at the heart of much anti-Jewish
feeling. There was a double-edged quality to Punch's portrayal of Montefiore as a "Hebrew of the Hebrews"—a blameless old man with a
bag full of charity, who looked nonetheless like the archetypal money-
grabbing Jew. The liberal *Spectator* had similarly grudging praise for
Montefiore: "the Jew philanthropist," who "attended to his own people
first, but . . . displayed no narrowness, or tribal exclusiveness."⁶ Oswald
Simon, a staunch Jewish "Liberal of the advanced school," protested at
the disparaging way in which his favorite periodical discussed both Jews
and Judaism.⁷ *The Spectator*'s editor replied with an article combining
praise and blame in equal measure:

> [W]e deny any disrespect for Judaism which, though now encumbered
> with a partly meaningless ritual, and chilled in its inner life by doubts of
> its own divine origin, is essentially a noble though insufficient creed . . .
> we have for a quarter of a century past contended for the total release of
> the Jews in all countries, and under all circumstances, from any disabili-
> ties whatever, holding that absorption will be the most rapid cure for
> their tribal exclusiveness, which, nevertheless, we have never denied their
> right . . . to maintain. We think them wrong, and wrong also in avoiding
> the usual occupations of mankind and seeking to live solely as distribu-
> tors; but that is their own affair. That they will in the end, as a new and
> exclusive caste of aristocrats, possessed of too large a share of wealth,
> exercising too much power, and adding too little to the world's resources
> in return, draw down on themselves the angry attention of the democra-
> cies of the world, is, in our judgment, certain . . .
>
> . . . Jews have now risen so high in Europe that . . . they are sensitively
> alive to any mention which implies that they are separate from other na-
> tions; but why not accept the separateness, and, as Sir Moses Montefiore
> has done . . . make it a claim to honour? . . . he would not as an ordinary
> philanthropic Englishman or American, have received half the honour
> paid to him last week. The wires did not quicken with telegrams when
> Mr. [George] Peabody died.⁸

Living at East Cliff, Montefiore was partly insulated from such invec-
tive. Everyone in Ramsgate knew old Sir Moses: his support for the life-

boatmen and local churches; his grand philanthropic gestures on patriotic occasions; his regular visits to schools and workhouses; the thoughtful gifts of food and money he distributed to the inmates and their children in person; the words of comfort and encouragement he gave the elderly. All this was legendary, and the locals loved him for it.[9]

Without him, Ramsgate would have been just an ordinary working port with little but sea and sand to recommend it. The white neo-Gothic house on the cliffs with its neighboring synagogue and college were famous the world over, while the glamor of Sir Moses brought crowds of well-heeled Jewish holidaymakers.[10] Tourists could pray in Montefiore's synagogue. They might even glimpse one of his exotic visitors—someone like the Persian Jew, who arrived in flowing robes and turban under the impression that Eastern standards of hospitality would guarantee him a bed in East Cliff Lodge.[11] Not for nothing was Montefiore's bust for sale in the Royal Albion Bazaar for 2s 6d.[12] The handful of Jewish schools, the growing number of Jewish boardinghouses, the weekly lectures at the Judith College: all gave the town an unexpected cachet.

It was here that Montefiore spent his belated retirement. If he had ever paid irregular visits to an illegitimate son, he was now too old to venture out alone.[13] Instead, his days passed regular as clockwork.[14] Awake with the dawn, he would drink a cup of tea, hear someone read a little—and fall asleep again until eight or half-past. Whereupon he dressed (carefully like the Regency buck he still was) in a skullcap, blue silk dressing-gown, and the frilled shirt and stiff collar fashionable fifty years earlier. First prayers, then breakfast: a cup of milk and bread, mixed with two raw egg yolks and a dash of rum. Next came the morning papers—current affairs, but also the financial markets in which he retained a compulsive interest; after that, a drive in his carriage and perhaps a walk on Margate pier. Then for lunch Montefiore would take beef tea and a few shredded vegetables, helped down by a couple of glasses of port. (He reputedly drank a bottle a day.)[15]

The afternoons were devoted to his extensive correspondence, a mammoth task that was regularly interrupted by social callers. A little soup, a mouthful of meat, fruit, more port, and at half-past nine he retired to bed. There, Montefiore wound up the day with a few slices of bread and butter sprinkled with grated cheese, and a cup of milk. Sometimes he wrote an entry in his diary, adding a few shaky words to the latest in the series of neatly bound red volumes kept locked in the Gothic Library alongside the busts and portraits of his friends.[16] Usually he read a favorite chapter of Cicero's *De Senectute* or a page of Christian Sturm's *Reflections on the Works of God*. Only then was it time for sleep.

Despite this seemingly monotonous existence, most who met Montefiore in his early nineties were struck by his extraordinary vitality. His secretary P. B. Benny attested that he was "in the very flower of a vigorous old age, hale and hearty, erect and strong, using ten-pound leaden dumb-bells every morning before putting the finishing touch to his toilet; still active and able to walk about, in something more than full possession of his faculties, his memory as retentive as ever, a capital talker, the very pink of courtesy—courtesy tinged with old-fashioned gallantry —and the very best of good company."[17]

Ten years later, his biographer Lucien Wolf recalled Montefiore "in the enjoyment of health, genial as ever, a cordial host, and a delightful conversationalist . . . His interest in public affairs is still intelligent and keen, and he is a wide reader of newspapers and periodicals. All his letters have his personal attention, and he directs every detail of the work of his secretaries."[18] But Montefiore's only surviving diary from these years gives a very different picture.

"Arthur M. Sebag came to remain a couple of days with me," he writes on February 14, 1879. "I am greatly depressed at the loss of my truly & painfully lamented dear Judith how I feel the loss more & more every hour." On March 20 he continues: "Week [sic] & poorly. Dr. Walter came at 4 O'Clock. Not to work so much." By April 17 he is more optimistic: "May the God of our Fathers Abraham, Isaac & Jacob renew my strength to enable me to perform good & worthy deeds for the benefit of my Co-religionists & all of God's Sons & Daughters. This day I had the happiness to leave the house the first time for some weeks but I feel extremely weak." His gloom has returned on April 25, when he is "very poorly all day & instead [of?] preparing for Sabbath was obliged to go to bed. I had invited the Gentlemen of Judith's College also [?] but sent them an apology." "I have been all day extremely poorly dreadfully weak," he writes again on May 5; "Arthur Cohen left at 8 Clock this morng & Jemima Guedalla at 1/2 past Eleven after Prayers. I regret I was far too poorly to entertain them as I could wish. I am old and weak & cannot bear sudden agitation & I must not expose myself to many visitors." A week later he is well enough to drive out in his carriage, but May 25 finds him once again "very weak & disquieted without thanks God any cause whatever for such feelings." Not until May 28 is he well enough to attend prayers in his own synagogue. "Praised be to the God of our Fathers Abraham Isaac & Jacob," he writes in an unusually full entry on May 29; "I had the great Happiness to attend our synagogue this morg & was called to the *Sefer Torah*. Dear Dear Jud how severely & painfully did I feel the heavy loss it had pleased God to afflict me, by Calling you[?] careful guide of me but the Lord gave the Lord hath taken away. Blessed be the name of the Lord."[19]

This was the reality of Montefiore's final years: a frail old man, who

The former Gothic Library at East Cliff Lodge, where Montefiore spent so many of his final years. The photograph was taken in the 1930s, shortly before the house was sold. (Courtesy of the Spanish and Portuguese Jews' Congregation, London)

hankered after his long-dead Judith and never failed to preach matrimony to his young visitors; an isolated old man, bereft of legitimate offspring, who had outlived his generation; a man so old that even his nephews were dying around him; a lonely man now, dependent on the devotion of paid subordinates, for whom the death of each longstanding acquaintance—friend, relative, neighboring Christian cleric—came as "a dagger" to his heart; a man who lived much in the past, regaling his greatnieces and -nephews and the descendants of long-dead business associates with tales of his adventures, "never altering details in the anecdotes," which he told over and over again.[20] Not that he was cut off from events: far from it. Sitting in the Gothic Library or, in later years, in his bedroom among the portraits of his beloved dead, Montefiore spent hours listening to letters from the leading Jews of the world. They brought bleak news.

For decades Montefiore had believed that his struggle for Jewish relief carried God's blessing; now the tide of history seemed to be flowing in reverse. The racist rhetoric that had plagued Disraeli during the Bulgarian atrocities and the patronizing sneers of *The Spectator* paled beside the vicious turn taken by German politics in the aftermath of unification and Jewish emancipation. Here, the crash of 1873 heralded a deeper malaise as Jews became the scapegoats of all that was wrong with the modern world: finance capitalism, political liberalism, materialism, and the infiltration of German culture by alien values. Respectable figures like the historian Heinrich von Treitschke declared that the "Jews are our misfortune." The court chaplain, Adolf Stöcker, fanned the flames of economic resentment and religious prejudice with his explicitly anti-Jewish Christian Social party. Even the word "anti-Semitism" was coined in Germany at this time by the radical political activist Wilhelm Marr.

Montefiore was a natural target for this new political movement. In 1882 the first International Anti-Jewish Congress at Dresden attributed Jewish control of the continental press to his malign influence, referring darkly to "the words of the Jew 'Montefiore,' uttered by him in a Rabbinical Assembly at Krakau in the year 1840." When Montefiore responded to ritual-murder accusations in Tisza-Eszlar by sending each member of the Hungarian Diet a copy of his Damascus *firman*, a theologian at the University of Prague claimed in return to possess a book "printed under the auspices of Sir Moses Montefiore so late as 1868, in which it is written (page 156a) 'that the shedding of the blood of non-Jewish maidens is considered among the Jews a very sacred act.'" Loewe published an elaborate refutation on both occasions. But for those inclined to believe such things, the mud probably stuck.[21]

Publicly, Montefiore was reluctant to abandon his faith in progress and in the gradualist approach to emancipation that he had made his hallmark. "Your communications referring to recent Sectarian movements and Anti-Semitic Leagues in your own country and other parts of Europe present cause of serious consideration," he wrote to Bleichröder in 1880; "I entertain, however, the hope that by prudence and discretion on our part, and increased enlightenment based on principles of humanity among non-Israelites, an improvement in the condition of our brethren will ultimately be effected." Privately, he was bitter and biblical.[22]

The year 1881 saw the outbreak of mass anti-Jewish violence in Russia. Rape, pillage, and assault were widespread: 20,000 Jews rendered homeless, 100,000 economically ruined, whole quarters burned to the ground. As in 1871, the atrocities heralded not a wave of sympathy for Jewish victims, but rather an intensification of hostile government policy and public opinion in Russia. The crisis was so pressing that the Board of Deputies and the Anglo-Jewish Association sent a joint deputation to the foreign secretary. Lord Granville was unforthcoming. Of course, he condemned Russian anti-Jewish legislation and the recent fearful riots, but he had no intention of intervening in the internal affairs of a fellow great power.[23]

The pragmatic realism of Gladstone's Liberal government compared badly with the crusading humanitarian rhetoric its leader had deployed during the Bulgarian crisis. Christians, it seemed, made more appealing victims than Jews. But even under Palmerston Montefiore's brand of diplomatic intervention had never really flourished in Europe. It was easy to preach humanity and civilization when this worked with the grain of British imperialism in North Africa and the Middle East; it was feasible (at least in theory) to enforce these values in the unstable states emerging in the Balkans; quite impossible to teach the pope Christian morality or to exert meaningful influence on the still all-powerful tsar.

An awareness of these realities had guided Montefiore's actions in 1846. In 1881 he agreed "perfectly" with Granville. "[I]t is only by mild and judicious representation—relying in advance, as it were, on their kindness and humanity—that you have a chance of your application reaching the throne of the Emperor," he advised Arthur Cohen, now president of the deputies. "If it be thought advisable, I am quite ready to go again to St. Petersburg, I should, in the first place, ascertain whether my visit would be thought agreeable or not to the Emperor and his Government; and in the next place, I should apply to the British Government for letters of recommendation to the British Minister, and thus equipped I should have every hope of smoothing the unfortunate position in which our brethren are placed in that country."[24] When his friends asked how he could contemplate doing so at ninety-eight, he replied that he could be carried there if necessary: nothing would prevent him from serving his brethren in distress. Prevented from going in person, he sent money to enable Jewish schools throughout the Pale to celebrate the coronation of the new tsar.[25]

This magnificent pigheadedness, this faith in the goodwill of the Romanovs and the ability of providence and the British government to promote his efforts, disguised a devout resignation. It found expression in a uniquely revealing letter to his great-great-niece, Lady Rosebery, wife of a Christian Liberal politician not known for his warmth to the Jews. "It is not . . . for Israel to speak," wrote Montefiore;

> his [Israel's] non-Israelite Friends [*deleted*: if there exist such in this country] ought to raise their voice and plead the cause of justice, truth and humanity . . .
>
> The treatment which Israel receives among the nations may be regarded as the barometer of the moral standing of their neighbours: truth, justice, and peace do not illumine yet the world; as long as this is the case, we

must always expect attacks similar to those which make you now apprehend great danger.

The present outcry is not new: Already Abimelech said unto Isaac "Depart from us for thou art become much mightier than we" (Genesis 26 v
16); it was a political system on which Pharaoh acted when he reduced
the Israelites to a state of bondage; and Balak, the King of Moab, at a
later period followed his example: "Now, Moab said unto the elders of
Midian shall this Company lick up all that are round about us, as the ox
licked up the grass of the field" (Numbers Ch 22. V. 4). These are precisely the words of our persecutors in Germany, Russia & Roumania.
Moab hired Balaam to curse, enlightened Berlin hired Stocker to do the
same; at the time of Moab, the man himself who was appointed to annihilate Israel by his word, was ultimately obliged to bless Israel, and thus,
I have no doubt, will be the case, one of these days, with those who are
against our Brethren [*deleted:* all over the world].

As long as Israel exists our forefathers have been placed among nations
such as those of Tyre, Canaan, Babel, Assyria, Greece and Rome, God
commanded them not to walk in their ordinances, not to do as they (the
above nations) did; all the time they observed that injunction they were
preserved in peace, the moment they deviated from it and commenced
bowing down to their idols and adopted the vices and abominations of
the land, God dispersed them. The only way by which we can secure permanent peace to ourselves is: the strict observance of our holy religion:
showing the world that neither wealth nor rank and station can estrange
us from the service of God.[26]

This was not the language of a man who had appealed confidently to
the decency of civilized Europe and pleaded the cause of his people before emperors, sultans, pashas, princes, queens, and cardinals. Here,
Montefiore relegated hopes of emancipation and tolerance to a messianic future, attributing the suffering of the present to the pressures of
secularization and assimilation that had led so many Jews to abandon
their faith.

If there were grounds for optimism in the 1880s, he saw them in the
fledgling Zionist movement. Like Montefiore, most religious leaders in
Russia and Poland had greeted the pogroms with traditional quietism.
Jewish intellectuals committed to the project of Russification were
forced into a more fundamental reassessment of their prospects under
the tsarist regime. As the St. Petersburg elite manifestly failed to rise to
the challenge, so the global Jewish public turned its thoughts to emigra-

tion—and the masses of the Pale began to vote with their feet. For most, the obvious destination was North America, where one group founded the small colony of Montefiore in Kansas. Others—more religious, or idealistic—thought instead of Palestine. In 1881 and 1882 small groups of Jewish students began to form in many important Russian cities, committed to emigration, united in the dream of Jewish political autonomy, divided only as to the relative merits of the United States and the Holy Land.[27] They found their ideologue and leader in the shape of Yehuda Leib Pinsker, a longstanding supporter of the integrationist Society for the Spread of Enlightenment among the Jews of Russia (OPE), whose faith in the Ginzburg worldview had been shaken to the core.

Confronted by intractable Jew-hatred in eastern and western Europe, Pinsker concluded that the Jews alone could rescue themselves from their condition of permanent alienation; the only viable solution was a territorial-political one in which Jews became masters of their destiny by achieving a Jewish state. His 1882 German-language pamphlet *Autoemancipation!* served as a manifesto for the inchoate movement in Russia. The Jews of Romania reached similar—if less theoretically sophisticated—conclusions once their hopes of mass citizenship under the Treaty of Berlin were gone. Brought up on tales of Montefiore's legendary generosity and love for Jerusalem, they looked naturally to Ramsgate for support.

Loewe tells us that the Zionist agitation of the 1880s captured the old man's imagination:

> They formed themselves into a society, adopting the name of "Chovevey Zion" (the friends or lovers of Zion) and had an excellent likeness made of him by a distinguished artist, which they sold in Russia, Holland, and Germany, the amount realised being intended for the benefit of Jewish colonists in the Holy Land . . .
>
> That for which he had been longing full sixty years of his life he now saw being realised by the strenuous efforts of the society *"Chovevey Zion,"* by the agricultural Hebrew associations in Roumania and elsewhere, and by private gentlemen, who individually exerted themselves for the good and great cause.[28]

But although Montefiore sent donations to the six Zionist colonies on his ninety-ninth birthday, the Hovevei Zion had limited expectations. Loewe confirmed Montefiore's enthusiasm for its initiative, but cautioned: "whereas the *sar* is very passionate about this matter, our leaders [in London] in their actions and their thoughts have different ideas." The delegate Chief Rabbi Hermann Adler, Arthur Cohen, and Joseph Sebag had all been present for his lecture at Judith College, but not a word about the Holy Land had found its way into public reports of the ninety-ninth birthday celebrations. Referring bitterly to the fiasco of the Testimonial Fund ten years earlier, Loewe added: "And this is their way: they first ask the Sar to tell them what he desires most, and the moment he expresses what he feels by saying that his heart and soul desires the Holy Land, they turn their faces from him."[29]

Montefiore's poor health was an added complication because his doctors forbade all discussion of such matters. David Gordon, editor of *Hamagid,* concluded that little could be expected from that quarter "apart from his admired name and past actions which we will always cherish in this matter."[30] Baron Edmond de Rothschild had already done more for Jewish agricultural settlements in the Holy Land than Montefiore had achieved in a lifetime, "and from him we could hope for far more in future whereas from the *sar* Moshe, may God lengthen his days, we have no hope for many reasons that he will do anything practical with his money while still alive (maybe we will see something from his action after his death)."[31] The Frenchman's star was now in the ascendant—and he was less hidebound than Montefiore, who would not take action to facilitate Jewish emigration to Palestine "until the time comes when the Sultan and Queen Victoria will dance together."[32]

Gordon recognized, however, that if Montefiore was a spent force his name remained a talisman. Sales of his portrait provided the activists with a basic income, enough for them to hope that naming a colony in his honor might generate further largesse—either from Montefiore or from his admirers.[33] And so it was that Gordon arrived in Ramsgate in person to present Montefiore with a tribute album, replete with over 1,300 signatures, while the first conference of the Hovevei Zion was scheduled in Katowice to mark the hundredth anniversary of his birth.[34]

The earliest calls for a grand commemoration of Montefiore's centenary came from New York in March 1883, but it was not until the old man had safely celebrated his ninety-ninth that plans really got underway. The disappointments of the Testimonial Fund were still a live issue. This time, Montefiore's well-connected relatives on the Board of Deputies joined forces with his Christian admirers to push through proposals for a convalescent home in Ramsgate for patients of all creeds. If the Testimonial Fund had been too traditionally Jewish for Montefiore's more Anglicized brethren, the Montefiore Centenary Movement provoked outrage among a different constituency, who had no wish to see a Jewish cause taken over by the Christian establishment.[35] Only three of the nine speakers at the grand public meeting scheduled to take place in the

Mansion House were Jewish, while the resolutions put forward by luminaries like Shaftesbury, the bishop of Bedford, and Cardinal Manning made no mention of Montefiore's religion, referring instead to his "philanthropic labours in the cause of Humanity, Justice, and Civilisation."[36] This was the glorification of Montefiore as universal humanitarian, not as Jewish patriarch. Whether fearful of another public humiliation, unwilling to tempt fate by making plans for his hundredth birthday, or simply exhausted at the prospect, he begged his greatnephew Nathaniel de Rothschild to cancel the meeting.[37]

Plans for another Ramsgate extravaganza were scaled down accordingly. It was clear by this time that Montefiore was fading. For the past year or so he had lived almost entirely on milk and port.[38] He still received regular visits from his doctor and his intimates, but he himself rarely left his room. The eminent physician Sir William Jenner considered Montefiore's pulse wonderful "for a man of his age" while stressing that his life was "hanging on a thread."[39]

The old man's frailty did not deter his many admirers. Rich men inevitably receive begging letters, and Montefiore had responded to innumerable personal appeals over the decades.[40] It is impossible to trace the scale of this most intimate form of philanthropy, but what survives suggests that he kept the undertaking made in 1828: "Never refuse to see and hear patiently, every one that applies to me for charity or assistance and to relieve them as far as prudence will permit."[41] Expressing his sense of giving as a religiously and socially appropriate form of thanksgiving, Montefiore regularly made ritual donations at moments of personal (and national) significance. Gifts of £79 to the Jewish poor of London and the Holy Land to mark his seventy-ninth birthday, of £95 to the Field Lane Ragged School on what would have been Judith's ninety-fifth birthday, and of £99 to the poor of the City to mark his own ninety-ninth birthday reflect the symbolic weight he attached to such donations.[42]

Montefiore's commitment to a highly individualized philanthropy was reflected in his penchant for face-to-face giving, his fabled Old World courtesy, and his nurturing of longstanding charitable relationships—in Ramsgate, London, and the Holy Land. And of course he gave readily to a myriad charitable causes, regularly and on an ad-hoc basis, both at home and abroad. The eclectic nature of this generosity and the small size of most donations do not render them unimportant. Their collective weight contributed substantially to Montefiore's reputation as a great philanthropist—both through the speeches, letters, and stories that found their way into print and, presumably, through word of mouth.

It was hard to settle on a single Montefiore memorial precisely because he had done a little for so many. His appeal transcended national and religious fault lines.[43] In Ramsgate, he was the local notable; in London, he remained a quintessential City figure; his brother Freemasons saw him as the perfect representative of their Craft. For Christian restorationists, Montefiore symbolized Old Testament virtue and the return to Zion; throughout the British Empire and North America, he represented the universal humanitarian values of Anglo-Saxon civilization and the imperial conscience. To many Jews in eastern Europe and the Muslim world he was a providential deliverer, a man of God who observed the commandments and did not forget the sufferings of his brethren. To their acculturated brethren in the West he stood rather for the dream of wealth, prestige, and acceptance by gentile high society. And to all—but most particularly the Hovevei Zion—he was the living embodiment of "national" unity in the Jewish world. It was this diversity of opinion that found expression in the global commemoration of Montefiore's centenary on 8 *Heshvan* 1884.

The international dimension of these celebrations was only partly expressed by the 2,500-odd telegrams, letters, and birthday addresses that reached Ramsgate.[44] The surviving testimonials include at least twenty-one from Austria-Hungary; two from Canada; one from Chile; ten from Italy; eighteen from Germany; fourteen from Great Britain; thirteen from Holland; two from New Zealand; three from the Ottoman Empire; one from Romania; twenty from the Russian Empire; four from South Africa; two from Sweden; one from Switzerland; and twenty-two from the United States.[45] Most but by no means all were Jewish in origin. Indeed, the worsening political climate ensured that Montefiore's interfaith appeal formed a key element in many Jewish accounts of the celebrations. Thus the *Jewish Chronicle* reported that the queen and the empress of Germany had sent congratulatory telegrams, that the lord mayor had attended one of the centennial celebrations in London, and that in New York the great clerical orator and social campaigner Henry Ward Beecher had himself given a birthday address. All this testified "to the high estimation in which the name MONTEFIORE is held outside the Jewish pale . . . We are so amazed by the unexpected recrudescence of medieval persecution in these days that we are apt to forget the revolution which has taken place in the relations of the Christian and the Jew."[46]

Such a widespread demonstration of admiration and respect was, in itself, remarkable. Yet there was no denying the peculiar charge attached to the occasion in Jewish circles. Synagogues all over the world held special services to mark Montefiore's centenary, and most of them adopted the liturgy specially written by Chief Rabbi Nathan Adler.[47] The *Jewish Chronicle* reported celebrations in Italy, Holland, Canada, South Africa, Australia, New Zealand, Jamaica, Morocco, Russia, Egypt, Turkey, Denmark, Palestine, Romania, Hungary, and Corfu.[48] Societies were founded in Montefiore's honor, prizes and professorships called after him. In North America alone, ninety-eight Jewish synagogues and charitable institutions would eventually carry his name.[49] Many of the birthday tributes sent to Ramsgate had been approved by public meetings, and some carried hundreds of signatures; this was, in a sense, the collective embodiment of the international Jewish public. Again and again, the sermons, poems, and addresses written by Jews to mark the occasion in places as far-flung as Kentucky and the Hasidic center of Medzhibozh in Ukraine demonstrated the authors' awareness that they were participating in a truly global Jewish movement.[50] Speaking at Bevis Marks, Rabbi Hermann Adler remarked tellingly that it was "without parallel in the annals of Judaism that this same festive service is being held simultaneously . . . throughout the world."[51] The sense of a powerful simultaneous experience binding the Jewish people closer together was almost palpable.

Yet only the Zionists chose to reflect more consciously on Montefiore's place at the heart of the nation. "Many were the defenders of the House of Israel in . . . the times of its wandering," wrote the Hovevei Zion of Pinsker's hometown, Odessa,

> but you surpassed them all. Like all advocates of the House of Israel, you too came to . . . save it from its miseries in its lands of crisis. But more than them all you acted also to alleviate the spirit of your people, its national spirit that its miseries almost extinguished . . . You were the first, as you traversed many countries to stand before kings and rulers to save your people, in so-doing you drew behind you all the people of Israel that lived in those countries and tied together the hearts of the sons of Jacob who lived in those countries, and the scattered house of people . . . became one nation in all the countries of its dispersal, and your honourable name was on the lips of all the people and at the heart of this united people.
>
> You were also the first that put your heart to build the ruins of Zion the land of our fathers, and your actions were the light beneath the foot of our people.[52]

This romantic assessment overlooked the contribution of men like Philippson, Crémieux, and Isaac Leeser. It did justice neither to the intellectual sophistication of its signatories nor to the complex global pro-

Testimonial to Montefiore on his hundredth birthday from the Association to Restore the Ruins of Zion, Odessa, October 11/23, 1884. Illustrated by the well-known Russian painter Isaac (later Leonid) Pasternak, it shows Montefiore as a bound slave, overlooking the glory of Jerusalem. A divine hand holds out a flag decorated with the number "100."
(Courtesy of the Montefiore Endowment, University College London Library Services, Special Collections)

cesses at work in the Jewish world. But it was not without truth for
all that.

With the centenary behind him Montefiore had nothing left to live for. A
small army of nurses and personal attendants tended him day and night,
but Loewe was the main prop of this, his very old age.[53] In public,
Montefiore attributed his achievements to Judith's blessed influence. Privately, he may have known that Loewe's contribution was greater. The
Prussian had shaped and shared his lifework since the 1840s. Such close
contact with an impeccably Orthodox east European *maskil* opened
new spiritual vistas for Montefiore. It gave the pragmatic English businessman an entrée into worlds that he might never have imagined existed—and circles that would influence the trajectory of international
Jewish politics in the decades to come. Older, and vastly richer, Montefiore was always the senior partner in their relationship; Loewe's rabbinical status, first-class intellect, and exposure to the currents sweeping
eastern European Judaism enabled him to mold his employer's agenda
in subtle but increasingly important ways.

Even now, Montefiore maintained the facade of ceaseless activity, but
as he grew weaker he seemed indecisive and overcautious. Always punc-
tilious in his recordkeeping, he gave special orders "never to allow any
of his letters to leave the house before an exact copy had been made of
them, however insignificant they might have been."[54] He still signed all
his checks personally. Yet he had begun to avoid making commitments,
putting decisions off until tomorrow and then changing his mind so that
the person who counted on him was disappointed.

His conversation alternated between the past and the future. "I have
endeavoured to do the best I could," he told Loewe, "no doubt I have
failed, but I rely on God's goodness; He forgives those who approach
Him with a contrite heart." But after contemplating his funeral and final
resting place, Montefiore's thoughts often turned back to earlier years.
"Do you remember when we crossed the Dwina near Riga, and the ice
broke under our feet?" he would ask Loewe. "We had many narrow es-
capes on our missions; praised [*sic*] be to God for His numerous mercies." Sometimes he recited a psalm or a favorite hymn. On other occasions he spoke of the great changes he had seen in Jerusalem, reflecting
that "after all, fifty years is but a short time, if we consider the number
of years it takes even in Europe to improve the condition of different
classes of people." And then he might turn his head and slip his hand
under his pillow, where he kept a stone from Jerusalem bearing the inscription "For thy servants take pleasure in her stones, and favor the

dust thereof." "This," Montefiore would tell Loewe, "you will put under my head when I am placed in my last resting place. Now go into the Gothic Library, take a good supper, and we shall have a glass of wine together in pleasing remembrance of what we have seen and endeavoured to do for our brethren."[55]

On April 24, 1885, the first bulletin about Montefiore's health appeared in the newspapers. By June he was so weak that he could hardly write a check. Banknotes and gold were brought in for small payments; when it came to large amounts he would try the strength of his hand on a sheet of paper, before asking someone to put the pen he held on the spot where his signature was required. "Have I anything more to do?" he would ask Loewe querulously. "If there is any cheque to be written for charitable purposes, tell me, and I will sign it the moment I am able." But he was strong enough to retain his interest in current affairs—to provide a dinner for the poor of Ramsgate in honor of the queen's birthday; to send a silver tea and coffee service to Princess Beatrice as a wedding gift; and to write a personal letter of congratulations when Victoria made his greatnephew Nathaniel de Rothschild the first Jewish peer.[56] If Montefiore knew that Shaftesbury had proposed his own name for this honor nearly twenty years earlier, he may finally have been too old to care.[57]

On July 27, when Loewe arrived at East Cliff to discuss the latest foreign correspondence, Montefiore clutched his hand and begged his "dear, dear" collaborator and traveling companion: "do not leave me; sleep here."[58] Montefiore spent his last hours in a haze of prayer, surrounded by his favorite niece and nephews, the rabbis of the Judith College, and the men and women who had served him so faithfully in Ramsgate over the years. Montefiore had thought long and hard about this moment. His affairs were in order; his will (which left £30,000 to the established Jewish communities in the Holy Land, £15,000 to charities in London and Ramsgate, and most of the rest to Joseph Sebag) was complete to the last personal bequest.[59] He was to be buried in the prayer shawl he had worn at his wedding, together with an olive wreath he had brought back from Mount Lebanon in 1827, some treasured mementos of Judith, soil from Jerusalem and the Tomb of Rachel, and a book containing an account of all the charitable deeds he had performed in his life. Loewe tells us that Montefiore died—like all good Jews—with the *shema* prayer on his lips. An alternative tradition has it that his last words were "Thank God!" Shops shut early as the news spread through Ramsgate and its surroundings, where flags flying from churches around the harbor were lowered to half-mast.

Conclusion

"History will not be ungrateful to Moses Montefiore," wrote one contributor to the *Archives Israélites* on his death. "It will register, and confirm, those panegyrics that every Jewish writer has compiled in honor of his illustrious memory."[1] But history was ungrateful, and the mass outpouring of popular enthusiasm that marked Montefiore's centenary proved ephemeral. Even so, this was a man with global impact. Rescuing his extraordinary life from obscurity brings to light aspects of the nineteenth century that have, until recently, entirely vanished from view.

The nineteenth century has rightly been seen as an age of nation-state formation, and Jewish emancipation has usually been studied within the framework of emerging nation-states. Montefiore's life highlights the international dimension of Jewish emancipation and the emergence of a new sort of Jewish politics, rooted in transnational Jewish activism. For Montefiore exploited the institutional apparatus of an emerging public sphere—the press, voluntary associations in civil society, and, increasingly in western Europe, representative governments—to mobilize opinion and diplomatic influence in the cause of international Jewish relief. These developments took place decades before the birth of Zionism, and on a scale that has never been properly appreciated. By focusing on the particular social and cultural experiences of different Jewish communities, historians have failed to appreciate the dynamic evolution of this interconnected world.

Voluntary associations, newspapers, pamphlets, books, and petitions took pride of place among the structures and strategies developed by Jews to meet the challenges of modernity in the West during the mid-nineteenth century. They proved key weapons in the struggle for emancipation and in the reformulation of relations between Jews and the non-Jewish majority. But civil society and the press also played a critical part in the internal transformation of Western Jewry. With the decline of officially sanctioned communal structures, voluntarism provided a fresh basis on which to build a religious community. With the rise of the press and the emergence of a Jewish public sphere, educated Jews found a fresh platform from which to elaborate new perspectives, debate with communal authorities, and question—or defend—the status quo. Montefiore's life reminds us that these developments had global resonance. The emergence of a world Jewish community reflected the internationalization of communal politics and the increasingly global nature of the Jewish public sphere. Yet for many the nation remained a primary point of reference. Both Montefiore and Crémieux identified powerfully with their native countries. Paradoxically, their commitment to rival imperialisms only intensified the impact of globalization in the Jewish world.

This internationalization of the Jewish question had important consequences for humanitarian politics. The evolution of diplomatic intervention by European states in the cause of international Jewish relief between the Damascus Affair and the Congress of Berlin has remained a largely untold story.[2] It matters because this was an example of intervention on behalf of a group who were not really "people like us"—unlike better-known military interventions in support of beleaguered Ottoman Christians.[3] Only a century earlier, Jews had been widely regarded as "oriental" aliens. Thanks to the efforts of activists like Montefiore, their condition—and the treatment of ethnic and religious minorities—would become a benchmark of European "civilization."

The prehistory of modern human rights has usually been traced to the French revolutionary tradition embodied by the Declaration of the Rights of Man, but it is generally accepted that in the century that followed, this humanitarian universalism gave way to an increasingly defensive and combative nationalism.[4] The story of human rights was, by this reckoning, a story of failure until the ratification of the Universal Declaration of Human Rights by the United Nations in 1948. This narrative ignores the existence of a rival humanitarian tradition epitomized by Montefiore. This was a profoundly religious tradition rooted in the Evangelical and nonconformist culture of British antislavery and the liberal interventionism of the Palmerstonian era. It was a tradition in which the cause of international Jewish relief came to occupy a privileged place. By integrating Jews into British humanitarian politics, Montefiore helped to universalize this more religiously inflected humanitarian agenda.

Unlike their French counterparts, British humanitarians united behind calls for "civil and religious liberty"—a slogan that reflected the prerevolutionary language of liberty rather than the language of rights "invented" by the French and symbolized by the Declaration of the Rights of Man. Like slaves, however, Jewish activists like Montefiore found postrevolutionary France consistently less ready than Victorian Britain to intervene diplomatically on their behalf in the name of "civilization" and "humanity." This contrast between what we might crudely term the theory and practice of human rights—between the aggressively secular tradition of the Rights of Man and the more religiously motivated tradition of humanitarian intervention elaborated in Britain—merits further reflection.

Until recently, the nineteenth century was seen as an age of secularization, but Montefiore's life underlines the role of religious ideology and conflict in the birth of the modern world. From papal Rome and tsarist Russia to Morocco and the Ottoman world, the issue of Jewish rights lay at the heart of the continuing battle between traditional religious institutions and the rise of the secular state. International causes célèbres like the Damascus Affair, the Mortara Affair, and the massacre of Syrian Christians heralded the globalization and mobilization of religious identities on the world stage. In the early twenty-first century, these issues are relevant as never before.

Appendices

Notes

Archives Consulted

Index

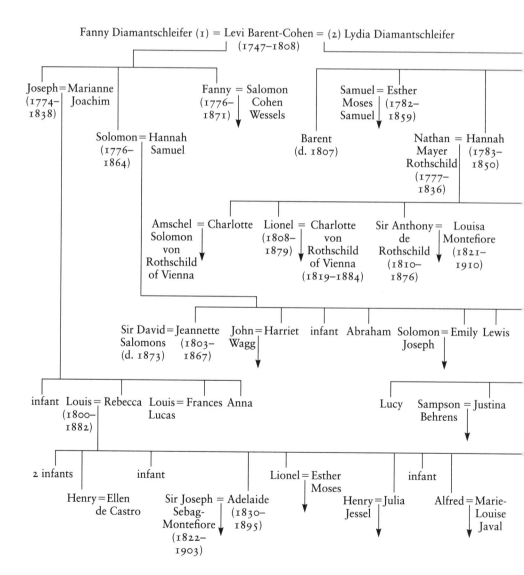

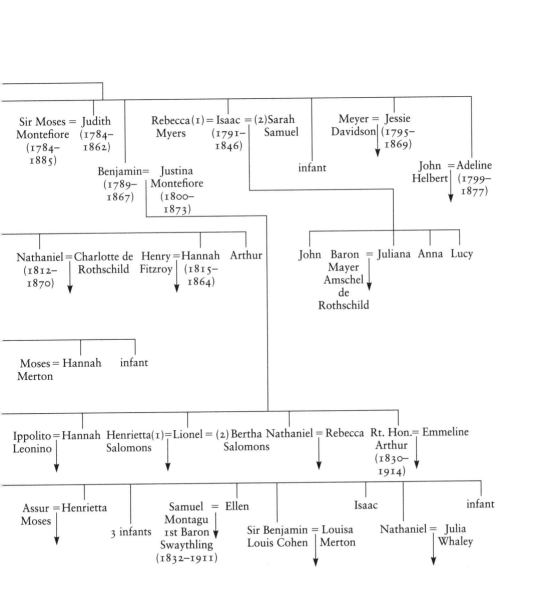

Appendix B: Montefiore Family Tree

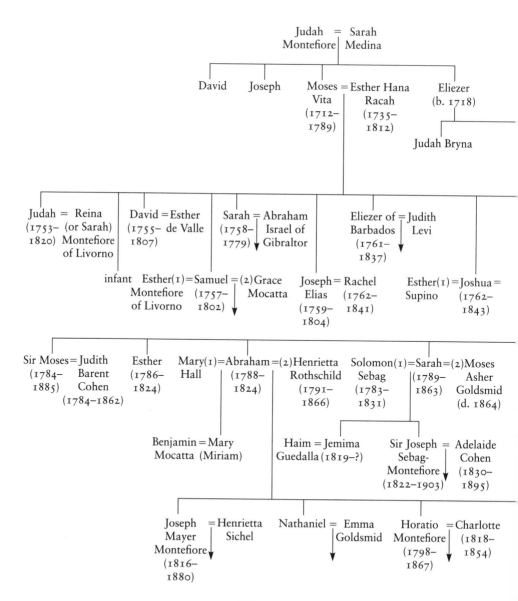

Judah = Sarah
Montefiore | Medina

David   Joseph   Moses = Esther Hana   Eliezer
                    Vita   Racah   (b. 1718)
                    (1712–   (1735–
                    1789)   1812)

Judah Bryna

Judah = Reina   David = Esther   Sarah = Abraham   Eliezer of = Judith
(1753– (or Sarah) (1755– de Valle   (1758– Israel of   Barbados | Levi
1820) Montefiore 1807)   1779) Gibraltor   (1761–
     of Livorno   1837)

     infant Esther(1) = Samuel = (2)Grace Joseph = Rachel   Esther(1) = Joshua =
         Montefiore (1757– Mocatta Elias (1762–   Supino   (1762–
         of Livorno 1802)   (1759– 1841)   1843)
                                    1804)

Sir Moses = Judith Esther Mary(1) = Abraham = (2)Henrietta Solomon(1) = Sarah = (2)Moses
(1784– Barent (1786– Hall   (1788– Rothschild Sebag (1789– Asher
1885) Cohen 1824)   1824) (1791–   (1783– 1863) Goldsmid
   (1784–1862)   1866)   1831)   (d. 1864)

             Benjamin = Mary   Haim = Jemima   Sir Joseph = Adelaide
             Mocatta (Miriam) Guedalla (1819–?) Sebag-   Cohen
                                        Montefiore (1830–
                                      (1822–1903) 1895)

         Joseph = Henrietta Nathaniel = Emma   Horatio = Charlotte
        Mayer Sichel   Goldsmid Montefiore (1818–
        Montefiore   (1798– 1854)
        (1816–   1867)
        1880)

Sarah = Judah de   Masshod =   Jael   David = ?Lea Rachel
(or   Moses Vita   Prospero   Montefiore   Vita
Reina)   Montefiore   of London

Abraham   Jael = Prospero   Hanna = Moses   Lydia (1771–   Lazarus
            (1766–   Massaod   (1768–   Ancona   1858)
            1815)   Montefiore   18?)   Converted to
                   of Livorno   Christianity

(2) American   Reyna = Abraham   Simha = Zacharia   Rachel = Moses   Jacob of
                  Ergos of   Levy   Castello   Barbados
                  Jamaica   of Barbados   (1773–
                                                        1863)

Benjamin = Abigail   Joseph = Rebecca   Benjamin = Justina   Sarah(1) = Horatio = Charlotte
Gompertz   (1790–   Salomons   (1793–   Cohen   (1795–   Mocatta   (1798–   Montefiore
(1779–   1871)   1869)   1873)   1867)   (1818–
1864)   See App. A   1854)

Sir Anthony = Louisa
de Rothschild   (1821–
(1810–   1910)
1876)

Notes

Abbreviations

AI	*Archives Israélites de France*
AN	Archives Nationales, Paris
ASM	Arthur Sebag-Montefiore Archive, Oxford Centre for Hebrew and Jewish Studies
AZ	*Allgemeine Zeitung des Judentums*
BD	Board of Deputies
BDMB	Board of Deputies Minute Book, London Metropolitan Archives
BL	British Library Manuscripts Collection, London
CMM	Sonia L. Lipman and Vivian Lipman, eds., *The Century of Moses Montefiore* (Oxford, 1985)
CPC	Correspondance Politique des Consuls, Ministère des Affaires Etrangères, Paris
FHG	Francis Henry Goldsmid
HAWL	Hodgkin Archive, Wellcome Library for the History and Understanding of Medicine, London
HBC	Albert Hyamson, *The British Consulate in Jerusalem in Relation to the Jews of Palestine, 1838–1914*, 2 vols. (London, 1939)
HL	MS259 A880, Montefiore Transcripts, Hartley Library, Southampton University
HLV	*Halevanon*
HM	*Hamagid*
ILG	Isaac Lyon Goldsmid
JC	*Jewish Chronicle*
JdR	James de Rothschild
JM	Judith Montefiore
JMM	Joseph Mayer Montefiore
JMPJ	Judith Montefiore, *Private Journal of a Visit to Egypt and Palestine* (London, 1836)
JMTD	Judith Montefiore Travel Diary
JNUL	Jewish National University Library, Jerusalem
JS	Joseph Sebag
JSS	*Jewish Social Studies*
LB	Letter Book
LC	Louis Cohen

431

LD   Louis Loewe, ed., *Diaries of Sir Moses and Lady Montefiore,*
                Comprising Their Life and Work as Recorded in Their Diaries from
                1812 to 1883, 2 vols. (London, 1890)
LDMS   Direct quotations from Montefiore's diaries, reproduced in LD
LJR   Lord John Russell
LL   Louis Loewe
MAE   Ministère des Affaires Etrangères, Paris
MB   Minute Books
MFA   Ministry of Foreign Affairs Archive, Ottoman Archives, Istanbul
ML   Mocatta Library, University College London
MLL   Montefiore List of Letters, ML
MM   Moses Montefiore
MMJ   Moses Montefiore Journal
MMSS   Montefiore MSS.; microfilms available in the London School of
                Jewish Studies, JNUL, Oxford Centre for Hebrew and Jewish Studies,
                and Jewish Theological Seminary, New York
NA   The National Archives, London
NMR   Nathan Mayer Rothschild
OAJA   *The Occident and American Jewish Advocate*
RAL   The Rothschild Archive, London
S&P   Spanish and Portuguese Jews' Congregation, London
SEGPC   Stock Exchange General Purposes Committee
SLC   Shandel-Lipson Collection, Oxford Centre for Hebrew and Jewish
                Studies
SvR   Salomon von Rothschild
TH   Thomas Hodgkin
TJHSE   *Transactions of the Jewish Historical Society of England*
VJ   *Voice of Jacob*

Introduction

1. The two best-known biographies of Montefiore are the authorized Lucien Wolf, *Sir Moses Montefiore: A Centennial Biography, with Extracts from Letters and Journals* (London, 1884); and the Zionist Paul Goodman, *Moses Montefiore* (Philadelphia, 1925). Two popular accounts are S. Umberto Nahon, *Sir Moses Montefiore, Leghorn 1784—Ramsgate 1885: A Life in the Service of Jewry* (Jerusalem, 1965); and Myrtle Franklin and Michael Bor, *Sir Moses Montefiore, 1784–1885* (London, 1984). Moshe Samet, *Mosheh Montifiori, ha'ish veha'agadah* (Jerusalem, 1989), is wildly revisionist. Most useful from a scholarly point of view are *CMM* and Israel Bartal, ed., *The Age of Moses Montefiore* (Jerusalem, 1987), but these examine only aspects of the life. Ruth P. Goldschmidt-Lehmann, *Sir Moses Montefiore, a Bibliography* (Jerusalem, 1984), provides a comprehensive guide to more arcane Montefioriana.

2. LD, 1: v.

3. Richard Barnett, "Sources for the Study of Sir Moses Montefiore," in *Sir Moses Montefiore: A Symposium,* ed. Vivian D. Lipman (Oxford, 1982), 4.

4. Oral tradition passed on by Adolf Schischa.

5. George Collard, *Moses the Victorian Jew* (Oxford, 1990), 11.

1. Livorno and London

1. Ernst Moritz Arndt, *Reisen durch einen Theil Teutschlands, Ungarns, Italiens und Frankreichs in den Jahren 1798 und 1799,* vol. 2 (Leipzig, 1804), 283, 284, 297–298.

2. George Bonnard, ed., *Gibbon's Journey from Geneva to Rome: His Journal from 20 April to 2 October 1764* (London, 1961), 230–231.

3. On the political and institutional history of the Livorno community see Renzo Toaff, *La Nazione Ebrea a Livorno e a Pisa (1591–1700)* (Florence, 1990). For the eighteenth century see Francesca Bregoli, "Mediterranean Enlightenment: Jewish Acculturation in Livorno, 1737–1790" (Ph.D. diss., University of Pennsylvania, 2007); Jean-Pierre Filippini, "Da 'Nazione Ebrea' a 'comunità Israelitica': La comunità ebraica di Livorno tra cinquecento e novecento," *Nuovi Studi Livornese* 1 (1993): 25–43; and Filippini, "La Nazione Ebrea di Livorno," in *Dall'emancipazione a Oggi,* vol. 2 of *Gli Ebrei in Italia,* ed. Corrado Vivanti (Turin, 1997), 1047–68. Filippini, *Il porto di Livorno e la Toscana (1676–1814),* 3 vols. (Naples, 1998), deals extensively with Jewish economic activities, notably in vol. 3.

4. The most recent overview of Italian Jewry is Vivanti, *Ebrei in Italia.* See also Attilio Milano, *Storia degli Ebrei in Italia* (Turin, 1963). For a general introduction in English see Arnaldo Momigliano, "The Jews of Italy," in *Essays in Ancient and Modern Judaism,* ed. Silvia Berti and Arnaldo Momigliano (Chicago, 1987), 1–37. Still worth reading is Cecil Roth, *The History of the Jews of Italy* (Philadelphia, 1946).

5. Lucien Wolf, *Sir Moses Montefiore: A Centennial Biography, with Extracts from Letters and Journals* (London, 1884), 4.

6. See Christian Fischer, *Reise von Livorno nach London im Sommer und Herbste 1818* (Leipzig, 1819), 10.

7. Filippini, *Livorno,* 1: 129–130.

8. Guido Bedarida, quoted in Flora Aghib Levi d'Ancona, "The Sephardi Community of Leghorn (Livorno)," in *The Sephardi Heritage: Essays on the History and Cultural Contribution of the Jews of Spain and Portugal,* vol. 2: *The Western Sephardim,* ed. Richard Barnett and W. M. Schwab (Grendan, Northants, 1989), 190.

9. Jonathan Israel, *European Jewry in the Age of Mercantilism, 1550–1750,* 3d ed. (Oxford, 1998), chaps. 1–3.

10. Arndt, *Reisen,* 287–288.

11. LD, 1: 9.

12. I draw here on LD; Wolf, *Montefiore;* and John Montefiore-Vita, "A Brief History of Montefiore Conca and the Montefiore Family," private research commissioned by the Montefiore family (1989).

13. Myrtle Franklin and Michael Bor, *Sir Moses Montefiore, 1784–1885* (London, 1984), 17. See also Paul Goodman, "Joseph Montefiore," in *Festschrift zu Simon Dubnows siebzigstem Geburtstag (2. Tischri 5691),* ed. Ismar Elbogen, Josef Meisl, and Mark Wischnitzer (Berlin, 1930), 259–261.

14. S. Umberto Nahon, *Sir Moses Montefiore, Leghorn 1784—Ramsgate 1885: A Life in the Service of Jewry* (Jerusalem, 1965), 14.

15. Wolf, *Montefiore*, 4.

16. Filippini, *Livorno*, 1: 63–71.

17. Ibid., 45.

18. Thomas Perry, *Public Opinion, Propaganda, and Politics in Eighteenth Century England: A Study of the Jew Bill of 1753* (Cambridge, Mass., 1962); and David Katz, *The Jews in the History of England, 1485–1850* (Oxford, 1994), 246–251, argue that the Jew Bill debate was essentially a party matter, underplaying the religious element. However, Todd Endelman, *The Jews of Georgian England, 1714–1830: Tradition and Change in a Liberal Society* (Philadelphia, 1979), 26, argues that though economically and politically motivated in part, opposition to the Jew Bill was successful because of its exploitation of outdated religious attitudes.

19. See Gedalia Yogev, *Diamonds and Coral: Anglo-Dutch Jews and Eighteenth-Century Trade* (Leicester, 1978).

20. Wolf, *Montefiore*, 5.

21. For more detail see Sonia Lipman, "The Making of a Victorian Gentleman," in *CMM*, 4.

22. Albert Hyamson, *The Sephardim of England: A History of the Spanish and Portuguese Jewish Community, 1492–1951* (London, 1951), 201.

23. Filippini, *Livorno*, 3: 284.

24. Lipman, "Victorian Gentleman," 4.

25. Filippini, *Livorno*, 3: 283.

26. For details of this journey see Richard Barnett, "Samuel Vita Montefiore's Diary," in *Explorations: An Annual on Jewish Themes*, ed. Murray Mindlin and Chaim Bermant (London, 1967), 245–263.

27. Lipman, "Victorian Gentleman," 4.

28. LD, 1: 22.

29. Barnett, "Samuel Vita Montefiore's Diary," 258–259.

30. LD, 1: 10–11.

31. See Paul Emden, *Jews of Britain: A Series of Biographies* (London, 1944), 87–89; and Wolf, *Montefiore*, 11–12.

32. On Anglo-Jewry see Katz, *Jews in England*; Todd Endelman, *The Jews of Britain, 1656–2000* (Berkeley, 2002); and Hyamson, *Sephardim of England*.

33. Endelman, *Jews of Britain*, 29.

34. On eighteenth-century Anglo-Jewry see Endelman, *Jews of Georgian England*.

35. On the Mocattas' business see Yogev, *Diamonds and Coral*, 50–53.

36. Will of Isaac Lamego, Sept. 16, 1754, Prob/11/925, NA. For the value of money in today's prices see www.measuringworth.com.

37. Lipman, "Victorian Gentleman," 6.

38. Hyamson, *Sephardim of England*, 170.

39. See Yosef Kaplan, *An Alternative Path to Modernity: The Sephardi Diaspora in Western Europe* (Leiden, 2000).

40. Johann von Archenholz, *A Picture of England: Containing a Description of*

the Laws, Customs, and Manners of England, Interspersed with Curious and Interesting Anecdotes (Dublin, 1791), 81–82.

41. See also Endelman, *Jews of Georgian England,* chap. 4.

42. Katz, *Jews in England,* 258.

43. Yosef Kaplan argues that tendencies toward assimilation and acculturation can be traced back to the earliest days of the Sephardi community. See "The Jewish Profile of the Spanish-Portuguese Community of London during the Seventeenth Century," in *Alternative Path,* 155–167. The community became more traditionally Jewish in the early 1700s, but the tendency to assimilation gained strength beginning in the mid-eighteenth century.

44. Todd Endelman, *Radical Assimilation in English Jewish History, 1656–1945* (Bloomington, Ind., 1990), 11, and more generally on conversion.

45. Certificate Authorising Joseph Montefiore to Kill Poultry According to Shechita, Tammuz 29, 5537, private collection of Robert Sebag-Montefiore.

46. Wolf, *Montefiore,* 13.

47. Rachel Montefiore to MM and JM, Jan. 28, 1839, ASM; see also Joseph Sebag to MM, with Sally Sebag to MM and JM, Jan. 28, 1839, ASM.

48. Articles on Marriage of Joseph Montefiore and Rachel de Mattos Mocatta, Aug. 4, 1783, ASM.

49. Lipman, "Victorian Gentleman," 6.

50. List of Finta Payments for the Following Three Years: Sept. 15, 1788, and Sept. 12 1791, all in MB Mahamad, Kislev 5548-1788 to Adar Rishon 5554-1794, MS. 107, uncat. B07/085, fols. 20–23, 148–151. Sept. 8, 1794, Sept. 4, 1797, Sept. 4, 1800, MB Mahamad, Kislev 5554-1794 to Adar Rishon 5563–1803, MS. 108, uncat. B07/085, fols. 1–4, 153–156, 282–285, all in S&P, London Metropolitan Archives.

51. Lipman, "Victorian Gentleman," 8.

52. W. D. Rubinstein, *Men of Property: The Very Wealthy in Britain since the Industrial Revolution* (London, 1981), 120.

53. Lipman, "Victorian Gentleman," 6. This along with Sonia L. Lipman, "The First Half of Montefiore's Biography," in *The Age of Moses Montefiore: Collection of Essays,* ed. Israel Bartal (Jerusalem, 1987), xxxv–xlii, provides the best account of Moses Montefiore's early years.

54. LD, 1: 11.

55. Rachel Montefiore to MM and JM, March 18, 1823, ASM.

56. Rachel Montefiore to MM and all my dear children, Feb. 16, 1840, ASM.

57. Wolf, *Montefiore,* 17–15; LD, 1: 12–13.

58. MM and JM to NMR, March 9, 1814, 000/651/1, RAL.

59. LD, 1: 12.

60. Wolf, *Montefiore,* 14–15.

61. Ibid., 10–11.

62. Joshua Montefiore, *An Authentic Account of the Late Expedition to Bulam on the Coast of Africa, with a Description of the Present Settlement of Sierra Leone, and the Adjacent Country* (London, 1804).

63. Reproduced in *CMM,* 365–368.

64. For additional information on the business activities of Eliezer and Jacob see Emden, *Jews of Britain*, 154–155.

65. Lydia converted to Christianity in old age; see Anon., *Bekehrungs-Geschichte der Lydia Montefiore, Tante des verstorbenen Sir Moses Montefiore* (London, n.d.).

66. On the Beberiscos of London see Daniel J. Schroeter, *The Sultan's Jew: Morocco and the Sephardi World* (Stanford, Calif., 2002), chap. 4.

67. MM to Moses Racah, Dec. 21, 1793, folder 1, HL.

68. On the role of "Port Jews" as agents of modernity see David Sorkin, "The Port Jew: Notes toward a Social Type," *Journal of Jewish Studies* 50 (Spring 1999): 87–97; and Sorkin, "Port Jews and the Three Regions of Emancipation," *Jewish Culture and History* 7, no. 2 (2001): 31–46. Also Lois C. Dubin, *The Port Jews of Habsburg Trieste: Absolutist Politics and Enlightenment Culture* (Stanford, Calif., 1999).

2. Making a Fortune

1. S. R. Cope, "The Goldsmids and the Development of the London Money Market during the Napoleonic Wars," *Economica*, n.s., 9 (May 1942): 188.

2. Levy Alexander, *Memoirs of the Life and Commercial Connections, Public and Private, of the Late Benj. Goldsmid, Esq. of Roehampton; Containing a Cursory View of the Jewish Society and Manners, Interspersed with Interesting Anecdotes of Several Remarkable Characters* (London, 1808), 95–101.

3. Lucien Wolf, *Sir Moses Montefiore: A Centennial Biography, with Extracts from Letters and Journals* (London, 1884), 16.

4. Paul Emden, *Jews of Britain: A Series of Biographies* (London, 1944), 235.

5. See the discussion in Sonia Lipman, "The Making of a Victorian Gentleman," in *CMM*, 7.

6. LD, 1: 13.

7. Quoted from Lipman, "Victorian Gentleman," 8.

8. For a general history of the City in this period see David Kynaston, *A World of Its Own: 1815–1890*, vol. 1 of *The City of London* (London, 1994).

9. See Larry Neal, *The Rise of Financial Capitalism: International Capital Markets in the Age of Reason* (Cambridge, 1990), chaps. 9–10.

10. See Ian P. H. Duffy, "Bankruptcy and Insolvency in London in the Late Eighteenth and Early Nineteenth Centuries" (Ph.D. diss., Oxford, 1974), 164–166.

11. SE Admission Applications, 1804, MS 17957/3, Guildhall Library, City of London.

12. See S. R. Cope, "The Stock Exchange Revisited: A New Look at the Market in Securities in London in the 18th Century," *Economica* 45 (Feb. 1978): 1–21; E. Victor Morgan and W. A. Thomas, *The Stock Exchange, Its History and Functions* (London, 1962). Also see Thomas Mortimer, *Every Man His Own Broker: Or, a Guide to Exchange-Alley* (London, 1762).

13. See P. L. Cottrell, "The Business Man and the Financier," in *CMM*, 24.

14. Wilfred Samuel, "Tentative List of Jewish Underwriting Members of Lloyd's

(from Some Time prior to 1800 until the Year 1901)," *Miscellanies of the Jewish Historical Society of England* 5 (1948): 188.

15. See Cottrell, "Business Man," 25; Wolf, *Montefiore*, 16. On Grigsby's see Bryant Lillywhite, *London Coffee Houses: A Reference Book of Coffee Houses of the Seventeenth, Eighteenth and Nineteenth Centuries* (London, 1963), 250.

16. Johann von Archenholz, *A Picture of England: Containing a Description of the Laws, Customs, and Manners of England, Interspersed with Curious and Interesting Anecdotes* (Dublin, 1791), 199.

17. Quoted in Kynaston, *A World of Its Own*, 17–18.

18. SEGPC, Feb. 27, 1815, MS. 14-600/8, fols. 98–99, Guildhall Library.

19. Lucien Wolf, "Lady Montefiore's Honeymoon," in *Essays in Jewish History*, ed. Cecil Roth (London, 1934), 241.

20. SEGPC, Oct. 22 and 30, 1806, and Jan. 21, 1807, MS. 14-600/5, fols. 238–239, 249, Guildhall Library.

21. SEGPC, Feb. 27, 1815.

22. 1823, LD, 1: 28; 1831, LDMS, 2: 85.

23. SEGPC, Feb. 27, 1815.

24. Cottrell, "Business Man," 25.

25. Stock Exchange Admission Applications, 1812, MS 17957/11; SEGPC, April 2, 1812, MS. 14-600/7, April 1810–March 1814, fol. 534, Guildhall Library.

26. See Todd Endelman, *Radical Assimilation in English Jewish History, 1656–1945* (Bloomington, Ind., 1990), 11–33.

27. Wolf, *Montefiore*, 18–19.

28. Rachel Montefiore to MM and JM, March 18, 1823, ASM.

29. Wolf, "Honeymoon," 241.

30. There is no S&P record of her.

31. Marriage certificate of Miriam Montefiore, a proselyte, and Benjamin son of Moses Mocatta, Heshvan 8, 5597, Bevis Marks Records, pt. 2, no. 1827, S&P.

32. See Sonia Lipman, "Judith Montefiore—First Lady of Anglo-Jewry," *TJHSE* 21 (1968): 287–303.

33. Quoted in Wolf, *Montefiore*, 21.

34. Will of Levy Barent-Cohen, June 17, 1808, Prob/11/1480, NA. More generally see Herbert Kaplan, *Nathan Mayer Rothschild and the Creation of a Dynasty: The Critical Years 1806–1816* (Stanford, Calif., 2006), 6–10.

35. List of Finta Payments for the Following Three Years: Aug. 28, 1806, and Aug. 24, 1809, MB Mahamad, Kislev 5563–1802 to Nisan 5571–1811, MS. 109, uncat. B07/085, fols. 149–153, 278–282; Sept. 3, 1811, MB Mahamad, Kislev 5571–1811 to Elul 5578–1818, MS110, uncat. B07/085, fols. 15–20, S&P, London Metropolitan Archives.

36. Lipman, "Judith Montefiore," 290.

37. Brother John M. Shaftesley, "Jews in English Freemasonry in the 18th and 19th Centuries," *Transactions of Quatuor Coronati Lodge No. 2076* 92 (Nov. 1979): 38.

38. On English marriage practices see Leonore Davidoff and Catherine Hall, *Family Fortunes: Men and Women of the English Middle Class, 1780–1850* (London,

1992), 222. On confusion over Judith's age, see Lipman, "Judith Montefiore," 287–288.

39. See the pencil drawing of Moses Montefiore c. 1812 in Myrtle Franklin and Michael Bor, *Sir Moses Montefiore, 1784–1885* (London, 1984), 17.

40. Lipman, "Judith Montefiore," 291, dismisses the possibility that a childhood injury had left her slightly deformed.

41. Franklin and Bor, *Montefiore*, facing 16.

42. LD, 1: 3.

43. MM and JM to NMR, March 9, 1814, 000/651/1, RAL; MM to JM, Sept. 21, 1837, 1837:1, SLC.

44. Lipman, "Victorian Gentleman," 13.

45. Journal entry, June 10, 1812, in Wolf, "Honeymoon," 241.

46. LD, 1: 4.

47. Lipman, "Judith Montefiore," 288.

48. Copy of the Will of Mrs. Lydia B. Cohen, ASM.

49. Journal entry, June 12, 1812, in Wolf, "Honeymoon," 242.

50. P. B. Benny, "Personal Reminiscences of Sir Moses Montefiore, I," *Jewish World*, Aug. 7, 1885, 5.

51. Journal entries, June 17 and 18, 1812, in Wolf, "Honeymoon," 245–246.

52. June 10, 11, and 13, 1812, ibid., 242–243.

53. June 15, 1812, ibid., 244.

54. June 29, 1812, ibid., 250.

55. The best account of Nathan's early business activities is Kaplan, *Rothschild*. More generally see Niall Ferguson, *The World's Banker: The History of the House of Rothschild* (London, 1998).

56. See Kaplan, *Rothschild*, chap. 4.

57. Quoted in Ferguson, *World's Banker*, 96. More generally see John Sherwig, *Guineas and Gunpowder: British Foreign Aid in the Wars with France, 1793–1815* (Cambridge, Mass, 1969).

58. Quoted in Ferguson, *World's Banker*, 53–54.

59. Montefiore Account Book 1827–29, Mocatta 11, ML.

60. LD, 1: 29.

61. Quoted in Ferguson, *World's Banker*, 113.

62. Wolf, *Montefiore*, 18.

63. Paul Goodman, *Moses Montefiore* (Philadelphia, 1925), 32.

64. Stanley Chapman, "The Establishment of the Rothschilds as Bankers in London," in *The Rothschilds: Essays on the History of a European Family*, ed. George Heuberger (Frankfurt am Main, 1994), 80.

65. Kynaston, *A World of Its Own*, 4.

66. MM and JM to NMR, March 9, 1814.

67. On the militia see J. W. Fortescue, *The County Lieutenancies and the Army, 1803–1814* (London, 1909).

68. Wolf, "Honeymoon," 245–246.

69. LD, 1: 25.

70. LD, 1: 17.

71. Kosher wine was imported to Britain but was probably never produced in Portugal.

72. LD, 1: 18.

73. Henry Thornton, 1802, quoted in Kynaston, *A World of Its Own,* 9.

74. Quoted in ibid., 10.

75. Quoted in ibid., 29.

76. LD, 1: 19.

77. Small Brown Book starting with MM's Will, Ellul 5, 5573, ASM.

78. See Kaplan, *Rothschild,* chap. 5.

79. MM to NMR, March 9, 1814, folder 1, HL.

80. Ibid., P.S. from JM.

81. Wolf, *Montefiore,* 23–24.

82. John Francis, *Chronicles and Characters of the Stock Exchange* (London, 1849), 303–304.

83. Certificate of Attestation, Feb. 1816[?], issued by Montefiore Brothers & Jo & Geo Van Sommer, Herries Papers, Add. 57380, fol. 70, BL.

84. JdR to NMR and SvR, Aug. 17, 1816, XI/109/5/2/130, tape 98, letter 7, RAL.

85. Ferguson, *World's Banker,* 126–129.

86. JdR to NMR and SvR, Aug. 17, 1816.

87. Lists of Finta Payments for the Following Three Years: Sept. 19, 1815, MB Mahamad, Kislev 5571–1811 to Ellul 5578–1818, MS110, uncat. B07/085, fols. 176–179, S&P, London Metropolitan Archives.

88. SvR and JdR to NMR, May 19, 1817, XI/T27/256, RAL.

89. JdR to NMR, May 19, 1817, XI/109/7, tape 107, letter 4, RAL.

90. SvR, P.S. from JdR to NMR, Dec. 29 1817, XI/109/8/2/134, tape 111, letter 15, RAL.

91. Carl von Rothschild to SvR and JdR, Nov. 11, 1815, XI/109/3/1/48, tape 20, letter 10, RAL.

92. JdR to NMR, May 19, 1817.

93. Quoted in Lipman, "Victorian Gentleman," 14.

94. LD, 1: 21.

95. MM to NMR, Feb. 10, 1818, folder 1, HL.

96. Aug. 8, 1836, loose leaf, MMJ, ASM.

97. JdR to NMR, P.S. from SvR, Nov. 27, 1818, XI/109/9/2/86, tape 184, letter 18, RAL.

98. Ferguson, *World's Banker,* 135.

99. Cottrell, "Business Man," 29–30.

100. Quoted in Chaim Bermant, *The Cousinhood* (New York, 1971), 25.

101. For context see Boyd Hilton, *Corn, Cash, Commerce: The Economic Policies of the Tory Governments, 1815–1830* (Oxford, 1977), chap. 2.

102. Kynaston, *A World of Its Own,* 53.

103. See for instance *An Essay on the Commercial Habits of the Jews* (London, 1809).

104. Ferguson, *World's Banker,* 278.

105. Lord George Byron, *Don Juan,* ed. T. G. Steffan, E. Steffan, and W. W. Pratt (London, 1996), 421.

106. "A New Court Fire Screen (1824)," reproduced in Ferguson, *World's Banker,* 296.

3. A World beyond Business

1. LD, 1: 21.

2. Quoted in Mona Wilson, "Travel and Holidays," in *Early Victorian England,* ed. G. M. Young, vol. 2 (Oxford, 1988), 297–298.

3. Journal entry, Dec. 25, 1825, in Lucien Wolf, "Lady Montefiore's Honeymoon," in *Essays in Jewish History,* ed. Cecil Roth (London, 1934), 255.

4. MM to NMR, March 9, 1814, folder 1, HL.

5. LD, 1: 24. The Shakespeare quotation comes from *Richard III,* act III, scene 4. The poem appears to have circulated widely: see for instance William Mavor, *The English Spelling-Book* (London, 1818), 94, which was first published in 1801 and sold over 2 million copies.

6. A number of MS. diaries survive: JMTD, 1816–1817, MS. Var 3/1-2, JNUL; JMTD, 1821 and 1830, ASM; JMTD, 1823 (transcript), 1823:1a, SLC; and JMTD, 1825, 1825:1, SLC.

7. Quoted in Sonia Lipman, "Judith Montefiore—First Lady of Anglo-Jewry," *TJHSE* 21 (1968): 292.

8. Aug. 19, 1821, JMTD.

9. Oct. 4, 1823, JMTD.

10. Oct. 16, 1823, JMTD.

11. MM to NMR, March 9, 1814.

12. July 17, 1825, JMTD.

13. July 18 and June 11, 1821, JMTD.

14. June 15, June 20, and July 26, 1821, JMTD.

15. JM to Hannah Rothschild, Nov. 21, 1823, folder 1, HL.

16. On traveling on the Sabbath see July 17, 1825, JMTD. Saturday prayers are mentioned repeatedly in MMJ 1827–28, ASM. On irregular synagogue attendance see Nov. 23, 1823, JMTD.

17. See Lipman, "Judith Montefiore," 293.

18. See Sonia Lipman, "The Making of a Victorian Gentleman," in *CMM,* 293–294; and LD, 1: 22.

19. MM to NMR, March 12, 1818, folder 1, HL.

20. 1817, 1823, 1827.

21. Oct. 7 and 9, 1823, JMTD.

22. Oct. 4, 1823, JMTD; April 13, 1837, loose Leaf, MMJ, ASM. On the Montefiores' interaction with Mazzara in Rome see May 9, 1859, TH LB, item 13, PP/HO/D/A2425, HAWL.

23. See Amalie Kass and Edward Kass, *Perfecting the World: The Life and Times of Dr. Thomas Hodgkin, 1798–1866* (Boston, 1988).

24. Quoted in Ben Gersehen, "The Quaker and the Jew," *Maryland Medical Journal* 40 (Sept. 1991): 764.

25. TH to Elizabeth Hodgkin, Nov. 12, 1823, PP/HO/D/A604, box 8, file 5, HAWL.

26. TH to John Hodgkin Jr., Nov. 12, 1823, ibid.

27. Dec. 2, 1823, JMTD.

28. Dec. 8, 1823, JMTD.

29. TH to John Hodgkin Sr., Jan. 11, 1824, PP/HO/D/A612, box 8, file 5, HAWL.

30. John Hodgkin Sr. to TH, Feb. 20, 1824, PP/HO/D/A291, box 7, file 2, HAWL.

31. LD, 1: 30, Psalms 103:15.

32. TH LB 1859, fol. 20, item 13, PP/HO/D/A2425, HAWL.

33. P. B. Benny, "Personal Reminiscences of Sir Moses Montefiore, IV," *Jewish World,* Aug. 28, 1885, 5.

34. Library Catalogue, 1842, ASM.

35. Guest List, 1812, ASM.

36. See John Shaftesley, "Jews in English Regular Freemasonry, 1717–1860," *TJHSE* 25 (1977): 150–209; also David Ruderman, *Jewish Enlightenment in an English Key: Anglo-Jewry's Construction of Modern Jewish Thought* (Princeton, 2000), 151–154. More generally see Jacob Katz, *Jews and Freemasons in Europe, 1723–1939,* trans. Leonard Oschry (Cambridge, Mass., 1979).

37. See LD, 1: 22, on the purchase of Tinley Lodge. See Lipman, "Victorian Gentleman," 14, on his heraldic application.

38. LD, 1: 6–7.

39. LDMS, 1:25; LD, 1: 14.

40. LD, 1: 20.

41. See Albert Hyamson, *The Sephardim of England: A History of the Spanish and Portuguese Jewish Community, 1492–1951* (London, 1951), 247, and 94 on the origins of this practice.

42. MB Mahamad 1818–1819, MS. 111 (uncat.), S&P, London Metropolitan Archives.

43. Meeting of Elders, Sept. 19, 1819, ibid.

44. LD, 1: 23; LDMS, 1: 26.

45. LD, 2: 27.

46. Lipman, "Victorian Gentleman," 9.

47. Journal entry, June 12, 1812, in Wolf, "Honeymoon," 242.

48. Wolf, "Honeymoon," 252–254.

49. July 19, 1821, JMTD.

50. See P. L. Cottrell, "The Business Man and the Financier," in *CMM,* 30–39.

51. G. Clayton, *British Insurance* (London, 1971), 100.

52. Sir William Schooling, *Alliance Assurance, 1824–1924* (London, 1924), 1–2.

53. On Barings see Peter Austin, *Baring Brothers and the Birth of Modern Finance* (London, 2007), chaps. 1–2.

54. D. M. Evans, *The City; or the Physiology of London Business; with Sketches on 'Change and at the Coffee Houses* (London, 1845), 20.

55. Sept. 18, 1821, JMTD.

56. Quoted in Cottrell, "Business Man," 31.

57. See Clayton, *British Insurance;* also D. T. Jenkins, "The Practice of Insurance against Fire, 1750–1840, and Historical Research," in *The Historian and the Business of Insurance,* ed. Oliver Westall (Manchester, 1984), 9–38.

58. On Catholic emancipation see G. I. T. Machin, *The Catholic Question in English Politics, 1820 to 1830* (Oxford, 1964). On O'Connell see Oliver MacDonagh, *The Hereditary Bondsman: Daniel O'Connell, 1775–1829* (London, 1988); and MacDonagh, *The Emancipist Daniel O'Connell, 1830–1847* (New York, 1989).

59. See MacDonagh, *Emancipist,* 110–115. O'Connell's published correspondence contains no reference to his purported involvement with the Provincial Bank, nor does MacDonagh, *Hereditary Bondsman.*

60. John Francis, *Chronicles and Characters of the Stock Exchange* (London, 1849), 263.

61. Clayton, *British Insurance,* 104–105.

62. Cottrell, "Business Man," 39.

63. Francis, *Chronicles and Characters,* 264.

64. JMTD, 1830.

65. July 23, 1827, MMJ 1827–28.

66. See Henry Malchow, *Gentlemen Capitalists: The Social and Political World of the Victorian Businessman* (London, 1991), 344; and R. J. Morris, "The Middle-Class and the Property Cycle during the Industrial Revolution," in *The Search for Wealth and Stability: Essays in Economic and Social History Presented to M. W. Flinn.,* ed. T. C. Smout (London, 1979), 91–113.

67. In 1824 he received 163 votes from an electorate of 278, but most other members of the committee won at least 275. Montefiore's support level remained almost unchanged in 1825, when a turnout of only 171 rendered his total of 164 votes unremarkable. A year later, however, he received only 146 votes out of a maximum of 216. SEGPC, March 26, 1824, March 28, 1825, and March 25, 1826, MS. 14-600/10, 05/1823–11/1826, fols. 92, 190, 267, Guildhall Library, City of London; SEGPC, June 9, 1823, MS. 14-600/10, 05/1823–11/1826, fols. 13–14, Guildhall Library; SEGPC, March 23, 1827, MS. 14-600/11, 04/12/1826–23/03/1829, fol. 53, Guildhall Library, contains details of his resignation.

68. W. D. Rubinstein, "Jewish Top Wealth-Holders in Britain, 1809–1909," *Jewish Historical Studies* 37 (2001): 138.

69. Edward Brayley, *London and Middlesex, or, an Historical, Commercial & Descriptive Survey of the Metropolis of Great-Britain: Including Sketches of Its Environs, and a Topographical Account of the Most Remarkable Places in the Above County,* vol. 2 (London, 1814), 5.

70. Wolf, "Honeymoon," 253–254.

71. Quoted in David Kynaston, *A World of Its Own: 1815–1890,* vol. 1 of *The City of London* (London, 1994), 68.

72. LDMS, 1: 34.

73. Cottrell, "Business Man," 29.

74. LD, 1: 34.

75. Kynaston, *A World of Its Own,* 45.

76. Journal entry, June 15, 1812, in Wolf, "Honeymoon," 244.

77. Lucien Wolf, *Sir Moses Montefiore: A Centennial Biography, with Extracts from Letters and Journals* (London, 1884), 25.

78. MM to JM, Oct. 29, 1825, ASM.

79. See Michele Klein, *A Time to Be Born: Customs and Folklore of Jewish Birth* (Philadelphia, 2000), chap. 2.

4. The Road to Jerusalem

1. May 1, 1827, Montefiore Account Book 1827–29, Mocatta 11, ML; May 1, 1827, JMPJ, 2; May 1, 1827, MMJ 1827–28, ASM.

2. Jacob Barnai, *The Jews in Palestine in the Eighteenth Century under the Patronage of the Istanbul Committee of Officials for Palestine*, trans. Naomi Goldblum (Tuscaloosa, 1992), 27–33.

3. Sonia Lipman, "The Making of a Victorian Gentleman," in *CMM*, 15.

4. He also contemplated a trip to Palestine in 1823; LD, 1: 30.

5. For an introduction to these issues see Lawrence Hoffmann, ed., *The Land of Israel: Jewish Perspectives* (Notre Dame, Ind., 1986).

6. P. B. Benny, "Personal Reminiscences of Sir Moses Montefiore, II," *Jewish World*, Aug. 14, 1885, 5.

7. See Michele Klein, *Not to Worry: Jewish Wisdom and Folklore* (Philadelphia, 2003), 49–50 and, more generally, chap. 5.

8. JMPJ. For an analysis of Judith's journal as literary text see Judith Page, "Jerusalem and Jewish Memory: Judith Montefiore's 'Private Journal,'" *Victorian Literature and Culture* 27, no. 1 (1999): 125–141. For a Jewish historian's perspective see Israel Bartal, "Introduction," in Judith Montefiore, *Private Journal of a Visit to Egypt and Palestine* (Jerusalem, 1975), i–iv.

9. MMJ 1827–28. This document may have been transcribed for Sir Joseph Sebag-Montefiore.

10. May 2 and 3, 1827, MMJ 1827–28.

11. June 5 and 7, 1827, JMPJ, 48, 51.

12. June 7, 1827, JMPJ, 51.

13. June 10, 1827, MMJ 1827–28.

14. June 12, May 3, and May 5, 1827, JMPJ, 55, 6–8.

15. June 16, 22, and 20, 1827, MMJ 1827–28.

16. June 25, 1827, ibid.; June 20 and Sept. 4, 1827, JMPJ, 62, 151.

17. See M. S. Anderson, *The Eastern Question, 1774–1923: A Study in International Relations* (London, 1966), chap. 3. On Egyptian involvement see Afaf Lufti Al-Sayyid Marsot, *Egypt in the Reign of Muhammad Ali* (Cambridge, 1984), 206–221.

18. June 25, 1827, JMPJ, 66.

19. June 28, July 1, and July 9, 1827, JMPJ, 70, 74, 91.

20. July 9, 1827, MMJ 1827–28.

21. K. Bonar and R. M. M'Cheyne, *Narrative of a Mission of Inquiry to the Jews from the Church of Scotland in 1839* (Edinburgh, 1842), 48.

22. July 16, 1827, MMJ 1827–28.

23. Aug. 1, 1827, ibid.

24. Aug. 1, 1827, JPMJ, 110–11.

25. Quoted in Al-Sayyid Marsot, *Egypt,* 208.

26. July 12, 1827, MMJ 1827–28.

27. Aug. 27 and 29, 1827, JMPJ, 131, 134.

28. Aug. 30 and Sept. 3, 1827, MMJ 1827–29.

29. Sept. 4, 1827, ibid. On Mehmed Ali see Al-Sayyid Marsot, *Egypt,* which has replaced the classic Henry Dodwell, *The Founder of Modern Egypt: A Study of Muhammad Ali* (Cambridge, 1931).

30. Quoted in Al-Sayyid Marsot, *Egypt,* 34.

31. Dr. R. Madden, *Travels in Turkey, Egypt, Nubia and Palestine in 1824, 1825, 1826 and 1827,* 2 vols. (London, 1829), 1: 243.

32. Quoted in Al-Sayyid Marsot, *Egypt,* 102–103.

33. Quoted in ibid., 28.

34. Sept. 5, 1827, JMPJ, 153.

35. Sept. 4, 1827, MMJ 1827–28.

36. Sept. 11 and 26, 1827, ibid.

37. Edward Barker, ed., *Syria and Egypt under the Last Five Sultans of Turkey: Being Experiences during Fifty Years of Mr. Consul-General Barker, Chiefly from His Letters and Journals,* vol. 2 (London, 1876), 62–65.

38. For an overview focusing especially on the Balkans, see Esther Benbassa and Aron Rodrigue, *Sephardi Jewry: A History of the Judeo-Spanish Community, 14th–20th Centuries* (Berkeley, 1993), chaps. 1–2. For more specific insights see Benjamin Braude and Bernard Lewis, eds., *Christians and Jews in the Ottoman Empire: The Functioning of a Plural Society* (New York, 1982).

39. Edward William Lane, *An Account of the Manners and Customs of the Modern Egyptians* (New York, 1973), 554. For a modern scholarly account see Jacob Landau, *Jews in Nineteenth Century Egypt* (New York, 1969).

40. Here I take issue with the argument made in Bartal, "Introduction," iii.

41. Sept. 21, 1827, MMJ 1827–28.

42. Sept. 22, 1827, ibid.

43. Sept. 20, 1827, JMPJ, 168.

44. In contrast with the attitudes depicted in Aron Rodrigue, *French Jews, Turkish Jews: The Alliance Israélite Universelle and the Politics of Jewish Schooling in Turkey, 1860–1925* (Bloomington, Ind., 1990); and Bettina Marx, *Juden Marokkos und Europas. Das marokkanische Judentum Im 19. Jahrhundert und seine Darstellung in der zeitgenössischen jüdischen Presse in Deutschland, Frankreich und Groß Britannien* (Frankfurt am Main, 1991), pt. 1, chaps. 1, 3.

45. Oct. 1, 1827, JMPJ, 174–175.

46. Sept. 23 and Oct. 1, 1827, MMJ 1827–28.

47. Sept. 30, 1827, JMPJ, 173–174. See the classic Edward Said, *Orientalism* (London, 2003); also Ivan Kalmar and Derek Penslar, eds., *Orientalism and the Jews* (Waltham, Mass., 2005).

48. Oct. 4, 1827, MMJ 1827–28.

49. Oct. 5, 1827, JMPJ, 177.

50. Oct. 18, 1827, JMPJ, 202–203.

51. Oct. 8, 1827, MMJ 1827–28.

52. See Madden, *Travels,* vol. 1, which includes several letters to the Montefiores. For evidence of their friendship see Project of a Spanish Tour for Sir Moses and Lady Montefiore, with the Kindest Regards and Best Wishes of Their Old Friend and Fellow Traveller Richard Robert Madden, 1859, Schischa Collection, London; MM to LL, Jan. 8, 1850, folder 2, HL; also MM to Madden, 1876, in *The Memoirs (Chiefly Autobiographical) from 1798 to 1886 of Richard Robert Madden, M.D., F.R.C.S.,* ed. Thomas Madden (London, 1891), 208.

53. Madden, *Travels,* 2: 385–395.

54. Oct. 10, 1827, JMPJ, 182.

55. Madden, *Travels,* 2: 395.

56. Oct. 9, 1827, MMJ 1827–28.

57. Oct. 16, 1827, ibid. On more customary English attitudes see Eitan Bar-Yosef, *The Holy Land in English Culture, 1799–1917* (Oxford, 2005), 81–85.

58. Oct. 17, 1827, JMPJ, 192.

59. Oct. 17, 1827, MMJ 1827–28.

60. Sonia Lipman, "Judith Montefiore—First Lady of Anglo-Jewry," *TJHSE* 21 (1968): 293.

61. On Jerusalem see Yehoshua Ben-Arieh, *Jerusalem in the 19th Century: Emergence of the New City* (Jerusalem, 1986). For a fascinating collection of contemporary images see Dan Kyram and Amos Mar-Haim, *Enduring Images: 19th Century Jerusalem through Lens and Brush* (Jerusalem, 5742 [1981–82]).

62. See Yehoshua Ben-Arieh, "The Population of the Large Towns in Palestine during the First Eighty Years of the Nineteenth Century According to Western Sources," in *Studies on Palestine during the Ottoman Period,* ed. Moshe Ma'oz (Jerusalem, 1975), 51–52.

63. See Usiel Schmelz, "Some Demographic Peculiarities of the Jews of Jerusalem in the Nineteenth Century," ibid., 121–126.

64. Oct. 18, 1827, JMPJ, 193.

65. See Adel Manaa, "Sandzak yerushalayim bein shetei pelishot (1798–1831): Minhal vehevrah" (Ph.D diss., Hebrew University of Jerusalem, 1986); also Mordechai Abir, "Local Leadership and Early Reforms in Palestine, 1800–1834," in Ma'oz, *Studies on Palestine,* 285–286. For longer-term context see Amnon Cohen, *Palestine in the 18th Century: Patterns of Government and Administration* (Jerusalem, 1973).

66. For a brief introduction to Jewish life in the city, see Tudor Parfitt, *The Jews of Palestine, 1800–1882* (Exeter, 1987), chap. 2. For an old-fashioned but still usable introduction to the Old Yishuv, of particular use in covering the early period, see Itzhak Ben-Zvi, "Eretz Yisrael under Ottoman Rule, 1517–1917," in *The Jews,* ed. Louis Finkelstein (London, 1961), 602–689.

67. Parfitt, *Jews of Palestine,* 180, 183.

68. Amnon Cohen, "Introduction," in *A World Within: Jewish Life as Reflected in Muslim Court Documents from the Sijill of Jerusalem (XVI Century)* (Philadelphia, 1994).

69. See Barnai, *Jews in Palestine*. On Pekam see Aryeh Morgenstern, *Hapekidim veha'amarkalim beamsterdam vehayishuv hayehudi be'erets yisra'el bemaḥatsit harishonah shel hame'ah hatesha-esreh* (Jerusalem, 1981).

70. Barnai, *Jews in Palestine*, 68.

71. Ibid., 27–29.

72. Ben-Zvi, "Eretz Yisrael," 650.

73. See Margalit Shilo, *Princess or Prisoner? Jewish Women in Jerusalem, 1840–1914*, trans. David Louvish (Waltham, Mass., 2005), 6–10.

74. See Ben-Zvi, "Eretz Yisrael," 649.

75. See Israel Bartal, "Yehudei mizraḥ eiropah ve'erets yisra'el (1771–1881): Ha'aliyot umivneh hayishuv ha'ashkenazi," *Cathedra* 16 (July 1980): 3–9.

76. May 13, 1827, MMJ 1827–28.

77. See Ruth Kark and Joseph Glass, *Sephardi Entrepreneurs in Eretz Israel: The Amzalak Family, 1816–1918* (Jerusalem, 1991), chap. 2.

78. Rev. Joseph Wolff, *Journal of the Rev. Joseph Wolff . . . in a Series of Letters to Sir Thomas Baring, Bart., Containing an Account of His Missionary Labours from the Years 1827 to 1831; and from the Years 1835 to 1838* (London, 1839), 214.

79. Oct. 18, 1827, MMJ 1827–28.

80. Oct. 19, 20, 1827, JMPJ, 205, 214.

81. See Mordecai Eliav, "Yaḥasim bein-edatiyim bayishuv hayehudi be'erets yisra'el bame'ah hatesha-esreh," *Pe'amim* 11 (1982): 118–133.

82. Montefiore gives the following figures: "Portuguese 500 families about 2000 individuals. Germans 40, or 160 persons, and near 2000 Old Widows in great distress"; Oct. 18, 1827, MMJ 1827–28.

83. Oct. 20, 1827, JMPJ, 214.

84. Oct. 20, 1827, MMJ 1827–28.

85. Oct. 20, 1827, JMPJ, 212.

86. Oct. 19, 1827, MMJ 1827–28.

87. Kyram and Mar-Haim, *Enduring Images*, 91. More generally, see Fred Strickert, *Rachel Weeping: Jews, Christians, and Muslims at the Fortress Tomb* (Collegeville, Minn., 2007).

88. Genesis 25:21.

89. See Susan Sered, "Rachel's Tomb: The Development of a Cult," Jewish Studies Quarterly 2, no. 2 (1995): 104–148. More generally see Shilo, *Princess or Prisoner?* 18–33. My thanks to Michele Klein for her help on this issue.

90. To JM, Fertility Amulet written by Yehudah Ben Yossef Nissim Burla, ASM (currently still with Mr. Robert Sebag-Montefiore). Rabbi Yehosha Burla the Elder (d. 1939) was the Sephardi *shamash* (guardian) of Rachel's Tomb for sixty years. He worked alongside the Ashkenazi *shamash* Rabbi Shimon Monzon (appointed and apparently paid by Montefiore) and the Ashkenazi Rabbi Jacob Freiman, *shamash* of Jerusalem's Hurvah synagogue and a deputy *shamash* at Rachel's Tomb. Rabbi Jacob inherited both these positions from his father; probably the Sephardi position was also hereditary and funded by Montefiore. R. Yehosha Burla's son was the well-known writer Yehudah Burla (1886–1969). In Sephardi tradition it is customary to

name sons after grandfathers, so the author of this amulet was probably the father of R. Yehosha Burla the Elder. For details see Eli Schiller, *Kever raḥel* (Jerusalem, 1977), 17, 32. R. Yossef Nissim Burla would be one of the first occupants of Mishkenot Sha'ananim, and we have evidence of his contact with Montefiore in MM to JMM, Aug. 28, 1866, BD, 3rd Half-Yearly Report, BDMB, ACC/3121/A/010, fol. 127.

91. Oct. 19, 1827, JMPJ, 206.

92. LD, 1: 182. But see also Petitions for Repairing the Tomb of Rachel, 5599, MMSS vol. 574 53B. On the Montefiores' involvement with Rachel's Tomb see Schiller, *Kever raḥel*, 25–25; and Sered, "Rachel's Tomb," 116–119. Montefiore's niece Jemima Guedalla attributed his interest in it to its association with his mother's name; Jemima Guedalla, *Diary of a Tour to Jerusalem and Alexandria in 1855 with Sir Moses and Lady Montefiore by the Late Mrs. H. Guedalla* (London, 1890), 48.

93. Oct. 21, 1827, MMJ 1827–28.

94. Oct. 24, 1827, ibid.

95. Oct. 27, 1827, ibid.

96. See Barker, *Syria and Egypt, 58–59*.

97. Nov. 4, 1827, MMJ 1827–28.

98. Quoted in Al-Sayyid Marsot, *Egypt*, 217.

99. Nov. 25, 1827, MMJ 1827–28.

100. Nov. 26, 1827, ibid.

101. See Hayim Schwarzbaum, *Shorashim venofim* (Beer Sheva, 1993), 157.

102. Nov. 26, 1827, JMTD, 1827–28, MMSS vol. 567, fol. 14.

103. Dec. 1, 1827, MMJ 1827–28.

104. Nov. 26, 1827, loose Leaf, MMJ, ASM. Numerous photocopies of this document are in circulation within the Sebag-Montefiore family.

105. Dec. 22, 1827, MMJ 1827–28.

106. Jan. 28, 1828, JMTD, 1827–28.

107. MM to duke of Norfolk, May 13, 1831, ASM.

108. Sept. 3, 1827, MMJ 1827–28.

5. Rise, Sir Moses

1. Quoted in G. I. T. Machin, *The Catholic Question in English Politics, 1820 to 1830* (Oxford, 1964), 115.

2. On Anglo-Jewish emancipation see M. C. N. Salbstein, *The Emancipation of the Jews in Britain: The Question of the Admission of the Jews to Parliament, 1828–1860* (London, 1982); and Abraham Gillam, *The Emancipation of the Jews in England, 1830–1860* (New York, 1982).

3. ILG to Wellington, May 9, 1828, in Lionel Abrahams, "Sir I. L. Goldsmid and the Admission of the Jews of England to Parliament," *TJHSE* 4 (1903): 133–134.

4. Wellington to ILG, April 24, 1828, in Abrahams, "Sir I. L. Goldsmid," 132.

5. On the origins of the Board of Deputies see James Picciotto, in *Sketches of Anglo-Jewish History*, ed. Israel Finestein (London, 1956), chap. 13; and Albert

Hyamson, *The Sephardim of England: A History of the Spanish and Portuguese Jewish Community, 1492–1951* (London, 1951), 123–139.

6. April 28, 1828, BDMB, ACC/3121/A/5/AA.

7. For the classic view of the two men as opposites see Salbstein, *Emancipation*, 85–94; Israel Finestein, "The Uneasy Victorian: Montefiore as Communal Leader," in *CMM*, 67–68.

8. On Goldsmid's philanthropy see Mordechai Rozin, *The Rich and the Poor: Jewish Philanthropy and Social Control in Nineteenth-Century London* (Brighton, 1999), 77–79.

9. Chaim Bermant, *The Cousinhood* (New York, 1971), 63.

10. On Francis Goldsmid see D. Wolf Marks and A. Löwy, *Memoir of Sir Francis Henry Goldsmid* (London, 1882).

11. Holland to ILG, May 18, 1828, in Abrahams, "Sir I. L. Goldsmid," 134–135.

12. LDMS, 1: 61.

13. On British philanthropy see David Owen, *English Philanthropy, 1660–1960* (Cambridge, Mass., 1964); also Frank Prochaska, *The Voluntary Impulse: Philanthropy in Modern Britain* (London, 1988). Specifically on this period see Joanna Innes, "State, Church and Voluntarism in European Welfare, 1690–1850," in *Charity, Philanthropy and Reform: From the 1690s to 1850*, ed. Hugh Cunningham and Joanna Innes (Basingstoke, 1998), 15–66; and other essays in this volume. More generally see Colin Jones, "Some Recent Trends in the History of Charity," in *Charity, Self-Interest and Welfare in the English Past*, ed. Martin Daunton (London, 1996). On what David Turley terms the "middle-class reform complex" see David Turley, *The Culture of English Antislavery, 1780–1860* (London, 1991), chap. 5.

14. On urban poor relief see Peter Mandler, ed., *The Uses of Charity: The Poor on Relief in the Nineteenth-Century Metropolis* (Philadelphia, 1990).

15. See Marcel Mauss, *The Gift: Forms and Functions of Exchange in Archaic Societies* (London, 1954); also Ilana Silber, "Modern Philanthropy: Reassessing the Viability of a Maussian Perspective," in *Marcel Mauss: A Centenary Tribute*, ed. Wendy James and N. J. Allen (Oxford, 1998), 134–150. On the role of philanthropy in interelite politics, see for instance Sandra Cavallo, "The Motivations of Benefactors: An Overview of Approaches to the Study of Charity," in *Medicine and Charity before the Welfare State*, ed. Jonathan Barry and Colin Jones (London, 1991), 46–62. For a stimulating critique of the functionalist approach to philanthropy, see Alan J. Kidd, "Philanthropy and the 'Social History' Paradigm," *Social History* 21 (May 1996): 180–192.

16. "Jews' Free School," *VJ*, March 31, 1843, 139.

17. For biographies of City figures see "London Mayors, Aldermen and Common Councilmen in the Victorian City of London," www.london-city-history.org.uk, accessed Dec. 20, 2008.

18. For an economic motivation rooted in middle-class capitalism see David Brion-Davis, *The Problem of Slavery in the Age of Revolution, 1770–1823* (Ithaca, 1973). But see also the critique provided in Thomas Haskell, "Capitalism and the Origins of the Humanitarian Sensibility," *American Historical Review* 90 (1985): 339–361, 547–566.

19. On proselytism see Mel Scult, *Millennial Expectations and Jewish Liberties: A Study of the Efforts to Convert the Jews in Britain, up to the Mid Nineteenth Century* (Leiden, 1978). For a comparative European perspective see Christopher Clark, *The Politics of Conversion: Missionary Protestantism and the Jews in Prussia, 1728–1941* (Oxford, 1995). On philo-Semitism in English Protestant thought see Todd Endelman, *The Jews of Georgian England, 1714–1830: Tradition and Change in a Liberal Society* (Philadelphia, 1979), 50–57. More generally, see William Rubinstein and Hilary Rubinstein, *Philosemitism: Admiration and Support in the English-Speaking World for Jews, 1840–1939* (Basingstoke, 1999).

20. See for instance Linda Colley, *Britons: Forging the Nation, 1707–1837* (London, 1996), 31–34.

21. See William Thomas Gidney, *The History of the London Society for Promoting Christianity among the Jews, 1809 to 1908* (London, 1908); also Robert Michael Smith, "The London Jews' Society and Patterns of Jewish Conversion in England, 1801–1859," *JSS* 42 (Summer/Fall 1981): 275–290.

22. Cited after Scult, *Millennial Expectations,* 132.

23. LD, 1: 60–61, 65.

24. On O'Connell's support for Jewish emancipation see Oliver MacDonagh, *The Emancipist: Daniel O'Connell, 1830–1847* (New York, 1989), 17–19.

25. Quoted in Niall Ferguson, *The World's Banker: The History of the House of Rothschild* (London, 1998), 156 and, more generally, 155–165.

26. LD, 1: 65–66.

27. Holland to ILG, April 12, 1829, in Abrahams, "Sir I. L. Goldsmid," 140–141.

28. *Hansard's Parliamentary Debates,* 3d ser., 20 (Aug. 1, 1833): 245.

29. March 17 and April 16, 1829, BDMB, ACC/3121/A/5/AA, fols. 7–10; LD, 1: 67.

30. LD, 1: 71.

31. May 3 and 5, 1829, BDMB, ACC/3121/A/5/AA, fols. 12–13.

32. Holland to ILG, May 4, 1829, in Abrahams, "Sir I. L. Goldsmid," 141–142.

33. Mr. Pearce's Report, June 11, 1829, BDMB, ACC/3121/A/5/AA, fols. 24–47.

34. On this episode see LD, 1: 76–79.

35. LDMS, 1: 79.

36. Quoted in Gillam, *Emancipation,* 79.

37. LDMS, 1: 79.

38. For details see April 26, 1830, BDMB, ACC/3121/A/5/AA, fols. 44–46.

39. Quoted in Ferguson, *World's Banker,* 191.

40. Frank Felsenstein, *Anti-Semitic Stereotypes: A Paradigm of Otherness in English Popular Culture, 1660–1830* (London, 1985), 232–235.

41. Quoted in Israel Finestein, "Anglo-Jewish Opinion during the Struggle for Emancipation, 1828–58," in *Jewish Society in Victorian England: Collected Essays,* ed. Finestein (London, 1993), 8.

42. *Hansard's Parliamentary Debates,* n.s., 23 (April 5, 1830): 1304, 1306.

43. See ibid., 32 (April 1, 1833), 221–246.

44. See especially Richard Brent, *Liberal Anglican Politics: Whiggery, Religion and Reform, 1830–1841* (Oxford, 1987). More generally see Norman Gash, *Reac-*

tion and Reconstruction in English Politics, 1832–1852 (Oxford, 1965); Peter Mandler, *Aristocratic Government in the Age of Reform: Whigs and Liberals, 1830–1852* (Oxford, 1990); Ian Newbould, *Whiggery and Reform, 1830–41: The Politics of Government* (London, 1990); and Owen Chadwick, *The Victorian Church,* vol. 1 of *An Ecclesiastical History of England* (London, 1966), chaps. 1–2. The importance of this wider context is overlooked by traditional accounts like Finestein, "Anglo-Jewish Opinion," 1–53.

45. Nov. 3, July 1, and Nov. 18, 1830, BDMB, ACC/3121/A/5/AA, fols. 71, 55–56, 73–75.

46. Jan. 5, 1831, BDMB, ACC/3121/A/5/AA, fols. 76–77.

47. Mocatta to BD, Feb. 9, 1831, BDMB, ACC/3121/A/5/AA, fols. 82–83.

48. LD, 1: 82.

49. LD, 1: 83.

50. Resolutions, 1828, ASM.

51. LD, 1: 86, 99.

52. Todd Endelman, *The Jews of Britain, 1656–2000* (Berkeley, 2002), 79. On the Sephardim see Montefiore's own estimate, LD, 1: 75.

53. LDMS, 1: 80. On Anglo-Jewish philanthropy see Rozin, *Rich and Poor;* and more generally Derek Penslar, *Shylock's Children: Economics and Jewish Identity in Modern Europe* (Berkeley, 2001).

54. On the changing view of poverty in this era see Gertrude Himmelfarb, *The Idea of Poverty: England in the Early Industrial Age* (London, 1984); for broader context, Boyd Hilton, *The Age of Atonement: The Influence of Evangelicalism on Social and Economic Thought, 1785–1865* (Oxford: Clarendon, 1988); on visiting the poor, Owen, *English Philanthropy,* 136–145.

55. Quoted in Owen, *English Philanthropy,* 102.

56. Montefiore was sufficiently engaged in the Quaker world to possess copies of Thomas Clarkson, *A Portraiture of Quakerism* (London, 1807); Joseph John Gurney, *Observations on the Religious Peculiarities of the Society of Friends* (London, 1824); and Gurney, *Notes on a Visit Made to Some of the Prisons in Scotland and the North of England in Company with Elizabeth Fry* (Edinburgh, 1819); Library Catalogue, 1842, ASM.

57. LDMS, 1: 81; LD, 1: 83.

58. For a history of the synagogue at Ramsgate see Rev. D. A. Jessurun Cardozo and Paul Goodman, *Think and Thank: The Montefiore Synagogue and College, Ramsgate* (Oxford, 1933).

59. June 16, 1833, loose leaf, MMJ, ASM.

60. June 17, 1833, loose leaf, MMJ, ASM. LD, 1: 91, omits the word "Christian."

61. On this see J. Mordaunt Crook, *The Rise of the Nouveaux Riches: Style and Status in Victorian and Edwardian Architecture* (London, 1999), 40–46.

62. See W. D. Rubinstein, "New Men of Wealth and the Purchase of Land in Nineteenth-Century England," *Past & Present* 92 (Aug. 1981): 125–147.

63. LD, 1: 72.

64. Thomas Walker, quoted in F. R. Cowell, *The Athenaeum: Club and Social Life in London, 1824–1974* (London, 1975), 35.

65. The classic account remains Michael Brock, *The Great Reform Act* (London, 1973).

66. MM to NMR, 1832, XI/109/27/4/66, RAL.

67. LD, 1: 92.

68. "Jewish Disabilities," *The Times*, May 28, 1833, 6.

69. Brent, *Liberal Anglican Politics*, 252.

70. Gillam, *Emancipation,* 83. On the role of public opinion in the campaign see Polly Pinsker, "English Opinion and Jewish Emancipation (1830–1860)," *JSS* 14, no. 1 (1952): 51–94.

71. "Supplement to the Jewish Chronicle: Biography of Sir Moses Montefiore," *JC*, Oct. 26, 1883, 1.

72. JM to Gompertz, Jan. 15, 1834, folder 1, HL.

73. Hannah Cohen, *Changing Faces: A Memoir of Louisa Lady Cohen by Her Daughter* (London, 1937), 23.

74. April 8 and May 11, 1835, BDMB, ACC/3121/A/5/AA, fols. 91–92, 93–96.

75. March 7, 1836, BDMB, ACC/3121/A/5/AA, fols. 99–101. For an alternative interpretation see Israel Finestein, "The Jews and English Marriage Law during the Emancipation," in Finestein, *Jewish Society in Victorian England*, 54–77.

76. LD, 1: 97.

77. See Turley, *Culture of English Antislavery;* Howard Temperley, *British Anti-Slavery, 1833–1870* (London, 1972).

78. Brent, *Liberal Anglican Politics*, chap. 7.

79. Quoted in ibid., 272.

80. LD, 1: 215. Montefiore owned a copy of Thomas Fowell Buxton, *The African Slave Trade and Its Remedy* (London, 1839), and a copy of the Life of Wilberforce. Library Catalogue, 1842, ASM.

81. LD, 1: 99.

82. Gillam, *Emancipation*, 27.

83. On Salomons see Albert Hyamson, *David Salomons* (London, 1939).

84. LD, 1: 97.

85. Spring-Rice to MM, Nov. 26, 1835, ASM.

86. Camden to Jas. Alexander, Nov. 30, 1835, ASM.

87. LD, 1: 96.

88. See Cecil Woodham-Smith, *Queen Victoria: Her Life and Times, 1819–1861* (London, 1972), chap. 3. For an alternative interpretation see Monica Charlot, *Victoria: The Young Queen* (Oxford, 1991), 56–57.

89. LD, 1: 96.

90. LD, 1: 96, refers only to visits by the duchess, not to those by Victoria; LD, 1: 138, gives more detail on Montefiore's subsequent interaction with the duchess at a time when she was persona non grata at her daughter's court.

91. Woodham-Smith, *Queen Victoria*, 103–108.

92. Victoria writes only of walking on the pier; Queen Victoria's Journal, 1835–1836, Royal Archives, Windsor. The same holds true for her subsequent visits.

93. Stanley Weintraub, *Victoria: Biography of a Queen* (London, 1987), 56. Weintraub gives no source for this story.

94. Cohen, *Changing Faces*, 22

95. For a variant of this motif see the discussion of an article in *The World* (1900) in Pauline Wengeroff, *Memoiren einer Grossmutter. Bilder aus der Kulturgeschichte der Juden Russlands Im 19. Jahrhundert,* vol. 2 (Berlin, 1908), 13.

96. "Sir Moses Montefiore," *JC,* Jan. 24, 1879, 12. Montefiore had no contact with the duke and duchess of Kent in this period, but there is a kernel of truth in this story. See Woodham-Smith, *Queen Victoria,* 19–25.

97. Rabbi Berol Futerfas told me this story in December 2003.

98. See LD, 1: 99; and "Christ's Hospital," *The Times,* Feb. 2, 1836, 3.

99. LD, 1: 106; and Sonia Lipman, "The Making of a Victorian Gentleman," in *CMM,* 19. See also Secretary of the Royal Society to MM, June 17, 1836, ASM. On Jewish Fellows of the Royal Society see Redcliffe Salaman, "The Jewish Fellows of the Royal Society," *Miscellanies of the Jewish Historical Society of England 5* (1948): 146–175.

100. March 7, 1836, BDMB.

101. April 12, July 9, 1836, BDMB, ACC/3121/A/5/AA, fols. 102–104, 125–127.

102. LDMS, 1: 111.

103. June 7 and 13, 1836, BDMB, ACC/3121/A/5/AA, fols. 106–107, 111–112.

104. LD, 1: 107; LDMS, 1: 108.

105. MM to JM, c. Sept. 21, 1837, 1837:1, SLC.

106. LDMS, 1: 116.

107. See Weintraub, *Victoria,* 110, perhaps based on LD, 1: 110.

108. Weintraub, *Victoria,* 134.

109. P. B. Benny, "Personal Reminiscences of Sir Moses Montefiore, II," *Jewish World,* Aug. 14, 1885, 5.

110. LD, 1: 127.

111. Montefiore's private library catalogue included the following references: "Government of Gaols," "Report of Prison Discipline," "Roscoe on Penal Jurisprudence," and "Gurney on Prison"; Library Catalogue, 1842, ASM.

112. LDMS, 1: 147.

113. Cohen, *Changing Faces,* 21. See also LD, 1: 142–144; Benny, "Personal Reminiscences, II." There is no evidence to link Montefiore's views with the Jewish tradition on capital punishment.

114. P. B. Benny, "Personal Reminiscences of Sir Moses Montefiore, IV," *Jewish World,* Aug. 28, 1885, 5. Benny apparently doubted the accuracy of this story, for it was "never trotted out except when certain visitors of the *nouveau riche* type were present."

115. Nov. 9, 1837, Queen Victoria's Journal.

116. LDMS, 1: 122.

117. Nov. 9, 1837, Queen Victoria's Journal.

118. MM to LJR, April 25, 1838, ASM.

119. Niall Ferguson, "'The Caucasian Royal Family': The Rothschilds in National Contexts," in *Two Nations: British and German Jews in Comparative Perspective,* ed. Michael Brenner, Rainer Liedtke, and David Rechter (Tübingen, 1999), 314–319, on the ennoblement of the Rothschilds.

120. MM to JM, c. Sept. 21, 1837.

6. The Land of Milk and Honey

1. LDMS, 1: 153.

2. Feb. 8, 1838, JMTD, 1838–39, MS. Var 3/1-2, JNUL. I have preferred, where possible, to use the original MS. rather than the privately published (and very slightly edited) Judith Montefiore, *Notes from a Private Journal of a Visit to Egypt and Palestine by way of Italy and the Mediterranean,* 2d ed. (London, 1885).

3. LDMS, 1: 151.

4. Ibid., 154.

5. Ferdinand Gregorovius, *Der Ghetto und die Juden in Rom, mit einem Geleitwort von Leo Baeck* (Berlin, 1935), 72.

6. See Raphael Loewe, "Louis Loewe: Aide and Confidant," in *CMM,* 105–117; and "Dr. Louis Loewe: Celebrities of the Day," www.kurrein.com, accessed Sept. 6, 2008.

7. Rabbi L. Rabinowitz, "Three Letters of Anglo-Jewish Interest," *Miscellanies of the Jewish Historical Society of England 5* (1948): 138, and, more generally, 135–146.

8. LDMS, 1: 102.

9. March 29, 1839, JMTD, 1838–39.

10. May 1, 1839, ibid.

11. LD, 1: 157.

12. May 1, 1839.

13. April 14, 1839, JMTD, 1838–39; LDMS, 1: 159.

14. Oct. 20 1827, in Montefiore, *Notes from Private Journal,* 212.

15. Sherman Lieber, *Mystics and Missionaries: The Jews in Palestine, 1799–1840* (Salt Lake City, 1992), 219, 336. See also Arie Morgenstern, *Hastening Redemption: Messianism and the Resettlement of the Land of Israel,* ed. Joel Linsider (Oxford, 2006), chap. 3.

16. See Shalom Bar Asher, "The Jews of North Africa and the Land of Israel in the Eighteenth and Nineteenth Centuries: The Reversal in Attitude toward Aliyah (Immigration to the Land) from 1770 to 1860," in *The Land of Israel: Jewish Perspectives,* ed. Lawrence Hoffmann (Notre Dame, Ind., 1986), especially 298, 306–308.

17. Petition of the Moghrabi Jews in Jerusalem, enclosed with James Finn to Stratford Canning, April 6, 1850, HBC, 1: 150.

18. On early Hasidic immigration to Palestine see Lieber, *Mystics and Missionaries,* chap. 3; more generally, Harry Rabinowicz, *Hasidism and the State of Israel* (London, 1982).

19. Quoted in Lieber, *Mystics and Missionaries,* 44.

20. See Immanuel Etkes, *The Gaon of Vilna: The Man and His Image,* trans. Jeremy M. Green (Berkeley, 2002), especially chaps. 3–6 on the struggle with Hasidism.

21. For a comparison of the different Ashkenazi Aliyahs in this period see Israel Bartal, "Yehudei mizraḥ eiropah ve'erets yisra'el (1771–1881): Ha'aliyot umivneh hayishuv ha'ashkenazi," *Cathedra* 16 (July 1980): 3–12. On the Perushim see Lieber, *Mystics and Missionaries,* chap. 4. The extent to which the followers of the Vilna *Gaon* were motivated by a messianic ideology is a matter of dispute. For a se-

lection of articles relating to this controversy see Richard Cohen, ed., *Vision and Conflict in the Holy Land* (Jerusalem, 1985), 141–189.

22. Quoted in Lieber, *Mystics and Missionaries,* 131.

23. On this conflict see ibid., chap. 6; and Aryeh Morgenstern, *Hapekidim veha'amarkalim beamsterdam vehayishuv hayehudi be'erets yisra'el bemahatsit harishonah shel hame'ah hatesha-esreh* (Jerusalem, 1981), chap. 3. For the Anglo-Sephardi angle see Miriam Rodrigues-Pereira, "Relations of the Mahamad of the Spanish and Portuguese Congregation of London with the Holy Land in the 19th Century," *Jewish Historical Studies* 31 (1988–90): 197–230; and Albert Hyamson, *The Sephardim of England: A History of the Spanish and Portuguese Jewish Community, 1492–1951* (London, 1951), 252–253.

24. Morgenstern, *Hapekidim veha'amarkalim beamsterdam,* 76, 192–193.

25. Quoted in Lieber, *Mystics and Missionaries,* 345.

26. Quoted in Israel Bartal, "Karka'ot vetokhniyot le'ibudan bimei bikuro hasheni shel montefiori be'erets yisra'el bishnat 1839," *Shalem* 2 (1976): 258.

27. LD, 1: 159.

28. May 14 and 15, 1839, JMTD, 1838–39; LD, 1: 160.

29. See E. Scott Calman, *Description of Part of the Scene of the Late Great Earthquake in Syria, in a Letter from E. Scott Calman, Beyrout* (London, 1837).

30. LDMS, 1: 160.

31. See Zvi Kargila, "Teudah: Igeret rav shemuel berabi yisra'el perets helir be'inyan bizat tsefat bishnat 1834," *Cathedra,* March 1983, 109–116 (Hebrew).

32. May 17, 1839, JMTD, 1838–39.

33. May 18, 1839, ibid.

34. Ibid. On Montefiore's agricultural plans and the Jewish response, see the seminal Bartal, "Karka'ot vetokhniyot"; Ruth Kark, "Karka'ot vetokhniyot le'ibudan bimei bikuro hasheni shel montefiori be'erets yisra'el bishnat 1839," *Cathedra* 33 (Oct. 1984): 57–92; and Lieber, *Mystics and Missionaries,* chap. 15.

35. For context see Yitzhak Hofman, "The Administration of Syria and Palestine under Egyptian Rule (1831–1840)," in *Studies on Palestine during the Ottoman Period,* ed. Moshe Ma'oz (Jerusalem, 1975), 311–333.

36. On Sachs see Lieber, *Mystics and Missionaries,* 225–227; and Morgenstern, *Hastening Redemption,* 153–157. On Sachs's agricultural project see also Morgenstern, *Hapekidim veha'amarkalim beamsterdam,* 175–178.

37. On Bak's press see Aryeh Morgenstern, "The Printing Press of Israel Bak in Safed—New Discoveries," *Books & People* 9 (June 1995): 7–8; on his experiences in the 1830s see Lieber, *Mystics and Missionaries,* 227–229.

38. Minutes of conversation with Jacob Meyer Ashkenazi, Rabbi Israel Drucker, and R. Josef Ben Shimeon Ashkenazi, 1839, MMSS vol. 574 67a. Here and below, names and organizations are rendered in accordance with the handwritten catalogue of these letters made by Louis Loewe. Many of the letters that Montefiore received demonstrated detailed knowledge of contemporary agricultural practices.

39. LDMS, 1: 167.

40. For a good example see Nahum Sokolow, *History of Zionism, 1600–1918,* vol. 1 (London, 1919), chap. 22.

41. He described two Jews living in Malta as troublemakers who "interfered very much in the nation"; Aug. 13, 1827, MMJ 1827–28, ASM. Similarly in MM to LC, Aug. 14, 1840, folder 1, HL. On the traditional Sephardi usage see Miriam Bodian, "'Men of the Nation': The Shaping of Converso Identity in Early Modern Europe," *Past & Present* 143 (May 1994): 48–76. But see Judith's somewhat different usage, when she described Egypt as "the land where our nation had, as it were, its cradle"; JMPJ, 130.

42. See Amalie Kass and Edward Kass, *Perfecting the World: The Life and Times of Dr. Thomas Hodgkin, 1798–1866* (Boston, 1988), chap. 15. Sussex and Bexley, both well known to Montefiore, were also leading patrons of the BACS. More generally see Claude Clegg III, *The Price of Liberty: African Americans and the Making of Liberia* (Chapel Hill, 2004).

43. LDMS, 1: 197.

44. Thomas Fowell Buxton, *The African Slave Trade and Its Remedy* (London, 1839), 519–521. Founding members of the Society for the Extinction of the Slave Trade and for the Civilization of Africa, almost certainly known to Montefiore, included Buxton, Hodgkin, William Allen, Joseph Gurney, Samuel Gurney Senior and Junior, John Henry Gurney, John Gurney Hoare, William Hoare, Charles Grant, and Charles Lushington. On Hodgkin's prepublication involvement see Kass and Kass, *Perfecting the World*, 401.

45. Library Catalogue, 1842, ASM.

46. On productivization and the *Haskalah* see Derek J. Penslar, *Shylock's Children: Economics and Jewish Identity in Modern Europe* (Berkeley, 2001), 81–90.

47. Minutes of conversation with Jacob Meyer Ashkenazi, Rabbi Israel Drucker, and R. Josef Ben Shimeon Ashkenazi, 1839. Bartal, "Karka'ot vetokhniyot," explores the differences between the original letters and the Loewe translations printed in Montefiore, *Notes from Private Journal*, first published in 1844.

48. May 18, 1839, JMTD, 1838–39.

49. See especially Morgenstern, *Hastening Redemption*, chap. 2.

50. Rabinowicz, *Hasidism and State of Israel*, 61.

51. See Aryeh Morgenstern, "Hadiyun bishe'elat ḥidush hakorbanot uvinyan hamikdash erev shenat 5600 (1839)," *Cathedra* 82 (Dec. 1996): 51–54.

52. The Montefiores left on Aug. 8, 1836. Kalischer's letter is dated Aug. 25.

53. See Niall Ferguson, *The World's Banker: The History of the House of Rothschild* (London, 1998), 316–318.

54. Library Catalogue, 1842, ASM.

55. June 1, 1839, JMTD, 1838–39.

56. For a discussion of these ideas see Shalom Rosenberg, "The Link to the Land of Israel in Jewish Thought: A Clash of Perspectives," in Hoffmann, *Land of Israel*, 154–156.

57. Letters and Petitions, 5599, MMSS vol. 575.

58. Zvi Hirsch ben Rabbi Sendr, Shmuel ben Rabbi Dov, and Shalom Turgeman to MM, Sivan 11, 5599, ibid., 3a.

59. Rabbi Haim Nissim Abulafia and the Portuguese Congregation of Tiberias to

MM, Sivan 9, 5599, MMSS vol. 574 35A. I am grateful to Asaf Pink for his work deciphering these manuscripts, and to my husband, Boaz Brosh, for helping me to translate them.

60. Kehillat Ashkenazim Habad Hebron to MM, 5599, MMSS vol. 574 61A.

61. May 27, 1839, JMTD, 1838–39.

62. K. Bonar and R. M. M'Cheyne, *Narrative of a Mission of Inquiry to the Jews from the Church of Scotland in 1839* (Edinburgh, 1842), 289–290.

63. For instance LD, 1: 174.

64. Ibid., 172.

65. Cadi of Tiberias to MM, 5599, MMSS vol. 574 39a.

66. William Young to MM, May 30, 1839, ibid., 45.

67. June 9, 1839, JMTD, 1838–39.

68. Holland to ILG, Feb. 10, 1829[?], in Lionel Abrahams, "Sir I. L. Goldsmid and the Admission of the Jews of England to Parliament," *TJHSE* 4 (1903): 135–137.

69. See Mayir Vereté, *From Palmerston to Balfour: Collected Essays of Mayir Vereté,* ed. Norman Rose (London, 1992), chap 3, and chaps. 4–5 on other aspects of British policy. On Palmerston see also Isaiah Friedman, "Lord Palmerston and the Protection of the Jews in Palestine," *JSS* 30 (Jan. 1968): 23–41. More generally see A. L. Tibawi, *British Interests in Palestine, 1800–1901: A Study of Religious and Educational Enterprise* (Oxford, 1961).

70. For a traditional view of Victorian Christian Zionism see Norman Bentwich and John Shaftesley, "Forerunners of Zionism in the Victorian Era," in *Remember the Days: Essays on Anglo-Jewish History Presented to Cecil Roth by Members of the Council of the Jewish Historical Society of England,* ed. John Shaftesley (London, 1966), 207–240; Michael Polowetzky, *Jerusalem Recovered: Victorian Intellectuals and the Birth of Modern Zionism* (London, 1995); Franz Kobler, *The Vision Was There: A History of the British Movement for the Restoration of the Jews to Palestine* (London, 1956). For a revisionist view see Eitan Bar-Yosef, *The Holy Land in English Culture, 1799–1917* (Oxford, 2005). For an exploration of the theological context see Sarah Kochav, "Shivatam shel hayehudim le'erets yisra'el vehatenuah ha'evangelit be'angliyah," *Cathedra* 62 (Dec. 1991): 18–36.

71. Cited after Polowetzky, *Jerusalem Recovered,* 11.

72. John Bidwell to Young, Jan. 31, 1839, HBC, 1: 2.

73. LD, 1: 178–179.

74. LDMS, 1: 182.

75. May 22, 1839, JMTD, 1838–39.

76. LD, 1: 180.

77. June 17, 1839, JMTD, 1838–39.

78. Nathan Netter Barhaf HaHasid et al., Directors of the New Building Called the Hurva of Rabbi Yehudah HaHasid, to MM, Tammuz, 5599, MMSS vol. 574 51C. On the Hurva campaign see Morgenstern, *Hastening Redemption,* chap. 6.

79. Gabbaim of the Gemilut Hassadim, and Hachnassat Orechim and Bikur Holim, of the Kollel of Ashkenazim Perushim in Jerusalem, to MM, 5599, MMSS vol. 574.

80. The Hon. Mrs. G. L. Dawson Damer, *Diary of a Tour in Greece, Turkey, Egypt and the Holy Land,* vol. 2 (London, 1842), 236–237.

81. For a full account of proceedings and subsequent negotiations, see LD, 1: 197–203.

82. "Alexandrien, 1. August," *AZ,* Sept. 9, 1839, 445.

83. LD, 1: 204.

84. Ibid., 206.

85. The classic account of the crisis of 1839–1841 is Sir Charles Webster, *The Foreign Policy of Palmerston, 1830–1841,* vol. 2: *Britain, the Liberal Movement and the Eastern Question* (London, 1951), chap. 8.

86. Palmerston to Henry Lytton Bulwer, Sept. 22, 1838: see Kenneth Bourne, *The Foreign Policy of Victorian England, 1830–1920* (Oxford, 1970), 233, and more generally. Specifically on the 1830s see Webster, *Foreign Policy of Palmerston,* vol. 2, chap. 7.

7. The Damascus Affair

1. "Revised Constitution of the Board of Deputies," *JC,* Feb. 8, 1856, 476.

2. See the seminal Jonathan Frankel, *The Damascus Affair: "Ritual Murder," Politics, and the Jews in 1840* (Cambridge, 1997).

3. See S. Posener, *Adolphe Crémieux, a Biography* (Philadelphia, 1940); and Daniel Amson, *Adolphe Crémieux: L'oublié de la gloire* (Paris, 1988).

4. Quoted in Frankel, *Damascus Affair,* 74.

5. For a good summary of the history of the blood libel see Helmut Walser Smith, *The Butcher's Tale: Murder and Anti-Semitism in a German Town* (New York, 2002), chap. 3.

6. JdR to A. Laurin, May 6, 1840, Bound Damascus Vol., fols. 393–398, ASM. On *shtadlanut* see François Guesnet, "Die Politik der 'Fürsprache'—Vormoderne jüdische Interessenvertretung," in *Synchrone Welten: Zeiträume jüdischer Geschichte,* ed. Dan Diner (Göttingen, 2005), 67–92; and François Guesnet, "Politik der Vormoderne—Shtadlanut am Vorabend der polnischen Teilungen," *Jahrbuch des Simon-Dubnow Instituts* 1 (2002): 235–255. For the relevance of this concept to Montefiore see Israel Bartal, "Nationalist before His Time or a Belated *Shtadlan?* —Guidelines for the Activities of Moses Montefiore," in *The Age of Moses Montefiore,* ed. Bartal (Jerusalem, 1987), 5–24.

7. Reprinted in "Horrible accusation contre les Juifs de Damas," *AI* 1 (March 1840): 164.

8. For an account of the meeting and transcripts of the letters received from Damascus, Constantinople, and Rhodes discussed in the following paragraphs, see Special Meeting, April 21, 1840, BDMB, ACC/3121/A/005/A, fols. 102–123.

9. On the economic advantages enjoyed by religious minorities in this period see Charles Issawi, "The Transformation of the Economic Position of the Millets in the Nineteenth Century," in *Christians and Jews in the Ottoman Empire,* vol. 1: *The Central Lands,* ed. Benjamin Braude and Bernard Lewis (New York, 1982), 261–285.

10. Frankel, *Damascus Affair*, 32.

11. For a hostile account of the episode, possibly compiled by Ratti-Menton himself, see Achille Laurent, *Relation historique des affaires de Syrie, depuis 1840 jusqu'en 1842*, vol. 2 (Paris, 1846).

12. Report of the Committee Appointed to Attend Lord Palmerston, May 12, 1840, BDMB, ACC/3121/A/005/3, fols. 131–136.

13. Palmerston to Wilkinson, May 25, 1840, F.O. 78/413, fol. 161, NA.

14. On British support for the Jews of Muslim lands see Abigail Green, "The British Empire and the Jews: An Imperialism of Human Rights?" *Past & Present* 199 (May 2008): 175–205.

15. Quoted in Ronald Haym, *Britain's Imperial Century: 1815–1914: A Study of Empire and Expansion* (London, 1976), 49.

16. Cochelet to Thiers, May 15, 1840, no. 189, Correspondance Consulaire et Commerciale Alexandrie, vol. 28, fols. 466–467, MAE.

17. Quoted in Frankel, *Damascus Affair*, 189.

18. See ibid., 198–199, 109–119.

19. Quoted in ibid., 216.

20. Article from *Morning Herald*, June 25, 1840, BDMB, ACC/3121/A/005/A, fols. 180–184.

21. There are interesting parallels with the alliance between Jewish activists and French liberals during the Restoration and July Monarchy outlined in Lisa Moses Leff, *Sacred Bonds of Solidarity: The Rise of Jewish Internationalism in Nineteenth-Century France* (Stanford, Calif., 2006), chap. 2.

22. All these figures either spoke at the meeting or were among 200 signatories to a petition published in *The Times*, calling for it to be held.

23. Article from *Morning Herald*, July 4, 1840, BDMB, ACC/3121/A/005/A, fols. 249–255. On the moral dimension of Victorian imperialism see Andrew Porter, "Trusteeship, Anti-Slavery, and Humanitarianism," in *The Oxford History of the British Empire*, vol. 3: *The Nineteenth Century*, ed. Andrew Porter (Oxford, 1999), 206–211; and John Cell, "The Imperial Conscience," in *The Conscience of the Victorian State*, ed. Peter Marsh (Syracuse, N.Y., 1979), 199–202. More generally Niall Ferguson, *Empire: How Britain Made the Modern World* (London, 2003), chap. 3; and Alan Lester, "Humanitarians and White Settlers in the Nineteenth Century," in *Missions and Empire*, ed. Norman Etherington (Oxford, 2005), 64–86.

24. Treasurer of the Damascus Mission to A. J. Jones, Aug. 8, 1842, ASM.

25. July 7, 1840, MMJ 1840, MS. Var 21 IIa, JNUL.

26. On Munk see Moise Schwab, *Salomon Munk, membre de l'Institut, professeur au Collège de France: Sa vie et ses oeuvres* (Paris, 1900).

27. MM to BD, July 13, 1840, BDMB, ACC/3121/A/005/A, fols. 277–279.

28. Sept. 9, 1840, Adolphe Crémieux Journal, Voyage accompli pour la défense d'Israélites accusés du meurtre d'un prêtre catholique, 369 AP/1, dr3, fol. 64, AN.

29. Aug. 18, 1840, ibid., fol. 17.

30. Ibid., fol. 21.

31. See LD, 1: 225–226. For Madden's account see Dr. Richard Robert Madden, *Egypt and Mohammed Ali: Illustrative of the Condition of His Slaves and Subjects* (London, 1841), 110–114.

32. Aug. 18, 1840, Adolphe Crémieux Journal, fol. 21.

33. LD, 1: 226.

34. Ibid., 240; MM to BD, Aug. 12, 1840, BDMB, ACC/3121/A/005/A, fols. 303–305.

35. Madden, *Egypt and Mohammed Ali,* 229.

36. MM to LC, Aug. 14, 1840, folder 1, HL.

37. Aug. 29, 1840, in Louis Loewe, "The Damascus Affair: Diary of Dr. Louis Loewe," *Yehudith: The Organ of the Judith Lady Montefiore Theological College, Ramsgate* 1 (Nov. 1940): 27.

38. MM to BD, Aug. 25, 1840, BDMB, ACC/3121/A/005/A, fols. 319–325.

39. Aug. 31, 1840, Adolphe Crémieux Journal, fol. 40.

40. AC to MM, n.d. [1840], ASM.

41. Aug. 31, 1840, Adolphe Crémieux Journal, fol. 43.

42. Ibid., fol. 44.

43. Ibid., fols. 47–48.

44. Sept. 9, 1840, ibid., fol. 55.

45. Ibid.

46. Lynn Hunt, *Inventing Human Rights: A History* (New York, 2007), chap. 2, argues that torture was a flagship issue for Enlightenment humanitarians.

47. Sept. 9, 1840, Adolphe Crémieux Journal, fol. 61.

48. See Nahum Sokolow, *History of Zionism, 1600–1918,* 2 vols. (London, 1919), 1: 124; 2: 231–232, 235.

49. See Frankel, *Damascus Affair,* 302–305.

50. Palmerston to Ponsonby, Aug. 11, 1840, HBC, 1: 33. See Isaiah Friedman, "Lord Palmerston and the Protection of the Jews in Palestine," *JSS* 30 (Jan. 1968): 23–41; Israel Friedman, "British Schemes for the Restoration of Jews to Palestine (1840–1850)," *Cathedra* 56 (June 1990): 42–69 (Hebrew); and Reeva Spector Simon, "Commerce, Concern, and Christianity: Britain and Middle-Eastern Jewry in the Mid-Nineteenth Century," in *The Jews and British Romanticism,* ed. Sheila A. Spector (Basingstoke, 2005), 181–194.

51. For a general account of the Ottoman reform era see M. Şükrü Hanioğlu, *A Brief History of the Late Ottoman Empire* (Princeton, 2008). On British policy and the Tanzimat reforms see Frank Edgar Bailey, *British Policy and the Turkish Reform Movement: A Study in Anglo-Turkish Relations, 1826–1853* (Cambridge, Mass., 1942); Allan Cunningham, "The Sick Man and the British Physician," *Middle Eastern Studies* 17 (June 1981): 147–173; and, more specifically, Frederick Stanley Rodkey, "Lord Palmerston and the Rejuvenation of Turkey, 1830–41," *Journal of Modern History* 2 (June 1930): 193–225.

52. See also Palmerston to Ponsonby, Feb. 17, 1841, HBC, 1: 37–38, which refers to Jewish settlement "in any part of the Turkish Dominions."

53. Grand Vizierial Note, Addressing the Chief Secretary at the Imperial Palace, and Requesting an Imperial Command, Djumada Al Awwal 28, 1256, Irade-Mesail-i Mühimme 1006/1, MFA.

54. Covering Summary, Grand Vizierial Note addressing the Chief Secretary at the Imperial Palace and Requesting an Imperial Command, Djumada Al Awwal 28, 1256, Irade-Mesail-i Mühimme 1006/1, MFA.

55. Oct. 22, 1840, in Loewe, "Damascus Affair," 50.

56. Draft of the 1840 *firman* provided by Montefiore to Reshid Pasha, Appendix, Irade-Mesail-i Mühimme 1005/2, MFA. This compares interestingly with the *firman* eventually granted.

57. MM to BD, Nov. 17, 1840, BDMB, ACC/3121/A/005/B, fols. 145–147.

58. Grand Vizierial Note, Addressing the Chief Secretary at the Imperial Palace, and Requesting an Imperial Command, Irade-Mesail-i Mühimme 1005/1, MFA.

59. Oct. 21, 1840, in Loewe, "Damascus Affair," 50. See also LD, 1: 269.

60. Grand Vizierial Note, Addressing the Chief Secretary at the Imperial Palace, and Requesting an Imperial Command, Irade-Mesail-i Mühimme 1005/1, MFA.

61. Ponsonby to Palmerston, Oct. 28, 1840, F.O. 78/398 no. 247, fol. 43, NA.

62. Oct. 28, 1840, in Loewe, "Damascus Affair," 53–54. For a contemporary description see Ludwig Frankl, *Griechenland, Kleinasien, Syrien*, vol. 1 of *Nach Jerusalem* (Leipzig, 1858), 145–163.

63. MM to BD, Oct. 28, 1840, BDMB, ACC/3121/A/005/B, fols. 99–102.

64. Ibid.

65. For the full text of the *firman*, as translated by Loewe, see LD, 1: 278–279.

66. MM to BD, Nov. 4, 1840, BDMB, ACC/3121/A/005/B, fols. 102–108.

67. MM to BD, Nov. 14, 1840, BDMB, ACC/3121/A/005/B, fols. 111–114.

68. MM to ILG, Nov. 13, 1840, folder 1, HL.

69. Ibid. On *dhimma* see Bernard Lewis, *The Jews of Islam* (Princeton, 1984). For an insight into the polemics surrounding this issue see Norman A. Stillman, "Myth, Countermyth, and Distortion," and Mark R. Cohen, "The Neo-Lachrymose Conception of Jewish-Arab History," *Tikkun* 6 (May–June 1991): 55–60, 60–64; also Mark Cohen, "Islam and the Jews: Myth, Counter-Myth, History," in *Jews among Muslims: Communities in the Precolonial Middle East*, ed. Shlomo Deshen and Walter Zenner (Basingstoke, 1996), 50–63.

70. Munk to his mother, Aug. 16 1840, in Schwab, *Salomon Munk*, 87.

71. Munk to Charlotte Danziger, Nov. 27, 1840, ibid., 112. On this initiative see Yaron Tsur, *Yehudim bein muslimim: bereshit tekufat hareformot*, vol. 2 of *Mavo letoledot hayehudim be'artsot ha'islama batekufah hamodernit 1750–1914*, provisional ed. (Open University, Tel Aviv), 222–227; revised version forthcoming with the Littman Library for Jewish Civilization, Oxford.

72. Sept. 13, 1840, in Loewe, "Damascus Affair," 35; Sept. 14, 1840, Adolphe Crémieux Journal, fol. 69.

73. See "Jewish Families in Alexandria in 1840," www.hsje.org; also "1840 Montefiore Alexandria Census online," www.sephardicgen.com, accessed Dec. 21, 2008. www.montefioreendowment.org.uk will publish a comprehensive online edition of the census in 2009.

74. Sept. 13, 1840, in Loewe, "Damascus Affair," 35.

75. Frankel, *Damascus Affair*, 370.

76. MM to ILG, Nov. 13, 1840.

77. Madden, *Egypt and Mohammed Ali*, 250.

78. MM to ILG, Nov. 13, 1840.

79. On alternative models of reformism see Tsur, *Yehudim bein muslimim,* 228–237.

80. "Turkey," *Morning Post,* Nov. 30, 1840, 5; also Nov. 4, 1840, in Loewe, "Damascus Affair," 59.

81. On the origins of this position see Mark A. Epstein, "The Leadership of the Ottoman Jews in the Fifteenth and Sixteenth Centuries," in Braude and Lewis, *Central Lands,* 101–115.

82. On the *millet* system see Benjamin Braude, "Foundation Myths of the *Millet* System"; Roderic Davison, "The *Millets* as Agents of Change in the Nineteenth-Century Ottoman Empire"; and Kemal Karpat, "*Millets* and Nationality: The Roots of the Incongruity of Nation and State in the Post-Ottoman Era," all in ibid., 69–88, 319–337, and 141–169.

83. For a good description of the religious, cultural, social, and economic institutions of Ottoman Jewry see Esther Benbassa and Aron Rodrigue, *Sephardi Jewry: A History of the Judeo-Spanish Community, 14th–20th Centuries* (Berkeley, 1993), chaps. 1–2; and Minna Rozen, ed., *The Last Ottoman Century and Beyond: The Jews in Turkey and the Balkans, 1808–1945,* 2 vols. (Tel Aviv, 2002). More generally, see Tsur, *Yehudim bein muslimim.*

84. "Mission of Sir Moses Montefiore," *Morning Post,* Dec. 12, 1840, 3.

85. See Aron Rodrigue, *French Jews, Turkish Jews: The Alliance Israélite Universelle and the Politics of Jewish Schooling in Turkey, 1860–1925* (Bloomington, Ind., 1990), 38.

86. See Carter Findley, "The Acid Test of Ottomanism: The Acceptance of Non-Muslims in the Late Ottoman Bureaucracy," in Braude and Lewis, *Central Lands,* 339–368.

87. See for instance "Mission of Sir Moses Montefiore."

88. MM to BD, July 21, 1840, BDMB, ACC/3121/A/005/A, fols. 279–282.

89. AC to MM, Oct. 16, 1840, Adolphe Crémieux Journal, fol. 114.

90. MM to LC, Sept. 27, 1840, folder 1, HL.

91. MM to BD, Oct. 15, 1840, BDMB, ACC/3121/A/005/B, fols. 88–91.

92. [Anselme?] de Rothschild to AC, undated, ASM.

93. MM to Hananel de Castro, Dec. 7, 1840, BDMB, ACC/3121/A/005/B, fols. 148–153.

94. MM to BD, Dec. 11, 1840, BDMB, ACC/3121/A/005/B, fols. 166–174.

95. LD, 1: 283.

96. See Frankel, *Damascus Affair,* 116–119, 368–369.

97. "Affaire de Damas," *Univers,* Oct. 8, 1840.

98. As outlined in JdR to mon cher frère, June 3, 1840, 000/87/2 (37), RAL.

99. Dec. 30, 1840, MMJ, File: Damascus 5610 Ref. To the Inscription on a Tombstone, ASM.

100. Dec. 29, 1840, ibid.

101. LD, 1: 155.

102. Dec. 31, 1840, MMJ, file: Damascus 5610.

103. Jan. 2 and 5, 1841, ibid.

104. Jan. 7, 1841, ibid.

8. Unity and Dissent

1. "London, 11. Januar," *AZ*, Feb. 13, 1841, 83.

2. "London, 15. März," *AZ*, April 10, 1841, 206.

3. D. A. de Sola, Discourse dedicated to MM, April 2, 5601, MMSS vol. 565.

4. Ibid.

5. Here and below see Michael Meyer, *Response to Modernity: A History of the Reform Movement in Judaism* (Detroit, 1988).

6. LD, 1: 69–70, 80. On the Ashkenazim, David Katz, *The Jews in the History of England 1485–1850* (Oxford, 1994), 334; on the Sephardim, Albert Hyamson, *The Sephardim of England: A History of the Spanish and Portuguese Jewish Community, 1492–1951* (London, 1951), 248–249.

7. Rev. D. A. Jessurun Cardozo and Paul Goodman, *Think and Thank: The Montefiore Synagogue and College, Ramsgate* (Oxford, 1933), 41, 43. The S&P retains the vestments.

8. Library Catalogue, 1842, ASM.

9. See Richard Barnett, "Haham Meldola and Hazan de Sola," *TJHSE* 2 (1968): 10–11. On the translation of Jewish liturgy and writings into English see David Ruderman, *Jewish Enlightenment in an English Key: Anglo-Jewry's Construction of Modern Jewish Thought* (Princeton, 2000), 214–272.

10. LD, 1: 80.

11. For an illuminating case study see Robert Liberles, *Religious Conflict in Social Context: The Resurgence of Orthodox Judaism in Frankfurt am Main, 1838–1877* (Westport, Conn., 1985).

12. Hannah Cohen, *Changing Faces: A Memoir of Louisa Lady Cohen by Her Daughter* (London, 1937), 27–28.

13. Dec. 12, 1836, loose leaf, MMJ, ASM; see also Katz, *Jews in England*, 334.

14. Horatio Montefiore to MM, Nov. 5, 1838, 1838:2, SLC.

15. Horatio Montefiore to MM, Dec. 10, 1838, Eric Lipson's handwritten notes of S/L 1838:5, 1838:5a, SLC.

16. See Horatio Montefiore to MM, Dec. 20 and 24, 1838, ASM. Horatio may have been referring to Alexander McCaul's weekly *Old Paths*, on which see David Feldman, *Englishmen and Jews: Social Relations and Political Culture, 1840–1914* (New Haven, 1994), 54–55.

17. Horatio Montefiore to MM, Dec. 24, 1838.

18. James Picciotto, *Sketches of Anglo-Jewish History*, ed. Israel Finestein (London, 1956), 367 and, more generally on the Reform movement, chap. 50.

19. LD, 1: 67–68.

20. June 30, 1840, and April 6, 1841, MB Mahamad, vol. 113, S&P.

21. April 29 and May 16, 1841, ibid.; May 16, 1841, MB Elders, 14 Hesvan 5598–2 Adar 5608, S&P.

22. LD, 1: 301.

23. On Hirschell's state of health in this period see "Death of Chief Rabbi Hirschel," *VJ*, Nov. 11, 1842, 57.

24. J. Barrow Montefiore, A. Mocatta Junr, Benjamin Mocatta, Elias Mocatta, John Mocatta, A. Lindo Mocatta, Abm Mocatta, J. G. Henriques, M. Mocatta, A.

Mocatta, Daniel Mocatta, Solomon Lazarus, D. L. Henriques, Emanuel Mocatta, David Mocatta, Jacob Montefiore. See Oct. 24, 1841, MB Elders, 14 Hesvan 5598–2 Adar 5608, 201, S&P. Rev. D. W. Marks, *Discourse Delivered in the West London Synagogue of British Jews, Burton Street, Burton Crescent, on the Day of Its Consecration Thursday 16th Sebat A.M. 5602–27th January 1842* (London, 1842), gives a useful insight into the religious agenda the Reformers pursued.

25. See Michael Meyer, "Jewish Religious Reform in Germany and Britain," in *Two Nations: British and German Jews in Comparative Perspective,* ed. Michael Brenner, Rainer Liedtke, and David Rechter (Tübingen, 1999), 67–84.

26. On the theological context for this see Feldman, *Englishmen and Jews,* 53–58. Steven Singer, "Orthodox Judaism in Early Victorian London, 1840–1858" (Ph.D. diss., Yeshiva University, 1981), 48–84, provides extensive discussion of this "Neo-Karaite" position.

27. For the text of this declaration see Arthur Barnett, *The Western Synagogue through Two Centuries (1761–1961)* (London, 1961), 180.

28. Oct. 24, 1841, MB Elders, 14 Hesvan 5598–2 Adar 5608, S&P.

29. LD, 1: 302. Loewe makes this comment in the context of his discussion of the 1841–42 crisis, and the words "any other institution" surely refer to Montefiore's position on the Mahamad at this time.

30. Picciotto, *Sketches of Anglo-Jewish History,* 374.

31. "P. S. Lazarus, Dec. 26, 1853, to the Editor," *JC,* Dec. 16, 1853, 112. Haim Sperber elaborates the case for Montefiore's responsibility in "Hanhagah yehudit behevrah petuhah: Shinuy behanhagah hayehudit be'angliyah beshanim 1828–1905" (Ph.D. diss., Bar Ilan University, 2005), 121–122.

32. LD, 1: 302.

33. FHG to MM, Feb. 2, 1842; MM to Rabbi S. Hirschel, Feb. 7, 1842; Hirschel et al. to MM, Feb. 7, 1842; MM to FHG, Feb. 8, 1842; MM to FHG, Feb. 9, 1842, all in folder 2, HL.

34. Rachel Montefiore to MM and JM, March 18, 1823, ASM.

35. P. L. Cottrell, "The Business Man and the Financier," in *CMM,* 28–29.

36. Ibid., 26, 39; LD, 1: 87; Horatio Montefiore to MM, March 1, 1830, 1839:2, SLC.

37. Abraham's children were wealthy enough anyway; see Resolutions, 1828, loose leaf, MMJ, ASM.

38. Feb. 25, 1842, MB Elders, 14 Hesvan 5598–2 Adar 5608, S&P.

39. JM to MM, Nov. 20, 1845, 1845:2, SLC.

40. On Montefiore's behavior at a family party see Charlotte's Diary, RAL 000/1066/1. For Sally Goldsmid's efforts to promote a reconciliation see May 8, 1861, loose leaf, MMJ, ASM.

41. MM to Horatio Montefiore, May 23, 1867, folder 4, HL.

42. "Tasteful Presentation," *VJ,* Oct. 28, 1842, 52; "Hamburg, den 31. Dezember 1841," *AZ,* Jan. 29, 1842, 54.

43. "Leitender Artikel: Magdeburg, den 25. August," *AZ,* Sept. 10, 1842, 545.

44. See *Puertas del Oriente,* Adar 5, 5606, 1, S&P; Pincherle would surely have known Montefiore from Bevis Marks. Thanks to Dov Cohen for this information.

45. "Great Fire at Smyrna," *VJ,* Sept. 16, 1841, 6.

46. See Andrée Aelion Brooks, *The Woman Who Defied Kings: The Life and Times of Doña Gracia Nasi—a Jewish Leader during the Renaissance* (St. Paul, Minn., 2002); Cecil Roth, *Doña Gracia of the House of Nasi* (Philadelphia, 1977).

47. See Baruch Mevorach, "Die Interventionsbestrebungen in Europa zur Verhinderung der Vertreibung der Juden aus Böhmen und Mähren, 1744–1745," *Jahrbuch des Instituts für Deutsche Geschichte* 9 (1980): 15–81; François Guesnet, "Textures of Intercession—Rescue Efforts for the Jews of Prague, 1744/1748," *Simon Dubnow Institute Yearbook* 4 (2005): 355–375.

48. See Derek Penslar, "Introduction: The Press and the Jewish Public Sphere," *Jewish History* 14 (2000): 3–8. Specifically on the Anglo-Jewish press see David Cesarani, *The Jewish Chronicle and Anglo-Jewry, 1841–1991* (Cambridge, 1994).

49. "The Conflagration at Smyrna," *VJ*, Oct. 29, 1841, 21.

50. "The Smyrna Jews," *VJ*, Dec. 10, 1841, 46.

51. 24 of the most distinguished Israelites in Bagdad to MM, Parashat Korakh 5602, folder 2, HL.

52. LD, 1: 300.

53. "The Montefiore Plate: Louis Loewe, Ramsgate, Sept 5603 (1842), to the Editor," *VJ*, Sept. 30, 1842, 29.

54. "Relief of the Sufferers at Mogador," *VJ*, Nov. 15, 1844, 33.

55. Ibid. On the Franco-Moroccan war of 1844 and its aftermath see Jean-Louis Miège, *L'ouverture*, vol. 2 of *Le Maroc et l'Europe (1830–1894)* (Paris, 1961), 202–210. For an analysis focusing on British diplomacy during the crisis see Francis Flournoy, *British Policy towards Morocco in the Age of Palmerston (1830–1865)* (Baltimore, 1935), chap. 4.

56. On Guedalla see Daniel Schroeter, *The Sultan's Jew: Morocco and the Sephardi World* (Stanford, Calif., 2002), 101–102, 145; on the Moroccan branch of the family see Samuel Romanelli, *Travail in an Arab Land*, trans. Yedida Stillman and Norman Stillman (Tuscaloosa, 1989), 124.

57. "The Late Judah Guedalla Esq.," *JC*, June 18, 1858, 214.

58. Guedalla's role is inferred since he was the recipient of Willshire's letter and a member of the Mogador relief committee; "Committee for the Relief of the Sufferers at Mogador," *VJ*, Nov. 15, 1844, 44. Guedalla played a similar role in a later appeal; see "The Famine in Morocco," *JC*, Aug, 23, 1850: 367. But Montefiore, too, received a letter dated May 29 from Mogador, containing "Accounts of the war," MLL 1844–51, letter 49, Mocatta 8, ML.

59. "Relief of the Sufferers at Mogador."

60. "Committee for the Relief of the Sufferers at Mogador." On gentile support for the Mogador campaign see William Rubinstein and Hilary Rubinstein, *Philosemitism: Admiration and Support in the English-Speaking World for Jews, 1840–1939* (Basingstoke, 1999), 17–18.

61. LD, 1: 320.

62. See, e.g., Carl von Rothschild to MM, Jan. 10, 1845, MLL 1844–51, letter 159, also letter 164.

63. LD, 1: 319–320.

64. MM to Aberdeen, Jan. 9, 1845, folder 2, HL.

65. Ben Idriss, Secretary, Commander of the Law & Wazeer of the Emperor of Morocco, to MM, Safer 16, 1261, ibid.

66. "The Emperor of Morocco," *VJ*, April 11, 1845, 139.

67. "London (V. of Jacob)," *AZ*, May 26, 1845, 325; "Jews of Morocco," *OAJA*, June 1845. Both newspapers effectively reprinted the *Voice of Jacob* article without further commentary.

9. Winds of Change in Russia

1. See Anon., *The Englishwoman in Russia: Impressions of the Society and Manners of the Russians at Home by a Lady, Ten Years Resident in That Country* (London, 1855), 20, 22, 242–243.

2. LD, 1: 327.

3. Marquis de Custine, *Journey for Our Time: The Journals of the Marquis de Custine*, trans. Phyllis Kohler (London, 1953), 98.

4. See Gershon Hundert, *Jews in Poland-Lithuania in the Eighteenth Century: A Genealogy of Modernity* (Berkeley, 2004).

5. On the origins of Russian policy toward the Jews see John Doyle Klier, *Russia Gathers Her Jews: The Origins of the "Jewish Question" in Russia, 1772–1825* (De Kalb, Ill., 1986). For an outstanding account of the impact of political change in the eighteenth and nineteenth centuries see Eli Lederhendler, *The Road to Modern Jewish Politics: Political Tradition and Political Reconstruction in the Jewish Community of Tsarist Russia* (Oxford, 1989).

6. See above all Michael Stanislawski, *Tsar Nicholas I and the Jews: The Transformation of Jewish Society in Russia, 1825–1855* (Philadelphia, 1983). On Nicholas see W. Bruce Lincoln, *Nicholas I, Emperor and Autocrat of All the Russias* (De Kalb, Ill., 1989).

7. The lachrymose view of conscription was first challenged by Stanislawski, *Nicholas I and the Jews*, chap. 1. More recently, see Yohanan Petrovsky-Shtern, "'Guardians of the Faith': Jewish Traditional Societies in the Russian Army: The Case of the Thirty-Fifth Briansk Regiment," in *The Military and Society in Russia, 1450–1917*, vol. 14, ed. Eric Lohr and Marshall Poe (Leiden, 2002), 413–439; and Olga Litvak, *Conscription and the Search for Modern Russian Jewry* (Bloomington, Ind., 2006).

8. On Kiselev see W. Bruce Lincoln, "Count P. D. Kiselev: A Reformer in Imperial Russia," *Australian Journal of Politics and History* 16 (1970): 177–188. On the Kiselev reforms see Stanislawski, *Nicholas I and the Jews*, 43–48.

9. For educational context see Patrick Alston, *Education and the State in Tsarist Russia* (Stanford, Calif., 1969).

10. See for instance Klier, *Russia Gathers Her Jews*, 62–63.

11. See David Philippson, *Max Lilienthal, American Rabbi: Life and Writings* (New York, 1915).

12. See Nicholas Riasanovsky, *Nicholas I and Official Nationality in Russia, 1825–1855* (Berkeley, 1959). On Uvarov see Cynthia Whittaker, *The Origins of*

Modern Russian Education: An Intellectual Biography of Count Sergei Uvarov, 1786–1855 (De Kalb, Ill., 1984).

13. See Julius Hessen, "Die russische Regierung und die westeuropäische Juden (zur Schulreform in Rußland 1840–44). Nach archivalische Materialien," *Monatsschrift für Geschichte und Wissenschaft des Judentums* 57 (July–Aug. 1913): 257–271, 482–500.

14. Quoted in Stanislawski, *Nicholas I and the Jews*, 76.

15. Lilienthal to MM, July 30, 1842, folder 2, HL.

16. Montefiore consulted Vilna communal leaders on this issue; MM to LC, Nov. 29, 1842, ibid. On Montefiore's contact with the Hasidic court at Ruzhin see David Assaf, *The Regal Way: The Life and Times of Rabbi Israel of Ruzhin*, trans. David Louvish (Stanford, Calif., 2002), 191. Yulii Gessen, "Graf P. Kiselev i Moisei Montefiore," *Perezhitoe* 4 (1913): 152, notes that Lilienthal advised the Jews of Grodno to appeal to Montefiore to come to St. Petersburg, and other such appeals may have been similarly orchestrated. On the appeal from Odessa, see "Russian Jews," *VJ*, Feb. 3, 1843, 108. The appeal from Mitau clearly emanated from government supporters; see Benjamin Schmahmann et al., Deputies of the Hebrew Congregation of Mitau to MM, Aug. 11–22, 1842, folder 2, HL.

17. Elders of Vilna to Lilienthal, quoted in Isaac Levitats, *The Jewish Community in Russia, 1772–1844* (New York, 1970), 84.

18. MM to LC, Dec. 18, 1842, folder 2, HL. D. K., "Montefiore w Warszawie," *Kwartalnik Poswiecony Badaniu Przeszlosci Zydow w Polsce* 1, no. 1 (1912): 76, confirms that the Polish conscription decree was Montefiore's major motivation. Thanks to Benedict Rundell for his help with this article and other Polish material.

19. See "Board of Deputies," *VJ*, Oct. 7, 1842, 36; and, more generally, Gessen, "Graf P. Kiselev," 152–153. Thanks to Svetlana Rukhelman for her help with this article and the translations of all Russian material.

20. "M. Cremieux and the Russian Jews," *VJ*, April 28, 1843, 155.

21. See Klier, *Russia Gathers Her Jews*, 147–155. For details of earlier policy in border areas and the expulsion of the 1840s, see Jacob Jacobson, "Eine Aktion für die russischen Grenzjuden in den Jahren 1843/44," in *Festschrift zu Simon Dubnows siebzigstem Geburtstag (2. Tischri 5691)*, ed. Ismar Elbogen, Josef Meisl, and Mark Wischnitzer (Berlin, 1930), 239, and more generally.

22. Elders of the Jewish Congregation, Konigsberg, to MM, June 29, 1843, folder 2, HL.

23. LDMS, 1: 316–317.

24. "Oppression of the Jews in Russian Poland," *VJ*, Aug. 4, 1843, 211. See also "The Morning Post and the Voice of Jacob," *VJ*, Sept. 1, 1843, 227.

25. *Journal des Débats* article reprinted as "English Sympathy with the Russo-Polish Jews," *VJ*, March 1, 1844, 88. See also Lewis Tonna to MM, Feb. 20, 1844, folder 2, HL; "The Ukase and Other Oppressions," *VJ*, March 15, 1844, 100; and, more generally, William Rubinstein and Hilary Rubinstein, *Philosemitism: Admiration and Support in the English-Speaking World for Jews, 1840–1939* (Basingstoke, 1999), 14–16.

26. See Jacobson, "Eine Aktion," 245.

27. "Ukase and Other Oppressions."

28. MM to J. A. Franklin, Jan. 21, 1844, Montefiore Collection, Arc 4 1746 124, JNUL.

29. See LDMS, 1: 317, 319. More generally, see Lincoln, *Nicholas I*, 219–223.

30. They first wrote to Montefiore from Sadgora on Av 24, 1845; see letter 233, MLL 1844–51, Mocatta 8, ML. The contact seems to have been mediated by R. Nissan Drucker; see letters 255, 258, 260, ibid. Here and elsewhere, all names taken from MLL use the transliteration original to the source. On the visit itself see LD, 1: 324.

31. Assaf, *Regal Way*, 197, and, more generally, 190–198. This biography provides a fascinating account of Rabbi Israel and the culture in which he lived.

32. "The Emperor of Russia and the Jews," *JC*, Jan. 9, 1846, 53.

33. LD, 1: 325.

34. "The Russo-Polish Jews," *VJ*, Feb. 13, 1846, 73; "The Emperor of Russia and the Jews," *JC*, Feb. 20, 1846, 78.

35. LD, 1: 330–331.

36. Custine, *Journey for Our Time*, 82.

37. See Myrtle Franklin and Michael Bor, *Sir Moses Montefiore, 1784–1885* (London, 1984), 63.

38. For accounts of this meeting see LD, 1: 333–334; MM to LC, April 13, 1846, folder 2, HL; also Lucien Wolf, *Sir Moses Montefiore: A Centennial Biography, with Extracts from Letters and Journals* (London, 1884), 149.

39. "Pesth—Two Days with Sir Moses Montefiore," *JC*, June 19, 1863, 5.

40. LD, 1: 334.

41. Henry Iliowizi, "Czar Nicholas the First and Sir Moses Montefiore," in *In the Pale: Stories and Legends of the Russian Jews*, ed. Iliowizi (Philadelphia, 1897), 261.

42. MM to LC, April 13, 1846.

43. Ibid. See also LD, 1: 334–336; Gessen, "Graf P. Kiselev."

44. See Stanislawski, *Nicholas I and the Jews*, 155–160.

45. Artur Eisenbach, *The Emancipation of the Jews in Poland, 1780–1870*, ed. Antony Polonsky, trans. Janina Dorosz (Oxford, 1991), 267–268.

46. See Louis Greenberg, *The Struggle for Emancipation*, vol. 1 of *The Jews in Russia* (New Haven, 1944), 47.

47. J. A. D. Bloomfield to Aberdeen, April 14, 1846, F.O. 65 321, no. 70, NA. Haim Guedalla later had no qualms about publicizing Montefiore's involvement; see Guedalla, *Some Account of the Two Journeys to Russia Undertaken by Sir M. Montefiore, Bart., in 1846 and 1872 to Further the Interests of the Russian Jews* (London, 1882), 13. Guedalla's pamphlet provoked surprise and anger among Russian Jews. See Israel Bartal, "Between Two Worlds: Reconsidering Sir Moses Montefiore," Paper presented at University College London conference on Britain and the Holy Land 1800–1914, 1989. Ephraim Deinard probably drew on Guedalla when he accused Montefiore of involvement in drafting the sorting decree, but did not mention Montefiore's subsequent change of heart; Ephraim Deinard, *Megilat setarim* (New York, 1928), cols. 11–12.

48. April 20, 1846, quoted in Guedalla, *Two Journeys,* 7–8.

49. MM to LC, April 13, 1846.

50. See LD, 1: 368; MM to LC, April 13, 1846.

51. MS. Enclosing Transcript of the Hebrew Tablet in the Soldiers' Synagogue at St. Petersburg, written shortly after 1867, MMSS vol. 520, 1. For an alternative description of this synagogue see "My Travels in Russia by Dr. Lilienthal," *JC,* Dec. 29, 1854, 2.

52. St. Petersburg: Intelligence about Montefiore, Montefiore police file, Fund 1 exponent, Inventory 1846, Case no. 89-3–89-4obv, in same file as Fund 109, Inventory 221 (86), Case no. 111, fols. 112–114obv, State Archive of the Russian Federation, Moscow; copies at Central Archive for the History of the Jewish People, Jerusalem.

53. MM to LC, April 13, 1846.

54. St. Petersburg: Intelligence about Montefiore.

55. April 24 and 25, 1846, loose leaves, MMJ 1846:?, SLC.

56. See Steven Zipperstein, *The Jews of Odessa: A Cultural History, 1794–1881* (Stanford, Calif., 1985).

57. Stanislawski, *Nicholas I and the Jews,* 72–73; more generally, Immanuel Etkes, "Immanent Factors and External Influences in the Development of the Haskalah Movement in Russia," in *Toward Modernity: The European Jewish Model,* ed. Jacob Katz (New York, 1987), 13–32.

58. Jacob Halevi Lifshitz, *Zikhron ya'akov* (Frankfurt am Main, 1924), 154.

59. See "Sir Moses Montefiore's Stay at Wilna in the Year 1846 (Translated from the 'Jüdische Volksblatt') (2)," *JC,* Oct. 18, 1861, 7. Alternative accounts of this encounter are given in Isaac Meir Dik, *Haoreḥ: Bo yesaper toledot hayamim haḥamurim asher avru aleinu toshvei vilna yibaneh ireynu amen me'az higiyah le'ozneinu habesorah mimasa ḥasar mosheh montifiori shelita vere'ato hagevirah ledi yehudit montefiori tihyeh le'irenu vilna ad tsetam mimenah ledarkam tsalḥah* (Vilna, 1846), 11–12; and Mordecai Aaron Ginzburg, "Al bikuro shel mosheh montefiori bevilna," in *Devir: Kolel kevutsot mikhtavim nifla'im ma'aseh aman* (Vilna, 1861), 100–102.

60. Ginzburg, "Montefiore bevilna," 102.

61. "Sir Moses Montefiore's Stay at Wilna (3)," *JC,* Oct. 25, 1861, 3.

62. MM to LC, April 13, 1846.

63. Col. Komayevsky to Count Orlov, April 26, 1846, Montefiore police file, Fund 1 exponent, Inventory 1846, Case no. 89-7/8, in same file as Fund 109, Inventory 221 (86), Case no. 111, fols. 112–114obv, State Archive of the Russian Federation.

64. "Sir Moses Montefiore's Stay at Wilna (3)." A similar account is given in Dik, *Haoreḥ,* 13.

65. LD, 1: 341–342. See also "Sir Moses Montefiore's Stay at Wilna (4)," *JC,* Nov. 1, 1861, 2; Dik, *Haoreḥ,* 15–16.

66. May 4, 1846, loose leaf, MMJ, SLC; Komayevsky to Orlov, April 29, 1846, Montefiore police file, Fund 1 exponent, Inventory 1846, Case no. 89-9, fol. 11obv, in same file as Fund 109, Inventory 221 (86), Case no. 111, fols. 112–114obv, State Archive of the Russian Federation, notes that Montefiore promised to give 100 ten-

ruble notes to the orphanage annually, and verbally promised to give 30 rubles each to those pupils who did best when studying Russian. See also Ginzburg, "Montefiore bevilna," 104.

67. On Salanter see Immanuel Etkes, *Rabbi Israel Salanter and the Mussar Movement: Seeking the Torah of Truth*, trans. Jonathan Chipman (Philadelphia, 1993).

68. "Sir Moses Montefiore's Stay at Wilna (5)," *JC*, Nov. 8, 1861, 2; also Dik, *Haoreḥ*, 25.

69. Dik, *Haoreḥ*, 27–28; and Ginzburg, "Montefiore bevilna," 104–105. Mordechai Aaron Ginzburg taught at the school. For Montefiore's impressions of the asylum see May 4, 1846, loose leaf, MMJ, SLC.

70. See the memoirs of Pauline Wengeroff, *Memoiren einer Grossmutter. Bilder aus der Kulturgeschichte der Juden Russlands im 19. Jahrhundert*, vol. 2 (Berlin, 1908), 8.

71. Isaac Baer, the Son of Rav. Moshe Epstein of Sharshev, to LL, Iyar 22, 5606, V.2717/13, JNUL.

72. Etkes, *Salanter,* 142.

73. Guedalla, *Two Journeys,* 11; "Sir Moses Montefiore's Stay at Wilna (4)."

74. MM to LC, April 13, 1846.

75. "Posen," *JC,* June 26, 1846, 162–163.

76. Ibid.

77. "Sir Moses Montefiore's Stay at Wilna (6)," *JC,* Nov. 15, 1861, 2.

78. Dik, *Haoreḥ*, 24, 27.

79. See the original diary entries, SLC.

80. Ginzburg, "Montefiore bevilna," 105–106.

81. See for instance Dik, *Haoreḥ,* 35.

82. May 9, 1846, loose leaf, SLC.

83. See Lifshitz, *Zikhron ya'akov,* 158.

84. Ginzburg, "Montefiore bevilna," 106; and LD, 1: 347.

85. See Lifshitz, *Zikhron ya'akov,* 157–158.

86. LD, 1: 347.

87. See Lilienthal's account, "A Visit to Wilna," *JC,* Jan. 25, 1861, 8.

88. LDMS, 1: 348.

89. See François Guesnet, *Polnische Juden im 19. Jahrhundert. Lebensbedingungen, Rechtsnormen und Organisation im Wandel,* (Cologne, 1998), 34; Eisenbach, *Emancipation of Jews in Poland,* 225. Both provide useful overviews of Jewish life in Poland in this period.

90. Quoted in Eisenbach, *Emancipation of Jews in Poland,* 42.

91. On cultural and religious currents in Polish Jewish society see Marcin Wodziński, *Haskalah and Hasidism in the Kingdom of Poland: A History of Conflict* (Oxford, 2005); and the conceptually outmoded Raphael Mahler, *Hasidism and the Jewish Enlightenment: Their Confrontation in Galicia and Poland in the First Half of the Nineteenth Century,* trans. Eugene Orenstein, Aaron Klein, and Jenny Malchowitz Klein (Philadelphia, 1985); for background also Glenn Dynner, *Men of Silk: The Hasidic Conquest of Polish Jewish Society* (Oxford, 2006).

92. Du Plat to Aberdeen, April 22, 1846, F.O. 65 325, no. 30, NA.

93. Du Plat to Aberdeen, May 16, 1846, ibid., no. 32.

94. LD, 1: 352–353.

95. See for instance "Sir Moses Montefiore . . . ," *Kurjer Warszawski*, May 27, 1846, 658. Thanks to Ursula Fuks and Ninel Kameraz-Kos for obtaining this material. All newspapers were subject to government censorship.

96. He was presumably referring to Abraham Buchner, whose son converted to Catholicism. See Mahler, *Hasidism and Jewish Enlightenment*, 218.

97. Assaf, *Regal Way*, 21–28, provides a helpful discussion of the problems involved in using this kind of source material.

98. See Harry Rabinowicz, *Hasidism: The Movement and Its Masters* (Northvale, N.J., 1988), 231. Rabinowicz includes Rabbi Isaac of Warka in the party, unlike Marcin Wodziński, "Hasidism, Shtadlanut, and Jewish Politics in Nineteenth-Century Poland: The Case of Isaac of Warka," *Jewish Quarterly Review* 95 (Spring 2005): 290–320.

99. Rabinowicz, *Hasidism*, 231.

100. LD, 1: 354–355.

101. On this see Rabinowicz, *Hasidism*, 203, 230; and Wodziński, *Haskalah and Hasidism*, 51–52.

102. LDMS, 1: 350.

103. "Mission of Sir Moses Montefiore to Russia," *VJ*, June 19, 1846, 150.

104. "Sir Moses Montefiore's Mission," *JC*, July 10, 1846, 178.

105. D. K., "Montefiore w Warszawie," 84.

106. "Aus dem Großherzogttum Posen, im Juli," *AZ*, July 6, 1846, 406–407.

107. "Mission of Sir Moses Montefiore to Russia."

108. MM to Peel, June 25, 1846; Peel to MM, June 28, 1846, Peel Papers Add 40594, fols. 259–262, BL; "Retrospect of A.M. 5606," *JC*, Oct. 16, 1846, 1.

109. For verbatim transcripts of Montefiore's letters to Kiselev see LD, 1: 360–373, 380–384.

110. Tsar Nicholas I's Comments on MM's Letter, May 26, 1847.

111. LD, 1: 360–373, 380–384.

112. Ibid. MM also wrote directly to Paskevich. Marcin Wodziński confirmed to me that extensive documentation exists in Polish archives. For a general discussion of responses to MM's comments on the situation in the Kingdom of Poland see D. K., "Montefiore w Warszawie," 78–84.

113. For a full transcript see LD, 1: 374–379.

114. Notes by Turkul', the Minister State-Secretary of the Polish Kingdom, on MM's Letter. Returned by Privy Councillor Turkul' to Kiselev Jan. 13/25, 1847, Document 2, fols. 6–32, delo 26: Po zamechaniiam Montefiroe o polozhenii evreev, Fond 1269 Evresiskii komitet, Russian State Historical Archive. For an alternative official view see Baron M. Korf, Member of the Government Council, State-Secretary, 19 April 1847, to His Excellency Count P. D. Kiselev, Document 6, fols. 58–59, 60–143, ibid.

115. Kiselev, May 29, 1847: Memo re. MM's Letter, Document 8, fols. 144–147, ibid. See also the argument in Gessen, "Graf P. Kiselev."

116. For an insight into the ways in which governmental structures obstructed

change see Daniel Orlovsky, *The Limits of Reform: The Ministry of Internal Affairs in Imperial Russia, 1802–1881* (Cambridge, Mass., 1981).

117. Kiselev, May 29, 1847, Memo re. MM's Letter. Nicholas added his comments directly to this memo.

118. Tsar Nicholas I's Comments on MM's Letter, May 26, 1847.

10. Trial and Error

1. MLL 1844–51, Mocatta 8, ML, also includes letters from Amsterdam (6), France (6), Portugal (1), Italy (including Nice and Lombardy-Venetia) (10), Berlin and East Prussia (15), other German cities (14), the Habsburg Empire (19), Russia (27, including 12 from Vilna), Malta (2), North Africa (including Tunis) (6), Ottoman lands (Syria, Iraq, Corfu, Dalmatia, etc.) (37), and Afghanistan (1). Letters from *shelehim* and Jerusalemites abroad are counted as Palestinian correspondence. The Schischa Collection, London, probably contains the best random sample of Montefiore's mailbag.

2. Aug. 18, 1840, Adolphe Crémieux Journal, Voyage accompli pour la défense d'Israélites accusés du meurtre d'un prêtre catholique, 369 AP/1, dr3, fol. 18, AN.

3. MM to LL, Dec. 26, 1844, folder 2, HL.

4. LL to MM, Aug. 10, 1848, ASM.

5. Yehiel Mendelssohn from Lublin to LL, Iyar 24, 5606, V.2717.17, JNUL.

6. Raphael Loewe, "Louis Loewe: Aide and Confidant," in *CMM*, 107, and more generally.

7. This account is taken from Finn to Palmerston, March 13, 1847, HBC, 1: 96–97. See also James Finn, *Stirring Times, or Records from Jerusalem Consular Chronicles of 1853 to 1856 by the Late James Finn, Edited and Compiled by His Widow*, vol. 1 (London, 1878), 108–110.

8. Inhabitants of der Alkiamar to the French Consul-General, March 21, 1847, CPC/Turquie/Beyrouth, vol. 8, fols. 73–74, MAE.

9. Bourré to Guizot, May 16, 1847, no. 38, ibid., fol. 88.

10. "Revival of the Damascus Calumny against the Jews of Beyrout and Its Refutation," *JC*, May 14, 1847, 129.

11. LD, 2: 1–2.

12. Beaudin to Sefata Pasha, April 22, 1847, CPC/Turquie/Damas, vol. 1, fol. 265, MAE.

13. Principal Leaders of the Hebrew Community at Damascus to MM, n.d.; Leading Members of the Hebrew Community at Damascus to MM, May 1847, ibid., fols. 264, 263.

14. MM to LC, Sept. 27, 1840, folder 1, HL; MM to Carl von Rothschild, Jan. 10, 1841, 000/87/2, RAL. See also LD, 1: 296–297.

15. LD, 2: 3.

16. See T. E. B. Howarth, *Citizen-King: The Life of Louis-Philippe King of the French* (London, 1961).

17. Quoted in ibid., 304.

18. Quoted in H. A. C. Collingham, *The July Monarchy: A Political History of*

France, 1830–1848 (London, 1988), 323; see chaps. 15–17, 23, on Orléanist foreign policy. On British foreign policy see David Brown, *Palmerston and the Politics of Foreign Policy, 1846–55* (Manchester, 2002).

19. LD, 2: 4–7.

20. "Phipps, Constantine Henry, First Marquess of Normanby," www.oxforddnb.com, accessed Dec. 27, 2008.

21. LDMS, 2: 4.

22. Quoted in Niall Ferguson, *The World's Banker: The History of the House of Rothschild* (London, 1998), 425; more generally, see 424–428.

23. P. B. Benny, "Personal Reminiscences of Sir Moses Montefiore, I," *Jewish World*, Aug. 7, 1885, 5.

24. MM to Louis-Philippe, Aug. 9, 1847, ASM.

25. LD, 2: 6.

26. Guizot to Vettier de Bourville (VdB), Aug. 6, 1847, no. 1, CPC/Turquie/Damas, vol. 1, fol. 245, MAE; Guizot to MM, Aug. 23, 1847, ASM; VdB to Guizot, Sept. 24, 1847, no. 3; and Guizot to VdB, Nov. 3, 1847, CPC/Turquie/Damas, vol. 1, fols. 272, 276, MAE.

27. Aug. 30, 1847, BDMB, ACC/3121/A/006, fols.67–82. See also 1st HY-R, recorded in ibid.

28. July 1, 1839, BDMB, ACC/3121/A/005/A, fols. 61–65.

29. Quoted in Israel Finestein, "Anglo-Jewish Opinion during the Struggle for Emancipation, 1828–58," in *Jewish Society in Victorian England: Collected Essays,* ed. Finestein (London, 1993), 8.

30. "Jewish Emancipation," *JC*, Feb. 7, 1845, 93.

31. "Jewish Emancipation," *JC*, March 7, 1845, 109.

32. July 5, 1847, BDMB, ACC/3121/A/006, fols. 64–67. For a discussion of Lionel's motivation see Ferguson, *World's Banker*, 526–532.

33. Lucien Wolf, *Sir Moses Montefiore: A Centennial Biography, with Extracts from Letters and Journals* (London, 1884), 162. On the changing public mood see Polly Pinsker, "English Opinion and Jewish Emancipation (1830–1860)," *JSS* 14, no. 1 (1952): 51–94.

34. Quoted in Ferguson, *World's Banker*, 542. See also M. C. N. Salbstein, *The Emancipation of the Jews in Britain: The Question of the Admission of the Jews to Parliament, 1828–1860* (London, 1982), 159.

35. LDMS, 2: 10.

36. See Franz Kobler, "Charles Henry Churchill," *Herzl Year Book* 4 (1962): 1–66.

37. "Damaskus," *Der Orient*, June 12, 1841, 181.

38. Quoted in Kobler, "Charles Henry Churchill," 22–24.

39. Churchill to MM, Aug. 15, 1842, folder 2, HL. See also Kobler, "Charles Henry Churchill," 40.

40. "London 14th October," *VJ*, Dec. 9, 1842, 77.

41. Churchill to MM, Jan. 8, 1843, ASM.

42. MM to LL, Aug. 4, 1848, MS259 A880, folder 2, ASM.

43. LL to MM, Aug. 10, 1848.

44. Kobler, "Charles Henry Churchill," 19.

45. See Salo Baron, "Abraham Benisch's Project for Jewish Colonization in Palestine," in *Jewish Studies in Memory of George A. Kohut,* ed. Salo Baron and Alexander Marx (New York, 1935), 72–85. See also John M. Shaftesley, "Dr. Abraham Benisch as Newspaper Editor," *TJHSE* 21 (1968): 214–231.

46. *Der Orient,* Sept. 19, 1840.

47. Benisch to Young, Jan. 3, 1842, HBC, 1: 42–46.

48. Quoted in Baron, "Benisch's Project," 83.

49. LD, 1: 308–309.

50. "Jerusalem Literature," *VJ,* July 22, 1842, 175.

51. "Jerusalem," *VJ,* Sept. 30, 1842, 30.

52. "The Press at Jerusalem," *VJ,* Nov. 25, 1842, 69; "The Holy Land and the Anglican Church (Concluded)," *VJ,* July 21, 1843, 201.

53. "Magdeburg, den 11. September. Leitender Artikel," *AZ,* Sept. 24, 1842, 573–574. On the origins of Jewish medical care in Jerusalem see Norbert Schwake, *Die Entwicklung des Krankenhauswesens der Stadt Jerusalem vom Ende des 18. bis zum Beginn des 19. Jahrhunderts,* vol. 1 (Herzogenrath, 1983), 193–228, and 108–192 on the missionary hospital.

54. "Frankfurt Am Main, 16. Februar," *AZ,* March 4, 1844, 138.

55. "Jewish Hospital at Jerusalem," *VJ,* Oct. 28, 1842. On Dr. Fränkel see Schwake, *Entwicklung,* 204–206.

56. Quoted in Schwake, *Entwicklung,* 132.

57. See Israel Freidin, "Bikur holim perushim birushalayim mihevrah leveit holim," *Cathedra* 27 (March 1983): 117–140.

58. Khayim Abr. Gagin et al., R. Moshe Rivlin et al., and Israel Drucker to MM, Sivan 9, 5604, MLL 1844–51, letter 27.

59. Khayim Abr. Gagin to MM, recd. Sept. 12, 1844, ibid., letter 64. On this initiative see Aryeh Morgenstern, "Beit haholim hayehudi harishon birushalayim," *Cathedra* 33 (Oct. 1984): 107–124; and Israel Freidin, "Beit haholim hasidim-sefardim birushalayim, 1844: shalav bemodernizatsiyah shel hayishuv hayashan," *Cathedra* 37 (Sept. 1985): 177–183. Both scholars appear unaware of the MLL. Also of interest is Shimon Stern, "Od al beit-haholim hayehudi harishon birushalayim," *Cathedra* 37 (Sept. 1985): 184–188.

60. Israel Drucker and Israel Moshe Khazan to MM, Ab 17, 5604, MLL 1844–51, letter 73.

61. Schwake, *Entwicklung,* 222.

62. "Jewish Hospital at Jerusalem," *JC,* May 16, 1845, 161. The committee was formed at the request of the emissary from Palestine Moshe Khazan, and the London Sephardim made an annual subscription to the hospital. See "The Jewish Hospital at Jerusalem," *JC,* Dec. 12, 1845, 42. Frankel to MM, Jan. 20, 1847, finally announced the move of the Montefiore dispensary to this hospital, MLL 1844–51, letter 102. Hirsch Lehren to MM, July 7, 1846, ASM, suggests that Montefiore had reservations about Khazan.

63. Judith Montefiore, *Notes from a Private Journal of a Visit to Egypt and Palestine by way of Italy and the Mediterranean,* 2d ed. (London, 1885). See the use

made of the appendix in an article by A. B. [Abraham Benisch?], "The Claims of Palestine," *VJ*, May 23, 1844, 146.

64. See Israel Bartal, "Karka'ot vetokhniyot le'ibudan bimei bikuro hasheni shel montefiori be'erets yisra'el bishnat 1839," *Shalem* 2 (1976): 231–296.

65. Kalischer to MM, Heshvan 16, 1844, and Shebat 29, 1845, MLL 1844–51, letters 146, 165. This is the only proof we have of Kalischer's preoccupation with the return to Zion at this time, predating his earliest known contact with Montefiore by ten years. On the later contact see Moshe Samet, "Kishrei montifiori im rav tsevi hirsh kalisher," *Cathedra* 33 (Oct. 1984): 54–56.

66. Turgemann to MM, Aug. 2, 5604; Mordekhay ben R. Shlomo Zalman, Sivan 2, 5604, and a second letter, recd. Sept 12, 1844, MLL 1844–51, letters 65, 25, 81.

67. "The Holy Land," *VJ*, Feb. 14, 1845, 102.

68. Mordekhai Salman, Ellul 13, 5605, MLL 1844–51, letter 243.

69. "Miscellaneous: We Hear from a Source . . . ," *JC*, May 30, 1845, 171.

70. MM to LL, June 27, 1845, folder 2, HL.

71. "Jerusalem," *JC*, June 26, 1846, 166.

72. "Jerusalem—Subscriptions to the Hospital—Emigration and Industrial School Bubbles," *JC*, Sept. 4, 1846, 207.

73. For a discussion of this see David Assaf, *The Regal Way: The Life and Times of Rabbi Israel of Ruzhin*, trans. David Louvish (Stanford, Calif., 2002), 191–193.

74. See, e.g., "Magdeburg, 16. Oktober. (Privatmitth)," *AZ*, Oct. 29, 1842, 645, which refers to articles published in 1840–41 in Jost's *Israelitische Annalen*.

75. "Frankfurt a. M. 24 September," *AZ*, Oct. 9, 1843, 609; "Palestine Relief Funds," *VJ*, Nov. 24, 1843, 35; "The Holy Land"; "Jerusalem, 1. November (O.P.A.Z.)," *AZ*, Jan. 13, 1845, 38.

76. David Hirschell Berliner, Samuel Slant, and Moses Khasbawitzer to MM, Feb. 15, 1847, MLL 1844–51, letter 106.

77. See Chayim Davidson, Chief Rabbi of Warsaw, Isaac Ettinger, Alexander Rosen, and Tiszel Lewenfisz, Collector of Contributions for the support of the poor in the Holy Land, to MM, July 1, 1849, and the many references to similar payments in MLL 1844–51. See also LD, 2: 16.

78. A. Loewe to MM, Jan. 29, 1847, ASM.

79. "Hebra Terumot Hakodesh," *OAJA*, March 1847; "Hebra Terumot Hackodesh, N.Y," *OAJA*, April 1847.

80. "Hebra Terumot Hackodesh, N.Y."

81. "The Jews at Tiberias," *JC*, Jan. 12, 1849, 115.

82. "Relief Fund for the Jews at Tiberias," *JC*, Jan. 19, 1849, 124; Jan. 26, 1849, 132; Feb. 2, 1849, 140; Feb. 23, 1849, 164.

83. "The State of Jerusalem, Letter II," *JC*, March 30, 1849, 200.

84. "The State of Jerusalem," *JC*, March 23, 1849, 193.

85. "The State of Jerusalem, Letter III," *JC*, April 4, 1849, 208. For some examples of Judith's personal giving see MLL 1844–51.

86. "Sephardim Synagogue" and "The Banquet," *JC*, Feb. 9, 1849, 143.

87. Jane Cox Gawler, *George Gawler, K.H., 52nd Light Infantry: A Life Sketch* (London, 1900), 22–23 , and more generally.

88. George Gawler, *Tranquillization of Syria and the East: Observations and Practical Suggestions in Furtherance of the Establishment of Jewish Colonies in Palestine, the Most Sober and Sensible Remedy for the Miseries of Asiatic Turkey* (London, 1845). On Gawler's restorationism see Menachem Kedem, "Pe'iluto shel dzordz gauler [George Gawler] lema'an hakamat moshavot yehudiyot be'erets yisra'el," *Cathedra* 33 (Oct. 1984): 93–106.

89. Memorandum in Connexion with "The Establishment of Jewish Colonies in Palestine," enclosed with Gawler to Aberdeen, June 26, 1845, MMSS vol. 513; Gawler to MM, July 4, 1845, SLC.

90. Charlotte Elizabeth Tonna, *Personal Recollections, Third Edition, Continued to the Close of Her Life* (London, 1841), 415.

91. Ibid., 421, 428–429. *Recollections* does not state explicitly that these words were directed at the Montefiores, referring only to "some dear Jewish friends." But the Montefiores can be inferred from J. H. Myers to MM, July 14, 1846, ASM.

92. "Formation of Jewish Colonies in Palestine," *VJ*, Feb. 13, 1846, 75.

93. J. C. Gawler, *Gawler*, 56.

94. LD, 2: 12.

95. J. C. Gawler, *Gawler*, 57.

96. See, e.g., Wood to Stratford Canning, Sept. 20, 1849, F.O. 78/801, no. 20, fols. 162–164, NA.

97. Wood to Canning, Feb. 14, 1849, ibid., no. 5.

98. Wood to Palmerston, ibid., no. 16, fol. 118; Wood to Canning, June 25, 1849, ibid., no. 14, fol. 120. This change was apparently implemented in 1850; see LD, 2: 20–21.

99. Wood to MM, July 7, 1840, File: Damascus 5610, ref. To the inscription on a tombstone, ASM. For broader context see Caesar E. Farah, *The Politics of Interventionism in Ottoman Lebanon, 1830–1861* (London, 2000), especially chaps. 3–16.

100. James Finn to Palmerston, Aug. 22, 1849, HBC, 1: 133–135.

101. On Montefiore's regular donations to the four holy cities "to be laid out in purchasing bread for the poor," see MLL 1844–51, letters 252, 257, 264, 267–269.

102. Beth Din Tzedek and the Heads of All the Ashkenazi Kollels [thirty-five signatories] to MM and JM, MMSS vol. 577.

103. But see also Avraham Ben Samhon and thirty-three other Sephardim, Tiberias, to MM, 5609, MMSS vol. 576; and Yitzhak, the Shamash of the Kollel and the Hevrat Bikur Holim of the Holy Community of Perushim Jerusalem, to MM, Tammuz 4, 5609, MMSS vol. 577. For the views of the German congregation see German Community Jerusalem to MM, 1849, ibid. On the productivist agenda pursued by Montefiore during this visit see Israel Bartal, "Shetei igrot mihudei hagalil lesir mosheh montefiori be'inyanei ḥaklaut, 1849," *Cathedra* 2 (1977): 141–152.

104. See the petitions and appointment documents collected in MMSS vols. 576–577.

105. Mordechai Ben Rav. Shlomo Zalman to MM and JM, Tammuz to the Parsha Vehayah ha'ish asher evḥar bo, Year Shalom uverakha, [5609], MMSS 577.

106. On the Finns see Mordechai Eliav, "Aliyato unefilato shel hakonsul haberiti

James Finn," *Cathedra* 65 (Sept. 1992): 37–81; Finn, *Stirring Times*; Elizabeth Finn, *Reminiscences of Mrs. Finn, Member of the Royal Asiatic Society* (London, 1929); Arnold Blumberg, ed., *A View from Jerusalem, 1849–1858: The Consular Diary of James and Elizabeth Anne Finn* (Rutherford, 1980).

107. Palmerston to the British Consuls and Consular Agents in the Turkish Dominions, Circular, April 21, 1841, HBC, 1: 39–40.

108. Aberdeen to Young, May 3, 1842, ibid., 46–47.

109. Finn to Palmerston, March 12, 1847; Lt. Col. Hugh Rose to Palmerston, March 27, 1847; Palmerston to Rose, April 2, 1847; Rose to Palmerston, Nov. 20, 1848, Letter from C. Basily received June 18, 1849, all in ibid., 95, 97–102, 109, 121–122. On Basily's opposition to Protestant missionary activities see Farah, *Interventionism*, 61.

110. Finn to Niven Moore, June 27, 1849, HBC, 1: 123–127.

111. For the first account of this incident see Finn to Palmerston, April 24, 1849, ibid., 112–115.

112. Finn to Moore, July 17, 1849; Moore to Palmerston, July 2, 1849, ibid., 123–127, 119–120.

113. Moore to Finn, June 18, 1849, ibid., 128–129.

114. Finn to Palmerston, Nov. 24 and Dec. 29, 1849; Moore to Palmerston, Nov. 25, 1849, ibid., 146–149, 158.

115. LD, 2: 18.

116. MM to JdR, Dec. 24, 1849, File: Damascus 5610.

117. Baroness JdR to MM, Feb. 12, 1850, ibid. On Betty see Laura Schor, *The Life and Legacy of Baroness Betty de Rothschild* (New York, 2006).

118. See MM to LL, Dec. 16, 1850, in which Montefiore details his preparations for this journey; and MM to LL, Dec. 30, 1850, folder 2, HL. Montefiore returned to Paris on this mission in 1855; see LD, 2: 39.

119. Baroness JdR to MM, Feb. 12, 1850.

120. MM to LL, March 22, 1850, MS259 A880, folder 2, HL.

121. See Geoffrey Alderman, *Modern British Jewry* (Oxford, 1998), chap. 1, for a demographic and socioeconomic overview.

122. On the continued importance of the communal oligarchy see Todd Endelman, "Communal Solidarity among the Jewish Elite of Victorian London," *Victorian Studies* 28 (Spring 1985): 491–526.

123. For the traditional view of Montefiore as communal leader see Israel Finestein, "The Uneasy Victorian: Montefiore as Communal Leader," in *CMM*, 45–70.

124. List of Deputies appointed 5610–1850, BDMB, ACC/3121/A/006, fols. 217–221.

125. Wolf, *Montefiore*, 288.

126. ILG to Parnassim & Vestry of the Great Synagogue, Sept. 26, 1838, BDMB, ACC/3121/A/005/A, fols. 33–45.

127. "The Board of Deputies of British Jews," *VJ*, Feb. 15, 1844, 87; "The Board of Deputies and the Manchester New Hebrew Congregation," *JC*, Oct. 22, 1847, 281.

128. Quoted in Brown, *Palmerston and Foreign Policy*, 33–34. Chap. 2 provides a

very sensitive discussion of the changing role of public opinion and the press in mid-Victorian politics.

129. For an excellent provincial study see Bill Williams, *The Making of Manchester Jewry, 1740–1875* (Manchester, 1976).

130. See Abraham Gillam, "The Burial Grounds Controversy between Anglo-Jewry and the Victorian Board of Health, 1850," *JSS* 45 (Spring 1983): 147–156.

131. For criticism of the board's lack of action see "Our Emancipation," *JC*, Jan. 3, 1851, 97.

132. "Educational Grant to the Jewish Schools," *JC*, April 16, 1852, 217. More generally see G. F. A. Best, "The Religious Difficulties of National Education in England, 1800–70," *Historical Journal* 12 (1956): 155–173.

133. "The Education Question: Important Meeting of the Board of Deputies," *JC*, Oct. 15, 9.

134. "The Board of Deputies. No. II," *JC*, Nov. 26, 1852, 61; "A.M., London, February 15th 1853, to the Editor," *JC*, Feb. 18, 1853, 158; "London, 24. November (Privatthmitth.)," *AZ*, Dec. 6, 1852, 599; "David, to the Editor," *JC*, Feb. 18, 1853, 157.

135. For details of attempts to repeal the *Herem* or to alter *Ascama* No. 1 within the Sephardi community see "The Sephardim Congregation—Repeal of an Obnoxious Law," *JC*, April 16, 1847, 116; "Sephardim Congregation," *JC*, April 30, 1847, 125; "Appeal to the Sephardim Congregation, for the Abolition of the Excommunication—Sent in by David Brandon, May 20th 1847: To the Yehidim of the Sephardim Congregation, Who Signed the Memorial Against Herem (Excommunication)," *JC*, May 28, 1847, 149; "Correspondence: To the Editor, December 22nd 1847, from David Brandon," *JC*, Dec. 24, 1847, 368; "Repeal of an Obnoxious Law," *JC*, Jan. 28, 1848, 407; "Repeal of an Obnoxious Law," *JC*, Feb. 25, 1848, 445; and "Sephardim Synagogue: Repeal of an Obnoxious Law," *JC*, Jan. 26, 1849, 129.

136. Elkin to the editor, *JC*, March 21, 1845, 120.

137. See, e.g., "Jews' Infant School," *JC*, Feb. 20, 1846, 92; "Jews' Infant School," *JC*, March 19, 1847, 102; "Jews' Infant School, A Ball," *JC*, Feb.1, 1850, 135; "Jews' Orphan Asylum," *JC*, April 26, 1850, 232.

138. "The Board of Deputies," *JC*, Dec. 9, 1853, 79.

139. For an excellent analysis of the religious politics of this period see Steven Singer, "Orthodox Judaism in Early Victorian London, 1840–1858" (Ph.D. diss., Yeshiva University, 1981); and Singer, "The Anglo-Jewish Ministry in Early Victorian London," *Modern Judaism* 5 (Oct. 1985): 279–299.

140. See List of Deputies appointed 5613–1853, BDMB, ACC/3121/A/007, fols. 164–171. For an account of this crisis see Israel Finestein, "The Anglo-Jewish Revolt of 1853," in Finestein, *Jewish Society in Victorian England*, 104–129; also David Feldman, *Englishmen and Jews: Social Relations and Political Culture, 1840–1914* (New Haven, 1994), 68–71.

141. The account in this paragraph and the next is drawn from "Meeting of the Board of Deputies, Extraordinary Proceedings," *JC*, Sept. 3, 1853, 380. Haim Guedalla provided an alternative version, "Haim Guedalla to the Editor," *JC*, Sept. 9,

1853, 389, which was disputed in turn; see "One Who Was Present, to the Editor," *JC*, Sept. 16, 1853, 398.

142. "The Board of Deputies," *JC*, Dec. 9, 1853.

143. See "Correspondence between Sir Moses Montefiore and Mr. Alderman Salomons," I and II, *JC*, Dec. 16, 1853, 90, and Dec. 30, 110; "Resignation of Mr. Alderman Salomons as Deputy of New Synagogue," *JC*, Dec. 16, 1853, 90.

144. "The Late Decision," *JC*, Dec. 12, 1853, 97.

145. "P. S. Lazarus, President, Sunderland, December 26th 1853, to the Editor," *JC*, Dec. 16, 1853, 112.

146. "London, 16. Dezember. (Privatmitth)," *AZ*, Jan. 2, 1854, 8.

147. See for instance reports of an official dinner held at Montefiore's home, "Makot yisra'el" *JC*, Jan. 20, 1854, 142.

148. LD, 2: 32-33.

149. "The Board of Deputies," *JC*, April 28, 1854, 254.

11. The Crimean War and After

1. On the rivalry between the two see Ehud Toledano, *State and Society in Mid-Nineteenth-Century Egypt* (Cambridge, 1990), chap. 1.

2. For an account of the visit see LD, 2: 26-30.

3. LDMS, 2: 28, 30.

4. LDMS, 2: 30.

5. On its origins see Sir John Marriott, *The Eastern Question: An Historical Study in European Diplomacy* (Oxford, 1940), chap. 10. The classic account remains Harold Temperley, *England and the Near East: The Crimea* (London, 1936).

6. Ludwig Philippson, "Die Juden im Orient," *AZ*, March 27, 1854, 151.

7. See Lisa Moses Leff, *Sacred Bonds of Solidarity: The Rise of Jewish Internationalism in Nineteenth-Century France* (Stanford, Calif., 2006), chap. 4.

8. Consistoire Central des Israélites de France to Napoleon III, March 24, 1854, BDMB, ACC/3121/A/007, fols. 253-254. See also Eliyahu Feldman, "The Question of Jewish Emancipation in the Ottoman Empire and the Danubian Principalities after the Crimean War," *JSS* 41 (Winter 1979): 41.

9. "The Jews in the East," *JC*, May 26, 1854, 292.

10. Clarendon to Stratford, May 15, 1854, F.O. 78/981, no. 255, NA.

11. "Colonel Gawler's Lecture on Palestine," *JC*, Nov. 16, 1849, 47.

12. MM to LL, Dec. 14, 1849, folder 2, HL.

13. "The Chief Rabbi's Visit to Portsmouth," *JC*, Jan. 11, 1850, 105.

14. George Gawler, *Syria and Its Near Prospects: The Substance of an Address Delivered in the Young Men's Christian Association Lecture Room, Derby* (London, 1853), 41-43.

15. "Yehudah Alkalai to the Editor, Sivan 15, 5612," *JC*, June 4, 1852, 278. On Alkalai see Israel Bartal, "Messianism and Nationalism: Liberal Optimism vs. Orthodox Anxiety," *Jewish History* 20 (March 2006): 5-17, esp. 13-14.

16. "Correspondence Relating to Palestine, IV," *JC*, July 23, 1852, 334; "Palestine," *JC*, Oct. 15, 1852, 14, 16; "Notice . . . Palestine Land Company," *JC*, April 12, 1854, 241.

17. See M. C. N. Salbstein, *The Emancipation of the Jews in Britain: The Question of the Admission of the Jews to Parliament 1828–1860* (London, 1982), 196; also "The Palestine Land Company," *JC*, June 9, 1854, 312.

18. See Arnold Blumberg, *Zion before Zionism, 1838–1880* (Syracuse, N.Y., 1985), chap. 8. The description of the Palestine famine is taken principally from James Finn, *Stirring Times, or Records from Jerusalem Consular Chronicles of 1853 to 1856 by the Late James Finn, Edited and Compiled by His Widow,* 2 vols. (London, 1878), 1: 435–443.

19. See Elizabeth Finn, *Reminiscences of Mrs. Finn, Member of the Royal Asiatic Society* (London, 1929), 74–76, 116–117.

20. For his account of these activities see Finn, *Stirring Times,* 1: 435–443 and 2: 60–76.

21. "An Appeal on Behalf of the Famishing Jews in the Holy Land," *JC*, May 19, 1854, 284.

22. See H. D. Schmidt, "Chief Rabbi Nathan Marcus Adler (1803–1890): Jewish Educator from Germany," *Leo Baeck Institute Year Book* 7 (1962): 289–311. On Adler's religious stance see Eugene Black, "The Anglicization of Orthodoxy: The Adlers, Father and Son," in *Profiles in Diversity: Jews in a Changing Europe, 1750–1870,* ed. Frances Malino and David Sorkin (Detroit, 1998), 295–325.

23. MM to LL, Dec. 4, 1844, folder 2, HL.

24. On communal centralization see Norman Cohen, "Non-Religious Factors in the Emergence of the Chief Rabbinate," *TJHSE* 21 (1968): 304–313; also Bill Williams, *The Making of Manchester Jewry, 1740–1875* (Manchester, 1976), 182–188. On Adler's educational initiative, see Albert Hyamson, *Jews' College, London, 1855–1955* (London, 1955). Israel Finestein, "The Uneasy Victorian: Montefiore as Communal Leader," in *CMM,* 58–59, argues that Montefiore's support was half-hearted.

25. Schmidt, "Adler," 11.

26. See the letters of appointment contained in MMSS vol. 576.

27. "Das heilige Land und seine jüdische Bevölkerung," *AZ,* March 20, 1854, 139; also "The Famine in Palestine: L. S. Magnus, Chatham, May 24th 1854, to the Editor," *JC,* May 26, 1854, 293. For Magnus' criticisms of Montefiore's behavior in 1853 see "The Late Decision," *JC,* Dec. 16, 1853, 97.

28. See, e.g., "The Famine in Palestine," *JC,* May 26, 1854, 293; "Western Synagogue, St. Alban's Place," *JC,* June 1, 1854, 302; "M. Davidsohn, to the Editor," *JC,* June 9, 1854, 310.

29. *Appeal Fund on Behalf of the Suffering Jews in the Holy Land: Report Released by Rabbi Nathan Adler and Moses Montefiore,* 1855, AK 76, pp. 16–18, Central Zionist Archives, Jerusalem. For more details see William Rubinstein and Hilary Rubinstein, *Philosemitism: Admiration and Support in the English-Speaking World for Jews, 1840–1939* (Basingstoke, 1999), 18–19.

30. "Appeal on Behalf of the Jews in the Holy Land (from the *Hampshire Independent,* June 3rd)," *JC,* June 9, 1854, 311.

31. On German contributions see "Erklärung hinsichtlich der Spenden für die Armen in Jerusalem und dem heiligen Lande," *AZ,* June 12, 1854, 293. On Italian support see Isidore Loeb, *Biographie d'Albert Cohn* (Paris, 1878), 87.

32. Quoted in Rubinstein and Rubinstein, *Philosemitism*, 19.

33. On Hasidic fund-raising see David Assaf, *The Regal Way: The Life and Times of Rabbi Israel of Ruzhin*, trans. David Louvish (Stanford, Calif., 2002), chap. 9. On the Anglosphere, see A. Mendelsohn, "Tongue Ties: The Emergence of an Anglophone Jewish Diaspora in the Mid-Nineteenth Century," *American Jewish History* 93 (June 2007): 177–209.

34. For the earliest example see Nathan Netter Barhaf HaHasid et al., Directors of the New Building Called the Hurva of Rabbi Yehudah HaHasid, to MM, Tammuz, 5599, MMSS vol. 574, 51C. See also the authorizations collected in vols. 576 and 577.

35. For details of the former see A. Loewe to MM and JM, Jan. 29, 1847, ASM. For details of Montefiore's contact with the Society for Improving the Condition of Our Brethren in the Holy Land, Cincinnati, see MM to Isaac Kubu and David Hirschell Berliner, Dec. 16, 1849, and other entries in MLL 1844–51, Mocatta 8, ML; also Samuel Bruel to MM, June 14, 1853, Schischa Collection, London. That Montefiore was appointed the London agent of the North American Relief Society of Palestine can be inferred from "Death of Judah Touro," *OAJA*, March 1854, 588. For details of other American contacts see, e.g., S. M. Isaacs, "The Jews of Palestine," *OAJA*, Jan. 1854, 502.

36. "Famine in Palestine: Letter from Sir Moses Montefiore, July 25th 5614 [1854] East Cliff Lodge Ramsgate, to the Rv. S. M. Isaacs of New York," *OAJA*, Oct. 1854, 373. For more detail on the American response see, e.g., "Distress in Palestine," *OAJA*, July 1854, 226.

37. MM to My dear Brethren of the House of Israel, Ellul 8, 5610, ASM; Rabbi Nathan Adler to Bury Anderson, Feb. 27, 1850, ASM. The Freemasons of San Francisco later named a lodge in Montefiore's honor; Montefiore Testimonials Provisional Catalogue, ML.

38. According to Raphael Loewe, Montefiore commissioned one Torah scroll from Hirsch Volozhin in Vilna every year, paying an annual retainer of £100; MLL 1844–51, letters 88, 104, 143, apparently refer to this. MM to LL, Oct. 7 and 11, 1850, folder 2, HL, suggest that Montefiore also employed at least one scribe in Palestine. For references to Montefiore completing or starting scrolls, see LD, 1: 27, 344 and 2: 134–135.

39. This is apparent from the generic inscription on the Montefiore Torah in Ballarat, Australia. Thanks to Prof. Jonathan Goldstein for this information.

40. On Touro see Leon Huhner, *The Life of Judah Touro* (Philadelphia, 1946).

41. "Death of Judah Touro."

42. See LD, 2: 25, 35–36. For a more detailed account see A. Schischa, "The Saga of 1855: A Study in Depth," in *CMM*, 278–285.

43. "Die Solidarität der Juden," *AZ*, April 24, 1854, 201; "The Condition of Our Brethren in the East, and How to Improve Their Moral Position," *JC*, June 16, 1854, 316.

44. "Lady Judith Montefiore," *AZ*, Sept. 27, 1862, 615.

45. Loeb, *Albert Cohn*, 52. See also "Zur jüdisch-orientalischen Frage (Fortsetzung)," *AZ*, June 19, 1854, 305.

46. "Zur jüdisch-orientalischen Frage (Schluß)," *AZ*, June 26, 1854, 219.

47. MM to LL, Jan. 6, 1851, folder 2, HL.

48. See Loeb, *Albert Cohn,* 74–75, for further details; also Finn to Stratford, July 27, 1854, HBC, 1: 228–229.

49. "Zur jüdisch-orientalischen Frage," *AZ,* Sept. 11, 1854, 463.

50. For details see Schischa, "Saga of 1855," 279–285.

51. On the civilizing aspirations of French Jewry see Aron Rodrigue, *French Jews, Turkish Jews: The Alliance Israélite Universelle and the Politics of Jewish Schooling in Turkey, 1860–1925* (Bloomington, Ind., 1990).

52. Finn to Stratford, July 24, 1855, HBC, 1: 233–235.

53. LD, 2: 37.

54. Oct. 19, 1854, loose leaf, MMJ 1854:9, SLC; MM to LL, March 27, 1855, folder 3, HL.

55. Caesar Farah, *The Politics of Interventionism in Ottoman Lebanon, 1830–1861* (London, 2000), 228.

56. On the Camondo family see Nora Şeni and Sophie le Tarnec, *Les Camondo, ou l'éclipse d'une fortune* (Actes Sud, n.p., 1997), esp. chap. 1; also Aron Rodrigue, "Abraham de Camondo of Istanbul: The Transformation of Jewish Philanthropy," in Malino and Sorkin, *Profiles in Diversity,* 46–56.

57. See Esther Benbassa and Aron Rodrigue, *Sephardi Jewry: A History of the Judeo-Spanish Community, 14th–20th Centuries* (Berkeley, 1993), 75–77.

58. Jemima Guedalla, *Diary of a Tour to Jerusalem and Alexandria in 1855 with Sir Moses and Lady Montefiore by the Late Mrs. H. Guedalla* (London, 1890), 27.

59. Stratford to Clarendon, June 20, 1855, F.O. 78/1081, no. 450, NA. More generally, see Allan Cunningham, "Stratford Canning and the *Tanzimat,*" in *Beginnings of Modernization in the Middle East: The Nineteenth Century,* ed. William Polk and Richard Chambers (Chicago, 1968), 245–264; and the official biography, Stanley Lane-Poole, *The Life of the Right Honourable Stratford Canning, Viscount Stratford de Redcliffe, from His Memoirs and Private and Official Papers,* 2 vols (London, 1888). For a colorful description of his personality see *Sir A. Henry Layard: Autobiography and Letters from His Childhood until His Appointment as H.M. Ambassador at Madrid,* vol. 2 (London, 1903), 83–85.

60. MM to LC, July 1, 1855, folder 3, HL.

61. Grand Vizierial Note, Addressing the Chief Secretary at the Imperial Palace, and Requesting an Imperial Demand, Shawwal 15, 1271, Irade hariciye 6042 OK, MFA.

62. Translation of the Memorandum Containing the Summary of a Petition Submitted to His Majesty by MM, July 1855, ibid.

63. For Montefiore's account of this encounter see LD, 2: 44; and MM to LC, July 1, 1855.

64. See the Humble Petition and Memorandum of those members of the Ashkenazim community of the House of Israel in Jerusalem the Holy City, who are under British protection, July 13, 1854, HBC, 1: 226–127. More generally, see Sherman Lieber, *Mystics and Missionaries: The Jews in Palestine, 1799–1840* (Salt Lake City, 1992), 127–131 and chap. 11.

65. See Finn to Stratford, July 13, 1854, HBC, 1: 225–226; and Memorandum Presented to the High Office of the Foreign Ministry of the Porte by the Ambassador

of England, Lord Stratford de Redcliffe, May 18, 1855, Irade hariciye 6044 OK, app. 1, MFA.

66. See *Samuel Gobat, Bishop of Jerusalem, His Life and Work: A Biographical Sketch Drawn Chiefly from His Own Journals* (London, 1884), 309–313; "Jerusalem," *JC,* July 13, 1855, 279.

67. "Appeal Fund on Behalf of the Suffering Jews in the Holy Land," Feb. 23, 5615, printed flyer, ASM.

68. For Montefiore's impressions see July 20, 1855, MMJ 1855, Transcript, Call no. Ms. Var. 21, JNUL. For Jemima's, see Guedalla, *Diary,* 44–45; and Finn, *Stirring Times,* 2: 325.

69. July 23, 1855, MMJ 1855.

70. See Finn, *Stirring Times,* 2: chap. 25.

71. See E. Finn, *Reminiscences,* 137–139; and Finn, *Stirring Times,* 2: 328–329.

72. The account and quotations that follow in the text are based on Schischa, "Saga of 1855," 305–306.

73. Accounts from MMJ 1855.

74. Schischa, "Saga of 1855," 305; Arnold Blumberg, ed., *A View from Jerusalem, 1849–1858: The Consular Diary of James and Elizabeth Anne Finn* (Rutherford, 1980), 212–213 n. 58.

75. Aug. 5, 1855, MMJ 1855; and Guedalla, *Diary,* 53–54. See also Blumberg, *View from Jerusalem,* 198–199.

76. It has generally been criticized as the latter; see Israel Bartal, "Nationalist before His Time or a Belated Shtadlan?—Guidelines for the Activities of Moses Montefiore," and Arieh Morgenstern, "Moses Montefiore and the Yishuv: General Lines of Approach for a New Consideration," in *The Age of Moses Montefiore,* ed. Israel Bartal (Jerusalem, 1987), 21–22, 31–39.

77. "Appeal Fund on Behalf of the Suffering Jews in the Holy Land," Feb. 23, 5615. Montefiore always insisted that the recipients of his generosity provided him with receipts. A representative sample remains in the Schischa Collection.

78. Ibid.

79. See the complaints of Rabbi Moshe Sachs in "Jerusalem," *JC,* July 13, 1855.

80. July 27, 1855, MMJ 1855. For an alternative account see "Migdal halevanon tsofeh penei yerushalayim," *HLV,* April 29, 1869, 1.

81. Aug. 14, 1855, MMJ 1855; also *Second Report: An Appeal on Behalf of the Suffering Jews in the Holy Land. The Rev. the Chief Rabbi, and Sir Moses Montefiore Bart., Trustees. The Rev. Aaron Levy Green Honorary Secretary* (London, 1856).

82. "Jerusalem," *JC,* March 21, 1856, 526; also *Second Report.*

83. Quoted in Margalit Shilo, *Princess or Prisoner? Jewish Women in Jerusalem, 1840–1914,* trans. David Louvish (Waltham, Mass., 2005), 86, and more generally for a fascinating account of women's lives in Jewish Jerusalem.

84. See ibid., 130. Montefiore and Adler claimed that Judith had taken the initative to establish this charity; see "Appeal Fund on Behalf of the Suffering Jews in the Holy Land," Feb. 23, 5615.

85. July 31, 1855, MMJ 1855.

86. Ludwig Frankl, *Nach Jerusalem,* 2 vols. (Leipzig, 1858), 1: 374.

87. Aug. 1, 1855, MMJ 1855.

88. Aug. 15, 1855, ibid.; Guedalla, *Diary,* 58.

89. See the argument made in Schischa, "Saga of 1855."

90. MMJ 1855.

91. MM to Stratford, Nov. 12, 1855, 1855:4, SLC. Montefiore rented one house for the girls' school and another for the weaving institution.

92. LD, 2: 51–52.

93. See MLL 1844–51, letter 42.

94. Aug. 1, 1855, MMJ 1855.

95. Aug. 2, 1855, ibid. This was not an unheard-of sum; see Ruth Kark, "He'arot lefarashat batei Touro," *Cathedra* 27 (Jan. 1981): 161.

96. Aug. 1, 1855, MMJ 1855; Finn, *Stirring Times,* 2: 336.

97. MM to Stratford, Nov. 12, 1855. For details of Montefiore's meetings with delegations from Safed and Tiberias see *Second Report;* July 30 and Aug. 1, 1855, MMJ 1855; and Accounts from MMJ 1855. These sources are somewhat contradictory.

98. LD, 2: 55.

99. "Palestine," *OAJA,* Jan. 1854, 483.

100. Quoted in Barbara Kreiger, *Divine Expectations: An American Woman in 19th-Century Palestine* (Athens, Ohio, 1999), 110. On Classen see also Frankl, *Nach Jerusalem,* 2: 5.

101. See Kreiger, *Divine Expectations,* 17, and more generally on Mrs. Minor. Also see Lester I. Vogel, *To See a Promised Land: Americans and the Holy Land in the Nineteenth Century* (University Park, Penn., 1993).

102. On the Artas project see Kreiger, *Divine Expectations,* pt. 1.

103. See "Warder Cresson," www.jewishvirtuallibrary.org, accessed Dec. 27, 2008.

104. "Aus Palästina," *AZ,* July 31, 1854, 383. See also "Relief by Agriculture for Palestine," *OAJA,* Oct. 1854, 351. On Leeser and Palestine see Maxine S. Seller, "Isaac Leeser's Views on the Restoration of a Jewish Palestine," *American Jewish Historical Quarterly* 58 (Sept. 1968): 118–136.

105. Aug. 27, 1855, MMJ 1855.

106. Aug. 28, 1855, ibid.

107. Ibid.

108. Quoted in D. De Sola Pool, "Some Relations of Gershom Kursheedt and Sir Moses Montefiore," *Publications of the American Jewish Historical Society* 37 (1947): 216–218. See also Guedalla, *Diary,* 66–70; and LD, 2: 56–57.

109. Ruth Sebag-Montefiore, *A Family Patchwork: Five Generations of an Anglo-Jewish Family* (London, 1987), 22; E. H. C. Moberly Bell, *The Life and Letters of C. F. Moberly Bell* (London, 1927), 17. The rumor is echoed in anti-Semitic websites; "Jewish press control," www.jrbooksonline.com, accessed Dec. 27, 2008.

110. Quoted in John Marlowe, *The Making of the Suez Canal* (London, 1964), 75; chap. 2 provides an excellent analysis of the broader context. On de Lesseps and Suez see George Edgar-Bonnet, *Ferdinand de Lesseps,* vol. 1: *Le créateur de Suez* (Paris, 1951).

111. LD, 2: 57.

112. Ibid., 25–26.

113. See Stanley Lane-Poole, ed., *The Life of the Late General F. R. Chesney, Colonel Commandant Royal Artillery, by His Wife and Daughter* (London, 1885), chaps. 12–15.

114. See ibid., chap 18. More generally, see Eliahu Elath, "A British Project for the Construction of a Railway between Jaffa and Jerusalem," in *Studies on Palestine during the Ottoman Period,* ed. Moshe Ma'oz (Jerusalem, 1975), 415–422.

115. MM to Kursheedt, April 25, 1856; De Sola Pool, "Gershom Kursheedt and Sir Moses Montefiore," 217–218.

116. MM Personal Bible, private collection of Rabbi Dr. Abraham Levy. These jottings are dated according to both the Jewish and the English calendars, and were made only in Jerusalem, Smithembottom, and Mont Cenis. They date from the mid-1840s, suggesting Montefiore may have used a different Bible in earlier life.

117. On earlier railway involvement see P. L. Cottrell, "The Business Man and the Financier," in *CMM,* 39–40.

118. March 10 or April 10, 1856, loose leaf, MMJ 1856:2a, SLC.

119. LD, 2: 58–60.

120. Ibid.; Eardley to Strzelecki, Jan. 22, 1857, MMJ 1857:2, SLC.

121. See Lane-Poole, *Chesney,* 453. Chesney dated this meeting to late 1856, but LD, 2: 63 indicates that it took place in Feb. 1857.

122. LD, 2: 68; Finn to Clarendon, June 6, 1857, HBC, 1: 246–248.

123. Lane-Poole, *Chesney,* 452–457; and LD, 2: 132–134.

124. See, e.g., the positive "Breslau, 5. November (Privatmitth)," *AZ,* Nov. 12, 1855, 587–588; the negative "Jerusalem, im Monat Ab," *AZ,* Sept. 1, 1856, 485; and Moshe Sachs's relatively enthusiastic letter, "Jerusalem," *JC,* March 21, 1856. For other responses, see "The Palestine Relief Fund," *JC,* Feb. 29, 1856, 500; "Hamburg, November. (Privatmitth.)," *AZ,* Dec, 24, 1855, 663; "Distress among the Jews in the Holy Land," *JC,* Jan. 4, 1856, 436.

125. *Second Report,* 10–11.

126. Feldman, "Jewish Emancipation," 45.

127. Dr. Lil, "The Jews in Palestine," *The Israelite,* Aug. 15, 1856, 44.

128. See the verdict of Loeb, *Albert Cohn,* 47, who compared its impact to that of the Damascus Affair.

129. Rodrigue, *French Jews, Turkish Jews,* 21.

130. "Welcome to Sir Moses Montefiore," *JC,* Oct. 5, 1855, 326.

131. Frankl, *Nach Jerusalem,* 1: 374. Montefiore has often been criticized for his failure to build lasting institutions. See the discussion in Bartal, "Nationalist or Belated Shtadlan?" 21–22; and Morgenstern, "Moses Montefiore and the Yishuv." Bartal argues that Montefiore did not see this as part of his role, but the letter to Loewe indicates otherwise.

132. MM to LL, March 24, 1857, folder 3, HL.

133. See MM to Stratford, Nov. 12, 1855; *Second Report;* Will Smith to MM, Jan. 14, 1856, ASM; Hodgkin's very open-ended ruminations in TH to MM, THLB, PP/HO/D/A2424, box 15, file 12 [back of the book], fols. 143–157, HAWL; MM to LL, March 24, 1857; MM to LL, Dec. 17, 1858, folder 3, HL.

134. LD, 2: 67–68; also Kursheedt to LL, June 12, 1857, folder 3, HL.

135. Frankl, *Nach Jerusalem,* 2: 111; Mary Eliza Rogers, *Domestic Life in Palestine* (London, 1862), 314–318.

136. LD, 2: 67.

137. "Jerusalem," *JC,* Nov. 13, 1857, 1211.

138. LD, 2: 78.

12. The Mortara Affair

1. Richard Barnett, "Sources for the Study of Sir Moses Montefiore," in *Sir Moses Montefiore: A Symposium,* ed. Vivian Lipman (n.p., 1982), 7.

2. MM to LL, March 5, 1857, folder 3, HL.

3. LD, 2: 75–77.

4. MM personal Bible, private collection of Rabbi Dr. Abraham Levy.

5. On Bologna see Steven Hughes, *Crime, Disorder and the Risorgimento: The Politics of Policing in Bologna* (Cambridge, 1994).

6. This account is taken from the standard history of the affair: David Kertzer, *The Kidnapping of Edgardo Mortara* (London, 1997), chap. 1. See also the popular Daniele Scalise, *Il Caso Mortara: La vera storia del bambino ebreo rapito dal Papa* (Milan, 1997). Gemma Volli, *Il Caso Mortara nel primo centenario* (Rome, 1960); and Volli, "Il Caso Mortara nell opinione pubblica e nella politica del tempo," *Bollettino del Museo del Risorgimento, Bologna* 5 (1960): 1087–1521, were pioneering in their day.

7. For a nuanced view of Jewish life under the papacy see Thomas Brechenmacher, *Das Ende der doppelten Schutzherrschaft. Der Heilige Stuhl und die Juden am Übergang zur Moderne (1775–1870)* (Stuttgart, 2004). See also Ermanno Loevinson, "Gli Ebrei dello Stato della Chiesa nel periodo del Risorgimento politico d'Italia," *La Rassegna Mensile di Israel* 8, no. 9 (1934): 512–538, 36–45, 159–174, 263–285, 422–439, 543–563; and Aram Mattioli, "Das letzte Ghetto Alteuropas. Die Segregationspolitik der Papst-Könige in der 'heiligen Stadt' bis 1870," in *Katholischer Antisemitismus im 19. Jahrhundert. Ursachen und Traditionen im internationalen Vergleich,* ed. Olaf Blaschke and Aram Mattioli (Zurich, 2000), 111–143.

8. See Cecil Roth, "Forced Baptisms in Italy: A Contribution to the History of Jewish Persecution," *Jewish Quarterly Review,* n.s., 27 (1936–37): 117–136.

9. Kertzer, *Kidnapping,* 34. There were at least eight cases of forced baptism after 1815: 1817 (Ferrara), 1824 (Genoa), 1826 (Ancona), 1836 (Modena), 1838 (Ferrara), 1840 (Rome), 1844 (Reggio d'Emilia and Lugo).

10. See Frank Coppa, "Realpolitik and Conviction in the Conflict between Piedmont and the Papacy during the Risorgimento," *Catholic Historical Review* 54 (Jan. 1969): 579–612.

11. Momolo Mortara and the Università Israelitica to Pius IX, with enclosures, Arch. Part. Pio IX, Ojetti Varii, 1433, Archivio Segreto Vaticano, Rome (hereafter ASV); see also ProMemoria Presented by Momolo Mortara, Segretaria di Stato, ep. moderna 1864, rubrica 66, fasc. 2 (7–69), ASV; for the papal response see Brevi Cenni e Riflessioni sul Pro-Memoria e Sillabo, Scritture Umiliate alla Santità di Nos-

tro Signore Papa Pio IX, Relative al Battesimo Conferito in Bologna al Fanciullo Edgardo Figlio degli Ebrei Salmone e Marianna Mortara, Arch. Part. Pio IX, Ojetti Varii, 1433, ASV.

12. "Lengthy Article from the Roman Correspondent of *Armonia*," *Tablet*, Oct. 30, 1858. For alternative versions see "Foreign Intelligence—France," *The Times*, Oct. 25, 1858, 8; and "The Mortara Case," *Morning Chronicle*, Dec. 7, 1858, 4. For the original account of his journey to Rome see Brigadier Agostini to Antonelli, Nov. 2, 1858, Segretaria di Stato, ep. moderna 1864, rubrica 66, fasc. 2 (2–3), ASV.

13. Quoted in the *Corriere Mercantile* of Genoa, "The Mortara Case," *Morning Chronicle*, Nov. 13, 1858, 3.

14. Gian Ludovico Masetti Zannini, "Nuovi documenti sul 'caso Mortara,'" *Rivista di Storia della Chiesa in Italia* 13 (1959): 264. For a psychological interpretation see Lita Linzer Schwartz and Nathalie Isser, "Some Involuntary Conversion Techniques," *JSS* 43 (Winter 1991): 1–10.

15. See Jean Maurain, *La politique ecclésiastique du Second Empire* (Paris, 1930).

16. On the press see Roger Price, *The French Second Empire: An Anatomy of Political Power* (Cambridge, 2001), 171–187.

17. On Risorgimento Italy see Stuart Woolf, *A History of Italy, 1700–1860: The Social Constraints of Political Change* (London, 1979); Harry Hearder, *Italy in the Age of the Risorgimento, 1790–1870* (London, 1983); Derek Beales, *The Risorgimento and the Unification of Italy* (London, 1981).

18. Cecil Roth, *The History of the Jews of Italy* (Philadelphia, 1946), 457.

19. On Cavour's philo-Semitism see Ermanno Loevinson, "Camillo Cavour e gli Israeliti," *Nuova Antologia di Lettere, Scienze ed Arti* 148 (July–Aug. 1910): 453–464.

20. Quoted in Giacomo Martina, *Pio IX (1851–1866)* (Rome, 1986), 35 n. 54.

21. Extract from *The Times*, Sept. 9, 1858, pasted in Sept. 6, 1858, BDMB, ACC/3121/A/18, fols. 290–297.

22. Reprinted in "L'Affaire Mortara de Bologne," *AI*, Aug. 1858, 557. On the European dimension of this conflict see Christopher Clark and Wolfram Kaiser, eds., *Culture Wars: Secular-Catholic Conflict in Nineteenth-Century Europe* (Cambridge, 2003).

23. For an excellent analysis of different Catholic ideological currents see Vincent Viaene, *Belgium and the Holy See from Gregory XVI to Pius IX (1831–1859): Catholic Revival, Society and Politics in 19th Century Europe* (Brussels, 2001), chap. 2.

24. Edmond About, *The Roman Question*, trans. H. C. Coape (London, 1859), 4–7.

25. Viaene, *Belgium and the Holy See*, 268–269.

26. *L'Univers*, Oct. 23, 24, 25, 15, and 16, 1858, quoted in Nathalie Isser, *Antisemitism during the French Second Empire* (New York, 1991), 34, 39. Conversely, see Rabbin E. Aristide Astruc, *Les Juifs et L. Veuillot* (Paris, 1859).

27. For a translation of the *Civiltà Cattolica* article see "The Little Neophyte—Edgardo Mortara," *JC*, Sept. 30, 1859.

28. On the modernity of Catholic anti-Semitism see Olaf Blaschke, "Die Anatomie des katholischen Antisemitismus. Eine Einladung zum internationalen Vergleich" and "Wie wird aus einem guten Katholiken ein guter Judenfeind? Zwölf Ursachen des katholischen Antisemitismus auf dem Prüfstand," in Blaschke and Mattioli, *Katholischer Antisemitismus,* 3–56, 77–110.

29. Police Report, Oct. 19, 1858, Correspondance Politique/Rome/1009 (77), MAE.

30. The best-known Catholic protest was L'Abbé Delacouture, *Le droit canon et le droit naturel dans l'Affaire Mortara* (Paris, 1858).

31. Extract from *The Times,* Sept. 9, 1858.

32. Circular letter from MM, Oct. 25, 1858, ACC 3121/B1/1, fol. 409, Board of Deputies Archives, London Metropolitan Archives.

33. Dec. 22, 1858, BDMB, ACC/3121/A/8, fols. 308–315; "The Mortara Case," *Morning Chronicle,* Oct. 16, 1858, 6.

34. MM to Malmesbury, Sept. 8, 1858, and Malmesbury to Cowley, Sept. 9, 1858, F.O. 881/811 (1–3), NA.

35. Gramont to Walewski, Oct. 5, 1858, Correspondance Politique/Rome/1009 (8), MAE.

36. Masetti Zannini, "Nuovi documenti," 273.

37. Cowley to Malmesbury, Oct. 13, 1858, and to Lyons, Oct. 4, 1858, F.O. 881/811 (13, 11), NA. See also Josef Altholz, "A Note on the English Catholic Reaction to the Mortara Case," *JSS* 23 (April 1961): 111–118; Raphael Langham, "The Reaction in England to the Kidnapping of Edgardo Mortara," *Jewish Historical Studies* 39 (2004): 79–102. More generally, see D. G. Paz, *Popular Anti-Catholicism in Mid-Victorian England* (Stanford, Calif., 1992); also E. R. Norman, *Anti-Catholicism in Victorian England* (London, 1968).

38. On the papal aggression see C. T. McIntire, *England against the Papacy, 1858–1861: Tories, Liberals and the Overthrow of Papal Temporal Power during the Italian Risorgimento* (Cambridge, 1983).

39. See, e.g., "Roman Proselytism," *Morning Chronicle,* Oct. 17, 1858, 6; conversely, "Leader: Practical Comment on the Mortara Case," *Tablet,* Dec. 25, 1858, for Catholic responses.

40. "France, Paris, Wednesday 6 Pm from Our Own Correspondent," *Morning Post,* Nov. 19, 1858, 5.

41. MM to Eardley, Oct. 5, 1858, Evangelical Alliance Committee of Council, MB, vol. 2, fols. 174–181. The Evangelical Alliance was founded to oppose government funding for the Catholic theological seminary at Maynooth, Ireland.

42. Twelfth Annual Conference, *Evangelical Christendom: Its State and Prospects* 12 (Dec. 1, 1858): 431–432.

43. "Evangelical Alliance and the Mortara Case," *JC,* Nov. 12, 1858, 4.

44. Memorial of the Committee of the Protestant Association, Memorial of the Committee of the Protestant Alliance, and Memorial from the Scottish Reformation Society, all to Malmesbury, F.O. 881/811 (20–21, 23), NA.

45. Hammond to Shaftesbury, Dec. 11, 1858 (reprinted in *The Times*); also Hammond to Lord, Protestant Association, Nov. 9, 1858, both in F.O. 881/811 (23),

NA. Malmesbury's view was probably shaped by his unsuccessful handling of an earlier episode with similar religious overtones. See Anna Lohrli, "The Madiai: A Forgotten Chapter of Church History," *Victorian Studies* 33 (Autumn 1989): 29–50.

46. "The Mortara Case: Correspondence between Sir Culling Eardley and Sir Moses Montefiore," *The Times*, Dec. 28, 1858, 5.

47. "Secret Baptism and Forcible Abduction of a Jewish Child by the Roman Inquisition," *JC*, Sept. 17, 1858, 316; "L'Affaire Mortara," *AI*, Nov. 1858, 618.

48. On the French intervention see Kertzer, *Kidnapping*, 86–87, and 123–124 on the Dutch intervention. The appeal of the Consistoire Central des Israélites de France was reproduced in *Journal des Débats*, Sept. 27, 1858. On the Prussian intervention see "Berlin, 27. Dezember," *AZ*, Jan. 3, 1859, 26. On the American response to the Mortara Affair see Bertram Wallace Korn, *The American Reaction to the Mortara Case, 1858–1859* (Cincinnati, 1957).

49. Philippson first proposed a German appeal in September; see "Die unglückliche Familie Mortara in Bologna," *AZ*, Sept. 6, 1858, 502. For the appeal itself see "Magdeburg, 27. September. Die Angelegenheit in Bologna," *AZ*, Oct. 10, 1858, 557.

50. Quoted in Korn, *American Reaction*, 63, 107. On the New York response see Board of Representatives of the United Congregations of Israelites of the City of New York to MM, Jan. 3, 1859, BDMB, ACC/3121/A/009, fols. 5–6.

51. Jan. 26, 1859, ibid., fols. 1–7.

52. "Prayers in the Synagogues for the Success of the Mission of Sir Moses Montefiore," *JC*, March 4, 1859, 4.

53. "Chronique du mois," *AI*, Feb. 1859, 99.

54. "Mélanges: Rapport de Sir Moses Montefiore sur sa mission à Rome, 2e article," *AI*, Oct. 1859, 573.

55. LD, 2: 88. See Alec Randall, "A British Agent at the Vatican: The Mission of Odo Russell," *Dublin Review* 479 (Spring 1959): 37–56; Noel Blakiston, ed., *The Roman Question: Extracts from the Despatches of Odo Russell from Rome, 1858–1870* (London, 1962); McIntire, *England against the Papacy*, 46–57; Karina Urbach, *Bismarck's Favourite Englishman: Lord Odo Russell's Mission to Berlin* (London, 1999), on his later diplomatic career.

56. Masetti Zannini, "Nuovi documenti," 266.

57. Quoted in Abraham Berliner, *Geschichte der Juden in Rom von der ältesten Zeit bis zur Gegenwart (2050 Jahre)*, vol. 2 (Frankfurt, 1893), 154. On Pius' attitude to the Jews in the 1870s see Giovanni Miccoli, "Santa Sede, questione ebraica e antisemitismo fra Otto e Novocento," in *Dall'emancipazione a Oggi*, vol. 2 of *Gli Ebrei in Italia*, ed. Corrado Vivanti (Turin, 1997), 1405.

58. Extract from *The Times*, Sept. 9, 1858.

59. Ibid.

60. On British attitudes see McIntire, *England against the Papacy*; F. A. Simpson, "England and the Italian War of 1859," *Historical Journal* 5 (1962): 111–121; Derek Beales, *England and Italy, 1859–1860* (London, 1961); Harry Hearder, "The Foreign Policy of Lord Malmesbury, 1858–9" (Ph.D. diss., University of London, 1954), 259–353.

61. McIntire, *England against the Papacy*, 100.

62. LD, 2: 89–90.

63. *Bolletino dei Conosciuti Avvenimenti dal Giorno*, April 25–26, 1859, Segretaria di Stato, ep. moderna, rubrica 155, fasc. 4 (72–74), ASV.

64. George Augustus Sala, *Rome and Venice, with Other Wanderings in Italy, in 1866–7* (London, 1869), 347–348.

65. Sir Edward Dicey, *Rome in 1860* (London, 1861), 10–11. On Catholic impressions see Viaene, *Belgium and the Holy See*, 248–277.

66. LD, 2: 91–92. On the political context for the Prince of Wales's visit see McIntire, *England against the Papacy*, 72–78. For a more personal account see George Plumptre, *Edward VII* (London, 1995), 39–41.

67. See, e.g., Dicey, *Rome in 1860*, 6–7.

68. Edmond About, *Rome contemporaine* (Paris, 1861), 92.

69. Ferdinand Gregorovius, *Der Ghetto und die Juden in Rom, mit einem Geleitwort von Leo Baeck* (Berlin, 1935), 65–67.

70. See Berliner, *Juden in Rom*, 167–172.

71. About, *Rome contemporaine*, 99–100.

72. See *Bolletino dei Conosciuti Avvenimenti dal Giorno*, April 15–16 and 17–18, 1859, Segretaria di Stato, ep. moderna, rubrica 155, fasc 4. (49–51, 52–54), ASV; Gendarmeria Pontificia, Commando della Compagnio, Avvenimenti dal Giorno, April 15–16, 1859, Miscellanea Rapporti Politica, Anno 1859, Busta 64 (15), Archivio di Stato di Roma.

73. LD, 2: 93, 95–96. See also *Bolletino dei Conosciuti Avvenimenti dal Giorno*, April 22–23, 1859, Segretaria di Stato, ep. moderna, rubrica 155, fasc. 4 (68–70), ASV.

74. LD, 2: 14.

75. "Varieta," *Il Vero Amico del Popolo*, April 16, 1859. For a fuller account of this incident see "Board of Deputies, the Galatz Outrages," *JC*, Aug. 19, 1859, 5.

76. LD, 2: 93. The punctuation makes it slightly unclear whether this was Montefiore's view or Loewe's.

77. *Bolletino dei Conosciuti Avvenimenti dal Giorno*, April 21–22, 1859, Segretaria di Stato, ep. moderna, rubrica 155, fasc 4. (65–67), ASV. See also Communità Israelitica di Roma to Communità Israelitica di Ferrara, April 29, 1859, Battesimi Forcati, Caso Mortara 1858 1UM, Communità Israelitica di Roma.

78. Quoted in Kertzer, *Kidnapping*, 136.

79. Report of MM to BD, BDMB, ACC/3121/B1/1, fols. 440–450.

80. See Frank Coppa, *Cardinal Giacomo Antonelli and Papal Politics in European Affairs* (New York, 1990).

81. "The Present Stage of the Mortara Affair," *JC*, June 10, 1859, 4.

82. For his account of the interview see LD, 2: 97–98; and Report of MM to BD.

83. R. de Cesare, *The Last Days of Papal Rome, 1850–1870* (London, 1909), 125.

84. Quoted in Coppa, *Antonelli and Papal Politics*, 3.

85. Report of MM to BD.

86. Ibid.; Lucien Wolf, *Sir Moses Montefiore: A Centennial Biography, with Extracts from Letters and Journals* (London, 1884), 112.

87. LDMS, 2: 98–99.

88. LD, 2: 98–99.

89. LDMS, 2: 99.

90. Report of MM to BD.

91. "Return of Sir Moses Montefiore," *JC*, May 27, 1859, 4; "Testimonial to Sir Moses Montefiore," *JC*, July 22, 1859, 2; "Commemoration of Sir Moses Montefiore's Philanthropic Exertions," *JC*, Aug. 5, 1859, 4; "Our Communal Weekly Gossip," *JC*, Aug. 12, 1859, 2; "Testimonial to Sir Moses Montefiore, Combined with the Jews' Hospital," *JC*, Aug. 19, 6; "Our Communal Weekly Gossip," *JC*, Aug. 26, 1859, 2; "Our Communal Weekly Gossip," *JC*, Sept. 23, 1859, 2.

92. See, e.g., "Our Communal Weekly Gossip," Aug. 26; also "Judith, Lady Montefiore, Memorial," *JC*, June 26. 1863, 4.

93. MM to BD, July 5, 1859, BDMB, ACC/3121/A/9, fol. 33. He had resigned in 1857 on grounds of Judith's poor health just before they set out for Jerusalem; "Resignation of the President of the Board of Deputies," *JC*, Feb. 6, 1857, 893. For details of his reelection see "Board of Deputies: Election of President," *JC*, Sept. 4, 1857, 1133.

94. Evangelical Alliance Committee of Council Minutes, May 13, 1859, MB, Evangelical Alliance, vol. 2, fol. 271; "The Mortara Protest," *JC*, Nov. 11, 1859, 7. For the text of the Protestant protest see LD, 2: 103.

95. Address of the Jews to the Pope, July 14, 1859, ACC/3121/B1/1, fol. 452, Board of Deputies Archives.

96. On Momolo's efforts see Kertzer, *Kidnapping*, chap. 23.

97. "The Mortara Protest."

98. "The Deputation to Lord John Russell," *JC*, Nov. 18, 1859, 2. See also "The Approaching Congress," *JC*, Dec. 9, 1859; "Meeting of the Board of Deputies: The Mortara Memorial," *JC*, Dec. 30, 1859, 5; "The Mortara Memorial," *JC*, Dec. 30, 1859, 4.

99. Dec. 26, 1859, BDMB, ACC/3121/A/009, fols. 71–76.

100. For an elaboration of this argument see Abigail Green, "Intervening in the Jewish question, 1840–1878," in *A History of Humanitarian Intervention*, ed. Brendan Simms and David Trimm (Cambridge, in press). Carole Fink, *Defending the Rights of Others: The Great Powers, the Jews, and International Minority Protection, 1878–1938* (Cambridge, 2004), pioneered study of this issue for a later period.

13. Grief and Sore Troubles

1. MM to LL, Feb. 1, 1860, folder 3, HL.

2. LDMS, 1: 16.

3. JM to MM, June 10, 1850, ASM.

4. Charlotte de Rothschild's Diary, 1846, fols. 102, 111–112; 1847, fol. 1, 000/1066/1, RAL. On Charlotte's religiosity see Niall Ferguson, *The World's Banker: The History of the House of Rothschild* (London, 1998), 522.

5. Rev. D. A. Jessurun Cardozo and Paul Goodman, *Think and Thank: The*

Montefiore Synagogue and College, Ramsgate (Oxford, 1933), 31; Lucien Wolf, *Sir Moses Montefiore: A Centennial Biography, with Extracts from Letters and Journals* (London, 1884), 115.

6. For involvement in Jewish charities see, e.g., "Jews' Infant School," *JC*, Feb. 20, 1846, 92; for involvement in non-Jewish charities see, e.g., British Syrian Relief Fund, Sept 1860[?], ASM. Judith was vice-president of the Ladies' Committee, alongside Lady Stratford de Redcliffe, the countess of Shaftesbury, and Florence Nightingale. More generally see F. K. Prochaska, *Women and Philanthropy in Nineteenth-Century England* (Oxford, 1980).

7. Kehillat Kodesh Ashkenazim, Kollel Perushim, to JM, June 24, 1849, MMSS vol. 577.

8. Judith Montefiore, *The Jewish Manual; or Practical Information in Jewish and Modern Cookery, with a Collection of Valuable Recipes and Hints Relating to the Toilette. Edited by a Lady* (London, 1846); see especially the Editor's Preface, i–vii. For a literary analysis see Sandra Sherman, "The Politics of Taste in the Jewish Manual," *Petit Propos Culinaires* 71 (Nov. 2002): 72–95.

9. Cardozo and Goodman, *Think and Thank*, 41.

10. See, e.g., JM to Charlotte de Rothschild, Jan. 11, 1843, 000/31/3, RAL.

11. LD, 2: 72.

12. Aug. 14, 1857, Queen Victoria's Journal, Royal Archives, Windsor.

13. LDMS, 2: 80–81.

14. MM to LL, Sept. 7, 1859, folder 3, HL.

15. LD, 2: 105.

16. MM to Sir Charles Beaumont Phipps, Nov. 7, 1858, VIC/Add J/1643, Royal Archives, Windsor.

17. MM to LL, Sept. 7, 1859.

18. See Amira Bennison, *Jihad and Its Interpretations in Pre-Colonial Morocco: State-Society Relations during the French Conquest of Algeria* (London, 2002), especially 15–41.

19. "Gibraltar . . . ," *JC*, Nov. 11, 1859, 5.

20. "Relief for the Jewish Refugees from Morocco," *JC*, Jan. 27, 1860, 2.

21. "Jews of Morocco Relief Fund—The Dublin Subscription List," *JC*, Dec. 9, 1859, 5. See also "The Refugees from Morocco," *JC*, Nov. 25, 1859, 4. Tudor Parfitt, "Dhimma versus Protection in Nineteenth Century Morocco," in *Israel and Ishmael: Studies in Muslim-Jewish Relations*, ed. Parfitt (Richmond, Surrey, 2000), 143, gives the final figure as over £40,000.

22. "Jamaica—Morocco Relief Fund," *JC*, March 9, 1860, 7.

23. For further details of the Anglosphere response see "Morocco Relief Fund: Meeting of the Committee," *JC*, Dec. 30, 1859, 7; "The Refugees from Morocco," *JC*, Feb. 10, 1860, 7; "Cape Town—Collection," *JC*, April 6, 1860, 7.

24. "Chronique du mois," *AI*, May 1860, 277.

25. "Chronique du mois," *AI*, Jan. 1860, 41.

26. See Leila Tarazi Fawaz, *An Occasion for War: Civil Conflict in Lebanon and Damascus in 1860* (London, 1994); Ussama Makdisi, *The Culture of Sectarianism: Community, History, and Violence in Nineteenth-Century Ottoman Lebanon*

(Berkeley, 2000); Caesar Farah, *The Politics of Interventionism in Ottoman Lebanon, 1830–1861* (London, 2000).

27. LDMS, 2: 112–113.

28. "Paris—the Massacre in Syria," *JC*, July 27, 1860, 8.

29. Ibid.

30. For details of the St. Petersburg and Moscow collections see "Russia—the Syrian Relief Fund," *JC*, Sept. 28, 1860, 3; and "Rusland," *HM*, Aug. 22, 1860, 131. For details of the *Aurora* article see "Ḥadashot shonot," *HM*, July 25, 1860, 114. On Italy see "Florenz, 14. August," *AZ*, Sept. 4, 1860, 535; "Rome—the Syrian Relief Fund," *JC*, Sept. 28, 1860, 5; "Italyen," *HM*, Oct. 16, 1860, 159. More generally, see Salo Baron, "The Jews and the Syrian Massacres of 1860," *Proceedings of the American Academy for Jewish Research* 4 (1933): 11–14.

31. See "Gibraltar—Syrian Relief Fund," *JC*, Sept. 14, 1860, 5.

32. "The Disturbances in Syria," *JC*, July 27, 1860, 4.

33. "Daytchland," *HM*, Sept. 20, 1860, 147. The Galatz blood libel and subsequent riots made Romania another newsworthy community.

34. "Florenz, 14. Aug."

35. "Die Sammlungen für die Maroniten," *AZ*, Aug. 14, 1860, 484. On the French response see also "Mélanges: Alliance Israélite Universelle," *AI*, Sept. 1860, 510.

36. "La souscription pour les victimes de la Syrie," *AI*, Aug. 1860, 434.

37. British Syrian Relief Fund, *Resolutions of Meeting of General Committee April 19th, 1861, with Recent Correspondence (Submitted to the Meeting) Relating to the Cultivation of Cotton in Syria and the Future Appropriation of the Fund*, pamphlet, April 23, 1861, ASM. The Executive Committee consisted of Lord Stratford de Redcliffe; Montefiore; the marquess of Lansdowne; the marquess of Clanricarde; the bishop of London; the earl of Malmesbury; the earl of Shaftesbury; Viscount Everley; Lord Calthorpe; Lord Ebury; Lord Stanley, M.P.; Sir Morton Peto, M.P.; Eardley; the lord mayor of London; Lionel de Rothschild; Admiral Sir Charles Napier; the Hon A. Kinnaird, M.P.; David Salomons; John Labourchere; P. Ralli; R. Monckton Milnes, M.P.; G. W. J. Repton, M.P.; H. Danby Seymour, M.P.; T. Baring, M.P.; Sir Jason Duke, M.P.; Sir Joseph Paxton; Sir J. V. Shelley, M.P.; S. Gurney; Darby Griffith, M.P.; W. Tite, M.P.; Adam Black, M.P.; General Peel, M.P.; G. Hadfield, M.P.; J. C. Ewart, M.P.; T. Bazley, M.P.; Edward Baines, M.P.; Sir J. Fergusson, M.P.; H. W. Freeland, M.P.; the Hon. William Ashley; Sir William James; J. P. Kennard; John Dillon; George Gawler; H. Austen Layard; W. Holt Yates; Colonel Walker, R.A.; Hodgkin; Fred Huth; R. N. Fowler; H. E. Gurney; Adate Crawfurd; Coleridge J. Kennard; James Cook; and Hugh E. Eardley Childers, M.P.

38. British Syrian Relief Fund, Sept 1860[?].

39. "British Syrian Relief Fund," *JC*, Sept. 14, 1860, 6.

40. "Sir Culling Eardley at Plymouth," *JC*, July 5, 1861, 5.

41. Quoted in Baron, "The Jews and the Syrian Massacres," 11.

42. July 16, 1860, BDMB, ACC/3121/A/009, fols. 86–91.

43. MM to LL, Aug. 5, 1860, folder 3, HL.

44. For a detailed account of this episode see Salo Baron, "Great Britain and Damascus Jewry in 1860–1861: An Archival Study," *JSS* 2 (1940): 179–208. Farah,

Interventionism in Ottoman Lebanon, 592, implies some justification for these rumors, but without elaborating.

45. MM to LL, [Oct. 1860?], folder 3, HL.

46. LDMS, 2: 115, 121–122.

47. Ibid., 128–129.

48. LD, 2: 131.

49. MM to JMM, July 2, 1862, folder 3, HL. See also the comments in "The Presidency of the Board of Deputies," *JC,* July 11, 1862, 5; and "Sir Moses Montefiore," *JC,* July 18, 1862, 4.

50. Inhabitants of St. Peter's and Broadstairs, to MM: Congratulations on 50th Wedding Anniversary, ASM. See also "The Jubilee at Ramsgate," *JC,* July 11, 1862, 5.

51. LD, 2: 135. For an alternative account of this event see "Ramsgate—the Golden Wedding," *JC,* July 11, 1862, 5.

52. LD, 2: 136–137.

53. Ibid., 138.

54. "Death of Lady Montefiore," *JC,* Oct. 3, 1862, 5. See also LD, 2: 139–140.

55. Wolf, *Montefiore,* 191.

56. See also LD, 2: 139–140.

57. "Pesth—Two Days with Sir Moses Montefiore," *JC,* June 19, 1863, 5.

58. MM personal Bible, private collection of Rabbi Dr. Abraham Levy.

59. Wolf, *Montefiore,* 212.

60. June 10, 1879, MMJ 1879, Mocatta 38, M4720, ML.

61. Ruth Sebag-Montefiore, *A Family Patchwork: Five Generations of an Anglo-Jewish Family* (London, 1987), 22.

62. The birth certificate of Joseph William Walden, May 11, 1863, describes his mother as "Louisa Thoroughgood Walden formerly Sherrin." The death certificate of Louisa Walden, Oct. 27, 1910, gives her age as sixty-five; George Collard Collection, Chester.

63. "1871 Census," www.1901censusonline.com., accessed Dec. 29, 2008.

64. Here and below I draw on my conversation with George Collard, as well as the following documents in his collection: Lizzie Arkell (née Walden), Poplar E14, to George Walden, c. 1920; Unidentified Child of Joseph Walden, Leeds[?], to George Walden; Notes about the Collard Family by George Collard; Notes Regarding the Recollections of Blanche Walden (Wife of George Walden, Son of Joseph Walden) by George Collard, March 20 1983. See also George Collard, *Moses the Victorian Jew* (Oxford, 1990), 138–139, although the reference to Louisa's "early death" indicates that this account has been somewhat romanticized and should be treated with caution.

65. "[T]he Soliciter [*sic*] said he was going to Leeds to see the brothers and thats the last I heard of it"; Arkell to George Walden, c. 1920.

66. Edmund Sebag-Montefiore to George Walden, Nov. 20, 1923, George Collard Collection.

67. "1861 Census," www.1901censusonline.com., accessed Dec. 29, 2008.

68. Both he and Judith would have been over fifty when Moberly Bell was born. We have no evidence either way regarding earlier infidelities.

69. This seems more probable than the claim that the teenage Louisa was Montefiore's housekeeper; Collard, *Moses,* 138.

70. JS to MM, Oct. 3, 1862, ASM. According to Robert Sebag-Montefiore, Joseph's mother was Montefiore's favorite sister. Sebag-Montefiore, *Family Patchwork,* 20, states that Montefiore thought Joseph's offspring more likely to remain Jewish than other branches of the family.

71. Eardley to MM, Sept. 20, 1862, fol. 153 of Condolence Correspondence to Montefiore, Mocatta 7, ML. Montefiore LB 1862, ML, which contains a wealth of similar letters.

72. MM to TH, Oct. 24, 1862, PP/HO/E/A447, box 35, file 2, HAWL.

73. MM to JS, April 21, 1863, ASM.

74. MM to Tooson Pacha [*sic*], Feb. 1, 1863, PP/HO/D/A2424, box 15, item 15, HAWL.

75. See MM to JS, April 21, 1863.

76. LDMS, 2: 142–144. See also "Sir Moses Montefiore," *JC,* June 19, 1863, 5.

77. "Nesiyat hasar mosheh montefiore hashem yishmerehu viḥiyehu le'erets hakedem," *HM,* Aug. 5, 1863, 241.

78. "Sir Moses Montefiore," *JC,* July 17, 1863, 4.

14. Mission to Marrakesh

1. On the Alliance Israélite see André Chouraqui, *Cent ans d'histoire: L'Alliance Israélite Universelle et la Renaissance Juive contemporaine (1860–1960)* (Paris, 1965). On its origins see Michael Graetz, *The Jews in Nineteenth-Century France: From the French Revolution to the Alliance Israélite Universelle,* trans. Jane Marie Todd (Stanford, Calif., 1996); and Lisa Moses Leff, *Sacred Bonds of Solidarity: The Rise of Jewish Internationalism in Nineteenth-Century France* (Stanford, Calif., 2006). On popular responses see Jonathan Frankel, "Jewish Politics and the Press: The 'Reception' of the *Alliance Israélite Universelle,*" *Jewish History* 14 (2000): 29–50.

2. "Morocco Relief Fund," *JC,* July 13, 1860, 7.

3. "Morocco Relief Fund—Meeting of the Committee," *JC,* Feb. 17, 1860, 5; "Morocco Relief Fund," *JC,* June 29, 1860, 5; "Jews of Morocco Relief Fund: London Committee of Deputies of the British Jews," *JC,* Aug. 17, 1860, 1; "Morocco Relief Fund," *JC,* Feb. 8, 1861, 5.

4. "Mélanges: La souscription Marocaine en France," *AI,* April 1860, 199; "Correspondance," *AI,* May 1860, 293.

5. On this episode see Mohammed Kenbib, *Juifs et Musulmans au Maroc, 1859–1948: Contribution à l'histoire des relations inter-communautaires en terre d'Islam* (Casablanca, 1994), 74–99. More generally, see Sarah Leibovici, *Chronique des Juifs de Tétouan (1860–1896)* (Paris, 1984).

6. "Morocco Relief Fund—Meeting of the Committee," *JC,* June 7, 1861, 5.

7. Chouraqui, *Cent ans,* 152–154.

8. On this see Aron Rodrigue, *French Jews, Turkish Jews: The Alliance Israélite Universelle and the Politics of Jewish Schooling in Turkey, 1860–1925* (Bloomington, Ind., 1990); also Rodrigue, *Images of Sephardi and Eastern Jewries in Transi-*

tion: The Teachers of the Alliance Israélite Universelle, 1860–1939 (Seattle, 1993). For the Moroccan angle see Michael M. Laskier, *The Alliance Israélite Universelle and the Jewish Communities of Morocco: 1862–1962* (Albany, N.Y., 1983), especially 61–62 on the Tétouan school.

9. On European economic penetration of Morocco see Jean-Louis Miège, *L'ouverture*, vol. 2 of *Le Maroc et l'Europe (1830–1894)* (Paris, 1961). For a general outline of the Moroccan state in this period see Edmund Burke III, *Prelude to Protectorate in Morocco: Precolonial Protest and Resistance, 1860–1912* (Chicago, 1976), chap. 1. On British policy see Francis Flournoy, *British Policy towards Morocco in the Age of Palmerston (1830–1865)* (Baltimore, 1935); and Khalid Ben-Srhir, *Britain and Morocco during the Embassy of John Drummond Hay, 1845–1886*, trans. Malcolm Williams and Gavin Waterson (London, 2005).

10. See L. A. E. Brooks, *A Memoir of Sir John Drummond Hay, Sometime Minister at the Court of Morocco, Based on His Journals and Correspondence* (London, 1896).

11. For a comprehensive account of the Safi Affair and its ramifications see Kenbib, *Juifs et Musulmans au Maroc*, 123–173. Also of interest, David Littman, "Mission to Morocco (1863–1864)," in *CMM*, 171–230.

12. Moses Pariente to MM, Sept. 17, 1863, enclosed with MM to Layard, Oct. 4, 1863, F.O. 99/119, NA.

13. Sultan Sidi Mohammed Ben Abderrahman to Mohammed Bargash, Rabi 17, 1280, Safi, DG, 4.715, Fonds de la Direction des Archives Royales, Rabat, Morocco. Thanks to Mohammed and Assia Kenbib for their help identifying and translating Moroccan documents.

14. On Jewish life in Morocco see above all Shlomo Deshen, *The Mellah Society: Jewish Community Life in Sherifian Morocco* (Chicago, 1989). For a Moroccan nationalist perspective see Kenbib, *Juifs et Musulmans au Maroc*. For a Zionist perspective see H. Z. Hirschberg, *From the Ottoman Conquests to the Present Time*, vol. 2 of *A History of the Jews in North Africa*, ed. Eliezer Bashan and Robert Attal (Leiden, 1981), chap. 11, esp. 301–326. For a more nuanced view see Daniel Schroeter, *The Sultan's Jew: Morocco and the Sephardi World* (Stanford, Calif., 2002), 4–10; and Bettina Marx, *Juden Marokkos und Europas. Das marokkanische Judentum im 19. Jahrhundert und seine Darstellung in der zeitgenössischen jüdischen Presse in Deutschland, Frankreich und Großbritannien* (Frankfurt am Main, 1991), 79–85.

15. For a sample of such views see the controversial Bat Ye'or, *The Dhimmi: Jews and Christians under Islam* (Rutherford, N.J., 1985), 291–323.

16. On the variations in Muslim-Jewish relations see Allan R. Meyers, "Patronage and Protection: The Status of Jews in Precolonial Morocco," in *Jews among Muslims: Communities in the Precolonial Middle East*, ed. Shlomo Deshen and Walter Zenner (Basingstoke, 1996), 83–97.

17. Hay to LJR, April 20, 1861, F.O. 99/105, no. 34; also F.O. to Hay, April 9, 1861 [draft], F.O. 99/104, no. 11, NA.

18. On the Jewish mercantile elite see Jean-Louis Miège and Michel Abitbol, in *Judaïsme d'Afrique du Nord au XIXe–XXe siècles,* ed. Abitbol (Jerusalem, 1980).

19. Thomas Hodgkin, M.D., *Narrative of a Journey to Morocco, with Geological Annotations* (London, 1866), 1.

20. MM to A. H. Layard, Oct. 4, 1863, F.O. 99/119, NA; also LD, 2: 145.

21. Hammond to MM, Oct. 5, 1863, F.O. 99/119; Thomas F. Reade to Bargash, Oct. 6, 1863, enclosed with Reade to LJR, Oct. 10, 1863, F.O. 99/117, no. 12, NA.

22. MM to Hammond, Oct. 28, 1863, annotated by LJR, F.O. 99/119, NA.

23. Hay to LJR, Nov. 12, 1863, F.O. 99/117, no. 7, NA.

24. MM to LL, Nov. [1?], 1863, folder 3, HL.

25. "Meeting of the Board of Deputies," *JC*, Nov. 6, 1863, 5.

26. MM to LL, Nov. 10, 1863, folder 3, HL.

27. LJR to Hay, Separate, F.O. 99/116, NA. This instruction must have been in response to a specific request from Montefiore.

28. "Cruelties by Spanish Officials," *JC*, Oct. 16, 1863, 4; see also "Le Maroc," *Univers Israélite*, Nov. 18, 1863, 143.

29. Reade's Memo of an interview with the Basha in Connection with the Bastina-doing of Two Jews on Oct. 26, also the covering letter, Hay to LJR, Oct. 29, 1863, F.O. 99/117, no. 3, NA; Reade to Hay, Oct. 28, also the covering letter, Hay to LJR, Nov. 1, 1863, no. 5, ibid.; LJR to Sir John Crampton, Nov. 16, 1863, F.O. 72/1054, no. 72, NA. LJR to Crampton, Nov. 20, 1863, no. 73, ibid., related the incidents involving Jews in Morocco, but instructed Crampton not to originate any discussion on the matter.

30. Hodgkin, *Journey to Morocco,* 11.

31. MM to JS, fragment [n.d.], ASM.

32. LD, 2: 148–149.

33. Crampton to LJR, Nov. 30, 1863, F.O. 72/1063 Separate, NA, describes the interview with Miraflores. For details of Miraflores' letter to Merry see Hay to Hammond, Dec. 16, 1863, F.O. 99/117, NA.

34. Hodgkin, *Journey to Morocco,* 23.

35. Captain G. Beauclerk, *A Journey to Marocco, in 1826* (London, 1828), 11.

36. One such banner survives in the possession of Robert Sebag-Montefiore. More generally, see M. Mitchell Serels, *A History of the Jews of Tangier in the Nineteenth and Twentieth Centuries* (New York, 1991).

37. Hay to Hammond, May 4, 1864, F.O. 99/121, NA.

38. Hodgkin, *Journey to Morocco,* 27–28.

39. Beauclerk, *Journey,* 14.

40. Hay to LJR, Dec. 15, 1863, F.O. 99/117, no. 14, NA.

41. Hay to MM, Dec. 20, 1863, ASM.

42. See the classic Vicomte Ch. de Foucauld, *Reconnaissance au Maroc: Journal de route conforme à l'édition de 1888 et augmenté de fragments inédits rédigés par l'auteur pour son Cousin François de Bondy* (Paris, 1939); also Heinrich von Maltzan, *Drei Jahre im Nordwesten von Afrika. Reisen in Algerien und Marokko,* vol. 4 (Leipzig, 1863).

43. Hodgkin, *Journey to Morocco,* 32.

44. Hay to LJR, Dec. 19, 1863, F.O. 99/117, no. 16, NA.

45. Béclard to Drouyen de Lhuys, Feb. 7, 1864, Correspondance Politique/Maroc, vol. 23, no. 2, fols. 234–237, MAE.

46. Hay to Hammond, May 4, 1864.

47. TH to JS, Jan. 1, 1865, ASM.

48. Hodgkin, *Journey to Morocco*, 40–42.

49. On Mogador see Daniel Schroeter, *Merchants of Essaouira: Urban Society and Imperialism in Southwestern Morocco, 1844–1886* (Cambridge, 1988).

50. Beauclerk, *Journey,* 232; but see "Mission of Sir Moses Montefiore," *JC,* Feb. 5, 1864, 5.

51. On Abraham Corcos see Schroeter, *Merchants of Essaouira,* 33–41.

52. Kenbib, *Juifs et Musulmans au Maroc,* 148–149.

53. "Edict of the Emperor of Morocco," *JC,* March 4, 1864, 5; MM to JMM, Feb. 24, 1864, BDMB, ACC/3121/A/009, fol. 291. For a description of the journey see Hodgkin, *Journey to Morocco,* 45–65.

54. Emily Gottreich, *The Mellah of Marrakesh: Jewish and Muslim Space in Morocco's Red City* (Bloomington, Ind., 2007), 2, and more generally on Muslim-Jewish coexistence. On Montefiore's stay here see also Hodgkin, *Journey to Morocco,* 69–70.

55. Hay to Hammond, May 4, 1864.

56. Reade to Hay, Feb. 7, enclosed with Hay to LJR, Feb. 20, 1864, F.O. 99/121, no. 16, NA.

57. On protection in Morocco see Earl Fee Cruikshank, *Morocco at the Parting of the Ways: The Story of Native Protection to 1885* (Philadelphia, 1935); and Mohammed Kenbib, *Les protégés: Contribution à l'histoire contemporaine du Maroc* (Rabat, 1996).

58. Reade to Prime Minister Seed Taib Ben Yamany, trans. Jan. 28, enclosed with Hay to LJR, Feb. 20, 1864, F.O. 99/121, no. 16, NA.

59. For accounts of this interview see MM to JMM, Feb. 24, 1864; and Hodgkin, *Journey to Morocco,* 79–82. For the text of Montefiore's address to the sultan see LD, 2: 153. For a description of Sidi Mohammed see Hay to LJR, July 22, 1861, F.O. 99/106, no. 104, NA.

60. Translation provided by Assia and Mohammed Kenbib, from the Arabic in Ahmed Naciri, *Al Istiqsa Li Akhbar Duwwal Al Maghrib Al Aqsa* (Casablanca, 1956), 113–114.

61. MM to JMM, Feb. 24, 1864.

62. MM to LJR, Feb. 23, 1864, folder 3, HL.

63. "Pesth—Two Days with Sir Moses Montefiore," *JC* June 19, 1863, 5.

64. "The Mission to Morocco," *JC,* March 11, 1864, 7.

65. LD, 2: 158. Those that survive can be found in Montefiore Testimonials, ML. A selection was published in "The Hall of Glory (An Album in Honour of Sir Moses Montefiore, Edited by Joseph Kohn, Lemberg, 1868)," *JC,* Jan. 22, 1869.

66. "Praysen," *HM,* March 9, 1864, 74; "Kingston, Jamaica—Thanksgiving," *JC,* July 22, 1864, 7; "Melbourne—Special Prayer and Thanksgiving," *JC,* Sept. 2, 1864, 2; "Esteraykh," *HM,* March 9, 1864, 74.

67. Avner Katvan Rosh Beth Din of Croieva to MM, Av 15, V. 2717/35, JNUL.

68. "Ir hamede'an," *HM,* Jan. 18, 1865, 20; "Azyen hamede'an," *HM,* Jan. 25, 1865, 28. For a copy of one of these addresses see "Jewish Persecution," *JC,* May 5, 1865, 5.

69. "Varsha," *HM*, Sept. 6, 1865, 275.

70. "New York—the Montefiore College," *JC*, May 6, 1864, 5; "Trieste—an Address to Sir Moses Montefiore," *JC*, April 15, 1864, 6 (Trieste was one of the towns visited by Montefiore during 1863); "The Mission to Morocco," *JC*, May 6, 1864, 5; "Nouvelles diverses: Etranger," *AI*, June 5, 1864, 544; Pester Verein zur Beförderung der Handwerke und des Ackerbaues unter den Israeliten in Ungarn: Creation of a Foundation in Honour of MM and JM, Aug. 1863, Montefiore Testimonials, ML; "Rusland," *HM*, Dec. 14, 1864, 379.

71. "Russia—Correspondence with Sir Moses Montefiore," *JC*, July 8, 1864, 5; "Esteraykh," *HM*, April 20, 1864, 122.

72. On this see "Address of Thanks to Sir Moses Montefiore from the Continent," *JC*, March 25, 1864, 5; "Kol kore," *HM*, March 16, 1864, 81–82; "Afrika: Hayehudim bemaroko," *HM*, March 30, 1864, 100; "Hegyonei hamagid," *HM*, April 20, 1864, 121; "Eleh hemah shemot he'arim asher ba'u al haḥatum al mikhtav hatodah lehasar mosheh montefiore," *HM*, June 8, 1864, 169. For Montefiore's letter of thanks see "Mikhtav me'et hasar mosheh montifiore," *HM*, June 22, 1864, 185.

73. The chief rabbi of Pressburg forwarded a circular to other Hungarian rabbis, suggesting a Hebrew-language address with as many signatures as possible; "Pressburg, Hungary—a Circular," *JC*, May 13, 1864, 6. This initiative should be seen within the wider context of bitter communal infighting; see Jacob Katz, *A House Divided: Orthodoxy and Schism in Nineteenth-Century Central European Jewry* (Hanover, N.H., 1998). Count Bentinck, the Dutch ambassador, presented Montefiore with an address from the Central Committee for the Affairs of the Jews in the Netherlands; "Sir Moses Montefiore," *JC*, July 1, 1864, 5.

74. "Sir Moses Montefiore—Proposed Demonstrations," *JC*, March 25, 1864, 4.

75. "Chronique Israélite de la quinzaine," *AI*, April 15, 1864, 319.

76. "The Jews in Morocco," *JC*, March 11, 1864, 7.

77. "Mr. Alderman Phillips' Motion in the Court of Common Council," *JC*, April 15, 1864, 3.

78. "The Mission of Sir Moses Montefiore to Morocco," *JC*, April 22, 1864, 5.

79. MM to JS, fragment [n.d.].

80. MM to LL, April 25, 1865, folder 3, HL.

81. Naciri, *Al Istiqsa Li Akhbar Duwwal*, 112–115.

82. Sultan Sidi Mohamed Ben Abderrahmane, Ramadan 2, 1280, to the Governor of Tétouan, Outaïq 4, fol. 294, Direction des Archives Royales, Rabat.

83. Bargash to Hay, enclosed with Hay to LJR, Aug. 7, 1864, F.O. 99/121, no. 55, NA.

84. "Morocco—Acts of Violence," *JC*, June 17, 1864, 6.

85. Hay to LJR, May 2, 1864, F.O. 99/121, no. 26, NA.

86. Hay to the British Vice Consuls & Austrian & Danish Con. Officers at the Western Ports of Morocco, April 20, 1864, enclosed with ibid.

87. Henri de Tallenay to Drouyen de Lhuys, May 14, 1864, Correspondance Politique/Maroc, vol. 23 no. 28, fols. 318–320, MAE.

88. On the contradiction at the heart of British policy toward Moroccan Jews see

Tudor Parfitt, "Dhimma versus Protection in Nineteenth Century Morocco," in *Israel and Ishmael: Studies in Muslim-Jewish Relations*, ed. Parfitt (Richmond, Surrey, 2000), 142–166.

89. LD, 2: 159–160.

90. Bargash to Hay, Aug. 7, 1864.

91. Hay to LJR, Aug. 7, 1864, F.O. 99/121, no. 55, NA.

92. MM to LJR, Sept. 7, 1864, F.O. 99/123, NA.

93. MM to the Jewish Authorities of Morocco, Sept. 7, 1864, ibid.

15. Building Jerusalem

1. "Pesth—Two Days with Sir Moses Montefiore," *JC*, June 19, 1863, 5.

2. Ibid.

3. On Kalischer see Jody Myers, *Seeking Zion: Modernity and Messianic Activism in the Writings of Tsevi Hirsch Kalischer* (Oxford, 2003).

4. See Moshe Samet, "Kishrei montefiore im rav tsevi hirsch kalischer," *Cathedra* 33 (Oct. 1984): 54–56.

5. Appeal from H. N. Abulafiah and R. Y. Abulafiah, *HM*, March 23, 1859, app., fol. 1.

6. "Lema'an tsiyon lo neḥshah," ibid., 45.

7. See "Levinyan batei maḥseh le'aniyim vehakhnasat orḥim al har tsiyon," *HM*, April 13, 1859, 58; "Al devar binyan batei maḥseh le'aniyim vehakhnasat orḥim al har tsiyon birushalayim," *HM*, June 7, 1859, 85. For more detail on the various aspects outlined see "Poh ir habirah london arba-esreh sivan 1859," "Hetakot mite'udot umelitsiyot ḥakhmei ha'amim hagedolim al odot binyan batim le'aniyei benei yisra'el al har tsiyon birushalayim," *HM*, June 29, 1859, app., fols. 1, 2; "Al devar binyan batei maḥseh le'aniyim vehakhnasat orḥim al har tsiyon birushalayim"; "Tirkiyah," *HM*, Nov. 7, 1860, 172; "Oystraliyen," *HM*, April 29, 1862, 132; and "Oystraliyen," *HM*, Dec. 4, 1862, 371.

8. "Yerushalayim," *HM*, Dec. 21, 1858, 192.

9. For a general overview of the "precursors of Zionism" debate see Gideon Shimoni, *The Zionist Ideology* (Hanover, N.H., 1995), chap. 2, esp. 55–60 on Hess and 78–80 on Natonek. See also Jacob Katz, "The Forerunners of Zionism," in *Essential Papers on Zionism*, ed. Jehuda Reinharz and Anita Shapira (London, 1996), 33–45; and Yosef Salmon, "The Historical Imagination of Jacob Katz: On the Origins of Jewish Nationalism," *JSS* 5 (Spring/Summer 1999): 161–179.

10. "Jewish Colonisation Society," *JC*, May 15, 1863, 6.

11. Quoted in Myers, *Seeking Zion*, 174.

12. Ibid., 186–187.

13. On Gordon's protonationalism see Yosef Salmon, "David Gordon and *HaMaggid*: Changing Attitudes towards Jewish Nationalism, 1860–1882," *Modern Judaism* 17 (May 1997): 109–124; and Salmon, "The Rise of Jewish Nationalism on the Border of Eastern and Western Europe: Rabbi Z. H. Kalischer, David Gordon, Peretz Smolenskin," in *Danzig, Between East and West: Aspects of Modern Jewish History*, ed. Isidore Twersky (Cambridge, Mass., 1985), 121–138.

14. "Beshuvah vanaḥat tivashe'un," *HM,* May 6, 1863, 137.

15. LD, 2: 107.

16. MM to Kursheedt, April 25, 1856, in D. De Sola Pool, "Some Relations of Gershom Kursheedt and Sir Moses Montefiore," *Publications of the American Jewish Historical Society* 37 (1947): 217–218. Note especially the messianic language used describing pilgrim festivals, the Jerusalem-Jaffa railway, and the impact of Judah Touro's legacy. MM to Sir Macdonald Stephenson, Oct. 1865, folder 4, HL.

17. LD, 2: 169. Loewe forwarded details to *Hamagid.* "England," *HM,* Aug. 16, 1865, 250.

18. Hyde Clarke to MM, Aug. 5, 1865, folder 4, HL.

19. MM to Clarke, Aug. 31, 1865, MLB 1865–70, fols. 57–59, Mocatta 9, ML.

20. MM to JS, Oct. 27, [1865?], ASM.

21. May 15, 1865, BDMB, ACC/3121/A/010, fols. 79–84.

22. "England," *HM,* Aug. 30, 1865, 267.

23. "Aziyen: Hodu hamizraḥit," *HM,* Aug. 16, 1865, 251.

24. For details of the board's appeal on behalf of the cholera victims see Aug. 28, 1865, BDMB, ACC/3121/A/010, fols. 85–87. For details of the Prussian committee see "Praysen," *HM,* Aug. 30, 1865, 266. On money sent through France see "Frankraykh," *HLV,* Sept. 8, 1865, 276.

25. Most donors in Bath were Christians; see "Bath—Holy Land Relief Fund," *JC,* Nov. 3, 1865, 5. But on North America see "The Collection for Palestine," *OAJA,* Jan. 1866, 468.

26. Reports of the money transmitted via Paris appeared regularly in *HLV;* see, e.g., "The Palestine Jews," *JC,* Jan. 19, 1866, 6; "Frankraykh," *HLV,* Nov. 17, 1865, 341. Similar reports also appeared in the *AI;* see, e.g., "Charité," *AI,* Feb. 1 and April 1, 1866, 132, 315. For details of eastern European activities see "Rusland," *HM,* Oct. 4, 1865, 308; "Nedavot le'aḥeinu benei yisra'el be'artsenu hakedoshah," *HM,* Oct. 18, 1865, 316.

27. "Cholera at Jerusalem," *JC,* Dec. 8, 1865, 5.

28. "Cholera at Jerusalem," *JC,* Nov. 17, 1865, 5.

29. "Cholera at Jerusalem," Dec. 8, 1865.

30. "Cholera at Jerusalem," Nov. 17, 1865.

31. Ludwig Frankl, *Nach Jerusalem,* 2 vols. (Leipzig, 1858).

32. "The Jews in the East," *JC,* June 17, 1859.

33. See for instance "Migdal halevanon tsofeh penei yerushalayim," *HLV,* Nov. 3, 1865, 321; "Frankraykh: et ledaber!" *HLV,* Dec. 1, 1865, 359; "Migdal halevanon tsofeh penei yerushalayim," *HLV,* Jan. 5, 1866, 4.

34. MM to Macleod, Dec. 24, 1865, MLB 1865–70, fol. 159; "Slanderous Attack of One of Her Majesty's Chaplains on the Palestine Jews," *JC,* Dec. 29, 1865, 5.

35. "The Palestine Jews," *JC,* Jan. 12, 1866, 2; "The Palestine Jews," Jan 19, 1866.

36. "Slanderous Attack on the Jews of the Holy Land," *JC,* Jan. 5, 1866, 5.

37. "The Palestine Jews," Jan. 12, 1866.

38. "Sir Moses Montefiore's Announced Journey to the Holy Land," *JC,* Jan. 26, 1866, 4.

39. "The Palestine Jews," *JC*, Jan. 19, 1866.

40. *Hamagid* also reported very positively; *HM*, Jan. 12, 1859, 7–8.

41. Letter from Mr. Smith[?], Nov. 24, 1859, ASM. On the mill see Shmuel Avitsur, "Wind Power in the Technological Development of Palestine," in *Palestine in the Late Ottoman Period: Political, Social and Economic Transformations*, ed. David Kushner (Jerusalem, 1986), 235–237.

42. The agreement with J. J. and T. R. Holman was for £1,450, but it is unclear if this included the stone tower; LD, 2: 63.

43. MM to Revd. J. K. Gutheim, Nov. 30, 1858, 1858:1, SLC. On the almshouses see Ruth Kark, "Notes on Batei Tora" (Hebrew), *Cathedra* 27 (Jan. 1981): 158–167.

44. J. W. Smith, Report re: Erection of a Building upon the Estate of MM at Jerusalem, [1858], ASM.

45. Mustafa Sureyya, Mutasarrif of the Holy Jerusalem, Rajab[?] 15, 1275, Irade hariciye 9332, app. 1, MFA.

46. Finn to Bulwer, Feb. 12, 1859, HBC, 1: 261–262.

47. Finn to Bulwer, Aug. 15, 1859, ibid., 265–266. On the earliest buildings outside the city walls see Yehoshua Ben-Arieh, *Jerusalem in the 19th Century: Emergence of the New City* (Jerusalem, 1986), 62–73.

48. Irade Hariciye Regarding the Petition Granted Montefiore to Build a Hospital in the Holy Jerusalem, Rajab 6, 1276, Irade hariciye 9332, MFA.

49. Smith to MM, April 28, 1859, ASM. For a progress report see "Jerusalem—Varieties," *JC*, Jan. 13, 1860, 6.

50. "A Jewish Traveller," *JC*, Feb. 6, 1857, 890.

51. LD, 2: 111.

52. Ben-Arieh, *Jerusalem*, 77, and 75, which refers to twenty or maybe twenty-four houses originally built here. But in 1859 John Mills spoke of "sixteen dwelling rooms"; see "Jerusalem—Varieties." *Hamagid* then reported the completion of eighteen houses, "Tirkiya," *HM*, Nov. 1, 1860, 167, estimating the number of inhabitants at around ninety; "Ḥadashot shonot," *HM*, Dec. 25, 1860, 198.

53. "From the Diary of Herr Adolph Neubauer," *JC*, March 22, 1861, 2.

54. MM to JS, Oct. 27, [1865?]; "The Palestine Jews," Jan. 19, 1866, also "News Item—Palestine," *OAJA*, March 1866, 561–565.

55. "Sir Moses Montefiore," *JC*, March 2, 1866, 3.

56. "News Item—Palestine." On North American involvement see "The Bnei Berith and Palestine," *OAJA*, Nov. 1865, 381; "The Bnei Berith and Palestine," *OAJA*, Dec. 1865, 431; and "The Collection for Palestine."

57. "Our Interest in Palestine," *OAJA*, Oct. 1862, 318–322.

58. Frankl, *Nach Jerusalem*, 2: 6; "Masa be'erets nod," *HLV*, Feb. 17, 1865, 55.

59. Moses Montefiore, *Report of Sir Moses Montefiore Bart. on His Mission to the Holy Land* (London, 1866), 10. See also H. Philip to MM, July 7, 1865, folder 4, HL.

60. "Migdal halevanon tsofeh penei yerushalayim," *HLV*, April 12, 1866, 113.

61. Montefiore, *Report on Mission to Holy Land*, 13–14.

62. March 27, 1866, Diary of Adelaide Sebag, 26/02/1866–10/05/1866, Pri-

vate Collection of Mrs. Ruth Sebag-Montefiore (hereafter ASMJ). Also "Sir Moses Montefiore at Jerusalem," *JC*, April 27, 1866, 6.

63. See "Jerusalem—Varieties." Montefiore had the slaughterhouse moved during his visit in 1855, see James Finn, *Stirring Times, or Records from Jerusalem Consular Chronicles of 1853 to 1856 by the Late James Finn, Edited and Compiled by His Widow*, vol. 2 (London, 1878), 333.

64. March 28, 1866, ASMJ.

65. Finn, *Stirring Times*, 60.

66. See the proposals made in TH to MM, THLB, PP/HO/D/A2424, box 15, file 12, fols. 143–157, HAWL. In 1865 Montefiore attended a meeting of the Syrian Improvement Fund Committee, which voted £100 toward excavations to improve Jerusalem's water supply; LD, 2: 166.

67. MM to Moore, March 17, 1868, MLB 1865–70, fols. 269–270.

68. Montefiore, *Report on Mission to Holy Land*, 42–43.

69. Montefiore had paved the area in front of the Wall some years earlier, and spoke of the need to protect worshippers from rain and sun; Montefiore, *Report on Mission to Holy Land*, 19. Auerbach raised the issue of garbage; see "Migdal halevanon tsofeh penei yerushalayim," *HLV*, April 26, 1866, 129.

70. April 2, 1866, ASMJ. For detailed accounts of this meeting see Montefiore, *Report on Mission to Holy Land*, 46–53; and "Migdal halevanon tsofeh penei yerushalayim," April 26, 1866.

71. "Sir Moses Montefiore at Jerusalem."

72. Montefiore, *Report on Mission to Holy Land*, 54.

73. March 30, 1866, ASMJ.

74. Thomas Hodgkin, M.D., *Narrative of a Journey to Morocco, with Geological Annotations* (London, 1866), vi–vii.

75. April 4, 5, 7, 15, 1866, ASMJ.

76. Montefiore, *Report on Mission to Holy Land*, 44.

77. April 16, 1866, ASMJ.

78. LD, 2: 188.

79. Montefiore, *Report on Mission to Holy Land*, 5.

80. Ibid., 14, 17–18.

81. Ibid., 38–39.

82. April 11 and 16, 1866, ASMJ.

83. Montefiore, *Report on Mission to Holy Land*, 77.

84. "Migdal halevanon tsofeh penei yerushalayim," *HLV*, Nov. 2, 1866, 321.

85. "Sir Moses Montefiore's Report to the Board of Deputies," *JC*, Oct. 5, 1866, 4.

86. "Al devar mikhtav hasar mosheh montifiori hashem yishmerehu vihiyehu," *HM*, Nov. 21, 1866, 354.

87. "Palestine Relief," *OAJA*, June 1866, 134.

16. Crisis in Romania

1. LD, 2: 189–191.

2. For a general introduction to Romania see Keith Hitchins, *The Romanians,*

1774–1866 (Oxford, 1996); Hitchins, *Rumania, 1866–1947* (Oxford, 1994); and Vlad Georgescu, *The Romanians: A History,* ed. Matei Calinescu, trans. Alexandra Bley-Vroman (London, 1991).

3. On Romanian Jewry see Carol Iancu, *Les Juifs en Roumanie (1866–1919): De l'exclusion à l'emancipation* (Aix-en-Provence, 1978), available in somewhat abbreviated form as *Jews in Romania 1866–1919: From Exclusion to Emancipation,* trans. Carvel de Bussy (New York, 1996). On the impact of the Crimean War in the principalities see above all Eliyahu Feldman, "The Question of Jewish Emancipation in the Ottoman Empire and the Danubian Principalities after the Crimean War," *JSS* 41 (Winter 1979): 41–74. In this context see also Mariuca Stanciu, "The Press as a Path to Self-Emancipation: Stages in the Evolution of the Jewish Press in 19th Century Romania," *Studia Hebraica* 2 (2002): 86–96.

4. Quoted in Iancu, *Jews in Romania,* 33.

5. Quoted in Feldman, "Jewish Emancipation," 59. For more detail, see Dr. Bluntschli, *Roumania and the Legal Status of the Jews in Roumania: An Exposition of Public Law* (London, 1879).

6. Beate Welter, *Die Judenpolitik der rumänischen Regierung, 1866–1888* (Frankfurt am Main, 1989), 51. By contrast there had been only 4,763 Jews under foreign protection in 1859. For general demographic statistics see Iancu, *Jews in Romania,* 26.

7. "The Jews of Jassy," *JC,* Sept. 7, 1866, 5. See also "Moldavia," *JC,* March 20, 1857, 938.

8. See Iancu, *Juifs en Roumanie,* 47.

9. "Wallachian Barbarism," *JC,* Sept. 27, 1861, 4. For reports of Cuza's expulsion orders see "Moldevei-Valakhiya," *HM,* Aug. 15, 1861, 204; "Moldevei-Valakhiya," *HM,* Sept. 3, 1861, 220; "Bucharest—a Pharaonic Decree," *JC,* Sept. 20, 1861, 5; "Der jüngste Vorgang in den Donaufürstenthümern," *AZ,* Sept. 3, 1861, 512. The order was rescinded in 1862—see "Moldevei-Valakhiya," *HM,* Feb. 26, 1862, 67—and the post-1866 historiography has largely ignored these precedents.

10. See "Moldevei-Valakhiya," *HM,* July 5, 1860, 104; and "Magdeburg, 16 Juli. An unsre Glaubensgenossen in den Donaufürstenthümern," *AZ,* July 24, 1860, 439.

11. "Aus der Wallachei, im Dezember," *AZ,* Dec. 25, 1860, 771.

12. See Iancu, *Jews in Romania,* 35; also "Bucharest," *JC,* Sept. 19, 1862, 2; and *Hamagid* reports, e.g., "Moldevei-Valakhiya," *HM,* Jan. 30, 1861, 20; "Moldevei-Valakhiya," *HM,* March 20, 1861, 47; and "Moldevei-Valakhiya," *HM,* Oct. 8, 1862, 314.

13. See Iancu, *Jews in Romania,* 35; "Moldevei-Valakhiya," *HM,* April 20, 1864, 124; "Hegyonei hamagid," *HM,* June 1, 1864, 162.

14. "Bucharest."

15. Iancu, *Jews in Romania,* 34–35.

16. On Carol see *Aus dem Leben König Karls von Rumänien. Aufzeichnungen eines Augenzeugen,* 4 vols. (Stuttgart, 1894).

17. This interpretation draws on Welter, *Judenpolitik,* 37–39. See also Frederick Kellogg, *The Road to Romanian Independence* (West Lafayette, Ind., 1995), 21.

18. Quoted in Iancu, *Jews in Romania,* 38.

19. See "Jassy, 16. Mai," *AZ*, June 5, 1866, 366; "Jassy, 16. Juni (Privatmitth),"
AZ, June 26, 1866, 415; "Jassy, 20. Juni," *AZ*, July 17, 1866, 463.

20. Jews of Servia to MM, March 20, 1856, 6th Half-Yearly Report 1856, 33–37,
BDMB, ACC/3121/A/008, fols. 133–134; "Serbiyen," *HM*, Nov. 1, 1859, 167;
"Serbiyen," *HLV*, May 10, 1866, 147. The parallels were not lost on contemporaries. See Isidore Loeb, *La situation des Israélites en Turquie, en Serbie et en Roumanie* (Paris, 1877).

21. Crémieux to Havin, July 1866, in Loeb, *La situation des Israélites en Turquie*,
154.

22. Quoted in Iancu, *Jews in Romania*, 38. More generally see Constantin
Iordachi, "The Unyielding Boundaries of Citizenship: The Emancipation of 'Non-
Citizens' in Romania, 1866–1918," *European Review of History* 8 (Autumn 2001):
157–186.

23. Iancu, *Jews in Romania*, 40.

24. On this see Iordachi, "Unyielding Boundaries," 161–162.

25. "Bonn, 20. Juli (Privatmitth)," *AZ*, July 31, 1866, 491. See Loeb, *Situation
des Israélites*, 149, for details of Crémieux's exchange with the French foreign minister. For the board's intervention see JMM to Clarendon, July 5, 1866, 3rd Half-
Yearly Report 1866, 20–21, BDMB, ACC/3121/A/010, fol. 127.

26. Telegram to Rabbi Nathan Adler, forwarded to Stanley, May 23, 1867; also
Israelite community at Jassy to MM, FHG, and Lionel de Rothschild, communi-
cated to Stanley, May 23, 1867, in *Principalities No. 1 (1877): Correspondence Respecting the Condition and Treatment of the Jews in Servia and Roumania 1867–
1876*, Parliamentary Accounts and Papers (London, 1877), 14.

27. Stanley to Green, May 24, 1867, in *Correspondence Respecting the Persecution of Jews in Moldavia, Presented to Both Houses of Parliament by Command of
Her Majesty*, Parliamentary Accounts and Papers (London, 1867), 2.

28. Quoted in Iancu, *Jews in Romania*, 73. See also Green to Stanley, May 26,
1867 (telegram); Green to Stanley, May 27, 1867, in *Correspondence Respecting
the Persecution of Jews in Moldavia*, 2–3.

29. "Jassy, 20. Juni."

30. 1867 saw the foundation of no less than thirty-one branch committees in Romania; see Welter, *Judenpolitik*, 161–164.

31. *Leben König Karls*, 1: 201.

32. "Persecution in the Danubian Principalities," *JC*, June 7, 1867, 2.

33. "Die Regierung der Donaufürstenthümer und die Juden, Bonn 2. Juni," *AZ*,
June 4, 1867, 469.

34. "The Minister Bratiano and the Jews," *JC*, June 14, 1867, 3.

35. On the Alliance Israélite Universelle (AIU) and Serbian Jews see André
Chouraqui, *Cent ans d'histoire: L'Alliance Israélite Universelle et la renaissance
Juive contemporaine (1860–1960)* (Paris, 1965), 82–84. On Goldsmid see D. Wolf
Marks and A. Löwy, *Memoir of Sir Francis Henry Goldsmid* (London, 1882). More
generally, on Jewish M.P.s see Michael Clark, "Identity and Equality: The Anglo-
Jewish Community in the Post-Emancipation Era, 1858–1887" (Ph.D. diss., Univer-
sity of Oxford, 2005), chap. 1.

36. FHG to Hammond, June 10, 1867, in *Principalities No. 1 (1877)*, 21.

37. Lionel de Rothschild to Hammond, June 17, 1867; FHG to Hammond, June 19, 1867, ibid., 27–28.

38. June 4, 1867, BDMB, ACC/3121/A/010, fols. 150–152.

39. Jesias Bhor, Chief Rabbi of Jassy, June 6, 1867, to MM, ibid., fols. 156–158. See also Bhor to MM, Sivan 15, 5627, ibid., fol. 158.

40. MM to JMM, June 30, 1867, ibid., fol. 157.

41. Minutes, July 3, 1867, ibid., fols. 156–158.

42. "Persecution of Jews in Moldavia," *JC*, July 8, 1867, 7.

43. "The Jews in Roumania," *JC*, July 12, 1867, 3.

44. Green to Golescu, Aug. 2, 1867, in *Principalities No. 1 (1877)*, 47. On the Commons debate see "The Jews in Roumania." For details of the Ottoman response see HR-SYS 1048/3, MFA. For the British response see *Further Correspondence Respecting the Persecution of Jews in Moldavia, Presented to Both Houses of Parliament by Command of Her Majesty*, Parliamentary Accounts and Papers (London, 1867).

45. *Leben König Karls*, 1: 213–214.

46. See Carol Iancu, "Adolphe Crémieux, l'Alliance Israélite Universelle et les Juifs de Roumanie au début du règne de Carol Hohenzollern-Sigmaringen," *Revue des Etudes Juives* 133 (Jan.–June 1974): 493–494. On Picot see N. Georgescu-Titsu, "Emile Picot et ses travaux relatifs aux Roumains," *Mélanges de l'Ecole Roumaine en France* 1 (1925): 181–276; also Georgescu-Titsu, "Correspondance d'un secrétaire princier en Roumanie: Emile Picot (1866–1868)," *Mélanges de l'Ecole Roumaine en France* 1 (1926): 102–215.

47. Bucharest AIU Committee to President of the AIU, Paris, July 12/24, 1867, Roumanie/IC 1-3/Situation Générale Intérieure des Juifs, Microfilm Bobine 14, AIU, Paris. See also LD, 2: 205–206.

48. [?] Jassy to MM, June 18, 1867, copy, 521/c, Central Archive for the History of the Jewish People, Jerusalem.

49. Carpel Lippe, "Moldevei: Yasi," *HL*, Aug. 16, 1867, 250.

50. Le Cler, 1866, quoted in T. W. Riker, *The Making of Roumania: A Study of an International Problem, 1856–1866* (London, 1931), 2. See also James Samuelson, *Roumania Past and Present* (London, 1882), 38–39.

51. "2004. Elisabeta-Cristina Constantin: Ethnicity and Urban Development in Bucharest at the End of the Nineteenth Century: Progress Report," www.iser.essex.ac.uk/furs, accessed Jan. 1, 2009.

52. Picot to Mme. Cornu, Nov. 2/14, 1866, quoted in Welter, *Judenpolitik*, 21.

53. Green to Stanley, Aug. 24, 1867, in *Correspondence Respecting Persecution of Jews in Moldavia*, 56. For an account of Montefiore's journey to Bucharest see LD, 2: 197–98; and "Sir Moses Montefiore," *JC*, Aug. 30, 1867, 5.

54. Iancu, *Jews in Romania*, 44.

55. LDMS, 2: 199–200; Green to Stanley, Aug. 24, 1867, in *Correspondence Respecting Persecution of Jews in Moldavia*, 56.

56. See Samuelson, *Roumania*, 259; *Leben König Karls*, 1: viii–xix.

57. See, e.g., Karl Anton to Karl, March 22, 1868, in *Leben König Karls*, 1: 260.

58. *Naţiunea Română,* July 29, 1867, 89. Thanks to Marius Turda for gathering and translating Romanian material.

59. *Naţiunea Română,* Aug. 24, 1867, 113, translated in LD, 2: 200–201.

60. LD, 2: 203. See also Green to Stanley, Sept. 2, 1867, in *Principalities No. 1 (1877),* 58.

61. Boyard to Drouyn de Lhuys, Sept. 3, 1867, CPC/Turquie/Bucharest, vol. 30 no. 174, MAE.

62. LDMS, 2: 205; more generally, LD, 2: 204–207.

63. LDMS, 2: 205.

64. LD, 2: 207.

65. LD, 2: 211–212.

66. LDMS, 2: 207.

67. Montefiore to Green, Aug. 30, 1867, in *Report Presented by Sir Moses Montefiore, Bart., to the London Committee of Deputies of the British Jews on His Return from His Mission to Roumania, September 5627–1867* (London, 1867), 9–11. He clearly gave the same account to the French consul; see Boyard to Drouyn de Lhuys, Sept. 3, 1867.

68. I. Pretor, "From Paris," *Naţiunea Română,* Sept. 5, 1867, 1.

69. "Mr. Montefiore and the Newspaper Naţiunea," *Sentinella Română,* Sept. 7, 1867, 314.

70. "Mr. Cezar Bolliac and the Jews" (in Romanian), *Sentinella Română,* Sept. 10, 1867, 318.

71. See for instance Montefiore's letter in "England: London," *HLV,* Oct. 17, 1867, 316; and Loewe's reply to criticism in "Bonn, 16. October," *AZ,* Oct. 22, 1867, 860.

72. "Esteraykh," *HLV,* Oct. 7, 1867, 315.

73. "Moldevei-Valakhiya," *HM,* Sept. 11, 1867, 283; "The Return of Sir Moses Montefiore," *JC,* Oct. 4, 1867, 4.

74. "Roumania—Further Expulsions," *JC,* Oct. 25, 1867, 5.

75. "The Mission of Sir Moses Montefiore," *TO,* Nov. 1867, 403.

76. See, e.g., Green to Stanley, Dec. 14, 1867, Jan. 3, 1868, and Feb. 4, 1868, in *Principalities No. 1 (1877),* 69, 70, 77.

77. Iancu, *Juifs en Roumanie,* 49.

78. "Frankraykh," *HLV,* Jan. 29, 1868, 74.

79. Golescu to MM, Feb. 7/19, 1868, in *Principalities No. 1 (1877),* 83. Montefiore published the correspondence in *The Times,* Feb. 29, 1868. The version published in LD, 2: 220, entirely omits the reference to Jewish guilt.

80. "The Jews of Roumania," *JC,* April 10, 1868, 4. More generally, see Welter, *Judenpolitik,* 39; and Iancu, *Juifs en Roumanie,* 89–90.

81. See MM to Hammond, April 10, 1868, in *Correspondence Respecting Persecution of Jews in Moldavia,* 92.

82. Green to Stanley, March 28, 1868, ibid., 91. See also Iancu, *Jews in Romania,* 53–54.

83. Stanley to Green, April 24, 1868, in *Correspondence Respecting Persecution of Jews in Moldavia,* 105.

84. Bonar to Stanley, Oct. 7, 1868, ibid., 130.

85. LDMS, 2: 223.

86. Ibid., 198.

17. Fading Glory

1. "Unveiling of the Portrait of Sir Moses Montefiore," *JC*, Nov. 20, 1868, 6.

2. Rev. D. A. Jessurun Cardozo and Paul Goodman, *Think and Thank: The Montefiore Synagogue and College, Ramsgate* (Oxford, 1933), 51; LD, 1: 307; 2: 141.

3. See, e.g., "Judith Montefiore," *JC*, Oct. 10, 1862, 4; "The Projected Lady Montefiore Endowment" ibid., 5; "Judith, Lady Montefiore, Memorial," *JC*, June 12, 1863, 5. For details of contributors and international resonance see, e.g., "Judith Montefiore Memorial Fund," *JC*, Nov. 13, 1863, 5; "The Lady Montefiore Memorial Fund," *JC*, Dec. 11, 1863, 8; "Judith, Lady Montefiore Memorial," *OAJA*, Nov. 1863, 376; "San Francisco, California—Judith Lady Montefiore Monument," *JC*, June 24, 1864, 3. On the difficulties encountered, "Judith, Lady Montefiore Memorial," *JC*, Dec. 14, 1866, 5.

4. Charlotte de Rothschild to Leopold de Rothschild, Oct. 16, 1866, RFamC/21 (66), RAL.

5. "Judith, Lady Montefiore Convalescent Home," *JC*, Feb. 5, 1869, 5.

6. Oct. 19, 1827, MMJ 1827–28, ASM.

7. Cardozo and Goodman, *Think and Thank*, 56, and more generally.

8. *Statutes for the Regulation of the College Ohél Moshé Vé Yehoodit in Ramsgate Established by Sir Moses Montefiore Bart., in Memory of His Beloved Wife Judith Lady Montefiore of Happy Memory* (London, 1867).

9. On a similar divide between traditional and "modern" models of charity in a different religious tradition see Adele Lindenmeyr, *Poverty Is Not a Vice: Charity, Society, and the State in Imperial Russia* (Princeton, 1996).

10. *Statutes.*

11. LD, 2: 260, 240.

12. *Statutes.*

13. "England," *HLV*, Nov. 28, 1867, 365.

14. Yitzhak Eisener, Rav of Neue Stupova[?], Menachem 24, 5629, to MM, V. 2717/28, JNUL.

15. Avner Katvan Rosh Beth Din of Croieva to MM, Av 15, V. 2717/35, JNUL.

16. Cardozo and Goodman, *Think and Thank*, 67–68.

17. "The Consecration of the Montefiore College at Ramsgate," *JC*, Oct. 22, 1869, 7. On the translation of Judith's journals see Israel Bartal, "Karkaot ve'tokhniot le'ibudan be'yamei bikuro shel Montefiore be'Eretz-Israel be'shnat 1839," *Shalem* 2 (1976): 231–296.

18. LD, 2: 231–232.

19. "The Late Mrs. Gompertz," *JC*, March 17, 1871, 6.

20. Charlotte de Rothschild to Leopold de Rothschild, Oct. 16, 1866.

21. To Moshe Montefiore Regarding the Forced Conversions in Meshed, 5603,

MMSS vol. 576. See also "The Jews in Persia and Bokhara," *VJ*, April 25, 1845, 149; "The Jews of Balkh," *VJ*, April 25, 1845, 149. On the Mashhad episode see Jaleh Pirnazar, "The Anusim of Mashhad," in *Esther's Children: A Portrait of Iranian Jews*, ed. Houman Sarshar (Philadelphia, 2002), 117–136. On the mission of Nissim bar Shlomo from Hamadan see Nov. 3, 1847, BDMB, ACC/3121/A/006, fols. 90–92.

22. On Persian Jews see Daniel Tsadik, *Between Foreigners and Shi'is: Nineteenth-Century Iran and Its Jewish Minority* (Stanford, Calif., 2007); also Hooshang Ebrami, "The Impure Jew," and Janet Afary, "From Outcasts to Citizens: Jews in Qajar Iran," in Sarshar, *Esther's Children*, 98–102, 139–174. On socioeconomic roles see Laurence Loeb, "Dhimmi Status and Jewish Roles in Iranian Society," in *Jews among Muslims: Communities in the Precolonial Middle East*, ed. Shlomo Deshen and Walter P. Zenner (Basingstoke, 1996), 247–260. Walter Fischel, "The Jews of Persia, 1795–1940," *JSS* 12 (1950): 119–160, is becoming outdated.

23. See Abbas Amanat, *Pivot of the Universe: Nasir al-Din Shah Qajar and the Iranian Monarchy, 1851–1896* (London, 1997).

24. Murray to Clarendon, Oct. 5, 1857, F.O. 60/219, no. 109, NA. Tsadik, *Between Foreigners and Shi'is*, 44–46, discusses British attempts to promote Jewish rights as part of a wider revision of inheritance law relating to Iran's religious minorities in 1851.

25. Sadr Azim to Murray, Feb. 22, 1858, enclosed with Murray to Clarendon, Feb. 28, 1858, F.O. 60/229, no. 27, NA.

26. LD, 2: 167–168. See also Hamadan Congregation to MM, Jan. 5, 1865, F.O. 60/293, NA.

27. Alison to LJR, Nov. 18, 1865, F.O. 60/291, no. 121, NA.

28. The Shah to Alison (trans.), enclosed with ibid.

29. Alison to Clarendon, Dec. 21, 1865, ibid., no. 134.

30. MM to JMM, Feb. 1, 1866, BDMB, ACC/3121/A/010, fols. 96–97.

31. Alison to LJR, Nov. 18, 1865.

32. Alison to the Sipeh Salar Aazem, May 29, 1866, enclosed with Alison to Clarendon, June 4, 1866, F.O. 60/297 (enclosed with no. 67), NA.

33. LDMS, 2: 190–191.

34. Draft to Alison, June 11, 1866, F.O. 60/295, no. 46, NA.

35. The First Monshee to Alison, Aug. 21, 1866, F.O. 60/298, no. 103, NA.

36. Alison to Stanley, covering letter to ibid.

37. W. J. Dickson to Alison, Aug. 18, 1866, enclosed with ibid.

38. Shelomo Bechor Husein, "Aziyen," *HM*, Dec. 19, 1866, 388.

39. "Hayehudim be'erets paras," *HM*, Nov. 4, 1868, 340.

40. Major R. M. Smith, Persian Telegraph, to Alison, May 3, 1871, enclosed with Alison to Granville, May 29, 1871, F.O. 60/334, no. 64, NA. More generally see Shoko Okazaki, "The Great Persian Famine of 1870–1871," *Bulletin of the School of Oriental and African Studies, University of London* 49, no. 1 (1986): 183–192.

41. LD, 2: 237–238, enclosed with MM to Capt. Jones, July 2, 1871; London Committee of Deputies of the British Jews, *Persian Famine Relief Fund: Report and Balance Sheet* (London, 1873), 10–11.

42. "*Hamagid* Persian Famine Donation Lists Donors from Lithuania, 1871–

1872," www.jewishgen.org, accessed Jan. 2, 2009; "Hayehudim be'erets paras," *HM*, Nov. 8, 1871, 337, contrasted the support of Russian Jews with lack of interest in Germany and Austria.

43. *Relief Fund Report*, 10–11. The deputies particularly commended the significant German contribution. "Current Gossip," *JC*, Oct. 1, 1875, 430, suggested that London Jews contributed only £1,000.

44. *Relief Fund Report*, 5. On demographic impact see Okazaki, "Great Persian Famine," 184–185.

45. "Eine schöne Erscheinung aus der neuern Zeit," *AZ*, Feb. 13, 1872, 119–122.

46. See Abigail Green, "Nationalism and the 'Jewish International': Religious Internationalism in Europe and the Middle East, c. 1840–c. 1880," *Comparative Studies in Society and History* 50 (April 2008): 535–558. On Montefiore's role see Green, "Sir Moses Montefiore and the Making of the 'Jewish International,'" *Journal of Modern Jewish Studies* 7 (Nov. 2008): 287–307.

47. See Lloyd P. Gartner, "Roumania, America, and World Jewry: Consul Peixotto in Bucharest, 1870–1876," *American Jewish Historical Quarterly* 58 (1968): 25–117; and Gartner, "Documents on Roumanian Jewry, Consul Peixotto, and Jewish Diplomacy, 1870–1875," in *Salo Wittmayer Baron Jubilee Volume*, ed. Saul Liebermann and Arthur Hyman, vol. 1 (Jerusalem, 1974), 467–490.

48. "*Hamagid* Persian Famine Donation Lists."

49. "Sir Moses Montefiore," *JC*, July 18, 1862, 4.

50. "The Late Joseph Mayer Montefiore," *JC*, Oct. 15, 1880, 10.

51. LDMS, 2: 236. "The Excesses at Odessa," *JC*, May 19, 1871, 6, took a similar line.

52. "Odessa," *JC*, June 23, 1871, 2.

53. "The Peril of Our Russian Brethren," *JC*, June 9, 1871, 7; June 29, 1871, BDMB, ACC/3121/A/011, fols. 12–22.

54. Sept. 7, 1871, BDMB, Acc/3121/A/011, fols. 33–39. On the AJA see Eli Bar-Chen, *Weder Asiaten noch Orientalen. Internationale jüdische Organisationen und die Europäisierung "rückständiger" Juden* (Würzburg, 2005).

55. "The Anglo-Jewish Association of the Universal Israelites Alliance," *JC*, July 28, 1871, 3.

56. "The Board of Deputies," *JC*, Sept. 22, 1871, 8.

57. For Philippson's response, see "Bonn, 20. August. Zustände in Rußland (Schluß)," *AZ*, Aug. 29, 1871, 689–692. On the impact of Odessa in Russia see John Doyle Klier, *Imperial Russia's Jewish Question, 1855–1881* (Cambridge, 1995), 358–363.

58. "Bonn, 14. August. Zustände in Rußland," *AZ*, Aug. 22, 1871, 669–671.

59. "The Jews of Roumania: Great Meeting at the Mansion House," *JC*, May 31, 1872, 124.

60. Ibid.; "Sir Moses Montefiore," ibid., 129.

61. "The Board of Deputies and the Czar of Russia," *JC*, July 12, 1872, 207.

62. "Was ist in Rumänien erreicht?" *AZ*, Aug. 6, 1872, 625. See also "The Mission of Sir Moses Montefiore," *JC*, July 19, 1872, 219.

63. LD, 2: 247; Loftus to Granville, July 22, 1872, F.O. 65/835, NA.

64. MM to LL, May 5, 1848, folder 2, HL.

65. See L. Mashbir, "Montefiore i Russkie Yevreii (K. Predstoiaschemu Yubil-eiu)," *Russkii Yevrei* 30 (1884): 25–29.

66. "Russia, April," *JC*, May 19, 1854, 283.

67. Brunnow to MM, Oct. 1/13, 1873, ASM.

68. Fritz Stern, *Gold and Iron: Bismarck, Bleichröder and the Building of the German Empire* (Harmondsworth, 1977), 379.

69. MM to LL, May 5, 1848.

70. On the relationship between Jews, Russian society, and the state under Alexander see Klier, *Imperial Russia's Jewish Question.*

71. See Benjamin Nathans, *Beyond the Pale: The Jewish Encounter with Late Imperial Russia* (Berkeley, 2002); and Yvonne Kleinmann, *Neue Orte—Neue Menschen. Jüdische Lebensformen in St. Petersburg und Moskau im 19. Jahrhundert* (Göttingen, 2006).

72. Nathans, *Beyond the Pale*, 87, 117.

73. *Report Presented by Sir Moses Montefiore Bart., President, to the London Committee of Deputies of the British Jews on His Return from His Mission to St. Petersburg, August 5632—1872* (London, 1872), 16.

74. Quoted in Nathans, *Beyond the Pale*, 144.

75. Pauline Wengeroff, *Memoiren einer Grossmutter. Bilder aus der Kulturgeschichte der Juden Russlands im 19. Jahrhundert*, vol. 2 (Berlin, 1908), 171–172.

76. Nathans, *Beyond the Pale*, 128.

77. On Gordon see Michael Stanislawski, *For Whom Do I Toil? Judah Leib Gordon and the Crisis of Russian Jewry* (Oxford, 1988). For his account of Montefiore's visit see Judah Leib Gordon, "Al nehar kevar, pirkei zikhronot, devar yom beyomo," in *Kitvei Yehudah Leib Gordon* (Tel Aviv, 1928), 33–37.

78. Eli Lederhendler, *The Road to Modern Jewish Politics: Political Tradition and Political Reconstruction in the Jewish Community of Tsarist Russia* (Oxford, 1989), 99.

79. See, e.g., Ephraim Deinard, *Megillat Setarim* (New York, 1928).

80. *Report Presented by Montefiore on His Return from St. Petersburg*, 18.

81. Mihail Dolbilov, "Russifying Bureaucracy and the Politics of Jewish Education in the Russian Empire's North West Region (1860s–1870s)," *Acta Slavica Iaponica* 24 (2007): 129.

82. *Golos* as reported in "Rusya," *HLV*, Dec. 31, 1872, 148.

83. "The Shah at Wiesbaden," *JC*, June 27, 1873, 214. On the shah's visit more generally, see Tsadik, *Between Foreigners and Shi'is*, 88–95.

84. LDMS, 2: 245–246.

85. LD, 2: 256.

86. For more detail see "Beritaniyah," *HLV*, Oct. 15, 1873, 68.

87. "The Shah of Persia and the Jews," *JC*, June 27, 1873, 217.

88. "The Shah of Persia and the Jews," *JC*, Aug. 1, 1873, 321.

89. Fischel, "Jews of Persia," 124.

90. "Presentation of Addresses to the Shah on Behalf of the Jews," *JC*, June 27, 1873, 213.

91. "The Board of Deputies and the Berkley Street Congregation," *JC*, May 2, 1873, 71.

92. "Constitution of the Board of Deputies: The Admission of Representatives of the Berkeley Street Synagogue," *JC*, Dec. 26, 1873, 648.

93. MM to Rabbi Nathan Adler, Dec. 19, 5634, Arc 4 1746 I/4, JNUL.

18. The Final Pilgrimage

1. LDMS, 2: 259–260.

2. April 15, 1874, BDMB, Acc/3121/A/011, fols. 219–221.

3. "Die Hungersnoth in Jerusalem," *AZ*, May 26, 1874, 363.

4. "Famine in the Holy City," *JC*, April 17, 1874, 41.

5. LDMS, 2: 261.

6. "The Jerusalem Jews," *JC*, June 26, 1874, 209; "The Palestine Jews," *JC*, July 10, 1874, 241.

7. "The Jerusalem Jews," *JC*, July 3, 1874, 209.

8. June 14, 1874, BDMB, ACC 3121/A/011, fols. 240–241.

9. LDMS, 2: 262.

10. July 9, 1874, BDMB, ACC/3121/A/011, fol. 258.

11. See "Al devar avodat ha'adamah umelekhet yad (5)," *Habazeleth,* Nov. 20, 1874, 2; and other articles in the series.

12. Moses Montefiore, *Translations of a Letter Addressed by Sir Moses Montefiore Bart., F.R.S., Member of the Most Noble Order of the Medjidie of the Second Class, to the Jewish Congregations in the Holy Land on the Promotion of Agriculture and Other Industrial Pursuits in That Country and of the Replies Received Thereto* (London, 1874), 35–38. On Schlesinger see Michael Silber, "Alliance of the Hebrew, 1863–1875: The Diaspora Roots of an Ultra-Orthodox Proto-Zionist Utopia in Palestine," *Journal of Israeli History* 27 (Sept. 2008): 119–147; and Silber, "Pa'amei lev ha'ivri be'erets hagar: rabi akiva yosef shelezinger—bein ultra-ortodoksiyah ule'umiyut yehudit bereshiton," in *Meah shenot tsiyonut datit,* ed. Avi Sagi and Dov Schwartz, vol. 1: *Ishim veshitot* (Ramat-Gan, 2003), 225–254.

13. Montefiore, *Translations,* 10.

14. "Board of Deputies," *JC*, Aug. 14, 1874, 2317.

15. See Dec. 22, 1863, BDMB, ACC/3121/A/009, fols. 277–284.

16. Rabbi Hirsch Salomon Berliner to LJR, May 12, 1865; James Murray, F.O. Departmental Note, Sept. 8, 1855, in HBC, 2: 336–340.

17. MM to Hammond, Dec. 18, 1867, and F.O. notes, ibid., 344–345.

18. "The Jews of Damascus," *JC*, Nov. 4, 1870, 10.

19. "The Jews at Damascus," *JC*, Nov. 11, 1870, 13.

20. Charles Kennedy to Granville, Jan. 11, 1871, in HBC, 2: 349–358; Geoffrey Alderman and Colin Holmes, "The Burton Book," *Journal of the Royal Asiatic Society,* 3d ser., 18, no. 1 (2008): 1–13, analyzes Burton's Judeophobia and fixation with the Jews of Damascus. But see also Isabel Burton, *The Inner Life of Syria, Palestine, and the Holy Land: From My Private Journal* (London, 1884), 264–272.

21. See Kennedy to Granville, Jan. 30, 1871; Burton to G. Jackson Eldridge, June

9, 1871; Sir Henry Elliot to Granville, May 30, 1872; Granville to Eldridge, July 1, 1872; Elliot to Granville, Sept. 1872, in HBC, 2: 360–361, 366–367, 374–375, 378–379.

22. MM to Granville, May 31, 1873; Alfred Green, Memo re. the grant of British Protection to Foreign Jews in Palestine, Jan. 16, 1873; Sidney Locock to Derby, May 12, 1874, ibid., 380–389, 393–394, 397–398.

23. "Board of Deputies," *JC*, Nov. 23, 1866, 6.

24. "Palestine Colonisation Scheme," *JC*, Jan. 4, 1867, 4.

25. See "Migdal halevanon tsofeh penei yerushalayim," *HLV*, March 15, 1867, 88; "Paris," *HLV*, May 10, 1867, 139; "Migdal halevanon tsofeh penei yerusha-layim," *HLV*, Jan. 14, 1869, 4.

26. This account is pieced together from "Azia," *HLV*, June 3, 1869, 174; "Azia," *HLV*, Aug. 5, 1869, 246; "Tsefat," *HLV*, Oct. 18, 1869, 318.

27. Charles Netter, "Rapport," *Bulletin de l'AIU*, July 1, 1868, 55.

28. March 23, 1869, BDMB, ACC/3121/A/010, fols. 274–279; "Jewish Agricul-turalists at Jaffa," *JC*, April 9, 1869, 2; "Jewish Agricultural Colony at Jaffa," *JC*, April 23, 1869, 3; "Migdal halevanon tsofeh penei yerushalayim," *HLV*, April 22, 1869, 121; "Migdal halevanon tsofeh penei yerushalayim," *HLV*, April 29, 1869, 129; "Migdal halevanon tsofeh penei yerushalayim," *HLV*, May 20, 1869, 153; "Migdal halevanon tsofeh penei yerushalayim," *HLV*, May 27, 1869, 162; "Migdal halevanon tsofeh penei yerushalayim," *HLV*, June 3, 1869, 169; as well as "Al devar beit sefer lilmod avodat adamah be'irenu hakadosh yafo," *HLV*, June 10, 1869, 177; and other articles in this extensive series.

29. "Aziyen," *HM*, Sept. 2, 1868, 276; "Tsarfat," *HLV*, Feb. 18, 1869, 59; "The Projected Agricultural Colonies in the Holy Land," *JC*, March 26, 1869, 4.

30. "Shelom yerushalayim," *Habazeleth*, Nov. 25, 1870, 17; "Shelom yerusha-layim," ibid., Dec. 23, 1870, 25.

31. "The Distress in Jerusalem," *JC*, March 11, 1870, 7.

32. *The Israelite*, March 25, 1870, 9.

33. "The Jaffa Agricultural Colony," *JC*, Oct. 27, 1871, 4.

34. "The Jaffa Colony," *JC*, Dec. 22, 1871, 3.

35. Dec. 15, 1874, BDMB, ACC/3121/A/011, fols. 304–306.

36. "The Montefiore Testimonial," *JC*, Jan. 22, 1875, 683.

37. "The Sir Moses Montefiore Testimonial," *JC*, Feb. 12, 1875, 738.

38. "The Moses Montefiore Testimonial," *JC*, Feb. 19, 1875, 748.

39. "England," *HM*, March 17, 1875, 91.

40. "The Condition of the Jews of Jerusalem," *JC*, Aug. 20, 1875, 339; "Condi-tion of the Jews of Jerusalem," *JC*, Aug. 27, 1875, 350. More generally see Cecil Bloom, "Samuel Montagu's and Sir Moses Montefiore's Visits to Palestine in 1875," *Journal of Israeli History: Studies in Zionism and Statehood* 17 (Autumn 1996): 263–281.

41. "Condition of the Jews of Jerusalem," Aug. 27, 1875.

42. "Sir Moses Montefiore," *JC*, May 28, 1875, 144.

43. "Sir Moses Montefiore," *JC*, June 11, 1875, 171.

44. Ibid.

45. Moses Montefiore, *Narrative of a Forty Days Sojourn in the Holy Land, Devoted to an Investigation of the State of Schools, Colleges, and Charitable Institutions, Given to the Well-Wishers of Zion* (London, 1877), 46, 53.

46. Ibid., 55, 66, 69.

47. "Leharamat keren yerushalayim vetosheveiha," *Habazeleth,* July 16, 1875, 298.

48. Montefiore, *Narrative,* 82–83.

49. "Yerushalayim," *HLV,* Aug. 25, 1875, 21.

50. See Israel Bartal, "From '*Kollel*' to 'Neighbourhood': Revisiting the Pre-Zionist Ashkenazi Community in Nineteenth-Century Palestine," in *Ottoman and Turkish Jewry: Community and Leadership,* ed. Aron Rodrigue (Bloomington, Ind., 1992), 203–224.

51. Montefiore, *Narrative,* 106–107.

52. Ibid., 103–106, 128–129, 136.

53. "Al devar yishuv erets yisra'el," *HLV,* Oct. 13, 1875, 73.

54. Montefiore, *Narrative,* 146.

55. Dr. Bernhard Neumann, *Die Heilige Stadt und deren Bewohner in ihren naturhistorischen, culturgeschichtilichen, socialen und medicinischen Verhältnissen* (Hamburg, 1877), 423–424, 427–428.

56. "Sir Moses Montefiore in the City," *JC,* Sept. 24, 1875, 418.

57. See "Current Gossip," *JC,* Oct. 1, 1875, 430. American Jews were similarly ambivalent; Ismar Elbogen, "The Montefiore Testimonial Fund and American Israel," *Publications of the American Jewish Historical Society* 37 (1947): 55–94.

58. "Barukh atah betsetekha," *Habazeleth,* Aug. 20, 1875, 2.

59. "Montefiore Testimonial Fund," *JC,* Nov. 5, 1875, 515.

60. W. D. Rubinstein, "Jewish Top Wealth-Holders in Britain, 1809–1909," *Jewish Historical Studies* 37 (2001): 146.

61. Simon Schama, *Two Rothschilds and the Land of Israel* (London, 1978).

62. LDMS, 1: 59.

63. Meyer Auerbach, Samuel Salant, and Moses Montefiore, *An Open Letter Addressed to Sir Moses Montefiore, Bart., on the Day of His Arrival in the Holy City of Jerusalem (May It Soon Be Rebuilt and Established), Sunday, 22 Tamooz, 5635, A.M.—July 25, 1875, Together with a Narrative of a Forty Days Sojourn in the Holy Land, Devoted to an Investigation of the State of Schools, Colleges, and Charitable Institutions, Given to the Well-Wishers of Zion* (London, 1877); "An Open Letter Addressed to Sir Moses Montefiore, &c., with a Narrative of 'Forty Days Sojourn in the Holy Land,'" *JC,* Feb. 11, 1876, 739; "Yamim yedaberu," *Habazeleth,* April 28, 1876, 199.

64. "Sir Moses Montefiore Testimonial," *JC,* Feb. 4, 1876, 719.

65. "Notes of the Week: Sir Moses Montefiore Testimonial," *JC,* March 3, 1876, 779.

66. "The Montefiore Testimonial Fund," *JC,* March 24, 1876, 833.

67. "Sir Moses Montefiore Testimonial Fund," *JC,* Oct. 27, 1876, 468.

68. On events in the Balkans see the revisionist Justin McCarthy, *Death and Exile: The Ethnic Cleansing of Ottoman Muslims, 1821–1933* (Princeton, 1995), chap.

3. On the British response see the classic R. T. Shannon, *Gladstone and the Bulgarian Agitation, 1876* (London, 1963).

69. "Lady Strangford's Bulgarian Peasant Relief Fund," *JC*, Dec. 1, 1876, 549.

70. Quoted in David Feldman, *Englishmen and Jews: Social Relations and Political Culture, 1840–1914* (New Haven, 1994), 100–101.

71. Feldman, *Englishmen and Jews*, 78–88, makes this argument in some detail.

72. LD, 2: 285–286.

73. "Colonization of the Holy Land," *JC*, Jan. 7, 1876, 652.

74. "The Montefiore Testimonial Fund," *JC*, April 7, 1876, 9.

75. "Jewish Colonization of Syria," *JC*, July 21, 1876, 251.

76. "The Canard of Purchasing Palestine," *The Israelite*, Jan. 24, 1879, 4.

77. For an analysis of the Treaty of Berlin in this context see Carole Fink, *Defending the Rights of Others: The Great Powers, the Jews, and International Minority Protection, 1878–1938* (Cambridge, 2004), prologue.

78. Fritz Stern, *Gold and Iron: Bismarck, Bleichröder and the Building of the German Empire* (Harmondsworth, 1977), 376–377.

79. T. P. O'Connor, *Lord Beaconsfield: A Biography* (London, 1879), 671.

80. Ibid.

19. End of an Era

1. For accounts of the ninety-ninth birthday celebrations see LD, 2: 316–319; and Joseph Fiebermann, *Internationales Montefiore-Album* (Frankfurt am Main, 1885), 13–16.

2. Fiebermann, *Internationales Montefiore-Album*, 42–55.

3. Ibid., 13.

4. "Sir Moses Montefiore," *JC*, Oct. 19, 1883, 7.

5. The *Times* biography was later reprinted as Israel Davis, *Sir Moses Montefiore, a Biographical Sketch, Reprinted, by Permission, from The Times, with Additions* (London, 1883). The 1883 and 1884 *Times* leaders are reproduced in *CMM*, 362–368.

6. *The Spectator*, Oct. 27, 1883, 1367.

7. "*The Spectator* and the Jews: Letters to the Editor: Oswald John Simon, October 27th, to the Editor," *The Spectator*, Nov. 3, 1883, 1409.

8. "Jewish Sensitiveness," ibid., 1407–1408.

9. "Ramsgate," *JC*, Feb. 2, 1872, 6.

10. Rev. D. A. Jessurun Cardozo and Paul Goodman, *Think and Thank: The Montefiore Synagogue and College, Ramsgate* (Oxford, 1933), 39–41, 99–101.

11. P. B. Benny, "Personal Reminiscences of Sir Moses Montefiore, IV," *Jewish World*, Aug. 28, 1885, 5.

12. "Sir Moses Montefiore Bart," *JC*, Nov. 3, 1882, 13.

13. George Collard, *Moses the Victorian Jew* (Oxford, 1990), 10.

14. P. B. Benny, "Personal Reminiscences of Sir Moses Montefiore, I," *Jewish World*, Aug. 7, 1885, 5.

15. Arthur Conan Doyle, *Memories and Adventures* (New York, 1924), 284.

16. Benny, "Personal Reminiscences, I," states that this was his invariable practice; LD, 2: 286, and MMJ 1879, Mocatta 38, M4720, ML, indicate otherwise.

17. Benny, "Personal Reminiscences, I."

18. Lucien Wolf, *Sir Moses Montefiore: A Centennial Biography, with Extracts from Letters and Journals* (London, 1884), 288.

19. MMJ 1879.

20. Davis, *Montefiore,* 34.

21. LD, 2: 309, 313–315.

22. LDMS, 2: 294.

23. LD, 2: 299.

24. LDMS, 2: 300.

25. "Sir Moses Montefiore and the Czar of Russia," *JC,* June 1, 1883, 4; "Sir Moses Montefiore and the Czar," *JC,* Aug. 17, 1883, 6. Some correspondence with individual communities survives in the Schischa Collection, London.

26. MM to Lady Rosebery, Nov. 7, 1881, 1881:6, SLC.

27. On Zionism see Ben Halpern, *The Idea of the Jewish State* (Cambridge, Mass., 1969); Walter Lacqueur, *A History of Zionism* (London, 1972); Gideon Shimoni, *The Zionist Ideology* (Hanover, N.H., 1995); David Vital, *The Origins of Zionism* (Oxford, 1975).

28. LD, 2: 326.

29. Letter 64, in A. Droganov, ed., *Ketavim letoledot ḥibat tsiyon vishuv erets yisra'el* (Odessa, 5679), 132.

30. Letter 79, ibid., 179.

31. Letter 93, ibid., 171.

32. Letter 97, ibid., 179.

33. *Hamagid* 1884–85 contains numerous lists of those who purchased the Montefiore portrait, and other articles relating to this initiative.

34. Barry Walfish, "The Hovevei Zion Tribute Album Presented to Moses Montefiore on the Occasion of His 100th Birthday," Paper presented at the Sixty-sixth IFLA Council and General Conference, 2000, www.ifla.org, accessed Jan. 4, 2009.

35. "Sir Moses Montefiore," *JC,* March 9, 1883, 7; "Sir Moses Montefiore," *JC,* Nov. 30, 1883, 11; "Sir Moses Montefiore's Centenary—the Proposed Memorial," *JC,* Nov. 30, 1883, 5; "Sir Moses Montefiore," *JC,* Dec. 14, 1883, 6.

36. Sir Moses Montefiore Memorial, Announcement of Public Meeting to Be Held at the Egyptian Hall, Mansion House, Jan. 22, 1884, Letters of MM 1869–1883, 2002/27 (43), Jewish Museum, London.

37. NMR, Chair, Jan. 21, 1884, circular, ibid. (44).

38. Davis, *Montefiore,* 33–35.

39. LD, 2: 326.

40. Benny, "Personal Reminiscences, IV."

41. Resolutions, 1828, ASM.

42. LD, 2: 144, 225; "Sir Moses Montefiore," *JC,* Jan. 25, 1884, 6.

43. This argument is expanded in Abigail Green, "Rethinking Sir Moses Montefiore: Religion, Nationhood and International Philanthropy in the Nineteenth Century," *American Historical Review* 110 (June 2005): 631–658.

44. James Weston, *Sir Moses Montefiore: The Story of His Life* (London, 1884), 86.

45. See Montefiore Testimonials Provisional Catalogue, ML.

46. "The Montefiore Commemoration," *JC*, Oct. 31, 1884, 9.

47. *Tephilat le Moshe: Service of Prayer and Thanksgiving to Be Used on the Occasion of Sir Moses Montefiore, Bart., Completing His Hundredth Year, 26th of October 5645–1884* (London, 1884).

48. "Sir Moses Montefiore," *JC*, Oct. 17, 1884, 10; "Sir Moses Montefiore," *JC*, Oct. 24, 1884, 7; "Sir Moses Montefiore," *JC*, Nov. 21, 1884, 10; "Sir Moses Montefiore," *JC*, Nov. 28, 1884, 12; "Sir Moses Montefiore," *JC*, Dec. 12, 1884, 12; "Sir Moses Montefiore," *JC*, Jan. 18, 1884, 5; "Sir Moses Montefiore," *JC*, Nov. 23, 1883, 10. A couple of these articles refer to 1883 celebrations, but it seems reasonable to assume that communities celebrating Montefiore's ninety-ninth very likely celebrated his hundredth birthday.

49. Moshe Davis, *Sir Moses Montefiore: American Jewry's Ideal* (Jerusalem, 1985).

50. Jewish Congregation of Medzhibozh to MM, 1884, Montefiore Testimonials Provisional Catalogue.

51. Quoted in Paul Goodman, *Moses Montefiore* (Philadelphia, 1925), 207.

52. Association to Restore the Ruins of Zion, Odessa, to MM, Oct. 11/23, 1884, with illustration by Isaac Pasternak, Montefiore Testimonials Provisional Catalogue.

53. LD, 2: 337–341.

54. LDMS, 2: 337.

55. Ibid.

56. Schischa Collection.

57. LD, 2: 224.

58. "Supplement to the Jewish Chronicle: Death of Sir Moses Montefiore," *JC*, July 31, 1885, 1, supplements the account given by Loewe.

59. This information comes from "Hatsava'ah," *HM*, Aug. 13, 1885, 279. See also "Will of Sir Moses Montefiore," *JC*, Aug. 28, 1885, 7, but since some of the money is left in shares, the exact total is hard to quantify here.

Conclusion

1. Joseph Fiebermann, *Internationales Montefiore-Album* (Frankfurt am Main, 1885), 179–180.

2. Carole Fink, *Defending the Rights of Others: The Great Powers, the Jews, and International Minority Protection, 1878–1938* (Cambridge, 2004), is a notable exception.

3. These form the bulk of examples discussed in Gary J. Bass, *Freedom's Battle: The Origins of Humanitarian Intervention* (New York, 2008).

4. See Lynn Hunt, *Inventing Human Rights: A History* (New York, 2007), 177–186, on the rise of nationalism. See also Micheline R. Ishay, *The History of Human Rights: From Ancient Times to the Globalization Era* (Berkeley, 2004), 4.

Archives Consulted

Alliance Israélite Universelle, Paris
American Jewish Archives, Cincinnati
American Jewish Historical Society, New York
Archives Nationales, Paris
Archives Royales, Rabat
Archivio di Stato di Roma, Rome
Archivio Segreto Vaticano, Rome
Board of Deputies Archives, London
British Library Manuscripts Collection, London
Cambridge University Library
Central Archives for the History of the Jewish People, Jerusalem
Central Zionist Archives, Jerusalem
Communità Israelitica di Roma, Rome
Consistoire Central des Israélites de France, Paris
Evangelical Alliance, London
Guildhall Archives, London
Hartley Library, University of Southampton
Hodgkin Archive, The Wellcome Library, London
Jewish Museum, London
Jewish National University Library, Jerusalem
Jewish Theological Seminary, New York
London Metropolitan Archives
Ministère des Affaires Etrangères, Paris
Ministerio de Asuntas Exteriores, Archivio General, Madrid
Ministry of Foreign Affairs Archive, Ottoman Archives, Istanbul
Mocatta Library, University College London
The National Archives, London
Office of the Chief Rabbi, London
Oxford Centre for Hebrew and Jewish Studies
Palestine Exploration Fund, London
Private Collection of George Collard, Chester
Private Collection of Rabbi Dr. Abraham Levy, London
Private collection of A. Schischa, London
Private collection of Robert Sebag-Montefiore, Switzerland
Private collection of Ruth Sebag-Montefiore, London
Romanian National Archives, Bucharest

The Rothschild Archive, London
The Royal Archives, Windsor
Russian State Historical Archive, St. Petersburg
Spanish and Portuguese Jews' Congregation, London
State Archive of the Russian Federation, Moscow

Index